Biographical revi County, Iowa;

Hobart Publishing Company. [from old catalog]

BIOGRAPHICAL REVIEW

OF

LEE COUNTY, IOWA

CONTAINING

BIOGRAPHICAL *and* GENEALOGICAL
SKETCHES *of*

MANY OF THE PROMINENT CITIZENS OF TO-DAY AND ALSO OF THE PAST

"*Biography is the only true history.*"—EMERSON.

ILLUSTRATED

CHICAGO
HOBART PUBLISHING COMPANY
1905

The history of a nation is best told in the lives of its people."—MACAULAY.

PREFACE

The present age is happily awake to the duty of writing its own records, setting down what is best worth remembering in the lives of the busy toilers of today, noting, not in vain glory, but with an honest pride and sense of fitness, things worthy of emulation, that thus the good men do may live after them. The accounts here rendered are not of buried talents, but of used ability and opportunity. The conquests recited are of mind over matter, of cheerful labor directed by thought, of honest, earnest endeavor which subdues the earth in the divinely appointed way. "The great lesson of biography," it is said, "is to show what man can be and do at his best." A noble life put fairly on record acts like an inspiration, and no more interesting or instructive matter could be presented to an intelligent public.

In this volume will be found a record of many whose lives are worthy the imitation of coming generations. It tells how some, commencing life in poverty, by industry and economy have accumulated wealth. It tells how others, with limited advantages for securing an education, have become learned men and women, with an influence extending throughout the length and breadth of the land. It tells of men who have risen from the lower walks of life to eminence as statesmen, and whose names have become famous. It tells of those in every walk of life who have striven to succeed, and records how that success has usually crowned their efforts. It tells also of those, who, not seeking the applause of the world, have pursued the "even tenor of their way," content to have it said of them, as Christ said of the woman performing a deed of mercy, "They have done what they could." It tells how many, in the pride and strength of young manhood left all and at their country's call went forth valiantly "to do or die," and how through their efforts the Union was restored and peace once more reigned in the land.

Coming generations will appreciate this volume and preserve it as a sacred treasure, from the fact that it contains so much that would never find its way into public record, and which would otherwise be inaccessible. Great care has been taken in the compilation of the work and every opportunity possible given to those represented to insure correctness in what has been written; and the publishers flatter themselves that they give to their readers a work with few errors of consequence.

Yours respectfully,

January, 1905. HOBART PUBLISHING COMPANY.

"A people that take no pride in the noble achievements of remote ancestors will never achieve anything worthy to be remembered with pride by remote generations."—MACAULAY.

BIOGRAPHICAL REVIEW

OF

LEE COUNTY, IOWA

SAMUEL ATLEE.

Samuel Atlee, honored and respected by all not alone because of his success, but by reason of the straightforward methods he has ever followed, has in a long and active business career developed ideas into commercial possibilities and transmuted immature plans into marketable commodities. The extent and importance of his business interests and connections at the present day render him one of the prominent factors in commercial, industrial and financial circles in southeastern Iowa, and his investments effect trade relations and promote business prosperity over a wide territory.

The name of Atlee has figured in the history of Lee county since 1836, when John C. and Emeline S. (Brooks) Atlee, established their home in Fort Madison. It was but two years later on the 29th of October, 1838, that their son, Samuel Atlee, was born. He acquired his preliminary education in the public and private schools of Fort Madison and afterward continued his studies in Pittsburg, Pennsylvania, where he pursued a business course that qualified him for entrance into the active career which has since claimed his time and energies. Returning to Fort Madison, he entered his father's mill not as the hampered son of a prosperous parent, but as an employe who made it his object to fully qualify himself for the business by a mastery of every detail in each department. Gradually as he acquainted himself with the trade in its various branches he assumed the management and eventually in 1868 was admitted to a partnership. Consecutive progress has marked his endeavors and as opportunity has offered and trade demanded he has enlarged the plant until it has a capacity of about twenty-five million feet of lumber annually, while employment is furnished to three hundred workmen. The mill is equipped with modern machinery and every facility to advance the business and the entire plant and yards cover thirty-five acres. Excellent shipping facilities have been secured, private tracks connecting the yards with all of the railroads entering Fort Madison. The business is largely conducted along wholesale lines, but a retail department is now in operation. Mr. Atlee owns lumber lands in Minnesota and Wisconsin, while during the winter months he gives employment to many men to prepare the timber for shipment to the mill to be manufactured into a product for the lumber market.

This is but one of the interests which claim the attention and have profited by the co-operation of Samuel Atlee. He was a prominent factor in the organization of the Lee County Saving's Bank, which was incorporated in 1889 and at the first meeting of this board of directors he was elected president, which position he still holds. The bank was capitalized for thirty thousand dollars, which amount has since been increased to fifty thousand dollars and the institution now has a surplus of $10,000 and deposits amounting to $500,000. In 1895 was erected the structure now known as the Lee County Savings Bank Building at the corner of Second and Market streets. It is 50x145 feet, is three stories in height, was constructed of brown sandstóne and is the best building in this section of the state. The bank occupies the rooms on the ground floor at the corner and the adjoining room is occupied by the postoffice. The bank is equipped with the latest devices for safety protection as well as for convenience in conducting the banking business. The second story of the building is devoted to offices and the third floor is utilized by the Masonic fraternity.

Mr. Atlee installed the electric light plant that is used in lighting the city and also for private lighting and in this enterprise was associated in the ownership with his father. The plant was established in 1887 and has been enlarged from time to time until it is now very extensive. Mr. Atlee is a director of the Street Railway Company, of Fort Madison, and is financially interested in the Fort Madison Canning Factory, which gives employment to many operatives during the season.

Public spirited in citizenship and a stanch Republican in his political views Mr. Atlee has, however, never sought nor desired office, but his position in the regard of his fellow townsmen was indicated by his election in the years 1893, 1895 and 1899 to the mayoralty. He gave to the city an efficient, business-like administration, conducting municipal affairs with the same spirit of industry and enterprise that has ever been manifested in his private commercial and industrial interests. It was during his terms in office that the sewer system was inaugurated and that much of the paving in Fort Madison was laid. Fraternally a Mason, he belongs to Stella Lodge, Free and Accepted Masons; Potowonok Chapter, Royal Arch Masons, and Delta Commandery, Knights Templar.

On the 20th of January, 1867, Mr. Atlee was married to Miss Nancy M. Wright, of Fort Madison, a daughter of Mrs. Rosanna Wright. Mrs. Atlee died March 29, 1904. Mr. Atlee has a beautiful home in the midst of attractive grounds at the corner of Fourth and Market streets, in the city which has been his place of residence throughout his entire life, save for a brief period in his boyhood, when his parents resided upon the farm in Lee county. To him there has come the attainment of a distinguished position in connection with important productive industries and financial enterprises. It is true that in early manhood he became interested in a business already established, but he had the foresight and capability to develop and enlarge this and has also extended his efforts into various other fields, his entire career proving that success is not a matter of genius, but the direct result of sound judgment, experience, commendable ambition and honorable purpose.

JOHN C. ATLEE.

John C. Atlee, of Fort Madison, now deceased, who as a pioneer in the development of the lumber industry of southeastern Iowa and an active promoter of railroad construction contributed in a large measure to the substantial upbuilding and progress of the state, his labors entitling him to classification with its founders and builders, was descended from English ancestry. A native of Maryland, he was born on the 22d of March, 1816, and spent his youth in that state, living with his paternal grandparents. Subsequently he removed to New York city, where he entered upon an apprenticeship to the carpenter's trade and when his term of indenture had ended he was employed as a journeyman in New York city for several years. The keen foresight which enabled him in later years to recognize and improve business opportunities led him to seek a home in the West and he went by way of the sea to New Orleans and thence to Mobile, Alabama, working in different cities at his trade. His sojourn in the South, however, was temporary and he made his way up the Mississippi river to Fort Madison, where he arrived in 1836, finding an embryo town with the development and upbuilding, with which he became closely associated. He continued his active connection with building operations until 1841, assisting in the construction of many of the more important of the early buildings of Fort Madison. In the year mentioned, however, he removed to Cedar township, where he purchased a tract of land and developed a farm, but after carrying on agricultural pursuits for eleven years he returned to Fort Madison in 1852 and began the lumber business. He dealt in the manufactured product until 1855, when in connection with a Mr. Bennett, under the firm name of Atlee & Bennett, he built a sawmill, which they operated for two years. On the expiration of that period he purchased his partner's interest, thus becoming sole proprietor. The mill was located on the present site of the extensive Atlee lumber enterprise of Fort Madison that is now conducted by his son, Samuel Atlee. The father enlarged the mill from time to time as the demand for his product increased and became the owner of the first extensive lumber industry of the city. He was also the first man to bring logs down the river to be manufactured into a marketable commodity and he carefully watched for indications pointing to success, enlarging and developing his business as he saw opportunity until its importance as a productive industry of southeastern Iowa was widely acknowledged. About 1868 he admitted his son Samuel to a partnership and the firm style of S. & J. C. Atlee was assumed. The relation between father and son was maintained for some time, but ultimately the father retired from active business life some years prior to his death.

Had he confined his attention alone to his lumber business he would have merited distinction as a citizen of southeastern Iowa who had won notable success, and yet he extended his efforts into other fields of activity that resulted to the great benefit of the state as well as to his individual prosperity. He was instrumental in securing the building of the St. Louis, Keokuk & Northwestern Railroad, now a part of the Chicago, Burlington & Quincy system through Fort Madison. He was likewise instrumental in the building of the Chicago, Burlington & Kansas City road and with B. W. Davis took the contract for building the section of the road from Fort Madison to Farmington. It was also largely through his influence that the narrow gauge road to West Point, now a branch of the Chicago, Burlington & Quincy Railroad, was constructed and his labors proved a potent factor in securing the extension of the Santa Fe Railroad to Fort Madison. No other element has done more to advance civilization and promote industrial and commercial activity than has railroad building and in this connection Mr. Atlee's service proved of direct and lasting benefit to his adopted state. A stanch advocate of Republican principles from the organization of the party to the time of his demise John C. Atlee, although without aspirations for public office, represented his ward in the city council and was also a member of the school board. He was especially interested in educational matters and township improvements and was a co-operant factor in many measures that resulted beneficially to Fort Madison and Lee county. Fraternally he was connected with the Independent Order of Odd Fellows, his association therewith dating back to the middle of the nineteenth century.

Mr. Atlee was married at Quincy, Illinois, in 1836, to Miss Emeline S. Brooks, of Boston, Massachusetts, a representative of the same family to which Philips Brooks, the noted divine, belonged. Mr. and Mrs. Atlee became the parents of four children who reached adult age: Samuel; Martha, the wife of Peter Okell, of Fort Madison; Margaret, the wife of G. M. Hanchett, and William H.

The life record of John C. Atlee forms no unimportant chapter in the history of Lee county, for along business, social, political, educational and moral lines his influence was felt as a directing force and his labors were of acknowledged benefit.

HON. EDWARD JOHNSTONE.

Edward Johnstone was for half a century one of the most prominent and distinguished citizens of Iowa, and was a leader in business and political affairs, as well as a man of most extensive information and versatile talents. No man in the State of Iowa was better known or more highly respected than was he. In almost every public enterprise he was a prominent figure, yet he never sought preferment, although he possessed qualifications for the highest offices.

Hon. Edward Johnstone was born in Kingston, Westmoreland county, Pennsylvania, July 4, 1815. His paternal ancestry was originally from Annandale, Scotland, and the first of his immediate family who emigrated to Ireland was Robert Johnstone. This was late in the seventeenth or early in the eighteenth century. Alexander Johnstone, the father of our subject, was born in Ireland in 1772, and came to this country in 1796, where he married Miss Elizabeth Freame, a native of the Keystone state though of Irish descent. Unto them were born ten sons and two daughters. The two eldest sons were educated in the United States Military Academy, West Point, New York, and served in the regular army. Another son, William F. Johnstone, was the third governor of Pennsylvania. Another, James, a scholar and a poet, was through the Mexican War and was one of the prominent military men of western Pennsylvania. Another brother, John W., served in the Mexican and Civil Wars, attaining the rank of colonel. The youngest son, Richard, was appointed to a lieutenancy in the regular army, and was killed in the Mexican War. The father, a man of fine physique, died at the age of one hundred years.

Our subject was educated in his native town, and also read law and practiced at Greensburg in the same county. Admitted to the bar at the age of twenty-two, he set out for the West, locating at Mineral Point, Wisconsin, where he remained until the fall of the same year, when he went to Burlington, then the capital of Iowa, and served as clerk in the territorial legislature. During that session he was appointed one of three commissioners to gather testimony regarding titles to what were known as "half-breed" lands. The discharge of this duty was facilitated by his removal to Montrose, where he remained for one year. In 1839, after the law under which he was appointed was repealed, he went to Fort Madison, having, together with General Hugh T. Reid, been employed by the St. Louis Land Company to institute proceedings to secure a division of the lands under the partition laws of the territory. This resulted in the Decree Title under which the lands are now held.

In 1839 Mr. Johnstone was elected to the legislature, and for two successive terms was speaker of the house. In 1840 he was elected to the council, and during President Polk's administration was United States district attorney for the judicial district of Iowa. In 1851, when the board of county commissioners was established, Mr. Johnstone was elected judge of Lee county, and served in that capacity until 1855, making the most efficient guardian of the community's interests to whom the public affairs of the county was ever intrusted.

In 1857 he was a member of the state constitutional convention, and as such assisted in making the present constitution of the state. He distinguished himself in that body by his eminent ability, took a prominent part in all its deliberations, and did much to secure the incorporation into the constitution of many of its most important provisions.

After the expiration of his term upon the bench Judge Johnstone engaged in the banking business, the title of the firm being McMurphy, Johnstone & Bacon, which was subsequently changed to Johnstone & Bacon. In 1868 he removed to Keokuk and to the management of the Keokuk Savings Bank, of which he continued the executive head until his death, which occurred May 17, 1891, and it is to Judge Johnstone's great business and financial ability that the success attained by this most prosperous institution is due.

Through his influence the first state insane asylum at Mount Pleasant was established, he being one of three commissioners. When Iowa's commission was appointed for the World's Columbian Exposition he was made a member and chosen president. In fact, he never entered a meeting of men assembled for deliberation that he was not called to preside.

When Mr. Cleveland was elected to the presidency for the first time there was a large and spontaneous movement to have Judge Johnstone called to the cabinet from the West, but he himself refused to consent. From public office he ever shrank. During the last years of his life he was president of the Pioneer Lawmakers' Association of Iowa.

In January, 1840, the first attempt formally to organize the Democratic party in Iowa was made, and with that end in view a document, which is still in existence, was prepared by Mr. Johnstone personally and signed by himself and sixteen others setting forth the necessity of at once taking steps toward bringing the party's members into line and electing Democrats to congress.

When Joseph Smith, the founder of Mormonism, met with those difficulties at Nauvoo which have become matters of history he at once wrote to Mr. Johnstone to defend him, and had not that gentleman been starting for his old home in Pennsylvania, he would have been counsel in that celebrated case. The letter from Mr. Smith is still in the possession of Judge Johnstone's family.

Judge Johnstone was greatly interested in the success of the Columbian exposition, and was especially anxious that Iowa's geological display should be full and complete. Had he been spared, there is no doubt that he would have been of great assistance to Iowa's exhibitors. To Judge Johnstone as much if not more than any other man is the city of Keokuk indebted for its fine government building, as well as for the dry docks, for his influence was exerted most effectively in behalf of these important improvements.

He was a close student as well as a great reader, and it was rare indeed that the moments between business hours did not find him engaged in reading. To his many other accomplishments was added the ability to compose poetry of superior merit. As early as 1857 he was awarded the prize offered by the management of a prominent St. Louis opera house for the best poem to be used on the occasion of their opening performance.

Judge Johnstone married Miss Elizabeth

V. Richards in April, 1849, the ceremony being celebrated in St. Louis county, Missouri, and to them were born three sons and one daughter. Alexander E., president of the Keokuk Savings Bank, of Keokuk, Iowa. Edward R., now residing in California. Hugo R., a resident of New York. Miss Mary M. makes her home with her brother at Keokuk.

Judge Johnstone was affable and friendly in conversation, and had the faculty of making friends. He numbered his friends among both political parties. He was a man of high culture and education, with all the instincts and fine sensibilities of a gentleman. No man in Iowa had more to do with the making and shaping of the commonwealth than he. During all the time of his residence here he was identified with all the great public movements. He had a wide acquaintance throughout the state, and many went to him for counsel and advice. It seems appropriate in this place to quote from an estimate of Judge Johnstone's character as made by a fellow citizen of Keokuk:

"A man of strong convictions, he was ready on all occasions to express them and conscientiously stand by them. Charitable in his judgment of others, fair to those who opposed him, considerate of the opinions of others, however widely they might differ from those entertained by himself, with a warm and sympathizing heart towards all who were in need and sorrow, with a loyalty to friends that was proverbial, the sum of such a life may find expression in the words, a good citizen, faithful public servant, true friend, kind husband and indulgent father. He was at all times an honest, honorable, kindly man. He flattered nobody, he persecuted nobody, he maligned nobody, but was always frank and open. He gave everybody his due. He was plain in his manner, plain in attire, plain in language. He was a man of the people."

JOSEPH M. CASEY, M. D.

Dr. Joseph M. Casey, one of the leading physicians of Fort Madison with offices in the County Savings Bank building, was born in this city August 3, 1865, and is a son of Hon. Joseph M. Casey, who is represented elsewhere in this work. The public schools afforded him his literary education and after completing the high school course by graduation he entered upon the study of medicine under the direction of F. C. Roberts, of Fort Madison, with whom he continued for some time. He then matriculated in Rush Medical College of Chicago and was graduated with the class of 1888. Returning immediately to Fort Madison, he again entered the office of Dr. Roberts, with whom he remained for about three years, during which time he gained valuable, practical experience, thus putting to the test his theoretical knowledge. He then opened an office and has since remained alone engaged in general practice, in which he has been very successful, viewing from both a business and professional standpoint. He has pursued a post-graduate course in the New

York Polyclinic and has been a constant student of the science of medicine, carrying his investigations far and wide in order that he might promote his efficiency and render his labors of greater value in the important calling which he has chosen as a life work. In 1893-4 he was the physician for the penitentiary located at Fort Madison and was also physician of the board of health of this city for three years. At one time he practiced in Old Mexico for a little more than a year, being located at Cedral Coahuila as mine physician. He belongs to the Lee County Medical Society, the State Medical Society, the American Medical Association and the Tri-State Medical Association, of which he is one of the charter members while at its organization he was elected the junior vice-president.

Dr. Casey was married December 23, 1895, at Fort Madison, to Miss Sarah Zillah Johnson, a daughter of Professor Nelson Johnson. She was educated in Fort Madison and is well known in social circles. She also received a musical education in St. Louis. Of the two children born of this marriage one died in infancy, while the other is Robert Sabert Casey, now seven years of age. Dr. and Mrs. Casey hold membership in the Episcopal church and he belongs to Claypoole Lodge, No. 13, Free and Accepted Masons; Potowonok Chapter, Royal Arch Masons, No. 28; Delta Commandery, No. 51, Knights Templar, and the Mystic Shrine. In politics he is a Democrat, but has never had aspiration for office. Community interests, however, elicits his attention and receive his support and he favors every movement calculated to benefit his city. He is now president of the board of trustees of the Cattermole Memorial Library of Fort Madison. His home located at No. 932 Fourth street is one of the handsome residences of the city.

REV. GEORGE D. STEWART, D. D.

Rev. George D. Stewart, D. D., who for fifty-five years devoted his life to the Christian ministry the greater part of this time being spent in promoting the work of the Presbyterian church in Iowa, resigned on the 1st of January, 1904, his pastorate in Fort Madison after twenty-seven years' connection therewith and is now living in the enjoyment of a rest well-merited. However, his life, growing broader spiritually and mentally year by year, still gives out of its rich stores, wisdom and experience, and his counsel is yet sought by many. His influence has long been a potent power for good in Iowa, and will continue after he has passed away for "Our echoes roll from soul to soul, and grow forever and forever."

Rev. Dr. Stewart is a native of Pennsylvania, his birth having occurred at Jenkintown, near Philadelphia, in Montgomery county, on the 30th of December, 1824. His boyhood was spent there and his early education was obtained in the Abington Friends' school. Subsequently he entered the Lawrenceville Classical and Commercial High School, of New Jersey, completing his course in that institution in September, 1842, and

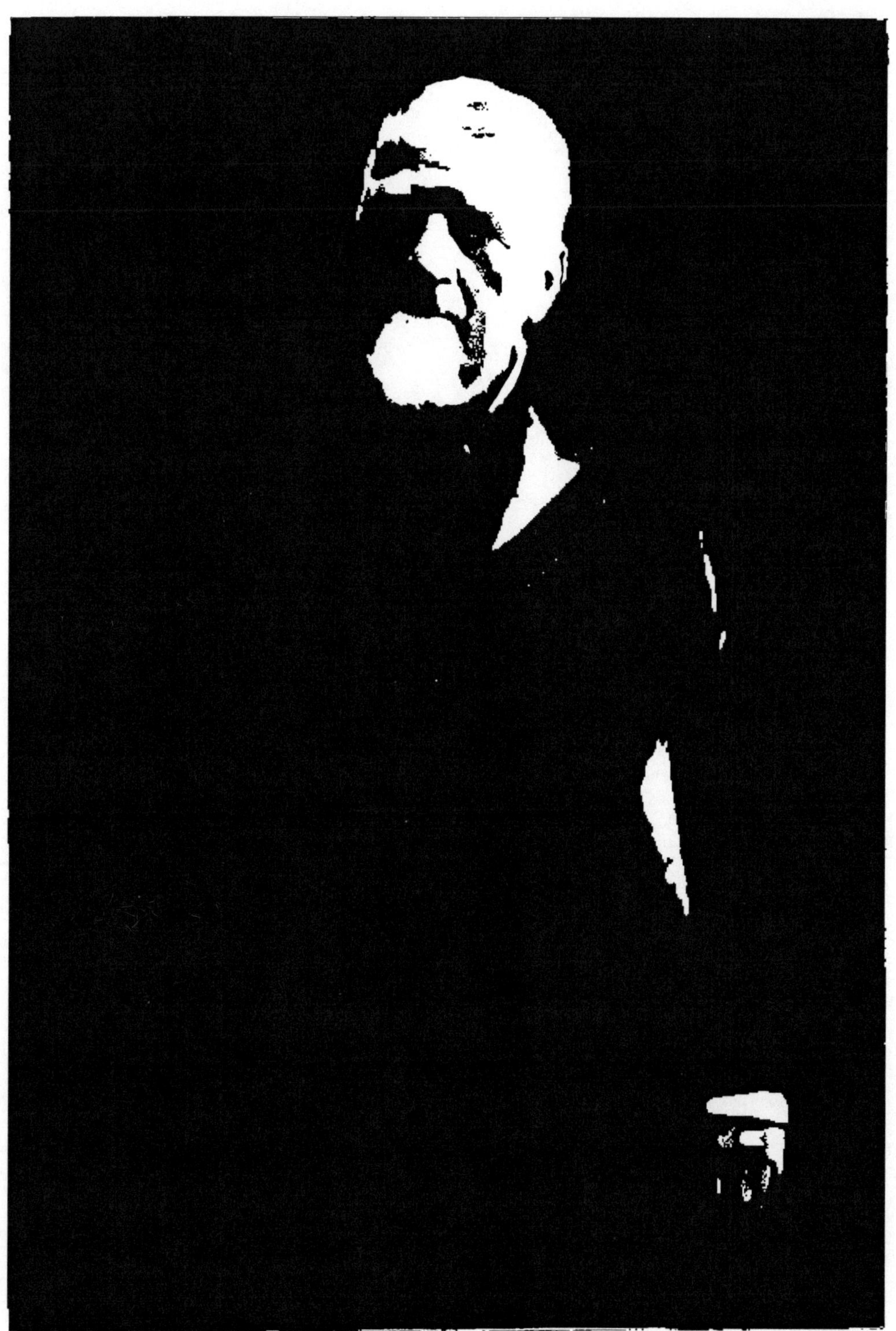

REV. GEORGE D. STEWART

is now one of the oldest living graduates of that famous institution of learning. He is likewise a graduate of Lafayette College, at Easton, Pennsylvania, of the class of 1845, and his literary training was supplemented by preparation for the ministry as a student in Princeton Theological Seminary, where he completed his studies in April, 1849. The previous year he had been licensed to preach and on leaving the seminary he immediately entered upon the active work of the ministry his first charge being a missionary field at Conquest, Cayuga county, New York, October, 1849, where he remained for two years. While there, in April, 1850, he was ordained by the Presbytery of Steuben, Synod of Western New York, at Port Byron. He then accepted a call from the First Presbyterian church of Bath, New York, where he labored as pastor of that church for eight years.

In the fall of 1859, Rev. Dr. Stewart came to Iowa to seek a drier climate for throat trouble, accepting the charge of the missionary circuit comprising West Point, Sharon, Pilot Grove, Primrose, Dover and Franklin in Lee county, Iowa. He continued that work for four and a half years. The minister, whose pastoral duties are now confined within a small circuit owing to the condensed population of our towns and cities, little realizes the arduous labors that devolve upon the pioneer minister, who braved the storms of winter and the hot summer's sun in order to carry the message of salvation into frontier districts, to proclaim the glad tidings of great joy in pioneer homes or to speak words of consolation and sympathy at the death bed. With marked consecration to his chosen field of labor, putting forth every effort in his power to bring the world into harmony with divine teachings and principles, Dr. Stewart rode for miles on horseback over a country where homes were widely scattered and where the journey was ofttimes fraught with danger as well as discomfort. His visits were eagerly welcomed and to this day his name is lovingly spoken in many a household, which he visited in pioneer times.

His next charge was the First Presbyterian church at Burlington, Iowa, where he remained for six and a half years, meeting with marked success and then accepted a call from the First Presbyterian church at Omaha, Nebraska, where he labored for a similar period, trebling the church membership. In June, 1872, the honorary degree of Doctor of Divinity was conferred on him by Hanover College, Indiana. In 1877 he was called to the pastorate of the Union Presbyterian church at Fort Madison, Iowa, entering on his duties on the 1st of April, of that year, and remained as pastor until January 1, 1904, when after a continuous service of twenty-seven years he resigned and is now leading a retired life. Fifty-five years he has given to the work of the ministry and his labors have not been denied the full harvest nor the aftermath. Every church with which he was connected made substantial progress, growing in spiritual growth and extending the various church activities. Under his pastorate the present house of worship at West Point was erected and the church edifice at Fort Madison was also built. Another material evidence of his labors is shown in the cemetery and church grounds at Sharon. The land was purchased through his instrumentality and the church located there. Upon the cemetery a large sum of money has been expended, amounting probably to about $85,000 the gift of the Seeley family according to the expressed wish of the youngest son and brother, George Seeley, and although this is a country cemetery the cities of the state can display no more beautiful resting place for the dead. The church at Primrose is also the result of the labors of Dr. Stewart, the First Presbyterian minister who preached there. Under his careful guidance and consecrated labors his congregations have developed a spiritual strength that has been a most potent element for good in the various communities mentioned. At length after more than a half century's active connection with the ministry, of which forty-five years have been passed in Iowa, and Nebraska, Rev. Dr. Stewart was honorably retired by his presbytery, at his own request. He still officiates occasionally, however, in the pulpit and at funerals and at weddings in response to the demands of those who have come to love him and desire his ministerial services on these sacred occasions.

Dr. Stewart was married in Fort Madison, Iowa, October 4, 1864, to Miss Emily Stewart Walker, the eldest daughter of Dr. J. C. Walker, one of the pioneers of this city who came to Lee county in 1836. Their union was blessed with one son and three daughters: George B., who is a practicing attorney of Fort Madison; Helen Walker, who died at Omaha, Nebraska, at the age of five years, her remains being interred in the city cemetery at Fort Madison; Anna residing with her parents in this city; and Miriam, now the wife of T. P. Hollowell, Jr., of Fort Madison. Mrs. Stewart's parents, grandmother and great-grandfather were pioneers of Lee county, coming to Lee county, May, 1834. The maternal grandmother of Mrs. Stewart was Mrs. Emily Stewart, widow of Dr. Abram Stewart, who was assistant surgeon in the United States army, and was stationed at Jefferson Barracks, St. Louis, Missouri, as early as 1809. He resigned his position in the army to enter upon the private practice of medicine in and near St. Louis, making his home at Florissant, a suburb of that city. There upon the 20th of January, 1820, Martha Maria Stewart, the mother of Mrs. George D. Stewart, was born. Dr. Joel Calvin Walker, the father of Mrs. George D. Stewart, was born in Springfield, Ohio, February 7, 1812, his parents having removed to that city from Rockbridge county, Virginia. He studied medicine in Circleville, Ohio, and afterward attended lectures in Jefferson Medical College, at Philadelphia. For a number of years he practiced his chosen profession and then retired. He held a number of the leading local offices in Lee county, Iowa, and was a prominent and influential citizen here, making his home in Fort Madison until 1888, when he passed away at the age of seventy-six years. His widow still resides in Fort Madison. The Union Presbyterian church of Fort Madison was organized in 1838 with a charter membership of seventeen and seven of this number were members of the Walker and Stewart families. Mrs. George D. Stewart was born in Fort Madison, Iowa, and acquired her early education in the private schools and public schools of Fort Madison, and in Denmark Academy, in Lee county, the oldest incorporated educational institution of the state. She afterward attended for three years, the Female Seminary at Steubenville, Ohio, where she was graduated with the class of 1860. She has been a most able, helpful and sympathetic assistant to her husband in all of his work and throughout Lee county the names of Dr. and Mrs. George D. Stewart are revered. Nature bestowed upon them many of her rare gifts. They possess minds of broad compass and industry that have brought forth and developed the talents which they received. Their humanitarian spirit and kindly sympathy have been continually manifest in their relations to their fellowmen and have made them honored and respected wherever they have gone.

Dr. and Mrs. Stewart spent three of the early months of 1904 at San Diego and Los Angeles, California, with great pleasure and profit to health. While this volume is passing through the press, they are arranging for a trip to the Southern Mediterranean in "the Bible Student's Cruize," on the White Star steamer, "Arabic." If permitted to carry out their purpose, they will visit Southern Spain, Gibralter, Algiers, Walta, Athens, Constantinople, Asia Minor, Palestine, Egypt, Italy, England and Scotland. This trip which Dr. Stewart has long desired to make will be a suitable and very pleasant conclusion to his many years of labor, and will show that as he enters his eighty-first year sufficient health, energy and courage remain to enable him to undertake, with Mrs. Stewart's companionship, a journey over the Atlantic ocean of 15,000 miles and which will take them from the center of this continent to visit the shores of Europe, Asia and Africa.

HON. C. A. KENNEDY.

Among the better known and most successful of the younger business men of Lee county, Iowa, is Hon. C. A. Kennedy, of Montrose, a native of that village, where his birth occurred March 24, 1869. He is the son of William Kennedy, who was born in the year 1830 in County Galway, Ireland, and the father of our subject on coming to America first located at Ogdensburg, New York, whence he removed to Keokuk, Iowa, and there in 1856 he married Miss Maria Williams, who was born in Dublin, Ireland, December 13, 1837, and on the death of her parents accompanied an aunt to the United States, living for a number of years in the State of New York and later removing to Keokuk, where she met Mr. Kennedy. William Kennedy, who learned in his native land the trade of shoemaking, worked in a shoe shop for a time in Keokuk, but in 1860 removed to Montrose, where he worked as a shoemaker until his death, which occurred June 22, 1885. He was a faithful member of the Episcopal church and fraternally was connected with the Masonic order and with the Independent Order of Odd Fellows, while his political allegiance was given to the Republican party, through which he took an active part in public affairs, being elected to membership in the municipal council and board of education. Mr. and Mrs. Kennedy were the parents of eight sons and daughters, as follows: John, now postmaster of Montrose, who married Miss Marjoie Ballou and has two children, Katherine and Margaret; William, who is engaged in the lumber business at Doty, Washington; Eva, who died in December, 1902, was the wife of N. J. Chapman, of Everett, Washington, and is survived by three children, George, Fred and Helen; Jennie, wife of F. D. Butzer, of Bucoda, Washington; C. A., the subject of this review; George, who is superintendent of the public schools of Montrose; Anna and Lilly.

For his formal education Hon. C. A. Kennedy is indebted to the public schools, but as the death of his father occurred when he was but fourteen years of age, and as this event necessitated his leaving school, he owes the extraordinary development of his mental powers to intelligent observation and the reading of good literature, combined with a constant interest in current affairs, as to which he keeps himself thoroughly informed. Since his fourteenth year he has been successfully engaged in the nursery business in association with his brother, John Kennedy, the firm being Kennedy Brothers, and they are proprietors of the Eagle Nursery, which they purchased in 1885 of H. M. Crouse, who had established the enterprise fifteen years previous to that date. Twenty-five to seventy-five men are employed during the spring and autumn, and Mr. Kennedy travels extensively in order to keep in touch with the work of similar establishments in other states, introducing all modern ideas as rapidly as it is possible to demonstrate their utility and availability. By these energetic and progressive methods a very large and constantly growing business has been built up, covering a very wide extent of territory and supplying dealers who are located at very great distances, even as far, in some cases, as the State of South Dakota, where the products of the Eagle Nursery are well known and highly appreciated. In addition, Mr. Kennedy personally owns the twelve-acre tract on which is located the old family home, where he resides with his invalid mother, and he occupies the position of assistant postmaster of Montrose, giving his attention to the office in the absence of his brother John, whose profession, that of the law, frequently requires his presence at other points.

Mr. Kennedy has always been active in local politics, serving the Republican party as chairman of its county committee at one time and also in various other capacities in which his energy and unwavering loyalty have been important factors in its success, for he is possessed of practical ability of an unusual order. He enjoys vast popularity in his own community and throughout Lee county, and is known to all the leading statesmen of Iowa as a man whose honorable record makes him a power in the state's affairs. He served as mayor of Montrose before he was twenty-one years of age, being then probably the youngest man to hold that office in the history of the United States, and a fact no less remarkable, his administration was equal in efficiency to that of many a more experienced man, and he was re-elected. He was elected city recorder and to many minor offices, and was treasurer of the board of education for many years. In the year 1903 he became a candidate for the Iowa legislature, and such is the esteem in which he is universally held by his fellow citizens that although his party in Lee county is normally in the minority, he overcame the usual large majority of his opponents, and was triumphantly elected, thus securing entrance into what his friends freely predict will prove new and still greater fields of honor and usefulness. Mr. Kennedy has fraternal connections with the order of the Knights of Pythias and with the Modern Woodmen of America, while his mother and four sisters are members of the order of the Eastern Star, of which Mrs. Kennedy has been Worthy Matron in the Montrose lodge. The career of Hon. C. A. Kennedy is one that should be full of inspiration for all young men, especially for those who depend for advancement upon their own efforts and devotion to duty.

SABERT M. CASEY.

Sabert M. Casey, occupying a prominent position at the bar and in public regard, was born at Sigourney, Keokuk county, Iowa, on the 28th of August, 1858, a son of Judge Joseph M. and Sarah J. Casey, who was only three years of age when brought by his parents to Fort Madison, where he continuously made his home up to the time of his demise. He arrived in the city about the hour that Fort Sumter was fired upon. His primary education was acquired in the public schools of Fort Madison and he was a member of the first graduating class in the high school. Subsequently he entered Fort Madison Academy and when his literary course was finished he began preparation for the bar as a student in the law office of Casey & Hobbs, the senior partner being his father, who carefully directed his reading and his thorough mastery of the principles of jurisprudence enabled him to successfully pass an examination that secured his admission to the bar on the 1st of November, 1879. On the 1st of May, following, he entered into partnership with his father under the firm style of Casey & Casey and this business relation was maintained until the elevation of Judge Casey to the bench in 1886. For about two years thereafter Sabert Casey was alone, but in 1888 entered into a partnership, whereby the firm of Casey & Stewart was formed. Its existence continued up to the time of Mr. Casey's death and he ranked as one of the leading representatives of the legal fraternity of Fort Madison. For more than twenty-three years he was identified with the legal profession for which by natural attributes and thorough preparation and research he soon proved his fitness. Realizing that in this calling more than in almost any other success depends upon the force of the individual and that an unusual degree of keenness, power of analyzation and logical summarizing of the chief points in a case are essential, he spurred himself on in the attainment of the supremacy which he enjoyed. His devotion to his client's interests was proverbial and yet he never forgot that he owed a higher allegiance to the majesty of the law. He prepared his cases with great fairness and exactness and a felicity and clearness in expression in the presentation of his case enabled him to make a deep impression upon the minds of his auditors.

Mr. Casey was actively concerned in matters of public affairs and in fact a deeper or more helpful interest in community affairs. He was opposed to misrule in municipal interests, favored reform and progress and at all times gave hearty cooperation to those movements which tend toward public good. In politics a Democrat, he held the office of city clerk in Fort Madison for several years, beginning in March, 1881. He was a candidate for congress in 1896, but could not overcome the strong Republican majority, although he polled a large and complimentary vote. For six years he was a member of the school board and the cause of education has materially advanced by his unremitting efforts in behalf of the schools. For several years prior to his death he was a member of the board of trustees and the president of the Cattermole Memorial Library. He was distinctively a man of affairs and the people acknowledged his ability and worth by electing him as the leading spirit in any movement that tended toward the advancement of the city, morally and socially. He was, however, compelled to refuse many positions of honor tendered him because his large law practice would not permit him to give the necessary time. However, to his enterprise and public-spirit are largely due the Cattermole library and the lecture courses as well as many other enterprises of literary merit and profit. He had the entire respect and esteem of his community and his friends recognized in him the possession of many sterling traits of character.

Socially Mr. Casey was a Knight Templar, belonging to Delta Commandery, No. 51, Knights Templar; the Mystic Shrine and the Order of the Eastern Star, acting as grand patron of Iowa in the last named for one year, and he belonged to Claypoole Lodge, No. 13, Free and Accepted Masons, and to Potowonok Chapter, No. 28, Royal Arch Masons. He was likewise a member of the Independent Order of Odd Fellows; the Knights of Pythias fraternity; Fort Madison Lodge, No. 347, Benevolent and Protective Order of Elks; the Modern Woodmen of America and others. He manifested in his life the beneficent, helpful and brotherly spirit which is the basic element of these various organizations. At his death which occurred on the 20th of August, 1903, resolutions of respect and sympathy were passed by many societies of which he was an honored representative. Meetings were held by the bar associations of both Keokuk and Fort Madison, at which the following resolution was reported and unanimously adopted:

"Whereas, the grim reaper death has again invaded our ranks and removed from among us our late brother and associate Sabert M. Casey, for many years a prominent, high-minded and exemplary member of our profession, therefore, we, the members of the bar at Fort Madison in conjunction with the bar at Keokuk, in joint meeting assembled at the court house at Fort Madison, Iowa, as expressive of our sentiments and feelings on the sad event do hereby adopt the following resolutions:

"Resolved, That we deeply mourn the death of our friend, associate and brother member of the Lee County Bar; that we recognize and bear testimony to his moral, upright life, his untiring activity and zeal as a citizen in all public affairs for the welfare of this city and county, his uniformly kindly disposition to all and especially to his associates in his profession.

"Resolved, That in his death our profession has lost a member who from his early manhood was prominent in our ranks; that our city has lost an active and progressive worker in its higher interests; that the county has lost one whom the people delighted to honor; and the great public has lost one who always sympathized with its best interests, who was active and efficient in the conduct of its affairs, and whose labors were made all the more effective by reason of his strong and noble character, his kind and charitable disposition and his willingness at all times to expend his strength and means for the public and private welfare of others."

No one is heard to speak of Sabert M. Casey except in terms of praise for in all life's relations he commanded the highest confidence. He used his power to the best ability and possessed laudable ambition, unfaltering courage and strong determination and in his calling he won success that ranked him with the leading members of the Iowa bar. He had a wide acquaintance in legal circles through the state and the Burlington Gazette said of him: "In the death of Mr. Casey the profession loses one of its brightest ornaments, the district one of its best citizens and the community in which he lived one of its most honored members. All who had the pleasure of his acquaintance knew him only to honor and respect him. He was a most courteous and agreeable companion, an intelligent and interesting associate and withal a highly agreeable and entertaining member of any society where his presence was met. Sabert M. Casey's memory will long be cherished and honored by those who knew him in this part of the state, because he was always courteous, and no one parted with his company without feeling that his association had cast a pleasant shadow upon the surroundings."

There is no standard by which man may be better judged than by the concensus of public opinion and all unite in bearing testimony to the lofty character, high principles and manly conduct of Sabert M. Casey. One who knew him long said of him: "We believe we are truthful in saying that the announcement of the death of no other man in Lee county would be received with the general sorrow that has been brought by the announcement of the passing away of Hon. Sabert M. Casey. We believe also that we are truthful in saying that there does not live in the broad State of Iowa a better man than was he. An intimate friendship with him for twenty-five years had endeared him to the writer as a brother. During these years we observed him in all manner of trying circumstances, especially in a political way and in conduct of legal battles where sometimes unfairness characterized those opposing him; and where others would have chafed and fumed and fretted and vented their ire or disgust in loud or angry words, he ever preserved a calm demeanor and calm, dispassionate judgment and speech—always permeated with charity for those offending. Resourceful and tactful, forceful and kind, he won the highest esteem of his countless friends. Socially he was a charming companion, well read, bright and witty—in business and profession as fair as the evenly balanced scales of justice. His life was as near faultless as it is possible for mortal man to live—and his fellowmen knew and appreciate it. His memory will linger long with them. May he rest in the utmost peace and may the fullest joys of whatsoever may come after this life be his."

WILLIAM R. TIMPE.

In this age of energy and success, when men of merit, industry and brains are irresistibly pushing their way to the front, those who by their own individual efforts have won favor and fortune may with propriety claim recognition. Mr. Timpe is an excellent representative of this class. His position in the business world is that of senior member of the firm of Timpe & Schroeder, leading dry goods and carpet dealers of Fort Madison. He was born in West Point township, Lee county, Iowa, September 4, 1859, and is the son of Jacob F. and Henrietta (Schultz) Timpe. Jacob F. was born in the village of East Lynn, province of Brunswick, Germany, January 18, 1824. The mother was a native of the same province, the date of her birth being March 26, 1823.

Jacob F. Timpe, in search of larger opportunities for self-advancement, emigrated from Germany in 1848, and came to Lee county, where he secured employment on a farm. The ordinary rewards of labor at that time were small, and the first wages he received were at the rate of five dollars per month. However, his work afforded him an opportunity to become acquainted with the business of farming and to familiarize himself with the language of the country which was to be the scene of his life and efforts. For six years he continued in this employment, and at the end of that time he had accumulated sufficient money to enable him to rent a farm to make an independent start in life, he having in the meantime married Miss Schultz, who had also come to this county directly from her native land. He rented a farm for eight years, and then purchased 120 acres in Pleasant Ridge township. This he continued to occupy and to increase by further purchases until, at the time of his death, June 12, 1902, he owned 900 acres, having, by care and untiring industry, became one of the most prosperous residents of that section. In politics he was a lifelong Democrat, although a firm believer in gold as the basis of our national currency, casting his ballot for Mr. Mc-

R. TIMPE

Kinley in 1896, and was honored by election to a number of township offices. He was one of the early members of the local congregation of the Lutheran church, and was a member of the building committee of the Cumberland Presbyterian church in his township. The wife and mother still resides on the old home farm in Pleasant Ridge township. To them were born six children. Four survive, and of these the subject of this sketch is the fourth, the others being Caroline; Sophia, wife of Isaiah Hosier, of Pleasant Ridge, and George S., who lives on the home farm.

William R. Timpe was educated in the common schools of Pleasant Ridge township and in Johnson's Business College at Fort Madison, after which he returned to the farm, and there remained until he was placed in charge of a business which came to his father through the failure of a man whom he had befriended in a financial way. Mr. Timpe assumed charge in 1886, and after six months he bought the store of his father. He continued the business in Fort Madison with great success for a number of years, and after several times changing to larger quarters he erected a fine two-story brick building in 1888 at No 731 Second street. The structure, the dimensions of which are 25x100 feet, is devoted exclusively to the business, and here he conducts the largest dry goods store in the city. In 1889 he admitted Henry L. Schroeder as a partner, the style of the firm being Timpe and Schroeder. By his own unaided effort Mr. Timpe built up a large and very successful business—one of the monumental institutions of Fort Madison—and of this achievement he has good reason to be proud.

Fraternally Mr. Timpe holds membership in Stella Lodge, Free and Accepted Masons; Potowonok Chapter, Royal Arch Masons, and in the local lodge of Benevolent and Protective Order of Elks. In politics he gives his support to the Republican party.

In 1891 he was married to Miss Eveline Baldwin, daughter of Isaac Baldwin, of Princeton, Illinois. They are members of the Episcopal church, of which Mr. Timpe is a vestryman.

In matters pertaining to the general good Mr. Timpe has always been progressive. At the same time he has so conducted his business affairs that they have returned to him an excellent financial reward. At once conservative and alert to the call of opportunity, he is today numbered among the prosperous citizens of Lee county, as well as one whose character should be an inspiration to all younger men who have the ambition to rise to heights of success and honor.

HON. JOSEPH MONTGOMERY CASEY.

Hon. Joseph Montgomery Casey, three times elected district judge of the first judicial district of Iowa, was a prominent representative of the judiciary of the state, but while his course upon the bench reflected credit and honor upon the district which honored him, it was his charming personality, his kindly spirit and abiding geniality that won him the friendship or love of all with whom he came in contact and causes his memory to be cherished by those with whom he was associated. He was descended from an old and distinguished southern family and the name figures in connection with the bench and bar of Kentucky. His grandfather, Col. William Casey, a native of Frederick county, Virginia, became a resident of Kentucky in the winter of 1779-80 and became one of the founders of Logan Station, near the present town of Stanford. His was a typical pioneer experience and he performed an important part in reclaiming the state from the domain of the Indian and converting it to uses of civilization. In the spring of 1791 he organized a party for colonization purposes and went down Green river to its mouth. Not far distant a settlement was made and though considerable trouble was experienced because of Indian attacks, the brave pioneer people maintained their homes in the wilderness and planted the seeds of present progress and prosperity. Colonel Casey was one of the most influential residents of his part of the state and not only aided in molding public affairs in his district, but also assisted in forming the policy of the state. He was elected by a large majority a delegate to remodel the constitution of Kentucky in 1799 and was also chosen to other important positions. He died at an advanced age.

Green Casey, only son of Colonel Casey, who, however, had several daughters, was the first white child born in Adair county, Kentucky, and was reared amid pioneer environment. He married Miss Jane Patterson, a native of Rockingham county, Virginia, and in 1836 they became residents of Sangamon county, Illinois. Not long afterward, visiting Iowa, then a territory, he secured a claim adjoining the tract on which the town of West Point was afterward built. He then returned, sold his Illinois home and was making preparations to become a resident of Iowa when his death occurred. Soon afterward, however, his widow carried out his plans of establishing the family home in West Point and with four of her children settled upon the land which her husband had secured. There she supervised the improvement of the farm and continued to make it her home until her death. Six children were born unto Green and Jane (Patterson) Casey, five of whom reached years of maturity: John A., who died in Kansas; Mary A., of this county; Margaret J., who became the wife of Albert U. Stone and died in Pekin, Illinois; William P., who died in Crawford county, Kansas, and Joseph M.

Joseph M. Casey was born in Adair county, Kentucky, March 25, 1827, and was therefore a young lad at the time of the removal to Illinois, while at the age of eleven years he came to Lee county. He suffered from ill health in his youth but managed to secure a good education, his public school course being supplemented by study in the academy at West Point where he was under the instruction of a celebrated Presbyterian clergyman, Rev. John Mark Fulton. Early forming a resolution to make the practice of law his life work, he became a law student with Judge John F. Finney as his preceptor, and also pursued his reading under the direction of Cyrus Walker, one of the ablest jurists of Illinois. His close application and strong mentality enabled him to readily master the principles of jurisprudence and secured his admission to the bar when he was but twenty years of age.

Visiting Keokuk county in search of a favorable location, Judge Casey was urged by his many friends to become a resident of Lancaster, then the county seat, and he was offered the position of prosecuting attorney. Then visiting Lee county and making arrangements for his removal to Keokuk county, he was soon installed in an office in Lancaster, and, as promised received election to the position of prosecuting attorney, in which capacity he served, by re-election, for about six years. His election to the position of county judge followed soon after the removal of the county seat to Sigourney, he became a resident of that place and remained upon the bench until April, 1861, his decisions being strictly fair and impartial and based upon a comprehensive understanding of legal principles so that he won high encomiums from the members of the bar. He had also become interested in journalism, as an editor of the Iowa Democrat, but when two years had passed, desirous of making Fort Madison his permanent home, he removed to this city, severing his connection with the journalistic and legal interests of Keokuk county. He had won success as a leading and gifted lawyer and the circle of his friends in that county had become an extensive one. Locating in Fort Madison, because of the lack of legal business, occasioned by the Civil War, he became editor of the Fort Madison Plaindealer, but when three years had passed, he withdrew from the field of journalism in order to devote his entire attention to his legal practice, which grew in volume and importance until he was called to the bench and retired from general practice. His knowledge of the law and experience in practice soon won him a leading position in the ranks of the legal fraternity. His reputation at the bar was won through earnest, honest labor and his standing at the bar was a merited tribute to his ability. He soon secured a large practice and his careful preparation of cases was supplemented by a power of argument and a forceful presentation of his points in the courtroom so that he never failed to impress court or jury and seldom failed to gain the verdict desired. Higher honors in his profession awaited him, for in 1886 he was elected to the bench of the first judicial district of Iowa, and after a four years' term was re-elected in 1890 and again in 1894, having just entered upon his third term when called from the duties of active life. On the bench as at the bar he won marked distinction. A man of unimpeachable character, of unusual intellectual endowments, with a thorough understanding of the law, patience, urbanity and industry, he took to the bench the very highest qualifications for the office, and his record as a judge was in harmony with his record as a man and lawyer, distinguished by unswerving integrity and a masterful grasp of every problem which presented itself for solution.

Casting his first presidential vote for General Cass Judge Casey remained an inflexible supporter of the Democratic party, but accorded to all the rights which he reserved to himself, of forming an unbiased personal opinion upon all questions affecting the state and national welfare, as well as concerns of public policy and expediency in his community. He enjoyed the highest confidence and esteem of those who differed from him politically, numbering many of his warmest friends among the adherents of the Republican party. In community affairs a leader, he wielded a wide and beneficial influence, and while serving as mayor of the city, to which office he was twice elected, he gave a practical, business-like and progressive administration. He was called to represent his district in the house of representatives in the eighteenth general assembly of Iowa and several years later was elected state senator. His friendship for the public-school system was demonstrated during his four years' service as president of the board of education. He was the champion of many progressive measures and his interest in his city was of so practical a character that its benefits are yet felt.

A member of the Masonic fraternity Judge Casey's connection was with Claypool Lodge, No. 13, Free and Accepted Masons; Potowonok Chapter, No. 28, Royal Arch Masons; Delta Commandery, No. 51, Knights Templar. He also belonged to Fort Madison Lodge, No. 157, Independent Order of Odd Fellows, and was honored with various offices in these different organizations.

In 1854 Judge Casey was married to Mrs. Sarah Jane Ward Hollingsworth, who was born in Wayne county, Ohio, in 1832, a daughter of Thomas and Jane Ward. In 1850 she became the wife of Mr. Hollingsworth, who died the following year, and the son of that marriage, Albert E., has always been known in Fort Madison by his step-father's name. Five children were born to them, of whom one died in infancy, the others being: Sabert M.; Belle V., wife of William S. Hamilton; Joseph M. and Sarah.

Judge Casey died suddenly February 9, 1895, having just entered upon his third term as judge of the first judicial district. Perhaps no better estimate of his character can be given than that contained in the journals of that date, one of which said: "Judge Casey was a man among men and his friends were numbered only by the limit of his acquaintance. He was big hearted, kind to everyone, pleasant in conversation and was loved by all. He was ever affable and obliging. As an attorney his opinions were highly valued. His aim has always been to put forth his best efforts for his clients and was ever opposed to the practice of dishonesty or deception for the winning of a case when it could not be won on its merits. In fact he was a man of principle. As a judge he was always fair and unbiased in his opinions and possessed rare legal ability. He was probably the greatest brain worker in the state of Iowa. Always at his office in the early morning he read his newspaper and kept well in touch with the doings of the world through that medium and would then sit for hours at a time looking up decisions and references or reading law and seemed to be wholly taken up with his profession. He was a deep reasoner; in argument forcible in expression, convincing in tone and impressive in manner. His sudden death is a severe loss to his family and friends, his constituency of the district, the bar of the state and the public in general."

S. T. Marshall, long his friend and admirer, knowing almost his every thought, expressed the following sentiment: "Judge Casey had marked virtues inherent in his nature. He was all merciful and a worshiper of truth and right. The judge adopted that grand Roman motto in all his practice, 'prodesse quam conspici' (to improve rather than be seen) He loved not display and had a contempt for those who tried to pass for more than they were worth. His integrity could not be shaken and his innate love of honesty and truth was proverbial and universally known."

Faultless in honor, fearless in conduct, stainless in reputation,—such was his life record. His scholarly attainments, his statesmanship, his reliable judgment and his charming powers of conversation would have enabled him to ably fill and grace any position, however exalted, and he was no less honored in public than loved in private life.

HON. ANDREW J. DIMOND.

Hon. Andrew J. Dimond, mayor of the City of Keokuk and proprietor of the Keokuk Milling Company, is a fair representative of the more progressive business element of Lee county. Mr. Dimond was born at Louisville, Kentucky, December 6, 1845, the son of John and Elizabeth (Rudy) Dimond. The father was born in Ireland, and came to Kentucky as a young man. Being a shoemaker by trade, he conducted a shoe business in Louisville for a number of years. Elizabeth Rudy Dimond was born in Pennsylvania, and removed when young with her parents to Maysville, Kentucky.

In 1854 the father of our subject sold his business in Louisville, and brought his family to Keokuk, where he continued in the shoe business until 1885, becoming one of the leading shoe dealers of the city. He died in February, 1893. The death of the mother occurred in May, 1897. They reared a family of seven children.

Andrew J. Dimond received his education in the public schools, and while growing to years of maturity gained some knowledge of business in connection with the enterprise conducted by his father. At the early age of nineteen years he volunteered for the service of his country in her struggle for the suppression of rebellion, enlisting in Company C of the Forty-fifth Iowa Volunteer Infantry in April, 1864. His regiment formed part of the Sixteenth army corps under General Smith, and was sent to Tennessee and Mississippi, where the young soldier served until the end of the war and was honorably discharged.

His military service ended, Mr. Dimond formed a partnership with his father, and they conducted a shoe business on Main street in Keokuk. By his energy, tact and talents he assisted in building up a very extensive volume of business. This enterprise they continued to conduct, with signal success, until 1885, when they sold it, and in 1887 Mr. Dimond bought what was then the Eagle Mills, changing the name to the

Dimond Mills. The firm is now known as the Keokuk Milling Company, of which he and his son are proprietors, he having taken his son into partnership in 1889. Since acquiring the business he has thoroughly remodeled the mills, installing the most improved equipment, modern in every respect, and the product has become celebrated throughout a very extensive territory as of superior excellence. The details of the work have his personal attention and supervision to a large extent, and he has cause to feel pride in what he has accomplished. Special lines manufactured are table meal, brewer's grits and meal, Pearl hominy and graham flour. The firm are also dealers in hay and feed, and Mr. Dimond holds real-estate interests in the city.

In his fraternal relations Mr. Dimond is a member of Puckechetuck Lodge, No. 43, Independent Order of Odd Fellows, of which he is Past Grand and trustee, and also a member of Puckechetuck Encampment, No. 7, Independent Order of Odd Fellows. He has been through the chairs, and has served as delegate to the Grand Lodge of the state. In the Grand Army of the Republic he is a member of Torrence Post of Keokuk.

In December, 1867, Mr. Dimond was married to Miss Carrie T. Kaltwasser, who was born in Germany and with her parents, Mr. and Mrs. William Kaltwasser, came to America when two years of age. They have two sons and one daughter, as follows: Harry C., who is associated with his father in business; Dr. Charles A., physician and surgeon of Keokuk, and Elizabeth C. The family residence is a commodious and handsome structure erected by Mr. Dimond at 718 High street.

Mr. Dimond has never been an aspirant for public office, but by reason of the general favor with which he is regarded and on account of the ability displayed in the conduct of his private affairs, he was elected in 1903 mayor of the city of Keokuk, and has proved easily equal to the trust, giving a strong and efficient administration. Among his official acts was the appointment of the first water commission, which has resulted in considerable improvement in the municipal water supply. He is a man of pleasing and genial presence, and enjoys wide popularity, while at the same time the substantial nature of his connection with the city's material interests has tended to inspire confidence and respect.

HON. JAMES A. JORDAN.

As the architect of his own fortunes Hon. James A. Jordan, mayor of the city of Fort Madison, Iowa, has builded wisely and well, and his efforts, too, have been of material benefit to the city. As a servant of the public and through his position as superintendent of the Iowa Farming Tool Company he has contributed largely to the improvement of Fort Madison, and while promoting individual prosperity has also advanced the general welfare. Practical in all he does, far-sighted and enterprising in his quick recognition of opportunity, he has used time, talent and means to the best advantage. A man of purpose, upright in intent and honorable in contact, his popularity is of the kind that comes to such a man naturally and unsought. He was born at Prattsville, Greene county, New York, May 18, 1849, and is the son of William R. and Dolly (Weismer) Jordan. William Jordan was in business in Prattsville for a number of years, being by trade a tailor. He later removed to Leonardsville, Madison county, New York, and there rounded out the full measure of a worthy and useful life, his lamented death occurring in 1871. There also passed away his helpmeet and companion, the mother of our subject, in the year 1880. She was born at Delhi, New York, the daughter of Walter Weismer, of that place.

James A. Jordan was educated at Leonardsville and the academy at West Winfield, and immediately upon the conclusion of his schooling entered the fork and hoe shop which was in operation at that time in Leonardsville, and, by hard and painstaking toil as a practical workman, attained a thorough mastery of the business of manufacturing the tools and implements of agriculture. He pursued the same line of endeavor for a time at Naugatuck, Connecticut, his services having been secured by the Tuttle Manufacturing Company of that place, and in 1875 he came west to the city of his adoption, taking employment as a foreman for the Iowa Farming Tool Company. With this company he has remained continuously for thirty years, and the proof of his ability and high integrity is that he has risen by merit alone to his present position. In 1894 he was also made superintendent of the company which manufactures farming tools at the state penitentiary, and in this capacity he has direction of the work of 140 to 200 men, this being in addition to his other duties. A number of other business enterprises have also profited by the impetus of his favor and substantial aid.

In politics Hon. James A. Jordan gives his allegiance to the Democracy. Beginning in 1891 he served his ward, the second, in the city council for three terms of two years each, being an active and zealous member of several important committees, and it was during this period that many of the improvements which now grace the city were consummated. In 1897 he received the highest honor within the gift of his city, that of the office of mayor, and his eminently business-like administration led to his renomination in 1899, at which time, however, he was defeated, but was again elected in 1903. The electric lighting, steam hauling and interurban railway franchises have all been granted during his term of office. Both his administrations have been notable in the history of Fort Madison.

In Claypoole Lodge No. 13, Free and Acepted Masons, and in Potowonok Chapter No. 28, Royal Arch Masons, Mr. Jordan has filled positions of honor and responsibility, and is also a member of the Benevolent and Protective Order of Elks.

On August 23, 1887, he married Miss Susanna R. Wild, a daughter of Walter Wild and a member of one of the older families of Fort Madison. They occupy the beautiful residence erected by Mr. Jordan at No. 608 Third street.

The career of Mr. Jordan illustrates

most happily the truth that the man who possesses the right qualities of mind and heart needs nothing but his own merit to carry him to success in the business world, and that one so gifted may confer great and lasting benefit in shaping the destinies of his community. And of him, as of few others, it may be said that had he never risen to the position which he now occupies, he would still be a man of marked and recognized distinction.

JOHN LACHMANN.

John Lachmann, a prominent farmer residing on the southeast quarter of section 18, Green Bay township, was born December 16, 1859, in Jefferson township, Lee county, and is the son of William H. Grubb. The mother and father of Mr. Lachmann died when he was but an infant, and when he was two years of age was adopted, though not formally, by Carl and Louise V. (Frank) Lachmann, whose home was in Green Bay township. As they had no children of their own, he continued a member of their household until his marriage. Learning after he had attained his majority that he possessed no legal right to bear their name of "Lachmann," he made application to the Circuit Court of Lee county for the privilege, which was granted.

Mr. Lachmann's foster father, Carl Lachmann, was born September 2, 1818, in Silesia, Prussia, and Mrs. Lachmann was a native of Saxony, near Leipzig, the date of her birth being September 11, 1830. They became acquainted in the State of New York, where both resided for a time, but were married in Chicago, coming then to Iowa. Carl Lachmann was a self-made man, having won his own way in the world. He was of rather retiring disposition, but possessed ability, and was respected by all. Both were members of the Lutheran church.

As a boy, our subject received a good education in the public schools, and later he spent three terms in a German private school. During his early years he learned the German language at home, and when he began attending school he knew not a single word of English. He soon learned it, however, and now possesses the advantage of being thoroughly acquainted with both languages.

In the German Evangelical church at Fort Madison, October 1, 1889, Mr. Lachmann was united in marriage with Miss Anna E. Schubert, a native of Green Bay township, Lee county, where her birth occurred June 15, 1865. The marriage ceremony was performed by Rev. Mr. Batrsch. Mrs. Lachmann is a daughter of Carl and Caroline Dorothy (Knospe) Schubert. She has received a good common school education, and reads and speaks both the English and German languages. To Mr. and Mrs. Lachmann have been born two daughters and one son, as follows: Louise Victoria, born in Green Bay township Tuesday, June 30, 1891; August Carl, born in Green Bay township Tuesday, January 2, 1894, and Alma Anna, born Thursday, August 23, 1900, at the present home of the family.

When about twenty-two years of age Mr. Lachmann purchased forty acres of land adjoining the Lachmann home farm and later added forty-eight acres to this, having eighty-eight acres at time of his marriage, and after his marriage he resided in the old home of his foster parents, they having moved, and had charge of the farm. On May 6, 1894, he moved on the Junge place, which he had bought a short time before. The death of Carl Lachmann occurred February 7, 1899, and that of his wife November 11th of the same year, and all the property they possessed they bequeathed to Mr. Lachmann, excepting $600, which went to other relatives of the Lachmann family. He now owns 190 acres of excellent land, on which are three residence buildings.

Mr. Lachmann acts in political matters with the Democratic party, and cast his first presidential ballot for Cleveland in 1884. He is popular, and has served his township two terms as its trustee. Indeed, he has at various times filled all the township offices except that of clerk. In the autumn of 1899 he was elected county supervisor, and was re-elected in 1902, serving as chairman of the board one year. Fraternally he is a member of the Knights of Pythias, and has been honored by election to all the offices of the local lodge at Wever, as well as delegate to the Grand Lodge of Iowa. He also has membership relations with Empire Lodge, Independent Order of Odd Fellows at Fort Madison, in which lodge he has passed all the chairs. He has attended the Grand Lodge, though not at the time serving as delegate. He is similarly connected with Claypoole Lodge, Free and Accepted Masons, at Fort Madison, and with Potowonok Chapter, Royal Arch Masons and the Benevolent and Protective Order of Elks at that place. He has hosts of friends, the result of his ability, well-known integrity and genial disposition. Still in the prime of life, he has achieved much.

JONAS RICE.

Jonas Rice, a venerable resident of Washington township, has had a long and useful career in this part of the state, and his name deserves honorable mention among those who have done so much to make it what it is. For more than sixty years his lot has been cast in Washington township, and here he has made an enviable name for himself, being widely known as an honorable, upright and industrious man, a kind neighbor and a good citizen.

Mr. Rice comes of good New England stock, and was born in Worchester county, Massachusetts, November 28, 1823, where his parents, Jonas and Grata (Partridge) Rice, were born and reared. In 1839 they removed to the West, and settled in Washington township, the journey in those days being both fatiguing and dangerous. It began by stage to Springfield, Massachusetts, and thence to Hartford by boat; to New York by steamer, and to Philadelphia by rail; thence to Pittsburg mainly by canal, and down the Ohio by a new steamer to St.

Louis; an old boat brought them to Fort Madison. The passengers had to walk around the Rapids, and take team for the Fort, a three days' trip, costing them twenty-five dollars. They arrived at the old hotel, the MacIntyre, in time for a late dinner, and in the afternoon paid a man five dollars to take them out on the prairie, where they quickly found a very desirable location.

E. A. Eaton, a brother-in-law, had located the previous year on section 6, Washington township, and was then living alone. His wife came on later. The elder Rice paid $400 for a claim on a quarter of section 5, in the same township, and a year or two after a land sale was made for Washington township, at Burlington. For the purpose of making a promising investment he borrowed two hundred dollars, for which he had to pay thirty-three and a third per cent. interest, building a log cabin, part of which is still in existence, being used in the house in which the subject of this sketch is still living.

The elder Rice was always a farmer, and was a thoroughly upright and patriotic citizen of his day. In the old state militia he took a deep and vivid interest, and for many years held rank as a lieutenant colonel in its organization. He was long known as Colonel Rice. He was over seventy-two years of age when he was called to the world beyond.

Mrs. Grata Rice lived to be a little older than her honored husband. She was one of a family of sixteen children, three of whom died young, and eleven lived to reach maturity. Three of her sisters are now living. Mr. and Mrs. Rice were members of the Christian church, and their remains are now at rest in the Denmark cemetery. He was a Whig in his earlier political life, and later became a Democrat, but voted for Abraham Lincoln on the occasion of his second election as president. After that he continued to vote the Republican ticket as long as he lived.

Jonas Rice, the subject of this article, was mainly educated in the district school in his native state, where he passed the first sixteen years of his life. On coming west he attended district school in the Denmark district one winter term, and was also a student for a time in a private night school taught by a Mr. Hobart in a neighboring church. He always lived at home, and after he had been of age several years his father deeded him a portion of the original homestead, on which he was engaged in farming several years. While he carried on a system of general farming quite successfully, he was one of the first to see the advantage of the dairy, and for many years he had large dairy interests which proved very remunerative.

Mr. Rice was married in June, 1849, to Miss Harriet Newell Cowles. She was a native of New York, and accompanied her parents to their settlement in Fort Madison in 1839. Her father, Josiah Cowles, was a botanic doctor, and practiced throughout the community in an early day, being remembered by the old settlers as a man of more than ordinary character and ability. To the union of Mr. and Mrs. Rice were born a family of six children, the oldest of whom, Oscar J., is now dead. The second child, Harriet Amanda, married William

Benbow, and died in Washington township. The third child, Phoebe Lillian, married Ira Dow, and is living in Denmark township. Lucy Ida, the wife of G. Henry Colvin, lives in Washington. John G. is a resident of the township. Edward Josiah is still under the parental roof.

Mr. Rice and his excellent wife are memsirable farm land, which he has well improved, and under a high state of cultivation. When he bought it, it was nearly all unbroken, and it has been the labor of a lifetime to bring it into its present condition. He is still actively engaged in farming, and takes immediate supervision of all that is done on his place.

Mr. Rice owns a half section of very debers of the Christian church, in which he has been an elder for many years. Politically he is a Republican, and has been trustee of his township many times, filing other local positions of trust and responsibility to the perfect satisfaction of all who have had to do business with him in his official capacity.

The many friends of Mr. and Mrs. Rice will be interested in this sketch of a career creditable alike to the heart and character of one of the oldest living settlers of Lee county.

HON. JOHN E. CRAIG.

John E. Craig is a prominent attorney of Keokuk whose efforts have had important bearing upon the legal history of his district, upon the progressive development of his city and upon the legislative annals of his state. He was born at Claysville, Washington county, Pennsylvania, March 14, 1855, his parents being Alexander K. and Sarah (McLain) Craig. His paternal great-grandfather, Alexander Craig, was the founder of the family in the new world, emigrating from the north of Ireland to Washington county, Pennsylvania. The family had originally been driven out of Scotland on account of the political troubles of the country and had taken refuge in Ireland. Alexander Craig settled near Claysville and there Hugh Craig, the grandfather, was born and reared. He spent his life as a farmer and upon the old homestead in Pennsylvania Alexander Craig, the father of John E. Craig, was born. He, too, spent his youth in that county and after arriving at years of maturity he devoted his energies to merchandising and farming. He took a prominent part in Democratic politics, proved an active and helpful factor in controlling the interests of his party in his district and though not accepting any local office he was elected in 1890 as a member of congress, occupying that position at the time of his death, which occurred in July, 1892. His wife, who bore the maiden name of Sarah McLain, was born in his home neighborhood and was a daughter of William and Margaret McLain, who were likewise of Scotch-Irish descent.

John E. Craig having pursued his preliminary education in the schools of Washington county, Pennsylvania, was subsequently graduated from the Washington and Jefferson College with the class of 1877. By teaching school through the winter months he had earned the money necessary to meet his college tuition and other expenses of his more advanced course. The degree of Bachelor of Arts was conferred upon him when he was twenty-four years of age and three years later he won the honorary degree of Master of Arts. He was for one year principal of an academy at Pittsburg and then came west to Keokuk, Iowa, in 1878. Entering upon the study of lay under the direction of his uncle, J. H. Craig, he was admitted upon examination to the bar in 1879 and at once opened an office for practice. A year later he formed a partnership with his uncle, becoming a member of the firm of Craig, Collier & Craig. They enjoyed an extensive practice and Mr. Craig was associated professionally with his uncle until the latter's death in 1893. There were changes, however, that occurred in the firm, A. J. McCrary succeeding William Collier as the second partner. Following the death of the senior partner Mr. McCrary and Mr. Craig remained together until the former's elevation to the bench, since which time Mr. Craig has practiced alone, maintaining a foremost position as a representative of the legal fraternity in his district. He is now considered one of the strongest members of the Keokuk bar, which has numbered many men of notable legal strength. He is a member of the State Bar Association, the Municipal Law League and the American Bar Association. He has been attorney for different corporate interests as well as a legal representative of many individuals and for many years his clientage has been of a very important and distinctively representative character. He was early identified with the Keokuk Electric Street Railway & Power Company, as one of its directors.

Fraternally Mr. Craig is connected with the Knights of Pythias lodge and with the Benevolent and Protective Order of Elks, in which he has served as exalted ruler. His political allegiance is given to the Democracy and he has been an active worker in its ranks. He was a member of the state legislature in 1886 and again in 1888 and during these sessions served on various important committees. He belonged to the judiciary committee and was one of the subcommittee that reorganized the present judiciary system of the state. He was also one of the council appointed to prosecute Auditor Brown during that session and he introduced a bill that later became a law, authorizing fidelity insurance companies to give bonds. He has also been prominent in community affairs and his deep interest in the welfare of his city has found tangible demonstration in the effective labor he has put forth for general progress and improvement. In 1889 he was elected mayor of the city and his first term proved so satisfactory to the people at large that he was re-elected in 1891. During this time the Union depot was built in Keokuk and the system of brick paving was inaugurated and an electric railway system built. The sewer system of the city was likewise established and rebuilt and there is no western city today that has a finer system of this kind than has Keokuk. From 1896 until 1900 he acted as county attorney, covering two terms and he has attended the higher conventions of his party and was assistant secretary at the National Democratic Convention held in St. Louis, was the nominee of the Democratic party for congress in 1902 and 1904, running far ahead of his party ticket in both contests. For eleven years he was a member of the school board and he was also identified with the establishment of the free public library and has been for some time president of the board of trustees under whose direction a splendid library has been developed which is indeed a credit to the city. Mr. Craig has likewise been a member of the Young Men's Christian Association from the time of its organization and he was for some years president of the Keokuk College of Physicans and Surgeons and professor of jurisprudence until the time of its consolidation with the Keokuk Medical College.

On the 7th of October, 1880, Mr. Craig married Miss Fannie S. Coulter, of Washington, Pennsylvania, and they have one son, M. Coulter. They hold membership in the Presbyterian church and occupy a fine residence at No. 208 Fulton street, its generous hospitality being one of its most attractive features. From early manhood a resident of Keokuk this city has been the scene of his entire professional labor and his life record is well known to his fellow townsmen. While he has striven for success, which is the legitimate goal of all individual endeavor, he has at the same time labored for higher ethical relations in the practice of law and in citizenship as well as in private life and in local and state office he has been the champion of many measures whose beneficial influence and far-reaching effect are now widely acknowledged.

ST. MARY'S CATHOLIC CHURCH.

St. Mary's Catholic Church, of West Point, Iowa, holds an honored position on the roll of the parishes of that faith in the state. Its history runs far back into the past, and its membership comprehends some of the best material to be found in that community. Its pastors have been scholarly and devoted, its officials faithful and conscientious, and its membership earnest and enthusiastic.

The beautiful location of West Point, on the southern border of Pleasant Ridge, and the fertile parishes stretching far and wide, attracted many Catholic settlers, and as early as 1836 their religious preferences began to attract attention. Such families as the Dierkers, the Fullenkamps, the Strothmans, the Rumps, and others could not be lightly treated and ignored in any community. They were men of character and women of devotion, and when for the first time they were visited by a priest from Quincy, Illinois, in 1838, it was the beginning of a work not yet ended. Father August Brickwedde, was so encouraged by the result of his visit here that year that he made West Point a mission station. The following year he returned, and baptized Mary E. Groner, Gerhard H. Hellman, Mary E. Rump and Barbara Ritt. At this time the double log house of Joseph Strothman was used as a chapel, and the officiating priest made his home with that family, or with the son, Casper, and later with Dr. Lowrey, who arrived in 1845.

Father J. G. Alleman was placed in

charge of the Catholic interests at West Point in 1840, and continued his ministry until 1851. During the years 1844 and 1845 he spent the most of his time here, and from this place made his pastoral visitations. The first church, a frame building, 21x40 feet, was erected in 1842, and dedicated the following year. It sufficed for the congregation some eight or ten years, which had now increased to fourteen families. In 1849 a clear-toned church bell was given to this movement by Bishop Loras, and it is the same bell which is now used in the school. It was hung on trestles near the front door, and for many years was regarded affectionately by the devout as it called them to song and prayer.

Father Alleman is everywhere spoken of with peculiar reverence by the pioneers who have survived to the present time. He was a man of broad character, and a priest of piety and devotion, and his insight into the wants and needs of the people of those days was singularly quick and accurate. When he gave up the mission, he was succeeded by Father Michel, and by Fathers Walterman, Reffe, Hattenberg, Johannes Orth, as well as other able and devoted priests. Father Jacoby, is now the priest in charge.

In June, 1855, Father Walterman was made resident pastor, and the oldest baptismal register, now preserved in St. Mary's was opened by him. About this time some of the members sent back to Hanover, their fatherland, and induced Henry Krebs, a finely educated young man, to come over and teach their children. In 1858, several families, removing to Minnesota, induced him to accompany them and teach their children. There remains in his beautiful handwriting, a list of the parish which he compiled in 1854.

In the spring of 1856 Father Hattenberg visited this parish, and he was followed by Father Michel for a time, and later by Father Reffe and Father Eusebius Kaiser. In December, 1858, Father Reffe became pastor, and was continued as such until 1864. That year Father De Cailly took charge, and under him was a period of great growth for the parish. He was a wise and exemplary priest, and as many families came over from Hanover and Westphalia, he was their one friend in a new and strange country. He enlarged and improved the parsonage, and secured the erection of a new church, which was dedicated in 1862. Father Michel, from St. Paul, cared for the interests of this progressive movement for a year, and Father Orth, from Fort Madison, for another year. Father Hattenberg was sent here in 1867, and remained for two years, and under his direction the present brick parsonage was constructed. To him succeeded Father Johannes, and when this faithful pastor and pious priest was called to Dubuque in 1871, his departure was felt as a personal loss by many who knew him well. After him came Father Orth, who remained until 1876, when he was called to Keokuk. The memorable mission of the Redemptorist Fathers Giessen and Jacobs must not be omitted in this hasty review.

Father William Jacoby arrived in March, 1877, and has been in charge to the present time. Under him all the loose ends of parish administration have been gathered up, and magnificent progress in building a church of the Master has been made. Under him the church has been completely remodeled and redecorated at a total expense of about $25,000. The parish has every modern facility for every department of its work, and all societies that it may need.

Its school work is very dear to the hearts of the congregation, and was a part of its field as early as 1846, and in 1850 was erected its first school house. In 1877 was built the present fine edifice, a brick building, 55x70 feet, two stories in height with a roomy basement. It is arranged with four school rooms, in which the children are taught by the Sisters of St. Francis, whose mother-house is at La Crosse, Wisconsin. German and English are taught, church history is made a study, and religious exercises are conducted in each room two hours a week by Father Jacoby.

Connected with the parish is a Young Men's Sodality for general literary work, a Young Ladies' Religious Society, and the Altar Society, to which married ladies are admitted.

St. Mary's parish has also an assembly hall, seating about four hundred people, and here is housed a large circulating library. There is also a handsome parsonage, the home of Father Jacoby for many years, and to which all who call are made welcome.

In 1903 the church began the remodeling of its building, and today it has one of the finest structures in this part of the state. The cost of the rebuilding exceeds $17,000. The redecoration, including the fixtures and windows amounts to $4,200, and the church is now valued at over $40,000, largely through the patient and persistent efforts of Father Jacoby, who has also installed in the church several valuable oil paintings and the first pipe organ the church has possessed.

St. Mary's in all its departments is equipped for work, and the work that it is doing reflects credit on its earnest and faithful members; but most of all upon its pious and consecrated pastor, Father Jacoby.

THE REV. FATHER WILLIAM JACOBY.

The unselfish and devoted labors of the Christian ministry have done much to elevate the manners, purify the hearts and quicken the moral powers of the people of the Nineteenth century, especially in the newer regions and on the frontier. The rush and stir of settlement is so immense in a new country, the material value of things so impressive if not overwhelming, that all the resources the unselfish life and the religious heart could command, were needed to the maintenance of the kingdom of God in this world. In this good fight the Catholic priesthood has always been conspicuous. Its members able and consecrated have always tried to keep alive in human society the sense of God and the obligation of duty. In this great work Father Jacoby has been by no means silent or inefficient. He has abundantly proved himself a loyal and trustworthy son of the Church, which has accepted his vows of consecration, and sealed him to its ministry.

Father Jacoby, who has been pastor of the Catholic church of the Assumption, at West Point, since 1876, was born in the city of Ettelbruck, Grand Duchy of Luxemburg, and was there reared. His parents, Peter and Catherina (Berg) Jacoby, were of pure German lineage, and their entire lives were passed in the old fatherland. The father was a successful shoe merchant.

Father Jacoby when a young man possessed but little means, and to a considerable extent paid his way through college by money earned in giving instruction to the younger students. For seven years he was librarian of the Luxemberg public library, containing over a hundred thousand volumes. He completed his classical and philosophical studies in Luxemburg, and came to this country unattended by relative or friend.

After his arrival in the United States the future priest became a student in the theological seminary at Milwaukee, Wisconsin, where he devoted two years to study, and was then admitted and ordained to the priesthood by Bishop Hennesy, of Dubuque, Iowa. The work of preparation had been well done, and the young priest had greatly profited by the rich opportunities afforded him; so that when he came to the West Point parish in 1876, it was with all the powers of a rich and generous mind, brought to a high degree of activity by a thorough and systematic training.

From 1876 to the present time West Point has continued the home of this scholarly and eloquent divine, whose influence has been great in the community. All his attention has been given to the St. Mary's church, which has greatly grown under his pastorate. When it began there were one hundred and forty-five families on the parish rolls. Today, in spite of the many removals from this region into the newer West, by those seeking cheaper lands and the opportunities found there, there are one hundred and eighty-five families still enrolled in the church.

The years of Father Jacoby have been full of hard labor as well as of rich attainment. Here he has built a large school, which is now under the charge of the Sisters of St. Francis from La Crosse, and has one hundred and ninety pupils in attendance. The building is a substantial brick structure, and is a monument to the zeal for education that has always moved and inspired the pastor of St. Mary's in his public work. Father Jacoby made a trip to Europe in 1890, and while there paid his respects to Pope Leo XIII., then the venerated and beloved head of the church.

In 1894 Father Jacoby erected the Mortuary, located at the cemetery, which was built at a cost of $1,700, and which is the pride of the community. It was erected in honor of the dead who rest there. The inscription inside says:

"Memento homo quia pulvis es et in pulverem reverteris."

Father Jacoby is a devoted student of church history, and takes a deep interest in every effort that looks to the improvement of society. He is much beloved and respected alike by his own people and those of all faiths, who comprehend the useful and beautiful work continually being accomplished at St. Mary's.

EDWARD C. LYNN.

The persistency of purpose which Superintendent E. C. Lynn displayed while acquiring his education indicates the elemental strength of his character, and gave early promise of his successful future; and his career since leaving school has been in harmony with the promise of his youth, while his present activities and earnest attitude toward the work to which he is devoting his life and energies bespeak still further development of his native talents and yet greater advancement to positions of honor, usefulness and public service. He is now superintendent of schools of Lee county, Iowa, and enjoys a rapidly increasing reputation as one of the rising educators of the southern portion of his state.

Superintendent Lynn, who is now a resident of Donnellson, Iowa, was born near Osage City, Kansas, and with his parents removed in 1878 to Henry county, Iowa, where he spent his boyhood days on a farm and began his education in the rural schools. He was graduated from the public schools at the age of sixteen years, and subsequently entered and was graduated from Howe's Academy, the Mount Pleasant Academy and the Henry County Normal Institute and also did considerable work along special lines bearing upon the teaching profession in the Iowa State Normal University. He holds a teacher's state certificate, and his career as a teacher extended over a period of nine years of highly useful service, beginning with two years in rural schools, followed by one year in the Mount Pleasant Academy, and the remainder of the time he was principal of graded schools, first at Primrose, then at West Point and the last three years at Donnellson. Meanwhile his personality and his brilliant work had attracted the widespread attention of older educators and of the general public, and in the autumn of 1903 he was elected to the important office of county superintendent of schools, resigning his position as principal of the Donnellson schools to accept the larger opportunities and responsibilities. While Mr. Lynn is one of the younger teachers of the county, his uniform success as a teacher, his energy, enthusiasm and natural ability have strongly appealed to the people, who placed him at the head of their schools with full confidence that these institutions would receive his most careful thought and conscientious attention in every detail relating to their highest welfare and efficiency—an expectation entirely realized during the comparatively brief period of his incumbency and one evidently destined to yet fuller fruition in due time.

In 1900 Mr. Lynn was united in marriage to Miss Mabel Harlen, a native of Lee county, and two sons grace their union, these being Harold and Max. Mrs. Lynn, who is a lady of liberal culture and of unusual social talents, is a member of the Christian church at Hillsboro, and Mr. Lynn is a member of the Presbyterian church at New London; and while there is no congregation of either of these denominations at Donnellson, and they have not become formally identified with any church in their present home, they nevertheless maintain close relations with religious progress in the community, and are helpful and valued supporters of the work of the church in its various departments. Mr. Lynn has shown himself to be public spirited in all the best senses of the word, and is a loyal worker in the ranks of the Republican party, in whose principles he is a thorough believer and on whose ticket he received the honor of election to his present office. His principal and almost exclusive care, however, is the welfare of the public-school system under his charge, which is a very extensive one, there being more than 200 teachers employed in Lee county, and in this field he finds worthy employment for his powers, for his work as principal of schools has shown him to be the possessor of executive ability of no mean order, and in all that relates to the purely technical aspects of education his superiority is undisputed. Moreover, he brings to his task that invaluable factor in the success of all public enterprises, the support and sympathy of the people, as he is highly popular, not only in the immediate vicinity of his home, but throughout Lee county and wherever he is known.

ALLEN T. ADAMS.

Allen T. Adams, one of the earlier settlers of Lee county, Iowa, and now numbered among the oldest residents of the county, was born December 16, 1826, in Adams county, Ohio, a member of one of the pioneer families of that state and son of Robert and Nancy (Oxchier) Adams. The father died in Ohio, but the mother came west and located in Whiteside county, Illinois, whence she later removed to Iowa and joined her sons in Lee county, and died in Scotland county, Missouri, at the remarkable age of 106 years. She was the mother of six children, of whom only three survive, the two others being Chambers Adams, of Whiteside county, Illinois, and Sarah A., wife of Thomas Walker, of near Kirksville, Missouri.

Mr. Adams was first married near Rome, Ohio, in 1846, to Miss Margaret McCandlass, who died in 1873, and was buried at Yellow Bank cemetery, she being the mother of eleven children of whom eight survive, these being Mary C., wife of Jacob M. Shook, of Mitchell county, Kansas, who has eight children; Mrs. Louisa Evans; Mrs. Anna Leckermeyer; Mrs. Allen Sharp; Mrs. Bertha Teten; Joseph M.; Francis R.; Walter E. and Ralph E.; Robert, who married Miss Margaret Danford, resides at Mooar, Iowa, and has four children, Mary, Cora, Katherine and Lydia; William, who married Miss Belle Sharp, resides in Pratt county, Kansas, and has three children living, Viola, Ruby and William; Joseph, who married Miss Belle Forsythe, resides at Pueblo, Colorado, and has two children, Nora and Ruby; Nancy, wife of Frank Croison, of New Mexico, has one child, Margaret: Allen, who married Miss Katherine Fletcher, resides at Fort Madison, Iowa, and has three children, Pearl, Allen V. and Lida M.; John, who married Miss Emma High, is a farmer of Jackson township; Lizzie, wife of William Lee, of Pratt county, Kansas, has one son, Joseph. On

April 27, 1876, Mr. Adams remarried, wedding Mrs. Amanda J. Blakemoore, of Fort Madison, Iowa, and to them have been born five children, of whom four are living, as follows: James, now residing in Pratt county, Kansas, who married Miss Jenett Sharp and has three children; Walter married Irene Oilar and resides at home; Ida, wife of Alonzo McCandlass, who resides at Mooar, Iowa, and has one child, and Margaret, wife of Charles Wright, of Keokuk, who has one child. Mrs. Adams also has one son, Edward Blakemore, a farmer of Jackson township, who married Miss Alice Wittich and has four children, Richard, Alberta, Charles and Louise.

Coming to Lee county in 1857, he was variously employed for four years, and in 1861 went to Scotland county, Missouri, where he soon after enlisted in Company B, First Northeast Missouri Regiment of the Home Guards under Colonel Moore and Captain James Best, and was engaged in the battle at Athens and in scouting and skirmish duty for five months. At the expiration of that period the regiment was regularly organized, and left the state, but Mr. Adams was then in such feeble health as to prevent his re-enlistment, and he returned to Iowa, locating in 1865 on his present farm in Jackson township, where he has ever since resided. Here he has been very highly successful, and occupies an enviable position among the leading agriculturists and largest land owners of Lee county, owning approximately 350 acres of fertile farming land well improved and unusually productive. The farm, which was originally all located in Jackson township, has been divided into two tracts by a change in the channel of the Des Moines river, so that a portion now lies outside the township.

Mr. and Mrs. Adams are well known throughout this vicinity as lifelong Methodists, and are members of the Valley Methodist Episcopal church, whose house of worship Mr. Adams helped to build and in whose welfare he has ever taken the deepest interest, contributing generously to its support and to its various charitable enterprises. All public movements of a worthy nature have commanded his attention and study, and he was in former years an active and helpful member of the Grange, which derived substantial benefit from his influential position and standing in the community, and he is also known as a prominent member of the Republican party in Jackson township. Although he has never aspired to the holding of public office, he has at various times consented to discharge the duties of several minor official positions with a view to serving the interests of the community in which he lives, and for this he deserves credit, for he has always amply justified the confidence of his fellow citizens. The public schools have been the especial object of his care and solicitude, and he has at times occupied the office of school director in order to keep more intimately in touch with this characteristically American institution, which is the foundation stone of the nation's liberties and one of the chief factors in her progress and continued greatness. In fact, every movement or institution calculated to promote the general welfare has elicited his sympathy and aid, and ever since casting his first ballot for General William Henry Harrison for president of the United States he has conscientiously observed all the duties of citizenship, and in consequence enjoys today the admiration and respect of those who know him for the uprightness and strict integrity which mark his life record, while his personal loyalty and the social virtues of his character have made him a host of friends.

DENNIS A. MORRISON.

Among the strongest forces that have contributed to the substantial upbuilding and development of Fort Madison has been the intelligently directed effort of the men who have promoted its business affairs. Prominent in this class stands Dennis A. Morrison, a leading financier of Lee county, whose association with important financial interests includes the presidency of the Fort Madison Savings Bank and the vice-presidency of the German-American Bank. With keen insight into business possibilities and opportunities he has likewise been a promoter of varied interests which have had important bearing upon the business outlook and prosperity of the city, while contributing as well to individual success and in this connection he is the president of the Fort Madison Street Railway Company, the Fort Madison Gas Company and the Fort Madison Canning Company.

Mr. Morrison was born at Frankfort, Ross county, Ohio, October 5, 1839, his parents being Samuel D. and Maria (Blacker) Morrison. The father, a native of New York, became a resident of Ohio in his boyhood days and in Chillicothe learned the blacksmith's trade, which he followed in that city and in Ross county for many years. He came to Fort Madison, Iowa, in 1848, and after residing here for one year removed to Augusta, Des Moines county where he made his home for five years, returning then to Fort Madison, where he continued to reside until his death. Prior to 1860 he established a plant for the manufacture of plows and although the enterprise was begun on a small scale he developed a business in later years to extensive and profitable proportions. After the close of the war his sons, J. B. and D. A. Morrison, who had been to the front as soldiers of the Union Army as had their two brothers, joined the father in business under the firm style of S. D. Morrison & Sons. The plant was then enlarged and its producing capacity increased from year to year as occasion demanded, it becoming one of the leading industrial concerns of the city.

Samuel D. Morrison was united in marriage to Maria Blacker, during his residence in Ohio and all of their children were born in that state. Mr. Morrison became one of the early members of St. Joseph's church of Fort Madison and was a generous contributor thereto, at the same time giving liberally to any movements having for their object the educational and material upbuilding of the city.

Dennis A. Morrison acquired his education in the common schools of Ohio and

Des Moines county, Iowa, and when seventeen years of age began working in his father's shop, gaining intimate knowledge of the practical methods of manufacturing plows as well as conducting the financial department of the business. After the inauguration of the Civil War, however, in response to his country's need he enlisted in September, 1862, as a member of Company D, Seventh Iowa Infantry. He joined the regiment at Corinth, Mississippi, and continued with that command until after the close of the war when he was honorably discharged at Washington, District of Columbia. He had participated in many important engagements, including the battles of the Atlanta campaign, the march to the sea under Sherman and the march from Savannah to Washington and in the capital city he took part in the grand review, which was the most celebrated military pageant ever seen on the western hemisphere. During the latter part of the war he acted as quartermaster sergeant.

Following his return from the army Mr. Morrison was admitted to a partnership in his father's business under the firm style of S. D. Morrison & Sons. He remained actively engaged therein until after the retirement of the father, when the business was continued under the firm name of Morrison Brothers and later was incorporated as the Morrison Manufacturing Company, with a capital stock of one hundred thousand dollars, D. A. Morrison becoming the president. This was one of the earliest of the productive industries of Fort Madison and its business development was one of continued progression in keeping with modern business methods. In the meantime Mr. Morrison has become an active factor in financial circles in Fort Madison as one of the organizers of the First National Bank and its president. He remained at the head of the institution until the bank closed and the Fort Madison Savings Bank was organized with a capital stock of thirty thousand dollars. He has been its president from the first and under his guidance it has become known as the leading commercial bank of Fort Madison with deposits of five hundred thousand dollars. In 1901 a fine bank building was erected and equipped with all modern conveniences and safeguards. For a number of years Mr. Morrison has been connected with the German-American Bank as vice-president and in financial as well as industrial circles his reputation has ever been such as any business man might be proud to possess. Having the prescience to discern what the future held in store for the city and recognizing the opportunities for its further development, Mr. Morrison has become a co-operant factor in other enterprises that have proved of marked benefit in promoting Fort Madison's progress and substantial upbuilding. He was active in the organization of the Fort Madison Street Railway Company, became a member of its first board of directors and in 1891 was made president since which time he has been in charge of its business affairs as manager. The cars were at first drawn by horses, but the motive power was changed to electricity by Mr. Morrison soon after he assumed the management of the road. He was one of the founders of the Fort Madison Canning Company and is president of this successful corporation which is now furnishing employment during the canning season to two hundred operatives. He early became identified with the Fort Madison Gas Company and for the past ten years has been its president. He is financially interested in other business concerns and his investments have been so judiciously placed as to win for him excellent financial results and at the same time proved important factors in business, progress and advancement in Lee county.

In his political views Mr. Morrison is an earnest Republican who regards it the duty as well as the privilege of every American citizen to exercise his right of franchise and support the principles which he believes contain the best elements of good government. He has, therefore, taken a public-spirited interest in party work, was sent as a delegate to the Republican National Convention at Minneapolis which nominated James G. Blaine for the presidency and is recognized as one of the Republican leaders of the city, although he has no political aspirations for himself. He belongs to both the Commercial Club and to the Grand Army of the Republic.

Mr. Morrison was married at Fort Madison in 1868 to Miss Emma A. Kennedy, a daughter of John Kennedy, one of the early residents of this city. Unto Mr. and Mrs. Morrison have been born three children: Maude, now the wife of Ralph R. Bradley, of Chicago; Edward, of Fort Madison, and Don D., of St. Louis, Missouri. Mr. Morrison erected a beautiful home at the corner of Third and Cedar streets, which has been the family residence for twenty-one years. His life record forms an integral chapter in the city's history and while his personal success is notable and gratifying his co-operation in affairs of public moment and importance also entitle him without invidious distinction to rank with the foremost residents of Lee county.

JAMES CAMPBELL BREWSTER.

James Campbell Brewster, president of the German-American Bank and vice-president of the Fort Madison Savings Bank of Fort Madison, was born November 19, 1860, in the city which is still his home, his parents being Charles and Eliza Jane (DeForest) Brewster. His early education acquired in the city schools was supplemented by study in Denmark Academy and in Bryant & Stratton's Commercial College of Chicago. He entered upon his business career in the Bank of Fort Madison, the predecessor of the First National Bank, which in turn was succeeded by the Fort Madison Savings Bank. He entered the institution as clerk, but his capability won ready recognition in successive promotions until he became cashier of the First National Bank. He acted in that capacity until compelled to resign his position in the active management of the institution on account of ill health. Subsequently the bank was merged into the Fort Madison Savings Bank, of which he was chosen vice-president and a director. Later in connection with D. A. Morrison he became one of the heavy stockholders in the German-American Bank, of which he was elected president. This has become one of the largest and most reliable banking institutions of the city, its deposits exceeding that of any bank here. The business is constantly growing under the capable management of Mr. Brewster and his colleagues, whose entire business career has connected him with banking interests, so that he has intimate and accurate knowledge of the business in its various departments. To other fields of labor Mr. Brewster extended his efforts, becoming the president of the Fort Madison Chair Company and at the present writing he is its vice-president. He is also interested in the Fort Madison Street Railway Company, of which he is the treasurer and his financial interests represent investments in other activities both mercantile and industrial.

Mr. Brewster was married to Miss Eliza A. Merrill, of Burlington, Iowa, who died in 1887, leaving two children: Eugenia Starr, now the wife of Alba Garrott, of Frankfort, Indiana; and Charles Merrill. In 1889 he wedded Miss Daisy McClurg, a daughter of Leander McClurg, a prominent attorney of that city. Mr. and Mrs. Brewster hold membership in the Presbyterian church of Fort Madison, of which he is a trustee. Theirs is one of the beautiful homes of the city situated on Third street. It was erected in 1895 and is justly celebrated for its generous and attractive hospitality. In matters of citizenship Mr. Brewster is progressive and public-spirited and although never an aspirant for political office he served for many years as school treasurer of Fort Madison and the cause of education has ever found in him a stanch friend. He votes with the Republican party and fraternally he is connected with the Benevolent and Protective Order of Elks.

JOHN W. PHILPOTT, M. D.

Dr. John W. Philpott, one of the leading physicians and surgeons of Lee county, located for practice at Fort Madison, for ten years surgeon of the Iowa State Penitentiary and also surgeon for several railroad companies, has risen to distinction through the avenue of opportunity which is open to all, and today stands in a commanding position that he has gained through close study and conscientious effort, resulting in marked capability. He was born in New London, Henry county, Iowa, December 24, 1857, and is a son of Dr. J. H. and Louisa M. (Farrar) Philpott. The father was born in Kentucky, where he spent his early years and as a young man he came to Iowa, completing his education in this state. Entering upon preparation for the medical profession he read under a preceptor in Burlington, Iowa, and subsequently entered the Miami Medical College at Cincinnati, from which he was graduated. He then located for practice in New London, Iowa, where his professional career covered a period of fifty years, during which time he long maintained a foremost place in the ranks of the medical fraternity, his acknowledged ability leading to a large patronage. His political support was given to the Republican party. In early manhood he married Miss Farrar, who was born near Ruthland, Vermont, and when a young lady came to Iowa with her parents, Mr. and Mrs. Philetus Farrar, who were pioneer residents of Henry county. Dr. and Mrs. J. H. Philpott are still residents of New London.

John W. Philpott is indebted to the public schools of his native city for the early educational privileges which he enjoyed. He read medicine with his father and pursued a course of lectures in the University of Vermont at Burlington, completing his studies there by graduation with the class of 1878. He afterward pursued a hospital course in New York city and then opened an office in Danville, Iowa, where he remained until 1887, during which time he built up an extensive country practice that brought him wide and varied experience and called into play an extended knowledge of the principles of medicine. While residing there he was a member of the Des Moines County Medical Society and was serving on its board of censors at the time of his removal from the county.

Dr. Philpott has been identified with the medical profession in Fort Madison since 1887. Seeking a broader field he established his office in this city, where he has progressed until he occupies a foremost position in the ranks of the medical fraternity here. In addition to an extensive private practice he has for ten years served as surgeon of the Iowa State Penitentiary and he is also surgeon for the Chicago, Burlington & Quincy Railroad Company, the St. Louis, Keokuk & Northwestern Railroad Company and the Fort Madison Street Railway Company. He is likewise examiner for several of the leading life insurance companies and he belongs to the Lee County Medical Society, of which he is one of the charter members, the Iowa State Medical Society, the American Medical Association and the Iowa Railway Surgeons' Association.

Dr. Philpott's study of the political questions and issues of the day has led to his earnest support of Republican principles. Fraternally he is connected with Delta Commandery, Knights Templar, and was at one time identified with the lower divisions of the order, but from this has demitted. He was married March 19, 1881, to Miss Lucy Bollinger, a daughter of Alexander Bollinger, of Burlington Junction, Missouri, and they now have one son, Dr. Austin Flint Philpott, who is a graduate of the College of Physicians and Surgeons at St. Louis, Missouri, and now city physician of Fort Madison.

Regarding his profession as a life work eminently worthy of his best efforts Dr. Philpott has given his time and attention almost exclusively to the practice of medicine and surgery and to the acquirement of further knowledge concerning the science until he now has accurate and comprehensive understanding of the great principles upon which it is based. A careful and conscientious performance of his professional duties and the obligations which devolve upon him have gained him the confidence of the public, while his professional brethren acknowledge his worth.

MILWARD H. ROGERS.

The life record of Milward H. Rogers covered more than eighty-one years, and the story of his life is that of an honorable man, who was active in business, loyal in citizenship and faithful to his friends. As the day with its morning of hope and promise, its noontide of activity and its evening of completed and successful effort ended in the grateful rest and quiet of the night, so was the life of this upright man. For six decades he remained a resident of Iowa, and while he won success through capably conducted business affairs, he was always mindful of his duty to his fellowmen and of his obligation to his Maker.

Milward H. Rogers was born in the city of London, England, March 19, 1819, the son of Thomas and Elizabeth Rogers, who were both of English birth. The son was christened in Saint Paul's church, London, and while an infant removed with his parents to Montgomery, in Wales, where he passed his early years and for a time attended school. In the fall of 1832 he accompanied his parents to America, remaining in New York until the following spring, when the family journeyed westward and settled in Delaware county, Ohio. There the father died a few months later,—in September, 1833. His wife survived him for a period of forty-nine years, her death occurring at the residence of her son in Lee county, Iowa, in the ninety-first year of her age. She was a woman of fine mentality, had traveled extensively, and possessed a character of true refinement and culture.

In 1840 Mr. Rogers removed from Delaware county, Ohio, to Lee county, Iowa, where for a time he rented land and engaged in farming, but later decided that he could more profitably employ his efforts in cutting and supplying wood for fuel for the Mississippi River steamboats, and accordingly devoted some years to that occupation with considerable pecuniary success. He also purchased wooded lands near the river and resold it to owners of boats, thus by his prompt grasp of a business situation gaining a foothold in the new country and obtaining the means necessary to give him a start in life. He first purchased land in section 13 of Green Bay township, and after a number of years devoted to other enterprises decided to give his entire attention to farming. This he did during the remainder of his life, and by his ability, care and unwavering fulfillment of duty he succeeded to an extraordinary degree and became one of the most extensive landholders of the township, owning 1,465 acres of fertile and highly improved lands in one of the most lavishly productive agricultural regions of Iowa. Here he erected a magnificent brick residence, introduced modern methods and processes in farming, and constructed numbers of barns, granaries and other buildings according to the most approved scientific ideas, being of a supremely enterprising disposition and always a friend of progress.

On March 24, 1842, he was united in marriage to Miss Susan Johnson, a daughter of Sheppard and Ann (McDaniel) Johnson. The father and mother of Mrs. Rogers were natives of Long Island, New York, and of Pennsylvania, respectively, and after their marriage settled in Hamilton county, Ohio, crossing the Mississippi in 1840 and locating in Green Bay township, where Mr. Johnson died two weeks after his arrival,—September 10, 1840. His wife survived him four years, her demise occurring April 23, 1844, at the home of her daughter, Mrs. Rogers. Mrs. Rogers, who was the second of a family of six sons and daughters, was born in Hamilton county, Ohio, October 21, 1819, and came with her parents to Lee county, Iowa, June 19, 1840. To Mr. and Mrs. Rogers were born seven sons and one daughter, of whom four sons still survive, as follows: Milward H., Jr., who married Miss Sarah E. Fry; Johnson; George E., and Arthur. Biographical notices of the last three will be found elsewhere in this volume. Those deceased are Milward S., Monroe, Rebecca A. and Thomas.

Always taking a keen interest in public affairs, Mr. Rogers early gave his support to the Democratic party, an allegiance which he continued through life, and as a young man was prevailed upon to accept a number of public trusts, including the offices of drain commissioner, justice of the peace and county supervisor, he performing the duties of these positions with that conscientious devotion to the welfare of the community in which he lived which characterized everything he did that could by any possibility affect his neighbors and friends. Ever ready to do the right as it was given him to see the right he, as also his devoted wife, was an active worker in the Christian church, and in that body he acted as an elder for many years. His last years found him faithful, even as his whole life had been one beautiful illustration of Christian faith. He departed mortal life December 19, 1900, the wife and mother having preceded him to the better world on May 21st of the same year, the remains of husband and wife being laid at rest in Beebe cemetery in Green Bay township. They left a memory fragrant with Christian charity and good deeds, and they so lived that the work they did shall not pass away. Mr. Rogers was a strong and significant character, combining business ability of a high order with humanitarian principles, and while achieving a large success and securing for himself much material wealth, he contributed in an important measure to the upbuilding of the county in which he passed the greater part of his life. He was widely known and respected wherever known, being regarded as a man of superlative integrity and vast business ability.

ANDREW J. WILKINSON.

So closely was the life work of Andrew J. Wilkinson interwoven with the history of Keokuk's commercial and intellectual progress that no record of the city would be complete without mention of him. No human character can be justly depicted with all his lights and shades duly touched and set forth in a thousand phrases or even in a few pages. How much more impossible to make clear the force of human character which has been involved in great affairs and upon which responsibilities have acted and re-acted and which a large and varied experience has modified, educated and developed and yet this is what the historian essays in attempting to portray the life of Andrew J. Wilkinson. He lived a life of his time amply, knew humanity in its many phases and had wide sympathy as well as varied interests.

A native of Rhode Island, he was born in Foster township, Provence county, May 20, 1830. After his father's death and when he was yet a young lad he removed with his mother to Lonsdale, later to Providence and afterward to Richmond, Rhode Island, and to provide for his own support he secured employment as a farm laborer near the last-named place. His educational opportunities were limited, but the few he had he improved to the best of his ability. When fourteen years of age he became an employe in his brother's store in Troy, New York, and subsequently spent some time in connection with mercantile interests in New York city, but the great and growing West attracted him and he wisely chose this section as his scene of action. Arriving in Keokuk in 1856 he invested the capital which he had previously secured through his unremitting diligence and careful management in the purchase of a wholesale and retail drug business, formerly the property of Horace Ayres. In this enterprise he was associated with a partner, Richard Marshall and the firm of Wilkinson & Marshall conducted the business for about a year. In 1857, however, he purchased Mr. Marshall's interest and was alone until 1864, when the firm of Wilkinson, Bartlett & Company was formed, his partners being George F. Bartlett and J. F. Kiedaisch. These gentlemen were together for seventeen years, when in 1887 Mr. Bartlett retired and the firm style of Wilkinson & Company was assumed, being maintained up to the death of Mr. Wilkinson, since which time the Wilkinson Drug Company has been incorporated. Ever watchful of indications pointing to success, Mr. Wilkinson conducted his mercantile affairs along progressive lines in keeping with modern thought and in touch with the wonderful business development that has been characteristic of this age. Moreover, his business integrity stood as an unquestioned fact in his career. He was ever liberal in his dealings, considerate of his employes and thoroughly reliable so that the drug house, with which he was connected ever sustained an unassailable reputation.

On the 13th of July, 1859, Mr. Wilkinson was united in marriage to Miss Willia Thompson, the wedding being celebrated at the home of her father, Colonel William Thompson, a distinguished son of Kentucky, who might well have been called one of nature's noblemen. He inherited an estate consisting of valuable property interests and many slaves, but being an opponent of the system of slavery he sent as many of his negroes as he could to Liberia, the expense of their transportation being forty thousand dollars in addition to the value of the slaves. In 1857 he removed to Keokuk and invested extensively in real estate, erecting the bank building at the corner of Second and Main streets now occupied by the Iowa State Insurance Company at a cost of twenty-two thousand dollars. He had previously been an agriculturist and was not used to northern business methods of loaning money, having up to this time lived in Kentucky, where "every man is believed honest until proven otherwise." He therefore loaned money unwisely and in the financial panic which swept over the country he lost all his possessions. After a time he removed to Palatka, Florida, where he engaged in the practice of law until his death, which occurred in 1901. His remains were brought back to Keokuk for burial and were interred in Oakland cemetery. He was a man of most kindly nature and broad humanitarian spirit and he was continually exerting his efforts to ameliorate the difficult conditions which are found in life. Unto Mr. and Mrs. Wilkinson were born four sons and two daughters, four of whom are yet living: Dr. George Wilkinson, a resident of Omaha, Nebraska; W. T. Wilkinson, of Ottumwa; Burton Wilkinson, of Keokuk; and Miss Mary J. Wilkinson, of this city.

The position which Mr. Wilkinson occupied in Keokuk aside from his business relations was one commanding the highest respect. His patriotism was a characteristic that led him to take deep interest in the welfare and progress of the nation as well as of his home locality. In 1861 when the country became involved in civil war, although he did not have the rugged strength required of those who went to the front he manifested his loyalty to the Union in many ways. He became one of the charter members of the old City Reserves and in that connection was frequently called upon to protect the border and was with his company at the battle of Athens, Missouri. His aid was never sought in vain in behalf of any movement which he believed would contribute to public progress or to the permanent good of Keokuk. His efforts in behalf of public education were particularly beneficial. He served for almost eighteen years as a member of the board of education and did all in his power to promote the efficiency of the schools and to raise the standard of public instruction for he justly considered the best educated man makes the best citizen. In 1871 he was chosen a member of the school board, serving at that time for three years and again in 1881 he was called to the office and continued therein until his death. Another matter of deep interest to him was the public library, which owed its existence in large measure to his efforts, for he was one of the originators of the plan and the organizers of the library in 1863. He was chosen its first president by election and re-elected both in 1864 and 1865. He continued a member of its board of directors throughout his entire life and when the library was made a free institution in the summer of 1894 Mayor Moorhead appointed him a member of the new board. By his fellow members he was chosen president and was acting in that capacity at the time of his demise. The first certificate of life membership was issued to him on the 1st of May, 1864, and it is now among the treasures in the custody of the librarian. His fellow citizens accorded him recognition of his personal worth, his public spirit and his devotion to the general good by electing him to the office of alderman, where he served in 1867-8. The following year he was elected mayor and thus controlled the municipal interests for one term. He held membership in Atlantic Lodge, No. 178, Free and Accepted Masons, of New York city, the Northwestern Traveling Men's Association, the Knights of Honor, the Loyal Legion and the Ancient Order of United Workmen, but the membership which claimed most of his time and energies was his church relationship. He was a communicant and vestryman of St. John's Episcopal church and aided in large measure in the development and growth of the church when it was established near his residence. His broad humanitarian spirit was manifest in his active and unostentatious charity. None knew the extend of his benevolences for while he gave freely he never boasted of his generosity and, in fact, there were times when not even the recipients of his bounty knew to whom they were indebted for timely aid. He was uniformly courteous and his gentlemanly demeanor made him a man whom to know was to respect and honor. He passed away after an illness of three months, although for only a few days was he confined to his home, his death occurring January 7, 1895. Resolutions of respect were passed by the various organizations with which he had been closely associated, including the lodges and the public library board. The city council passed the following resolutions:

"In the broad sweep which it is making among those who wear a crown of honor in our city the scythe of death has reached and cut down the faithful, courteous and conscientious Andrew J. Wilkinson.

"It is no mere formal manner that we take this occasion to show our respect for him. When a man who has lived as Mr. Wilkinson has, who has, through long years, constantly chosen the right, the good, the honest, the sincere, and who, as a result, carries the honor, the confidence and the favor of his fellows—when such a man is taken men do not merely show the outward garb of sorrow. He carries down with him men's hearts. In the lack of his counsel and example men feel that they have sustained a loss.

"The influence of Mr. Wilkinson's life has for many years been strongly felt in the religious, educational, political and social work of Keokuk. In 1869 he was thought worthy of the honor and was elected mayor of the city. For years he has been a zealous worker for the public library and when that institution was by the city made free to all the mayor appointed Mr. Wilkinson a member of the board of trustees, of which body he was chosen to be president, and which office is vacated by his death.

"In respect to him, who, through so many years and in so many ways has served his city and his fellowman, be it

"Resolved, That this council do now rise until Thursday evening, January 10, after the body of ex-Mayor Wilkinson has been laid to rest."

One who knew him well, said: "He had been for many years one of the chief business men of Keokuk. He was a good and lovable man. He lived his life in 'the beauty of holiness;' not cant or religious pretense; there was not a particle of that in him; but all his life he simply did to others as he would have them do to him. He seemed incapable of selfishness. He was gentle, gracious, kindly, courteous, considerate, obliging, helpful and yet fixed and resolute in his convictions. He could say 'no' as firmly as any man we ever knew. We have many times had occasion to admire the high and punctilious sense of official duty, exactness and thoroughness he took to the discharge of any public trust that fell to him. His pervading integrity, sincerity and dignity made him do all his work without paltriness or slighting. It was a delight to be associated with him on the school board or anywhere. His high courtesy, kindness, calm but fixed regard for justice and the properties of life made it so that his respect for the personality of every one pervaded any meeting with the atmosphere of good will and gracious comradship. Human nature is a rather lofty matter after all or there would not be so many really noble men and women as there are. We say what is simply true when we say that the parting breath of Andrew J. Wilkinson ended one of the best and most beautiful lives that have ever been in Keokuk."

THOMAS J. MAXWELL, M. D.

Dr. Thomas J. Maxwell, one of the most eminent surgeons of Iowa, one of the organizers of St. Joseph's Hospital of Keokuk and professor of surgery and clinical surgery in the Keokuk College of Medicine, College of Physicians and Surgeons, of Keokuk, was born in New Athens, Harrison county, Ohio, March 6, 1837. His parents were John and Jane (Orr) Maxwell. The father was born near Wheeling, West Virginia, was a representative of one of the old families there and in 1804 accompanied his father, Thomas Maxwell, on his removal to Ohio, where he attained his majority and was married to Miss Orr, who was born in Washington county, Pennsylvania, and had gone to New Athens, Ohio, with her father, Robert Orr, and his family. In early life John Maxwell mastered the trades of a wheelwright and cabinetmaker and followed those pursuits in Ohio. In 1842 he visited Iowa on a prospecting tour and in 1844 he brought his family to this state, locating in Crawfordsville, Washington county, where he continued to work at the millwright's trade, building many mills throughout that section of the state. There his death occurred in 1871 and his wife passed away in 1885. They were members of the United Presbyterian church and their influence was strongly felt on the substantial and moral development of the community in which they made their home.

Dr. Maxwell, when seven years of age, accompanied his parents to Iowa and pursued his literary education in the district schools and in the academy of Crawfordsville, after which he engaged in teaching in Washington county. While thus engaged he determined upon the practice of medicine as a life work, and to this end began studying with Dr. J. D. Miles, a highly educated and skillful physician, as his preceptor. He pursued lecture courses in Keokuk, in what was then known as the medical department of the University of Iowa, and was graduated in February, 1861.

Dr. Maxwell located for practice in Washington county, Iowa, but in 1862 he was commissioned assistant surgeon in the Third Iowa Cavalry, continuing in charge of the field practice with that regiment until 1865. The command participated in many hotly contested engagements, resulting in the necessity for much surgical treatment. In 1865 Dr. Maxwell was transferred from the Third Iowa Cavalry to the One Hundred and Thirty-eighth colored regiment as surgeon, with the rank of major, and he was mustered out under order given by the war department in January, 1866.

Returning to Washington county, Iowa, Dr. Maxwell then made arrangements to remove to Olena, Henderson county, Illinois, where he built up a large country practice, that made his labor financially as well as professionally successful, but in 1882, desirous of putting aside the very arduous duties involved in such a practice, he removed to Keokuk and opened an office. Although he began here as a general practitioner the demands made upon him for surgical work soon made him a specialist in that line, and his superior skill gained him eminence that has since ranked him with the leading surgeons of the state. He has performed many capital operations and has the honor of having first successfully performed the operation for the removal of an ovarian tumor in Iowa, resulting in the recovery of the patient. He continued to enjoy a very large and important surgery practice until 1885, since which time his attention has been given chiefly to education labor in the line of his profession. In that year he became lecturer on state medicine and hygiene in the College of Physicians and Surgeons and subsequently was given the chair of clinical surgery, while later he was made professor of anatomy and occupied that chair for four years. His next position was the professorship of obstetrics and gynecology, but on the return of the former occupant of the chair he gave up the department of obstetrics, continuing, however, to lecture on gynecology and anatomy.

In 1890, in connection with Dr. Jenkins and a few other noted members of the profession, Dr. Maxwell assisted in founding Keokuk Medical College and became professor of surgery and clinical surgery, occupying that position until the Keokuk Medical College bought out the College of Physicians and Surgeons and the two institutions were consolidated, the new school being known as the Keokuk Medical College, College of Physicians and Surgeons. Dr. Maxwell continued to fill the chair of surgery and clinical surgery and at the same time has contributed in substantial measure to the success of the school through his efforts to advance its standard and promote its efficiency. He has seen old methods superseded by new and improved ones and the college has kept pace with the universal progress that has marked the medical profession, no greater advancement being made in any line of scientific research and investigation. Dr. Maxwell is also connected with the dental department of the college and has seen great growth in the attendance in recent years, a fact indicative of its rank as an institution for the training of those who desire to become active members of the profession.

Dr. Maxwell was a member of the Illinois State Medical Society and the Military Tract Medical Society and now belongs to the Keokuk Medical and Iowa State Medical Societies, both of which he has been the president. He likewise belongs to the American Medical Association and is the author of various papers of merit and of value to the profession which he has read before these different organizations. He is now preparing a book for publication upon the treatment of intra-capsular fractures, such as fractures inside the hip joint, having devised a method of healing which was previously thought to be an incurable fracture of the hip joint. He has treated many cases successfully and his discovery has proven of the greatest benefit in surgery. He was active in founding St. Joseph's Hospital and since its establishment has been surgeon-in-chief.

Dr. Maxwell married Miss Elizabeth Riley, who was born in Ohio, in 1866, and they became the parents of six children, but Mabel died at the age of twenty years and two died in early childhood. The living children are Maude, Helen and John R. The son is a graduate of the Illinois University at Champaign and of the Keokuk Medical College and is now professor of anatomy and clinical surgery in the Keokuk College of Medicine. The Doctor has a beautiful and hospitable home at No. 727 North Ninth street, in Keokuk. He is a member of Torrence Post, Grand Army of the Republic and of the Loyal Legion and in his political views is a Republican. He took an active part in politics while in Illinois and was there candidate for senator but the district was strongly Democratic. The demands of his profession now leave him little time for outside interests, and his labors as medical and surgical practitioner, lecturer and author have made his life work of marked value to his fellowman.

JOHN R. DIMOND.

In various official positions John R. Dimond has demonstrated his loyalty and his public-spirited citizenship and at the present writing is capably serving as city, county and state assessor for Keokuk and Lee county. He was born in Louisville, Kentucky, June 17, 1841, his parents being John and Elizabeth (Rudy) Dimond. The father was born in Londonderry, Ireland, in May, 1806, and there learned the shoemaker's trade. When twenty-one years of age he left his native country and crossed the Atlantic, establishing his home in Buffalo, New York, but soon afterward he removed to Louisville, Kentucky, where he followed his trade for some time and was also engaged in the shoe business. He likewise conducted what was known as a shoemaker's boarding house, the third story being fitted up as a shop for the boarders, to which they might take their custom work

MR. AND MRS. JOHN R. DIMOND

and finish it. Mr. Dimond, taking an active part in Democratic politics in the South, was made turnkey or jailer for Louisville, and occupied that position for a number of years. At length he disposed of his business interests there and in the spring of 1854 removed with his family to Keokuk, where he worked for a time as a journeyman, but in 1858 he again entered business for himself. At one time he was the owner of three farms in Hancock county, Illinois, but on selling this invested the money in Keokuk property and opened a custom shop on Main street, where he continued in business until his retirement in 1890. He also improved considerable city property here and in his investments and different business ventures displayed the possession of strong sagacity, able management and unabating energy. His political views undergoing a change, he voted the Republican ticket from 1860 until in his later years, when he gave his allegiance to the Greenback party.

In early manhood he wedded Elizabeth Rudy, who was born in Philadelphia, Pennsylvania, March 12, 1806, a daughter of John and Susan (Lusley) Rudy. During her girlhood her parents removed to Maysville, Kentucky, where her father engaged in contracting and building. Her maternal grandfather, Capt. Robert Lusley, was a soldier of the Revolutionary War and was a member of the Lusley family that was established in Philadelphia in 1734. He is mentioned in the history of the landing of the Palatines at that period. Mr. Dimond passed away February 2, 1892, his wife surviving him until the 7th of May, 1896. They were members of the Unitarian church and they left a family of five children. John R. Dimond having acquired his education in the city schools of Louisville and Keokuk, Iowa, entered upon his business career in the employ of General Brown, at the age of thirteen years, keeping the first toll gate on the plank road from Keokuk to Charleston. He was afterward for some years employed in a brick yard and this business experience brought him splendid physical development. He afterward learned the shoemaker's trade and in 1858 he enlisted in the regular army for service on the plains, but his father objected to this course and he was thereby compelled to remain at home. Military service, however, was not denied him for at the outbreak of the Civil War he responded to President Lincoln's call for 75,000 troops, joining the first three-year regiment which enlisted in response to that call. He was about the tenth man in Keokuk to be enrolled. The troops drilled for some time but they missed being accepted in the first regiment, as only one Iowa regiment was called for the three months' quota. On replying to a telegram to the war department they were informed that they would be accepted for three years in a call soon to be made. Having enlisted on the 19th of April, 1861, they were sworn in for three years' service on the 27th of May, 1861, Mr. Dimond being a member of Company A, Second Iowa Infantry. This was the first regiment, however, to leave the state. They went to St. Joseph, Missouri, and did guard duty on the Hannibal & St. Joseph Railroad for two months, when they were sent to Bird's Point, Missouri, and from there to Sulphur Springs, and on to

Pilot Knob. Joining Fremont, they started on a march to Cape Girardeau and in October, 1861, arrived at Benton Barracks, St. Louis, in order to recruit, for there were only 200 men in the regiment who were not ill. Mr. Dimond was sent home on a furlough, after which he reported at McDowell's College, St. Louis, and guarded rebel prisoners through the winter. In February he went to Fort Donelson and was in the famous charge at that place on the 15th of the month, where the Union troops captured and held the rifle pits. Mr. Dimond being frozen during the night was sent to the hospital and was there detained as a nurse. He returned to his regiment about a week after the battle of Shiloh, which was the only battle of his command in which he was not an active participant. He was at Corinth in 1862, the battle of Iuka, the second battle of Corinth and afterward went to Pulaski, Tennessee, under General Dodge, where he was detained as scout and was thus serving until he went to Chattanooga, where he joined Sherman's army. He took part in the battles of Dalton and Resaca and made the first crossing at the Oustenola river. He was also in the engagements at Peach Tree Creek, Crab Orchard, Dallas and at Atlanta, the Second Iowa Regiment occupying the position on the extreme left of the army. He was also in the seige of Atlanta and after the engagement at Rome, Georgia, went on the celebrated march to the sea and participated in the various military movements around Savannah. Later the regiment started northward on the campaign through the Carolinas and Mr. Dimond was in all of the engagements up to the close of the war. He was the first man who veteranized from the State of Iowa and was then made corporal. He participated in the grand review at Washington, District of Columbia, and received an honorable discharge, July 19, 1865, after four years and three months of meritorious service in the South. He has every reason to be proud of his military record, for he never faltered in the performance of any duty and bravely took his place on the lonely picket line or on the firing line. He suffered the usual hardships and rigors of war and cheerfully gave his services to his country that the integrity of the Union might be preserved.

Mr. Dimond after being discharged started for Rockford, Illinois, and was married to Miss Sarah Carpenter of that place, the wedding being celebrated July 31, 1865. They traveled life's journey together for more than a quarter of a century and Mrs. Dimond then passed away on the 9th of June, 1891, leaving seven children: Mrs. Alice Mundy; James H., of Evansville, Indiana; Nellie, the wife of Thomas McGinnis, of Indianapolis, Indiana; Oscar C., of St. Louis; Jessie, of Mount Pleasant, Iowa; George L., of Quincy, Illinois, and Sadie, also of Mount Pleasant, Iowa. On the 7th of November, 1900, Mr. Dimond was again married, his second union being with Mrs. Dorothy Jester, a daughter of Abel Morris, of Wayland, Missouri. She was the mother of two children by her first marriage, Mabel and Leota, who reside at home.

Reaching Keokuk after his marriage, Mr. Dimond was employed by his father in the shoe business and in 1867 engaged in business for himself, continuing in that line for twelve years. He afterward turned his attention to the grocery business and for five years was storekeeper for the workingmen's co-operative grocery and for eight years conducted a grocery store of his own. He next turned his attention to the insurance business and was afterward variously employed until 1898, when he was elected state and county assessor for Keokuk. He has since occupied that position and has also been state and county and city assessor for the City of Keokuk since 1900. Other local offices he has filled, having been a member of the city council from 1878 until 1880. No public trust reposed in him has ever been betrayed in the slightest degree and now for six years he has served in his present office, discharging his duties in a manner creditable to himself and satisfactory to his constituents. At the general election of 1904 Mr. Dimond was elected, without opposition, again to the office of state and county assessor. He is a member of Belknap Post, No. 515, Grand Army of the Republic, of which he is now serving as Commander and he has attended both the state and national encampments. He has a pleasant home at the corner of Ninth and Palean streets and throughout Lee county has a wide and favorable acquaintance. He is today as true to his duties of citizenship as when he wore the blue uniform of the nation and followed the starry banner on the battlefields of the South. His integrity as a citizen and as a business man have never been called into question and he commands the uniform confidence and good will of all with whom he has been associated.

JOHN MENZ.

A successful business man of Keokuk and one of the most prominent political leaders of Lee county, is John Menz, now serving his third term as county treasurer. Mr. Menz was born near the village of Suhl, Prussia, Germany, January 12, 1829, and is the son of Christopher and Elizabeth (Munk) Menz. Leaving their native land to seek the superior opportunities of a new and undeveloped country, the family came to America, landing at New Orleans November 28, 1853. They ascended the Mississippi river to St. Louis, and located at Highland, Illinois, where the father passed the remainder of his life.

John Menz received a good general education in Germany, and in addition attended a training school and was educated as an architect, but in America found little demand for the work of his profession. For a time, however, he was associated with his father in his business as a contractor, but began his independent business career as the proprietor of a general store at Highland, Illinois. In this venture he was quite successful, but sold out in 1876, and removed to Keokuk, where he purchased the Eagle hotel, which he conducted for a number of years. This proved to be very profitable enterprise.

In 1889 Mr. Menz was elected, against his own expressed wish, by the Democratic party as county and city assessor. He accepted the office, and continued to perform its duties with credit to himself until 1893. In September, 1893 he was appointed by the board of supervisors to fill an unexpired term as deputy county treasurer. This position he held until 1899, when he received the nomination for county treasurer at the hands of the Democratic party, was elected, and has been twice re-elected, a fact which speaks loudly for his capability and integrity, as well as his popularity. The position is one of the highest importance, large amounts of money, approximately $160,000 each year, passing through his hands.

Mr. Menz is influential in Democratic circles, and has often served the party as delegate to the state conventions. He was at one time prominently connected with various fraternal organizations, but being frequently elected to offices in these orders, and finding the demands upon his time interfered with his public duties, he has allowed these relations to lapse.

Mr. Menz was united in marriage to Miss Christina Steiner of Highland, Illinois, a native of Switzerland, and they are the parents of six children, as follows: Mrs. Louisa Haines; Mrs. Emily Kraft, of Burlington, Iowa; Mrs. Milda Kraft, of Keokuk; Ella, who is now living at her father's home; Mrs. Ida Atwood, deceased, and Robert J., president of the Menz Lumber Company, a prominent business house of Minneapolis, Minnesota.

Coming to the United States without resources, unaided and by his own efforts and talents climbing the ladder of success, the achievements of Mr. Menz form a lesson in self-help worthy of studious consideration by all younger men. Of strong character and unbending integrity, he is honored and respected by all.

LEWIS WALTER.

Lewis Walter, a leading citizen of Donnellson, Iowa, and postmaster at that place, was born March 31, 1842, in Venango county, Pennsylvania, the son of P. H. and Mary (Cole) Walter. Although both his parents were born in Pennsylvania, the father was of German and the mother of Irish extraction, and, combining in themselves many of the highest and best characteristics of their respective nationalities, they successfully overcame the adverse conditions of pioneer life in the West, and while acquiring a competence, at the same time they achieved for themselves a position of recognized standing in the community, being respected by all who knew them. Early forming a resolution to bear a share in the conquest of the vast and wealthy region west of the Mississippi river, they set out from their eastern home in the year 1857, and after an arduous wagon journey of twenty-eight days arrived in Des Moines county, Iowa; and in the fall of that year they purchased a farm of 160 acres in Franklin township, Lee county. There they improved the land and pursued the vocation of farming until the early seventies, when they disposed of their holdings in order to purchase a farm near Dover in the same township, on which they resided for a number of years, selling it later, however, and buying a small farm in that neighborhood on which the remainder of their days were passed in the enjoyment of the well-earned fruits of their long and faithful toil. Much honor is due them for the part they played in the early development of Iowa, and it is with eminent fitness that a record of their lives and deeds is here inscribed in loving remembrance and veneration. Mr. Walter attained to quite a degree of prominence in local public affairs, being an active worker in the ranks of the Democratic party and having held the office of assessor and a number of minor elective positions of trust and honor, and enjoying a wide acquaintance and popularity. Ever striving for the triumph of humanity's higher interests, he and his wife were active members of the Methodist Episcopal church, and did much to advance its welfare. The remains of both rest in Clay Grove cemetery.

Two brothers and two sisters of Mr. Walter, our subject, attained to years of maturity. Jesse Carroll, the eldest, is now deceased. He was a prominent member of the Lee county bar, and at one time held the office of county auditor, and was a veteran of the Civil War, having served with the Thirteenth Iowa Volunteer Infantry. He was a man of brilliant endowments and extraordinary ability. Mary A., the elder sister, is the widow of Henry Jefferson, and resides at Cedar Falls, Iowa. Kate G., who is the fourth in order of birth, is the widow of Francis H. Semple, formerly a prominent attorney of Keokuk, and is a resident of Chicago. George R., the youngest, is also deceased, his demise having occurred in 1903.

The early educational advantages of Lewis Walter were limited to those of the public schools in his native state of Pennsylvania, and practically ended in his fifteenth year when he accompanied his parents to Iowa, but being of a studious disposition he made the most of his opportunities, and by following an instinctive love of knowledge qualified himself for many positions of honor and usefulness in his later life. The days of his youth were devoted to the exacting duties of his father's farm, in which he continued until the call of patriotism drew his attention from peaceful pursuits and he went forth to serve his country in the cause of freedom, justice and national unity. In 1862 he enlisted in company "E," Nineteenth Iowa Volunteer Infantry, at Fort Madison under Captain William Adams. The first nine months of his service were spent in the department of the Frontier, and it was during this period that he participated in the famous battle of Prairie Grove. Later he participated in the siege of Vicksburg, after which he was transferred to the department of Gulf, and on September 29, 1863, the entire regiment, consisting of 206 men, were captured by a superior number of Confederate forces at Sterling Farm, Louisiana, and held as prisoners of war, first at Tyler, Texas, and later at Shreveport, Louisiana. At the latter place they were exchanged on July 22 of the following year, after suffering many hardships in prison, and rejoined the Union army under General Canby, taking part in the numerous engagements of the campaign which culminated in the fall of Mobile, at which place our subject was honorably discharged with the rank of sergeant, having earned that military grade by meritorious service in camp and on the field of battle.

Upon the close of hostilities Mr. Walter returned home, and shortly after was united in marriage to Miss Martha Adeline Walker, daughter of Milton Walker, a highly respected citizen and early pioneer settler of Iowa. For a year after his marriage he cultivated his father's farm, but owing to the low state of his health, which had been much impaired by the life of southern prisons, camps and fields, he was compelled to abandon the work, and for a number of years followed successfully the profession of teaching. Later he was interested at intervals for the space of ten years in mercantile enterprises at West Point and at Dover, and also completed a course of reading in law, but did not apply for admission to practice in the courts. On removing to Donnellson he spent two years in teaching, and subsequently became the first editor of the Lee County Record, published at this place, of which he afterward became owner but which he has since sold. At one time he was also an editorial writer for the Plain Dealer, of Fort Madison, and in these positions he exercised a very considerable influence in public affairs, acquiring a wide reputation as a clear and consistent thinker and forceful writer, whose pen was ever employed on the side of justice and sound policy.

To Mr. and Mrs. Walter have been born the following children who reached maturity: Alice R., who is the wife of Charles H. Scheurs, at the present time a rural mail carrier of Donnellson, and has two children, Walter and Karl; John, who died at the age of eighteen years; Elva and Kathryn, who reside with their father. In March of 1903 the mother of this family passed to the higher life, and was laid at rest in Clay Grove cemetery. Although reared in the Presbyterian faith, in which denomination her father was a prominent and leading worker, she was a member of the Methodist Episcopal church. She was a woman of many rare qualities, a consistent Christian, a devoted wife and loving mother, and to those who, by the intimacy of family relations, it was permitted to know the depth and truth of her affections, the sweet aroma of her memory will remain ever precious.

To Mr. Walter has fallen many public duties. During a year of his residence at West Point he held the office of justice of the peace, for a period of thirty years he acted as notary public, in the village of Donnellson he has been elected by his fellow citizens to the offices of alderman, recorder and mayor, and during the administration of President Harrison he was appointed postmaster, a position to which he was reappointed on the inaguration of the late President McKinley. Also he was at one time made its secretary by the Lee county agricultural association. In 1892 he was one of the prime movers in the organization of the People's Mutual Fire Insurance Company, and was its first secretary, a relation which he has ever since sustained. In fraternal affairs he has assumed a prominent place, being a past chancellor of the local lodge of the Knights of Pythias, and a member of the Masonic order and Sedgewick post Grand Army of the Republic of Maryville, Missouri. His political faith is that indicated by the part he has borne in public affairs—that of the Republican party, in which for a long term of years he has been a valued worker.

both on account of his large personal influence and his advice in the councils of the party. Mr. Walter's life work has been one of broad and lasting usefulness, and the varied abilities he has displayed in differing occupations, together with his honorable and strictly upright course in all relations of life, fully entitle him to that universal respect which he has long enjoyed. He is well known, by reputation and personally, throughout Lee county, and has a host of friends who honor him for his character and his long record of duty conscientiously and nobly performed.

HON. CHARLES H. FINCH.

Success which comes from capability and the honor which is accorded in recognition to true worth are today enjoyed by Hon. Charles H. Finch, auditor of Lee county and ex-mayor of the city of Fort Madison. He was born in Fort Madison November 17, 1860, and is the son of Hiram and Jane (Jenkins) Finch. Hiram Finch was born at Montrose, Susquehanna county, Pennsylvania, May 27, 1824. The family came to America from England at an early date, the grandfather, Hiram Finch, being an early resident of Montrose, Pennsylvania, where he secured a grant of land. He was one of the prominent men of his day, a sheriff of the county, and a successful real-estate operator. Hiram Finch, the father of our subject, followed the sea for many years, as mate of a sailing vessel. On retiring from the life of an ocean sailor he became, in 1857, mate and captain on the Mississippi river, and was one of the well-known rivermen during the days when the river traffic was large and important. He continued in this line of activity until 1872.

The parents of Charles H. Finch were married at Swansea, South Wales, and came to Fort Madison in 1857. After retiring from the river the father was connected with the state penitentiary at this place, holding various positions in the institution until about one year prior to his death. He was one of the early members of the Masonic order at Dallas City, Illinois, being a charter member of Dallas City Lodge, Free and Accepted Masons. He died July 8, 1900, the demise of his wife having preceded his own by a year. Five children survive them.

The subject of this sketch, after the completion of his education in the public schools of his native city, entered the employ of the Iowa Farming Tool Company of this place, serving a regular apprenticeship of three years, in order to acquire the trade of a machinist. As a master mechanic he remained with the same company until June, 1900, when he became manager of the Hotel Anthes. This connection was continued until April, 1904.

In politics he has been an active worker in the Democratic ranks ever since attaining his majority. Twice he has been elected to serve his ward in the city council, but resigned the office during his second term on account of having changed the place of his residence. In the first term of his tenure he was chairman of the Light and Park committees, and it was at this time that Old Settlers' Park was graded and filled and otherwise beautified and improved. In 1901, the year following his resignation, he was called by his fellow citizens to the highest office within their gift, and it was during his administration as mayor of the city of Fort Madison that the floating debt of the municipality was materially reduced.

Prior to the expiration of his term of office as mayor he was elected auditor of Lee county, assuming his new duties in January, 1903. He has discharged the obligations and responsibilities of this position with credit to himself and in such a manner as to reflect honor upon the constituency which has seen fit to repose in him a trust of such importance and magnitude.

Fraternally he is Master of Stella Lodge, No. 440, Free and Accepted Masons, and as a Past Master of the lodge has been its representative in the Grand Lodge. In Potowonka Chapter, No. 21, Royal Arch Masons, he holds membership, and has occupied the positions of High Priest and representative to the Grand Chapter. In the Masonic craft, especially, has he been prominent. He is a member of the council and of Dallas Commandery No. 51, of Fort Madison, of which latter he has been Eminent Commander. In the Mystic Shrine his membership is in Kaba Temple, Davenport, Iowa.

April 10, 1894, Mr. Finch married Miss Elizabeth Anthes, a member of one of the prominent families of Fort Madison. She is a daughter of George and Anna Anthes. Two sons grace their home—George H. and Charles A. Mr. Finch gives his active support to the Episcopal church, in which he was reared, and Mrs. Finch is a member of that denomination. In Fort Madison and throughout Lee county the name of Hon. Charles H. Finch stands for many things of which any man might feel justly proud. Among these are honor, integrity and an unswerving faithfulness to duty.

GEORGE RANSON.

George Ranson, an old and honored pioneer of Cedar township, Lee county, Iowa, who is living upon his magnificent estate of four hundred and eighteen acres and after a long and useful career is passing his last years in a well-deserved peace and quiet.

Mr. Ranson was born in Yorkshire, England, March 3, 1831, a son of James and Elizabeth Ranson. The following year his parents crossed the ocean in an old sailing vessel, and made their way to Jacksonville, Illinois, where they maintained their home until 1841. That year they removed to Henry county, Iowa, where the father bought a two-hundred-acre farm, to which he later added thirty acres, on which he spent the balance of his life. There was only a log cabin and stable upon the place and made such other improvements as the needs of the place demanded. He was the father of six girls and two boys. Three of the girls are dead, and the subject of this sketch was the fourth member of the family in order of birth.

George received but a limited education in the old log school houses of Illinois and Iowa, under the instruction of the frontier pedagogues, but he has made the most of the instruction that he did receive. By close observation and wide reading he has supplied many of the defects of his early training, and has become a well-educated man in the great school of life. He lived at home until he reached the age of twenty-five years when his father died. In March, 1861, he was married to Miss Romelia Hyde, who was born near Columbus, Franklin county, Ohio, a daughter of George W. and Sarah (Hart) Hyde. Her father was born in New York city, and her mother in Ohio, but her people were of Southern origin. About 1849 they settled in Cedar township, Lee county, bought a farm of two hundred acres, on which her father was engaged in farming his remaining years.

Mr. Ranson made his home with his father-in-law, for one summer, then bought the place where he now resides on which he built a fine house and barn, making many other improvements, such as setting out a fine orchard, and bringing the entire place up to the most exacting requirements. After his father-in-law's death he bought out the other heirs' interest.

To Mr. and Mrs. Ranson have come the following children: Elizabeth and Laura died young; Eva is dead; Luella, the wife of George E. Powell, has four living children—Howard, Lena, Nellie and Vern; Frank, a resident of Big Mound, Lee county, married Miss Olive Crawford, and they are the parents of two children—Roland and Martha; Ellen married C. W. King, a farmer in Cedar township, and is the mother of four children—Ellen, Henry, George Marion and Velda; Walter married Grace Zigler, and is a farmer near Salem; Florence Magnolia married Richard Dodsworth, and is a resident of Marion township; Martha is at home; Charles and Wallace died young.

Mr. Ranson is Republican in his political sympathies, and though he has never sought official honors he has acted as treasurer of his school district for many years. In religion he is a member of the Methodist Episcopal church, and has well squared his life by the principles of honesty, brotherhood and square dealing. Among the old settlers his name is well known, and he is the most respected and esteemed by those who have known him the longest.

JAMES M. GARDNER.

James M. Gardner, who was for many years a resident and large landholder of Franklin township, Lee county, Iowa, was born at Hillsboro, New Hampshire, May 11, 1835, a son of William and Sophronia Gardner, with whom he removed to Jackson county in what is now West Virginia, when he was but four years of age, and there he received his education in the rural schools and grew to years of maturity as his father's assistant on the farm, but in 1865 he decided to broaden the field of his labors, and entered the employ of the Louisville Bridge

& Iron Company as a bridge builder. He remained in the employ of this company throughout the remainder of his life, and having early displayed remarkable aptitude for the work of his chosen profession, was given charge of the bridges of the Louisville & Nashville Railroad during the disturbed period which marked the close of the Civil War, and was captured a number of times by the Confederate guerrillas who then infested that section, but being a non-combatant, was always released. He soon took high rank as a superintendent of bridge building, and in that capacity did a great deal of construction work on various railroads, being thus engaged in nearly all the states of the Union, and building a large number of bridges. He possessed mechanical ability of a high order, and was a man of strong executive force, possessing in an unusual degree the talent for governing and directing men, and it was this quality that caused his services to be always in demand and brought him unusual appreciation from his employers, together with the fact that he was always thorough in his work and never failed to insist upon the same conscientious observance of detail from those under his command.

On December 15, 1879, Mr. Gardner wedded Miss Amanda Peoples, of Ohio, who was born in Steubenville, Meigs county, that state, July 8, 1838. In 1874 he purchased a farm of 160 acres in Franklin township, Lee county, Iowa, and in 1876 he brought his family from West Virginia and established them in this new home, he having great faith in the possibilities of the West as a field of opportunity for his children, to whom he desired to furnish all the advantages in his power. Later he added to his real-estate holdings until he owned 364 acres of fertile lands, which was cultivated by his sons, he himself being constantly absent upon the duties of his profession. To Mr. and Mrs. Gardner were born the following children who survive them: William S., of Central City, Nebraska; Lucinda H., wife of A. L. C. Wolf, of Central City, Nebraska; Harry A., of Cushing, Iowa; Mary E., wife of Laurence Ray, of Central City, Nebraska; Robert A., postmaster at West Point, Iowa; and John E., practicing the profession of dentistry at Newman's Grove, Nebraska. Two sons, James C. and Edwin E., are deceased.

Mr. Gardner's death occurred July 11, 1886, his demise having been preceded by that of his wife, which occurred March 7, 1884, and both are buried in Clay Grove cemetery. While Mr. Gardner was enthusiastically devoted to his work, his first consideration was ever that of his duty as a citizen, and he was an intelligent student of public affairs in their more general aspects, and a consistent member of the Republican party, which he supported in all important contests. He believed in an overruling Providence, to which he owned allegiance, and holding firmly to the tenets of the Christian faith, he held membership in the Christian church, as did also his devoted wife, and they observed a lifelong fidelity in their religious relations as embodying the most exalted conception of which the human mind is capable. He was a man of resolute and determined character, yet kind and gentle in disposition, one who made friends easily and retained their regard without effort as belonging to him by natural right, and was respected by all with whom he came in contact.

CHARLES E. RUTH, M. D.

Dr. Charles E. Ruth, physician, surgeon and educator, now holding the professorship of surgery and clinical surgery in the Keokuk Medical College, College of Physicians and Surgeons, of Keokuk, was born in Johnson county, Iowa, on the 17th of August, 1861, his parents being Alexander and Sarah Jane (Funk) Ruth. The Ruths are of old Pennsylvania stock. The great-grandfather of Dr. Ruth was brought from England to America when only a year old, the family home being established in Washington county, Pennsylvania, prior to the American Revolution. There he was reared, becoming a farmer and stockraiser. His home was located about two miles south of West Alexandria, Pennsylvania. His wife, a native of Ireland, was also brought to America when about a year old and was reared in the same neighborhood as her husband. They became the parents of ten children. Their son, Hugh Ruth, the grandfather of Dr. Ruth, died in Winterset, Madison county, Iowa, at the advanced age of eighty-seven years. He was married twice and had twelve children. His first wife, a Miss Jacobs, was the grandmother of Dr. Ruth. She died in 1845, age thirty-four.

Alexander Ruth was born in Washington county, Pennsylvania, in 1836, and came to Iowa when twenty years of age, settling in Johnson county, where he has since made his home. He enlisted in Company G, Fourteenth Iowa Volunteer Infantry, and served in the Indian war on the border under General Sully, participating in all the engagements of his regiment. Later he was transferred to the Forty-first Iowa Volunteer Infantry and subsequently to the Seventh Iowa Cavalry, and remaining at the front until after the close of the war, he then received an honorable discharge and has since lived in Johnson and Muscatine counties and at present is a resident of Winterset, Iowa. In 1860 he married Miss Sarah J. Funk, who was born in Greene county, Pennsylvania, in 1840, a daughter of Joseph Funk, also a native of that county, where the family was established in pioneer times, and where the descendants are now very numerous. Her father was a shoemaker and later a farmer. Six children were born to Alexander and Sarah Ruth, of whom four are living: Charles E., Oliver J., Carrie B. and Lizzie J. The elder daughter became the wife of Walter Braham, who was killed by a falling timber in 1894, while living at Croxton, Nebraska, and she is now the wife of J. H. Mark. Lizzie J. is engaged in deaconess work in Mother's Jewels Home, in York, Nebraska. Mrs. Ruth died in July, 1896.

Charles E. Ruth, reared upon his father's farm, acquired his early education in the district schools and afterward attended the high school of Iowa City. Determining upon practice of medicine as a life work he pursued a three years course of study in the Medical department of the Iowa State University, from which he was graduated, March 7, 1883. He at once began practice in Atalissa, Muscatine county, Iowa, where he remained for four years and then removed to the city of Muscatine. While there he became a member of the County and State Medical Societies and the American Medical Association. Finding that Muscatine did not offer him the field of labor he desired and which was demanded by his constantly developing powers. Accordingly he came to Keokuk in 1892. Two years prior to this time he had been elected professor of anatomy in the Keokuk Medical College, while in 1893 he was elected professor of clinical surgery at St. Joseph's Hospital, at Keokuk. His connection with the Keokuk Medical College began in 1890. He was elected vice president of the institution in 1896, and his connection therewith has since been continuous. In 1903 he became secretary of the faculty of the Keokuk Medical College, College of Physicians and Surgeons, and in July, 1904, was elected professor of surgery and clinical surgery in the college. In the same year he was made chairman of the section of surgery of the Iowa State Medical Society. He has also served for one term as president of the Tri-State Medical Society, embracing Illinois, Iowa and Missouri. In 1898 he was chosen chairman of the section of obstetrics and diseases of women of the Iowa Medical Society, and in June of that year he was appointed brigade surgeon, with the rank of major, in the United States volunteer army, but on account of illness was obliged to resign his commission the following month. Among later societies organized for the dissemination of knowledge among the members of the profession, of which Dr. Ruth has become a representative are: The Western Surgical and Gynecological Society, the Military Tract Medical Society, the Southeastern Iowa Medical Society and the Southwestern Iowa Medical Society. His prominence and ability are widely acknowledged by the profession, and not only in private practice but also as an educator his labors have proven of far-reaching benefit to mankind.

On the 3d of October, 1883, Dr. Ruth married Miss Adella Tantlinger, an accomplished daughter of John L. and Louisa (Warren) Tantlinger, born in Johnson county, Iowa, August 28, 1864. The Tantlingers located in Iowa City as early as 1840 when the site was nearly all uncultivated prairie or timber land. Joseph Stover, a native of Kentucky and a descendant of Daniel Boone, was the great-grandfather, in the maternal line, of Mrs. Ruth. He was a broad-shouldered, powerful man, intensely loyal and was well fitted to cope with pioneer conditions, which undoubtedly he enjoyed, for he became a frontiersman in four states. He became wealthy through investment and well-directed business activity and died at the advanced age of ninety-seven years, leaving his farm, two miles southwest of Iowa City, to his son, who still resides there. His wife died at the age of eighty-eight years. His daughter, grandmother of Mrs. Ruth, was a widow when she went to Iowa

City with her father. Her name was Mrs. Sarah (Stover) Warren and she had six children.

Dr. and Mrs. Ruth have three children: Verl Alton, Una Gertrude and Zana. The parents are members of the Methodist Episcopal church, to which Dr. Ruth has belonged from the age of ten years. He is also a member of the Masonic fraternity and is deeply interested in all that pertains to the betterment of mankind. It would be almost tautological in this connection to enter into any series of statements as showing him to be a man of strong intellectuality and progressive ideas, for these have been shadowed forth between the lines of this review. Those who have profited by his professional service have also recognized in him a broad humanitarian spirit and a kindly sympathy which have won him the entire respect of the general public as well as his fellow members in the profession.

RUDOLPH H. KREHBIEL.

In order to properly and fully understand the greatness of the country in which we live it is necessary to make a study of the various sources from which that greatness arises, to analyze its elements, and to appraise, with what accuracy we may, the value and importance of its several constituent parts; and in any inquiry of this kind it invariably appears that a very great measure of credit is due to families of Germanic origin, and that the energy, enterprise and keen mentality of this class of citizens has entitled the part played by them in the material, moral and civic advancement of the nation to be considered highly excellent, praiseworthy and broadly significant. A representative of this class of estimable citizens in Lee county and a member of one of its old and prominent families, is Rudolph H. Krehbiel, of Franklin township, where he resides on a large and highly improved farm in section 29 and successfully conducts a business of general farming and stockraising.

Mr. Krehbiel is a native son of Lee county, having been born March 19, 1866, in the home which he now occupies, and is the son of Christian and Mary (Schnebele) Krehbiel, who were both of German birth and an account of whose lives will be found elsewhere in this work. He received his education in both the German and English languages, attending the public schools and a German institution in his district, the latter being maintained by families of that nationality in order that their children might enjoy superior advantages and that the most cherished and valuable traditions of the Fatherland might be perpetuated for their influence on the characters of their descendants. He also took an active share in the work of the farm, learning the details of management and operation under the direction of his father, and in his twenty sixth year he began his independent work in life by renting one of his father's farms in Franklin township, which he conducted with great success until the death of his father in 1899, when, receiving the bequest of the home farm, he removed here and has since made it his place of residence. Here he has profitably continued his work of farming, and devotes a great deal of attention to the raising of high-grade stock, a subject on which he is a recognized authority. Besides the farm of 100 acres on which he resides he owns 80 acres in section 30 and 35 acres of fine timber land in section 30. He has brought his land to a high state of cultivation, has introduced many modern improvements, thus demonstrating his thorough confidence in up-to-date ideas and proving by his success in their application that enterprise is as valuable in agriculture as in any other line of business, and at the same time he has observed a legitimate conservatism which gives full respect to the results of past experience.

On May 15, 1892, Mr. Krehbiel was united in marriage to Miss Mary Lowenberg, a native of Lee county and a daughter of Valentine and Kate (Krehbiel) Lowenberg. Mrs. Krehbiel's father was born in Germany, and when only fourteen years of age came to America, locating in Lee county, where he successfully engaged in farming throughout his active life. To Mr. and Mrs. Krehbiel have been born eight sons and daughters, as follows: Hilda, Edgar, Robert, Mary, Rudolph, Kurt, Lillian and Homer, who died at the age of two months. All had Franklin township for their place of birth, and are being educated in the public schools of that township.

Mr. Krehbiel is a member of the Mennonite church and an active supporter of its work as of all movements calculated to secure the welfare of his community. While an advocate of all progressive measures and taking a great interest in public affairs, he has never aspired to public office, but contents himself with conscientious effort in his capacity of private citizen to promote honest and efficient government. In his partisan relations he is a member of the Democratic party, believing the principles and declared policies of that organization to be the highest embodiment of American political science, but usually maintains an independent attitude in affairs of local government, casting his ballot according to his individual estimate of the men and measures involved. Always public spirited and ready to aid all worthy enterprises, he was at one time a stockholder in the Bank of Donnellson during the earlier history of that institution, but has not maintained the connection. Mr. Krehbiel's position among the progressive and substantial citizens of Lee county is one of the very highest, and by reason of his successful career, his representative character and his wide acquaintance he is well deserving of a prominent place in a work of the present nature.

JOHN C. COURTRIGHT.

A careful and methodical farmer, a conscientious citizen, a good neighbor and friend, and a sincere Christian, John C. Courtright has left behind him a record which will long keep his memory in the hearts of those who knew him best. From he comforts and pleasures of the home which he had built up as the result of years of faithful effort he was called to the higher life on July 9, 1900, aged fifty-four years, four months and eleven days. A brief sketch of his career is here given among the lives of the representative men of Lee county.

Mr. Courtright was born in Franklin county, Ohio, February 28, 1846, and came to Lee county with his parents when five years of age, they settling in Franklin township. After the death of his father and mother he made his home with Edward Courtright near Clay Grove, remaining there until his marriage May 4, 1867, to Miss Virginia Jarrett. Mrs. Courtright was born in North Carolina, and came to Lee county with her parents in her girlhood. She is the daughter of Elias and Fanny (Lantz) Jarrett, both natives of North Carolina, and is one of a family of thirteen brothers and sisters, all but one of whom attained years of maturity and were married. The father died in this county at the age of eighty-two years, having spent the greater part of his life as a farmer near West Point. The mother is still living, at the age of ninety-seven years, and resides with her daughter, Mrs. Courtright, in Fort Madison.

To Mr. and Mrs. Courtright were born eight children, as follows: Otho C.; Lulu Edith, who is the wife of Dudley Barnes, and resides on the old Courtright home farm; Edward E., dentist, of Fort Madison; Viola Belle, wife of R. A. Gardner, of West Point, this county; Myrtle; Hugh L.; Pearl C.; Lilly, deceased.

Mr. Courtright was educated at Denmark Academy at Denmark, Lee county, and engaged in general farming and stock-raising in Franklin township, continuing these occupations until the time of his death. He owned a farm of one hundred acres which he inherited from his father, being part of the original estate, and in addition he purchased eighty acres, which he improved and placed under a high state of cultivation. He was a member of Clay Grove Methodist Episcopal church, of which he was trustee and steward for a long period of years, and was one of its active workers and a devout Christian. He served as township trustee of Franklin township for eleven years. In politics he was a Democrat, but never sought public office. He was, however, a public-spirited man, in the highest sense of the term, and was one who enjoyed the profoundest esteem of those who knew him.

Otto C. Courtright, eldest of the children of John C. Courtright, is engaged in the business of photography at Fort Madison. Born on the home farm near West Point, he was educated in Whittier College at Salem, Iowa, and Howe's Academy of Mount Pleasant, and later this was supplemented by a course of study in a business college at Burlington. He assisted in the work of the farm until about twenty-one years of age, when he began his present business, locating first at Salem, Henry county, Iowa. After two years spent at that place he removed to Farmington, but remained there only a short time before taking up his present location in Fort Madison, where he has been continuously since. Here he has a modern and unusually well-appointed studio, and conducts a large and successful business. He was united in marriage at Fort Madison to Miss Birdie Marsh, and they have one son, Lazarre. Mr. Courtright has made many friends here, and is rapidly assuming a substantial position in the business world of Fort Madison. He is a member of the Methodist Episcopal church.

LAWRENCE E. DENMIRE.

Lawrence E. Denmire is a man whose career illustrates the value of sound business principles applied to every undertaking. He is a general farmer, the proprietor of a fine estate consisting of 200 acres of very choice land in section 25, Montrose township, Lee county, and has risen to a very prominent place in his chosen calling by the use of precisely the same principles that make for fame and fortune wherever manly character and business integrity manifest themselves. He has studied the situation in which his interests are involved, has determined what is right and proper to do, and then has gone ahead with boldness and enterprise, to work out great problems in his own life and field of labor. In general, that problem is to bring the finished product with the least intermediary expense the closest to the consumer. The principle is the same, whether applied to the affairs of a nation, or the humble efforts of the individual tiller of the soil, to cut off as far as possible the exactions of intermediate agencies, and bring the producer and the consumer as close together as possible. In the establishment and the development of a very important canning factory, Mr. Denmire deserves to rank with the "captains of industry," and while his name may never appear on the rolls of the great, it deserves and receives an important place in the annals of Lee county.

Mr. Denmire was born on the farm where he now lives May 5, 1857, a son of Edward and Emily K. (Kyle) Denmire, natives respectfully of Preble and Trumbull counties, Ohio. They were married in Dayton, Ohio, and removed to Lee county in 1853, where they led a farming life until the death of the husband and father in 1888. There is a sister of Mr. Denmire, Altha E., who is living at home and is unmarried. She has been a very successful school teacher.

The subject of this review left school when he was only fifteen years of age and applied himself for some years to the work of the farm. For fifteen years he held an important position as contracting and receiving agent for the Burlington Pickling Works at Ballinger Station. He has a naturally mechanical turn of mind, and is quite an expert blacksmith and iron worker. For several years he was quite busily engaged in blacksmithing, and all the machinery in his canning factory was installed by himself. This was an enterprise which he began in 1894; and he has enlarged it year by year until it now has an output of three thousand cases of tomatoes yearly, besides other goods. He himself raises about a fourth of the tomatoes he uses and contracts for the rest, which of course makes business in the neighborhood. During the season about thirty-five women are employed in the factory as well as from three to eight men. It now represents a total investment of about $5,000, of which about $1,400 has been put in this season in the form of new machinery and other needed improvements. Everything in the factory is done under the personal direction of the proprietor, and he has proved himself in this notable business undertaking an exceedingly careful as well as enterprising manager. In 1904 he had a tomato-field that covered over thirteen acres with an unusual abundant yield. His goods are of a high grade, and the wholesale grocers of Burlington and Keokuk are glad to handle all they can secure of his make.

Mr. Denmire was married October 24, 1888, to Miss Maude Burt. To this union have come six children: Helen Coe; Leta E.; Burt E.; Dorothy J., Frederick S., who is dead, and Lawrence, Jr. He is a charter member of the Summitville Camp, No. 4594, Modern Woodmen of America, and is an enthusiastic and devoted friend of the fraternity. Years ago he was a member of the Independent Order of Good Templars. It was a country lodge, and had at one time some forty members. During its existence he was one of its most active workers, and much of the time occupied official station.

Mr. Denmire is a member of the Christian church at Sandusky, Lee county, and for years has been one of its deacons as well as a member of its financial committee. He was a liberal contributor to the building of the first church, and is now one of the trustees of the organization. In politics he is a Republican, and is generally regarded as one of the prominent and influential citizens of the county.

Benjamin Coe Burt, the father of Mrs. Denmire, a native of Orange county, New York, spent his last years in the village of Sandusky, Lee county, where he died in 1888. His widow is still living, and makes her home with her son, Harvey, of Washington. Her children, other than Mrs. Denmire, are as follows: Howard, Charles, Frank, Harry and Mrs. William Jessup, now residing in Florida, New York.

The Denmires are very highly esteemed in the community where their helpful and useful lives are swiftly passing in a round of good deeds and quiet fostering of all that is generous and inspiring in life around them.

HENRY F. EPPERS.

Probably no agriculturist of Lee county enjoys a greater degree of prominence and influence than the subject of this sketch, and certainly none has borne a more important part in shaping the destinies of the county than he. Sagacity, discrimination and keen foresight are the qualities that have raised him to a commanding position, and of him it may be justly said that his natural talents have not been used merely for purposes of self-aggrandizement, but have always been employed for the public good. Although not a native of the county, he has been a continuous resident here since 1856, and his record has been honorable and significant. Mr. Eppers was born in Brunswick, Germany, January 4, 1848, the son of Henry and Wilhelmina Eppers. He came with his parents to America when eight years of age, and settled on a farm in Jefferson township, and here his father spent the remainder of his life. Our subject received his early education in the public schools of his township, and later he attended the village school of Franklin. During vacations, however, he assisted in the work of the farm, learning those lessons of useful labor that were destined to prove of value in later life.

With that independence which characterizes the best young American manhood, Mr. Eppers immediately began his active career on his own account as soon as he attained to the age of twenty-one years, securing employment at rafting and with lumber boats on the Mississippi river. He followed this occupation very successfully for a number of years. He then bought a farm of forty acres in Jefferson township, but finding after a time that he was able to make a handsome profit from the pursuit of agriculture, he decided to enlarge his holdings, and therefore traded his farm for one of eighty acres in same township, that which he now owns and on which he has resided for twenty-five years. By industry, economy and care he has here made for himself a pleasant home, one in which are to be found many modern conveniences, and in which his family enjoy the comforts of life.

On April 23, 1874, Mr. Eppers was united in marriage to Miss Minnie Knemeyer, of Fort Madison. Mrs. Eppers is of German parentage, but was born in America, being a native of Illinois. Of this union have been born four sons and one daughter. They are: Frederick, Edward, Minnie, Charles, Roy.

In matters of politics Mr. Eppers has given his support with unswerving loyalty to the Democratic party, and has been an active worker for the triumph of its principles. To him the party in southern Iowa owes much, and has often rewarded his efforts in its behalf by elevating him to positions of honor. His first public trust was that of township clerk of Jefferson township, which post he held for ten years, and later he was elected to the office of assessor and for a period of eight years he performed its duties with signal success and to the satisfaction of his constituents. He has served his party as delegate to every state convention for the last ten years, and as delegate to every county convention for thirty years—a remarkable record. For several years he was chairman of the county central committee, and it was during his tenure of office that the Democratic party received the largest majorities at the polls that it ever enjoyed—before or since. Of recent years he has been serving as a member of the congressional committee of his district, and is at the present time chairman of that body, having been elected in 1902 and re-elected in 1904. It will thus be seen that Mr. Eppers's part in shaping the policies of the great party to which he belongs has been one of no limited extent. In 1880 he accepted the nomination for county recorder, and as a result of his popularity he reduced the normal majority against him more than 1,100 votes. Long practical experience in politics gives great weight to his voice in Democratic councils, and he deserves honor from the fact that his influence has always been on the side of protecting the purity of the ballot and safeguarding the popular liberties. On account of his ability and integrity he enjoys the universal confidence and respect, and his pleasing manner and personality have made him a host of loyal friends.

CHARLES JEFFERSON HAGAN, M. D.

Death often removes from our midst those whom we can ill afford to lose, men whose lives have become an integral factor in the history of their communities, because of an unselfish spirit which prompts effort for the general good as well as for individual progress. Brave in the presence of danger, calm in the midst of excitement, at all times using his faculties to the utmost along progressive lines, giving of his labors for his fellowmen not only in his profession but also in other walks of life, Dr. Hagan commanded the respect and confidence of all and won the sincere friendship and deeper love of many. He was a man of scholarly tastes and attainments devoted to his family and in his daily conduct displayed those sterling traits which cause his friends to say:

"He was a man; take him for all in all,
I shall not look upon his like again."

Dr. Hagan was a native of Tuscarawas county, Ohio, born on the 10th of February, 1842, his parents being Charles and Margaret (Bailes) Hagan, the former a native of Pennsylvania and the latter of New York. In his native county he spent his youth and acquired his education, obtaining fair knowledge of the sciences and the languages. Throughout his entire life, however, he continued a student, constantly broadening his mind by research and investigation. Taking up the study of medicine in 1859, he was graduated from Starling Medical College, of Columbus, Ohio, in 1863, about the time he attained his majority. In 1862, however, when he was but twenty years of age and while yet a college student he was appointed acting assistant surgeon in the United States Army and after his graduation was commissioned assistant surgeon in the Forty-sixth Ohio Infantry, with which he remained until after the close of hostilities. His was a noble and commendable service. Ever forgetting all personal danger he made his way to the battlefield again and again to relieve the suffering of his wounded comrades. He was one of the few army surgeons wounded in the war, being severely wounded in Sherman's famous campaign to Atlanta, Georgia. He came to be loved by all to whom he ministered, because of his kindly, genial spirit as well as his professional skill.

When the war was ended Dr. Hagan returned to his old home in Ohio and there practiced his profession until 1867, when he came to the Mississippi valley and opened an office in Alexandria. Almost immediately he attained success as a practitioner there, his knowledge and skill being recognized and continually demonstrated in his alleviation of human suffering. He was appointed postmaster of Alexandria, serving in 1868-9 and afterward conducted the office for three years for C. H. Grumman. He continued a resident of Missouri until April 5, 18[illegible] when he removed to Keokuk, where he gave his attention to the practice of his profession and the supervision of his private interests until his death, which occurred on the 30th of November, 1903.

Dr. Hagan was married on the 29th of June, 186[illegible] Miss Louise G. Conway, and they became the parents of two daughters, but the elder, Nona, died February 3, 1896. The younger, the wife of Dr. H. A. Gray, is living in Keokuk. The death of his daughter was a blow to Dr. Hagan, from which he seemed never to recover. He was deeply attached to his family, his interests centering in his home and the best traits of his character were there daily displayed. Although he was not demonstrative in its expression his love for his wife and children was the ruling element in his character. He took little part in public life, dividing his attention between his family and his practice. While living in Missouri he had become a member of Memphis Commandery, Knights Templar, and was in full sympathy with the beneficent spirit of Masonry. He also belonged to the Northeastern Missouri Medical Society. He was always conscientious, never yielding one iota in a matter of principle or duty, yet he had ready sympathy for the mistakes of others and was ever willing to extend a helping hand to those who were finding it difficult to climb upward. He was of calm temperament, kindly spirit and genial disposition, possessing much of chivalry and entirely free from ostentation or display. He was a great lover of books, devoting much of his leisure hours from his profession to the study of history, biography, science and general literature. He read only the best and had the power of assimilating the great ideas of the master minds. He was a companionable man, although the circle of his friends was select rather than large and those who gained his friendship prized it as a rare jewel.

JAMES H. ANDERSON.

James H. Anderson, classed as one of the ablest lawyers that has ever practiced at the bar of Keokuk, has been a member of the legal profession for forty years and while his clientage has been extensive and of an important character he has at the same time found opportunity to assist in the substantial development of the city, his tangible labors in behalf of Keokuk rendering him a valuable and forceful factor in community affairs. His life work has won the admiration and respect of his fellow men and he receives the deference which the world instinctively pays to the man whose success has been worthily achieved. Born in Cincinnati, Ohio, on the 30th of May, 1842, he is a son of Robert James and Mary J. (Whitney) Anderson. Although his father was born in Dublin, Ireland, on the 5th of March, 1813, the ancestral history of the family can be traced back to an early epoch in Scottish annals. Robert Anderson, the founder of the family on the Emerald Isle, went with William the Conqueror, to the north of Ireland, and in the general confiscation which was there made according to the customs of war at that time he was given three small farms in the county of Cavan—property which remained in possession of his descendants for one hundred and forty years. His namesake, Robert Anderson, the grandfather of James H. Anderson, left the ancestral home in the north of Ireland and went to Dublin, where he married Constance Hoare, a daughter of a prominent lawyer of that city and a member of the same family to which belongs George F. Hoar and the London bankers of that name. Robert Anderson was an accountant at Dublin for a number of years and subsequently emigrated with his family to Canada in 1831, locating in Greenville. After his son, Robert James Anderson, emigrated to Cincinnati, he and his wife also made their way to the United States and spent their last years in Covington, just across the river from the Ohio city.

In the schools of Ireland, Robert James Anderson acquired his education and he, too, became an accountant there, but his business connection with his native country was of short duration as he came with his parents to the new world and in 1838 he went to Cincinnati, where he became bookkeeper for and a member of the firm of James Beatty & Company, extensive pork-packers of that city. It was during his residence there that he wedded Mary J. Whitney, a daughter of William W. Whitney, whose ancestors came to America with a Massachusetts Bay colony in 1635. Severing his business relations in Ohio Robert J. Anderson came to Keokuk in 1857 and remained an active factor in business circles of this city until his death in 1891. His widow still survives him and has reached the advanced age of eighty-one years. Both were consistent and active members of the Methodist Episcopal church.

Acquiring his early education in the public schools of Cincinnati, James H. Anderson continued his studies in the high school of Keokuk, from which he was graduated. His loyalty stood the test of the Civil War and was demonstrated by his active service with the First Northeast Missouri Regiment of Volunteers and which afterward became the Twenty-first Missouri Volunteer Infantry. He continued with the latter command for six months and was taken prisoner on the 14th of September, 1861, after which he was paroled and returned to his home. The regiment re-enlisted before he was exchanged, but with a characteristic feeling of honor he would not break his parole, and later re-enlisted in Company C, of the Forty-fifth Iowa Infantry. The regiment was assigned to Tennessee in 1864 and he remained with that command until mustered out at the close of his term of enlistment.

Subsequent to his return to civil life James H. Anderson entered upon the study of law in the office and under the direction of John H. Craig and was admitted to the bar by examination at Keosauqua, Iowa, on the 11th of March, 1866. On the 11th of November, 1867, he entered into partnership with Mr. Gilmore, an attorney of Keokuk, having a very large practice. This association under the firm name of Gilmore & Anderson was continued until the death of the senior partner August 31, 1881, and they were classed with the most prominent law firms of the city and of southeastern Iowa. Mr. Anderson has at different times been associated in practice with his brother and with James C. Davis, but is now alone. He is a forcible and convincing speaker, a fluent writer and trusted office adviser, having accurate and comprehensive knowledge of the principles of jurisprudence. He has ever prepared his cases with great fairness and care and his analytical mind and gift of oratory has enabled him to present his case so that his deductions have followed in logical sequence and with a force of a strong climax. He is one of the few members of the bar who have practiced here continuously since 1867 and his legal business extends to the higher courts and to the supreme court of the United States.

Had Mr. Anderson accomplished nothing save what he has done in connection with the conduct of important litigated interests he would be entitled to representation in this volume as one of the leading professional men of Keokuk, but his labors have been extended to other fields of activity resulting in great benefit to the city. He may well be termed a promoter in this connection, for with ready recognition of needs and possibilities he has so utilized the means at hand as to produce results whose far-reaching and beneficial influence will be ever found in later generations. Figuring in financial circles, he was for ten years a director of the State National Bank of Keokuk. He was also the organizer and the president of the Keokuk Water Works Company that built and put in successful operation the water works system of the city. He was vice-president and manager of the Keokuk & Northwestern Railway when it was built. He was one of the original promoters of the Keokuk Street Railway and was president at the time of the building of its line. He has also erected many residences in the city and purchased the land and laid out the Keokuk public park, which after he had greatly improved it and which today is one of the handsomest public parks in the West, he sold to the city for less than its cost to him. In connection with W. S. Sample he purchased, fenced and laid out the property and made a boulevard around Keokuk, which was afterward donated to the city, public-spirited citizens assisting him in this worthy enterprise by generous subscriptions. Mr. Anderson has frequently been solicited to accept public office and undoubtedly could have received any political preferment within the gift of his fellow townsmen, but he has no aspirations in that direction preferring that his service in behalf of Keokuk should be done as a private citizen. He has always been deeply interested in educational affairs and was president of the school board for three years, during which time the fine high school building was erected, the work receiving his earnest endorsement and co-operation.

On the 12th of March, 1868, occurred the marriage of James H. Anderson and Miss Anna Riggs, who was born at Brookville, Indiana, and they have five children, of whom three are living: Edwin G., who is an agricultural implement manufacturer of Council Bluffs, as a member of the firm of E. Children & Sons; Elizabeth, the wife of John W. Atwood, manager of the Big Four Implement Company at Council Bluffs, Iowa; and David F., who is a bookkeeper for his brother. Mr. and Mrs. Anderson are members of the Unitarian church, in which he has held various offices. From the age of twenty-one years he has been a Mason and was at one time identified with the Knight Templar Commandery. He belongs to Torrence Post, No. 12, Grand Army of the Republic. In 1870 he erected a fine residence at Fourth and Morgan streets, which he has since occupied and in the social life of the city as well as in its professional circles and public interests he was prominent. He stands today among those who are building for themselves lasting monuments in the success which they accomplish through capability and merit and in the effective effort which they put forth along lines that result beneficially to their fellowmen as well.

LAWRENCE SMITH.

A young man who has within a few years attained for himself an enviable position in the financial circles of Lee county is Lawrence Smith, of West Point. Mr. Smith was born in Hancock county, Illinois, October 1, 1874, the son of Riley Smith. He received his early education in the district school, and later attended college at Quincy, Illinois, from which he was graduated in the classical and commercial courses in the class of '93. Shortly after his graduation he began his independent career by removing to West Point, Iowa, and identifying himself with the private bank known as the Bank of West Point, having a capital of $15,000, with Riley Smith as president, Frederick Kriekenbaum vice-president and Mr. Smith as bookkeeper and assistant cashier, acting in this capacity until November, 1896, when he became the cashier and has since filled this position.

In 1896 Mr. Smith was united in marriage to Miss Anna Hutchinson, a native of West Point, and they have one daughter, Muriel. Mr. and Mrs. Smith attend the Methodist Episcopal church, of which Mrs. Smith is a member. In matters pertaining to politics Mr. Smith maintains an independent attitude, never casting his vote according to partisan distinctions, but giving his support to those who in his opinion are individually best qualified for the public service. He enjoys the general esteem in the county and town of his adoption, and in 1904 was elected to the office of Mayor of West Point on an independent ticket. Fraternally, he is a member of the Modern Woodmen of America.

Mr. Smith devotes his entire time during office hours to the banking business, and his experience here has been one of unbroken success. This being the only bank in the northwestern part of Lee county, it draws from a very extensive and resourceful tributary territory, and the choice of location reflects credit upon the founder. Mr. Smith's residence in West Point is an artistically designed edifice of impressive proportions, modern in its appointments and of pleasant surroundings, and is the centre of a refined and cultured social circle. He possesses talents of no mean order, and by virtue of his well-known character of high-minded integrity and frankness, qualities which mark his contact with others in all relations of life, he is accorded respect wherever known, and is justly considered one of the rising young men of Lee county.

THEODORE B. SNYDER.

Theodore B. Snyder, a resident of Fort Madison, where he has been successfully engaged in general legal practice for a number of years, is a native of Des Moines county, Iowa, the date of his birth being 1845. Mr. Snyder began his education in the public schools, and later entered Iowa Wesleyan University at Mount Pleasant, where he pursued the classical course of study, being graduated with the degree of Bachelor of Arts with the class of '69. He then began reading law in the city of Burlington, and afterward entered the law department of Iowa State University, from which he was graduated in 1871. He located in Burlington, and continued in the practice of his profession there until his removal to Fort Madison in 1891, where he has met with a very gratifying measure of success.

Shortly after his graduation from Iowa State University Mr. Snyder was elected, although a young man, to the position of county superintendent of schools of Des Moines county, and on the expiration of his term was re-elected. He was also elected, while a resident of that county, to a number of minor offices.

Mr. Snyder is a son of Andrew and Sarah (Baker) Snyder. The father was a native of Ohio, but being of an enterprising disposition, came west in 1844 with the object of sharing the more abundant opportunities of a new country, and settled near Burlington, where he continued his business of farming for the remainder of his life. He died at his country home August 3, 1885, at the age of eighty-two years and nine months. The death of his wife occurred December 24, 1882, in her seventy-fifth year. He was a successful farmer, and by the exercise of energy, care and ability attained to a very prosperous condition. He was the father of ten children, four of whom survive.

On February 25, 1880, Mr. Snyder was united in marriage to Miss Mary L. Dorgan, who is a native of Massachusetts. Mrs. Snyder is the daughter of C. P. Dorgan, now deceased, and Mary J. Dorgan. Her father was engaged in the shoe business at Brockton, Massachusetts, near which his widow still lives.

Mr. and Mrs. Snyder are the parents of four children, all of whom were born at Burlington and all survive. They are: Marie L., who is a graduate of Brockton, Massachusetts, high school; Garnet L., and Arleen L., who are graduates of Fort Madison high school; and Erlon L., who is at the present time in California. All have received advantages of excellent schooling and education.

Mr. Snyder is a member of the Iowa State Bar Association and of the Lee County Association. In his fraternal relations he is connected with the Masonic order, being a member of Stelle Lodge, 440, Free and Accepted Masons, and of Potowonok Chapter, No. 28, Royal Arch Masons. He gives his entire attention to the line of effort with which he is directly connected with the prosperity and progress of the community, and it may justly be said of him that he is a valued and valuable member of his profession. His ability has won him admirers, and his tact and social qualities, together with the confidence inspired by his well-known integrity in all relations, have made him many friends.

JOHN B. UNDERWOOD.

In taking up the history of the representative men of Lee county, especial mention must be made of John B. Underwood, an early settler of the county, a representative of one of its most prominent pioneer families and a well-known and influential citizen. A native of the Empire state, the date and place of his birth being Columbia county, New York, April 5, 1828, he removed with his parents when eight years of age to Chenango county, where he remained until 1853, when, having attained to years of maturity, and being possessed of an ambition to achieve for himself a career of honor, usefulness and independent success, he decided in favor of the great West as the scene of his future labors, and coming to Iowa, located in Lee county. Here he engaged in the lumber business at Montrose, meeting with much success in this pursuit.

Later Mr. Underwood returned to his native state for a short time, but came again to Lee county in 1857, purchasing a fine farm of 160 acres in Van Buren township and there establishing a home which has ever since been his place of residence, improving the wild land and adding to his real-estate holdings until he now owns 240 acres of fertile and productive lands, almost all of which he has placed under cultivation. Here he makes a specialty of stockraising, limiting his attention to the finer and more choice varieties, and conducts general farming on a large scale. A thorough believer in modern methods, he has equipped his farm with the latest and most approved apparatus, has introduced new ideas into its operation, and by the exercise of sound and practical business judgment has succeeded in securing a most gratifying return for his time and thought, having achieved a success which must be considered extraordinary even in this land of large successes. He has erected a large and substantial dwelling house in the midst of beautiful grounds, and here enjoys in well-earned ease the fruits of his care and toil.

Mr. Underwood is able to trace much of his success in life to early training and the advantages derived from sturdy New England ancestry, he being the son of Artch and Rhody (Chapin) Underwood, both of whom were born in Berkshire county, Massachusetts. The father was a farmer all his life, with the exception of teaching at Livingston Manor for four years and the son was his assistant in the work until he reached manhood, meanwhile receiving a good common-school education in the public schools of Chenango county, New York. The death of the father occurred in the seventy-sixth year of his age, and the mother attained to the age of seventy-seven years. They were the parents of nine sons and daughters, of whom Mr. Underwood, our subject, was the youngest and is now the sole survivor.

At Keokuk, on February 16, 1859, Mr. Underwood was united in marriage to Miss Almeda Baldwin, who was born in the State of New York and there received her early education. She was the daughter of Stephen Baldwin, was a member of an excellent family, and manifested in her life high qualities of Christian character, being a devoted wife and a kind and loving mother, of an altogether unselfish disposition, and always placing the welfare of her family and others before her own. She died May 7, 1898, at the age of sixty-two years, and was laid at rest in Croton cemetery in Van Buren township.

To Mr. and Mrs. Underwood were born during their residence in Van Buren township five sons and two daughters: George Allen, born May 8, 1860, died at the age of twenty years; Orlena, born August 4, 1862, died July 1, 1863; Jeremiah H., born April 17, 1864, now residing with his father, married Miss Capitolia Kinnick, and has five children, John Earl, Nellie May, Carl, Hilton and George; Ralph W., born April 5, 1867, died June 13, 1869; Philinda Estelle, born April 11, 1870, is the wife of Perry McPherson, of Clark county, Missouri; Isha Morell, born July 25, 1872, and now residing in the State of Washington, married Miss May Belle Starr and has one child, Roy; and Charles F., born May 11, 1877, died July 4, 1878.

Mr. Underwood was a member and active worker in the Presbyterian church, while the church was here, but of late years there has been no church here of that denomination, as was also the late partner of his joys and sorrows, and has always given of his worldly goods in the cause of religion and supported all worthy charities, welcoming all opportunities to do good in a quiet and becoming manner. He has served the community in which he lives in various public capacities, having for a time acted as school director and treasurer and for a number of years past holding the office of justice of the peace of his township. Politically, he affiliates with the Republican party, and his voice carries weight in its councils. By reason of his long residence here, his well-known ability, his success in whatever he has attempted, his honorable share in advancing the moral and material welfare of the community, his steadfast devotion to the cause of right and justice and his admirable Christian character he has become known, by reputation at least, throughout Lee county, enjoys amicable intercourse with a large number of friends, and is esteemed and respected wherever known.

ROBERT AINSLEY GARDNER.

Robert Ainsley Gardner, postmaster at West Point and a rising and popular young man of this community, is a native son of Lee county, having been born at Dover, Franklin township, September 16, 1874, a son of James M. and Amanda Gardner, an account of whose lives and ancestry appears upon another page of this work. It was in the district schools that Mr. Gardner received his early education, which he has since supplemented, however, by wide reading and study, and in 1892 he matriculated in the Gem City Business College at Quincy, Illinois, from which institution he was graduated in 1893 with the degree of Master of Accounts. He began his independent career utterly without capital or other resources except his own native ability, borrowing money to pay the expenses of his college course, and has always depended solely upon his unassisted personal efforts for the success which he has achieved.

After his graduation from business college Mr. Gardner entered the photographic business in partnership with a Mr. Courtright, under the firm style of Gardner & Courtright, with studios both at West Point and Fort Madison, and lived at West Point until 1895, following which he removed to Fort Madison, but returned, at the expiration of a period of one year, to West Point, where he has since resided. Here he continued in the photographic business for a number of years with very gratifying success, but in 1900 he sold his interest to his partner, and purchased a half interest in a drug store at West Point in association with Dr. W. S. Carpenter. This relation continued for only six months, however, and was terminated by his election at the end of that time to the position of superintendent of the West Point public schools, whose many and complex responsibilities he met with eminent credit to his own ability and satisfaction to the public until the spring of 1901, when he resigned to accept the office of postmaster, which he still holds. He took the oath of office on April 1, 1901, and it was in July of that year and under his administration that the three rural delivery routes were established which have added so materially to the efficiency and satisfactory service of the West Point office. On December 17, 1895, he was united in marriage to Miss Belle Courtright, whose family history is given in full under the name of J. C. Courtright elsewhere in the present volume, and to them have been born two daughters, Gertrude and Violet. Mr. and Mrs. Gardner are members of the Methodist Episcopal church of West Point, in which they are active workers, and contribute to the support of its regular work and numerous charities and philanthropic movements, holding the advancement of ethical ideals to be equally important with the attainment of material success in life.

In fraternal circles Mr. Gardner is recognized as occupying a leading position, sustaining membership relations with Claypoole Lodge, No. 13, of the Masonic order at Fort Madison; with the Modern Woodmen of America at West Point, of which he is Past Venerable Consul; and with the Woodmen of the World in Rover Camp of Omaha, of which he is Past Counsellor Commander of the West Point Camp, now out of existence. He has occupied a prominent place in all organizations of which he has been a member for any considerable time, and in 1896 was vice-president of the Photographic Association of Iowa, while he was the first president of the Commercial League of West Point, a club of which he is a charter member, and held that office during the first two years of its existence, during which time the organization was placed upon a firm footing and started well upon the road to that prosperity which it now enjoys. Politically, he is a believer in the principles of the great Republican party, for whose success he has worked with unfailing energy, tact and judgment, and the weight of his personal popularity and influence has been of distinct advantage to the party in this section, while it has made his name known throughout Lee county as a positive force in affairs of local government. In 1904 he served as delegate to the state convention at Des Moines, and has also served several terms as township committeeman with signal ability. Mr. Gardner is one of those young men characteristic of America who, working their way upward from humble beginnings, have attained honored places among their fellowmen by the practice of the old-fashioned virtues of perseverance, integrity and courtesy, and while his present standing is in all respects an enviable one, it is safe to predict for him still greater things in future.

JOHN H. SMUTZ.

One of the more successful farmers and rising young men of Cedar township, Lee county, Iowa, is John H. Smutz, who was born November 28, 1870, in Van Buren county, Iowa, the son of Benjamin R. and Sarah Jane Smutz. During his boyhood he received a good education in the public schools of his native county, a preparation for active life which he has since supplemented by extensive reading, and until attaining his majority he assisted materially in the work of his father's farm, acquiring a familiarity with the underlying principles of agriculture and farm management and making a study of the various problems which must be understood and mastered in order to achieve success in this line of endeavor.

On March 10, 1891, Mr. Smutz was united in marriage to Miss Cora McCracken, who was born in Harrisburg township, Van Buren county, Iowa, and they removed to Lee county, where Mr. Smutz purchased 105 acres of land forming a portion of his present farm, which original purchase he has increased until he now owns a tract of 159 1-2 acres. Here he conducts general farming and stockraising, and by the exercise of energy, enterprise, care and attention to the details of management he has been very successful in securing from the soil large returns for labor, time and thought expended, and has proved himself fully capable of grappling with this particular industry in its complex modern phases. While the land was originally unimproved, it is now in a high state of cultivation, and all the improvements, which are of the latest designs, are the work of Mr. Smutz, including the farm buildings and the handsome and commodious new residence building. The home has a pleasant atmosphere of hospitality, and is the scene of much social intercourse of an enjoyable nature, Mr. and Mrs. Smutz being very popular young people in their community and having many friends. Mrs. Smutz has enjoyed considerable educational advantages, and is a lady of unusual ability, having been for five years a teacher in the schools of Van Buren township previous to her marriage. She comes of an old and well-known Van Buren county family, her parents being still residents of that county, and is the third of a family of seven brothers and sisters. The father of Mr. Smutz also still continues to reside in Van Buren county, although the wife and mother is now deceased; and he is the second of a family of three. To Mr. and Mrs. Smutz have been born three sons and two daughters, Craig, Merle, Harley, Ralph and Gladys.

Mr. Smutz has ever shown sympathy with all movements calculated to advance the material and moral interests of the community in which he lives, and attends and supports the Baptist church, of which Mrs. Smutz is an active member, and while he has never sought for himself the adventitious honor which attaches to public office, he has given much thought to political questions as affecting the prosperity of country, state and nation, and early united with the Republican party as the best means of expressing his views on current issues in a practical manner. He is widely known throughout this section, as a young man of marked business ability, and has many friends who predict for him a future bright with honor and success as the reward of conscientious effort.

HENRY HELLING.

Prominent in the business and political life of Lee county is Henry Helling, of Fort Madison, a native son of the city. The date of his birth was January 23, 1863, and he is of German extraction, his parents having come from Germany in 1852. His father, Theodore Helling, was a teamster, and while living in Fort Madison was employed by Atlee & Wilson, lumber dealers. The mother was Theresa (Shoemaker) Helling. Her death occurred here in March, 1903. To Theodore and Theresa Helling were born nine children, six of whom are still living. They are: Barney, of Fort Madison; Mary, wife of Theodore Plesser, of Dubuque, Iowa; Anton, of Fort Madison; Theresa, wife of M. F. Dettmer, of Dallas, Illinois; Henry, the subject of this sketch, and Katherine, of Fort Madison.

Mr. Helling received his education in Saint Mary's parochial school, and in 1876, after leaving school, he entered the employ of the Weston Lumber Company, working in the planing mill, where he remained four years. This was followed by a period of three years spent in the planing mill of S. & J. C. Atlee, and then he accepted a position at Davenport, Iowa, with the J. S. Keater Lumber Company, but returned to Fort Madison at the expiration of a year. At the end of a further three years of active experience he was promoted to the position of foreman of the Knapp Stout Lumber Company's planing mills, in which position he continued successfully for five years.

In 1891 he began an independent business career by the purchase of a general store at the corner of Fourth and Arch streets. The style of the firm was Nelle & Helling, the partner being Miss Minnie Nelle.

On June 6, 1889, Mr. Helling was married to Miss Mary Nelle, who was born at Fort Madison September 12, 1865. Unto them have been born seven children, as follows: Evelyn, born February 28, 1890; Henry, born September 11, 1892; Herman, born June 18, 1894; Walter, born October 25, 1896; Celina, born November 10, 1898; Vincent, born January 5, 1901, and Dorothy, born April 28, 1904. Mrs. Helling is a daughter of Herman and Theresa (Kempker) Nelle, both deceased. They were born in Germany, but were married in Fort Madison. Mr. Nelle was a porkpacker and general merchant, and was a very prominent business man. In his religious affiliation he was a Catholic, and in politics a Democrat, and was a member of the board of aldermen. His death occurred at nine o'clock on the evening of November 29, 1881, at which date he had attained the age of fifty-three years. Mrs. Nelle, who was born December 28, 1830, died March 11, 1901. They were the parents of nine children, six of whom grew to maturity. Those living are: Bernard, of Fort Madison; Minnie; Mary; Theresa, wife of George Lohman, and Frank, of Fort Madison, who married Miss Rose Wagner. Katherine, second of those who attained years of maturity, is now deceased.

Mr. Helling, by reason of his natural gifts, takes a prominent part in social affairs, as well as in business and civic life. He is president of Saint Joseph's Society, a benevolent organization, a member of the Iowa Mutual Protective Society, and of the Benevolent and Protective Order of Elks. In his religious faith he is a member of Saint Mary's Catholic church. For twenty years he has been a member of the volunteer fire department and for two years its chief. He has been a lifelong supporter of the Democratic party, its principles and its leaders, and has borne an important part in the service of his party in public capacities. He is at the present time a member of the county central committee, representing the fourth ward of Fort Madison, and has served in state and congressional conventions. For four years he acted as alderman from the fourth ward, having received the office at the hands of his fellow citizens on account of his general popularity and representative character, and during the last year of his incumbency was president of the board of aldermen. He was formerly a director of the Fort Madison Building and Loan Association, but is now less active in that work.

Mr. Helling began life at the bottom of the ladder, without aid and without capital, and all he has acquired has come to him by virtue of his own frugality, industry, care and natural talents. He is, in a word, a self-made man, and his success under such conditions is a more fitting commentary on his character than any tribute that might be framed in words.

JAMES MAXWELL.

James Maxwell, the postmaster of Primrose, Harrison township, and also holding the office of clerk of the township, was born in Franklin township, Lee county, December 31, 1864, and has lived in this county all his life. Still in the prime of life, though the shadows are beginning to creep a little backward, he is a striking example of what Iowa can do in the way of building manhood, strong and vigorous, clear-eyed, and bearing himself with the unabated strength of full maturity. The record of his life shows that on many occasions he has sought the public good at the expense of his own personal welfare, and he has ever been ready to sacrifice himself and his own interests to advance the fortunes of his friends and improve the neighborhood. Such men have many friends, and richly merit the kindly feeling in which they are held by those who know them best. Mr. Maxwell well deserves the affectionate regard of a wide circle of friends and acquaintances, who hold him high as a man, a citizen and a friend.

James Maxwell was educated in the public schools of Primrose, and in due time he graduated from the local high school. In his earlier years he assisted his father in his farming enterprises, and was engaged in farming until five years ago; when he came to town and opened a confectionery store, and at the same time establishing a barber shop. Almost immediately he found a wave of popularity running his way, and he was able to obtain the office of postmaster, when a change became due about a year ago. This position he still holds, and its duties are administered to the pre-eminent satisfaction of the patrons of the office.

Mr. Maxwell is a son of Joseph and Sarah Jane (Williams) Maxwell. The father was born in Ireland, and the mother in Pennsylvania. He left Ireland when he was but nineteen years of age, and coming to the United States, spent some years in Ohio. In 1862 he located in Lee county, Iowa, buying a farm in Cedar township, which, however, he occupied only two years, when he sold it, and buying a place in Harrison township, made that his home in 1870, dwelling there until his death, April 6, 1872, at the early age of forty-five years. He was a weaver by trade in the old country; but after his arrival in this country devoted himself to the cultivation of the soil. His widow survived him many years, and entered into the life immortal January 9, 1901, at the age of seventy-one. She was the mother of eight children; of whom only four are now living. Both father and mother were buried in the Sharon cemetery, Harrison township. Of the four living children of Joseph and Sarah Jane Maxwell brief mention may be made: Sarah is the wife of Henry L. McMillan. They live in Milton, Van Buren county, Iowa. Joseph A. is a school teacher, and has his home in Canton, Illinois; Nannie is the wife of Alonzo J. Warson, a noted farmer of Harrison township, and they are now living on the old Maxwell home farm. The fourth surviving member of the family is the one whose career forms the subject of this writing. Those who are dead are as follows: Esther died at the age of three years, and hers was the first body to be interred in Sharon cemetery. Elizabeth died when only six months old. Maggie and John Francis were drowned in Sugar Creek, three miles west of West Point, their grandfather losing his life in the water at the same time. The three had been trading in West Point one day in the early spring, and upon returning found the Creek had greatly increased in volume. When they attempted to cross, they were swept away and drowned. This was a sad day, and long remembered in the family, March 22, 1874.

Personally Mr. Maxwell is a genial and delightful gentleman, and his is a welcome presence in the various fraternal circles with which he is connected, the Knights of Pythias, of Donnellson, and the Primrose Camp of the Modern Woodmen of America, of which he has been clerk since its organization. In politics he is a Republican, and has filled the office of town clerk for the last two years. In religion he belongs to the Presbyterian church, and his daily life and doings have brought no shame to his professions.

AUGUST BRODT.

One of the oldest living citizens of Lee county is August Brodt, of Green Bay township, who has passed the ninety-third anniversary of his birth, and claims Germany as the land of his nativity, where, during the earlier part of his life he pursued the profession of forestry with marked success and considerable pecuniary profit. Thence with his family he emigrated to America in 1853, taking passage from Bremen in the first steam vessel that ever cleared from that port, landing after a voyage of twenty-six days' duration, at New York, and proceeding at once to Green Bay township, Lee county, Iowa, where he arrived in September of that year, and shortly after purchased a tract of 360 acres of fine farming lands, together with much farm stock and the household furniture of the previous owner, for all of which he paid $7,000 in cash. Here he has passed the greater number of the succeeding years, although he has spent not a little time in travel, having crossed the Atlantic ocean nine times, in company with his wife, and on one of their trips to the Fatherland they passed two

AUGUST BRODT

years there, while at another they prolonged their stay to ten years, returning to America in 1895. He has given much attention to agricultural matters, taking rank among the most enterprising farmers of the county, as he is also one of the most successful, confining his efforts to general farming and stockraising, but for a number of years he has been living in retirement from the active life of business.

Before leaving Germany Mr. Brodt was united in marriage to Miss Caroline Schurbert, who was the constant companion of his labors and cares until 1897, when her death occurred, in the seventy-seventh year of her age, and she was buried in Claypoole cemetery, which is located on the farm formerly owned by her husband and now the property of their daughter, Mrs. Laura Langerbeck. To them were born eight children, four of whom came with them to America, as follows: Laura, who is now the sole survivor of the number; Bertha, who died at the age of twenty-six; Robert, who was accidentally shot and killed at the age of sixteen, and one child which died in infancy. Laura, who was in her fifteenth year when she accompanied her parents to America, was first united in marriage to Peter Mueller, who was of German birth, and to their union were born a son and a daughter: Harry F., the present clerk of Green Bay township, who married Miss Alma Pachley, and has five children: Edgar, Robert, Laura, Arnold and Margaret, and Ellen, the wife of Robert Lange, a sketch of whose family is given elsewhere in this volume. Mr. Mueller being in feeble health, he returned to Germany in hope of receiving relief, but in this he was destined to disappointment, and in 1867 he died, and was buried in his native land. His widow was afterward remarried, her second husband being Max Langerbeck, also a native of Germany, and to them were born two children, the elder of these being Edgar, now residing on his mother's farm, who married Miss Alma Lange. Their second child is Emma, who first married Mr. Krekel, by whom she had one daughter, Thea; she is now the wife of Paul Bufe. They have a very pleasant home in the village of Wever, Iowa, and are the parents of one child, Esther.

Mr. Langerbeck is now deceased, his death having occurred in 1894, and he is buried in Claypoole cemetery. He was a man generally respected wherever known, and was quite prominent in local political affairs as a worker in the Democratic party, being at one time elected to the office of township clerk. Mrs. Langerbeck is a cultured lady of many social talents and graces and pleasing conversational powers, and has had the advantage of considerable travel, including a trip to Europe nine years ago, when she visited Germany in order to accompany her parents on their return. She is the owner at the present time of 376 acres of highly productive farming lands, with modern improvements and a beautiful and commodious brick dwelling, a home which she has made notable as the center of a profuse and kindly hospitality.

Mr. Brodt, the subject of our sketch, is very well known throughout Lee county, and while he has never cared to take an active share in public affairs, always acting independently in politics and not as a member of any party, he has ever shown an interest in advancing the higher welfare of his community, he being a faithful member of the Lutheran church, in which denomination his deceased wife was also an honored worker, and manifesting in all the varied relations of life a spirit of the highest integrity and justice. His large success has been fairly and honestly won by the exercise of native ability and conscientious application to duty, and the wealth he has acquired has made no man poorer, but has rather been a blessing to many, and for these reasons his name is held in respect by all.

JAMES W. QUICKSELL.

James W. Quicksell, deceased, was a respected citizen of Keokuk for many years and was an honored veteran of the Civil War. He was born in Philadelphia, Pennsylvania, February 17, 1842, pursued a common-school education and came to Keokuk some time before the inauguration of the Civil War. Watching with interest the progress of events that presaged that great struggle, he resolved that if the South attempted to overthrow the Union he would strike a blow in its defense, and in April, 1861, enlisted as a member of Company A, Second Regiment of Iowa Infantry. He was a brave soldier, displaying his valor on many battlefields, and at all times and in all places did his full duty as a soldier. Three times he was wounded. The first injury was the result of an accident, a bayonet being thrust through the fleshy part of his arm when he was at Benton Barracks, St. Louis, in the fall of 1861. The second wound was received at Shiloh, April 6, 1862, the ball entering the right shoulder blade near the spine and there remaining imbedded until his death. It was this wound, in fact, that eventually caused his demise. He was again wounded when his regiment made its celebrated charge at Fort Donelson on the 15th of February, 1865. That was a most hotly contested engagement, the regiment losing two hundred and fifty-nine men and officers in killed and wounded, out of six hundred and fifty. At Shiloh Mr. Quicksell was taken prisoner and confined by the Confederates in the hospital at Jackson, Mississippi. He received kind treatment and good care from the enemy and the surgeons made every effort to extract the ball, but failed. Mr. Quicksell was parolled as soon as he was able to travel and re-entered the Union lines at Corinth, Mississippi, but because of his injuries was discharged from the service and returned to his home. His patriotic spirit, however, was not quelled by the suffering he underwent and in January, 1864, he re-enlisted as a member of Company C, Third Iowa Cavalry, and served throughout the remainder of the war as a veteran recruit of the regiment. His father was also a soldier of the Civil War and at the age of eighty-four participated in the "grand review of the old soldiers" at the national encampment of the Grand Army of the Republic, held in Philadelphia, where he was living.

When the war was over James W. Quicksell returned to Iowa and continued a resident of Keokuk until his death. He was a painter by trade and his capability in the line of his chosen vocation and his reliability in business were indicated by the fact that for thirty years he occupied the position of foreman with George Hill, painter and decorator, of Keokuk.

At Fort Madison, Iowa, on the 12th of March, 1868, Mr. Quicksell was united in marriage to Mrs. Emma (Ackley) Hayward. Her parents came to Iowa in 1856, from the vicinity of Cleveland, Ohio. Her father, Charles Ackley, was a teamster before the war, when there were no railroads in this locality. When the country became involved in hostilities growing out of the slavery question, he became a "graybeard soldier," enlisting at St. Louis, Missouri, in the Seventeenth Missouri Infantry, with which he served for about two years, and then passed away October 2, 1863, dying of illness while in the army. His wife, who bore the maiden name of Elizabeth Bunyan, and was born near London, England, died in Paducah, Kentucky, June 16, 1902. In their family were seven children: Franklin, of St. Louis, Missouri; William, living in Kansas City, Missouri; Mrs. Quicksell; Homer, of Keokuk; Mrs. Ellen Benson and Mrs. Minnie Meyers, both of Keokuk, and George, a resident of Fort Worth, Texas. There is also an adopted brother, Charles Ackley, living in Hamilton, Illinois.

Mr. and Mrs. Quicksell became the parents of but two children: Alonzo P., who was born November 16, 1872, and is a cooper, married Effie Lee Watson, of Paducah, Kentucky. Bessie May, born January 16, 1880, became the wife of John Wacker, now a resident of Paducah, Kentucky, and her death occurred July 31, 1901. There is one grandchild—Selma Louise Wacker, who was born July 28, 1900, and lives with her grandmother, Mrs. Quicksell.

Mr. Quicksell was a member of the Grand Army of the Republic and his widow is a member of Torrence Woman's Relief Corps, No. 100. In May, 1880, he erected a residence at No. 724 Paleau street, where his widow now resides. His death occurred August 16, 1898, and was deeply felt in the immediate circles of his friends, where he was held in high esteem for his personal worth. Within the last three years Mrs. Quicksell has lost her husband, two sisters-in-law, a brother-in-law, her daughter and her mother. She is now living in the home which her husband built for her almost a quarter of a century ago, devoting herself to the care of her little granddaughter and to charitable work.

EDGAR K. TOWNSEND.

The last half century in Lee county is a period of great change. The untravelled prairies have been transformed into peopled regions, and the few and scattered hamlets, thin lines of frontier settlement, have become prosperous and crowded centers of trade, while some very considerable cities have risen, prophecies of a still more crowded population and more pressing industrial development. Men who were born and reared in this county, and who are still enjoying an unabated manhood, have seen such a transformation. Like Caesar, they can say, "All of which I saw, and part of which I was." They have watched the growth of the county, and have done much to help things onward, as they have had strength and opportunity. Mr. Townsend, whose name appears above, has done his full share in the development of the community, in the history of which his own career forms an integral part.

Edgar K. Townsend, one of the highly respected citizens of Lee county, and now residing on his farm of 247 acres in sections 30 and 31, Harrison township, is a native of this county, and was born in the house he now occupies as a home, November 9, 1850. His early education was secured in the district schools of his native township, and while quite young he assisted his father in the cultivation of the home farm. His father, Clark Townsend, was born in Putnam county, New York, January 19, 1823, came to Iowa in 1845, spending the following winter in Farmington, and then purchasing the farm on which the subject of this sketch is now residing. It consisted of 160 acres, and here he made a home for himself, engaging in general farming, and also in stockraising to a limited extent. Politically he was a Democrat, though he never held office. In religion he was a member of the Baptist church, which he served as deacon many years. About ten years before his death he left the farm and moved to Farmington, Iowa, where he led a retired life, and died April 25, 1899, when over seventy-five years old.

The mother of Mr. Townsend, Sarah Elizabeth (Kelly) Townsend, was also born in Putnam county, New York, September 11, 1822. She died in Farmington, Iowa, on August 5, 1898, and her remains, with those of her husband, are at rest in the Farmington cemetery. Three of the four children to her marriage with Mr. Townsend are still living: Francis is a farmer in Harrison township; he was born in New York; Edgar K.; Albert is now engaged in the real-estate business in Farmington, Iowa, where he holds the position of justice of the peace. Carrie married Benton Pool, and is now dead; a sketch of Mr. Pool appears on another page of this work.

Edgar K. Townsend remained on the home farm, and after the death of the father, purchased it from the other heirs. From time to time he had added to his farm holdings until he now owns 247 acres of exceedingly choice land, all of which is highly improved and brought to an advanced stage of cultivation. Mr. Townsend is devoting much attention to stockraising and has more than a local reputation as a breeder of fine strains of stock, which attract much attention wherever exhibited.

In politics Mr. Townsend is a Democrat, and takes an intelligent and thoughtful interest in public affairs. He is much esteemed by his friends and neighbors, and takes a leading part in all local affairs.

Mr. Townsend was married December

11, 1873, to Miss Mary John, daughter of Griffith John. She was born in Henry county, Iowa, and her father, who was a native of Ohio, came to Henry county, Iowa, at an early day. There he engaged in farming and stockbuying, and when he died at Salem, Iowa, he was seventy-eight years of age.

Mrs. Edgar K. Townsend was reared in Henry county, where she was given a good education and well prepared for the duties and responsibilities of life. To her marriage with Mr. Townsend have come two children to bless the union: Walter C., who was born on the home place in Harrison township, and educated at the district school, and in the Farmington school, was married December 11, 1901, to Miss Ella Anders, a native of Primrose, Lee county, and a daughter of John Anders, an early settler, and now deceased. To their union have been born two children: Dorathy M. and John Edgar. Normal C., born at the home place in Harrison township, is at home.

Griffith John, the father of Mrs. Townsend, was married October 17, 1830, to Miss Caroline Brantover. He died March 26, 1899. They were honorable and upright people, and are kindly remembered by the old pioneers.

Clark Townsend and his good wife were superior people. They were faithful and devoted in their religious life, and made their faith a matter of daily living.

Edgar K. Townsend and his faithful wife stand in the place of good men and women, and that they fill these places is no exaggerated praise. Their character is high, their word is good.

JOSEPH H. D. CHENOWETH.

Joseph H. D. Chenoweth, of Keokuk, for thirty years in the postal service, a record which stands as incontrovertible evidence of his ability and fidelity, was born in Jackson township, Lee county, Iowa, on the 15th of February, 1842. He was named in honor of Joseph Hamilton Davies, who was killed in battle with the Indians near Lafayette, Indiana, in 1811—a great Indian fighter and pioneer for whom Thomas Jefferson Chenoweth, the father of our subject, had the greatest admiration. The Chenoweth family for many generations, both in its direct and collateral branches, has been distinctively American. The great-grandfather, Richard Chenoweth, was a native of Virginia. He came west with George Rogers Clark to Kentucky. He was at the head of a colony that settled on the site where Louisville now stands. The Indians were troublesome and killed many of these pioneers. Richard was the first sheriff of Jefferson county, Kentucky. Not far from Louisville the Indians attacked Richard's home while the men folk were away. They scalped his wife, wounded one of the boys, two girls hid in the spring-house and escaped being seen by the Indians, the spring is called the "Chenoweth" spring to this day. His wife recovered from her injuries and lived for many years afterward. The grandfather was taken prisoner by the Indians, but his life was spared on account of his black hair, which the Indians admired very much. He was a soldier of the Mexican War. Thomas Jefferson Chenoweth, father of the subject, was born near Louisville,

Kentucky, January 12, 1809, and was reared upon the frontier and for many years lived the life of a pioneer. He was married near Franklin, Indiana, in 1833, to Miss Mary Wright, who removed to that state from Ohio. Mr. Chenoweth became a farmer by occupation and carried on agricultural pursuits in the Hoosier state until 1837, when he came to Lee county, Iowa, and developed a farm in Jackson township, upon which he continued to reside until his death, which occurred on the 21st of April, 1880. His wife passed away July 16, 1878. In their family were eight children and those who reached adult age are Amanda, who died February 15, 1868; Henry Clay, a resident of California; Ruharna, who became the wife of Senator John Downey and died March 29, 1887, and Melvina.

Joseph H. D. Chenoweth, of this family, pursued his education in the public schools such as were common at that day, the little temple of learning which he attended being a log structure. He was trained to habits of industry, economy and integrity upon the home farm, worked in the fields through the months of summer and until crops were harvested in the late autumn and remained upon the old homestead until nineteen years of age, when he joined the Union Army, serving for three years. He enlisted on the 28th of July, 1861, as a member of Company E, Seventh Iowa Infantry under command of Captain James C. Parrott and Colonel J. G. Lauman, of Burlington, Iowa, being with the Sixteenth Army Corps at the close of the war. His services during the greater part of the time were in the vicinity of Corinth, Mississippi, and Pulaski, Tennessee. He participated in the battle of the Shiloh, the siege of Corinth, and in many lesser engagements. He was mustered out August 10, 1864, at Chattanooga, Tennessee, after three years' service and reached home on the 19th of the same month.

Not long after his return Mr. Chenoweth began learning the marble cutter's trade, serving a regular apprenticeship and worked in that line until 1871, when he entered the postal service on the 19th of October, as a clerk under Postmaster James C. Parrott. On the 26th of August, 1874, he was appointed railway postal clerk by the late Judge George W. McCrary, then congressman from the first district. His run is on the Chicago, Rock Island & Pacific Railroad between Keokuk and Des Moines, known as the Des Moines & Keokuk Railway postoffice. In 1884, when the present fast mail was put on the Chicago, Burlington & Quincy Railroad from Chicago to Council Bluffs an increase in the postal force was needed on that line and men of marked efficiency were chosen. Mr. Chenoweth was among the number, but he found that the long run and heavy work were aggravating physical afflictions sustained because of his army life and he, therefore, returned to his original run. He has been most capable during all this long period and now his active connection with the railway postal service covers thirty years.

On the 15th of October, 1873, in Keokuk, Mr. Chenoweth was united in marriage to Miss Ida A. Pollard, who was born in Keokuk, September 27, 1852. They became the parents of five children, of whom four are living: Melroy Milton married Elizabeth

Boudewyn and is a plumber of Keokuk; Cora died at the age of twenty-five years; Joseph Downey, a graduate of Keokuk Dental College and is now practicing at Waverly, Illinois; Eva Maude, a graduate of the Keokuk high school, and Roy Logan. The family home is at No. 1206 High street and in addition to this property Mr. Chenoweth owns a half interest in a building in the downtown business district. He belongs to Torrence Post, No. 2, Grand Army of the Republic, to the Unitarian church and is a Republican in his political views. Fidelity to duty and to principal has ever been one of his salient characteristics and has won him unqualified confidence and respect. The same trait of character is manifest in his friendships and in the county in which his entire life has been passed he is held in the highest regard by those who know him.

ETHAN L. TREVITT.

To pursue a career of service to humanity and to rise by virtue of talent and integrity to a position of honor is an ambition well worthy of the most aspiring. Such has been the life history of Dr. Trevitt. He was born near Pittsburg, Pennsylvania, November 12, 1862, the son of Rev. John Trevitt, a Baptist minister, and Emma (Bevins) Trevitt. Both parents were born at Birmingham, England, and were married in England just before John Trevitt entered the ministry. The mother died in Pennsylvania when Ethan L., who is the youngest of a family of eleven, was but three years of age. The following sons and daughters survive her: Enoch J., of Birmingham, England; Mrs. Kizie Logan, of Washington, Pennsylvania; Mrs. Anna Moorman, of Fort Madison; Miss Sadie, of St. Louis; John E., of Fort Madison; Henry C., of Burlington, Iowa; Samuel W., of Alaska; Dr. Alfred W., of Wausau, Wisconsin. Those deceased were Lizzie and Minnie, who died in girlhood.

The father removed with the family to Lee county in 1865, locating on a farm in Pleasant Ridge township. He died in February, 1871, at Bonaparte, Iowa, while conducting a revival meeting. The subject of this sketch received his education in the public schools of Fort Madison and the Denmark Academy at Denmark, this county, from which institution he was graduated in 1879. In Fort Madison he became a tinner's apprentice, learning the trade and being employed at that work for four years, and then in September, 1884, he entered the Eclectic Medical Institute, of Cincinnati, Ohio, from which he was graduated June 7, 1887. The two years immediately following his graduation were spent in further preparing for the work of his profession at a Minneapolis hospital, and for two years he was an interne of the hospital at Wausau, Wisconsin. In 1891 he returned to Fort Madison, and here established himself in the practice of his profession. He devoted his time exclusively, and with rather more than the ordinary measure of success, to the work of his profession until September 1, 1897, when he was appointed by President

McKinley to the office of postmaster of Fort Madison, which position he still holds, having received reappointment from President Roosevelt January 31, 1902. Despite the duties of his office he continues to give considerable attention to his medical practice.

In his fraternal connection Dr. Trevitt is a member of the Brotherhood of American Yoemen, and in politics has all his life loyally supported, as in his opinion most consistent with the general welfare, the Republican party and its principles. In 1896 he was president of the McKinley and Hobart club of Fort Madison, and served his party as delegate to the congressional and state conventions, and was also in attendance at the national convention. For a term of two years he served the city as physician to the board of health.

On April 20, 1897, Dr. Trevitt was united in marriage at Burlington, Iowa, to Miss Minnie W. Knoch, who was born at Franklin, Lee county, August 20, 1876, and they have their home at 1115 Third street. To them has been born one daughter, Evelyn L., her natal day being July 20, 1900. Mrs. Trevitt is the daughter of John Knoch, a carpenter. He died in Louisville, Kentucky, to which place he had removed from Iowa. Mrs. Trevitt is one of a family of four sisters. The others are: Mrs. Harry Kent, who lives on a farm in Madison township; and Misses Emma and Valley Knoch, who live with their mother in Fort Madison.

During Mr. Trevitt's incumbency as postmaster the revenues of the office have been increased from approximately $10,000 annually to nearly $14,000 per annum, three rural routes have been established, the salary of the assistant postmaster has been advanced from $700 to $1,100, that of the money order and register clerk from $600 to $800, the salary of the general delivery clerk has grown from $300 to $600, and an additional general delivery clerkship has been created, carrying a salary of $600 per annum. Moreover, there are not wanting those who affirm that the general efficiency and tone of the service rendered to the public have been constantly improved. Personally, Dr. Trevitt enjoys a gratifying degree of popularity. He is a man of much force of character and strong individuality, and his pleasant, social manner has won him a host of warm friends.

JOSHUA O. BEALL.

Joshua O. Beall, prominent ex-railroad man and now justice of the peace in Fort Madison, was born in Washington county, Pennsylvania, July 4, 1828, the eighteenth of a family of twenty. He is the son of Zephaniah Beall who was born in 1773 in what is now the District of Columbia. The grandfather, who was also named Zephaniah, was in the Revolutionary War, and at its close was serving under General Crawford. He was a farmer, and in addition made a business of buying farm produce to the amount of about $5,000 for shipment to New Orleans. While on one of these expeditions he and his party, about six in all, were murdered, and were never afterward heard from. The mother of our subject was Mary Purcell, who was born in Greene county, Pennsylvania, about 1788 or 1790, the date not being definitely known, and died in 1860.

Mr. Beall is proud of the fact that men of his blood have been engaged in every war within the present borders of the United States since the Indian massacre at Jamestown. His father served for thirteen months in the Indian War of 1790. In the War of the Rebellion two of his sons and two of his grandsons were members of the Federal Army, while three of his grandsons were in the Confederate forces. Some of his brothers were engaged in the War of 1812, and Reason Beall, a relative, was a member of Gen. William Henry Harrison's staff in that conflict.

Zephaniah Beall, the father, was twice married, and ten children were born of each marriage. He removed with his parents to Pennsylvania in 1774, and lived and died within three miles of the family's original place of settlement. Our subject was reared amid primitive conditions, attending school in a log building in which "slab" benches without backs did duty for seats, and receiving but six weeks of schooling each year, consisting of the traditional "three R's." He grew to maturity in the business of farming, and also for a time drove a wholesale and retail stoneware wagon, and bought beeswax, feathers, hides, etc.

True to the spirit and traditions of his forefathers, the Civil War had no sooner begun than he was ready and anxious to go to the front, and on November 14, 1861, he enlisted at Washington, District of Columbia, in Company I of the Fourth Pennsylvania Volunteer Cavalry, in which he served as a second lieutenant, under Col. David Campbell, of Pittsburg. After two months of provost duty at Washington he was sent to join the Army of the Potomac took part in the seven days' fight before Richmond, the second battle of Bull Run, Fredericktown, Maryland; South Mountain, Maryland; Antietam and finally the battle of Fredericksburg under General Burnside. But the constant hardships were too great for his constitution to bear, and he suffered a complete physical collapse, and was honorably discharged December 25, 1863, on account of disability.

Returning to his home in Pennsylvania, he came west in 1866, and was for a time at Streator, Illinois. From there he proceeded to Monroe City, Marion county, Missouri, where he remained for seven years, then returning to Streator, whence he removed to Fort Madison in 1888, and here he has since resided. At Streator he was "first hand" in the roundhouse of the Santa Fe Railroad, having full charge under the master mechanic, Henry Randels, now deceased. He was with the same company, all told, about fifteen years. Prior to that engagement he had held positions with the Hannibal & Saint Joseph, the Chicago, Pekin & Southwestern, and the Chicago, Burlington & Quincy Railroad Companies, being employed while with the Hannibal & St. Joseph Company on the wrecking train. The aggregate of his railroad experience amounts to nearly thirty years. On December 24, 1902, he retired from railroad work, and being elected by his fellow citizens justice of the peace for Madison township., has since held that office.

December 14, 1853, Mr. Beall was married at Fredericktown, Pennsylvania, to Elizabeth A. Donahho, who was born at that place in 1831. To them were born six children, as follows: Cyrus D., of Colorado; Mary, who died in 1889; Charles M., supposed to be deceased; John D., deceased; Mary B., dressmaker, who is at home, and Joshua L., of Albia, Iowa. The other members of the family are of the Presbyterian faith, while Mr. Beall is a Catholic. He is a member of the Grand Army of the Republic at Streator, Illinois, and of the Ancient Order of United Workmen, in which order he has passed through the chairs and has twice served as delegate to the Grand Lodge at Galesburg and at Springfield, Illinois. His first vote for a president of the United States was cast in 1848 for Zachary Taylor, and he has always been a loyal Democrat, although related by ties of kinship with the "peerless leader" of the Republican party, James G. Blaine. The grandmother of James G. Blaine was a sister of Mr. Beall's mother, Mary Purcell. Mr. Beall was personally acquainted with the famous statesman, and last saw him in Washington in 1861.

By reason of his honorable and upright life Joshua O. Beall is entitled to a prominent place in this volume, and for service rendered to his country in time of her need, the gratitude of all is his by right. It is with confidence that a sketch of his life is here presented, assured, as it is, of many interested readers.

CHARLES MARTIN.

Charles Martin, a widely known and prominent retired merchant of West Point and one of the present supervisors of Lee county, Iowa, was born in the Kingdom of Prussia October 20, 1839, of pure German ancestry, the son of Henry and Barbara (Geib) Martin, who were the parents of nine children, all born in Prussia, and who with their family emigrated to America. The voyage was made in a sailing vessel, and lasted sixty days, at the end of which they landed at the Port of New York and came thence directly to West Point, locating near the village in the year 1854. The father was a surgeon, but almost before he had time to begin the practice of his profession he was overtaken by an epidemic of typhoid fever, which was then raging, and died soon after his arrival here, and this terrible calamity was followed a few weeks later by the death of his wife, and this by the death of the eldest son, all of whom succumbed to the same dread disease.

Charles Martin, our subject, was the youngest of the family thus bereaved at one blow of its natural protectors and dearest earthly ties in a new and strange land. He had, however, received an excellent education in Germany, and so was not without means of self-support. After the death of his father he secured a position in a drug store in the village of West Point, which he retained for two years, and at the end of that time he entered the employ of W. R. Stewart, proprietor of a drygoods store, with whom he continued for a number of years, learning the details of the business and American methods. Later he established a store of his own, which he conducted for the long period of forty years, with very marked success, his energy, tact and careful business judgment enabling him to win the good will of the public, and the same qualities making it possible for him to tide his business over the numerous financial panics and seasons of depression which have caused the ruin of so many commercial houses during the last half century. At the close of this successful career he sold the store to Mr. John Schroder, and has since been living in retirement from active life, enjoying in well-earned ease the declining years of a life worthily spent in useful service to his fellowmen and in devotion to noble causes.

On November 1, 1860, Mr. Martin wedded Miss Fannie L. Jarrett at her father's home in West Point township. Mrs. Martin was born August 10, 1836, in North Carolina, of Southern ancestry and came with her parents to Iowa in 1850. Unto them have been born three sons and four daughters, as follows: Nettie, wife of E. T. Alter, of West Point township; Edward C., of Chicago; Hattie, wife of William H. Smith, of Oak Park, a suburb of Chicago; William H., of Seattle, Washington; Emma E., wife of F. C. Daube, who resides with her parents; and Ira and George, who died in childhood. To each of these, now so widely separated, was given a careful home training and a finished education such as would fit the recipient for the battle of life and for a high and worthy success in whatever part it may be necessary to play.

The extent of Mr. Martin's material achievements may be gauged by the fact that he is the owner of two fine farms, one in Marion township and the other in West Point township, as well as valuable residence property in the village, having erected a very pleasant dwelling house in which he receives his many friends and passes much of his time in reading. He was at one time largely engaged in real estate operations in the village of West Point, having built fifteen houses here, and thus contributed materially to the advancement of the community in which he lives and displayed a very commendable public spirit as well as individual initiative and enterprise. These traits of his character have also manifested themselves in other ways, for he has borne an aggressive part in promoting the fortunes of the Republican party in this section, and such is the confidence reposed in him by his fellow citizens that he was the first Republican ever elected to the office of county supervisor in Lee county, and received the remarkably large majority of 873 votes. His first election to that position was in 1895, and in 190[illegible] he was re-elected, each time for a term of three years, and holds the office at the present time. He also served the village as recorder for a number of years, and for a term of years was secretary of the West Point Agricultural Society, and thus his life has been one of constant usefulness and of continued activity, having for its object the general welfare without hope of personal aggrandizement or reward. His nature is fundamentally religious, and he is a believer in the efficacy of the Christian faith to elevate the ethical standards of society, and for this reason is a faithful member, as is also his wife, of the Presbyterian church at West Point, of which he is a deacon and the treasurer. He has done much to extend the influence of the church, and has given to its cause much thought and earnest effort, while his private life has been a true reflection of its teachings and has given no man cause to speak ill of the creed which he professes. The keynote of his life and character is integrity and fidelity to his obligations in all his relations with his fellowmen, and such has been the strict uprightness and unswerving directness of his course that to him all accord admiration, respect and genuine regard.

IRA STEPHEN SIMS.

Ira Stephen Sims, now living retired from active business life on his farm of 120 acres on section 7, Jackson township, Lee county, Iowa, is a man who owes his success entirely to his personal and unassisted effort—who, from his early years has depended upon his own energy, enterprise and judgment for the increase of his fortunes. He is, therefore, deserving of being called a self-made man, and few if any have borne that high title with greater propriety or honor than he, while at the same time his modesty leads him to ascribe a large share of the credit to our American institutions and spirit of equality, which enable every man of ability to do as he has done, and achieve for himself an important and highly respected position in the community in which he lives.

He was born June 14, 1836, in Wayne county, New York, and at the early age of sixteen years, after obtaining a good education in the public schools of the Empire state, he set out to begin his career in the world, having in view as the field of his labors the great undeveloped country known as the West. He located in Illinois, where he became a trusted agent for a contractor engaged in the construction of the Illinois Central Railroad between Centralia and Vandalia. His employer, Mr. Brigham, was so favorably impressed with his ability and soundness of judgment that in 1850 he persuaded him to come to Lee county, where he owned a farm, and here Mr. Sims was connected with the work and management of the farm for a period of six or eight years, at the expiration of which he went to Keokuk. Later he was entrusted with the superintendency of the Hines farm in Jackson township, in which capacity he met with his usual success. While thus engaged, he also became superintendent of the freight lighter business in the Des Moines rapids of the Mississippi river, during the fall of the years when the water was low until the present canal being at that time unbuilt, and it being necessary to transfer freight from packet to packet in boats of light draught which plied between Keokuk and Montrose. In 1870 he purchased his present farm of 120 acres of fertile land, on which he has since continuously resided, and by constant, energetic and determined effort has transformed the tract from a wilderness covered with original forest to one of the most thoroughly cultivated and productive farms in Lee county. Here he has conducted general farming on an extensive scale, and has given attention to stockraising, especially to fine horses, of which he has sold a number at very unusual prices. In the purely agricultural branch of his work he has been very successful, both in a pecuniary way and in furthering the upbuilding and development of this section of Iowa, for which he deserves much credit.

On June 14, 1859, Mr. Sims was united in marriage at Keokuk to Miss Eliza Thompson, who was born in Birmingham, England, in 1840, came to America in 1848 with her parents and settled in Bond county, Illinois, where she lived for five years before removing to Iowa. The father, who was in his native country a hardware merchant, but was engaged as a bookkeeper during his entire residence in this country, was a man of much ability, and was generally respected for his talents and his character. The family after a time removed to Des Moines, where the deaths of both parents occurred. Mrs. Sims has borne an active share in the management of the farm, has made her home the center of a much prized hospitality, and by many is her name spoken in tones of esteem and affection. To Mr. and Mrs. Sims have been born five sons and two daughters, as follows: George, now a resident of Montana; Clara, who is engaged in dressmaking at Colorado Springs; Ira Lambert, employed in the powder works at Mooar; James, who is a farmer and resides near Mooar; Samuel, who is also employed in the powder works; Lucy Elise, wife of George C. Bold, and resides near Mooar; and Fred, who died at the age of five years. They have also adopted one son, Leo.

Twelve years ago Mr. Sims suffered a stroke of paralysis, and since that time he has been unable to perform active labor and has been taking a well-earned rest from toil but his mind retains undimmed all its former lustre, and he relates many entertaining incidents of his earlier life and struggles and of pioneer times in the West. Although the aboriginal inhabitants had departed before his settlement in this region, he has collected much information in regard to their habits and customs, and relates that Sugar creek, which flows through Jackson township, was so named from the fact that its banks were formerly a noted camping ground for Indians who resorted thither for the purpose of making maple sugar, and that a large boulder, which is still pointed out, formerly supplied the Indians with the material for the manufacture of arrow and spear heads.

Mr. Sims has devoted much time and thought to reading along the lines of public questions, and has always taken a part in affairs of government as a member of the Republican party, of which he is a valued counselor in this township. He has also manifested throughout his life a deep interest in the moral and ethical advancement of society, and both he and Mrs. Sims have long been earnest and faithful members of the Baptist denomination, which they have supported liberally from their means, both in the regular work of the church and in its many enterprises of Christian charity and benevolence. Mr. Sims has a wide acquaintance, and to write the chronicle of his life, his work and his success is a pleasure which will be shared as readers by many friends, whose respect and esteem he has won in full and generous measure.

HENRY SCHMIDT.

It is always of interest to examine into the life history of a self-made man to know the methods he has followed and to take cognizance of the business plans and opportunities which have enabled him, perhaps, to pass many who started out in business life better equipped. Mr. Schmidt is eminently deserving of the praise that is conveyed in the term of a self-made man and his life is a splendid illustration of the force of character and the power of determination and unremitting energy. Born in Germany on the 20th of May, 1831, he there acquired a common-school education and in youth learned the trade of a carpenter and joiner. He followed that pursuit in the Fatherland until 1852, when at the age of twenty-one years he came to the United States, boarding a westward bound vessel on the 5th of September and arriving in the harbor of New Orleans on the 24th of October, following. Proceeding up the river to St. Louis, Missouri, he reached that place on the 7th of November. The journey across the Atlantic had been made in a sailing vessel "Sarah," which was seven weeks en route. After spending a few months in St. Louis Mr. Schmidt came to Keokuk, Iowa, in 1853 on the steamer "Kate Kearney," making the trip in April. Here he worked in various ways that would yield him an honest living and gain him a start. In 1856 he built a small shop in which to do carpenter work. He labored very industriously, but made little money. When the war broke out he began work on the railroads, helping to build bridges at Ottumwa and Rock Island. He afterward was employed at shop work in Eddyville, but subsequently turned his attention to contracting and building. When he arrived in Keokuk he was entirely without capital and had no friends in this locality, but he possessed laudable ambiton and firm purpose and these qualities have enabled him to steadily work his way upward. He commenced contracting and building in 1857 and was thus engaged for two years in New Orleans. The year 1880 was the beginning of his present business, for with two hand machines he at that time began the manufacture of screens. This proved a profitable venture, his trade gradually increasing and in 1886 he installed a steam engine, which was in operation until 1894. In the meantime he had extended the field of his labors not only making screens, but also sash, doors and various kinds of building fixtures. In the year mentioned he erected a building 50x102 feet and two stories in height. It is a solid brick structure and was equipped with machinery valued at from six to eight thousand dollars. The company now makes not only screens, doors and windows but all kinds of building work to order, including the best bank fixtures. Employment is furnished to twenty-five people and the payroll in 1903 for labor alone was $15,000. The capital stock was increased in the same year by $25,000 and the buildings and machinery are worth an equal amount. The business was begun under the name of Henry Schmidt, but later he admitted his son to a partnership and in 1894 the Henry Schmidt & Sons Company was incorporated. The enterprise has become one of the leading productive industries of the city and a large and profitable business is now carried on. Mr. Schmidt was also engaged in a contracting business from the close of the war until 1894 and has erected many of the fine business blocks of Keokuk, evidences of his handiwork being seen in a large number of the fine structures of the city.

Mr. Schmidt was married soon after his arrival in Keokuk to Miss Philipena Wiegner, who was born in Germany. The same year he built a home which he still occupies, but his wife died on the 21st of March, 1894, leaving three children. The eldest, Alfred J., survived only until June 1, 1895. He was manager of the business and he left a wife and five children, the eldest of whom, Alfred C. Schmidt, is now shipping clerk in the factory. Charles O. Schmidt, the present manager of the business, is married and has four children. Henry E. is connected with the Wilkinson Drug Company, being a graduated pharmacist of the College of St. Louis. He is also married and has three children.

Fraternally Mr. Schmidt is connected with the Odd Fellows Society, in which he has held all of the offices and has been a delegate to the Grand Lodge. He has never taken an active interest in politics because of the heavy demands made upon his time and attention by his business affairs. He belongs to the German Evangelical church and is one of its oldest and most valued members. He held office in the church until sixty years of age, serving as president, trustee and treasurer. He was largely instrumental in the erection of the original church in 1858 and in the newer house of worship of 1874. Upon coming to America in early manhood he was unfamiliar with the habits and customs of the people and with their language, but adapting himself to circumstances and making the most of his opportunities he gradually overcame all difficulties and obstacles in his path, these seeming to serve as an impetus for closer application and more earnest effort. He has led a busy and useful life, standing today as one of the leading representatives of industrial interests in his adopted city and at the same time he has been neglectful of no public duty that has devolved upon him. He has been particularly active in church work and he commands the unqualified confidence of all who know him.

FRANCE C. ROBERTS, M. D.

The field of medical practice has ever enlisted among its representative men of the strongest mental capacity and of broad humanitarian principles, who recognizing the great responsibility which devolves upon the practitioner puts forth his strongest and best effort, making his labors therefore a blessing to mankind as well as a source of individual profit. Dr. France C. Roberts, acknowledged as one of the most capable physicians and surgeons of Fort Madison, was born in Otsego, Allegan county, Michigan, on the 10th of January, 1855, his parents being Abel and Emma (Cole) Roberts. His father was born in Rensselaer county, New York, and the mother at Ovid, that state. The Roberts family is of Welsh lineage, the original American ancestors having come to the United States in early colonial days. Abel Roberts became a pioneer resident of Michigan, establishing his home near Adrian and later he was married at Ann Arbor to Miss Cole, who had accompanied her parents, Mr. and Mrs. Nelson Cole, to that state. Abel Roberts subsequently removed to Otsego, Michigan, where he was engaged in the practice of medicine. He was a graduate of the first class that completed the course in the medical department of the University of Michigan. Prior to that time he had spent a few years in California subsequent to the discovery of gold on the Pacific slope. He came to Fort Madison, Iowa, in the spring of 1859, and continued in practice here until his death, being one of the ablest representatives of the medical fraternity in the city at an early day. He was also prominent in politics and filled the position of county treasurer of Lee county for three terms. He was likewise the owner of the Democrat and erected the Democrat Building, a substantial brick block in which he began the publication of his paper. His efforts touched the general interests of society along many lines and proved of marked value in promoting public progress and substantial advancement. He died in Fort Madison in the year 1901, while his wife passed away in 1898.

France C. Roberts pursued his education in the private schools and in Fort Madison Academy. He was reared in an atmosphere of medical learning and whether environment, inherited tendencies or natural predilection had most to do with his choice of a profession it is difficult to determine, but at all events he resolved to make the practice his life work and entered upon a full course of preparation. He pursued his first two courses of lectures in the University of Michigan at Ann Arbor and afterward matriculated in the Louisville Medical College of Kentucky, from which institution he was graduated in the class of 1876. He then began practice in Fort Madison, where he has followed his profession continuously for twenty-seven years, becoming one of the best known and prominent physicians of this portion of the state. He is a member of the Lee County Medical Society, of which he was the first president and he also belongs to the Des Moines Valley Medical Association, of which he has also been president. He is a member of the State Medical Society and the American Medical Association. He is likewise an honorary member of the Santa Fe Railway Surgeons' Association and each year attends its meeting at Topeka, Kansas. He is also identified with other medical societies. He has been president of the Lee county commission of insanity for about twenty years. He is likewise local surgeon for the St. Louis, Keokuk & Northwestern Railway Company, the Chicago, Burlington & Kansas Railroad and the Chicago, Burlington & Quincy Railroad, occupying these positions since 1878. He was assistant surgeon of the Second Regiment of Iowa National Guards, afterward the Fiftieth Iowa Regiment. His practice has long been large and of a lucrative character and in his career has been manifest celerity of mental actions combined with a correctness of conclusions that have made him accurate in the diagnosis of a case and rendered his labors of much value in checking the ravages of disease.

Although the practice of medicine and surgery has been his real life work, Dr. Roberts has also done a large amount of newspaper writing and has long taken a deep interest in political questions, his support ever being given to the Democracy, and he has labored for local successes both as a private citizen and as chairman of the county central committee and of the congressional committee. He has, however, never aspired to office, desiring only to see the adoption of the principles in which he believes without wishing for office as a reward for party fealty. He is a member of Claypoole Lodge, No. 13, Free and Accepted Masons; Potowonok Chapter, No. 28, Royal Arch Masons, and Delta Commandery, No. 51, Knights Templar. His prominence in Masonry and the regard which the brethren of his fraternity entertain for him is indicated by the fact that he has served as Master of the Lodge, High Priest of the Chapter and Eminent Commander of the Commandry. He has likewise been a trustee of the different Masonic bodies. He is a charter member of the Benevolent and Protective Order of Elks.

In January, 1882, was celebrated the marriage of Dr. Roberts and Miss Ella Layton, who died in 1884, leaving one son, Edward Layton, who is now studying mining engineering in the University of California at Berkeley, that state. In 1889 Dr. Roberts wedded Mrs. Anna Burch, a daughter of A. J. Cowell, of Moulton, Iowa. They have one child, Katharine, and they occupy a fine residence at No. 1611 Fourth street. In 1887 Dr. Roberts spent the summer in Berlin, Germany, as assistant to Professor Koester in the surgical department of Queen Augusta Hospital and also traveled over the continent for a year. He has likewise been an extensive traveler in his own country and is a gentleman of scholarly attainments and broad culture, whose naturally strong mind enriched by reading and study and also by many reminiscences of his journeys in his home land and abroad, renders him an entertaining and agreeable companion.

LEONARD MATLESS.

One of the most successful, influential and highly esteemed citizens of the city of Keokuk during the last half century was Leonard Matless, whose ability, enterprise and strong, kindly character made him repected wherever he was known, and he enjoyed a wide acquaintance among the best people throughout Lee county and in many of the more important cities of the West. He was born in Norfolk, England, November 11, 1823, and there was united in marriage to Miss Matilda Gobel in 1840, and there he also inaugurated his independent career by acquiring the then highly lucrative trade of shoemaking, in which he became unusually proficient. To Mr. and Mrs. Matless four children were born in England; one died young and with their small family of three children they set out for the

New World in 1853, seven years subsequent to their marriage, being convinced that in America lay broader fields for business enterprise, more abundant opportunities of advancement and above all superior educational facilities for the benefit of their children. They made the voyage in the sail-ship "Golconda;" were overtaken by a storm that lasted for a number of days and resulted in the voyagers suffering shipwreck; were compelled to spend two weeks in refitting the vessel, and finally, as the crowning exasperation of their experience, were becalmed and lay motionless in midocean for two weeks, thus prolonging the trip to a total duration of ten weeks, at the end of which time, however, they arrived safe at New Orleans and proceeded up the Mississippi river by steamer to Keokuk. Here Mr. Matless began his business career by purchasing an interest in a shoe manufacturing business owned by a Mr. Odell, with whom he continued in partnership until the retirement of the latter from business, when he formed a partnership with Mr. Huiskamp, who came to Keokuk from St. Louis for the purpose, and conducted a wholesale and retail shoe business for a number of years. For twenty years, from 1853 to 1873, he was actively engaged in the shoe business in Keokuk, and then went west to Ft. Madison, where he acted as superintendent of the large factory which the firm had established in that city, continuing very successfully in the position for another period of almost twenty years, or until 1893, when his health failed, and he returned to Keokuk and here lived in retirement from active affairs for the remaining years of his life, which were devoted to the enjoyment of domestic and social intercourse and the well deserved fruits of labor and care.

To Mr. and Mrs. Matless were born ten children, all deceased but two sons and two daughters, as follows: Alfred E., Leonard, Jr., Kate, and Mrs. Henry A. Knights, all residents of Keokuk. The two sons have won very prominent positions in the business world of Keokuk, and are widely known men of ability and business foresight, worthy representatives of the influence formerly wielded by the distinguished father. Mr. Matless was well known in Masonic circles in this section, and the date of his being made a Master Mason was in 1875, he being a member of Hardin Lodge of this city, which afterward conferred upon him its supreme honor, that of Worshipful Master, in 1880. He was witness to many changes and improvements in the industry to which he devoted his life, and it was during the time of his association with the firm of Huiskamp Brothers that the transition was accomplished from handwork, which had previously prevailed universally, to modern machine manufacture in its most highly perfected and marvelous forms. He was capable of great and sustained effort of body and mind, owing much of his success to this quality, and while he passed the greater part of his life in the successful operation and management of large enterprises, his character was one of particular fineness and self-suppression. Quiet, reserved, kindly, the personification of cheerfulness, always ready to sacrifice his own convenience and pleasure to the happiness of others, even when under the shadow of feeble health he was everywhere respected for the strength of his personality and loved by all his friends for the unobtrusive beauty of his character and the virtues which made him in the best sense of the word a gentleman and a true man. Gifted with the keen discrimination, unerring foresight and decision of temperament, which enabled him to work out gigantic projects to their terminations and to acquire for himself and family a very substantial fortune, he was at the same time a kind, thoughtful husband, an indulgent and provident father, a loyal friend, hospitable and generous, and a citizen of the most worthy and admirable type. He died Monday evening, August 25, 1902, and was laid at rest in Oakland cemetery, followed by the benedictions of a multitude who felt that his loss was, indeed, a serious one for the community thus bereft. Mrs. Matless still survives him, and continues to reside at the family home at No. 911 Franklin street, the center of a refined and cultured circle of friends.

FREDERICK KREIKENBAUM.

Frederick Kreikenbaum, of West Point, vice-president of the West Point Bank, and one of the most extensive landowners of Lee county, Iowa, was born in the Province of Hanover, Germany, February 8, 1836, a son of Henry and Hannah Kreikenbaum and the fifth of a family comprising five daughters and one son, of whom all are now deceased but two. When only twelve years of age he emigrated with his parents to America, crossing the ocean in a sailing vessel, and after a voyage of eight weeks landed at New Orleans, whence they ascended the Mississippi river to St. Louis, where for a year Henry Kreikenbaum worked in a foundry, then in 1849 brought his family to Lee county, Iowa, locating at the village of Franklin. At that place he established a blacksmith shop, which he continued to conduct for the remainder of his active life, meeting with great success, and winning the esteem of all who knew him, and there occurred his death at the advanced age of ninety-three years.

Our subject received few educational advantages in his native land, and after coming to the United States he attended school for the space of only one month, this being a night school, and altogether his accomplishments in this line proceeded no further than the mastery of the alphabet during his early years, but he learned while still quite young the invaluable lessons of industry and self-reliance, and in time easily overcame the handicap of limited schooling. The first work which he performed for a cash consideration was digging potatoes for a wage of twenty-five cents a day, and when he was twelve years of age he became assistant to his father in the blacksmith shop, doing the hard and heavy work which was required with a determination to succeed in spite of all unfavorable circumstances, thus learning the trade of blacksmith under parental direction, and he feels today that he could have had no better instructor. He lived with his father until he was twenty-six years of age, at which time he was united in marriage to Miss Elizabeth Hefner, by whom he had three sons and two daughters, all of whom still live, as follows: Eliza, Edward, John Albert, Amelia and Frederick, Jr. The mother of the family, however, is deceased, and Mr. Kreikenbaum has been married, the second time wedding Miss Barbara Lutz.

After the retirement of his father Mr. Kreikenbaum assumed entire charge of the business, which he conducted with great ability and skill until the time of his own retirement in 1891, after working at his trade for more than forty-two years, and throughout this long period he was unfailingly successful. Beginning his independent career at the age of twelve years entirely without capital and with no education, not even understanding the language of the country in which he lived, he has by care, economy and good management achieved much, owning at the present time over 1,100 acres of excellent agricultural lands in Lee, Washington and Buchanan counties, Iowa, as well as a half interest in the West Point Bank, and having residence property in the village of West Point, upon which he erected in 1893 a magnificent modern dwelling, surrounded by beautiful and well-kept grounds. Here he has set out vines and fruit trees, and the large lawn is decorated with flowers and shrubbery artistically grouped and massed, so that the home of Mr. and Mrs. Kriekenbaum is one of both comfort and beauty. Upon closing his blacksmith shop in Franklin, Mr. Kriekenbaum removed to the city of Fort Madison, but after two years' residence at that place he came to West Point. His present condition contrasts very favorably with that of his first few years in Lee county, for when his father came to Iowa and located at Franklin the family occupied a small house which was covered with clapboards for protection from the elements, and had for a floor only hewed logs. Later, however, the father of our subject signalized his success in material matters by erecting a commodious and comfortable house, in which he passed his declining years.

The name of Frederick Kreikenbaum has been well known in every community in which he has resided, as his interest in public affairs and his devotion to the general welfare have always made him a prominent figure. For many years he has been actively engaged in the work of the Democratic party, and has held many positions of honor and trust, being at the present time one of the trustees of West Point township, and having held the office of mayor of Franklin; also serving his constituents as a member of the common council of that village, in all of which positions he has demonstrated himself to be the possessor of considerable practical ability, and has performed the duties that came to him to the eminent satisfaction of his fellow citizens and with much honor to himself. And in promoting the moral and spiritual interests of those who came within the circle of his influence he has been equally zealous. Himself and wife are members of the Evangelical faith, but as there is no church of that denomination in their community they attend the Presbyterian church, to which he is a very generous contributor. Thus he has shown himself to be a man of broad and liberal views, as indeed, a man must be who has succeeded in face of the obstacles which confronted him at the outset of his career; and successful he has certainly been in all his enterprises, his connection with the bank at this place proving especially helpful to that institution, which holds very high rank in the financial world of southern Iowa. No biographical record of Lee county would be complete without a full review of his career, and this account is offered with entire confidence that it will prove deeply interesting to his many acquaintances and friends, among whom he is admired for his conscientious work in life and respected for the the strength and unfailing uprightness and integrity of his character.

JOHN C. DANIELS.

John C. Daniels, whose intense and well directed activity made him a forceful factor in community interests in Keokuk, where for twenty-six years he figured prominently in commercial circles, was an opportunist—readily recognizing his chance and utilizing conditions for practical, resultant ends. With no special technical training for the business world he made for himself a position prominent in the trade circles of southeastern Iowa, winning at the same time an honored name because he followed no other road to success save the path of rectitude.

A native of Chenango county, New York, Mr. Daniels was born March 23, 1840, a son of Martin and Alice (Allen) Daniels, also natives of Chenango county. The father followed merchandising in New York while later he established his home in Richmond, Virginia, where he was engaged in the lumber business, and afterward removed to Canada. He next removed to Eau Claire, Wisconsin, in 1857 and figured prominently in the business circles of that place for many years. He was also a recognized leader in political circles there and for many years he held the office of county clerk and other local positions, wherein he furthered the interests of the community, fostering many measures for the general good. He was a man of much tact as shown in both his business and political relations, possessed a most cheerful disposition and benevolent spirit and was thus enabled to shed around him much of the sunshine of life. The kindly disposition of his wife made her his able assistant in many good works. They had two sons, John C. and Conway B. Martin Daniels died at the age of fifty-eight years and his wife passed away about six years later.

John C. Daniels acquired a common-school education and while living in Canada learned to speak the French language. He displayed much energy and business ability while yet a young man and at the age of seventeen years was operating a sawmill at Eau Claire, Wisconsin, in which he employed twenty men. At the outbreak of the Civil War it was his desire to enter the army, but his mother opposed this and he went instead to the northwest, where he remained from 1861 until 1866. It was a wild and unimproved district in which he located and in that locality he engaged in mining, merchandising and in lumbering, cutting and sawing lumber or doing anything that his hand found to do. It was this ready adaptability to any task that lay nearest him and seemed to promise the best results that made him an opportunist.

Returning to Wisconsin, Mr. Daniels went into the wholesale lumber commission business, selling rafts of lumber along the river. After living at Hannibal, Missouri, for three years, he settled at Keokuk, Iowa, in 1872 and continued in the wholesale lumber business at this point for twenty-six years, handling a large amount of lumber annually and conducting an extensive and profitable business. He also owned the steamboats "Lumberman," "Lumber Boy" and "Kit Carson" and was familiarly known as Captain Daniels. His steamers towed rafts from Reed's Landing and down the Mississippi river as far as Louisiana, Missouri. His raft boats were the first of their kind to use search lights on the Mississippi. In 1893 Mr. Daniels entered into partnership with William Garten, inventor of the Garten lightning arrester, a device for use on street cars, and they founded the Garten-Daniels Lightning Arrester Company, of which Mr. Daniels became the president. In 1902 the present Garten-Daniels Company, manufacturers of electric specialties, was organized, and Mr. Daniels was elected president, in which capacity he served up to the time of his death.

In 1869 John C. Daniels married Mrs. Cordelia May Hamer, daughter of Levi Munson and Sophia (Galbraith) Munson, whose early life was passed in Lawrence county, Indiana. Ida May, an adopted daughter is now the wife of E. L. Chamberlain, of Jonesville, Louisiana.

Mr. Daniels was a Republican in politics and a member of the Masonic fraternity, having attained the Knights Templar degree, and was also a member of the Mystic Shrine. He held membership in the First Congregational church of Keokuk, of which he was a trustee for many years, and while his attention was chiefly given to his business affairs, he yet took cognizance of the conditions of life which wrought for good to the individual and to the community, and was the champion of many helpful and progressive measures. He held friendship inviolable and was kindly and sympathetic, but the very best elements of his character were reserved for his family and for the relation of an ideal home life. He passed away at Eau Claire, Wisconsin, October 25, 1903. Mrs. Daniels, also a member of the Congregational church, occupies a beautiful home overlooking the river, and in Keokuk, where she has now lived for nearly a third of a century, she has a very large circle of friends.

JACOB HANDRICH.

One of the older residents of Franklin township, Lee county, Iowa, and at the same time one of the most enterprising and successful farmers of this part of the county, is Jacob Handrich, who now resides on his farm of 166 acres on section 8. Mr. Handrich was born February 18, 1838, in Germany, the son of Jacob and Katherine (Neff) Handrich, and with his parents came to America in 1844, taking passage in a sailing vessel and landing after a stormy voyage of sixty-five days' duration at New Orleans, whence the family traveled by way of the Mississippi river to St. Louis. From that city they crossed over to Madison county, Illinois, where the father, who was a farmer by occupation, purchased a farm of 100 acres, and this he cultivated with success until his untimely death, which occurred only six years later. In 1852 the mother brought her children to Lee county, locating in Franklin township, where the remainder of her life was passed and where her own death occurred. She was a member of the Mennonite church, while her husband was of the Presbyterian faith, and both were people of the most admirable character, highly esteemed by all who knew them, and many friends who prized them for their rare qualities.

Mr. Handrich, our subject, enjoyed in his youth only the most limited educational advantages, and when but twelve years of age began working out as a farm hand, and thus at a very early age commenced to acquire that hard and practical experience which proved so useful to him in later life and which has constituted in no small degree the basis of his success. During the years 1859 and 1860 he was employed in Davis county, Iowa, but in the latter year he returned to this county and married Miss Mary Dieffenbach, who was a native of the same German province as himself. She is a member of an enterprising family and the daughter of Jacob and Mary Katherine (Nauert) Dieffenbach, who emigrated from Germany with their children in 1851, and in their progress to the New World they encountered many discouraging circumstances. After embarking they discovered that the ship upon which they had taken passage was old and unseaworthy, being then on its last voyage and requiring the constant use of pumps to keep it from sinking, occupying the long period of seventy-eight days, and after landing at New Orleans the passage up the Mississippi river occupied three weeks, during which their boat was frequently frozen fast in the ice. Arriving at St. Louis, eight more days were consumed in coming up the river to Keokuk, whence they drove to Franklin township, where they made their home for three years and then removed to Davis county, both parents completing in that county the span of their lives and passing to the life beyond. To them were born nine sons and daughters, of whom Mrs. Handrich is the fourth, and the others now living are as follows: John, a resident of Davis county, Iowa; Martin, who resides in the same county; Jacob, of California; Phoebe, wife of Mr. Layman, of California; and Anna, wife of Mr. Look, also of California.

Prior to his marriage Mr. Handrich had purchased a farm of 100 acres in Franklin township, on which he built substantial barns and a fine dwelling house, improving the property in many ways, and later traded it for his present farm of 122 acres, to which he has since added forty-four acres. Here he has erected a magnificent residence and many necessary buildings, besides installing all the most modern improvements, and maintains throughout the entire establishment an atmosphere of scrupulous neatness that bespeaks careful supervision and practical efficiency. To Mr. and Mrs. Handrich have been born eleven children, of whom ten survive, as follows: Jacob, of Davis county; Anna, wife of Henry Rings, of Franklin township; Mary, wife of John Frueh, of this township; Katie, wife of Phillip Dieffenbach, of Davis county; Henry, of Franklin township; Emma, wife of August Gram, of West Point township; Laura, wife of John Specht, of this township; Lydia, wife of Edward Loewenberg, of Donnellson, Iowa; and Elizabeth and John, who reside with their parents.

Mr. and Mrs. Handrich are lifelong members of the Mennonite church, in whose work they have always taken an active and helpful part, and doing much to advance the cause of religion among those who have come under their personal influence, both by precept and by the high and noble example of their lives. Mr. Handrich has also borne a share in the shaping of public affairs as a supporter of the Democratic party, but he has never sought public office, preferring to devote his attention and abilities principally to the work of his farm, and in this he has been extremely successful by reason of his constant care, sound judgment and business foresight, achieving a very gratifying degree of prosperity. In all his relations with his fellowmen he has observed the strictest integrity, and the history of his life is a chronicle of honor, honesty and fair, impartial dealing that has earned him the admiration of all, while at the same time his whole-hearted and genial good nature have been the means of winning many friends.

REUBEN C. STONER.

Reuben C. Stoner, at the present time an engineer on the Santa Fe Railway and residing at No. 2621 Webster street, Fort Madison, was born in Henry county, Iowa, on January 26, 1870, and removed to Lee county with his parents when five years of age. The family coming to Lee county, located about four miles north of West Point in Pleasant Ridge township. There our subject received his early education in the public schools of his township, and was his father's assistant in the work of the farm until attaining his seventeenth year, when he hired out as a farm hand for three years, thus beginning his independent career at a very early age. He then came to Fort Madison, where he went to work for the Santa Fe Railway Company as call boy, and at the end of one year became a fireman. After ten years of conscientious service in this capacity he was promoted, in 1901, to the position of engineer, which he still retains. In the three years of his connection with the freight service as an engineer he has never been concerned in a wreck, nor indeed, in any serious accident, and is rapidly coming to be recognized as a valuable factor in the system.

Mr. Stoner is a son of John and Malinda (Lyle) Stoner. The father is a native of Ohio, but early came west, locating in Henry county, Iowa, and is now a resident of Lowell, that county. He was a farmer throughout his active life, but is now retired. Malinda Stoner, the mother, died when her son Reuben C. was thirteen years of age.

At Fort Madison on April 22, 1891, Mr. Stoner was married to Miss Nettie Davis, who was born near Burlington, Des Moines county. Mrs. Stoner is a daughter of John C. Davis, who was a farmer until 1890, at which time he removed to Fort Madison, where he now resides and is in the employ of the Santa Fe Railroad Company. Mr. and Mrs. Stoner are the parents of one child, Clarence William.

Mr. Stoner is the third of a family of six brothers and sisters, as follows: Clara E., now deceased, was the wife of Charles Miner, teamster, of Fort Madison; Emma L. is the wife of Charles G. Tull, farmer, of Bertrand, Nebraska; Reuben C., the subject of this review; William, who was in the men's furnishing business in Chicago, died at the age of twenty-seven years; Samuel resides in St. Louis, Missouri; Ida E., is the wife of Alfred Canaday, farmer, of Lowell, Iowa. Mrs. Stoner is the elder of a family of two sisters. Susan B., her sister, is the wife of John B. Sibert, formerly of Fort Madison but now of San Bernardino, California, where he is a carpenter for the Santa Fe Railroad Company of that place.

Mr. Stoner is affiliated with the Brotherhood of Locomotive Firemen, and in his strictly fraternal relations has been a member of the Ancient Order of United Workmen since 1891. He holds membership in the Methodist Episcopal church, in the work of which he takes a very active part. He bestows a portion of his time upon the study of public questions, and from considerations of the general welfare has allied himself with the Democratic party. He has not, however, aspired to any public offce, being only careful to cast his vote in the interest of good government. In 1894 Mr. and Mrs. Stoner built a pleasant home at 2621 Webster street where they now reside.

HARRY FULTON.

Harry Fulton, the oldest continuous resident of Keokuk, who for many years had figured prominently in local political circles and in this connection also had a wide acquaintance throughout the state, was born in Watertown, Jefferson county, New York, March 29, 1825, his parents, Nathan and Philena (Hastings) Fulton, the former born in Vermont and the later in Massachusetts. They were married in New York and became the parents of eight children—Harry, Lucretia, who became the wife of of M. T. Langdon and died of cholera in 1849; Amanda, married William Hunt and died at his home in Jefferson county, New York, in 1902; Caroline, married Orrin Webb and died in California; Philena, died in childhood; Albert, living in Vilisca; Cynthia, the wife of William Sprague, of Lakeview, Wisconsin, and Elwin, who died in Kansas in 1903. The mother died in 1857, while visiting in New York and was buried at Watertown.

Harry Fulton pursued his early education in the schools of his native city and afterward continued his studies in Keokuk. He came west in 1842 with his father, mother and their seven children. They left the Empire state on the 24th of August, traveling after the primitive manner of the times, and arrived at their destination on the 19th of October. Leaving Watertown they passed through Rochester, Buffalo, Cleveland, Dayton, Columbus, Indianapolis, Springfield, Illinois, and thence to Nauvoo, from which point they crossed the river to Keokuk. The father purchased a farm three miles west of the present city of Keokuk, and in 1844 died of small-pox, from which disease the entire family suffered. The loss of the father threw the responsibility of caring for the family upon Harry, who was the eldest son. He remained upon the home farm until 1847, when he sold the property and removed to Keokuk, where he has since resided. Here he began clerking in the wholesale dry goods house of Cox & Shelley, with whom he remained for three years, when he turned his attention to merchandizing on his own account, conducting both a wholesale and retail clothing business until 1860. The following year he was appointed deputy United States marshal for the southern district of Iowa by H. M. Hoxie, the first United States marshal in this State, his appointment having been received from Abraham Lincoln. Mr. Fulton continued to serve in that capacity for fifteen or sixteen years and was deputy provost marshal for Lee county during the period of the Civil War. He had also been deputy sheriff in 1847 under Peter Miller. In 1848 he was a candidate for the state legislature on the Whig ticket, but was defeated on account of the overwhelming Democratic majority that the district gives. He served for two years as coroner, and at one time was candidate for sheriff, but was defeated. Other official positions, however, he has filled. He was appointed by Judge Love as jury commissioner and acted in that capacity for a long period. He served under different United States marshals, for two years under H. M. Hoxie, for two years under Peter Melinda, four years under G. W. Clark, one year under Ed. Campbell, a Democrat, four years under David Miller, two years under E. P. Bradley, also a Democrat, two years under Col. R. Root, and four years under George M. Christian. In this capacity he has been called forth into active, arduous and ofttimes dangerous service. During the Santa Fe Railroad strike in Madison in 1894, he was on duty and again during the Wabash Railroad strike at the time of President Cleveland's first administration. In this connection he did considerable official business in the matter of making arrests. He has ever been prompt and fearless in the discharge of his duty and has the entire confidence and good will of the law-abiding community. In local affairs he has also been prominent and for five years he served on the city council from the second ward. His first election came to him in a singular manner. He was at that time in Cincinnati buying goods for his mercantile establishment and when he returned home he found he had been elected to the office. The ticket on which he was nominated was placed in the field only on the morning of the election, and was called the Know-Nothing ticket. On this occasion D. W. Kilburn was elected mayor of the city. None of the candidates on the ticket knew that their names had been placed there when the ticket was put in the field, but a number of the leading business men of the city desiring a clean, practical and progressive administration planned the movement, which was successfully carried out. This was the only election which Mr. Fulton has missed in fifty-seven years. For thirty years he has continuously been a delegate to state conventions, attending even at a time when he had to go by stage to Des Moines. He attended the national conventions at which Lincoln, Grant, Garfield, Blaine, Harrison, McKinley and Roosevelt were nominated; also the Democratic convention at Kansas City, which made Bryan its standard bearer and at the last Republican national convention at Chicago he was assistant sergeant-at-arms, his badge and appointment being now among his treasurer possessions.

Mr. Fulton was appointed by the court receiver of the plank road from Keokuk to New Boston and managed this for several years, or until it was sold, the purchasers being H. W. Sample, James M. Shelley and Harry Fulton. These gentlemen conducted the road for a time, but afterward sold it to Lee county. In 1862-3 Mr. Fulton purchased horses to the value of $42,000 for the government, and he also bought and sold some fine matched teams for private parties and some to the St. Louis fire department. During a period of ten or twelve years he was appointed assignee in nearly all bankruptcy cases that occurred in Keokuk.

In his own business career Mr. Fulton met with some reverses, but his characteristic purpose, unfaltering diligence and unquestioned integrity enabled him to overcome all difficulties and again work his way upward. After coming to this county he invested in real estate, but the financial panic of 1857 came on and he became involved as did thousands of others, so that he was left without a home, he and his wife giving up the residence which he had built, together with all their other property. At a bankruptcy sale of land he purchased 800 acres. Although he had not a dollar of his own to pay for this, friends came to his assistance and the wisdom of his investment was shown in the fact that within six months he sold 160 acres of the land for $500 more than the entire 800 acres cost. He has rarely been at fault in matters of business judgment, and he now own a farm of considerable value, comprising 110 acres within the city limits of Keokuk. He also has forty acres adjoining Hamilton, and he owns residence property in Keokuk, at the corner of Sixth and Franklin streets, and his home at No. 227 High street. He is a charter member of Eagle Lodge, No. 12, Free and Accepted Masons, has been prominent in the ranks of Masonry and has served as Senior Warden of the Grand Lodge.

On the 29th of August, 1846, Mr. Fulton was married in Keokuk to Miss N. E. Patterson, who was born in Guernsey county, Ohio, in 1828. Her parents were R. M. G. and Nancy (Phillips) Patterson.

The father, a native of Ohio, was a boat builder and farmer and came to Keokuk in 1839 on a boat which he had built, the trip being made down the Ohio river and up the Mississippi. Within an hour after they boarded the steamer it burned with all its contents and Mr. Patterson lost all of his possessions in this disaster, and one man was burned to death, while another was drowned. The family proceeded to St. Louis, and on another boat to Warsaw, where Mr. Patterson worked at carpentering for a year. In 1840 he moved across the Mississippi river, living in the midst of a heavy timbered district, in which Indians were still seen. R. M. G. Patterson, the father, became a leading and influential factor in the early development of Lee county and served in the territorial legislature before the admission of Iowa into the Union. He had a son who served as sergeant-at-arms in the house for two years, beginning in 1844. In 1849 Mr. Patterson removed with his family to Montgomery county, where he conducted a grocery store, and both he and his wife died in that county. They were the parents of four children, but only two are now living—John W., previously mentioned as sergeant-at-arms in the territorial legislature, died in Vilisca, Iowa, in 1895. Susanna is the widow of James Dunn and lives in Montgomery county, Iowa. J. T. died in February, 1904, in a hospital in Kansas City, Missouri.

Unto Mr. and Mrs. Fulton have been born seven children, but only one is now living: Ida C., the wife of Willis H. Davis, a dealer in surgical instruments at Keokuk. They have one son, Harry Fulton, born May 30, 1887. The children of the Fulton family who passed away in childhood are: Charles S., Albert H., Maggie, Harry S., Willis D. and one died in infancy. Mrs. Fulton is a member of the Congregational church and belongs to the Ladies' Aid Society, and Mr. Fulton contributes to the support of the church. They are probably the oldest married couple who have had continuous residence in Lee county. They have celebrated as the years have gone by by their tin, wooden, silver and golden wedding anniversaries. Theirs has been a happy married life, not without its sorrows and disappointments, for they come to every individual; but there has, nevertheless, been much of pleasure and prosperity in their careers, and their mutual love and confidence has increased as time has gone by. They have a most intimate knowledge of the events which have become matters of history in Lee county, being among the earliest settlers of this portion of the state. They have watched the county as it has merged from pioneer conditions to take its place among the leading counties of the commonwealth, with all its splendid improvements and its great business activities. Mr. Fulton has been particularly well known in business and political circles and has wielded a wide influence. In the evening of life he receives the respect and confidence of all with whom he has been associated, for his upright life and honorable purpose have gained to him the good will and trust of those with whom he has been brought in contact.

Mr. Fulton passed to his eternal home October 30, 1904.

FRANK M. BALLINGER.

Frank M. Ballinger, a member of the Keokuk bar, was born in Sandusky, Lee county, Iowa, May 2, 1867, his parents being Frank M. and Florence (Fatio) Ballinger. The family is of English lineage and was first planted on American soil in Virginia, whence representatives of the name removed to Kentucky, where the family is now very numerous. Many who bear the name have become prominent in that state, including distinguished representatives of the Kentucky bar. Frank Ballinger, grandfather of F. M. Ballinger, of this review, was a prominent lawyer of Harrodsburg, Kentucky, where he was judge of both the circuit and appellate courts and an intimate friend of Cassius M. Clay. Removing to Iowa in the early fifties he settled at what is now Ballinger's Station, Lee county, and became an extensive landowner. He built a large stone house, which is still a prominent feature of the landscape and in excellent state of preservation. Its construction was superintended by Steve Green, one of Judge Ballinger's former slaves, who was afterward a prominent contractor and builder of Ottumwa, Iowa, where he is now living, aged and feeble.

Frank M. Ballinger, a son of Judge Ballinger, came to Iowa and bought land for his father in the "half-breed tract" of the Sac and Fox reservation. He became an agriculturist with extensive landed holdings, well known in Lee county. He married Florence Fatio while in the government service in Washington, D. C. She was the daughter of a naval officer, a native of Spain, who served in both Spanish and English navies. He afterward came to the United States, settling at Washington, D. C., and he married a Miss Birch, of Virginia, a member of a prominent Southern family of that name. He served in the United States navy and died of yellow fever off the coast of Brazil, while in command of a government vessel. Mr. Ballinger, father of our subject, died in Keokuk, in November, 1889, and the following year his widow returned to Washington, D. C., where she now resides.

Frank M. Ballinger, their son, was educated in the schools near Sandusky and Keokuk, and following the completion of his literary course he entered upon the study of law, pursuing his reading in Colorado and in Keokuk. He was admitted to practice May 13, 1896, by the supreme court of the state, at Des Moines, and was admitted to practice in the United States circuit and district courts of the southern district of Iowa in 1896, and to the supreme court of the United States April 12, 1901. Following his admission to the bar he entered the office of Hon. John E. Craig, of Keokuk. At first he had a large mercantile practice, representing at different times nearly all the wholesale merchants of Keokuk. His later years have been devoted more largely to the practice of criminal and corporation law, and in this branch of jurisprudence his clientage is large. He is particularly well fitted for his specialty, because he not only has a comprehensive knowledge of legal principles, but is also forceful in argument, logical in his reasoning, clear in his deductions and presents his cause with the force and power of oratorical ability. The bar and the courts always listen attentively and his clear presentation of his cause, based upon the correct application of the law, has won him many notable forensic victories.

Mr. Ballinger is a stanch Republican, and in 1899 was a candidate of his party for the state legislature, but as the district is Democratic he was defeated. He is a valued member of several fraternal organizations, including the Benevolent and Protective Order of Elks, the Fraternal Order of Eagles, the Independent Order of Odd Fellows, the Modern Woodmen of America and the Sons of Veterans.

On the 13th of February, 1888, Mr. Ballinger was married to Miss Eliza S. Carpenter, of Sandusky, Iowa, daughter of Charles L. and Mary J. (Sawyer) Carpenter, he being one of the early settlers of the county. Mr. and Mrs. Ballinger now have a daughter, Hazel, and their acquaintance is wide and favorable in their native county. Having always made his home within the borders of Lee county the life record of Mr. Ballinger is well known to his friends, who recognize in his salient characteristics those traits which make for good citizenship, for high professional ideals and for ethical relations in private life.

HENRY HARMON DEIMAN.

Henry Harmon Deiman, deceased, long one of the prominent citizens of Lee county and for a number of years a successful pork packer in Fort Madison and later a farmer of Pleasant Ridge township, was born in Hamburg, Germany, in 1813, and came to America as a young man, crossing the ocean in a sailing ship and taking six weeks for the voyage. Landing in New Orleans, he proceeded by way of the Mississippi river to St. Louis, where he remained some three or four years, and there he was married to Miss Elizabeth Jansen, a native of Hanover, Germany. He engaged in farming, and was very successful, so much so that he was able to surround his family with the comforts and many luxuries of life, and to give them a fine home. The beautiful residence building, however, was destroyed by fire, a loss which was very considerable and was keenly felt. Mr. Deiman then removed with his family to Quincy, Illinois, where they lived for a number of years, and about 1848 came to Fort Madison, taking up their residence in the western part of the city. In Fort Madison Mr. Deiman engaged in pork packing, building up a very extensive business and giving employment to a large number of workmen, thus greatly assisting in the material progress of the city and contributing in an important measure to its prosperity at that time, as well as doing much, by encouraging an industry which was then in its infancy, to secure the present welfare of a community which still honors his memory. In 1879, however, he relinquished his work here, exchanging his packing business for a farm of 320 acres in Pleasant Ridge township. There he passed the remainder of his life in supervising the work of his farm, which he made one of the finest in the township, introducing modern improvements in both equipment and methods, and erecting buildings according to the latest and most approved models.

The death of Mr. Deiman occurred at his home in Pleasant Ridge township January 1, 1894. He was a man of great ability and strong but gentle character, and his passing was mourned by a large circle of acquaintances and friends, neighbors and former business associates who held him in affection for his genial but just disposition, respected his qualities of high honor and integrity and honored him for those traits of heart and mind which set him apart as a notable man, one of those rare personalities which appear but once in a generation, uplifting all those with whom they come in contact. Many hold him in grateful remembrance, and the record of his life is a precious possession to those left to mourn his loss. Mrs. Deiman survived her husband only one month, her demise occurring February 1, 1894. She was a woman of saintly character, universally beloved for her many virtues, and left a family which has done her credit through the testimony borne by their lives to her careful, conscientious and pious teachings and training. Both Mr. and Mrs. Deiman were members of St. Mary's Catholic church at West Point.

They are survived by a son and a daughter, these being Joseph, now a resident of South Dakota, and Elizabeth, who was born in Fort Madison November 1, 1854. There she received a very superior education in a private school and academy, thus fitting herself for the conspicuous position she has since occupied in refined and cultured social circles. At Fort Madison in January, 1874, she was united in marriage to Lawrence Figgen, who was born in the city of St. Louis, and who was a very successful young business man, and they took up their residence in Chicago, where Mr. Figgen was associated with his father in the candle business. In 1884 they decided to remove to the country, and returning to Lee county, they located in Pleasant Ridge township, residing near the Deiman home for one year, at the end of which time they accepted the invitation of Mr. and Mrs. Deiman to share their home and care for the old people during the remainder of their years. The death of Mr. Figgen, however, preceded theirs, that sad occurrence taking place May 10, 1887, and his remains were laid at rest in Saint Mary's cemetery at Fort Madison. He was a member of Saint Mary's Catholic church at West Point, and ever faithful to the teachings of his religion and the highest attributes of his nature. He possessed great ability and the most admirable character, and was very popular, having the good will of all who knew him. In his death his wife and children sustained a loss which is too great to be calculated and which no favor of fortune or circumstance can ever repair.

To Mr. and Mrs. Figgen were born three sons and three daughters, as follows: Lawrence, now residing at Leadville, Colorado, who married Miss Nellie Murdock and has one son, Lawrence James; Lillian, who married Frank McKibben, of Winfield, Kansas, and has two sons, Lawrence and Harold; Harry, who died in Chicago when only one year of age; Marie, who is the wife of George Krehbiel and has one son Lawrence; Joseph, who operates Mrs. Figgen's farm; and Emma, who also remains at home.

Lawrence and Marie are members of Saint Mary's Catholic church at Fort Madison, while Mrs. Figgen and her youngest two children are members of the West Point congregation. Mrs. Figgen has disposed of part of the original farm, but retains the ownership of 120 acres, which she devotes to general farming, in which she has had remarkable success. In addition to her abilities of a more practical nature she is a pleasant and accomplished lady of charming conversational powers, is widely celebrated for her hospitality and her social qualities, and is gifted with exceptionally brilliant intellectual endowments.

JOHN DOWNS, M. D.

Dr. John Downs, whose thorough preparation and resourceful effort in the practice of medicine have gained him prominence as one of the ablest representatives of the profession in Fort Madison, was born on the farm near what is now Reeseville, in Highland county, Ohio, April 15, 1854, his parents being James and Mary (McKernertny) Downs. He was only a year old when his parents removed to Fayette county, Ohio, and in October, 1863, they became residents of Ralls county, Missouri, settling near Saverton, where the father purchased land. His death there occurred in 1865, and in 1868 the mother married again. Dr. Downs was the eldest in the family of six children, of whom only two reached mature years, one sister dying at the age of twelve years, while a brother, James, was injured in a railway accident and soon afterward died. Following the mother's second marriage the property was sold in Ralls county, and the family removed to Marion county, Missouri, settling on a farm, there living until 1870, when they went to Shelby county and again established their home on a farm, Dr. Downs remaining with the family there until twenty years of age.

Having acquired a fair common-school education he started out in life on his own account. He began work as a farm hand in Knox county, being employed by the month, and in the succeeding winter he entered the high school in Edina. He completed the high-school course, and when twenty-one years of age began teaching. While thus engaged he also took up the study of medicine under the direction of Dr. Cornelius O'Brien, with whom he made his home for three years while following the teacher's profession. In the fall of 1876 he entered Rush Medical College, of Chicago, and in 1877 became a student in the medical school in Keokuk, the College of Physicians and Surgeons, now the Keokuk Medical and College of Physicians and Surgeons On his graduation in the spring of 1878 he received the degree of Doctor of Medicine, and immediately afterward entered upon the practice of his profession in Edina, Missouri, where he remained until June, 1882. He met with a fair measure of success, and he soon saved enough to pay for his medical education. In the year mentioned he removed to Fort Madison, and almost immediately entered upon a large and lucrative prac-

JOHN DOWNS, M. D.

tice that, indeed, made greater demands upon his time than he could meet. He has since resided continuously in Fort Madison, and although in recent years he has retired somewhat from active professional duties, his services are yet in demand by many who are loth to call in another family physician. Throughout his professional career he has made it his purpose to keep well informed concerning the advancement that is being continually made by the medical fraternity, and while quick to adopt any new method which he believes will prove of genuine value in his practice, he is, nevertheless, slow to discard the old and time-tried methods whose value has been proven through many years.

His first venture in real estate was in taking a twenty-year lease of a lot at No. 220 Pine street, on which he built an office. In 1887 he made his first purchase of acreage property in the west part of Fort Madison and improved it. In the same year he was named a member of the Soliciting Committee to raise money to bring the Santa Fe Railroad to this city. In that movement the committee was successful, raising $30,000. Dr. Downs was one of the guarantors of the right-of-way through the town. He aided in getting a charter for the bridge across the river, and the building of the railroad and the bridge proved a splendid impetus to the growth of the city, bringing about what is in popular parlance termed a "boom." He began to invest in real estate, and was among the first to build in the western part of town. In 1892 he assisted in raising a $50,000 bonus for the building of a slaughter house and meat packing establishment, although he lost considerable money in that deal, everything was done in good faith to advance the interests of Fort Madison. In 1895 he built the Marguette Building as a memorial to pioneers of the northwest. It was originally intended as an educational and club center, but is now used for office purposes, Dr. Downs maintaining his own office therein, and also the top floor being used as the home of the Knights of Columbus, the building thus, to a degree, reverting to its original purposes. He built his first residence at the corner of Third and Cedar streets, and there made his home until 1897, when he sold and removed to his present residence at No. 804 Third street. Dr. Downs has likewise been identified with the improvement of the city aside from his real estate operations. He was one of the incorporators of the Fort Madison Street Railway, but afterward sold his stock.

After coming to Fort Madison Dr. Downs was married on the 16th of October, 1883, in this city, to Miss Caroline Schwartz, a native of Fort Madison, and a daughter of John G. and Catharine (Strethman) Schwartz. Six children have been born unto them: John C., who has had a business education and is now with his father as a member of the firm of John Downs & Sons, manufacturers of concrete, Portland cement, stone and dealers in cement, sand, coal and building supplies, with factory and warehouse at Fort Madison; James L., who is now a stenographer for the chief clerk of the Santa Fe Railroad

Company, at Fort Madison; Marie Catharine, Anna Marie, who died in infancy; Catharine Isabella, and Joseph Garrett.

While yet a boy Dr. Downs became deeply interested in questions of politics, and has always kept well informed on the issues of the day. He cast his first ballot but a week after he attained his majority, and in 1876 he championed the cause of Cooper, but lost his vote on account of being in Chicago at the time of the election. In 1880 he supported Hancock, and has since been an advocate of Democracy in national politics. He has never been an office seeker, but was appointed County Physician, and has served as health officer of Fort Madison. Free and untrammeled in the expression of his views and unfaltering in his advocacy of what he believes to be right in matters of citizenship as well as in other relations of life, he accords to others the privilege which he reserves for himself, of forming an unbiased opinion. In manner he is pleasant and genial, and has gained a large circle of friends by his unfailing courtesy and deference for the opinion of others. Subsequently he has been called upon to serve as a delegate to the various county, congressional and state conventions. He was reared in the Catholic faith, and was confirmed in the church at Edina, Missouri, by Rev. P. J. Ryan, coadjutor of Archbishop Kendrick, of St. Louis. Rev. Ryan is now archbishop of Philadelphia. Dr. Downs is identified with St. Joseph's church, at Fort Madison, and was one of the building committee at the time of the erection of the house of worship, in 1885. In that year he became a charter member of the Fort Madison St. Joseph Benevolent Society, and also of the Knights of Columbus, of this city, having, however, become a member of the latter at Burlington, Iowa. This was called the Gallitzen Council, No 739, Knights of Columbus, and was organized in October, 1903. Dr. Downs's influence has often been exerted for the upbuilding and improvement of Fort Madison, and is widely known as the champion of many measures that have been of great benefit to the state. He did all he could to influence the school board to erect a school house in each ward, instead of having a central building and the wisdom of this plan has been fully demonstrated. He was likewise in favor of a good sewerage system and advocated the planting of shade trees. Fort Madison has, indeed, benefited by his efforts and his progressive and loyal citizenship stands as an unquestioned fact in his career.

HAZEN I. SAWYER.

Hazen I. Sawyer, who is an attorney at law practicing as a member of the firm of Hughes & Sawyer, of Keokuk, was born in this city October 10, 1868. He is a son of I. A. Sawyer of the Irwin-Phillips Company, of Keokuk, one of the prominent representatives of commercial circles in Lee county. He was at one time a lieutenant in the regular army and enlisted as a private in the Third Iowa Infantry at the commencement of the Civil War. He married Miss Mary Irwin, a daughter of Stephen Irwin, one of the founders of the Irwin-Phillips Company, and a sister of John N. and Wells M. Irwin, of that corporation. In the Sawyer family were four children: Stephen L., with the Irwin-Phillips Company, of Keokuk; Hazen I., Mrs. T. R. Board, of Keokuk, and Mrs. John A. McElroy, of Chicago.

Hazen I. Sawyer began his education in the public schools of Keokuk and afterward spent three years in Parsons College, at Fairfield, where he completed his literary course. Preparing for the bar as a student in the University of Michigan at Ann Arbor, he was graduated there with the class of 1892. During his school and college days he spent the period of vacation in the wholesale house of the Irwin-Phillips Company. Following his graduation he entered upon the practice of law at Aurora, Missouri, and in the fall of 1893 returned to Keokuk, where he opened an office, practicing alone until 1900. He then became associated with James C. Davis, now general attorney for the Chicago & Northwestern Railroad Company, at Des Moines, this connection being continued until 1902, when he entered into his present professional relation with Judge Felix T. Hughes. He is local attorney for the Iowa State Insurance Company, and the firm of Hughes & Sawyer represent locally the Chicago, Burlington & Quincy, the Wabash, Santa Fe and Chicago, Rock Island & Pacific Railway Companies. Mr. Sawyer is also attorney for the Keokuk Savings bank and in addition represents many private interests, having a distinctively representative clientage. He is a student, preparing his cases with great care and thoroughness and presenting his cause in the strong, clear light of reason. He was city attorney for Keokuk from April, 1896, until April, 1899, and was a second time elected to that position in April, 1902, serving until April, 1904. From August 1898, until his second election to the office of city attorney he served as referee in bankruptcy, being appointed by Federal Judge John Woolson. Strong in argument and clear in expression he bases his statements upon a thorough knowledge of the fact and correct application of the law to the points in litigation and has gradually advanced to a position prominent in the ranks of the local fraternity in his native city.

Mr. Sawyer is also recognized as a leader in the ranks of the Republican party, taking a very active interest in county politics. He has served as a member of the Republican county central committee, as chairman of the city committee and as chairman of the county delegation, attending the state convention. He is a close and earnest student of the signs of the times and of the questions which divide the country into two great parties and his championship of Republicanism is the result of honest convictions, based upon a thorough and comprehensive understanding of the issues of the day.

On the 8th of February, 1899, Mr. Sawyer was married to Miss Marcia Louise Jenkins, a daughter of Dr. and Mrs. George F. Jenkins, of Keokuk, and they occupy a pleasant residence at No. 522, Orleans street. Fraternally Mr. Sawyer is connected with Keokuk Lodge, No. 13, Independent Order of Odd Fellows, and Morning Star Lodge, No. 5, Knights of Pythias. He has passed all of the chairs in the former organizations and he likewise belongs to the Sons of Veterans. He also holds membership in the Keokuk Country Club, in which he served as a director for about four years. In connection with his profession he holds various membership relations, belonging to the Keokuk Bar Association, the Iowa State Bar Association, in which is serving as a member of the Committee on Grievances, the American Bar Association and the Commercial Law League of America. While his is a well-rounded character, his record presenting a commendable interest in social life, in politics and in many of the questions which have bearing upon the conditions of the locality and the nation, his efforts are chiefly directed toward the calling which he has chosen as a life work and in which through individual merit, close study and application, supplementing strong intellectuality, he has won noble and gratifying success.

ROBERT R. BULLARD.

Robert Rolla Bullard, for many years a prominent agriculturalist of Green Bay township and a representative of one of the older families of Lee county, occupies a pleasant home on the southwest quarter of section 16 of his township. Here he owns 280 acres of productive bottom lands, forty acres being in timber. He was born in Jefferson township, Lee county, Iowa, October 11, 1856, son of James and Sarah A. (Wallace) Bullard. James Bullard, father of our subject, was born at Jacksonville, Morgan county, Illinois, and the mother was born in Northumberland county, Pennsylvania. When James Bullard was nine years of age he came to Des Moines county, Iowa, with his father, Theophilus Bullard, and a year later came to Lee county. They located in Jefferson township, entering a "homestead" of government land there. The date of James Bullard's birth was 1825.

Robert Bullard's maternal grandfather, Joseph Wallace, came west at an early day, and located in Jefferson township, where the parents formed their acquaintance. Before his marriage James Bullard bought 160 acres of land in Jefferson township, where the greater part of his life was passed, and there Robert Bullard was born and grew to manhood, receiving, meantime, a good education in the public schools. At the age of twenty years he began his independent career by farming part of his father's land, and on the twentieth day of the following February, 1877, he was married in Jefferson township to Miss Nellie J. Shay, daughter of Patrick and Mary (Waters) Shay.

Mrs. Bullard's parents were both born and reared in County Clare, Ireland, and after their marriage emigrated to Canada. Later they removed to Ohio, where the father was employed in a brick yard near the City of Cleveland. Thence they came to Iowa.

After his marriage Mr. Bullard continued farming his father's land, and their interests were largely in common until the latter's death, which occurred in 1898. Sarah Bullard, the mother, died in 1885.

Unto Mr. and Mrs. Bullard have been born two sons, Robert Edward, who died at the age of about nine years, and one other who died in infancy. One child, Marie Bullard, they have adopted. She was born in St. Louis, May 26, 1900.

Mr. Bullard conducts a general farming business on a small scale, renting most of his land. He is a student of public questions, and in his political faith is a consistent supporter of the Democratic party, believing its principles to be in accord with the spirit of American institutions. Personally, however, he has always refused to accept public office. In a fraternal way he is a member of Wever Lodge, No. 552, Independent Order of Odd Fellows. He is well known in this section of Lee county, has made friends by his geniality and hospitality, and is esteemed for the uprightness and justice that characterize all his dealings.

ARTHUR ROGERS.

Arthur Rogers, who is one of the younger farmers of Green Bay township, is a native son of the township, having been born September 9, 1861, on section 16. It is recalled, as a reminder of pioneer times and in contrast to the present highly developed condition of the county, that his birth occurred in a log cabin. He is the son of Milward Rogers, a sketch of whose career and ancestry appears elsewhere in this review. Mr. Rogers, our subject, received his early knowledge of books in the public schools of his district, but may be said to be largely self-educated, as his home mental training, in connection with natural talent, has enabled him to assume his present place in the community.

Until his twenty-second year Mr. Rogers assisted in the work of the home farm, acquiring the familiarity with the details of practical agriculture, which has since stood him in good stead and has been a most valuable factor in his success. On December 28, 1884, he was united in marriage to Miss Florida Marsh, who was born in Wayne county, Iowa, the daughter of Benjamin and Sarah (Baldwin) Marsh. Mr. and Mrs. Marsh were among the earlier settlers of the present State of Iowa, and both of eastern birth. Mr. Marsh died in 1897, at the age of sixty-five years, and was laid at rest in Cherry Grove cemetery, in Washington township, Lee county. Mrs. Marsh, who still survives at the age of seventy-three, resides in Green Bay township. She was born in Delaware, and as a girl came with her parents west and located at Nauvoo, Illinois.

After his marriage Mr. Rogers rented a portion of his father's farm, which he cultivated and upon which he continued to reside until 1898, when he moved to his present place of residence. This farm consists of fine farming land, and is in two tracts of sixty-five and 140 acres, respectively. He has improved the original buildings on the farm, and made the entire establishment thoroughly modern, having installed, among other conveniences, a private gas plant for his own use. The residence building is a handsome and commodious structure situated amid pleasant surroundings.

Mr. and Mrs. Rogers are members of Good Hope Rebecca Lodge, No. 267, at Wever, and Mrs. Rogers is a member of the Christian church. To Mr. and Mrs. Rogers have been born two daughters and one son: Ethel Rebecca, Sarah Jane and Harold Arthur. Fraternally Mr. Rogers is a member of the Independent Order of Odd Fellows, No. 552, at Wever, of which he is Past Grand, and of Benevolent and Protective Order of Elks, No. 374, at Fort Madison. In political affiliation he is a free thinker and considers well before casting his ballot. He is thoroughly progressive in his ideas, both as a farmer and as a citizen, and by his loyalty to his convictions and his capacity for friendship has won the regard and respect of those who know him.

ANDREW J. EIDSON, M. D.

Dr. Andrew J. Eidson, whose scholarly attainments, professional skill and broad humanitarianism made him a man among men, standing as one of the representative citizens of Fort Madison, where he won the honor and respect of all, was born in Butler county, Ohio, on the 26th of October, 1837. He was the eldest in a family of four sons and two daughters born unto William M. and Catherine (Daugherty) Eidson, the former born in North Carolina in 1814 and the later in Ohio in 1817. They were married in Butler county, Ohio, to which place William Eidson had removed in early manhood. They afterward became residents of Adams county, Illinois, where the mother died in 1858, but the father, long surviving her, passed away in 1886. After the death of his first wife he was united in marriage to Mrs. Eliza Nelson. During the Mexican War he offered his services to his country, but was not mustered into the army. His was an honorable and useful career, and late in life he became identified with the Congregational church.

Dr. Eidson accompanied his parents on their removal to Adams county, Illinois, in his early boyhood days and was reared upon the home farm there. He attended the common schools and by close application qualified himself for teaching, which profession he followed in the district schools for several years. He regarded this, however, merely as an initial step to other prefessional labor, for it was his ambition to become a member of the medical fraternity. Needing further preparation for this, however, he entered Quincy College, wherein he won the degree of Bachelor of Arts, and thus with broad literary knowledge to serve as the foundation upon which to rear the superstructure of professional learning he entered the McDowell College at St. Louis, Missouri, in 1859. Subsequently he matriculated in Rush Medical College, of Chicago, from which he was graduated in January, 1865. The following month he enlisted for service in the Civil War, becoming a private of Company D, One Hundred and Forty-eighth Illinois Infantry. Illness, however, soon compelled him to go to the hospital, and after partially recovering he was made ward master of the hospital and its acting surgeon, which position he filled until discharged on account of his own physical disability.

When his military service was over Dr. Eidson returned to Illinois and settled in McDonough county, where he resided until 1871, when he removed to Coatsville, Missouri. There he enjoyed a large and lucrative practice and his wife was the owner of a drug store there. He continued a resident of Coatsville until 1893, when he removed to Fort Madison. He afterward lived a retired life, devoting his attention to literary pursuits, for his practice in former years had brought to him a very desirable remuneration that enabled him to spend his last days without further recourse to professional labor. He had more than a local reputation as a writer and his poems have appeared in various periodicals from time to time. It was his intention to have these published in book form, but death cut short his work, but his widow intends publishing the volume of her husband's poetic productions, many of which have received favorable comment from the press.

Dr. Eidson was a member of the Masonic fraternity and for a number of years served as tyler of Stella Lodge, No. 440, Free and Accepted Masons, of Fort Madison. He was also a member of the Odd Fellows Lodge at Fort Madison. In politics he was a Republican and held the office of alderman from the first ward for two years. He held membership in the Methodist church, and during his life, prior to taking up the study of medicine, he studied theology and was known as a boy preacher, although he was never ordained. His influence was ever on the side of right, progress, reform and improvement and his career was a most honorable and straightforward one.

Dr. Eidson was married twice. In February, 1863, he wedded Miss Lucinda M. Monroe, of Cass county, Illinois, and by this marriage there were two children: Araminta A., the elder, is the wife of Charles C. Dean, a son of the late Hon. Henry Clay Dean, and they reside in Schuyler county, Missouri, where Mr. Dean is following the occupation of farming. They have become the parents of four children, all of whom are living: Charles Cass, Leo, Alice and Edith. Lillie Maude Eidson died the wife of Frank Waters, a son of Dr. Waters, of Salem, Arkansas, her remains being interred in the cemetery at that place. She left three children: Eidson, deceased, and Annie and Cecil, who live with grandmother at Salem.

For his second wife Dr. Eidson chose Bethany M. Wheeler, a native of Van Buren county, Iowa, and a daughter of Henry M. and Bethany M. (Charles) Wheeler. Mrs. Eidson was born August 8, 1850, and resided at the place of her birth until seven years of age, when she accompanied her parents to Missouri, where they lived until 1861. Her father was a mechanic and followed pursuits along that line throughout his entire life. He served as a member of the Home Guard and during the early part of the Civil War herded cattle for the government. About 1862 he removed to Illinois, locating at Huntsville. He died, however, at Coatsville, Missouri, and his wife passed away at Birmingham, Illinois, some years prior to his death. In their family were twelve children, of whom Mrs. Eidson was the youngest. In Huntsville Mrs. Eidson acquired a part of her education. She also attended school in Birmingham, Illinois, and it was there that she formed the acquaintance of Dr. Eidson. Their marriage was celebrated in Brooklyn, Schuyler county, Illinois, March 1, 1871, and they afterward went to Missouri, locating at Coatsville, where they remained until their removal to Fort Madison. Unto Dr. and Mrs. Eidson were born three children, all of whom are living. Marcus M., a resident of Manhattan, Illinois, is agent for the Wabash Railroad Company at that place. He is a member of the Masonic order and also of the Methodist church, South. He married Miss Ethel Seymour, of Sturgeon, Missouri, whose father is a merchant of that place. Edmond E., who was born in Coatsville and acquired his education there and in Fort Madison, is a machinist with the Iowa Farming Tool Company in the latter city and fraternally is connected with the Masonic Lodge of Fort Madison and also the Benevolent and Protective Order of Elks. Catherine E. is the wife of Benjamin J. Bothe, a resident of Fort Madison and a foreman of the finishing shop of the Iowa Farming Tool Company. He was born and reared in Fort Madison, being a son of Casper and Margaret Bothe, his father leading a retired life on Fifth street in Fort Madison. Unto Mr. and Mrs. Benjamin J. Bothe has been born one son, Charles Lewis, born at Fort Madison and now three years of age.

Dr. Eidson departed this life on the 4th of September, 1903. He had during the period of his residence in Fort Madison gained many warm friends who valued him not only because of his professional ability, literary skill and scholarly attainments, but also because of his kindly spirit, his generous sympathy and his genial companionship. He was a man of local prominence for whom his fellowmen entertained high regard because of his fidelity to duty and honest convictions. He possessed keen sensitiveness to the humor and pathos of life, its pain and its pleasures and his keen appreciation of the beautiful and the ideal was manifest in his writings.

WILLIAM FULTON.

William Fulton, a resident of Keokuk, is a representative of one of the old families of Pennsylvania, tracing his ancestry back to Abraham Fulton and on back to Ireland. Abraham became the founder of the family in America and was a man of upright character as is indicated by a paper which he brought with him from his native country and which reads:

"Whereas, Abraham Fulton, with his wife and family are now moving from this country to the Continent of America, this is to inform whom it may concern that they were born and lived until the date hereof in ye parish and behaved in a sober and Christian manner and now leaves us free from any publick scandal or other censure. Certified at Articlav, in the Kingdom of Ireland, this 26th day of May, 1772, by

M. KNOX, V. D. M.,
H. CALDWELL,
ROBERT GUTHRY,
Elders."

Abraham Fulton was the father of Robert Fulton, who was the father of William Fulton, Sr., who served in the Revolutionary War. William Fulton, Sr., was born in Westmoreland county, Pennsylvania, and became a volunteer for service in the War of 1812, having charge of wagons and transportation. He married Miss Nancy Peairs, who was born in 1791 and they became the parents of three sons who reached manhood, but William Fulton, of this review, is the only son now living. The father died in Westmoreland county, Pennsylvania, in 1851, and his remains were interred there. The mother, however, long survived him and coming west, passed away in 1882 in her ninety-second year, the burial being in the Keokuk cemetery.

William Fulton, the subject of this sketch, was born in Westmoreland county, Pennsylvania, June 4, 1829, and in his youth received but moderate school privileges. However, he afterward attended Washington College in Pennsylvania, and was graduated with the class of 1854. While in college he was chosen as essayest in a contest and was awarded the favorable verdict as preparing the best essay among those in the two literary societies contesting. This contest was an annual event and he chose as his subject the "Elements of American Literature." When twenty three years of age he left home and went South. He did not leave, however, until after election day, when he cast his first presidential ballot for Franklin Pierce. Mr. Fulton spent about two years in teaching school in private families in Louisiana, being located in Concordia Parish and elsewhere in that state. He also read law while in the South with a Mr. Perkins, who afterward became a member of Jefferson Davis's cabinet during the Southern Confederacy.

In 1856 Mr. Fulton returned to the North and spent the winter in teaching in his home district in Pennsylvania. In April, 1857, however, he came to Keokuk and read law with the firm of Hornish & Lomax for a year. He was admitted to the bar at Albia, Iowa, and practiced with his preceptor, John P. Hornish. In 1862, however, he turned his attention to the insurance and real estate business and on account of defective hearing he has not been actively connected with the legal profession for twenty years. His time and energies instead have been devoted to the building up of a good insurance and real estate business and in this he has met with fair success. He has acted as special adjuster for the Phoenix, Hartford, Liverpool, London and Globe Insurance Companies in Missouri, Iowa, Kansas, Nebraska and Illinois.

During the period of the Civil War Mr. Fulton was a member of the City Rifles, which was afterward merged into the state militia. It was an organization preparing men for active service and seventy-two men were enlisted from the City Rifles. Its purpose was for local defense and for the protection of ammunition and supplies stored here. Mr. Fulton was in the battle of Athens, was promoted to the rank of sergeant and served as secretary of his company.

He served as alderman from the fourth ward for two years and was school director of Keokuk for four years. His interest in community affairs is deep and sincere and has been manifested in active co-operation in many measures for the general good. He was secretary of the public library for eight or ten years, and has been co-operant factor in the promotion of religious interests in his city. He has twice been sent as a delegate to the general assembly of the Presbyterian church, attending its conventions in Washington and Cincinnati, and has served as deacon and elder in his church continuously from the time that he was admitted as a member in 1866. He was largely instrumental in securing the erection of the Presbyterian house of worship in 1872, acting as secretary of the building committee. Fraternally he is connected with the Independent Order of Odd Fellows. His influence can always be counted upon in behalf of right, progress, reform and improvement and in good citizenship his strong qualities are such as commend him to the good will and confidence of all.

On the 22d of June, 1865, Mr. Fulton was married at Keokuk to Miss Elizabeth Dalzell, who was born in Pittsburg, Pennsylvania, in 1832. They have four children: Nannie Peairs, who is librarian in the public library; Robert Dalzell, who is with the Northwestern Paint Company, of Portland, Oregon; James McQueen, now employed in the freight department of the Wabash Railroad at Keokuk, and Mary Elizabeth, an employe of the Iowa State Insurance Company, living at home.

NELSON COMMINS ROBERTS.

The modern newspaper, wherever it aspires to be anything more than a village newsletter, demands both business skill and intellectual ability in its management. Especially is this true of those publications that are somewhat metropolitan in their character, and undertake to enforce ideas and advance policies as well as to disseminate the news. The editorial profession is a field where character, ability and integrity are factors of success in no small degree; and he who occupies the editorial chair largely sways the destiny of the country. And while it is true he may not far outrun public opinion, still he leads. Day after day, and week after week, he leads, exhorts and entreats, and gradually the people follow him. They respect his moral character, yield to his fervid appeals, and adopted his opinions as their own.

A striking illustration of the editor at his best estate is presented in the life history and personal character of the gentleman whose name introduces this article. Mr. Roberts, the editor of the Fort Madison Daily Democrat and Fort Madison Weekly

Democrat, enjoys more than a local reputation as a master of the editorial art. His thought is clear and deep, his style modeled upon the masters, and admirably calculated to impress his readers, while his English is pure and simple. He has taken a very high rank in his chosen profession and is very popular in the community where his work is done.

Nelson Commins Roberts was born in Otsego, Michigan, October 11, 1856, and is the second son of Dr. Abel C. and Emily A. (Cole) Roberts. His parents removed to Fort Madison in 1859, and here he was given such liberal educational advantages as the times afforded and the finances of his parents permitted. He graduated from the Fort Madison Academy in 1872, and for a time was a student in the high school (the preparatory school of the University of Michigan) at Ann Arbor. In 1874 he became connected with the Fort Madison Democrat, where he mastered the printer's trade in all its details. Later on he was an assistant in the business end of the administration of the paper. Here he also did editorial work until his appointment as postmaster of Fort Madison by President Cleveland in 1893, took him out of the sphere of active newspaper work. He entered upon his official duties June 1, 1893, and continued to discharge the functions of that position until September 7, 1897, to the very great satisfaction of the Fort Madison public. At that time he gave way to a Republican successor.

Mr. Roberts removed in November, 1897, to Keokuk, where he became business manager of the Constitution-Democrat. In this capacity he remained in Keokuk until December 31, 1898, when he came back to Fort Madison to take charge of the Democrat, which he had acquired by lease from his father, Dr. Roberts. In 1901 he purchased the entire plant, which has greatly expanded under his very capable management into a very extensive business. It is now one of the influential publications of the state, and its editorials are freely quoted on all matters of general interest.

Mr. Roberts is a prominent member of the Masonic fraternity, and is well versed in its mystic lore. He is a member of Claypoole Lodge, No. 13, Free and Accepted Masons, Potowonok Chapter No. 28, Royal Arch Masons, and Delta Commandery No. 51, Knights Templar, all well-known Fort Madison fraternities. He is also connected with Zeraphath Consistory (thirty-second degree), Valley, of Davenport, Iowa, Kaaba Temple, Ancient Arabic Order Nobles Mystic Shrine, also of Davenport, and Fort Madison Lodge, No. 374, Benevolent and Protective Order of Elks. At one time he held membership in Gem City Lodge, No. 21, Knights of Pythias, and Fort Madison Lodge, No. 157, Independent Order of Odd Fellows, and is a non-resident member of the Chicago Press Club. For three years he was a member of the school board, and is now on the board of directors of the Cattermole Memorial Library.

Mr. Roberts's zeal and his ability as a political leader were early recognized by his party and he was soon called to the front. For some years he served on the Democratic county central committee, of which he was chairman two terms. From 1900 to 1904, he was on the Democratic State Central

Committee, of which body he was secretary the last two years. In this connection his services have been very valuable throughout the state, and the loyal workers of the party have everywhere been glad to meet and know this capable exponent of Jeffersonian Democracy.

The wedding ceremonies of Mr. Roberts and Miss James Preston were celebrated September 23, 1880. To this very happy union have come three children: Preston E., Ruth E., and Dorothy V. Mrs. Roberts is an accomplished lady and is a worthy associate of her gifted husband. They have many friends wherever they are known, and are esteemed and beloved alike for their strength of character, general intelligence and social spirit.

EDWARD M. BUCK, M. D.

That success is the result of individual merit is true of the learned professions to an extent that does not obtain in any other field of human effort, and the prominence which Dr. E. M. Buck is achieving as a practicing physician at Montrose, Iowa, is especially creditable to him because he owes his present position to his own energy, determination and desire to accomplish a useful work in the world, and has pursued this laudable object in spite of many obstacles that would have meant defeat had he been possessed of a less forceful character. Dr. Buck was born September 5, 1865, near Kahoka, Missouri, the son of A. Y. and Mary (Helmick) Buck and the third of a family of six brothers and sisters, the others being as follows: Mrs. Eleanor Brenn, of Fort Madison; Mrs. Clara Fleming, of Wayland, Missouri; Ella F., deceased; Effie, wife of William Buckley, of New Winchester, Missouri; John W. and Orvey C. A. Y. Buck, who is a native of Indiana and by occupation a farmer, came to Lee county with his father in 1858, and the family was living in Montrose township when the disturbances which drove the church of the Latter Day Saints from the Mississippi valley culminated in the burning of the Mormon temple just across the river in Nauvoo, Illinois. Thence he removed to Green Bay township, and in 1861 to Clark county, Missouri, where the doctrine of secession was then very popular and the situation was one full of danger for supporters of the Union cause, and there he still continues to reside on a farm of 160 acres. During the closing year of the Civil War he was in active military service for a time, being a member of the militia.

Our subject grew to years of maturity in the work of his father's farm, and in 1890 he heeded the call of ambition and returned to Lee county to take employment in Huiskamp Brothers' shoe factory at Keokuk, and at the same time to enter his name as a student in Keokuk Medical College. For six years he was engaged in the work of the factory and in the pursuit of his medical studies, and on March 3, 1896, he was graduated from Keokuk Medical College. While at Keokuk he wedded Miss Virginia Spicer in 1892, and she died November 13, 1895, survived by one child, Earl. On May

20, 1897, he was united in marriage to Miss Pauline Strong, a native of Keokuk, and to them have been born four children, as follows: Morris, who died at the age of two years; Theodore, born December 14, 1900; Carroll, born October 7, 1902; and Eulalia, born September 9, 1904. Immediately upon his graduation Dr. Buck removed to Montrose, March 5, 1896, and here established himself in the general practice of medicine and surgery. In his work here the perfection of his scientific preparation, the high qualities of his mind and heart—his sound, practical judgment and genial disposition—have endeared him to the people and won for him an enviable place in the affairs of the community in which his useful career is being passed. Among the members of his profession he is widely known, and is a member of the Lee County Medical Society and of the Iowa State Medical Society, while in fraternal circles he holds membership in the local lodge of the Independent Order of Odd Fellows and in Camp No. 853 of the Modern Woodmen of America and is examining physician for the Mutual Protective League and for the Bankers' Life Association of Des Moines. In his political faith he is a believer in the doctrines of the Republican party, and while he does not aspire to the honor of public office, he acts as official physician to the municipal board of health. His own interests are closely allied with those of the community, as he considers this his permanent home, having erected a substantial dwelling here in 1900, and is a stockholder in the Montrose Savings Bank, of which he was one of the incorporators.

ASA TURNER HOUSTON.

As a worthy representative of one of Lee county's sturdy and capable pioneer families the name of Asa Turner Houston may well be chosen, for it stands high upon the list of younger farmers who have made themselves felt in the affairs of the community. Mr. Houston was born on the farm on which he now resides, located on section 34, Denmark township, Lee county, Iowa, on August 18, 1868, and is the son of John, Jr., and Maria (Sturges) Houston, his father being a native of Lyndeboro, New Hampshire, where he was born December 15, 1823; and John Houston, Jr., was the son of John, Sr., and Zerviah (Fields) Houston. John Houston, Sr., was born June 5, 1787, and on March 21, 1811, married Miss Fields who was born November 1, 1784, and to them were born the following sons and daughters: Albert F., born January 15, 1812; Laura, who married William Davis, was born August 13, 1813. Abigail, born April 2, 1812, became the wife of Dr. George Shedd, a pioneer physician of the village of Denmark; Sarah, born October 7, 1816, married Warren Henderson; Zerviah, who became the wife of Mr. Bell, was born July 13, 1821; John, father of our subject, born December 15, 1823; Joseph, born September 13, 1826, now resides in Burlington, Iowa, and is the only survivor of his father's family; and Mary Jane, born May 28, 1820, married Joseph Ingalls. When ten years of age John Houston, Jr., removed with his parents to Lowell, Massachusetts, where his father was a mechanic in a woolen factory, and there he pursued his education in the city schools preparatory to entering college, but before the time for his graduation the family again removed, having resolved to locate in the West, and traveling by rail to Albany, New York, where they took the Erie canal to Buffalo, thence by the lakes to Chicago, and from Chicago westward by wagon, they arrived in Lee county after a long and trying journey. Upon their arrival here they took up their residence with Ira Houston, brother of John Houston, Sr., with whom they continued to reside until a dwelling could be erected upon the farm which they had purchased, they having bought eighty acres of land at $1.25 an acre with money earned by the daughter Laura as a school teacher before leaving the East. Upon this farm the father and mother of the family passed the remainder of their lives in the pursuit of their vocation and in devotion to the higher needs of the community, they being faithful workers in the Congregational church. Both were buried in the Denmark cemetery.

After coming to Iowa John Houston, Jr., taught school for a number of years, and in 1849 he was united in marriage to Miss Maria Sturges, daughter of Isaac and Sarah Sturges, both natives of Connecticut who joined the colony from that state at Granville, Ohio, where their daughter was born April 20, 1827, and came to Lee county with her brother, Albert A., who was the first teacher in the Denmark Academy and one of the three who established the mission at the Island of Micronesia. Soon after their marriage Mr. and Mrs. Houston took up their residence on the old Houston homestead, to which Mr. Houston eventually added another eighty acres, and here he gave his attention to farming and cheesemaking, always maintaing a large dairy, which was the source of considerable profit. He was very successful in his business, and attained to much prominence in public affairs as a loyal supporter of the Republican party and its doctrines, being elected to the office of assessor and to a number of minor official positions, in which his faithfulness to the interests of others was always conspicuous and was the determining factor in all his public acts. He was also an active worker in the Congregational church of Denmark, in which he was a deacon, continuing this connection until his death, which occurred on December 23, 1898. He is buried at Denmark, survived by his widow, who now resides in the village of Denmark, and by a numerous family. To them were born the following children: Albert S., born July 6, 1851, who was graduated from Denmark Academy, from Grinnell College and from the Theological School of Chicago, and for a number of years acted as a missionary at the Island of Micronesia, but is now deceased; Servia J., born September 8, 1853, who is the wife of Charles A. Swift and is a resident of Oregon; Warren H., born November 23, 1854, who was educated at Oberlin College and is now a Congregational minister in Kansas; Laura M., born November 27, 1856, who was a successful teacher prior to her marriage, is the wife of Fred Bement, of Sioux Falls, South Dakota; Mary E., born January 25, 1859, who is a teacher and resides in Denmark; Hattie A., born August 7, 1862, wife of William Hitchcock, professor in Jaffna College, Ceylon, India; John J., born May 23, 1865, who died at the age of four years; and Asa Turner, the subject of this review.

Mr. Houston received his formal schooling in Denmark Academy, a training which he has since supplemented by extensive reading and observation, and has always resided on the home farm, which is known as the Fairview farm and which he purchased after his father's death. In 1899 he wedded Miss Mary Leverett, of Denmark, and one son, Clyde Leverett, and one daughter, Florence Sturges, grace their union. Mr. Houston is engaged in stockraising and in general farming, in both of which he has gratifying success, having been trained to work since his early years and having made a study of the problems involved under the direction of his father and later independently, keeping abreast of modern progress by reading along the line of scientific investigation which has a bearing upon his occupations as a farmer and stockraiser. He gives his support consistently to the Republican party, as embodying in its principles the fundamentals of political science as necessarily applied to American conditions, and is widely known in this portion of the county as a representative of agricultural interests. He is at the present time one of the trustees of Denmark Academy, a position for which he is eminently fitted by business ability and by his training and well-known devotion to the cause of education, while the connection is of benefit to the institution by reason of his prominent standing in the community. Mr. and Mrs. Houston are members of the Congregational church, being active and helpful in its various departments of endeavor, and their beautiful home is a prominent center of social life on a high plane, for they have many friends who yield them respect and esteem.

HUGH H. CRAIG.

Although a young man and a comparatively recent addition to the legal fraternity in Keokuk, Hugh H. Craig in the short space of three and a half years has demonstrated himself to be the possessor of unusual aptitude and enthusiasm for his chosen profession, in which he has already achieved a gratifying degree of success and if past attainment be a criterion for prophecy is destined to genuine distinction and a high plane of usefulness. A native of Keokuk, he was born October 1, 1874, the son of John H. Craig, now deceased, a sketch of whose career and lineage appears elsewhere in these pages. His preliminary education was obtained in the public schools of this city, and he is a graduate of Keokuk high school, class of 1892, but being ambitious for further training, he entered Parsons College, at Fairfield, Iowa, in which institution he pursued a thorough course of classical study and was graduated in 1896 with the degree of Bachelor of Arts.

Mr. Craig early determined in favor of the law as a lifelong vocation, and on his graduation entered the law offices of John E. Craig in this city, where he studied for several months, but with a view to obtaining a variety of experience he then accepted a position as city editor of the Gate City, a leading daily newspaper of Keokuk, continuing in that line of work with marked success for three years, at the expiration of which period he resigned and resumed the study of law. Shortly afterward, in September, 1899, he was appointed by the county board of supervisors a justice of the peace, and after serving in that capacity until the following November was elected to fill the unexpired term for which he was originally appointed, and discharged the duties of the office in an acceptable manner until January 1, 1901. Meantime he had continued his legal studies, and in May, 1901, he was admitted to the bar, since which time he has devoted his attention to general practice.

Mr. Craig has shown himself to be a young man loyally devoted to the general welfare, and has assumed a prominent part in local politics as a member of the Democracy, having served his party for four years as secretary of the county central committee and for two years as secretary of the Keokuk committee, while he is also an active member of the board of directors of the Associated Charities of Keokuk, and since March of the past year has served the public as a member of the municipal board of education. He maintains substantial relations with industrial interests in Keokuk, being secretary of the Keokuk Improvement Company, and in the fraternal world of this city and of Iowa he is conceded a leading position, being Past Exalted Ruler of Keokuk Lodge, No. 106, Benevolent and Protective Order of Elks, an office to which he was elected after a membership of only ten months in the order, at present trustee of the Keokuk Lodge and member of the Grand Lodge, to which he has been twice elected representative, and having attended the session of the Grand Lodge at Baltimore in 1903; while he sustains membership relations with the National Union and with Morning Star Lodge, No. 5, of Keokuk, Knights of Pythias. Connected thus at many important points of contact with the varied interests of his native city, his rapid advancement is viewed with pleasure by many an experienced leader who, having played a worthy role in the upbuilding of the community, now looks about him to discover younger and stalwart shoulders upon which to cast his honored mantle.

GEORGE B. SMYTH.

The life record of George B. Smyth has been an important factor in shaping the policy, promoting the upbuilding and advancing the permanent development of Keokuk. He has by his far-sightedness and business sagacity upheld the city integrity and his efforts have also extended to measures of moment to state and nation. He has left the impress of his individuality upon Keokuk's annals and is today one of her venerable citizens, respected and honored for what he has accomplished and for the straightforward methods he has ever pursued in both business and public life. His father, George B. Smyth, Sr., was a native of Roscommon county, Ireland, and married Annabel I. McDonough, who was born in New York. Her father, Francis McDonough, was a native of Galway county, Ireland, while his wife was born in England.

George B. Smyth was born in Rising Sun, Ohio county, Indiana, October 14, 1828, and his early education was supplemented by study in the seminary of that place, his tutors being Professor McGuffey, the compiler of the McGuffey text-books and Professor Barwick. The former was a one-legged man, with whom Mr. Smyth had some schoolroom difficulty. Becoming incensed at the course taken by the professor he threw an ink bottle at him, which struck his leg and went through a knothole in the floor, while the professor fell over on the floor. Mr. Smyth then made his escape but afterward returned to the institution. In his early life his parents removed to Bayou Sara, West Feliciana Parish, Louisiana, where he continued his education, remaining there until the death of his parents, one passing away in August, 1840, and the other in December of the same year. Upon the death of his mother, his uncle, Lawrence McDonough, was appointed his guardian by the State of Louisiana and being then tired of school life Mr. Smyth entered the employ of John C. Morris, who was an intimate friend of his parents and who was conducting a large general store and two plantations in Louisiana. He was a man of considerable wealth and Mr. Smyth remained with him in the store for about two years, after which he returned to Rising Sun, Indiana, in 1843, and completed his education at the seminary. He there pursued higher branches of study and during the last year of his own course he also taught nine classes in the seminary. When his education was completed he accepted a position in the extensive dry goods establishment of Zeillar Brothers, and was afterward for two years with the firm of C. Garber & Company. He then became purchaser for their clothing department and acted in that capacity until April, 1849, when he came to Keokuk, Iowa, continuing in a clerical position with the firm at this place. He afterward formed a partnership with A. L. Connable in 1852 and went into the wholesale grocery business and continued with that establishment for twenty years, when the firm purchased five acres of ground in West Keokuk and erected a large stone packing house, costing with its equipment $125,000. In one year after the cold storage plant had been installed, 100,000 head of hogs and 2,500 head of cattle were killed and stored therein. In 1880 A. L. Connable retired from active business and Mr. Smyth purchased his interest in the packing house, which was then conducted under the firm name of George B. Smyth & Company, and for some time an extensive and profitable business was carried on.

It was during this time that the city of Keokuk, having endorsed largely the bonds of the Keokuk, Fort Des Moines, Minnesota Railway, afterward the Des Moines Valley Railroad, as well as the bonds of the Keokuk, Muscatine & Minnesota Railroad and the Mississippi & Wabash Valley Railroad, found itself facing a difficult financial problem. The interest upon the bonds had been due for many years and the question was decided in the supreme court of Iowa that the city was not responsible for the bonds not having received proper consideration for same. The supreme court of the United States, however, ruled that the holders of said bonds were innocent purchasers thereof and that the city of Keokuk was responsible to them for the bonds. During this litigation the interest on the bonds accrued until with the principal there was an indebtedness against the city of $3,000,000, a part of which was in judgment, the city being totally unable to pay the amount. At this juncture in 1869 Mayor A. J. Wilkinson called a meeting of about forty prominent men for the purpose of considering and debating a form of settlement through compromise of the large city debt. After full consideration of the question by the assembled citizens George B. Smyth was recommended for appointment as commissioner to the the city council and was appointed as acting commissioner for Keokuk for the settlement of the debt through compromise. The other commissioners were Samuel F. Miller, associate justice of the United States supreme court; George W. McCrary, congressman, secretary of war under President Hayes, United States district judge and solicitor of the Santa Fe Rairoad; and William Timberman.

Mr. Smyth had plenary authority to settle the debt as if it was a private business interest, the compromise to be by contract with the city, three per cent. on the first $200,000, four per cent. on the next $200,000 and five per cent. on the third $200,000 and all necessary expenses to be paid by the city. As it would be difficult to keep such matters out of politics Mr. Smyth adopted the following manner of settlement. In each settlement made with a holder of a city bond a descriptive receipt of such settlement was written by Mr. Smyth in a bound receipt book, showing the terms and conditions of the settlement and upon the payment of the conditions the holder of the bond signed that receipt, under which there could be no collusion of interest. Mr. Smyth represented the interests of the city of Keokuk and succeeded to a large extent in making settlements. Referring to his report as fiscal agent made to the mayor and council of Keokuk April 1, 1877, it is seen that there was a settlement of bonds to the value of $405,341.18 and $394,240.43 in judgments. Many settlements were made thereafter and Mr. Smyth deserves the greatest credit for what he accomplished for the city in this direction.

Mr. Smyth was appointed receiver of the Des Moines Valley Railroad Company by Judge John Mitchell, of Polk county, in 1876, and was discharged on the 19th of September, of that year. He was appointed receiver for Ayer & Sellew, hardware dealers, by Judge W. J. Jeffries, of the circuit court of Lee county in 1883 and gave bond for $10,000. When he had fulfilled the duties of the position he was discharged September 5, 1883. He received appointment from Judge George W. McCrary, of the United States circuit court, as receiver of the St. Joe & Western Railroad, a line of 252 miles and in its receivership he gave bond for $100,000. He had complete control of the road until relieved January 16, 1884. He was president of the Des Moines Valley Railroad Company, a member of its board of directors, one of its stockholders and one of the official executives of the road for many years.

In public affairs Mr. Smyth has been prominent and influential. He was president of the Keokuk Library Association for three years and then refused positively to serve longer. He was mayor of Keokuk in 1863 during the exciting period of the War of the Rebellion and municipal interests have claimed his attention and received his active co-operation when he believed that his endorsement of any measure would contribute to the general good. He was made chairman of a committee appointed by the Mississippi river convention held in Keokuk and was instructed by the convention to visit St. Louis and co-operate with the appointee of the Merchants' Exchange, which appointed D. A. January, president of the St. Louis Chamber of Commerce as its representative to prepare a memorial in connection with Mr. Smyth to be presented to both branches of congress and secured maps of the river at the Des Moines Rapids that an appropriation might be made for the building of a canal commencing at Keokuk and extending northward for eight miles at an expense of $4,000,000. All this was done and the subject presented so clearly and convincingly to congress that an appropriation of upwards of $4,000,000 was made for the building and equipment of the canal and lock system now used for the passage of river steamers. Mr. Smyth was appointed by Rutherford B. Hayes as government director of the Union Pacific Railway on the 2d of March, 1878. For two years he was a member of its finance committee in connection with Russell Sage and for one year was on the executive committee with J. Gould. There were four regular meetings held in New York or Boston each year and occasionally a called meeting and these Mr. Smyth attended. The duties of the committee were to examine into the physical condition of property and make reports to the Secretary of the Interior and the entire report for the year 1880 was made by Mr. Smyth. After the sale of the Des Moines Valley Railroad it was necessary for the land grant bondholders to take lands in northwestern Iowa, the land grant covering more than 700,000 acres. It was arranged that a portion of the land grant bondholders were to fund their bonds into land in northwestern Iowa at a valuation placed upon the land by the land commission of the road and the balance of the land grant bondholders were to take the railroad which they did, reorganizing it as the Des Moines & Fort Dodge Railway Company. As the vice-president of the road Mr. Smyth signed deeds for nearly the entire 700,000 acres of land and his work in this connection covered several years' time. On one occasion Mr. Smyth was a trustee and a member of the commission for the location of Parsons College at Fairfield, Iowa. Although closely associated with the railroad negotiations and municipal affairs he at the same time carried on his private business interests and in 1877-8 was president of the Pork Packers' Convention of the United States, which in that year convened in Keokuk.

Mr. Smyth had a personal acquaintance with Samuel S. Clemens, "Mark Twain," when he was devil in a printing establishment and afterward when he was pilot on the river steamers. He sold over 500 copies of Twain's book "Following the Equator, a Journey Around the World." He was also a personal acquaintance of Henry Clay Dean, the eloquent lawyer of "Rebel's Cave."

Mr. Smyth was married in Fort Madison, Iowa, October 1, 1850, to Miss Martha M. Chambers, who was born October 23, 1829, and died April 21, 1903. The following tribute was paid her by the officers of the Presbyterian church "A Mary in the house of God, a Martha in her own." They were the parents of five daughters and one son: Belle, now deceased; Sallie C.; Mrs. D. A. Collier, whose husband is with the Blom-Collier Company, of Keokuk; Mrs. John D. Rubidge, of Keokuk; Mrs. Samuel Edwards, of Rock Island, whose husband is a civil and hydraulic engineer with offices at Rock Island, having been in the government employ for many years and now acting as assistant superintendent of the river between Rock Island and Dubuque; and George B., Jr., who is living in Ogden, Utah. Since 1858 Mr. Smyth has been a leading member of the First Westminister Presbyterian church and for a number of years served as one of its elders, but afterward resigned. He has been a frequent contributor to newspapers, being asked to write upon various subjects. His political allegiance was given to the Democracy until the outbreak of the Civil War, when he became a stanch Republican. For thirty-one years the family home has been at the corner of First and Concerts streets in Keokuk. In the course of an active career Mr. Smyth accumulated a handsome competency, but unfortunate investment and decline in the price of land grant bonds lost him over $150,000, these financial reverses coming to him in 1876. He afterward engaged in the real estate and insurance business which he still continues. His has been, however, a very active and useful career, his labors proving of benefit to his city and state in large measure so that his name should be engraven deeply upon its history.

ARTHUR CHARLES CATTERMOLE.

Arthur Charles Cattermole, now deceased, was in his active life one of the prominent citizens of Fort Madison, taking such a part in the various affairs of that city as his high character, striking business ability and large mental endowments would demand and justify. From a very early day he was associated with important commercial and business enterprises of the city, and on all occasions proved himself a reliable and trustworthy gentleman. Beginning in a modest way, he rose to a commanding position in the city of his adoption, and became popular with a wide circle of friends and acquaintance, who learned to appreciate his many excellent qualities, and to prize him for his real worth.

Mr. Cattermole was a native of London, England, where he first inhaled the vital air July 29, 1829, a son of James C. Cattermole, a native of Suffolk, England, whose father was a farmer the most of his life.

James C. Cattermole came to the United States in the spring of 1832, and made his home in Cincinnati, Ohio, then a lively frontier city, where he remained four years, taking an active part in its busy life. From Cincinnati he removed to a farm in Hancock county, Illinois, where he was engaged in the cultivation of the soil until 1851. That year he settled in Fort Madison, Iowa, which continued to be his home until his death in 1862, at the advanced age of eighty-one years. When a young man he was married to Miss Naomi Tillett, a native of the English county in which his birth occurred. She died in Fort Madison when seventy-five years old, leaving tender memories of a wife, mother and friend, and was known in the community as a worthy Christian woman. She was the mother of nine children, of whom the subject of this sketch was the youngest child. Elizabeth, a daughter, married Henry Cattermole, whose sketch may be found on another page of this volume.

Arthur Charles Cattermole came with his parents to this country when he was only three years old, and continued with them, devoting himself to their welfare, until their settlement in Fort Madison, when he became a clerk in the store of Peter Miller, then a noted establishment in that city. In 1852 he retired from Mr. Miller's employ, and going to Alexander, Missouri, took entire charge of the wholesale and retail dry goods and grocery business of Thomas Fitzgerald, a position which he held until 1859, in which he not only demonstrated large ability for commercial lines but also integrity and honesty in a degree not often encountered.

In 1859 Mr. Cattermole returned to Fort Madison and formed a partnership with his cousin and brother-in-law, Henry Cattermole, who had married his sister Elizabeth, as noted above. They engaged in a pork-packing and grocery business under the firm name of H. & A. C. Cattermole, a business that long continued and became very prosperous. In 1871 Henry Cattermole retired in favor of his partner, who carried on the entire enterprise until 1882, when he retired from active life. After becoming sole owner of the business Mr. Cattermole disposed of the grocery trade, and devoted himself entirely to the packing interest, in which he was very successful, and became quite wealthy.

Upon the organization of the German American Bank of Fort Madison, Arthur C. Cattermole became one of its stockholders and was chosen vice-president. Here his conceded business abilities had full play, and to him this bank, now one of the solid financial institutions of the city, is very largely indebted for its splendid organization and building. Its management has been careful and conservative, but at the same time always ready to help the city and aid every laudable enterprise. Mr. Cattermole was an official of the bank until the day of his death. Arthur C. Cattermole was married November 11, 1869, to Miss Caroline Wilson, a native of Cincinnati, Ohio, and a daughter of Robert and Mary Wilson, of Scottish nativity, and the parents of a family of twelve children, of whom Mrs. Cattermole is the only one now living. The marriage of Mr. Cattermole and Miss Wilson was celebrated in St. Louis, Missouri, and to it have come two children: Robert W., who received a high-school education in Fort Madison, Iowa, having graduated with high honors from the local school, and also having been a student at two commercial schools, is a young man who displays the sterling worth and business ability that were so prominently indicated in the father's career. He is now with the Wisconsin Central Railroad, as division engineer, with headquarters at Abbotsford, Wisconsin. The position he holds is a responsible one, but he is proving himself more than equal to its varied demands. He was married in Fort Madison to Miss Nettie Atlee, a native of Memphis, Tennessee. Their only child, Charles A., died at the untimely age of two years.

In politics Mr. Cattermole was a Democrat, but he never suffered a narrow and partisan view of the situation to guide his action at the polls. He sought for the best men and the wisest measures asking for the largest good to all the people, and not simply partisan schemes and political advantages. In religion he was a believer in the Lord, Jesus Christ, and though not a member of any church was a devoted attendant and liberal supporter of the Episcopal church. In whatever looked to the uplifting and improvement of the community he was deeply interested, and to such measures always ready to lend a helping hand.

Mr. Cattermole died at Arrow Head Spring, California, July 31, 1888, whither he had gone on account of his health, having recently been ill with typhoid fever, from the effects of which he had not entirely recovered. His remains rest in the old city cemetery at Fort Madison. The funeral services were held from the Episcopal church, and were very largely attended by those who knew and honored him alike for his high character, business ability and sterling manhood. It was the general expression that in his death the city of Fort Madison had lost one of its very best friends; and that take him all in all, it would be difficult to find his like again.

Mrs. Cattermole, his widow, is a most charming woman, of pronounced Christian character, and of deep interest in all the moral and religious organizations of the city. After the death of her husband she built a lovely home at the corner of Fourth and Chestnut streets, in which she was but carrying out his plans, as he had desired to build there on his return from California.

OLIVER D. WALKER, M. D.

Prof. Oliver D. Walker, engaged in the practice of medicine and surgery at Keokuk, has attained high standing as a representative of the profession because of his excellent qualifications and his devotion to the duties which devolve upon him in this connection. He was born in Emporia, Kansas, December 3, 1860, the son of George Morton and Zipporah (Maxwell) Walker. His father, who was by profession a civil engineer, was born in Western Pennsylvania, and in early life removed to Washington, Iowa. Later he located at the present site of Emporia, Kansas, which city he himself platted and surveyed. His eldest son, John M., was the first white child born in the city. George Morton Walker became an extensive property holder, and remained at Emporia until the beginning of the Civil War, when he sent his family back to Iowa, and volunteered for the service of his country. He went to the front as a lieutenant in the Eleventh Kansas Cavalry, with which he served for more than four years. Some time after the close of the war he removed to Lawrence, Kansas, and there he gave increased attention to civil engineering, he having located and surveyed the entire route of the Missouri, Kansas & Texas Railway, from Junction City to Dennison, Texas. Since then he has given his time exclusively to locating and building railroads, and at present he is an engineer for the Kansas City Belt Railway, with his home at Kansas City, Missouri. The mother of our subject is a sister of Dr. Thomas Maxwell, of Keokuk, and an account of her genealogy will be found in the review of his life which appears elsewhere in this volume.

Dr. Walker made it his first care in life to secure a thorough schooling and education, and with that object in view entered the University of Kansas at Lawrence. He was graduated from that institution with the class of '83, earning the degree of Bachelor of Science, and having determined to devote himself to the practice of medicine, began reading soon after in the office of Dr. T. J. Maxwell. In 1884 he matriculated in the College of Physicians and Surgeons at Keokuk, and was graduated in 1886. On his graduation he began the practice of his profession in Lawrence, Kansas, remaining there for a year and a half, then locating at Keokuk, where for two years he was associated in practice with Dr. Maxwell. During this period he also acted as demonstrator of anatomy in the College of Physicians and Surgeons, for the purpose of perfecting his own knowledge of anatomy. In 1889 he was elected to the chair of chemistry in the College of Physicians and Surgeons, but before the beginning of that year's session received a government appointment in connection with the Indian service as physician in charge at Haskell Institute near Lawrence, Kansas, and occupied that post four years. In 1893 he resigned in order to associate himself with Dr. Maxwell under the firm style of Maxwell & Walker, this partnership continuing for four years. During that time he was engaged in general practice and the practice of surgery, and also had charge of the surgical clinic at St. Joseph's Hospital at Keokuk. He took a post-graduate course in 1894 at New York Polyclinic Institute. Since 1897 he has been engaged in general practice in Keokuk, and gives special attention to nervous diseases.

In 1894 Dr. Walker was elected to the chair of physiology and nervous diseases in Keokuk Medical College, which he held until the consolidation of the two medical schools of Keokuk, and also later in the consolidated school. He was secretary of Keokuk Medical College and the College of Physicians and Surgeons from 1897 till 1903, when he resigned on finding that there was danger of his official duties interfering with his private practice. At the present time he has charge of the neurological clinic at St. Joseph's Hospital.

Dr. Walker is in close touch with all progressive tendencies in the work of his profession. He is a member of Keokuk, Lee County, Eastern Iowa, and Iowa State Medical Societies and of the American Medical Association, and is a member and the secretary of the board of pension examiners. He also holds a directorship in the Lee County Building and Loan Association. Religiously he is a member of the Congregational church, and was a director and secretary of the board of directors of the Young Men's Christian Association at the time of the erection of the magnificent building now occupied by that society. In his fraternal affiliations he is a member of the Knights of Pythias and the Greek society of Beta Theta Pi.

Professor Walker was united in marriage to Miss Mary L. Simpson, of Lawrence, Kansas, and they have two daughters, Genevieve and Margaret. The family home is a beautiful residence erected by the Doctor at No. 528 Morgan street. Doctor Walker takes rank as one of the foremost practitioners of Lee county. He has continually broadened his knowledge of reading and original investigation, and few men of his profession in this section have made more thorough preparation for their task. He is well equipped for his work of alleviating human suffering.

WILLIAM H. WYATT.

William H. Wyatt, trustee of Jackson township, Lee county, Iowa, of which he is the oldest resident and settler, and now residing on his farm in section 27, was born April 2, 1843, in Fayette county, Ohio, the son of Zebulon and Elizabeth (Rowe) Wyatt. The family is an old one in America, and is descended from Governor Wyatt, royal governor of Virginia about the beginning of the eighteenth century, while both grandfathers of Mr. Wyatt were soldiers in the Revolutionary War, the father of Zebulon Wyatt fighting on the side of the king and the father of Elizabeth Rowe being in the Continental Army. The first Wyatt that they have any record of was Sir Thomas Wyatt, of England, who was born in 1503. The Rowe family came into direct contact with the Indians in the early days of the frontier settlements, and an uncle of Mr. Wyatt was shot by the savages while at work in a cornfield and his heart impaled upon a fence picket as an act of defiance from his murderers. Zebulon Wyatt was a man of considerable distinction in Ohio, having served as a captain in the Mexican War, and was appointed deputy sheriff and later elected sheriff of Fayette county, although he never held office after coming to Iowa, with the exception of township offices. He was a man of great force of character, and took a lively interest in public affairs, always supporting the Republican party after its formation, until his death, which occurred in 1872. His wife survived him until 1884, when she passed to the world beyond, mourned by all who knew her.

Mr. Wyatt, the subject of this review, accompanied his parents to Iowa in 1840, when only six years of age, crossing the Mississippi river on the ice at Nauvoo, after having been within sight of the great Mormon temple at that place for two days, as they made the journey overland by wagon. The father rented land near Keokuk, which he continued to cultivate during the remainder of his life, and there our subject passed the early days of his boyhood, assisting his father until sixteen years of age, when he left home, and was from that time employed in the neighborhood of Keokuk until 1861, when at the call of duty and patriotism he entered the service of his country, enlisting in Company A, First Iowa Cavalry, Captain Torrence and Colonel Fitz Henry Warren, the regiment forming part of the Ninth Army Corps. As a soldier of the Union Mr. Wyatt saw long and arduous service on Southern fields, as will be shown by the following, which is a partial list of his battles: Booneville, Jefferson City, Blackwater, Silver Creek, Lone Jack and Springfield, Missouri; Prairie Grove, Bentonville, Little Rock, Biameter, Poison Springs and Camden, Arkansas. In addition he served in the states of Florida, Louisiana, Texas, Mississippi, Kentucky and Tennessee, and during the Red River Expedition under Gen. A. F. Steele he was wounded in the right temple by a flying splinter shot from a tree by a cannon ball, being rendered for a long time unconscious by the blow. From the effects of this wound he apparently recovered completely, but a stroke of paralysis by which he was visited in the year 188[illegible] was attributed to the shock which his system received at that time. He was mustered out on March 16, 1866, and as he enlisted on June 13, 1861, he was thus a member of the army during the long period of four years, nine months and three days, during all of which he was actively engaged in the field, for the first year as a corporal and for the latter three and three fourth years as commissary sergeant.

At the close of hostilities Mr. Wyatt returned to farming as an occupation, conducting agricultural operations for the first two years in Clark county, Missouri, after which he removed to his present residence in Lee county, where he has since lived, and here he has been highly successful as a farmer, acquiring by careful management and the exercise of sound, conservative judgment 110 acres of very productive farming lands, of which thirty-five acres, on which stands his residence, is located in section 27, and seventy-five acres on section 32 in the Des Moines river bottoms.

The marriage of Mr. Wyatt took place at Keokuk in 1873, at which time he was united in holy matrimony with Miss Caroline Loomis, a native of Lee county, the date of her birth being April 17, 1849. Mrs.

Wyatt was descended from an old English family which came to America in 1639 and settled in Windsor, Connecticut, and she was a woman in whose character appeared many of the virtues of those early Pilgrims, discharging with ability the duties of her household and being tenderly faithful to all domestic and friendly ties until her death, which occurred on September 16, 1889. To Mr. and Mrs. Wyatt were born two sons and four daughters, as follows: John L., a resident of Keokuk, who married Miss Ida O'Blenness and has one child, Mildred; William H., Jr., residing on a farm in Jackson township, who married Miss Lena Haisch; Carrie L.; Laura Loomis; Alice Rowe, and May Loomis, and all are at home. The members of this family are the only representatives of the name in Lee county, but Mr. Wyatt has one brother, Thomas C., and a sister, Margaret M. Brinkley, who are residents of Winchester, Ohio.

Mr. Wyatt holds membership in Torrence Post, Grand Army of the Republic, Keokuk, and has attended the national encampments of the order at Columbus, Ohio, and St. Louis, Missouri, the state encampments at Des Moines, Dubuque and Davenport, as well as the reunions of his regiment at Cedar Rapids, Dubuque, Davenport, Ottumwa and Keokuk. He has given much attention to advancing the prosperity of the community in which his useful career has been passed, as well as to all matters of public interest, and it was mainly owing to his efforts, in association with Mr. Fred Lindner, which brought about in 1903 the establishment of the rural delivery route No. 1, which now serves the residents of this neighborhood so efficiently. He has been a loyal and zealous supporter of the Republican party ever since casting his first ballot for Abraham Lincoln when a member of the United States Army and stationed at Little Rock, Arkansas, and for eight years he served his party as chairman of its township committee, although he refused for personal reasons to continue in the position beyond that period. For an unbroken term of seventeen years he acted as road supervisor, during which time the highways of the township were maintained in a uniformly excellent state of repair under his direction, and at present he occupies the highest office in the gift of his township, that of trustee, in which his business ability is of conspicuous advantage to his constituents.

AUGUSTUS SCHERFE.

Augustus Scherfe, after a very active business career, crowned by successful accomplishment, is now living retired at his pleasant home in Fort Madison. He was born in Hartzfeld, Germany, on the 14th of December, 1843, and when about a year old was brought to the United States by his parents, Augustus and Wilhelmina (Luer) Scherfe. They came at once to Iowa, locating at Fort Madison, where Mr. Scherfe followed the occupation of butchering, continuing in that business for a number of years, after which he engaged in weaving, having learned the trade prior to his emigration to the new world. Thus his time was occupied until his death, which occurred at Fort Madison, when he was fifty-two years of age. He died in 1856 and his remains were interred in the Fort Madison cemetery. He was a member of the German Lutheran church, as was his wife, who survived him until 1882, passing away at the advanced age of eighty-four years, her remains being then buried by her husband's side. They were the parents of two children: Minnie became the wife of Nicholas DeKlotz, and after her husband's death she died at Portland, Oregon, at the age of sixty-one years, leaving a family of four daughters and one son.

Augustus Scherfe acquired his early education in the German Lutheran schools of Fort Madison, and as soon as old enough, after the death of his father, he assisted upon the home place and engaged in gardening. In 1861, when he was seventeen years of age, he enlisted in Company F, Fifth Iowa Cavalry and served during the war. He took part in some of the principal battles of Tennessee, Alabama and Georgia, and was honorably discharged at Clinton, Iowa, in 1865. He was corporal of his company and was always found at his post, displaying much valor in times of danger. Since the war he has maintained pleasant relations with his old army comrades through his membership in James B. Sample Post, No. 170, Grand Army of the Republic, of Fort Madison, of which he has twice been commander while for a number of years he has occupied the position of adjutant.

After receiving his discharge from the army Mr. Scherfe returned to his home at Fort Madison and was appointed a guard at the Iowa penitentiary, serving in that capacity for two years when his health failed and he gave up the position. He then removed to Burlington, Iowa, where he lived for nine years, acting as shipping clerk in a grocery house. He next removed to Lincoln, Nebraska, where he spent two years and then returned to Fort Madison, where he again became guard in the penitentiary, thus serving for thirteen years. On the expiration of that period he was appointed by the government, in 1890, to the position of census enumerator at Fort Madison, and after the completion of this task illness prevented his further work for a period of eight months. He then engaged in the fire insurance business to which he devoted his time and energies until 1899, when he retired from active life on account of ill health and the business established by him is now conducted by his son, William A. Scherfe, who is represented elsewhere in this volume. He has since been leading a quiet life.

Mr. Scherfe is a member of the German Lutheran Evangelical church of Fort Madison and was one of its trustees for a number of years. In politics he is a Republican, and he has always been deeply interested in the welfare of his country and the substantial upbuilding of his city.

On the 28th of April, 1866, Mr. Scherfe was united in marriage to Miss Amelia Sprenger, who was born in Odessa, Russia, and came to this country when five years of age with her parents, who located at Burlington, Iowa, where they lived and died.

Her father, George W. Sprenger, was a painter by trade and followed carriage painting and trimming. He died at the age of seventy-four years, while his wife, who bore the maiden name of Magdalene D. Faul died in Burlington, Iowa, May 8, 1895, at the age of seventy-nine years. Unto Mr. and Mrs. Scherfe have been born three children, and the family circle yet remains unbroken by the hand of death. The eldest, William A., is mentioned elsewhere in this volume. Amelia A. is the wife of Fred A. H. Soechtig, a retail grocer of Fort Madison. Matilda is the widow of Victor R. Egermayer, late of Tacoma, Washington, and she now makes her home in Fort Madison with her parents. The family home is at No. 214 Third street and its hospitality is enjoyed by their many friends.

ALVIN C. MORRIS.

Of the more successful and better known farmers of Lee county, a worthy representative is Alvin C. Morris, now residing on his farm of 201 acres in Cedar township. Mr. Morris was born September 28, 1861, in Cedar township, Van Buren county, Iowa, the son of George F. and Matilda (Ebert) Morris. The family is a very old one in Iowa, the father of Mr. Morris having come to Lee county with his parents in 1836 and located at Sugar Creek, where he remained, however, only a short time before removing to Van Buren county, Cedar township, at which latter place he received his education, grew to manhood and passed his life as a farmer. He was quite successful in a pecuniary way, and at his death in 1894 at the age of sixty-two years he owned 160 acres of well-improved farming land. He was a member of the Methodist Episcopal church, was very public-spirited, taking part in political affairs as a worker in the Republican party, and held a number of public offices. He was a native of Kentucky, as was also his father, the grandfather of our subject, who was Henry T. Morris. The latter purchased land in Van Buren county in 1836, and there spent the remainder of his life, his death occurring in his eighty-sixth year. The mother of Alvin C. Morris was born in Pennsylvania, came to Iowa as a small child, and passed practically the whole of her life as a resident of Van Buren county, her demise occurring about six years before that of her husband. She was the mother of ten sons and daughters, all of whom are still living.

Mr. Morris gained his early knowledge of books in the public schools of his native county, receiving a good common-school education, and learned the principles and methods of agriculture in his father's farm, assisting in the work until his marriage November 15, 1888, to Miss Lenora Jordan, a native of Cedar township, Van Buren county, and daughter of Johnson Jordan. Mrs. Morris's father was a pioneer of Van Buren county, but died at the age of only twenty-five years, leaving the care of the family of two girls to his wife, who still resides in Van Buren county. She again married after seven years of widowhood to Mr.

Benjamin Syferd. The other daughter was Eliza Jane, now Mrs. J. W. Shepherd, of Van Buren county, Iowa. To Mr. and Mrs. Morris have been born four sons and one daughter, the birthplace of the eldest being Van Buren county and that of the remaining four Cedar township, Lee county. They are: Rex, Everett, Mary, Leo and Alva.

For two years succeeding his marriage Mr. Morris continued a resident of his father's farm, but at the end of that period he removed to Lee county, purchasing and locating upon the farm he now owns and occupies, which, by the application of energy, perseverance and sound judgment he has greatly improved, introducing scientific methods and apparatus and making it in many respects a model farm, considered either with regard to appearance, convenience or producing power. Here he engages in general farming and stockraising, making a specialty, in the latter branch of the business, of the raising of Durham cattle.

Mr. Morris, as an extensive reader, careful thinker and active business man, has manifested considerable interest in public affairs, and believing in the duty of every citizen to exercise his political privileges according to his best understanding of his own needs and those of the county, state and nation, early united with the Republican party, in which he has ever since been a worker. Although he has not aspired to the holding of public office, he has served his community as director of the public schools for a number of years, and last election he was honored by his fellow citizens who gave him the highest township office within their power—that of township trustee, and, indeed, he has always shown himself ready to accept any duty or to support any movement calculated to advance the general welfare, and this readiness is usually held to indicate the possession of qualities of high civic value. Fraternally he is well known, being a member of both the Masonic order and that of the Modern Woodmen of America. He is a man of unusual force of character, is possessed of much business ability, has been very successful in the conduct of his affairs, and enjoys the universal respect of his friends and acquaintances.

F. W. ANSCHUTZ.

Among the sons of the Fatherland who came to America and won success and prominence in business and at the same time were recognized as valued and worthy citizens of the communities in which they lived was numbered F. W. Anschutz, who was born in Germany, May 28, 1835, and died in Keokuk on the 1st of April, 1889. He possessed great energy, strong determination and laudable ambition and in the years of an active business career he worked his way steadily upward contributing to public progress as well as individual prosperity. His father was in comfortable financial circumstances and provided him good educational privileges. He pursued a commercial course of study in his native land, and afterward was apprenticed to a merchant. Subsequently he entered his father's factory, sawmills and smelters, but not finding these lines of business congenial he was sent to America that he might enjoy the business opportunities of the new world. He came to America in 1847, locating first in Wisconsin and while there he learned the brewing trade. In 1852 he was married in Sauk City, Wisconsin, to Miss Augusta R. Diemar, who was born in Germany on the 19th of September, 1830. Following his marriage he engaged in farming for two years and then removed to Madison, Wisconsin, where he conducted a gun store. In 1858 he removed to Keokuk and established a brewery. He had great faith and energy in the new city and displayed a brave spirit and many of the qualities of a pioneer about entering the first and building a brewery in a new and almost undeveloped district. Everything had to be hauled by team and much work was required in the establishment of the brewery, but in course of time it became a paying investment and he continued to operate it successfully until 1881, when it was destroyed by fire, entailing a loss of $30,000. He never rebuilt the plant. Up to that time he had a large annual output, shipping much of his product. He employed a foreman and five or six other men about the place and developed his business in accordance with modern ideas, making the enterprise an excellent source of income. In 1881 he also suffered loss by fire, the interior of his home being badly damaged in that way. This house was erected by Mr. Anschutz in 1870 at the foot of Anschutz hill and the fire was caused by a spark from the furnace which ignited the roof.

Unto Mr. and Mrs. Anschutz were born five children: Adelaide, the wife of George Hassell, of the Keokuk Medicine Company, of Keokuk, Iowa, by whom she has two children, George and Melvina; Henry; Otto, an engineer at the middle lock, who married Susie Celtner and has two children, Mildred and Felix; Leo, at home; and Herman, a photographer, of Keokuk, who married Grace Smith and has one daughter, Adelaide. In 1858 the family home was established at its present location at the foot of Anschutz hill. It was through the efforts of Mr. Anschutz that the road along the hillside was opened up and it has since been known as Anschutz road. The hillside was covered with timber and it was a great undertaking and in the project Mr. Anschutz met with much opposition, but he persevered and the value of the road to this district of the city has long since been acknowledged. It now affords the main entrance to Keokuk from the north or upriver country. Toward its construction Mr. Anschutz gave $100 and a months' work with his team. He also raised the money for the construction of the road by solicitation of others and though he was strongly opposed he continued in the work and in due course of time his labors were crowned with success. An excellent bust of Mr. Anschutz adorns the family home, it being made by the youngest son, Herman Anschutz, the photographer. In his political views Mr. Anschutz was a Democrat, and he served as clerk on the registration board. He possessed the strong sturdy German spirit, with its admirable national characteristics, was found reliable in business, progressive in his ideas and at all times ready to aid in the promotion of the welfare of the city. His co-operation could always be counted upon in support of any measure for the general good, and his pleasant genial manner made him well liked by all and caused his death to be deeply deplored. His widow still occupies the old home, having lived at this place since 1858, while the home was built in 1870. She takes great interest in church work and is a lady of many excellent traits of character of heart and mind.

ISAAC W. TRAVERSE, M. D.

A prominent and successful representative of the medical profession in Fort Madison is Dr. I. W. Traverse, who was born on a farm near Nauvoo, Illinois, October 22, 1871. He is the son of W. F. and Emily (Wilsey) Traverse. The father died October 4, 1901, and at the close of his career he was possessed of a very considerable estate, comprising over 400 acres of land, as the result of a life which combined energy, carefulness and extraordinary ability. The death of his wife preceded his by a period of several years, having occurred in June, 1878. They were the parents of four children, as follows: John, now deceased; William, who resides at the old home farm; Isaac W., the subject of this sketch; and Jean, wife of Curt Silberschmidt, secretary and treasurer of the tannery and shoe factory at Santa Rosa, California.

The education of I. W. Traverse was begun in the public schools, but the ambition which led to his subsequent rise to a high and useful plane of activity has been a factor in his life since his earliest years; and in 1890 he became a student in Keokuk Medical College, determined to fit himself, by hard study and intense application, for the work of a physician. He was graduated from that institution March 7, 1895, immediately established himself in the practice of medicine in this city, and, with the exception of a temporary location at Wapello during the first year, has since been engaged continuously in the work of his profession in Fort Madison. If success is a criterion of ability, his rapid rise to his present position in the community would seem to indicate talents of a rare order.

Dr. Traverse devotes himself to general practice and to surgery, but makes a specialty of gynecology, and in all his work makes extensive use of the X-Ray apparatus. He acts as examining physician for the Metropolitan Life Insurance Company, of New York, the Union Mutual Life Insurance Company, of Portland, Maine, and for a number of beneficiary orders. In his fraternal connection he is a member of Claypoole Lodge, No. 13, Free and Accepted Masons, and in the same order has taken the degrees of the Royal Arch and Knights Templar, and of Kaaba Temple Mystic Shrine. He is also affiliated with Benevolent and Protective Order of Elks, No. 374, Modern Woodmen of America, No. 641, the Mutual Protective League and the Knights and Ladies of Security. He is a member of Lee County Medical Society, and has held the official position of physician to the Fort Madison Board of Health. In politics he is a believer in the principles advocated by the Democratic party, and consistently supports its nominees.

At Fort Madison December 19, 1891, Dr. I. W. Traverse was united in marriage with Miss Daisy L. Ehart. One child graces this union, a son, John William, born December 29, 1892. Mrs. Traverse is the daughter of Phillip and Sarah (Jarrett) Ehart. Phillip Ehart, who was by trade a wagonmaker, was born in Germany, and his death occurred July 30, 1876, interment being in the Fort Madison city cemetery. Mrs. Ehart, who is a native of North Carolina, makes her home with Dr. and Mrs. Traverse. The grandmother, Mrs. Fanny Jarrett, who is in the ninety-seventh year of her age, is a resident of West Point, Lee county. Mr. and Mrs. Ehart were the parents of three children, the others being John, who is an express agent at Fort Madison, and Maggie, wife of Frank Swanson, foreman in the Santa Fe railroad shops at this place.

Mrs. Traverse is a member of the Presbyterian church and of its missionary society, in which she is an active worker. She was graduated from the Fort Madison high school in the class of 1891, and has been a teacher in the schools of West Point and Fort Madison.

At a cost of $7,000 Dr. Traverse erected in 1901, a commodious and handsome residence at 907 Fifth street, and here he devotes to his home life the time which may be spared from the exacting demands of public and professional duty. He is a man of attractive personality, and in his technical equipment very thorough. We bespeak for him an increasing measure of the popular favor.

VALENTINE J. KREHBIEL.

One of the prominent younger farmers of Franklin township, where he owns 215 acres of farm lands, as also seventy-five acres in Harrison township, is Valentine J. Krehbiel. He was born on a farm adjoining that on which he now resides September 16, 1862, the son of Christian and Mary (Schnebele) Krehbiel, both natives of Germany. Their portraits appear upon opposite page. The father was a man of enterprising spirit, and came to America in 1850, at about twenty years of age, locating in Ohio. The following year, 1851, he came west and located in Franklin township, Lee county, Iowa. His future wife came to the township about the same time, with her parents. Here he took employment as a farm hand, in which he continued for about five years, when he married, and having saved his earnings, was able to purchase a farm. This consisted of eighty acres of unimproved land, upon which stood a log house. This tract he cleared and made it productive, occasionally adding to it by further purchases, until finally he was the owner of 415 acres in this township, besides a great deal of land in Kansas and forty-five acres in Harrison township. He was a self-made man, and by his own efforts came to be one of the most successful farmers in this section of the county. He was also an important factor in the township's affairs, and was for a number of terms trustee of the township. He was a lifelong Democrat, and often served the party in county conventions. His death occurred in 1899, and that of his widow in 1902. Both were early members

MR. AND MRS. CHRISTIAN KREHBIEL

of the Mennonite church, and helped in the building of the first church edifice for that denomination in Lee county. The father was for many years speaker of the church.

Valentine J. Krehbiel, the subject of this review, received his education in the schools of his township, and during his early years was his father's assistant on the farm. He continued in this work until the time of his marriage, April 27, 1890, to Miss Christina Hirschler, of Franklin township, when he purchased eighty acres where he at present resides, and there began his active business life as a farmer. That he has succeeded is evidenced by the fact that he now owns a fine home, with a farm of 215 acres, together with seventy-five acres in Harrison township, and also conducts a very extensive live-stock business, shipping in carload lots. He is engaged largely in general farming, but makes stockraising and dealing his specialty. Mr. Krehbiel, besides his private business, takes a prominent part in township affairs, acting politically with the Democratic party. He was elected trustee of his township in 1899, and was honored by reelection in 1902, being the present incumbent of that office. He is a man of unusual ability, and has performed the duties of his office in a highly efficient and satisfactory manner. The family occupies a large and handsome residence, which Mr. Krehbiel remodeled and improved a few years ago. To Mr. and Mrs. Krehbiel have been born two sons and five daughters, as follows: Della, Ruth, Leona, Carl, Hulda, Bertha and Adolph. Mr. and Mrs. Krehbiel are both active members of the Mennonite church, of Franklin township, and teachers in the Sunday school. Mr. Krehbiel is possessed of a genial and generous disposition, which, together with the reputation he enjoys for strict uprightness and integrity in all his dealings, has won for him the friendship of many and the respect of all who know him.

WILLIAM A. SCHERFE.

William A. Scherfe, a native son of Fort Madison, was born July 24, 1867, his parents being Augustus and Amelia Scherfe. He has continuously resided in this city, save for a brief period spent in the city of Burlington. His early education was obtained in the schools of this city, but when twelve years of age he put aside his textbooks and began working as a delivery clerk in a grocery store. He was afterward a salesman in a hardware store for Joseph Ehart & Son, of Fort Madison, with whom he continued for two years, and then at the age of eighteen he became an apprentice in a machine shop, where he remained for four years, thoroughly mastering the trade. When twenty-two years of age he became a locomotive fireman on the Chicago, Fort Madison & Des Moines Railroad and at the age of twenty-six he met with an accident that incapacitated him for manual labor. In 1894 he entered the insurance business with his father and this relation was continued until 1899, when the father retired and William A. Scherfe has since remained in the business alone. He does a general insurance business, which extends throughout Lee county and he is also assistant special agent for the German American Fire Insurance Company of New York. He is also buying and selling real estate and has secured a good clientage in both departments of his business.

Mr. Scherfe was married, on the 16th of June, 1892, to Miss Mary A. Young, a native of Cincinnati, Ohio, born December 13, 1870, a daughter of Jacob Young, a harness-maker of Troy, Iowa. In 1894 Mr. Scherfe was elected secretary of the independent school district of Fort Madison and still holds that position. He is a member of Fort Madison Lodge, No. 374, Benevolent and Protective Order of Elks, and belongs to the Presbyterian church, while in his political faith he is a Republican. One of the enterprising young business men of the city, he has gained well-merited success and the methods he has pursued are such as have won for him high regard and confidence. Dependent upon his own resources from an early age his history stands in evidence of what can be accomplished by strong and honorable purpose.

GEORGE W. SMITH.

George W. Smith, editor of the West Point Bee, of West Point, Lee county, Iowa, was born at Waterloo, Illinois, February 10, 1858, the son of George and Caroline Smith. He received his education in the common schools of St. Louis, having removed to that city in his early childhood. He remained a resident of St. Louis until 1871, during which time he learned the printing trade, which as a young man he followed for a number of years. After 1871 he worked at his trade in all the principal cities of the United States, his longest connection with any one publication being that with the Chicago Herald, which covered a period of fifteen years.

In 1894, Mr. Smith located in West Point, purchasing the Bee, a Democratic paper which had been established in 1892. At the time of the purchase the publication had but a small circulation, but under the thoughtful and enterprising management of Mr. Smith has greatly improved in character and appearance, and now enjoys a circulation of more than one thousand copies per week, a remarkable achievement. This is the only newspaper in the northwestern part of the county, where it occupies a peculiarly influential position. Mechanically it is of a high grade of excellence, and consists of four pages of well-written articles of local and general interest.

In 1887 Mr. Smith was married to Miss Kate R. Carroll, a native of Chicago, and to them have been born two daughters, Ernestine and Consuelo.

Mr. Smith is at the present time director of the public school, and a new and modern brick building has been erected for the accommodation of the schools. He has no other outside interests, however, and devotes all his time to the newspaper, including job printing, and in this enterprise has met with financial and professional success of very gratifying proportions. He is well known throughout Lee county, and his force of character and genial temperament have made him universally popular.

REUBEN CREPS.

One of the most public-spirited citizens of Fort Madison is Reuben Creps, who has been a resident of this city and actively connected with its growth and development for a great many years. Mr. Creps was born in Dixon township, Cumberland county, Pennsylvania, September 22, 1822, and there grew to years of maturity. In 1845 he made a trip to the West, going to Burlington, this state. After a year spent there he returned to his home in Pennsylvania, where he remained until 1851. He then came to Iowa a second time, arriving at Fort Madison June 21, 1851, and here he has made his home ever since.

Mr. Creps received a good education in the public schools at the place of his birth, and for several years was a teacher in that state. In Pennsylvania he also learned the carpenter's trade, which he was destined to follow for the greater part of his active life, and as carpenter and contractor he has been connected with the construction of nearly all the principal buildings, public and private, of Fort Madison, among which are the state penitentiary at this place, the Episcopal church, the court house, the jail and the city power house. He also attained some reputation as a millwright, and was connected with the building of the McConn mills and most of the other larger mills in this section. During the last six years he has been leading a retired life at his pleasant home at the corner of Fifth and Chestnut streets. He doubtless owes much of his success to the fact that he early had a rigid training in the school of hard work and business management. Born on a farm, he was his father's assistant until the latter's death, when he assumed the management of the farm, which he continued until he came west.

Mr. Creps was married in Pennsylvania to Miss Catherine Mower, who was born in Germany and came to the United States in her girlhood. She died, leaving one son and one daughter. The daughter is now deceased. The son, La Fayette, is a resident of Idaho, where he is engaged in the lumber business, and has achieved very considerable success. The wife and mother is buried at Fort Madison, her death having occurred in this city.

Our subject is a son of David and Elizabeth (Clippinger) Creps. His father was during his early life a farmer and for some time engaged in the mercantile business, but later returned to the farm.

Mr. Creps was originally a member of the Democratic party, but has since assumed an independent position in politics. In his religious connection he is affiliated with the Methodist Episcopal church, of which he has been a member ever since arriving in Fort Madison, and of which he has served as trustee for many years. He has been active in good works, and was one of those who organized, in about the year 1851, the first Sunday school formed in Fort Madison. Throughout the course of a long residence here he has been witness of all the more important steps in advance taken by his adopted city, and has borne his full share in securing for Fort Madison the enviable position which it now occupies. He has been an advocate of improvement, and has always taken an interest in everything calculated to forward the real welfare of the community in which he lives. By his character of integrity and strict justice in his dealings he has won the general respect, and his capacity for friendship has brought him into close relations with many who prize his acquaintance.

Mr. Creps again married, his second wife being Mrs. Lizzie Bock, on the 29th of April, 1890, his first wife having died in 1884. She was born in Fort Madison, a daughter of Henry and Elsie (Meier) Bock, both of whom were born in Germany, and came to Fort Madison about 1851.

Here Mrs. Creps grew up and has spent her life here, and is well-known.

FRANK TROJA.

One of the prominent and well-known agriculturalists of Lee county is Frank Troja, who resides just outside the corporate limits of the City of Fort Madison. Mr. Troja was born in Germany, November 20, 1835, there he was reared on a farm, acquiring in youth the habits of industry and frugality which made him successful in after life, and at the age of twenty-nine years came, in company with his brother Joseph, to America.

Locating in Fort Madison, the first year was spent in the work of a brick yard, at the end of which time he took employment in the Atlee sawmill. Here he remained continuously for seventeen years. Three years he was in the employ of his brothers, Joseph and John, who conducted an egg business in Fort Madison.

In 1886 he took up his present location, buying a tract of seventy-two acres of timber land just outside the city limits of Fort Madison. Twenty acres of this farm he has cleared and placed under cultivation, and here also he has built a comfortable and commodious home, and is now enjoying the fruits of a life of labor and continuous and conscientious toil. The farm is considered a valuable piece of property.

In 1865 Mr. Troja was married at Fort Madison to Miss Lizzie Putmeyer, who was born in Germany and came to America in the party of which Mr. Troja was a member. Unto them have been born eight sons and daughters, of whom six still live under the parental roof. They are as follows: Joseph, born August 15, 1869; John, born December 11, 1872; Benjamin, born March 4, 1876; George, born October 27, 1877, married Margarette Lackery; Lizzie, born September 25, 1879; Katie, Mrs. George Larkey, of Madison, born September 16, 1882; Annie, born January 15, 1870, wife of Barney Heiling, of Fort Madison; and Maggie, born November 10, 1874, wife of

Frank Heiling, of Fort Madison. All the children were educated in Saint Mary's Parochial School.

Mr. Troja is a member of Saint Mary's Catholic church, and in politics he early decided, after a careful study of political questions in the United States, to associate himself with the Democratic party. In his religious duties he has been active, having assisted in the building of Saint Mary's church, taking part in the labor of construction. Although now in his sixty-ninth year, he still assists in the work of the farm, and does some gardening, supplying garden truck, small fruits and milk to a number of city customers.

Frank Troja is the second of a family of eight children, of whom the only other survivors are Joseph, of Fort Madison, and Barney, who still lives in Germany. He is a self-made man, owing his success entirely to his own efforts; and his integrity, strong character and genial disposition have won for him many admirers and friends.

GEORGE E. ROGERS.

An enterprising citizen and agriculturist of Green Bay township is George E. Rogers, residing on section 16. He was born in a log cabin located on section 15, of this township, October 7, 1858, son of Milward H. and Susan Rogers, an account of whose lives and genealogies appears elsewhere in this volume. He acquired his early education and early knowledge of books in the public schools of his district, and grew to manhood in the acquirement of useful training as an assistant to his father. In fact, this training began very early. When only eleven years of age he was impressed into the hard service of caring for the year's harvest, his one elder brother having suffered from sunstroke. It is to such duties well and courageously performed, however, that many a man, like Mr. Rogers, has been able to trace his success in after life, and often what appears to many as mere good fortune is the result of years of training in the school of experience.

Mr. Rogers made his home beneath the paternal roof until the year 1880, when he was united in marriage with Miss Cordelia May Vogt, daughter of Samuel H. and Elizabeth (McGregor) Vogt. The father of Mrs. Rogers was a native of Switzerland, and emigrated to America when seventeen years of age, making the voyage by sailing vessel and taking twenty-three days to cross the ocean. He located at Nauvoo, Illinois, and was there married before the Civil War. At the beginning of the war he enlisted in the Seventeenth Iowa Volunteer Infantry, serving his country as a soldier for the long period of three years and four months, four months of which were spent as a prisoner of war, and was for a time detained in the famous Andersonville prison. He removed some time after his marriage to Montrose township, Lee county, and in 1880 again removed, taking up his residence in Green Bay township, where he bought a small farm in the southeast corner of section 15. There he died December 5, 1899, at the age of sixty-five years and twenty-seven days. Mrs. Vogt was a native of Coshocton county, Ohio. She died February 22, 1903, aged seventy-one years, five months and twenty-one days. The remains of both rest in Beebe cemetery, this township. They were active and valued members of the Christian church, and were universally esteemed and respected. To them were born four children, of whom Mrs. Rogers is the only survivor.

Mr. and Mrs. Rogers are the parents of six sons and daughters, two of whom died in infancy. Those living are: Roy V., Cora E., Frank K. and Charles Bruce. The sons remain at home, and the daughter is the wife of William Sweeney and resides at Macomb, Illinois.

Mr. Rogers owns 185 acres of fine farming land, on which he conducts general farming operations and the usual amount of stockraising. Here he has built a beautiful dwelling in the midst of fine grounds ornamented with shade trees, and has erected other buildings to meet the necessities and provide the conveniences of modern farm life, installing many improvements which combine the advantages of city and country. He supports the Christian church, of which Mrs. Rogers is a member, and in his political views is a Democrat, believing the policies to which that party stands pledged to be in accord with the fundamental principles of American government. Fraternally he has membership relations with the Independent Order of Odd Fellows, being Past Grand of the Wever Lodge and having serve'd as representative to the Grand Lodge; is a member of the Knights of Pythias at Wever and holds in that order the rank of Past Grand Deputy; and is a member of the Benevolent and Protective Order of Elks at Fort Madison. He is a gentleman of unusual ability, is thoroughly informed as to topics of current interest, and is accorded a position of high standing and great influence in his community. Although of the most modest pretentions as to his own worth, he is everywhere respected for the sterling qualities of his character ,and has many friends.

JACOB M. RISSER.

Jacob M. Risser, a leading and influential citizen of Sawyer, Lee county, Iowa, and a descendant of one of the early pioneer families of the West, was born in West Point township, Lee county, November 2, 1847, the son of Jacob and Amelia (Miller) Risser. Jacob Risser, Sr., was born in Bavaria, Germany, December 12, 1815, a son of Daniel Risser, who was born August 25, 1794, and of Elizabeth (Smith) Risser, his wife, a daughter of Henry Smith, and the date of the marriage of his parents was May 26, 1811. When a boy of sixteen the father of our subject worked his passage to America on a sailing vessel, and located at Cleveland, Ohio, where he learned the trade of cabinetmaking, and later established a cabinetmaking shop of his own, a venture in which he was very successful, and it was in that city on December 8, 1842, that he married Amelia Miller, who was like himself a native of Bavaria, where she was born May 16, 1821. In May, 1845, Mr. Risser, together with his father-in-law and his wife's sister and husband, accompanied by their families, came to Lee county, settling in the southwest part of West Point township, where they moved into a log cabin; and it was in this house that Mr. Miller and his son-in-law, Henry Leisey, on May 10, 1845, became the victims of the celebrated "Mormon murder," for which the perpetrators of the crime, who were members of the Hodges family, paid the penalty with their lives in July of the same year at Burlington, Iowa, where they were hanged.

Soon after coming to Iowa Jacob Risser purchased a farm of eighty acres, which he cultivated for a time, and later he owned a sawmill in the village of West Point, operating it with considerable profit until some time in the eighties, when it was destroyed by fire. He achieved success in all he undertook, and was respected for the fact that he was what is called a self-made man, having accumulated a competency by his own efforts and entirely without aid of any kind. He was a Democrat in matters of politics, and in his religious connection he was a member of the Mennonite church, together with his wife, continuing in that faith until his death, which occurred in 1896, followed by that of his wife in 1902, they both being buried in the West Point cemetery. To them were born the following sons and daughters: Daniel F., who resides in Pleasant Ridge township, this county; John, who is a resident of Kansas; Jacob M., our subject; Abraham, who died when young; Mary A.; and Anna, whose death occurred in childhood.

Jacob M. Risser, the subject of this review, received a good education in a select school at West Point as well as being thoroughly trained in the work of the farm, and was employed as his father's assistant until the twenty-third year of his age, when he wedded Miss Elizabeth Schantz, a native of Pleasant Ridge township and daughter of Peter and Anna Schantz, who settled in the township in 1846. At the time of his marriage Mr. Risser, in company with a brother, worked the land belonging to the family, Jacob Risser, Sr., of 340 acres, in partnership for six years, after which he bought a farm in Pleasant Ridge township of eighty acres, where he resided until 1891, when he again disposed of his land and purchased 120 acres in the northwestern part of Washington township. At the latter place he resided for twelve years, or until 1903, in the spring of which year he removed to the village of Sawyer, there entering into a partnership with G. W. Van Hyning to conduct a mercantile business, the style of the firm being Van Hyning & Risser, but the connection has since been dissolved, Mr. Risser retiring in 1904.

Mr. Risser is widely known in Lee county as a progressive and enterprising farmer who has achieved large and lasting success in his work by virtue of business qualifications of an unusual order, and his political activities have also brought him a large circle of acquaintances and friends, as he is a prominent member and worker in the Democratic party, and has received public honors at the hands of the people, having been twice elected to the important office of county supervisor and added much to his popularity. He has also taken an active and helpful interest in promoting the progress of religion and morals in his community, he and Mrs. Risser being consistent followers of the Mennonite faith and rendering much assistance in the labors of their denomination in this section. They are the parents of a family of two sons and one daughter, to whom they have given the advantages of modern education and excellent home training, and who occupy an honored place in the society in which they move. These are: Jona G., a resident of Montrose township, this county, who married Miss Ella Claypoole and has one son, Clay; and Elma E., and Irving P., who are members of the parental household.

Mr. Risser in November, 1904, purchased a home in Danville, Iowa, where he is now residing. Irving P., in partnership with Charles Burton, purchased the general mercantile business of L. R. Kelley & Company, of Danville, in October of 1904, and are now doing business under the firm name of Burton & Risser. Miss Elma E. Risser acting as their chief clerk.

SABRET T. MARSHALL.

Sabret T. Marshall, a practicing attorney at the Keokuk Bar, was born in the city which is yet his home, November 20, 1869, his parents being Samuel Taylor and Louisa Davis (Patterson) Marshall. The father was born in Butler county, Ohio, February 26, 1812, and was a son of Gilbert and Mary (Hueston) Marshall, native of Pennsylvania and Virginia, respectively. The paternal great-grandfather, James Marshall, was a native of Washington county, Pennsylvania, and a farmer by occupation. His wife's father was a pioneer settler of the Keystone state and was killed by the Indians. He lived in a block house in order to secure protection against possible dangers, but was shot while trading some tobacco.

Gilbert Marshall had a family of ten children, all of whom lived to mature years and reared families. This number included Samuel Taylor Marshall, who spent his boyhood days upon his father's farm within sight of the old Oxford College of Ohio. When he had completed his course in the country schools he entered the preparatory department of Oxford and in due course of time was graduated on the completion of a full classical course in July, 1839. He wrote the first constitution and by-laws for the Beta Theta Pi, a Greek letter society and was one of the founders of this organization which now numbers hundreds of members. In early manhood he became very patriotic and joined the army called The Patriots, which served at the time of the Canadian invasion. In recognition of his zealous activity he was commissioned a lieutenant colonel and the document indicating his soldierly rank was chewed and swallowed by him when he was captured by the British troops. He and a comrade were captured and were thrown into prison. They were then tried, pronounced guilty of invasion, sentenced to be fined and transported to Vandiemans Land. Mr. Marshall on account of the indifference with which he viewed the situation was set free, but his friend and comrade was sent into banishment. During his term of imprisonment, however, Mr. Marshall suffered great hardship and exposure and this brought on a severe illness. On reaching home he entered the law office of Timothy Walker, of Cincinnati, and after a season there passed, resumed his reading in the office of Pettit & Orth, of Lafayette, Indiana, where he completed his studies. In December, 1842, Mr. Marshall arrived in Lee county, Iowa, and entered upon the practice of law at West Point, then the county seat, continuing there until 1847, when he removed to Keokuk. Here he became one of the leading representatives of the early bar, securing a good clientage and in public affairs was prominent and influential, winning not only success as a reward, but also becoming a recognized leader in movements that advanced the general progress and upbuilding. At one time he was associated with the Nip & Tuck paper, published at a very early day in Lee county. In politics he was a recognized leader of the Democracy of this part of the state, and in his fraternal relations he was a Mason. He married Miss Louisa Davis Patterson, a native of Kentucky, their wedding being celebrated at West Point in 1846. Her father, Colonel William Patterson, was one of the honored pioneer settlers of Iowa, and served in the first territorial legislature and several succeeding ones. He was a son of Joseph Patterson, a native of Virginia, who espoused the cause of the colonists in the Revolutionary War and served in the battle of Utah Springs, South Carolina. Colonel Patterson was a very prominent man in early times and carried on business in Iowa as a pork packer. In official life he was a recognized leader, serving as postmaster, as alderman and as mayor of his city. His religious faith was that of the Presbyterian church and he assisted materially in erecting the house of worship, furnishing all the stones from his [illegible] quarry. His death occurred in 1888, and his wife passed away a few years prior. Mrs. Marshall passed away on the 28th of March, 1904, and his death occurred June, 1895, in the city of Keokuk. Their children were as follows: Robert M., who resides in Keokuk, and is county attorney of Lee county and has held the office twice previously; A. Tom, who is engaged in the practice of law with his brother, Sabret; C. H., who is engaged in painting and paper-hanging in Keokuk; Maude M., and Sabret.

At the usual age Sabret T. Marshall entered the public schools of Keokuk and passed through successful grades until he had become a high-school student. Determining to make the practice of law his life work he began reading with his father and brother, and in January, 1895, was admitted to the bar at Des Moines, passing an examination in open court before the supreme court of Iowa. Soon afterward he began practice in his native city, but he spent the years 1896-7-8 in Denver, Colorado, and El Paso, Texas, on account of the failure of his health. In 1898, however, he returned to Keokuk and resumed his law practice here. He also became an active factor in political circles and in 1899 he was nominated on the Democratic ticket for the office of legislature. He was elected and served so capably during his first term that he was reelected. He was an active working member and though he did not seek to figure before the house in brilliant public debate he did effective service for his party and for his state in the committee rooms, being instrumental in securing the passage of a number of important bills. He belonged to the committees on judiciary, railroads and commerce, municipal corporations, compensation of public officers, buildings and loan, hospital for insane, woman's suffrage and rules. During the campaigns he has delivered many addresses and is a forceful, earnest and logical speaker, who keeping well informed on the questions and issues of the day, is able to support his position by intelligent arguments and to present it in the strong light of clear reasoning. Mr. Marshall was one of a family of ten children, of whom five survive. None of these are married and they all reside at the old family homestead at No. 730 Grand avenue. One brother, W. P. Marshall, also an advocate of the Democracy, died in 1890 while serving his second term as county sheriff. Sabret T. Marshall is accorded a position of leadership in political circles in his native county, and has also attained a creditable position as a member of the Lee County Bar, having gained a clientage which is constantly growing in extent and importance, and which has in recent years connected him with much of the notable litigation in his district.

WILLIAM M. CONLEE.

William M. Conlee was for many years a prominent farmer of Lee county, and well deserves mention among the leading residents of this community who in the past were loyal to its best interests and largely promoted the general good. Although some years have come and gone since he passed to his final rest, his influence still remains as a potent factor in the world, and the memory of his life and character is a precious heritage to his descendants. He was a native of Kentucky, having been born near the celebrated Mammoth cave in that state, November 9, 1821. There he obtained his education in the public schools, and at the age of nineteen he removed with his parents to Burlington, Iowa. After a short stay at that place the family came to Lee county, locating upon the farm on which Mrs. Conlee, the widow of our subject, still resides.

He was the son of Reuben and Nancy (Doyle) Conlee. On removing from Burlington to Lee county, Reuben Conlee, his father, purchased sixty acres in Jefferson township, composing part of the present estate, and here passed the remainder of his life as a farmer. He died in his fifty-sixth year, December 23, 1846, while at Iowa City attending the session of the first legislature of the State of Iowa, he being a member of the lower house. He is buried in Wilson cemetery in Jefferson township. He was a man of prominence, and in addition to his other honors he for many years held the office of justice of the peace in this county. His widow survived him for five years, her death occurring in April, 1856. Reuben and Nancy Conlee were the parents of eleven sons and daughters, only four of whom are living at the present time.

William Conlee, after the death of his father, remained on the home farm, purchasing the interests of the other heirs, and increasing his holdings until they consisted of 160 acres of fertile land which is now virtually all under cultivation. He continued general, farming and stockraising until his death, which occurred September 23, 1896, at the old farm home. His remains rest in the Wilson cemetery. He was a consistent Christian, and a faithful member of the Baptist church. Politically he was a believer in the principles for which the Democratic party stands, and was loyal to its best interests. For nearly fifty years he was a justice of the peace in Lee county, and held that office at the time of his death. His last illness was of long duration, and because of the low state of his health he tendered his resignation from the office, but this was rejected. He was also at one time elected trustee of Jefferson township. He was a public-spirited man, an advocate of all measures tending to improve conditions in the community of which he was a valued and valuable member. He was profoundly respected by all who knew him, and a reference to his long career as a public servant will indicate the honor in which he was held by the general public. Many were accustomed to seek his advice and counsel in regard to matters of importance, and this was always freely given.

On December 6, 1863, in Van Buren county, Iowa, at the home of the bride's parents, he was united in marriage with Miss Sylvia Jane Standley, daughter of Robert and Catherine (Bray) Standley. Mrs. Conlee's father, Robert Standley, was born in Kentucky, and coming to Iowa in pioneer days, located in Van Buren county, where he died while his daughter was yet a child. His wife survived him several years, her death occurring in Van Buren county in 1866.

Unto Mr. and Mrs. William M. Conlee were born five sons and four daughters at the family home in Jefferson township, and all are still living. They are: Laura, wife of Fred Naylor, a farmer of Jefferson township, has two children, Sylvia Eunice and Lawrence; Mary, wife of William Woodside, a farmer, of Van Buren county, Iowa; George W., a resident of Keokuk, where he is a clerk in the postal service, married Nancy Davis, and has two children, Mildred and Anita; Robert, who operates the home farm, on which he resides; Nora, wife of Noah Hewitt, a machinist in the Santa Fe shops at Fort Madison, has three sons and three daughters, Roy, Cecil, Arthur, Alice, Walter and Gladys; Reuben, who is at home, is at the present time holding the office of clerk of Jefferson township, and is secretary and treasurer of the Viele Telephone Company; Elvira, wife of Fred Bullard, a farmer of Warsaw, Illinois; Linza is living at home; Andrew A., farmer of Jefferson township, married Miss Anna Christianson.

On the original purchase which formed the nucleus of the present Conlee homestead the grandfather of our subject, following the custom of the time, built a large log house. This reminder of pioneer days was in use until about six years ago, when Mrs. Conlee and her sons erected the present frame structure, which is a very pleasant and commodious residence. They have also made other improvements.

William Conlee was an interested witness of the development of Lee county from primitive conditions, and did his full share toward making the county what it is today, one of the richest agricultural sections of the state. A kind and loving husband and father, a good citizen and a true man, his was a life without a stain and a character that was rich in traits of native nobility.

CHARLES H. HENNEMANN.

The name which introduces this review is one familiar to the residents of Keokuk, and it is one which suggests to the honest man a feeling of confidence and security, while to the evil doer it betokens a power which is feared as the instrument through which he is most likely to meet with apprehension, and therefore pay the penalty of his crimes against the laws, which are the stable foundation of the peace and prosperity of his fellow beings. As city marshal, Mr. Hennemann has made a most honorable record, and one which reflects credit upon his unfaltering allegiance to duty and the right.

Charles H. Hennemann was born in Keokuk, Iowa, February 15, 1866, the son of Charles George and Elizabeth (Schroeder) Hennemann, and his father was a native of Eversberg, Westphalia, Prussia, the date of his birth being March 17, 1836. The mother of Charles G. Hennemann died when he was but six weeks old, survived by her infant son and a daughter, Matilda, who passed the greater part of her life in St. Louis, but is now deceased, and his father was later married a second time. Father and son were coppersmiths by trade, and when Charles G. Hennemann was twenty years of age, in 1856, he decided to seek the broader opportunities of the New World for the exercise of his skill, and accordingly took passage in a sailing vessel to New Orleans, and landing there, ascended the Mississippi river to St. Louis, where he took employment as a copper smith. Later he was joined by other members of the family, including his father, who worked at his trade in St. Louis, and whose death occurred there four or five years after his coming to America. In St. Louis the father of our subject married Miss Schroeder, who was born in Hamburg, Germany, September 17, 1843, and came to America with her parents and settled in St. Louis in 1846 or 1847, and to them were born ten sons and daughters, as follows: Bertha, who first married Sylvester Betts, by which union she had four children, and who is now the wife of James Carss; Charles H., the subject of this sketch; Addie, wife of Frank Sheldon, who resides in St. Louis, and has one child; Albert, a resident of Keokuk; John, who died at the age of thirteen; Willis, of Quincy, Illinois; Matilda, who died at the age of twenty-four years; Frank, who died in infancy; Henry, who died in childhood; and George, who resides in St. Louis. The father of the family was foreman of the copper smith department of the Missouri Pacific Railway in St. Louis from 1861 to 1865, in which latter year he removed to Keokuk, where he was for a time employed by the Chicago, Rock Island & Pacific Railroad Company, but later established himself in independent business, which he continued until 1880, when he retired from active life, and his death occurred in this city on November 25, 1888.

The formal education of Charles H. Hennemann was received in the public schools, and when only fourteen years of age he began to learn the trade of cigarmaking by taking employment as a tobacco stripper in a factory, continuing in this work for two years, after which he served a regular apprenticeship of three years, and from 1885 to 1887 was a journeyman cigarmaker. During this time he traveled to San Francisco, thence by an ocean voyage of twenty-eight days' duration, and crossing the Isthmus of Panama by rail, he reached New York, and worked at his trade in Albany, Troy, Lockport, Rochester, Erie, Pennsylvania; and Chicago, whence he returned to Keokuk, and here he formed a partnership with Edward Smith to conduct a business of cigar manufacturing and dealing. At the end of a year, however, this connection was dissolved, and for the following six months he was in the manufacturing business at Nauvoo, Illinois, and from 1890 to 1895 he was engaged in the pursuit of his trade in St. Louis, but in the latter year returned to his native city, and for four years conducted a successful business here. He then became a member of the Keokuk police force, and two years later was elected to the office of city marshal, which he holds at the present time, this being the fourth year of his incumbency, as he was re-elected at the close of his first term. Under his administration the City of Keokuk has enjoyed remarkable immunity from crime, especially from the violence and depredations of habitual offenders, while those who have had the hardihood to tresspass against the majesty of the law have been brought promptly and sharply to account. Every effort has been put forth to suppress crime in any form, and the law-breakers of the city are beginning to understand that they can not with impunity abuse the rights and privileges the law accords to their fellowmen. Mr. Hennemann certainly deserves credit for what he has accomplished in the way of suppressing vice, and his course has the endorsement of all the best citizens of Keokuk. He has made arrests of many desperate characters, notably that of Walter Dorman, who was afterward the companion of the Biddles, bandits of Pittsburg, who were executed for murder.

To mention merely his physical development, Mr. Hennemann is a magnificent specimen of manhood, being six feet, three and a half inches in height and weighing 265 pounds, while he holds rank as one of the leading and best-known athletes of the United States, and holds many important championship medals, as well as having broken a number of the world's records in athletic performances. Among his better known feats of strength may be mentioned the winning of the championship for putting the fifty-six-pound weight in 1892, when he made a record of twelve feet, ten inches, and also won the Western Athletic Association medal by throwing the sixteen-pound hammer, 121 feet. In 1895 he won a championship by throwing the fifty-six pound hammer twenty-nine feet, and in the Central

Athletic meet of the same year made the champion shot put of forty-one feet, ten inches, and the champion sixteen-pound hammer throw of 127 feet. In 1897 he accompanied the Chicago Athletic Association team to New York, where he won the national championship for putting the sixteen-pound shot, forty-two feet, seven and three-fourths inches, and at the same meet took second place for throwing the fifty-six-pound shot, while on the same day he won the world's record for the classical sport of discus throwing, making a distance of 118 feet, nine inches, the best previous record being 106 feet. This remarkable record was made on August 28, 1897, and the following month Mr. Hennemann again went to New York to participate in a meet between the Chicago Athletic Association and the New York Athletic Club, and won the discus throw at 113 feet, and second, the sixteen-pound shot put with a distance of forty-one feet, and won second place in the sixteen-pound hammer throw with a distance of 136 feet. At the Olympian games at St. Louis in 1904, he was awarded fourth place, throwing the fifty-six-pound weight thirty-two feet, one inch.

On September 26, 1888, Mr. Hennemann wedded Miss Mary A. Gallett, daughter of Eseph Gallett, a native of Paris, France, and an early settler of Keokuk, and previously of Nauvoo, Illinois. Mr. Gallett is now deceased, and his widow has since married Louis Cobelena, and resides in Keokuk. To Mr. and Mrs. Hennemann have been born two children, Charles M. and Mary A.

Politically, Marshall Hennemann is a Democrat and a loyal worker for the success of his party. In his fraternal relations he has numerous connections, being a member of Hardin Lodge, No. 29, Free and Accepted Masons; Knights of Pythias, No. 5; Keokuk Camp, No. 622, Modern Woodmen of America; the local lodge of Ancient Order of United Workmen; Keokuk Assembly No. 105, American Benevolent Association; Keokuk Lodge, No. 106, Benevolent and Protective Order of Elks; Keokuk Lodge, No. 544, Knights of Honor, and the local lodge of the Order of Eagles. It is scarcely necessary to say that Mr. Hennemann is a man endowed with the strongest individuality, intrepid bravery when in the face of the most desperate situations, and a remarkable coolness and presence of mind under all circumstances. As a man among men he holds the esteem of those with whom he comes in contact, either in an official or a social way.

WILLIAM M. DOOLEY.

William M. Dooley, a retired business man of Keokuk whose careful management and the husbanding of his resources in former years now enables him to rest from further active labor, was born in Bath county, Kentucky, May 9, 1862. His father, Jefferson Dooley, also a native of Bath county, was a farmer by occupation and engaged in the raising of horses. He married Elizabeth Boyd, who died June 23, 1881, at the age of forty-five years, while his demise occurred March 1, 1899, when he was sixty-nine years of age. They were the parents of six children: Sanford N.; Lavona, the deceased wife of J. B. Walker, of Bath county; Alice, deceased; William; Charles R., a farmer of Bath county, and Nannie, wife of Edward Speckman, of Quincy, Illinois.

William Dooley was educated in the country schools of Kentucky and remained at home until twenty-two years of age assisting his father in his farm labors, after which he began farming on his own account. Two years were thus passed in Bath county and in 1887 he came to Keokuk, where he went into the livery business in connection with William Smith. After a year the partnership was dissolved and Mr. Dooley was alone in business until he sold out in 1899. He conducted a good stable at Nos. 18 and 20 Third street, keeping twenty horses for livery purposes, and his earnest desire to please his patrons, combined with his reliability in all business transactions, secured him a good patronage. Thus as the years passed he added to his income and now is living retired.

In 1886 Mr. Dooley was united in marriage to Miss Lois O. Smith, a daughter of John W. and Eliza (Yenowine) Smith, natives of Kentucky but at the time of their daughter's marriage living upon a farm in Hancock county, Illinois. They were the parents of eight children. Mr. and Mrs. Dooley are members of the Christian church and in his political belief he is a Democrat but has never had political aspirations. The years of his residence here have brought him warm friendships and high regard.

HENRY C. GERBOTH.

H. C. Gerboth, retired engineer, who is now living at his home in Montrose, Lee county, Iowa, was born October 11, 1848, in Saxony, Germany, and when about six years of age came with his parents to America, embarking at Bremen and landing at New York, after a voyage of six weeks' duration. Here the family first went to La Salle, Illinois, but later returned east to Pittsburg, Pennsylvania, where our subject was apprenticed in a steamboat machine shop, and acquired the trade of a machinist. The parents, however, went to Nicollet county, Minnesota, where they engaged in farming, and there the father was shot and killed by Indians while working in the field, and there also the death of the mother occurred. They were the parents of five children besides our subject, these being Frederick, Charles, Augusta and William, all of Minnesota, and Emma, of Des Moines, Iowa.

Mr. Gerboth first came to Iowa in 1856, as engineer on a steamboat, which went down the Ohio river to its mouth and ascended the Mississippi river, he making his headquarters at Keokuk, and in 1863 he married and established his home at Montrose. For forty-six years he followed his profession on the Mississippi river—from 1856 to 1902 continuously—about four years of this time being spent as assistant engineer and forty-two years as chief engineer, and in all this long period of time he met with but one accident of importance, which occurred in 1865, when he was making the trip up the river on the boat,

"Island City," with a cargo of corn belonging to the Federal government, and destined for the garrison at Fort Union. The cargo becoming wet, it swelled and burst the hull of the vessel, thus causing the boat to sink, and while the machinery was saved and towed back to the City of St. Louis on barges, the hull of the boat was left in the river, as all efforts to raise it failed. The second engineer on this trip was William Oldenburg, now deceased, a sketch of whose career is given on another page of this volume. Mr. Gerboth's experience as an engineer has been extremely varied, and included during the Civil War considerable work on transport boats, he also acting as engineer of the dispatch boat, "Adam Heine," which was in the service of General Grant, at Millikin's Bend, near Vicksburg, from which the general viewed the maneuvers of the army and fleet. His first regular employment on the Mississippi river was as engineer of a towboat plying over the Des Moines rapids, after which he was engineer on the Northern line, which ran daily packets between St. Louis and St. Paul, and for three years he was employed on the ferryboat "Keokuk," plying between Keokuk and Hamilton, this being before the Keokuk and Hamilton bridge was constructed, while from 1880 to 1885 he run a sawmill at Montrose for the firm of Healy, Felt & White. During the latter period of his work he was engineer of the Kit Carson raft boat, owned by John C. Daniels, of Keokuk, and engaged in towing lumber and logs from Stillwater, Minnesota, to Hannibal, Missouri, and to other points, and among the principal boats on which he has filled the position of chief engineer are the "Reserve," the "Canada," the "Kit Carson," and the "Savannah."

On September 9, 1863, Mr. Gerboth was united in marriage to Miss Harriet Patterson, who was born in Ohio, and came to Montrose in her girlhood, and to them have been born three sons, as follows: Edward, who died at the age of thirty-eight years; Charles, of Deeth, Nevada, who married Miss Ida Bane, and has four children, Charles, Ruth, Albert and Eloise; Albert, groceryman, of Davenport, who married Miss Nellie Reeves, of Montrose. Husband and wife are faithful members of the Presbyterian church, in which they are devoted workers, and to whose support and charities they have always generously contributed, and fraternally Mr. Gerboth is a member of Joppa Lodge, No. 136, of the Masonic Order, being Junior Warden of the Lodge, and Mrs. Gerboth is a member of the Order of the Eastern Star. He has done his full share in attending to the public affairs of his community, having served as a member of the common council, and of the board of education, and being a helpful worker in the ranks of the Republican party, in whose principles he is a thorough and conscientious believer, although bound by no hard and fast ties of partisanship. In a pecuniary way he has been very successful, owning at the present time the ranch of 240 acres in Nevada, managed by his son, Charles, the store building in Davenport, Iowa, occupied by his son Albert, residence property in East Moline, Illinois, and the pleasant home in Montrose, where he enjoys in retirement from active duties of life the ease which he has well earned by a life of conscientious labor, frugality and economy. His place in the esteem of his neighbors is an enviable one, and the honor in which he is held has been fully merited by the life record which he had made for the inspiration of future generations, for his achievements are entirely the result of his own efforts, unassisted by family, kindred or friends.

SARAH J. THOMPSON, M. D.

Dr. Sarah J. Thompson, who, since 1869, has engaged in the practice of medicine, and is now devoting her attention exclusively to the treatment of chronic diseases, in Keokuk, was born in Delaware county, Indiana, July 7, 1834, her parents being Joseph and Elizabeth (Pope) Bentley. The founder of the Bentley family in America was Jonathan Bentley, who came from England and settled in Virginia. He was the father of Dr. Joseph Bentley. The latter married Elizabeth Pope, a daughter of Nathaniel Pope, a native of England, and a son of Sir Walter and Lady Isabella Pope, of England. Lady Isabella was shipwrecked while on a voyage to America in colonial days to visit members of her family in this country, and was lost at sea. Nathaniel Pope was a resident of Ohio at the time his daughter, Elizabeth, became the wife of Dr. Joseph Bentley.

Dr. Bentley was born near Richmond, Virginia, and became a physician and surgeon. He practiced many years and was a resident of Indiana while the Red Men were still living there. There he reared his family, numbering one son and five daughters: Lydia and Sydia, twins; Sarah Jane, Julia Ann, Nathaniel, and Mary. In 1852 Dr. Bentley made the overland trip to the Pacific coast, accompanied by his daughter, Dr. Thompson, who was then sixteen years of age. He drove an ox team and she rode a pony. Their road lay through Council Bluffs, up the Platte river and through the Black Hills country, striking the Columbia river at The Dalles, Oregon. Indians were numerous in the Western districts, but did them no harm. Dr. Bentley's oxen died on the road, and he and his daughter were assisted by a Mr. Huntington to the John Day river, where they found William L. Thompson, who had a mule team, and took them to The Dalles. From the cascades of the Columbia they went to Portland by boat, thence up the Willamette to Oregon City, and from September Dr. Bentley and his daughter made their home with his cousin, a Mr. Jennings, who had been the first school teacher in Iowa, and who then lived a mile and a half from Oregon City.

On the 2d of December, 1852, Sarah Bentley gave her hand in marriage to William Lytle Thompson, the wedding taking place in Oregon City. Mr. Thompson was born in Huntingdon county, Pennsylvania, August 18, 1823, and was a descendant of Thomas Thompson, who was born December 7, 1744. He was of Scotch-Irish lineage, and settled in Pennsylvania about 1768. He married Eleanor Lindsey, who was born May 4, 1767, and they settled on government land in Carter county, Pennsylvania, which was then an almost unbroken wilderness. Twelve children were born unto them there, eleven of whom reached adult age. They were: William, Elizabeth, Abraham Thomas (who died in infancy), John, Thomas (second of the name), Israel, Amos, Nathan, Mary, Jonathan and Joseph. All of the sons, with one exception, were over six feet in height, and were strong and active.

Amos Thompson, father of W. L. Thompson, was born October 27, 1783, and was the smallest of the family—being five feet and ten inches in height—but was the most active, and the finest shot, not only in his own, but also in adjoining counties. For several years he wore the champion belt as a fist fighter, surpassing all others in that part of Pennsylvania. In later years he left behind him the games of youth and became an active member of the Methodist Episcopal church. In 1812 he married Miss Elizabeth Bateman, of Center county, Pennsylvania, who was born July 4, 1790. She was a member of the Methodist Episcopal church for over sixty-six years. Amos Thompson died in Morgan county, Ohio, March 18, 1851, and his widow passed away in Keokuk, Iowa, March 4, 1871. They reared four sons and five daughters: Thomas B., Eleanor, Hannah, John W., William L., Rachel M., Joseph L., Jane E., and Drusilla.

William Lytle Thompson acquired a common-school education, and in 1852 went to Oregon. There he ran a wharfboat and transported goods up the Willamette twenty miles to the Falls, assisted by Dr. Bentley. In 1854 he and his wife and her father returned to "The States," by way of Portland, proceeding by steamer to Frisco, where they boarded another boat for Panama. After landing there Mrs. Thompson rode a mule, carrying her baby in her arms, over the rough trail to the end of the railroad, which transported them to the Atlantic coast, where they boarded a steamer for New York, and from the Eastern metropolis returned to Muncie, Indiana. Soon afterward they made their way to Keosaqua, Iowa, where they settled. Mrs. Thompson's mother and the other members of the family had gone to Kansas, and there they were joined by Dr. Bentley. Both he and his wife died in that state.

In 1861 Mr. Thompson enlisted in the Third Iowa Cavalry for service as a defender of the Union cause, but was soon transferred to the hospital corps as a nurse. He remained on active duty until the close of hostilities, and was discharged at the close of the war with health shattered. He had been in the hospital service in Missouri, Arkansas, Georgia, and Kentucky, and was discharged in Louisville in 1865. Mrs. Thompson also went to the front as a nurse, and was in the field service until 1863, enduring all the privations and hardships of marches through the heat of summer and the cold of winter. She was in the hospitals at Fulton, Pilot Knob, Houston, and Mexico, Missouri, and also spent some time in the hospital at Keokuk. She was in the hospital in the Ozarks one winter, then returned to Pilot Knob, and later to Keokuk, being in the Simpson House Hospital for two years. When the war ended Mrs.

Thompson continued in hospital work, becoming matron of the hospital conducted by Dr. J. C. Hughes, of Keokuk, and there, in addition to her duties, she attended three courses of lectures daily in the Keokuk Medical College for five years, at the end of which time she stood the examination and obtained a certificate to practice from the State of Iowa. She has engaged continuously in practice since 1869, and her long hospital experience, as well as her thorough preparation as a medical student, well qualfied her for the work which she chose and in which she won creditable success. She has now retired from general practice, treating only chronic diseases. Her husband, following his return from the war, was unable to engage in any business on account of a sunstroke which he had sustained. He was a Republican in politics. His death occurred June 28, 1904.

Mrs. Thompson became the mother of twelve children, but only one is now living: Joseph C. Thompson, who was born in Oregon City, Oregon, and is now a mail carrier in Keokuk. He was graduated from Jamison's school and Miller's Commercial College, of Keokuk. He married Mamie McDonald, a daughter of Michael and Katherine McDonald, who were natives of Ireland, while their daughter was born in Keokuk. Unto Mr. and Mrs. Joseph Thompson six children have been born: Mary Alice, the wife of Edward G. Singleton; Virginia Ellen, the widow of Clifton Floyd, of Texas; Grace Elizabeth, deceased; James C., Mamie L., and Laura Ruth. Dr. Thompson has one great-grandchild, Clifton T., son of Clifton V. and Virginia E. Floyd, of Keokuk.

Dr. Thompson receives a pension for her services in the war. Hers has been an eventful life, full of unusual experiences that have developed her latent powers and brought out splendid traits of character. Leaving home at the age of sixteen to accompany her father on the arduous journey across the plains, she became familiar with life on the Pacific coast during the period of its pioneer development, and later returned to the West to soon afterward render effective aid to her country in caring for its sick and wounded soldiers. The ill health of her husband prompted her to become a factor in professional circles, and as a physician she has won notable success, at the same time ever displaying those womanly qualities which have made her a strong factor socially as well as professionally, winning her the unchanging respect and esteem of many friends.

ROBERT KERR.

Any work which has for its object the philosophical exposition of the history of a community, with a view to its adoption by the present or future generations as a guide or inspiration in the daily affairs of life, must in a large measure deal with the origins of that society, with the primeval condition of the land and with the careers and characters of the men and women who, urged by the stimulus of some supreme conviction, waged war with hostile nature, pushed back her borders, and reclaimed her hitherto wild and untamed forces to the uses and purposes of civilization. Of one of the well-known pioneer families which made Lee county what it is today—one of the richest argricultural sections of the Mississippi valley—Robert Kerr was a worthy representative, and a record of his life, showing the relation in which he stood to the early development of Iowa, will be valuable as illustrating man's power over environment, and as an example of high achievement through noble and inflexible resolve.

Robert Kerr was born near Pittsburg, Pennsylvania, and on coming west with his parents, settled near Peoria, Illinois, but later, when the lad was fifteen years of age, the date being 1840, the family removed to Lee county and purchased a farm in Jackson township, where a house of logs was erected, and the pioneers settled down to the long fight with the wilderness, which was to issue in such splendid triumph in later years, and whose object was to secure "the glorious privilege of being independent." Theirs was a life of many cares, and was necessarily much concerned with the acquirement of worldy wealth, not because they considered material benefits as the highest good in life, but because they saw that these might be made the means to spiritual ends, and that the successful tiller of the soil has the strength to resist the march of Wrong and to help forward the cause of Right.

Mr. Kerr grew to years of maturity on the farm in Jackson township, and near Charleston, on May 9, 1852, he was united in marriage to Miss Ruth Caldwell, who was born May 19, 1832, near Monmouth, Illinois, the daughter of Thomas and Mary (Carruthers) Caldwell, of near Mount Pleasant, Ohio. To Mr. and Mrs. Kerr were born six sons and two daughters, all of whom are still living, as follows: Alex D., who married Miss Laura Wright; William C., who married Miss Anna Hempstead; Olive C., now the wife of William C. Kite; Robert C., who married Miss Lilly Van Ausdal; Walter B., who married Miss Lucille O'Blennis; Isaac B., Thomas E., and Mary Isabel, wife of C. M. Snodgrass, of Albia, Iowa. The roll of family names also contains those of eight grandchildren.

Mr. Kerr was a lifelong member of the United Presbyterian church, as was also his father, and was for a long term of years an elder of the Summitville congregation, and always by the influence of his life doing much to advance the cause of Christianity. On his farm one of the early church edifices was erected, consisting of logs, and he and his father and brothers assisted in hewing the logs for the structure, which occupied the present site of the "Hickory Grove" school-house. The "Hickory Grove" cemetery is also located on his farm, and has always been cared for by the family. He gave careful and detailed attention to the management and operation of his farm, which was a fertile tract of 200 acres, well-improved and cultivated, but he never neglected his duties to the public, discharging the functions of director of the public school nearly all his life after attaining his majority, and holding the important office of trustee of his township for a great many years. Enjoying as he did the fullest confidence of his neighbors and of all who knew him—confidence in his ability, soundness of judgment and the absolute rectitude of his every act—his administration of public interests was always vigorous and effective, though at the same time cautious, conservative and economical. Politically he acted with the Republican party, and was one of its highly valued members in his township, possessing much influence in its counsels, which was used in accordance with the purest dictates of integrity and honor. He passed his life in the practice of the cardinal virtues, and upon all with whom he came in contact he left his impress for good, and this was strengthened by his genial and generous temperament and admirable social qualities. His death occurred at the home farm, July 21, 1884, in the fifty-ninth year of his age, and he was laid at rest in Hickory Grove cemetery beside his father, mother, brothers and sisters, who preceded him to the better life beyond. His mother's death occurred in her ninety-first year, and she is also interred in Hickory Grove cemetery, leaving a memory rich in records of good deeds. Mr. Kerr was a man of great force of character, and is entitled to credit for what he accomplished, for while achieving a private business success of no small proportions, he contributed in a material degree to the general advancement and upbuilding of the community.

EUGENE S. BAKER.

The more important financial and business interests of southern Iowa are worthily represented by Eugene S. Baker, of Keokuk, who has for a number of years been actively and substantially connected with most of the large enterprises having their inception in this section of the state. Mr. Baker was born at Waukegan, Illinois, April 10, 1850, and is the son of Silas F. and Weltha G. (Buell) Baker. His father was born at Sandy Creek, Oswego county, New York, and coming west as a young man, became a farmer in Lake county, Illinois. There he married Miss Buell, who was also a native of New York, but removed to the West with her parents. S. F. Baker made several changes of residence, and finally settled in Keokuk, where he engaged in the proprietary medicine business, achieving, by the exercise of energy, care and ability much above the ordinary, a very gratifying measure of success. He formed some connection with purely financial interests, being at one time a director of the State Central Bank. For fifteen years before his death, which occurred in 1898, he lived retired from active life. Mrs. Baker, mother of our subject, died in 1891.

Eugene S. Baker received his education in the public schools of Iowa, and on coming to Keokuk in 1868 engaged in business, first with his father, under the firm style of S. F. Baker & Son. The name was changed to S. F. Baker & Company, and has since been continued as such. A large and well-equipped manufactory is maintained at Seventh and Johnson streets, placing upon the market a general line of family remedies, and a force of traveling salesmen is employed, sufficiently numerous to cover thoroughly all the states of the entire Middle West.

Mr. Baker is at the present time a director in the Blom-Collier Company, wholesale grocers, of Keokuk; the Drake Carpet &

Furniture Company, of Burlington; the Collins-Heaslip Company, of Keokuk; the State Central Savings Bank, of Keokuk; the Lincoln Trust Company, of St. Louis; the Gate City Printing Company, of Keokuk, and of the Taber Lumber Company, and vice-president of the Keokuk National Bank.

Keokuk is pre-eminently a city of beautiful homes, and one of the finest is the magnificent edifice erected by Mr. Baker, at the corner of Fourth and Orleans streets, on the bluffs overlooking the Mississippi river. Both the situation and the structure are all that might be desired. In 1874 Mr. Baker was united in marriage to Miss Mary E. Cochran, of Keokuk, and to them have been born three sons, as follows: E. Ross, who married Miss Upham, and has one son, E. Ross, Jr.; Jesse E., who married Miss Adelaide La Taste, of Montgomery, Alabama, and Myrle F., who is at present a student in Yale College. Jesse E. and E. Ross Baker are associated with their father in the medicine business.

Mr. Baker has beeen prominently associated with the various charities and philanthropic movements of Keokuk, and was a director of the Young Men's Christian Association during the erection of the present large and beautiful building. Fraternally he is a member of the Independent Order Odd Fellows and the Knights of Pythias. In political affiliation he is a Republican, but has never engaged in partisan activities, nor aspired to public office. His position and standing in the community, however, together with the signal ability displayed, is shown in the conduct of his private affairs. Self-respecting, of known integrity and strong character, he has risen easily equal to all trusts reposed in him, he has made himself known and felt throughout a wide circle of action, and wherever known enjoys the respect and esteem which rewards success honorably achieved.

WILLIAM SCHNEIDER.

William Schneider, one of the early settlers and highly respected citizens of Fort Madison, now leading a retired life at his pleasant home, at No. 1736 Fifth street, was born in the Kingdom of Hanover, Germany, on the 16th of March, 1837, and was a son of Francis Schneider, who was in the English service at the time the Duke of Wellington checked the progress of Napoleon in his conquest of Europe. He received a medal in recognition of the aid which he thus rendered, and the medal bears the inscription "Francis Schneider, Third Land Battalion, K. G. L., Wellington, Waterloo, June 18, 1815." He had one son, Fred Schneider, who came to America ten years before the emigration of William Schneider, and who was a very successful man, his estate being valued at about $100,000 at the time of his death, which occurred in 1893.

When sixteen years of age William Schneider, bidding adieu to home and friends, crossed the Atlantic to the new world, and he never saw his parents afterward. He brought with him the medal just mentioned and it is one of his cherished possessions. When he reached the United States he had only a few cents and one set of clothing. He made his way westward to Chicago, and there found employment at seventy-five cents per day. After a year spent in that city he came to Lee county, Iowa, locating at St. Paul, where he arranged to work as a farm hand at sixty dollars per year. He continued to reside at that place and within a short time purchased forty acres of land near St. Paul, making his home there. He engaged in farming until his removal to Fort Madison, about fifteen years ago, after which he accepted a position as guard at the penitentiary, acting in that capacity for twelve years. He has since lived a retired life, doing just enough gardening upon his own place to occupy his attention, for idleness and indolence have ever been utterly foreign to his nature, and he could not content himself without some occupation. He purchased his pleasant home about eleven years ago, and it is the visible evidence of his life of thrift, economy and enterprise.

Mr. Schneider manifested his loyalty to his adopted country at the time of the Civil War by enlisting in 1864 as a member of Company F, Twelfth Iowa Infantry, with which he served until the close of hostilities. He was in Alabama and Louisiana, and followed Sherman through the Atlanta campaign, being honorably discharged at Montgomery, Alabama, where he was also mustered out. He is now a member of the Grand Army of the Republic, and thus maintains pleasant relations with his old army comrades. His interest in matters of citizenship and of local and national progress is deep and sincere, and he manifests the same loyalty to his country in days of peace that he displayed when he wore the blue uniform and followed the stars and stripes on the battlefields of the South.

On the 3d of November, 1867, in St. Paul, Lee county, Iowa Mr. Schneider was married to Miss Maggie Van Tiger, who was born in Germany and came to the United States in 1862, being a resident of St. Paul at the time of her marriage. Her father was a farmer, and following his emigration to the new world lived and died in St. Paul. Mr. and Mrs. Schneider have become the parents of eleven children, seven sons and four daughters: Gertrude, the wife of Barney Korte, a farmer residing at Salisbury, Missouri, by whom she has six children: John, Margaret, Katherine, Benjamin, William and Louise; Frank, who is now living in Omaha, Nebraska, and married Bertha Leach, by whom he has four children: Lydia, Eva, Rubie, and Margaret; Kate, the wife of Rudolph Pletscher, of Davenport, Iowa, and the mother of two children: Waldemar and Elsa; Lizzie, who died at the age of seventeen years; William, who conducts a saloon in Fort Madison; Henry, at home; Stephen, of Seattle, Washington; Martin, also of Seattle; John, of Hannibal, Missouri; Joseph, who is a member of a railroad construction corps and resides in Indiana, and Margaret. All of the children were born in Lee county, and have been educated in the Catholic schools, both Mr. and Mrs. Schneider being communicants of the Roman Catholic church. In politics he is a Republican, and has been a member of the registration board. Having long been a resident of Lee county, he has witnessed many important changes here and has seen the work of improvement carried on, bearing his full share in the labor of developing the county and promoting its substantial progress. Having lived in the United States from the age of sixteen years, dependent entirely upon his own resources since he left the Fatherland, his life record is today an exemplification of what may be accomplished when one has a strong will, a persevering spirit and unfaltering energy. These being numbered among Mr. Schneider's salient characteristics he gradually won for himself successes in the business world and in his adopted county has gained many friends.

CHARLES OFF.

Charles Off, proprietor of the bakery in West Keokuk, was born in Wurttemberg, Germany, on the 11th of March, 1866. His parents, Gottlob and Christina (Dannenhauer) Off, are still living in their native country. There were eight children in the family: Mrs. Carrie Sturm, John and Charles, being in America; and those in Germany are Christina, Christian, Rosina, Gottlob and Ernest.

Charles Off obtained his education in the schools of his native country and when fifteen years of age came to America, landing at Philadelphia on the 25th of May, 1881. There he learned the baker's trade, which he followed for five years and in 1886 he removed to Peoria, Illinois, where he spent eight months. In August, 1887, he came to Keokuk and after working for others for ten weeks he began business on his own account at No. 918 Main street. This was on the 1st of November, 1887, and on the 8th of the same month he was married. After three years he purchased property at No. 501-3 A street, building there a residence and bakery. He improved the property to the value of four thousand dollars and has since been at this place, conducting business here for fourteen years. He is now proprietor of a general baking establishment, employing three bakers and using three horses and two delivery wagons in sending out his goods to his customers. His is entirely a local trade and there is a large demand throughout the city for the products of his establishment. His business has reached very gratifying proportions, owing to his thorough knowledge of the trade and his reliability in all transactions.

On the 8th of November, 1887, Mr. Off was married to Miss Minnie Traenkle, who was born in Germany in 1865. They became acquainted in Philadelphia and their marriage has been blessed with six children, three sons and three daughters, Carrie, Minnie, Charles, Gustaf, Gertrude and Ernest. Charles Off was reared in the German Evangelical Lutheran church, to which he belongs. He is also a member of the Independent Order of Odd Fellows, the Woodmen of the World, the Ancient Order of United Workmen and is the president of the Liederkranz Singing Society. He possesses in common with the majority of his countrymen great love of music and has considerable talent in that direction. In his political views he is a Democrat and is now serving as alderman from the fourth ward. He is an active working member of the council and is now in the committees on finance, railroads, board of health and streets. He is deeply interested in local politics, doing all in his power to promote the growth and insure the success of his party and has frequently been a delegate to county conventions. Time has demonstrated the wisdom of his choice of Keokuk as a place of residence for in this city he found the business conditions he sought and through close application and capability in the control of his trade interests he has gradually advanced toward success and is one of the substantial representatives of industrial life in Keokuk.

MRS. GRACE REBO.

Mrs. Rebo was born on a farm near Fort Madison September 20, 1864, and is the daughter of Wilson and Gertrude (Wallace) Bullard, being the only child. The mother died in the child's infancy, but the father is still living. At the age of sixteen years she was married to Bernard Rebo, who was born near Waterloo, Iowa. He was of French descent. To them were born three children, as follows: John, born December 14, 1883; Ray, born September 13, 1887, and Gertrude, born February 7, 1889.

Mrs. Rebo's main characteristic is self-reliance, and for many years she has supported herself and the family by her own efforts. Fifteen years she spent as a pioneer in the West—in Kansas, Nebraska, Colorado and South Dakota. She has taken, held and sold two "claims" or homesteads of government land, one in Hitchcock county, Nebraska, and the other in Cheyenne county, Kansas. At Wano in the latter state she conducted an ice-cream parlor for a year. It was here also that she became the proprietor of a house and eleven lots, trading for this property a farm of eighty acres. But the town is now of the past, as when the railroad was constructed through that section it passed through Saint Francis, one mile east. By this important change the Rebos lost everything they then possessed. At Loop City, Nebraska, Mrs. Rebo earned a living by exercising her skill in dressmaking.

The life of Mrs. Grace Rebo furnishes for her children and for all who read its history an example of constant, earnest and noble endeavor. All the hardships and heartbreaking trials of pioneer life have been hers to endure. In her travels over the western plains she has suffered, even to tears, for a drink of water; she has fought the terrible prairie fire; in Hitchcock, Nebraska, had her home torn from its foundations by cyclone; at Loop City in that state, suffered from visitations of terrific hailstorms and cloudburst; she has lived in a dug-out where, night after night, the only sound outside was the dismal howling of the coyote; has defended herself and family from rattlesnakes; has helped in the "round-up" of the cattle ranch, doing the hard work that usually falls to the lot of a man.

In 1900 she returned to Fort Madison where she bought a house and three lots. She also rents thirty-five acres of land, which she cultivates, hiring the necessary help. She keeps a half-dozen cows of the finest Jersey stock, eligible for register, and furnishes milk to customers. The products of the land are principally tomatoes, sweet potatoes and peas, which are sold to a canning factory. On a tract of four acres she, this year, raised 401 5-8 bushels of peas—the largest yield ever known in Lee county. By careful study and planning she has brought the whole thirty-five-acre tract to a marvelous degree of productiveness. It is exclusively devoted to truck farming, and the success with which it is being operated should be an encouragement to others to make attempts in the same direction. On February 24, 1901, Mrs. Rebo purchased her present home, giving her note for the full amount. She owned at that time one horse and one cow, and these were her entire assets. Since then her success has been phenomenal, and of her achievements she has every reason to be proud.

CHARLES SCHULTZ.

To one who has shown his readiness and ability to serve his community and his country in the walks of useful industry and on the field of battle, certainly there should belong a place on the roll of the distinguished men of Keokuk, Iowa. In this class belongs Mr. Charles Schultz. He was born at Kupferzell, Wurttemberg, Germany, November 13, 1839, the son of John Schultz, who was by trade a butcher and also was engaged in business as proprietor and manager of a hotel. The family landed at New York November 13, 1851, and located at Philadelphia, where the father was employed in a bark shed, near the navy yard, until May 4, 1857, at which time they started west for Keokuk, arriving in this city May 11th. Here the father was employed as a sausagemaker. His death occurred in 1866. The mother, who was Susanna Schulz, also died in Keokuk.

Charles Schulz is the only living representative of his father's family, although there were five brothers and sisters besides himself. He received his education in the public schools of Philadelphia, and in that city also he began his active career as an employe in a factory which produced nails and wooden letters and figures for sign lettering. During the last two years of his residence in Philadelphia he was employed in a metallic-cap factory. On coming to Keokuk he began, in the summer of 1857, to acquire the trade of cabinetmaking. From 1859 to 1897 he combined his work with mercantile business, having established a high-class furniture store, but at the present he gives his time to his trade of cabinetmaking.

July 7, 1863, Mr. Schulz married Miss Barbara Schmied, daughter of John Schmied, and to them have been born seven sons and daughters, all of whom are living.

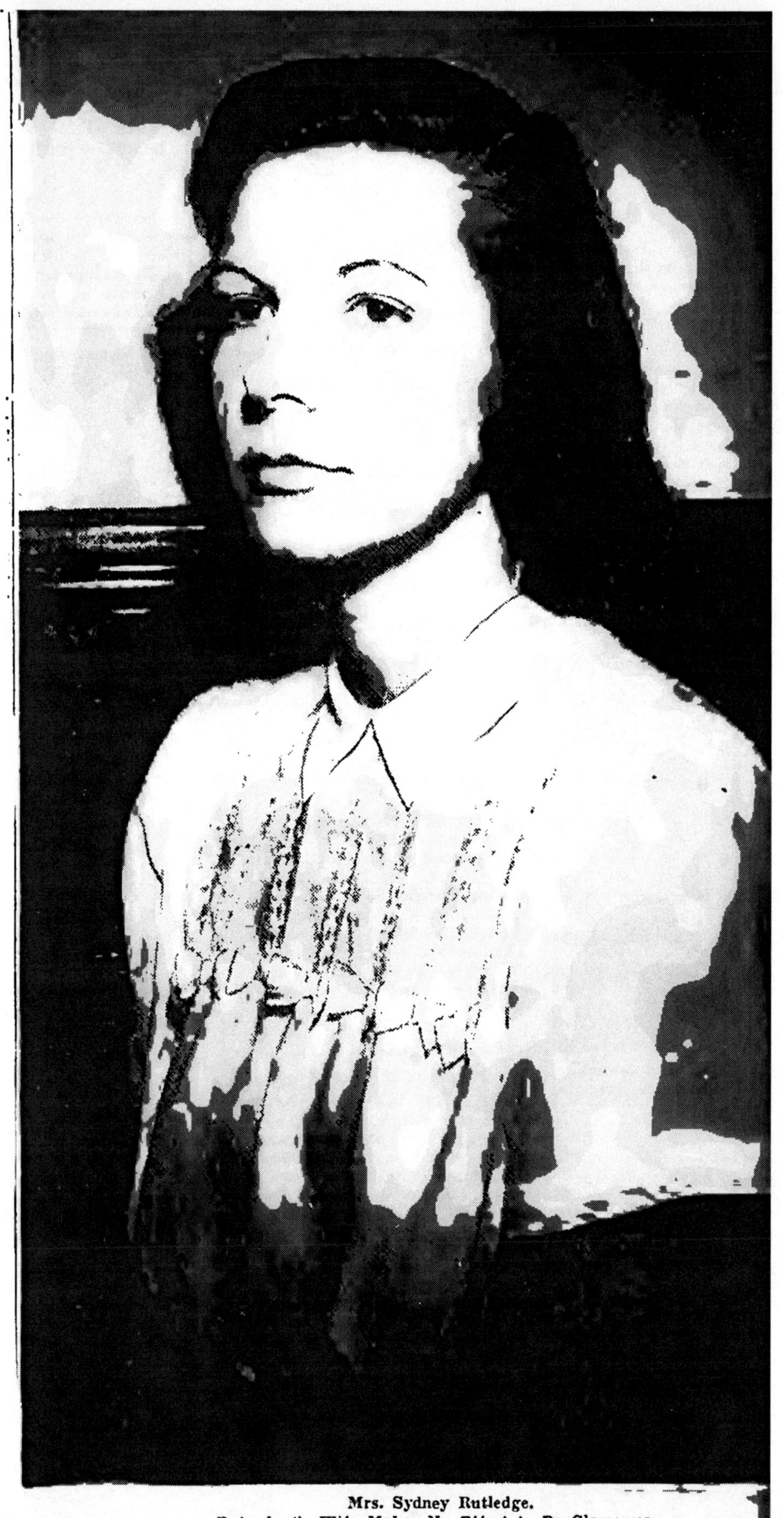

Mrs. Sydney Rutledge.
Defendant's Wife Makes No Effort to Be Glamorous.

...h operat-
...s 860 high
...are widely
...din' and GAMMACK.
...temper, he may profit by it
...stalemate: A husband who

...bet you that he can pull
...ck of cards in three tries.
...that he can . . . *The Wall*
...*nti-Semitism has been of-*
...rns of Toledo suggests this
...wer to the question, "How
...l," means not so good while

...of 732 Eighteenth st. *Their*
Fort Des Moines' is 3-1161
...*tor Freight Terminal's is*
...the daytime, Mrs. Lund
...that are intended for one
...ed about five times a week
...calls intended for one of

...cture of Britain's Princess
...partment in Vatican City
...The Vatican Swiss guard
...own in the picture accom-

...President Carl Cacciatore,
...of Commerce just after

...placed persons, as told by
...A New York surgeon en-
...to work in his home. *The*
...*nely happy in free Amer-*
...*oth the man and his wife*
...*e in the United States.*

...'t have two people of his
...domestics. But the Euro-
...ntent with their lot. Next
...re arranged for you to be
...finished, you'll be able to
...that you remain as guests

...crat, Charlie Gebhardt,
...a national scoop during
...ge. When Grange com-
...editor inquired casually

5 to 3 decision handed down in February, 1948. The state obtained a rehearing. The Iowa supreme court then reversed itself last December and upheld the act by a 6 to 3 decision. Later, the court refused to rehear the case again.

Meanwhile, the state comptroller's office is withholding payment of $4,500,000 in credits under the act. Another $5,000,000 would become available next November, and a similar sum in November of 1950.

Thus $14,500,000 will go to farmers as tax credits within a year if the act finally is declared constitutional.

The 1945 legislature provided $500,000 to pay that portion of school taxes on agricultural lands of 10 acres or more where the levy is more than 15 mills. The money was to be refunded for taxes paid in 1947.

Challenged Act.

Mrs. Laura Dickinson of Epworth challenged the act in the Dubuque county district court, in a suit filed Sept. 24, 1945. She lost in the district court, and appealed to the Iowa supreme court.

State Comptroller Ray Johnson said that at the present level it would take about six million dollars a year to pay in full the obligation taken on by the state.

The $500,000 available for refunds on taxes paid in 1947 would pay only about 18 per cent of each claim on a pro rata basis, Johnson said. The two million dollars available for 1948 payments would pay only about 38 per cent. About the same percentage could be paid on claims for taxes paid this year, when two million dollars also was made available.

S.U.I. School of Religion Meeting

IOWA CITY, IA.—Nearly 200 Iowans representing the Protestant, Jewish and Catholic faiths will attend the annual meeting of the State University of Iowa school of religion here Monday.

A board of trustees meeting will be held in the afternoon, according to Dr. M. Willard Lampe, director of the school. He will present his annual report and 13 positions on the board of trustees will be filled by election.

The board is composed of 40 representatives of the University of Iowa religious groups. Delegates will be guests at a luncheon.

tion at the same time with another car traveling at right angles to you. Who has the right of way?

If the other car is coming from your right, then it has the right of way. Notice that this rule applies only when the cars would arrive at the intersection at the same time. If

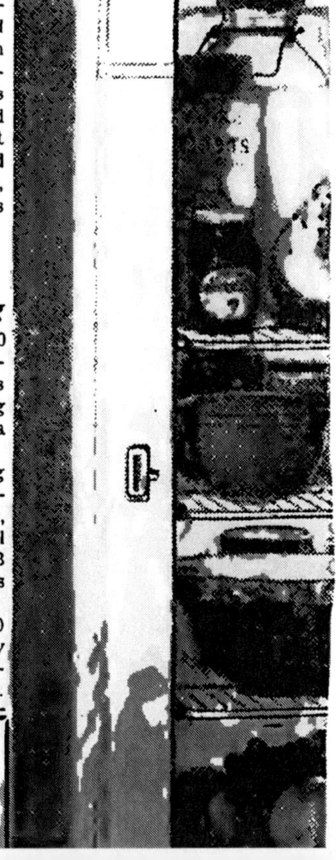

Of these Lizzie, wife of Charles Schmidt, lives in Keokuk; Charles J. married Miss Martha Weil, daughter of Jacob Weil, and he is employed in a shoe factory in this city; Minnie is the wife of Ed. Loewenstein, a traveling salesman of Keokuk; Julia is the wife of Harry Wolf, of this place; Anna married George Mayer, and has her home here, and Edward is at home with his father at the family residence, 1205 Exchange street, as is also Albert C.

When the first call for volunteers was issued at the time of the Civil War Charles Schulz enlisted in Company D, of the First Regiment Iowa Volunteer Infantry, under Captain—afterward General—Mathies, and after going into camp at Keokuk was sent to Hannibal, Missouri, Macon City and Booneville, and thence to Springfield, Missouri, where he was engaged in the battle of Wilson's Creek, which was an extremely severe engagement in its consequences to the Union troops. Later he took part in several skirmishes but was shortly incapacitated by illness from which he still continues to suffer after the lapse of so many years, and was compelled to quit the service, having been discharged about August 20th.

Mr. Schulz is not without some of the tastes of the collector and virtuoso, and among other articles of value he possesses a chiffonier that holds rather an odd and amusing interest on account of its peculiar dating, which reads: "Tschermantaun (Germantown), Pa., 1776." The lettering is in German characters.

A careful consideration of the basic principles of government early led our subject to affiliate himself with the Republican party, and he has acted with that organization all his life. He has never asked for office, but his popularity has caused him to be elected to various positions of trust in his township, among them that of township trustee. He is a consistent member of the German Evangelical church, and fraternally he holds membership in the Independent Order of Odd Fellows, the Iowa Workmen, Knights of Honor and the Grand Army of the Republic, in all of which he has held offices of honor. In the latter order he is a member of Torrence Post. He at one time organized two lodges of the Knights of Pythias, but has since dropped his membership in that order. He is a self-made man in all senses of the word, and has a wide circle of acquaintances and friends. He is truly a representative citizen.

JOHN DE ROSEAR.

John De Rosear, a representative of one of the old and highly honored pioneer families of Lee county, Iowa, was born April 19, 1854, in Cedar township, the son of William De Rosear, a native of France. On coming to America William De Rosear first located in the State of Kentucky, and later removed to St. Louis, where he was united in marriage to Miss Sarah Ann Bristow, who was born in London, England, and they came to Lee county, he purchasing a farm of 170 acres in Cedar township, and it was there that his death occurred on June 25, 1892, and his wife died in October, 1895. He was a highly successful farmer, being possessed of unusual business ability, as well as of high moral qualities that made him esteemed and respected wherever known, and enjoyed in a marked degree the confidence of his fellow citizens, being elected to a number of township offices, although he never sought public favor. He was a veteran of the Mexican War, and when the great war between the States cast its shadow over the land of his adoption, he enlisted in the year 1862 in the regiment known as the "Old Gray Beard," at Keokuk, and for a period of approximately three years he fought the battles of liberty on Southern fields. He and his wife were the parents of fifteen sons and daughters, as follows: Mary Jane, now deceased; Sarah, wife of James Nicholson, of California; William, of Colorado; David and Jane, twins, of whom the former is a resident of Kansas and the latter of Colorado; John, our subject; Ellen, wife of Armenus Irwin, of Ringgold county, Iowa; Alice, wife of M. Holmes, of Lee county; Isaac, of Lee county; Clara Holmes, of Lee county; James, of Arizona; Zephyr, deceased; Charlotte Lunsford, of Illinois; Isabelle, deceased, and Albert, of Lee county.

For his early education John De Rosear studied in the public schools of Cedar township, at the same time being engaged in the work of the home farm under the direction of his father and as his assistant, continuing in this occupation until about the year 1887, when he entered the employ of the United States government, and for sixteen years assisted in the operation of the guard lock of the Des Moines rapids canal. During this latter period he resided at Galland, but in October, 1903, he removed to Montrose, where he has engaged in the meat business, and at the present time is expecting to take up farming in a short time, for which purpose he will remove to Harrison township, where he owns a farm of eighty acres, as well as property in Galland and in Montrose. In this enterprise he will, no doubt, achieve the same success which has been his in other ventures, as he enjoys the advantage of an early training in the work and also farmed independently for a number of years in Cedar township with gratifying results after leaving his father's employ and before entering the government service.

Mr. De Rosear has been a prominent worker in the Republican party in Lee county, having a decided taste for affairs of a public nature, and for nine years was a member of the township board of trustees, and also has done much to advance the welfare of the public schools in the capacity of director. Fraternally, he is a member of Cascade Lodge, No. 66, Independent Order of Odd Fellows of Montrose, in which he is Past Noble Grand and as whose representative he attended the Grand Lodge at Burlington in 1881, and he, with his wife, is a member of the local lodge of Daughters of Rebekah, in which Mrs. De Rosear has held official rank. He attends and supports the Presbyterian church of Harrison township, and both his parents are buried in the Presbyterian cemetery at that place, which is universally conceded to be the most carefully maintained and most artistically appointed cemetery in the State of Iowa, being supported by endowment.

On February 19, 1880, at Galland, Iowa, Mr. De Rosear was united in marriage to Miss Emma Lyons, who was born in Lee county, the daughter of David Lyons, a farmer of Montrose township. The mother of Mrs. Rosear, whose maiden name was Henrietta Young, was first married to Mr. I. Bain, who died, leaving two children, and later she married Mr. Lyon, and they are both now deceased, having died several years ago. They were the parents of nine sons and daughters, of whom five are still living, as follows: George Lyons; Emma, wife of our subject; Warren Bain, and Etta Johns and Viola Hemmingway, the latter two being twins. To Mr. and Mrs. De Rosear have been born two sons, these being David Everett, who died at the age of eighteen months, and Charles Earl, born September 30, 1892.

PATRICK H. FINERTY.

Patrick H. Finerty, a dealer in groceries and notions in Keokuk, who is also serving as oil inspector by appointment of the governor, is one of the worthy citizens that Ireland has furnished to the new world and in his life record he displays the ready adaptability, executive force and energetic characteristic of people of his race. His birth occurred in County Galway, Ireland, March 14, 1844. His father, Patrick Finerty, was a stone mason and contractor which occupation he pursued until he retired from business life on account of advanced age. He wedded Mary Logan, also a native of Ireland and his death occurred on the 9th of March, 1876, while his wife passed away on the 26th of January, 1890, the remains of both being interred in the Catholic cemetery. They were members of St. Peter's Catholic church and in their family were four children: Mrs. Bridget McGrath; Mary, the wife of H. J. Mills; John F., deceased, and Patrick H. The living members of the family are all residents of Keokuk. John F., the deceased brother, was a soldier of the Civil War for four years and five months, serving with the gallant Second Iowa Infantry, which stormed Fort Donelson. He also went with Sherman on the celebrated march to the sea and participated in the grand review at Washington, following the close of hostilities.

Patrick H. Finerty was only three years of age at the time of his parents' emigration to the new world. They located first at Halifax, Nova Scotia, where they remained for eighteen months and then went to Maine, settling in the town of Gardner on the Kennebec river, where they passed seven years. On the expiration of that period they removed to Madison, Indiana, but six months later came to Iowa, arriving at Keokuk on the 1st of April, 1855. Mr. Finerty accompanied his parents on these various removals. He acquired his education in the public schools of Maine and in the public and parochial schools of Keokuk and in 1858, when but fourteen years of age, he was apprenticed to learn the shoemaker's trade, at which he worked for a number of years. In 1869, however, he went to San Francisco by way of New York city, the Isthmus and up the Pacific. It was a delightful trip and he was in California at the time the completion of the Union Pacific Railroad was celebrated. He worked in San Francisco for about eight months as a cutter in a shoe store and then returned over the newly completed railroad. At that time he resumed work as a shoemaker in Keokuk, but again his labor in that direction was interrupted for in 1864, when twenty years of age, he responded to the call of his adopted country and enlisted at Keokuk as a member of Company C, Forty-fifth Iowa Infantry, under command of Capt. C. K. Peck and Col. A. H. Berryman. He was too young to enlist at the outbreak of the war, but after he joined the army he displayed his unfaltering loyalty to the government and the cause which he espoused. The regiment was attached to the Western Army, forming a part of the Sixteenth Army Corps commanded by General Washburn, and was largely engaged in guard duty, holding forts and defending garrisons. It was for this purpose that the regiment was organized, it being intended that the Forty-fifth Iowa should take the place, in the garrisons, of the soldiers who went into battle. Mr. Finerty was in Gayosha House Hospital, at Memphis, Tennessee, for two weeks with typhoid fever contracted while in the swamp districts of Tennessee. He was then sent home by reason of the expiration of his term of enlistment. As a boy he had served in militia companies in Keokuk, during the turmoil on the Missouri border, these companies being ordered to stop any threatened invasion.

Resuming his work at the shoemaker's trade, Mr. Finerty was thus engaged until 1876, when he entered the employ of the Constitution Democrat as superintendent of the city circulation, acting in that capacity for four years. He then began clerking in a dry goods store for John Zerr, now of Fort Madison, with whom he continued for four years and on the expiration of that period he entered the employ of Brinkman & Company, dealers in dry goods. He was made manager of the dry goods department, continued in the establishment for about twenty years and during much of the time was a partner. When this business was closed out Mr. Finerty spent six months with the Central Dry Goods Company and then on account of failing health rested from further business labors for six months. In April, 1900, however, he established his grocery and notion store at 316 South Tenth street and has since carried on business. Here he has built up a good trade, having constantly enlarged his stock to meet the growing demands of his business. His long and practical experience in connection with mercantile interests had well qualified him to conduct an enterprise of this character and he is now meeting with very gratifying success. For two years Mr. Finerty has also been deputy oil inspector through appointment of Governor Cummins. He was selected from out of ten applicants and he tests all the refined oil that is shipped to Keokuk, Fort Madison and Farmington. He tests by the car tank, visiting the different points regularly.

His principal business is with the Standard Oil Company, of Keokuk.

On the 2d of May, 1873, in Keokuk, Mr. Finerty was married by the Rev. Father Travis to Mary R. Flood, who was born in Haverstraw, New York, August 4, 1853. She is of Irish descent, was reared in Keokuk and pursued her education here, attending the common schools and afterward St. Vincent's Academy. Unto Mr. and Mrs. Finerty have been born four children who are yet living: Mary Josephine, who was born March 7, 1876, and is now employed as a bookkeeper; Alice Julia, who was born August 4, 1882, and assists her father in the store; Arthur Logan, born April 30, 1892, and Leon Patrick, born February 28, 1895. They also lost two children: Henry Francis, who was born April 10, 1874, and died October 20, 1878, and Clara Belle, born July 26, 1884, and died February 2, 1887.

In his political views Mr. Finerty is a Republican. He belongs to the Catholic church, and is fraternally a member of the National Union, an insurance order. During the past two years he has been a member of the Soldiers' Aid Commission, a county office secured by appointment of the county board. In 1903 this commission disbursed $1,740 in this locality among soldiers who were ill or deserving, widows and orphans. This amount was secured from a fund raised by special taxation of four mills. The commission consists of three members and Mr. Finerty is now president of the board. He belongs to the Grand Army of the Republic, in which he has served as commander. In his business career and in his public and private life there are many elements worthy of commendation and emulation. With no family or pecuniary advantages to aid him when he started out in life, he has progressed through his own efforts and his utilization of circumstances and possibilities. He has long figured as a representative of commercial interests in Keokuk and is known for his straightforward dealing in business and his reliability in discharging every public trust reposed in him. He has a wide and favorable acquaintance in Keokuk and throughout the county and many friends esteem him for his genuine worth.

BENJAMIN FRANKLIN HAGERMAN.

Benjamin Franklin Hagerman was born September 18, 1823, at Cool Springs, near Aldie, Loudoun county, Virginia. His father, Capt. Benjamin Hagerman, was a prominent man, and occupied a high rank in the Masonic order. The subject of this sketch came with his widowed mother and his sister to Missouri in 1833, settling first in Lewis and afterward in Clark county, and it was in the latter county that he was married, in 1848, to Miss Ann Staunton Cowgill, a daughter of Missouri pioneers who had removed thither from Kentucky. The legendary history of the Hagerman family relates that three brothers of the name emigrated from Holland and settled in New Jersey, whence one brother, and later another, removed to Virginia.

Mr. Hagerman came to Keokuk in 1864,

and here passed the remainder of a life rich in good deeds—a career whose reward was the enviable reputation that crowns a beautiful character. His death occurred February 6, 1900. The death of his wife preceded his own, the date of her demise being August 19, 1897. Husband and wife were interred in Oakland cemetery, Keokuk.

In his early days in Missouri Mr. Hagerman passed through all the hardships and vicissitudes of pioneer life, and was in turn farmer, school teacher, merchant, real estate and collecting agent and a large land-holder. He was a man of powerful mind and overwhelming force of character—self-reliant, honest, brave, truthful, frank and unselfish, a true man, a majestic personality; to his family, kindred and friends, loving and devoted. Upon his children he bestowed those advantages which he himself was not privileged to enjoy. Three sons and one daughter survive him. Of these, James, who was educated at Christian Brothers' College, is a resident of St. Louis. He is a member of the legal profession, and although a young man, is one of the leading lawyers of the West. He is president of the National Bar Association and general counsel for the Missouri, Kansas & Texas Railway Company. Frank Hagerman, of Kansas City, Missouri, the second son, is also eminent in the profession of law, and is adding to the glory of the family name. He is universally conceded to be one of the most brilliant lawyers ever produced west of the Alleghanies. George C. is a resident of Hot Springs, Arkansas, and Miss Linnie Hagerman, the daughter of this accomplished and distinguished family, makes her home in one of the most desirable and pleasant localities of Keokuk. She was educated at Visitation Convent, St. Louis, and is a woman of literary tastes and accomplishments.

In politics Mr. Hagerman was a lifelong Democrat, ever devoted to his party, its principles and its chosen leaders. He was one of the best-known citizens of Keokuk. He enjoyed the friendship and confidence of a large number of eminent men throughout the West, especially in Missouri and southern Iowa. The circle of his acquaintance was wide, and co-extensive therewith was the circle of those that honored him for what he was and no more.

D. NELSON COON, M. D.

The name of Dr. D. Nelson Coon is enduringly inscribed on the pages of Lee county's history, for he located in this county at an early date, and has continued one of its most honored and valued residents until the present time. His life has been devoted to labors wherein wealth and influence are of little avail, the measure of success depending upon mentality, ability—both natural and acquired—and the broad culture of the individual. Possessing all the requisite qualities of a physician, Dr. Coon advanced during his active career to a prominent place among the representatives of the medical fraternity in Lee county.

A native of New York, he was born in Chenango county on March 24, 1841. His

D. NELSON COON, M. D.

preliminary education was obtained at the academy at De Ruyter, New York, a Seventh Day Baptist institution. On leaving the academy he resolved to take up the study of medicine, and pursued courses of reading with various practitioners in the Empire state, as well as for a time in Wisconsin, whither his parents had removed. During the years 1860 and 1861 he attended the College of Physicians and Surgeons, in New York city, and in 1863 passed the examination of the United States Medical Board, at Washington, and was appointed hospital steward and acting assistant surgeon at Lincoln Hospital, of Washington, which position he held until the assassination of President Lincoln. He was then sent to Hart Island, in New York harbor, and continued in the government service there until discharged in August, 1865. After some time spent at his home in Syracuse, New York, he removed, in 1866, to Green Bay, Wisconsin, and there established himself in the practice of medicine, continuing at that place for about two years. At the expiration of that period he came to Iowa, locating at Olin(then called Rome), and after a short stay there, and two years of residence at Carmen, Illinois, he removed, in 1875, to Fort Madison. The following year he began the practice of medicine in this city, devoting himself to general practice, in which he was eminently successful. By his ability and by his constant fidelity to the welfare of those who depended in times of need upon his knowledge and skill, he secured a great patronage, his services being in demand throughout a territory having a radius of fifteen to twenty miles in all directions from Fort Madison. This work he continued until 1902, when, on account of failing health, he brought his active career to a close, and is now leading a retired life at his pleasant home in this city.

Dr. Coon was married in 1878 to Miss Josephine Sprague, of Des Moines county, Iowa, who died July 19, 1897, leaving two children: Harry, who was born in 1879, and is a professional musician, residing at Milwaukee, Wisconsin, and Esther, who is living with her father. He wedded on September 12, 1899, as his second wife, Mrs. Emma Krehbiel, who was born at West Point, Lee county, the daughter of George Linhard, one of the early settlers of that place, now deceased. His death occurred five years ago, in his seventy-fifth year. He was a prominent and very prosperous farmer. Mrs. Coon, at the time of her second marriage, was the widow of Christian W. Krehbiel, and had one child, Elsie. Her mother, who has for the last seventeen years been an invalid, is still liviing, and resides at 1401 Sixth street, Fort Madison. Mr. and Mrs. Linhard have always been members of the German Lutheran church.

Dr. Coon is the son of Abram and Esther (McCall) Coon. His father, who was a farmer, was born in the State of New York in 1804, and there remained until 1857, whence he removed to Fond du Lac, Wisconsin. He continued farming near that place until the time of his death, which occurred in his eightieth year. The mother of our subject survived her husband, and died January 1, 1903, age ninety-three years. Both are interred at Fond du Lac.

Dr. Coon is a member of the Christian

church, and in his political affiliations has always acted with the Republican party. At one time he permitted the use of his name as a candidate for the legislature, but suffered defeat in common with the remainder of his ticket. For ten years he served the City of Fort Madison as city physician. He is a member and has held all the offices of James B. Sample Post, Grand Army of the Republic, of Fort Madison, and in his fraternal relations he is similarly connected with the Benevolent and Protective Order of Elks. He is also an honorary member of Lee County Medical Association.

Dr. Coon early qualified himself thoroughly for the work of his profession, realizing the great responsibility which devolves upon a physician. Moreover, he possesses a sympathetic, kindly nature that has prompted him to put forth every effort in his power to aid his fellowmen. All his strong traits of character are such as commend him to the confidence and good will of the public, and he enjoys the warmest regard of all with whom he has associated.

HENRY WENDE.

Henry Wende, who was for many years connected with the business interests of Keokuk, was born November 15, 1833, in Germany, and there acquired his early education, attending school until his thirteenth year. Arrived at that age he formed the resolution, remarkable in one of such tender years, to emigrate to America and make his own way in the new world without aid or encouragement from family or friends. Accordingly he set out alone, taking passage in a sailing vessel, and after a voyage of eight weeks' duration arrived in New Orleans, whence he proceeded to the City of St. Louis and began working at the trades of cabinetmaking and carpentering, continuing there until 1849, when he removed to Quincy, Illinois. There he took up and pursued the trade of wagonmaking for a few years, but desiring to secure a more desirable location, he again removed, in 1854, this time to Keokuk, Lee county, Iowa.

In Keokuk Mr. Wende established a wagon shop at Thirteenth and Main streets, where he continued in business for a period of twenty years, being very successful and by his workmanlike skill, his integrity, uprightness and straightforward methods in all his dealings attracting a large and profitable patronage. As one of the pioneer wagonmakers of the West, he occupied a very prominent position, was well known throughout a wide extent of territory, made many friends and contributed in a very important degree to the development and more rapid upbuilding of the country in which he made his home. For a portion of this period he was associated in partnership with Jacob and Charles Frank, the firm being known as Wende & Frank, and for two years engaged with his partners in the manufacture of plows, conducting quite an extensive enterprise and sometimes employing as many as ten workmen simultaneously. Mr. Wende has been identified with many significant movements in the history of the West since an early day, and recalls that his manufacturing enterprise in Keokuk received a substantial impetus from the discovery of gold in California and the resulting emigration to that place. He built many of the famous "prairie schooners" in which the argonauts of '49 crossed the continent of North America to pluck wealth and untold treasure from the mountains and streams along the golden shores of the Pacific ocean. For one man he built a train of twelve wagons, using extra heavy construction on account of the length and difficulty of the journey.

In 1882 he disposed of his shop and acquired his present farm of forty acres on section 21, Jackson township, where he has since continued to reside, conducting general farming operations and working at his trade in a small way, building a few wagons and doing a great deal of repair work, being still in the full enjoyment of all his faculties and remarkably vigorous and active for one of his years. Mr. Wende was married at Quincy, Illinois, in 1854, to Miss Amelia Lang, who was also of German birth, and to them were born seven daughters who still survive. They are: Katherine, wife of Henry Peters; Mollie, widow of Leonard Siebold, of Keokuk; Minnie, wife of George S. Merriam, of Keokuk; Etta; Cora, who has been for five years a teacher in the public schools of Keokuk; Emma, who is acting as clerk in a store at Keokuk, and Elizabeth, who married O. F. Peterson, of Keokuk, Iowa. Three sons and one daughter are deceased, and the mother of the family passed to her eternal rest on the 1st of April, 1895, and is buried in Oakland cemetery. She preserved throughout her life the quiet beauty of a true Christian character, and left many friends who deplore her loss.

Mr. Wende was formerly an active member of the German Lutheran church of Keokuk, and assisted in the actual work of constructing the present church building, being at the time of its erection one of the four trustees of the church and at present the only one of the four living. He has always been interested in public affairs, and believing it to be the duty of the private citizens to bear a share in the work of government, he has made a study of political questions, and in matters of public polity has acted with the Democratic party. While never aspiring to political office, he has shown a willingness to accept the responsibilities of public trusts, and since removing to Jackson township has acted as school director at the solicitation of friends. His life has been one long exposition of business and personal rectitude in its highest forms, and furnishes an excellent chapter of proof that the practice of these virtues is no bar to the achievement of success in the best sense of the term. A self-made man, he has worked his way from humble beginnings to a position of honor in the community, and enjoys the respect of many friends, who value him for the strength and sincerity of his character.

ST. JOSEPH'S CATHOLIC CHURCH.

The history of the Catholic church in Fort Madison runs far back into the midst of the years, and begins with ancient and honored names. Here came Father Marquette in 1673. On the 17th day of June, of that year, his eyes first rested on the waters of the Mississippi river, at the mouth of the Wisconsin river. Floating down the stream on the 25th day of the same month he reached what is now Lee county, Iowa, and here he spent six days. He was followed by Father Hennepin in 1680. No doubt there were others, ardent and impulsive spirits, consecrated to the church and devoted to the cross, to penetrate the wilderness, and proclaim the victorious Christ. History is silent, however, as to their names and deeds, and it was until Father Mazzuchelli said mass in Fort Madison in 1839 that the story of the Catholic church in that city may be said to really begin. The same year mass was celebrated by Father Broedwegge.

The first resident priest in Fort Madison was Father J. G. Allemann, who came here in 1840. At that time he was the only priest within a hundred miles and his work was to gather into the fold the various Catholic families scattered through a wide range. Wherever the number would warrant he established churches and schools. He was a generous and kind-hearted man, and would divide his last farthing with any one who would ask assistance. He built a small brick church, sixteen feet square, on the property where now stands the spacious and attractive edifice occupied by St. Joseph's congregation. He built again in 1844, this time the church being 30x50 feet. To this structure Father Hattenberger made an extensive addition in 1854. In 1886 the present church building was erected under the pastorate of Father Louis DeCailly, a native of France, and the pastor of the congregation from 1884 to 1898, when he was killed in a railroad accident. He left behind him inspiring memories as a man greatly devoted to his sacred calling. Under his administration the present structure was erected, and it is expected that it will shortly be greatly enlarged and beautified.

The following priests have officiated in St. Joseph's church: Fathers Allemann, Hattenberger, Michael, Weikmann, Orth, Gane, Greiser, DeCailly and Father Zaiser, who is now its rector.

The parish has from its beginning maintained a school, which is now under the management of the Sisters of Humility, of Ottumwa, Iowa. Five Sisters act as teachers of the various grades. The school has always been highly regarded by the public, and during its more than sixty years of history has had an extended patronage.

Associated with St. Joseph's church are some of the most prominent families of Fort Madison, and it is noted for its liberality in all good works and beneficial undertakings.

THE REV. FATHER ARTHUR J. ZAISER.

Father Arthur J. Zaiser, pastor of St. Joseph's church in Fort Madison, Iowa, is a worthy successor of those consecrated and devoted clergymen who have given their lives to the cause of Christ as exemplified in the work of this noble church. The priesthood is a great calling, and its interests were never more transcendant than at the present time when socialism, atheism and materialism are making for the ravage of society. The Catholic priest occupies an especially onerous and responsible position. As a faithful shepherd, he must guard his people not only against the wiles of evil habits, protect them against the insidious temptations of luxury and selfish ease, and point them to the better life it is possible for them to live, but expose to them also the dangers of modern intellectual conceit and skepticism which mock at religion and decry all authority. He is a sentinel upon the outer wall, and his vigilant eye must sweep every point of danger. In this vast work, so pressing upon the modern priest, Father Zaiser is by no means incompetent or unready. In his own pulpit he is heard with reverent affection, and in the city he is a leader in every good work and noble enterprise. Father Zaiser was born near Quincy, Illinois, January 25, 1862, a son of John and Margaret (Funk) Zaiser, who are now residents of Burlington, Iowa. To that city the subject of this sketch was taken by his parents when he was only five years of age, and here he received his first instruction in a private Methodist institution, which he attended from the age of seven years until he was ten. At that age he entered the Burlington public school, graduating from the high school of the city when he was sixteen. For three years following he was a student in the Wesleyan University at Mt. Pleasant, Iowa, after which he taught instrumental music for a year or more. This was in 1880 and 1881. For another year he was employed in a bank at Burlington, Iowa. After this, he was moved by great considerations, and seeking the Catholic priesthood as a life profession, he entered the Jesuit College at Prairie du Chien, Wisconsin, where he spent four years in the study of the classics. Another year was spent in the Jesuit College, Buffalo, New York, where he devoted himself to the study of philosophy. Three years were spent by him at St. Francis Theological Seminary, a noted institution of the church at Milwaukee, and there he made a special study of theology in its various divisions. There he was admitted to the priesthood, being ordained by the Most Reverend Archbishop Katzer, now of saintly memory, and assigned to the teaching of language and mathematics in St. Ambrose College, Davenport, Iowa. There he remained three years, and was then assigned to a new work at Exira, Iowa, there being called upon to establish a parish from the very beginning. In this work he was quite successful and gathering a new congregation, erected a handsome church and school and drawing to the new parish the friendly attention of the community in a marked degree. In 1898, when a pastor was needed at Fort Madison, to succeed the lamented Father DeCailly, his zeal and devotion marked him as a fit man to take up this work. He was accordingly called to Fort Madison, and the work put into his hands. It is no flattery to say that from the first his success has been pronounced and immediate. As a preacher his sermons are simple and clear, enunciating the great central truths of the church: and as a pastor and administrator of all the varied interests of the parish his work is beyond criticism. In the city at large he is regarded as a public-spirited citizen, who may be depended upon to help every good cause. He was largely instrumental in the establishment of St. Elizabeth's Hospital, one of the humane enterprises of the church, which has done much good and was opened September, 1901, being under the auspices of the Franciscan Sisters. The hospital is located at the corner of Third street and Broadway, and is very efficient in its work. Father Zaiser is a pleasant and courteous gentleman, after the manner of his profession and well sustains the dignity of his sacred calling.

THOMAS H. JOHNSON.

One of the more distinguished members of the bar in southern Iowa, widely known by reason of professional standing and long public service, is the subject of this review, who is at the present time county attorney of Lee county. Mr. Johnson was born at Bonaparte, Iowa, March 29, 1858, the son of William J. and Mary J. (Christy) Johnson. His parents were natives of Ohio, and in Bonaparte his father was for a time a miller and merchant, but is now engaged in banking, in association with one of his sons, J. A. Johnson. They conduct the Farmers' and Traders' State Bank of Iowa. The mother died in 1899.

Mr. Johnson is one of a family of four brothers and four sisters, as follows: James J., who died at the age of eighteen years; Mrs. Nannie B. Warde, of Chicago; Mrs. Clara J. Smith, of Keosauqua, Iowa; Mrs. Maggie Meek, of Denver; Miss Ella M., who died at the age of thirty-four; Thomas J., our subject; Joseph A., of Bonaparte, Iowa, bank cashier, and George B., of Fort Worth, Texas, for twenty-one years train dispatcher for the Missouri, Kansas & Texas Railway Company.

In 1873, at the early age of fifteen years, Mr. Johnson was graduated from Howe's Academy, at Bonaparte, and in further preparation for a life of useful activity immediately began a special academic course of two years' study in Iowa State University, at Iowa City. His university course completed, he returned to Bonaparte in 1875, and engaged, together with his brother-in-law, George F. Smith, in the publication of the Van Buren Democrat, continuing in this work for nine years. He began with the duties of an apprentice in the mechanical department, familiarizing himself with the business in all its details, and at the time of severing his connection with the paper had attained to the position of manager.

While engaged in newspaper work at Bonaparte he continued his studies, reading law with the law firm of Knapp, Lea & Beaman, of Keosauqua, and in 1882 was admitted to the bar. In 1885 he removed to West Point, Lee county, where he established himself in the practice of law, also assisting for a time in the publication of the West Point Appeal. His residence in

Fort Madison dates from 1890, when he removed from West Point to this city. Here success and honors have been his to enjoy. For six years he was city attorney for the municipality of Fort Madison, for a similar period he acted as assistant county attorney, and he has served Lee county four years as county attorney. The city also claimed his services for six years as a member of the board of education.

In politics Mr. Johnson is a thorough-going Democrat, and in every political contest that has arisen within the borders of Lee county for the last fifteen years, or during the whole time of his residence here, he has never failed to advocate the principles of the party from the stump, and to hold up the hands of her chosen leaders. A natural orator and a profound student, his services along this line are always in demand. And in the more obscure but no less useful work of the caucus and the convention his aid and counsel are valuable. He has served as alternate delegate to the national Democratic convention, and has many times acted as delegate to the state and congressional conventions, often serving as chairman of the latter. Twice he has presided over the county convention, and for the last seven years has been central committeeman for the Third ward. In the Democratic state convention of 1903 he was a member of the committee on resolutions. His interest in politics is eminently practical, while at the same time directed toward the attainment of higher ideals of government.

Mr. Johnson is a member of the First Presbyterian church, and fraternally he is connected with the Benevolent and Protective Order of Elks, of which he has held the chair two terms; the Ancient Order of United Workmen, holding in this order the rank of Past Master Workman, and the Loyal Americans.

On his twenty-fourth birthday, March 29, 1882, Mr. Johnson was united in marriage with Miss Beatrice E. Strickling, of Keosauqua, Iowa. She is the daughter of the late Judge Henry Strickling, for two terms county judge of Van Buren county, prominent in the Masonic order, and highly esteemed as a judge, as a physician and as a man. He died in 1902. The mother, who was Sarah A. (Kinkead) Strickling, died in 1877, and rests in the Keosauqua cemetery. Both were members of the Methodist Episcopal church. The date of Mrs. Johnson's birth is January 11, 1858.

Unto Mr. and Mrs. Johnson have been born two children, a son and a daughter. Daisy M., born October 22, 1883, is acting as stenographer in her father's law offices, and William Harry, born March 12, 1885, is city editor of the Gem City, of Fort Madison. Both are graduates of Fort Madison high school.

If it is true, as it probably is, that success in the learned professions depends solely upon talent and individual merit, Thomas H. Johnson has demonstrated that he is the possessor of natural gifts of a high order, and a genial disposition and pleasing manner, combined with the elemental strength of his character have made for him many friends and admirers in Lee county, as well as in the larger fields of action in which he is known.

Mr. Johnson passed away some time after this sketch was written, September 25, 1904, and was buried at Bonaparte, Iowa.

EUGENE LA BARRON MATTESON.

Peace of mind and a contented spirit belong to the farm. Close to the heart of nature may be found true wisdom, and in the tillage of the fields may be nurtured the noblest philosophy of life. Under the shadow of the great trees with the blue skies above, and the waving grain before the eye, there is little room for envy and bitterness. The country life is good for the largeness of the soul and helps men cultivate and strengthen the things that belong to God and immortality and the free soul. More and more does it become evident that the men of this generation who keep close to the soil are wise. They escape the heart worry and the nerve exhaustion the strenuous and utter abandon to business cares and interests that so strongly characterize the present life; and while no less earnestly laboring in their appointed fields of work, do so in that steadiness and patience that make men strong and mighty in their day.

Eugene La Barron Matteson, whose name introduces this article, is a good illustration of the wise farmer and the upright citizen, who prefers the airs of nature and the fragrant odors of the meadow to the turmoil and commotions of the city pavement. He is an honorable and successful farmer, and is widely regarded as a good citizen and a man of unimpeachable character.

Mr. Matteson, whose pleasant and spacious residence is on his farm in section 4, Green Bay township, Lee county, was born at Central Falls, Rhode Island, July 3, 1847, a son of Isaac A. and Joan (Gage) Matteson. The father is known as one of the early settlers of Lee county, coming into this part of Iowa as early as 1854, when he secured a fine farm of 240 acres in section 4, of Green Bay township. He was born in East Greenwich, Rhode Island, April 14, 1819, and was a son of Greene and Sallie (Fowler) Matteson, both natives of Rhode Island, where they spent their entire lives. They were the parents of a family of eleven children, of whom Isaac A. was the fourth in order of birth. When he was a boy he became an employe of the cotton and woolen mills in his native town, and there continued at work until he reached the age of twenty-six years. His tastes were for a more open and out-of-door life, and he became a carpenter and machinist, in which occupation he rose to positions of trust and responsibility, soon attaining place as a foreman in railroad bridge construction. In this work he continued until 1851, when he removed to the West. While constructing two or three bridges he spent a year in Chicago, then giving but little promise of its future greatness. The following year Mr. Matteson went on to Kankakee, where he constructed a railroad bridge. Returning to Chicago, where he stayed until 1854, when he came into Lee county, where he bought his farm and on which he spent his remaining years, with the exception of a period of three years, when he was a resident of Fort Madison. When he made his first purchase of land he contracted for 240 acres, but part of this he later sold.

Isaac A. Matteson was married in Southfield, Rhode Island, May 20, 1840, to Miss Joan Gage, a daughter of Benjamin and Isabella (Randall) Gage, natives of Massachusetts and Rhode Island, respectively. She was born in Cranston, October 22, 1818, and was the mother of one child, Eugene La Barron. Mr. Matteson was appointed a member of the county board of supervisors in 1883, and was re-elected for three successive terms. He filled the office of justice of the peace for many years, and was called upon from time to time to fill other minor positions. In politics he was a Democrat, and enjoyed more than a local reputation as an upright citizen. His death occurred February 9, 1899, his wife having passed to her rest October 11, 1887.

Eugene La Barron Matteson was educated in the public schools, and in a commercial school at Fort Madison, which he attended one winter. He remained at home until 1880. That year he went to Colorado, where he found a profitable business in the gold and silver mines. For three years he remained in that state, and then returned to his Iowa home, having met with very fair success in his western ventures.

Mr. Matteson was married in 1867 to Miss Eliza Speaks, a daughter of Thomas and Sarah (Haynes) Speaks. Mrs. Speaks is still living, and has her home with her daughter, Mrs. Matteson. She has reached the age of ninety-four years, and is a bright and well-preserved old lady. To Mr. and Mrs. Matteson have been born two children: Joan, who married Frank Carr[illegible]eth, and has her home in Denmark township, and Arion, who married Miss Nettie Osborn, and still has his home with his father.

Mr. Matteson is much interested in stockfarming. In this line he has done a large business, and is known far and wide as a reliable and trusty dealer. Politically he is a Democrat, and is an intelligent and thoughtful student of the times, preferring, however, to follow the peaceful avocation of agriculture to the turmoil and disturbance of active political cares and ambitions. The farm to him is a field large enough for all noble aspirations, and he has lived in the enjoyment of the full privileges of the modern agriculturist, studious, public spirited and industrious. He is wide-awake and enterprising, ready for business at any time, and keeping his hands clean and clear of taint in all transactions.

WILLIAM OLDENBURG.

William Oldenburg was a resident of Keokuk the greater part of his long life, was well known to the majority of her people, and was closely associated with many of the men who played the most important parts in her history. He was born at St. Louis, October 22, 1832, of a family belonging to the religious body known as Pennsylvania Quakers, although his father was a native of Oldenburg, Germany. Mr. Oldenburg, the subject of our sketch, removed to Keokuk with his parents on April 1, 1841, five years before the admission of the territory to the Union as the State of Iowa, and received his education in the public schools, was the schoolmate of George E. Kilbourne, Frank McGavic and many others whose names were in after years linked with the development of the city and county. Being very ambitious, he began at the early age of fourteen years to fit himself for his work in life, and took up the profession of steamboat engineering, a field of endeavor which in that pioneer community was very well calculated to appeal to the adventurous and enterprising instincts of aspiring youth, and which offered pecuniary rewards of tempting proportions.

Mr. Oldenburg progressed rapidly in acquiring knowledge and skill in his chosen work, which he continued to follow for a great many years, and had a vast and varied experience, being employed on most of the principal boats plying on the Mississippi river, working below St. Louis in the winter season and on the upper course of the river in the summer. During the Civil War he was often engaged in transporting United States troops, and in many other ways was connected with important and interesting events and movements in the history of the West and the nation. For a period of four or five years subsequent to 1877 he was half owner of the steamer "Plowboy," which plied between Keokuk and Warsaw, making three trips daily, and in this enterprise he had very gratifying success, and added very considerably to the small fortune which he had amassed by his previous efforts. Indeed, he proved himself in all he undertook to be the possessor of sound business judgment and foresight, and also exhibited qualities of absolute faithfulness and rectitude in all positions which he was called upon to occupy. For sixteen years he was in the employ of the national government, and these qualities gained for him the praise and regard of his official superiors, as they gained for him the trust and admiration of all who came into contact with his personality in the various relations of life. His later years were spent in retirement from active business, and during this time he resided in Keokuk, where he enjoyed the comforts of his pleasant home and the society of his many warm friends. Here he owned residence property, but contracted no new business relations. A year before his death he had the misfortune to be overcome by heat, from the effects of which he never recovered, and he died September 17, 1902, his mortal remains being laid at rest in Oakland cemetery.

Mr. Oldenburg never neglected the duties of citizenship, and while he did not consider it within his proper province to seek public office, he was a consistent member of the Democratic party, and gave to that organization his unfailing support in all matters of importance. He was also a believer in fraternal societies, and was enthusiastically devoted to the work of Oddfellowship, being for thirty-five years a member of Puckechetuck Lodge of Independent Order of Odd Fellows. He was twice married, first at Middleton, Missouri, in 1856, to Miss Sarah Jane Hogue, who died in 1870, leaving three daughters, Mrs. Leola A. Lucas, of Whitewater, Colorado; Mrs. Mollie F. McGrew, of Denver, Illinois, and Mrs. Willie Cornelia Shoel, of Keokuk. In 1875 he wedded at Monterey, Kentucky, Miss Sarah Isabella Sparks, who survives him, and continues to reside at the family home overlooking the Mississippi river, at No. 102 Concert street, Keokuk. Mrs. Oldenburg is a daughter of Ivison Sparks, who was born in Owen county, Kentucky, and died there at the age of fifty-seven years, and his wife, Mary (Calvert) Sparks, whose death occurred in Owen county in the thirty-third year of her age. She came west when only eight years old, making her home with her brother in-law, E. Hardin, and pursuing her education in the public schools, but returned to Owen county, Kentucky, in 1868, and there remained until her marriage, which was celebrated at her brother's residence, the old home of the family. She then came with her husband to Keokuk, where she has since resided, and here she has witnessed many of the improvements which have made the city what it is at the present time, it even having been her good fortune to see the first railroad train cross the Mississippi river at this point—an event of historical significance. She has also borne a prominent part in social affairs in Keokuk, and is a member of Colfax Lodge, No. 4, Daughters of Rebekah, in which she has occupied all the positions of honor, and has also attended meetings of the Grand Lodge at Burlington and at Keokuk. A pleasant lady of gracious presence and unusual ability, her friends in Keokuk are many.

WILLIAM H. NEWLON, M. D.

Dr. William H. Newlon, a man of rare capacity, whose intense and well-directed activity and strong intellectual force have made him one of the ablest representatives of the medical fraternity in Fort Madison and Lee county, was reared in [illegible] fostered any natural predilection [illegible] ited tendency which he may have had in the practice. His father, Dr. Benjamin Franklin Newlon figured for many y[illegible] one of the prominent early physicians of Illinois and not only along professional lines, but also in many other ways [illegible] a active and helpful factor [illegible] community interests. He was born in Louisville, Kentucky, July 27, 1833, and during his infancy his parents removed to Edgar county, Illinois, establishing their home near Paris where he was reared. His literary education was completed by study in the Edgar County Academy, [illegible] began preparation for the practice of medicine in P[illegible] Illinois, with Dr. Shubal York [illegible] his preceptor. He was one of the few graduate physicians of the West at an early day, and after completing his training he located [illegible] practice in Hancock county, Illinois [illegible] in 1845. About two years later [illegible] 1847 he settled at Dallas City and [illegible] one of the founders [illegible]. He entered into partnership with [illegible] brother, Dr. John F. Newlon, and the business relation between them was continued for five years, after which Dr. B. F. Newlon was alone in business. He was one of the most capable and therefore one of the most successful of the pioneer physicians of western Illinois, and he enjoyed a very large and important practice until 1862, when his health failed him and he temporarily put aside the arduous duties of the profession. On recovering his health he entered into a partnership with the younger brother, Dr. William S. Newlon, which was maintained for five years.

Dr. Benjamin F. Newlon was a moving spirit in many of the enterprises which led to the substantial improvement and upbuilding of Dallas City. He was present when the town was surveyed and laid out, and he wrote the charter of the city, and in connection with Colonel Rolloson, in 1859, went to Springfield, in order to secure its passage through the legislature, which mission he successfully accomplished. He also prepared the ordinance of the city when it was first chartered; was chosen its first mayor, serving for two years, and for five terms was supervisor. His political support was given the Democracy, and he labored earnestly for the advancement of the party's growth. As a Mason he also won more than local distinction. He was the founder of Dallas City Lodge, No. 235, Free and Accepted Masons, and its first Worthy Master, occupying that position for many years. He was also a charter member of Dallas Chapter, No. 111, Royal Arch Masons; was its High Priest and was District Deputy Grand Master, and a representative to both the Grand Lodge and the Grand Chapter. He had comprehensive and accurate knowledge of Masonry, its teachings and its tenets, and did much to inculcate its beneficent spirit among his fellow townsmen. At one time he edited the Dallas City Democrat, and was a frequent correspondent for publications of the country, his articles appearing under the non de plume of Don Osso, being greatly appreciated by the reading public. He held membership in the Universalist church, and thus his activities touched almost every line affecting the general interests of society in his part of the state. He yet managed his professional and business interest most successfully and accumulated a large amount of property, although at a later date he met with financial reverses.

Dr. Newlon was married three times, first to Mary Walker, of Dallas City, who died within a year; afterward to Almira A. Richards, who at her death, left three daughters and a son; and third, to Mrs. Katherine McCarty, daughter of James Gassaway, of Dallas City, by whom he had a son and daughter. His living children are: Hattie, now the widow of Dr. W. V. English and a teacher in the schools of Keokuk; Melissa, wife of C. Lee, of Berkeley, California; William H.; Benjamin F., a physician of Leger, Oklahoma, and Katherine, wife of R. C. Barnett, of Kansas City. Dr. Newlon died March 2, 1882, and was survived by his widow for two years. The mother of our subject was a Methodist.

Dr. William H. Newlon, who was born in Hancock county, Illinois, November 10, 1862, began his education in the public schools of Dallas City, and supplemented his preliminary advantages by study in the Dallas Academy. Interested in the practice of medicine from early boyhood because of his father's connection with the profession he pursued his early professional studies under the direction of his father, but his course in medicine was not continuous, owing to his financial circumstances, which made it necessary that he provide the means for continuing his education. After leaving school he engaged in clerking for a time and with his earnings defrayed his college expenses, for in the meantime his father had met with business reverses, and the son was forced to start out in life without financial assistance. Matriculating in the College of Physicians and Surgeons, of Keokuk, Iowa, Dr. Newlon was graduated with the class of 1890, and soon located for practice in Fort Madison, Iowa, where he soon secured a good patronage and his business has since been increasing in volume and importance. He is also registered to practice in several states in addition to Iowa, including Illinois, Missouri, Kansas and Oklahoma. He belongs to the Lee County Medical Society, the Missouri Valley Medical Association, the Tri-State Medical Society, the Atchison, Topeka & Santa Fe Medical and Surgical Society, and is local surgeon for the Atchison, Topeka & Santa Fe Railroad Company, and surgeon in charge of its dispensary. He is also examiner for a large number of the most reliable old-line insurance companies. His office is a very fine suite of rooms, Nos. 12, 13, 14 and 15, in the Lee County Savings Bank Building, and in addition to this the Doctor has large property interests in Fort Madison, including a beautiful residence at the corner of Market and Third streets.

On the 13th of March, 1895, Dr. Newlon was married to Miss Mary Hogeboom, of Topeka, Kansas, a daughter of Dr. George W. and Sophia (Buckmaster) Hogeboom. Her father was born in Northampton, Fulton county, New York, in 1832, and in early youth his educational privilege was limited to three months' attendance annually at the common schools. At the age of thirteen he entered Kingsboro Academy, where he prepared for college, and then engaged in teaching in order to meet the expenses of a course in the Berkshire Medical College, of Pittsfield, Massachusetts, from which he graduated in 1853, when twenty-one years of age. He became a practitioner at Gloversville, New York, where he remained until failing health compelled him to seek a change of climate, and in May, 1857, he removed to Leavenworth, Kansas, which place he called his home for eight years, but during five years of that time he served as assistant surgeon of the Eighth Kansas Infantry and surgeon of the Eleventh Kansas Regiment, in the Civil War. In 1863 he was commissioned by President Lincoln as staff surgeon, with the rank of major, and at the close of the war he was brevetted lieutenant-colonel for faithful and meritorious service.

Dr. Hogeboom removed to Oskaloosa, Jefferson county, Kansas, in 1866, and while engaged in practice there also figured prominently in public affairs affecting not only the community, but also having marked influence upon the welfare of the state. In 1869 he was chosen state senator by popular suffrage for a term of two years, and in 1878 was elected to the house of representatives. He then removed to Topeka, and until his retirement from professional life was accounted one of the most prominent and able physicians and surgeons of the capital city. In 1881 he was appointed chief surgeon of the Santa Fe Railroad, which position he ably filled until March 15, 1897, when he resigned. The present hospital service of the Santa Fe Railroad was organized by Dr. Hogeboom in 1882, and the company hospitals in Colorado and New Mexico were built the following year. The erection and equipment of the finest railroad hospital in the West is due to the efforts of Dr. Hogeboom, who early in his labor as chief surgeon of the Atchison, Topeka & Santa Fe Railroad, recognized the necessity for such an institution, where every medical and surgical attention could be paid to those who were wounded, crippled or sick while in the company's service. All plans for the railroad hospital at Topeka were made under his personal supervision, with the result that this model institution is a lasting monument to his extensive and lengthy service as chief surgeon of that railroad line.

Dr. Hogeboom was married on the 4th of May, 1861, to Sophia Buckmaster, the eldest daughter of Dr. Henry Buckmaster, a physician of much more than local reputation, and who was a member of the first house of representatives of the State of Kansas. He served through the War of the Rebellion as staff surgeon, with the rank of major, and he and Dr. Hogeboom were the only surgeons of United States Volunteers commissioned by President Lincoln from the State of Kansas. To Dr. and Mrs. Hogeboom were born four sons and three daughters, and his belief in education has been shown by the liberal opportunities he has provided his children. The three sons are graduates of the high school of Topeka and completed their studies in the University of Kansas. Denton is now a druggist and Henry B. and Roch W. are graduates of Rush Medical College, of Chicago, and have attained more than local repute as successful practitioners. The daughters—Kate, Mary and Helen—completed their educations in the College of the Sisters of Bethany, at Topeka, and the second daughter has become the wife of Dr. Newlon and the mother of one child, Helen, who was born June 4, 1898.

Dr. Newlon has attained high rank in Masonry, belonging to Dallas City Lodge, No. 235, Free and Accepted Masons; Dallas Chapter, No. 111, Royal Arch Masons; Delta Commandery, No. 51, Knights Templar, and Kaaba Temple of the Mystic Shrine, at Davenport, and also a member of Fort Madison Lodge, No. 374, Benevolent and Protective Order of Elks. Hardly yet in the prime of life, he is nevertheless recognized as one of the prominent men of the city, of a strong and forceful individuality, of laudable ambition and of earnest and conscientious purpose in his profession.

DAVID WHITE McELROY.

This is pre-eminently the age of industrial and commercial activity and the business conditions afford excellent possibilities for the achievement of success to the man of keen discernment and unfaltering energy.

It is also true that in the development and control of a prosperous business enterprise there must be close application and unfaltering purpose and the rewards of labor are sure. We are led to this train of reflection by examination into the life history of D. W. McElroy, who today stands at the head of one of the leading productive industries of Keokuk, and who has risen to a position of prominence in business circles through his own unaided efforts.

A native of Armstrong county, Pennsylvania, he was born on the 1st of March, 1842. His father, John McElroy, was a native of Belfast, Ireland, and throughout his entire life carried on merchandising. He was married in 1837, in Washington county, Pennsylvania, to Miss Julia Anna White, a native of that county, and in 1840 they removed to Armstrong county, where they resided for about twenty-nine years. In 1869 they became residents of Adams county, Illinois, where the father spent his remaining days, passing away in 1879, while his wife spent her last days with her sons in Keokuk, dying at the home of John A. McElroy, in 1892. Our subject has but one brother living, John A. McElroy, who was a soldier of the Civil War and is now with S. Hamill Company, of Keokuk.

D. W. McElroy was reared in the county of his nativity until seventeen years of age, and acquired his education under the direction of his father, attending school not more than six months. However, his father was a man of learning and he carefully directed the studies of his son, and Mr. McElroy was preparing to enter Washington and Jefferson College, of Pennsylvania, when his patriotic spirit was aroused and he enlisted in the United States Army from Kittanning, Pennsylvania, becoming a member of Company A, Seventy-eighth Pennsylvania Infantry under Capt. William Cummins, and Col. William Sirwell. He joined the army August 27, 1861, and served until November 3, 1864. The regiment was attached to the Fourteenth Army Corps and he participated in the engagements at Stone River, Chickamauga, New Hope Church, and the Atlanta campaign as far as the City of Atlanta. He was also in many skirmishes, and he was wounded at Stone River by a gunshot in the leg. This incapacitated him for active field service for six weeks, but he would not go to the hospital. Prior, however, he was taken to the hospital with typhoid fever, in December, 1861, and was in a Louisville hospital for about two months. During a period of his service the regiment did provost duty at Murfreesboro, Tennessee.

Following his discharge from the army on the expiration of his term of service Mr. McElroy returned to his home in Pennsylvania, and in 1867 became a resident of Keokuk. He entered the employ of Sample, Armitage & Company, iron workers, in 1869, in the capacity of bookkeeper, and the following year purchased an interest in the business. He became purchasing agent and has so continued in various changes in the firm. In 1880 he and Mr. Armitage purchased the interest of the other partners and in 1898 Mr. McElroy became sole owner and has so continued. He does all kinds of architectural work and drafting; employs sixteen men in the shop and turns out some splendid specimens of architectural iron work, manufactured in his plant. His connection with the business covers more than a third of a century, and his efforts have been largely instrumental in its substantial development. The plant is valued at $25,000, and the annual output of these products amounts to $35,000. A specialty is made of steam generators and rendering tanks, which for twenty-five years had been manufactured after designs made by Mr. McElroy.

On the 17th of January, 1872, in Keokuk, Mr. McElroy was married to Miss Mary Bailey, and they have three children who are living: John A., who is now cashier in a bond and stock office in Chicago, and who married Elizabeth Sawyer, of Keokuk; Margaretta, the wife of H. R. Collison, of Keokuk, local agent of the Iowa State Insurance Company, and David W., at home. Fraternally Mr. McElroy is connected with the Royal Arcanum, and is prominent in the Grand Army of the Republic Post, at Keokuk, in which he has filled all of the offices. He has served for two terms as commander, three terms as adjutant and has been assistant adjutant general of the State Department for one year. His political allegiance is given the Republican party, but while keeping well informed on the issues of the day his business affairs have left him little time for active political work. He belongs to the Westminster Presbyterian church, in which he has served as deacon since 1871, and his labors in the line of various church activities have contributed to its upbuilding and the extension of its influence. In 1875 he erected his present home at No. 619 High street, occupied by his family. He thoroughly enjoys home life and takes great pleasure in the society of his family and friends. He is always courteous, kindly and affable, and those who know him personally have for him warm regard. A man of great natural ability, his success in business, from the beginning of his residence in Keokuk, was uniform and rapid. As has been truly remarked, after all that may be done for a man in the way of giving him early opportunities for obtaining the requirements which are sought in the schools and in books, he must essentially formulate, determine and give shape to his own character, and this is what Mr. McElroy has done. He has persevered in the pursuit of a persistent purpose and gained the most satisfactory reward. His life is exemplary in all respects and he has ever supported those interests which are calculated to uplift and benefit humanity, while his own high moral worth is deserving of the highest commendation.

RICHARD EDMUND SMITH.

R. E. Smith, who died in Keokuk in February, 1892, was a man of marked business energy and personal popularity, and his death was the occasion of deep regret throughout the city in which he had long made his home and in which he had come to be recognized as a man whom to know was to respect and honor. He was born, reared and educated in Maryland and in early manhood removed from that state to Pennsylvania, where he became a sub-contractor in the building of a tunnel a mile and a quarter in length through the Alleghany mountains. This was a difficult piece of engineering and indicated his superior skill in that direction.

Mr. Smith arrived in Iowa in 1854, at which time he took up his abode in Davenport, but not pleased with that city he came to Keokuk in 1855 and purchased property here with the intention of making his permanent home in Lee county. He then returned to Loretta, Pennsylvania, where on the 4th day of May, 1856, he was married. He then brought his bride to his new home and here began contracting and building, his attention being given to the construction of houses. Later he was made assistant superintendent on the Des Moines Valley Road, occupying that position for sixteen years, when his health failed and he turned his attention to the building of county bridges for Lee county. He was employed as county supervisor and afterward took small contracts up to the time of his death, doing whatever his health permitted. He enjoyed the unqualified confidence of the business community because of his fidelity to the terms of a contract and his strict conformity to the ethics of business life. He constructed the first freight car ever built in the State of Iowa and the tree is still standing under which he did his work, for that was before any shops were built. Later he gave his attention to the building of passenger coaches. As stated, Mr. Smith was married, in Loretta, Pennsylvania, the lady of his choice being Miss Catherine A. Myers, who was born in that city April 18, 1832. Her parents were John B. and Catherine (Meyers) Myers. Her parents were natives of Germany and came to the United States soon after their marriage, locating in Loretta, Pennsylvania, where Mr. Myers carried on farming. Subsequently he turned his attention to hotel keeping at that place. Mrs. Smith is related to the Schwab millionaires, of Pittsburg, and is an aunt of Charles M. Schwab, of steel fame. Unto Mr. and Mrs. Smith were born six sons and two daughters: Charles, now living in Hannibal, Missouri; Frank, who died in 1899, at the age of thirty-seven years; Edward, a resident of Pender, Nebraska; George, who is living in Omaha; William, who is with the Frankel-Frank & Company, wholesale milliners, of Kansas City, Missouri; John, a member of the firm of Cherry, Sither & Company, stoves and tinware, of Keokuk; Mrs. Anna White, a widow residing with her mother, and Mary Grace, the wife of W. Winger, a dry goods merchant of Keokuk. Mrs. Smith now has ten grandchildren.

Mr. Smith held membership in St. Frances De Sales Roman Catholic church, to which all his family belonged. He was a man of many estimable traits of character, was very generous and kind to the poor and needy, sympathetic with those in distress and had a ready understanding that enabled him to enter into the feelings and realize the conditions of others. His benevolent spirit prompted him to give assistance wherever it was needed and yet he was always unostentatious in his charity. He was a wise coun sellor in business, giving his advice freely when it was sought, and his judgment was rarely, if ever, at fault. In his family, however, his best traits of character were shown. He was a devoted husband and father, doing everything in his power to promote the welfare and happiness of his wife and children. His relations to his employes is shown by the fact that while he was serving as railway superintendent the employes of that road bought and presented to him a horse and saddle, the former valued at $250. His popularity with his friends was proven by the gift of a gold-headed cane, which was voted to him at a Catholic fair as the most popular railroad man of the city He left his family in comfortable circumstances, having his home and other city property in addition to considerable life insurance. He died at the age of sixty-two years, respected by all who knew him and his memory is yet cherished not only by his immediate family, but also by the many friends whom he won during the years of his residence in Keokuk.

L. H. PHINNEY.

Deeds of valor have been the theme of song and story throughout all the ages, and while memory remains to the American people they will hold in grateful recognition the men who fought for the preservation of the Union, in one of the most sanguinary struggles that has ever been recorded in the annals of the world. During the most trying period of that trying time L. H. Phinney was one of "the boys in blue," and yet he was no more loyal to the duties of citizenship in time of war than he is in days of peace. Mr. Phinney claims Ohio as his native state, having been born at Kirtland, Geauga county, June 2, 1838. He is the son of Horatio and Emily (Kent) Phinney, they being of New England birth, but early settlers of Ohio, where the father was a farmer. In 1855 the family decided to emigrate to the more distant West, and removed to Lodi, Wisconsin, and there they spent the remainder of their lives, their later years especially being rich in works of piety and good deeds. The father was a very prominent member of the Methodist Episcopal church at that place, acting as class leader for many years, and being ever active and zealous in support of the church and her charities. In politics he was a Whig, and on the formation of the Republican party he became a member of that organization.

It was in Ohio that L. H. Phinney received the major portion of those educational advantages which he has been privileged to enjoy, but it was in Wisconsin that he formed many of the important connections that were largely to determine the course of his after life. There he was united in marriage, on November 1, 1859, to Miss Martha J. Hill, of Lodi, and there he began and for three years pursued the study of veterinary surgery, which work was to constitute the principal activity of his career. At the very beginning of the Civil War, however, he gave up his chosen work, and in July, 1861, enlisted in Company A, of the Seventh Wisconsin Volunteer Infantry.

Proceeding to Madison, where the regiment was organized, he joined the Army of the Potomac, under Gen. George B. McClellan. He continued in active service up to and including the battle of Antietam, where he was wounded, in consequence of which he was later dischargel for disability.

After recovering in some measure from the effects of wounds he began the practice of veterinary surgery at Lodi, and after a short but successful experience at that place, he removed to Iowa, locating at New Hampton, Chickasaw county. It was shortly after this that he was appointed deputy sheriff, an office which he filled for two terms. This was followed by his removal to Butler county, where he acted as constable, and in this capacity he traveled extensively, making the record of arresting more criminals than, in all probabliity, can be credited to any other officer in the state, if not even the United States. After a residence of eleven years at New Hampton he removed to Iowa Falls, in Hardin county, and there discharged simultaneously the duties of veterinary surgeon, liveryman, city marshal and constable, continuing a successful business career until 1898, by which time he had built up a large veterinary practice that claimed his entire attention. In 1894 he came to Fort Madison, and rapidly acquired the leading veterinary practice of the city, at the same time that he was taking rank as one of the leading and most representative citizens.

To Mr. and Mrs. Phinney have been born six children, five of whom still live: Endora, wife of F. E. Brown, died at Brooklyn, New York, in 1903. Those living are: Alfred H., of Iowa Falls; Ida, now married and living in Oskaloosa; J. H., of Chicago; Myrtle, wife of John Ramsey, of Oskaloosa; Lena May, wife of Bert Vermeer, of Lucas, Iowa.

Mr. Phinney was a member of the Grand Army of the Republic at Iowa Falls, but has allowed the connection to lapse. In politics he has always given his allegiance to the Republican party, believing that the best interests of the nation are conserved thereby. Genial, upright and thoroughly loyal to his friends, he is universally respected and honored.

LEWIS CONLEE.

One of the well-known farmers of Lee county and at the present time trustee of Jefferson township, where he owns 175 acres of valuable land, is Lewis Conlee, who was born in this township, November 4, 1862, the son of Paris and Amanda (Hewit) Conlee. Paris Conlee was born in Greene county, Illinois, and came to Iowa with his parents when only one year old. His father, the grandfather of our subject, was a man of prominence, and at the time of his death was a member of the state legislature at Iowa City. The family, which had located at Burlington, removed to Jefferson township when Paris Conlee was five years of age, and here he grew to manhood, but after his marriage he continued farming near Veile, spending there the greater part of his active life, and acquiring a good farm of 100 acres. He was quite prominent in local Democratic politics, being several times elected township assessor and always an active worker in the interest of the party. Mrs. Conlee was born in Jefferson township, her parents having early removed here from Pennsylvania. Both were early members of the Baptist church. They were the parents of three children, as follows: Levi T., Lewis, and Ella, wife of H. C. W. Eppers, of Montrose township. The father is still living, but the death of the mother occurred in March, 1886.

Lewis Conlee, the subject of this review, obtained his early knowledge of books in the public schools of his township, and on his father's farm learned the lessons of useful labor. His time was thus employed until his twenty-first year, when he went to Dakota territory. Failing to find there the opportunities he had expected, he returned after two years to this township and rented a farm. After a few years, being very successful in this venture, he bought his present farm in 1903, and has since added to it until now he owns a tract of 175 acres. He has increased the productivity of the soil since purchasing it, and has added many improvements.

On November 4, 1886, Mr. Conlee was united in marriage to Miss Rosa Applegate, daughter of Andrew J. Applegate, of this township. To this union have been born two sons and three daughters, as follows: Julia G., Harry, Ruth P., Esther, and Charles P.

Mr. Conlee early allied himself with the Democracy, believing its principles to be more consistent with American ideas of liberty and popular government than those of any other party. He has been an active worker in politics, and to him is due much of the party's success in this section. He has served as delegate in a number of conventions, and his first public office was that of road supervisor. During his term the roads under his care were much improved, and needed bridges were installed. In the autumn of 1894 he was elected trustee of Jefferson township, and having performed the many duties of the position with great credit to himself and the satisfaction of the public, has since been twice re-elected, being now in his third term. He has also been active in educational matters, realizing that the greatness and continued prosperity of the nation depend upon the faithful administration of the public schools, and has acted as treasurer of school district No. 7, of Jefferson township, of the last ten years. By virtue of these facts and in view of his public spirit manifested in many other ways, Mr. Conlee is justly known as one of Lee county's most progressive and enterprising citizens. He has many friends who delight to do him honor, and his sphere of usefulness will probably grow larger as his ability and merits become more widely known.

CAPTAIN WILLIAM WILSON.

Capt. William Wilson, an honored veteran of the Civil War, who for more than half a century has been a resident of Keokuk, arrived in Lee county, February 22, 1852. He was born in Gallia county, Ohio, on the 10th of May, 1829. His father, Robert G. Wilson, was born in Washington, Pennsylvania, and was a representative of an old Pennsylvania Dutch family. He died at Point Pleasant, Virginia, and his widow, who bore the maiden name of Laura Barnes, afterward came to the West, and passed away in Iowa, in 1880. They were the parents of five sons and four daughters: James L., who served in the Civil War in the Second Iowa Infantry, and is now bridge engineer with the Keokuk & Hamilton Company; Matilda, now Mrs. Mason, who has been three times a widow, and lives in Keokuk; Maria, who is the widow of John Douglas and resides with her brother, Captain Wilson; Lucretia, the widow of John Richart, of Montana, and Mary, the wife of Robert Harrington, and a resident of Boone, Iowa; Charles, Henry Clay are both deceased as is also George W., who was a private in the Regular Army and died in Omaha and is buried at Keokuk, Iowa.

The other member of the family is Captain Wilson, who was reared to manhood in the state of his nativity and acquired his education in a private school, at one time being a pupil of Rev. Stewart Robinson, afterward a Presbyterian minister and at the time of the Civil War a well-known Confederate leader. Captain Wilson desired to enter the service at the time of the Mexican War, but was rejected on account of his youth. He afterward learned the carpenter's trade with an uncle in Pittsburg, Pennsylvania, and continued to follow that pursuit until 1856. He arrived in Lee county, Iowa, on the 22d of February, 1852, and while en route he heard Kossuth speak in Cincinnati. He made his w[illegible] westw[illegible] by the Ohio river from K[illegible] wh[illegible] West Virginia, and on up the Mis[illegible]ppi, and after following carpentering in Keokuk fo[illegible] three or four years he purchased the [illegible] depot, which he conducted until 18[illegible]

In that year he put aside all b[illegible] and personal considerations and responded to his country's call for aid, his patriotic spirit prompting his enlistment with the boys in blue, of Company C, Third Iowa Cavalry. He enlisted as a private, was made orderly sergeant when the regiment was organized and successively became second and first lieutenant, while at Helena, Arkansas, on the resignation of Captain Anderson, he was promoted to the command of the company. He continued in that rank until November, 1864, when he was mustered out through special order issued by General Grant, that all officers who had served for three years should be released from duty, if they so desired. Captain Wilson was offered the position of major, if he would remain, but he decided to return home, having already served for three years and four months. He participated in the battle of Pea Ridge, and went on the march from the mouth of the Black river to Helena, Arkansas, which was known as the "lost army." They foraged through the country, obtaining all their provisions in that way, and were upon the march for about five weeks, during which time the regiment was lost from the department, in fact being cut off from all communication with the outside world. They celebrated the 4th of July, 1862, at

Augusta, Arkansas. Following the engagement at Helena the regiment went to Vicksburg, and following the capitulation of that city, to Jackson, Mississippi. Later they returned to Vicksburg and destroyed all the stock on the railroad from Yazoo to Memphis. At length the regiment was reunited at Little Rock, Arkansas, and was stationed at the Benton outpost until December, when it was ordered back to Little Rock. Captain Wilson returned home on a veteran furlough, in February, 1864, and at this time the regiment was recruited to its full strength in Keokuk. Captain Wilson afterward went to St. Louis and thence by steamboat to Memphis, Tennessee. Only on one occasion did the regiment suffer defeat, and that was at the first battle of Guntown. They met reinforcements, however, at Collirsville, then entered Memphis and went out under Gen. A. J. Smith, again meeting the Rebels under Forrest, at Guntown, and this time scoring a splendid victory. Later the troops returned to Memphis and Captain Wilson was detailed to bring the non-veterans home. This closed his military service, he arriving in Keokuk, November 1, 1864, after more than three years of active duty in defending the stars and stripes. He was never wounded, but was twice seriously ill and on one occasion he was ordered home, it was thought to die, but he refused to leave the front and ultimately recovered his health.

After his return from the war Captain Wilson filled several civic offices. He was police judge for four years, city collector two years, clerk of the district court two years, and in his election to the last office he overcome a usual Democratic majority of between 800 and 900, being elected by a majority of twenty-seven. For a second term, however, he was defeated. In 1875 he turned his attention to the grocery business, in which he engaged for twenty-five years. Later he served as justice of the peace for two years, and is now living retired.

In Keokuk, Iowa, in 1852, Captain Wilson was united in marriage to Miss Lydia Barrett, who was born in Ohio, and died February 9, 1903, her remains being interred in Oakland cemetery. They had but one child, James R., who was born in April, 1854, and died in infancy, age two months and nine days. However, they reared Mrs. Wilson's niece, who lived with them twelve years, and then became the wife of Joseph Tanner, a cousin of the late Governor of Illinois. She died in Evansville, Indiana. Mrs. Wilson was a member of the Methodist Episcopal church, and he contributes to the support of the church, although he is not a member. His political support has always been given to the Republican party, and in matters of citizenship he is as true and loyal to his country as when he followed the old flag upon Southern battlefields.

JOHN WALLACE.

John Wallace, who proved his loyalty to the Union cause by active service on Southern battlefields in the Civil War, and is now a resident of Keokuk, was born in Bennington county, Vermont, in 1838. With his parents he removed to Pennsylvania, and the mother died in Sparta, that state. Later the family came to the Mississippi valley, settling in Wisconsin, and the father afterward went to Kansas, where his death occurred, he being whipped until he died by cowboys who wanted his property. He owned 160 acres of land on the Vermilion river, and after the assassins had succeeded in their dastardly deed they drove off all of his cattle and took his blacksmith tools. He had learned the blacksmith's trade in early life, and had followed that to a greater or less extent throughout his active business career.

John Wallace had no opportunity to get an education and only attended school but three days, and began to make his own way early in life. When eighteen years of age he was bound out to Tom Murray, of Atkinson, Kansas, who became, however, a border ruffian, and Mr. Wallace remained with him only about a year. He afterward earned a few dollars by sawing wood, and later returned to Wisconsin, where he worked as a farm hand until he entered the pineries, being thus employed in the lumber regions up to the time of his enlistment. It was on the 15th of December, 1863, at Ripon, Fond du Lac county, Wisconsin, that he enrolled his name among the boys in blue, of the First Regiment of Wisconsin Cavalry. He was mustered into the United States service at Camp Randall, Madison, Wisconsin, on the 19th of December, as a private, belonging to the company commanded by Capt. Charles Pettibone, while Col. O. H. LaGrange was in command of the regiment. He enlisted for three years, or during the war, and the regiment was assigned to the Twentieth Corps of the Army of the Cumberland, and participated in the engagements at Bloomfield, Clark Bluff, West Prairie, Jonesboro, Jacksonville, Carterville, White Water, Cape Girardeau, Caster River, Middleton, Chickamauga, Anderson Crossroads, Maysville, New Market, Mossy Creek, Dandridge, Cleveland, Fair Garden, Big Shanty, Kenesaw Mountain, Harpers Ferry, and Chattahoochee River, and the pursuit of Wheeler, in Tennessee. He was also in the battles of Hopkinsville, Elizabethtown, Centerville, Scottsville, Montgomery, Columbus Road, and Fort Taylor. He had three ribs broken by accident when near Atlanta, while hauling batteries, and on one occasion he was captured near Bowling Green, Kentucky, but succeeded in making his escape and rejoined his regiment. He was one of the detachment under command of General Herndon that captured Jefferson Davis, at Irwinsville, Georgia, May 10, 1865, and there he sustained a buckshot wound in the side, the troops being fired upon by Colonel Pritchard's men when they went to capture the president of the Southern Confederacy. Mr. Wallace was honorably discharged August 26, 1865, at Madison, Wisconsin, following the close of the war, and he returned to his home with a most creditable military record, for he had always been true to the duty assigned him, notwithstanding it frequently called him into the thickest of the fight. He was ever brave and loyal and was a creditable member of the great army whose sacrifices preserved the Union.

In 1866 Mr. Wallace was united in

marriage to Miss Hannah Vest, who died in Keokuk in 1890. In 1892 he was again married, his second union being with Laura M. Wheeler. They have three children, Olivet Myrtle, Gordon N. W., and Lyman W.

Mr. Wallace worked at the blacksmith's trade for thirteen years. He now draws a pension of thirty dollars per month, but he still engages in active labor to some extent. He has a comfortable home at 416 South Eleventh street, and enjoys the respect of many of his fellow citizens. His political allegiance is given to the Republican party, and he belongs to the Grand Army of the Republic. He is as true today to his duties of citizenship as when he followed the old flag upon Southern battlefields.

CHARLES BREWSTER.

Charles Brewster, deceased, the period of whose residence in Fort Madison—from 1844 to 1893—covered the era of its great growth and substantial development, figured prominently in public affairs, especially along the lines of business progress. The self-made man is particularly a product of America, for no other country affords the opportunities that the new world does for the exercise of native talent and ability. Of this class Charles Brewster was a representative, entering upon manhood without capital, yet finding opportunity for business advancement and seeing in each transition stage of his business career a chance for an onward step. While he won notable success he also worked for higher ethical ideas in the business world, realizing that honor and truth are as valuable in trade relations as in other walks of life.

Charles Brewster was born in Ireland in 1813, and when twelve years of age came to America with his grandfather. He went to live with an uncle in Philadelphia, with whom he remained until twenty-three years of age. He had expected pecuniary assistance sufficient to enable him to engage in business on his own account on attaining his majority, but his uncle failed, and Mr. Brewster, at the age of twenty-three years, found himself without capital. This seeming obstacle, however, called forth his latent powers and native resources. Seeking a favorable field for the exercise of his talents he went to Indiana, where he obtained employment in the government land office, at Vincennes. Subsequently he engaged in merchandizing there, and in 1844 came to Fort Madison. Here he again established a mercantile enterprise, and for a number of years successfully continued his connection with the dry goods trade. He confined his attention solely to this line for many years, or until his prosperity was an assured fact, and then extended his efforts into other fields. In 1876 he became associated with Dr. Joseph A. Smith in the banking business, purchasing the Bank of Fort Madison, of which he became the president. On the control of this institution he manifested the same close application, discriminating judgment and unfaltering enterprise which were notable in his career as a merchant. He was still with the bank when it was merged into the First National Bank, of Fort Madison, and with the latter institution became a member of the first board of directors. Later, when that bank was succeeded by the Fort Madison Savings Bank, he was chosen president, and the comprehensive knowledge which he had gained through practical experience concerning the banking business enabled him to make this new moneyed enterprise one of the solid financial concerns of Lee county. There were few enterprises of importance in Fort Madison that did not receive from him substantial assistance, while his wise counsel proved a valued factor in their successful conduct. He was one of the founders of the Fort Madison Chair Company, at the time of its organization, which is still profitably conducted, and while promoting his individual prosperity he thus contributed in large measure to the commercial development and substantial upbuilding of the city.

Upon the organization of the Republican party Charles Brewster became an advocate of its principles, but never sought office, although never remiss in the duties of citizenship. His religious faith was that of the Presbyterian church, to which he contributed generously; also giving of his time and energies to the various church activities and the extension of its influence.

Mr. Brewster was married twice. In early manhood he wedded Miss Margaret Badollet, a native of Vincennes, Indiana, who died in 1852, leaving one child. For his second wife he chose Eliza J. DeForrest, of Sharon, Pennsylvania, and they were the parents of three children, who reached mature years: Martha J., James C., and William J. Mrs. Eliza Brewster passed away in 1879, and the death of Charles Brewster occurred on the 13th of November, 1893, after a residence of nearly half a century in Fort Madison. Under the stimulus of necessity in early manhood his powers developed and his keen mentality enabled him to equally recognize the possibilities of a business situation. He found in the young but growing city of southeastern Iowa the opportunities he sought and, prompted by a laudable ambition which had for its objective point the acquirement of large success through honorable methods, he gradually worked his way upward from humble position until he ranked with the leading financiers of the state, thus proving by his life's record that prosperity and an honored name may be won simultaneously.

JAMES CONARO.

James Conaro, of Denmark, Iowa, one of the largest landowners and most widely known retired farmers of Lee county, was born September 15, 1824, in Schoharie county, New York, the son of Jacob Conaro, and was reared by his grandmother and by an uncle, his mother having died when he was but a small child in his seventh year. For six years he worked as a farm hand, first receiving nine dollars a month for eight months' work, and when he was about twenty-four years of age he went to Ashtabula, Ohio, and with his brother, conducted a dairy farm for two years, learning, during that time, the trade of cheesemaking, which he followed intermittently throughout the remainder of his active career. He next engaged in partnership with others in renting a large dairy farm, and in that enterprise he continued until 1855, when he decided to begin business independently, and after considering various locations, resolved to try his fortunes in the West, and accordingly came to Denmark township, where he purchased ninety acres of land at twenty dollars an acre; but, being at that time almost without resources, other than his individual strength and energy, he was compelled to depend upon his personal efforts to pay for the farm. This he was able to do after ten years of hard and faithful work and careful planning, although the scarcity of ready money in those days placed him under the necessity of paying ten per cent. interest upon his original indebtedness for about six years, when he got it reduced.

Here in Iowa Mr. Conaro devoted his time to his trade of cheesemaking and to general farming, for the former business keeping a dairy of twenty-five to thirty cows and making up the milk and cheese on his own farm, selling in Burlington his entire product, for which he always received the highest current prices. He became probably one of the largest cheese manufacturers in this part of the state, and certainly one of the most successful, while on the other hand he displayed remarkable ability in the conduct of his agricultural interests, continuing to increase his original purchase until he now owns 350 acres of valuable land in a high state of improvement and cultivation, equipped with labor-saving appliances and many modern buildings. Thus he followed farming and dairying with great profit until 1884, when he purchased a pleasant home in the village of Denmark, and here he has since resided in retirement from active business, renting his lands to farmers.

Mr. Conaro has been twice married, first in 1847, to Miss Emily Montgomery, who was a woman of beautiful Christian character and a faithful member of the Congregational church. She was the mother of two daughters, who survive her, the elder of these being Adella, wife of O. R. Lippet, of Duluth, Minnesota, who has six children: Chester, Walter, Dunbar, LeRoy, Fannie and Agnes; and the younger Adelia, who now resides with her father, being the widow of George Humphrey, a soldier of the Civil War, who died three years after the close of that great conflict. Mr. Conaro's second marriage was to Mrs. Henrietta (Sackett) Wilder, who was first married in 1862 to Hermon D. Montgomery, brother of the first Mrs. Conaro, a farmer of Denmark township, whose death occurred in 1875, and she later became the wife of George Wilder, a native of Lemonington, Massachusetts, who, with his parents, was among the very earliest pioneers of Lee county and of Iowa. Mrs. Conaro is a daughter of Cassander and Henrietta (Beach) Sackett, the mother being a native of Connecticut and the father of Ohio, where they celebrated their marriage, and whence they came to Denmark in 1849 and engaged in farming. Both were active members of the Congregational church here, and here they passed the remainder of their lives, and were buried in the Denmark cemetery, survived by children, as follows: Mercy, since deceased, who was the wife of William Hornby; William Lloyd, who resides in California; George C., and Mrs. Conaro.

Mr. and Mrs. Conaro are both very active in the work of the Congregational church, at Denmark, of which Mr. Conaro is a trustee; are devoted to the doctrines and practice of the Christian faith, and have ever been generous in the support of charitable and benevolent movements. Mr. Conaro has made a study of most of the public questions which have agitated the nation during the past half century, and has taken considerable interest in matters of politics, acting with the Republican party, and has given much thought and effort to the upbuilding of his own immediate community, having been one of the prime movers in the organization ten years ago of the Lee County Mutual Fire Insurance Company, and having served as its president throughout the entire term of its existence. The company is in a highly flourishing condition, and for this much of the credit is conceded to its president, who has been very self-sacrificing in his efforts to bring the company to a level with the very best in the state. In fact, every enterprise of which he has had the exclusive management has been conducted with care, fidelity and large business ability, combined with the most scrupulous rectitude, and the success which he has achieved is the result of a rare union of qualities. His position has always been that of a leader, for which he is pre-eminently fitted by nature, and in all affairs affecting the public welfare which have been favored by his participation, his upright and honorable course has made him many friends and admirers, who will, without doubt, be interested in this modest review of his career.

PETER HOTT.

Peter Hott, an old and much esteemed resident of Cedar township, Lee county, Iowa, was born in Pickaway county, Ohio, September 29, 1834, a son of George and Jane (Dean) Hott, both of whom were of German descent. The parents left Ohio with their family September 6, 1839, and drove through with team and wagon to Harrison township, Lee county, where the husband and father bought a claim of forty acres, which he later entered from the government. The wife and mother died the following March, leaving four children: Isaac, Peter, whose name introduces this article; Aaron died at the age of six years, and Henry, who died a baby. She was buried near their farm on the old Poole place. The father afterward married Mrs. Jane Warren, and moved to Cedar township, to settle on the farm now occupied by the subject of this sketch. There he died January 19, 1889, full of years and honor. He was seventy-seven at the time of his death, and his ashes rest in the Bayles cemetery, as does those of his wife, whose death occurred February 27, 1885. Politically he was a Democrat, and is remembered as a man of much character and energy. He was born in Pickaway county, Ohio, February 22, 1812, and his wife was born in Robinson county, Tennessee, September 6, 1811.

Mr. Hott helped to develope a large farm, and he built a home on his forty-acre claim in Cedar township. He also bought out the different heirs to his wife's first husband, Mr. Warren. At the time of his death he owned 425 acres. He started out poor in this world's goods, though he was blessed with indomitable courage and a mighty persistance that carried him safely through all difficulties. Handicapped by a lack of education, when he began for himself he could not even sign his name, but he became a well-informed citizen, and mastered every detail of his calling. For some years he was engaged in the cooper trade, and was engaged in that work at Farmington, Iowa. The cultivation of the soil was his master passion, and he devoted his life to general farming. At the time of his second marriage he had but ten acres under cultivation. All the rest was wild prairie and timber and he patiently and persistently worked at it until it was all under the domain of the plow and the harrow.

Peter Hott attended school for a little time, when the building was burned with all the school books, and as his father would not buy more he had to go to work. This was known as the Bayles school, and when he did attend it he and his brother took turns going on alternate weeks. They found it a hard school of instruction, but what they learned they prized, and it became the nucleus of a wider knowledge as the years passed until as they entered manhood they were able to take a stand as upright and intelligent citizens.

Mr. Hott has devoted his life to farming, and at the present time is the proprietor of a fine rural estate of six hundred acres all in one piece except as crossed by the public highway. This land has cost him on the average a little over thirty dollars an acre, but could not be bought for several times that price. Here he has six houses and other conveniences for advanced and progressive farming, and by common repute is said to be worth more than $50,000.

Peter Hott and Miss Mary Harlan were married January 18, 1855. She was a native of Ohio, and after a brief matrimonial career passed to her rest, March 6, 1865, leaving two children: Dora, who married William Shaw, they had one child, Florence M. She married Lute Hixon, and has one child, Lester. Mr. Shaw is deceased and his wife's second marriage was to Mr. Samuel Huddleston, and they live upon part of her father's farm. To this union has been born the following children: Ora J., who married Samuel Maloy, and has one child, Kenneth; Sherman M., deceased; Cyrena M.; George P.; Blanche; Mary H.; Merle and Olive. The second child of Mr. Hott was Cyrena, who died at the age of twenty-eight. She was not married.

Mr. Hott contracted a second marriage, December 7, 1865, when Miss Anna Lane became his wife. She was a native of Highland county, Ohio, and a daughter of Jacob and Charlotte Lane. Her parents drove through from Ohio, and settled on a farm a half mile only from the present home of Mrs. Hott. Later on they removed to Clark county, Iowa, where Mr. Lane secured eighty acres under government entry. They spent their last days with Mr. and Mrs. Hott, and died under their roof. Their remains rest in the Bayles cemetery.

To the second marriage of Peter Hott was born one child, Isaac Henry, who has his home on part of the paternal estate. He married Miss Elizabeth Yargus, who died, leaving two children, Boyd and Edith.

Mr. Hott is a Republican, though he has never consented to take office, and has devoted his life to his farm. He is a member of the Christian church, of which he is an elder, and has been a deacon. Mr. and Mrs. Hott were burned out May 6, 1903, with the total loss of everything above the first floor. He has since erected a new and handsome residence. It contains all the modern improvements, and is a model farm residence. Five years prior his son, Isaac Henry, burned out, losing everything, and Mr. Hott erected a fine large residence.

LOUIS A. HECHLER.

Louis A. Hechler, proprietor of a meat market in Keokuk, was born in Warsaw, Illinois, December 26, 1862, his parents being Carl Frederick and Margaret (Wagner) Hechler. The father was born at Nordheim, Wurttemberg, September 5, 1821, and was a stonemason. He also learned the weaver's trade, but his father had owned a stone quarry, and had educated his sons with reference to the business and its kindred industries. He first married Elizabeth Wagner, who died a year later, leaving no children. He afterward married Margaret Wagner, who was born at Badenheim, Wurttemberg, March 3, 1832. After his second marriage he became discontented with regard to the treatment of his family and came to America with his father-in-law, George Wagner, a tailor. They left Germany in 1854 and crossed the Atlanta to New Orleans, thence proceeded up the river to Warsaw, Illinois, where they remained in the fall of 1854. Carl Hechler had been a healthy, strong man until seasickness left him a dyspeptic, he never being well after the voyage to the United States. Following his arrival in this country he worked in a brewery in Warsaw. His wife died February 17, 1868, and his death occurred January 18, 1871. Their children were as follows: Fred C., who was born October 20, 1853, and is now in California; Caroline C., who was born April 6, 1856, and is now the wife of George Lowenstein, a cigar manufacturer and city collector, of Keokuk; Elizabeth M., who was born August 21, 1858, and is the wife of Charles Sayller, of Keokuk; Catherine Helen, who was born January 2, 1866, and was adopted by Dr. Knowles, and is the wife of J. G. Koon, of Vinemount, Alabama.

Louis A. Hechler was left an orphan when eight years of age. He lived with his guardian, Charles Barney, until sixteen years of age and then worked for S. P. Pond & Company, dealer in eggs, for eight years. He was later a porter for Collier, Robinson & Hamilton, wholesale grocers, for two years, and subsequently spent one year with the firm of J. Burke & Company, bottlers of mineral waters. Throughout these years he was saving money as he found opportunity, and in 1889, when his capital had sufficiently increased to permit of the venture, he opened a butcher shop in Keokuk, which he has since conducted, being now one of the well-known meat merchants of the city. He always carries a good line of meats, and his earnest efforts to please his customers, combined with straightforward dealing, has secured to him a liberal and profitable patronage.

Mr. Hechler married Miss Mary Heine, a daughter of Charles E. Heine, a farmer residing west of Keokuk. They have two children, Grace and Ralph. Mr. Hechler is a member of Hardin Lodge, No. 29, Free and Accepted Masons; Keokuk Lodge, No. 13, Independent Order of Odd Fellows; Aerie Lodge, No. 683, Fraternal Order of Eagles, and Keokuk Lodge, No. 256, Ancient Order of United Workmen, and has many warm and admiring friends among his brethren of these fraternities. He votes with the Republican party, but has never aspired to office, preferring to concentrate his energies and attention upon his business affairs. Starting out in life for himself at an early age, he has steadily worked his way upward through persistency of purpose, which he would allow nothing to swerve, and his business capacity and energy have made him one of the substantial citizens of his ward.

FRED H. OHNING.

In Lee county are many inhabitants of foreign birth who, attracted by more progressive institutions, broader educational facilities and the superior advantages offered for making a living, have come here with their families and means for the purpose of founding homes in the new country. These valuable additions to the native population have by their industry, economy and honorable methods become essential factors in the growth of the county. A member of such a family is Fred H. Ohning, of Franklin township, who was born in Hanover, Germany, November 2, 1864, the son of Frederick and Dorothy v. Alm Ohning. His parents were both natives of Hanover, and removed to America in 1873, sailing from Hamburg and landing at New York. Proceeding directly to Lee county, Iowa, they located at Primrose, where the father opened a shop and established himself in his trade of tailoring. The following year he removed to Franklin township, and here he continued to work at his trade for some years. Later he became a veterinary surgeon. In this profession he was highly successful, and attained a wide reputation, his services being in constant demand. He is a member of the Evangelical church, and in questions of political policy has always supported the Democratic party. He owns residence property in the village of Franklin, where he has erected a substantial brick dwelling house. Being of an original and investigating turn of mind, he discovered some six years ago a method of curing the dreaded disease of cancer which entitled him to rank as a benefactor of the human race. The process is one which does not require a surgical operation, and has proved very successful. This achievement alone would constitute a life work of which any man might well be proud.

Mr. Ohning, the subject of this sketch, received a good education in the public schools, and remained a member of his father's family until he was twenty years of age, when he began active life on his own account, determined to achieve success for himself by his unassisted efforts. Comparing all available fields of honorable endeavor, his choice was made in favor of the West, and he located at Nebraska City, Nebraska. There he secured employment for a time as a laborer, but in 1883 took up the trade of printing, which he followed for eight years. In 1892, returning to Franklin township, he began farming, having long felt an inclination for that sort of work, and the following year purchased a farm of forty acres. Later he purchased his present home in the village of Franklin. Here he carries on general farming, in which he has met with much success.

On September 22, 1887, Mr. Ohning was united in marriage with Miss Louise Karte, a native of Hanover, Germany, who removed from the Fatherland to Nebraska City, Nebraska, at the age of twenty-five years, the date of her birth having been July 30, 1859.

Mr. Ohning is an active worker in the ranks of the Democratic party, and has served his party and the public in various positions of honor and importance. In 1899 he was appointed to fill an unexpired term as justice of the peace, and since that time has been twice elected to the office for terms of two years each. Such has been the high judicial character of his rulings on all points of law in matters submitted to his decision, that during this period no decision of his court has been reversed by a superior jurisdiction. For nine years he was clerk of the village of Franklin, and for the past six years has been secretary of the school board, a position which he occupies at the present time. This official record speaks loudly of the esteem he enjoys in the community in which he has his home. In a business way, he is a stockholder of the German-American Telephone Company, of Houghton, Iowa. In all his enterprises he has been very successful, and the ability thus displayed, combined with his well-known character of integrity and frank and open methods in all his dealings, has made him many friends who give him their confidence and profound respect.

W. G. DOERN, M. D.

Among all the callings and professions into which human activity is divided, probably a census of opinion would award the distinction of greatest and most direct usefulness to the practice of medicine. Certainly no profession is held in higher honor or is more deserving from the viewpoint of the self-sacrifice involved. One of the younger physicians and surgeons of Lee county who have shown greatest promise of future distinction is Dr. W. G. Doern, of Fort Madison, who has been established in practice in that city since June 1, 1902.

Dr. Doern is a graduate of Keokuk Medical College and of Rush Medical College, now affiliated with the University of Chicago.. At the time this was written he was professor of pathology and of clinical diagnosis in the College of Physicians and Surgeons at Keokuk. Formerly he was lecturer on diseases of the stomach in the same school. As part of the preparation for his life work he at one time pursued a course of special surgical work under the direction of Doctors Murphy and the famous Nicholas Senn, of Chicago, and also spent two years in Saint Joseph's hospital at Keokuk with Dr. Ruth. He is now devoting himself to surgery and general medical practice, and his enthusiasm and high respect for the work have led him to install one of the most extensive office equipments to be found anywhere. A thorough believer in modern ideas, he has spared neither money nor pains to secure all the latest appliances, and the mere mastery of the mechanical conveniences by which he has surrounded himself would seem to indicate ability of an unusual order.

Dr. Doern was born at Fond du Lac, Wisconsin, of which place his parents are still residents, and there began his education. The credit of his achievements is exclusively his own, and he has throughout manifested a fixity of purpose that may be considered remarkable. At the time of entering upon his course of the study of medicine he possessed but three hundred dollars in cash, and no other property, but considerations of difficulty were not allowed to interfere with the determination to succeed, and the position he has assumed here is an indication of satisfactory progress. Fraternally Dr. Doern is connected with the Brotherhood of American Yeomen and with the Benevolent and Protective Order of Elks, and he is a member of the Congregational church. He enjoys a gratifying measure of the public respect and esteem, and it is here ventured to predict for him a high place on the roll of Lee county's distinguished and useful citizens.

Mr. Doern resigned the chair of Pathology and Clinical diagnosis in the Keokuk Medical College September 1, 1904, to accept the chair of Anatomy and Clinical Surgery in the Milwaukee Medical College, Milwaukee, Wisconsin, to which place he removed.

CAPTAIN WASHINGTON GALLAND.

While it is impossible to determine what would have been the fate of Fort Madison had not the Galland family established its home within the borders of the city, the history of Lee county plainly indicates the value of the labors of Captain Galland, of this review, and of his honored father. From pioneer times down to the present their efforts have had beneficial and far-reaching effect upon the public life, upon substantial upbuilding and consecutive prog-

WASHINGTON GALLAND

ress, and looking beyond the exigencies of the moment to the possibilities of the future they have wrought along lines that have benefited present generations and will prove most helpful for years to come.

Captain Galland, whose office is located in the Hesse Building, Fort Madison, was born, according to an account left by his father in the fly-leaf of the family Bible, at Lower Yellow Banks, now Oquawka, Henderson county, Illinois, July 20, 1827. An account given by a maternal uncle, George W. Kinney, says that he was born there when his parents were on their way by water from Yellow Banks to the present site of the City of Nauvoo, or at this place after the arrival of the parents, which was the home of his maternal grandfather, Peter Kinney, who was then residing at a point now known as the Hibbard Spring or Smith Grove, about a mile below the present City of Nauvoo. His parents were Dr. Isaac and Hannah (Kinney) Galland. In the winter of 1827-8 the father hired men to build a store house and dwelling on the west side of the Mississippi river a few miles down the stream from Nauvoo, at what is now called Galland, the place being then known as the head of the Des Moines Rapid of the Mississippi river, the Indian name being Ah-wi-pe-tuck, signifying beginning of the cascades. This was the first building erected at that point. There was an Indian village about three miles above composed of the Sac and Fox tribes. The Indians had not yet relinguished their title to the land, and the white race, therefore, could not locate there except by permission and for this Dr. Galland applied. It was about the latter part of 1828, or early in 1829, however, before the papers granting him permission reached him, and, therefore, it was not until that time that his family was installed at his new home. He was to have the privilege of establishing a trading post for trade with the Indians, and also that he might supply steamers with wood, and in addition to his labors in these directions he was to practice medicine in the pioneer community. In the winter of 1830 several other families settled in the same district. Dr. Galland, with his white neighbors, realizing the need of educational privileges for their children, built a log schoolhouse, which was the first "temple of learning" in the territory of Iowa. The first teacher was Berryman Jennings, a scholarly gentleman, who was clerking in a store for Dr. Galland, and also studying medicine with him. There were about sixteen or eighteen pupils, some of whom came from the Illinois side of the river, crossing the water either in canoe or on the ice, for at that time the river was frozen over for a much longer period each year that the present. In fact, the ice was so thick over the Father of Waters that teaming could be done on the river from Quincy to Fort Madison. Captain Galland was one of the pupils in this little school, but of the number that attended at that early day only four are known to be living now. Captain Galland and Capt. J. W. Campbell, who are residents of Fort Madison; Benjamin Galland, a cousin, now living in central Iowa, and a half-sister, Eliza Sturdevant Galland, now Mrs. Eliza S. White, who lives at La Crosse, Wisconsin.

In 1831 Dr. Galland's second wife died

and was taken across the river into Illinois, being buried in a cemetery within the present limits of the City of Nauvoo. About twenty years later, however, her remains were removed to Fort Madison cemetery. By Dr. Galland's first marriage there were three daughters, and by the second union there were two children: Washington and a younger sister, Eleanor, was unquestionably the first white child born in the territory now occupied by the State of Iowa, her birth occurring at Ah-wi-pe-tuck January 3, 1830. After the death of the second wife, two daughters by the first marriage came to live with Dr. Galland, the elder taking charge of the household affairs.

In 1832, on the breaking out of the Black Hawk War, Dr. Galland and many others fled to Fort Edward, now Warsaw, Illinois, and his property was left in the care of a young man, Samuel Brierly, who afterward married the Doctor's eldest daughter. Most of the men joined the militia, and Dr. Galland rose to the rank of colonel, and was stationed at Fort Edward. Captain Galland has seen the commission which was issued to his father.

In 1833 Dr. Galland was again married, wedding Miss Elizabeth Wilcox, of Warsaw, a sister of his warm personal friend, Maj. John R. Wilcox, who was a graduate of West Point and an officer of the Regular Army, at one time in command of a detachment of troops at Fort Edward. He afterward retired from military service and settled permanently at Warsaw, Illinois, where he was married. A daughter of that marriage, Mrs. Virginia W. Ivins, now lives at the corner of Second and Bloudeau streets, in Keokuk. After his third marriage Dr. Galland removed to Carthage, Illinois, where he remained a short time. Later he traded that for a large stone house, two stories in height, on the bank of the Mississippi river, now the present site of Nauvoo, which was known as the property of Capt. James M. White, the maternal grandfather of Capt. James W. Campbell, now of Fort Madison. There Dr. Galland lived until 1839, when he sold that property and other property to Sidney Rigdon and the Mormons. On the 4th of July, 1839, taking with him his family and household goods, Dr. Galland became a passenger on the steamer Brazil, bound for St. Louis, Missouri. There the party changed to an Ohio river boat and went to Portsmouth, Ohio, and thence by canal to Chillicothe, where they remained for several months.

Washington Galland was only seven or eight years of age when the family located in Illinois, and up to the time of their removal to Ohio his education had been only such as could be obtained in log schoolhouses at different places. One year Dr. Galland had employed a private tutor, but after reaching Chillicothe our subject had the privilege of attending an academy. Dr. Galland was at that time interested with others in a tract of land of 120,000 acres in the south side of Lee county, known as the half-breed tract or reservation. While in Chillicothe he published a book and map, entitled "Iowa Emigrant's Guide," which was intended to give information and to induce emigrants to the west side of the Mississippi river. The result of his efforts was that a large number of people emigrated to and settled in Iowa, many establishing homes in or near Keokuk. In 1840 Dr. Galland and his family returned to this state, locating at Keokuk, where he continued in the practice of medicine, which business he had never abandoned during all these years. He made his home in Keokuk until 1854, when, with his family, he went to California, making a trip overland with ox teams, and reaching his destination after several months of travel. In 1856, however, he again came to this state and located in Fort Madison, where he died two years later, his remains being interred in the Fort Madison cemetery, where has been erected a monument to his memory, and his second and third wives are also buried there. As a pioneer of Iowa his name is inseparably associated with its history, and not only did he establish one of the first homes and built the first school in Lee county, but he contributed in large measure, through his published work to its settlement, and along many lines aided in its substantial upbuilding, laying the foundation for its present progress and prosperity. On leaving Chillicothe, Ohio, Captain Galland came to Iowa, but later his father took him back to Ohio, placing him in school in Akron, which was then a village of about 2,500 population. On leaving school he again came to Iowa, and when sixteen years of age he became a clerk on a river steamer plying between St. Louis and points on the upper Mississippi. After two years he began working in a store at Alexandria, Missouri, and in the spring of 1847, at St. Louis, Missouri, he enlisted as a private of Company A, Third Missouri Mounted Volunteers, under Capt. George W. Lafayette McNair and Col. J. Ralls. On the march to Fort Leavenworth he stood guard one night over the horses, and was then detached as a clerk in the adjutant's office. After about a year he was appointed sergeant-major of a battalion and was continued until after the last battle of the war was fought at Santa Cruz. He participated in that engagement, which, however, was the only battle in which he took part. He was under fire there through the greater part of the day. This occurred in the State of Chihuahua, where he remained until the fall of 1848, when his regiment returned to Independence, Missouri, where he received an honorable discharge.

Following his leaving the military service Captain Galland returned to his father's home in Keokuk, and in 1849 he again became a clerk on a steamer on the Mississippi, plying in its upper waters. Next year with the same employers, but on a new steamer he entered the Missouri river, going to points as far as St. Joseph. There was an immense business being done, as California emigration made travel heavy. He followed the river until 1856, and then, at his father's solicitation, located in Fort Madison. After a short time, however, he went to Montrose, where he accepted the agency for the sale of town lots, the owners living in St. Louis. Captain Galland began the study of law while living in Montrose, and completed his reading under the direction of Rankin, Miller & Enster, a leading firm of attorneys, of Keokuk. In 1858 he was admitted by examination to practice in all of the courts of the state, and in the federal courts, and he opened a law office in Montrose, and also engaged in practice in Keokuk and Fort Madison.

In April, 1861, at the first three years' call for men, Captain Galland recruited, organized and drilled a company for service, and at his own expense, quartered and fed them for two months until they were accepted by the national government and ordered to Burlington to be mustered into the United States service as Company H, of the Sixth Regiment of Iowa Volunteers. They were sent to Jefferson Barracks and later to St. Louis. They did not get supplies and arms, however, for two months. At the end of that time they became a part of General Fremont's army, and took part in his campaign through southwestern Missouri to Springfield. After General Fremont was superceded they were sent to Sedalia, Missouri, and during the winter of 1861-2 guarded railways and bridges between that place and Syracuse, Missouri. In March, 1862, they were ordered to St. Louis and taken by transport to Cairo, Illinois, thence up the Ohio and Tennessee rivers to Pittsburg Landing, becoming part of Sherman's division of Grant's Army. There they had their baptism of fire on the memorable 6th of April, 1862. During the engagement Captain Galland and sixteen of his own company and thirty-two members of the regiment were captured, being taken South as prisoners of war. At Memphis he became ill, and was sent to the Confederate Hospital. After being at Mobile for ten days he was transferred to Tuscaloosa; was for one week at Macon, Georgia, and for one month at Madison, Georgia, where he and his comrades remained until they received notice that they were ordered to Richmond for parole and transportation within the Union lines. This was in November, 1862, after having been held as a prisoner for seven months. Captain Galland passed through the capitals of South Carolina, Georgia and North Carolina, and when in Richmond was for one night in Libby prison. He suffered many hardships incident to Southern prison life, but at Aikens Landing he saw again the stars and stripes, and for the first time in months drank good coffee with real sugar in it. They were sent to Fortress Monroe, thence to Annapolis, Maryland, and on to Washington, and after a few days received notice that they could go home and there await the notice of exchange and further orders. About a month later he was told to rejoin his command at Grand Junction, Tennessee, under Gen. Sooy Smith, confronting General Chalmers. In June, 1863, on account of disability and being informed that he would have to submit to a dangerous operation, Captain Galland concluded to resign, and by special order of General Grant his resignation was accepted, to date from June 20, 1863. He then returned to his home in Montrose, Iowa. At Shiloh he had received a slight wound in the left wrist, caused by a fragment of shell.

After recovering his health Captain Galland resumed the practice of law and soon won creditable success at the bar. In the fall of 1863 he was elected to the general assembly from Lee county for a term of two years. He served on several committees and introduced a number of bills, some of which were passed. Some also failed, including one for the establishment of a reformed school for boys for each congressional district, but at a later date this became a law of the state. After the close of that legislative session he engaged to go to southwestern Missouri to close up the affairs of several branches of a St. Louis bank. He took a contract for five counties, and this work required five years. His health becoming impaired during that time, he went to California by order, remaining four years on the Pacific slope, during which time he was greatly benefited. Upon his return to Iowa in 1880 he located in Montrose. He was in Washington, District of Columbia, when President Garfield was shot and saw him carried out on a stretcher. He also saw Guiteau, the assassin. Since his return to Lee county he has continuously engaged in the practice of law, real estate and loans, and stands today as one of the most capable members of the Lee County Bar, and also successful as a real estate dealer.

Captain Galland has been a stanch Republican since the war. His father was a Whig in early life, and when he became a supporter of Fremont Captain Galland gave his allegiance to Democracy, but soon afterward changed and voted the Republican ticket. In his religious faith he is an Episcopalian. He became a member of the Masonic fraternity at Montrose, filled all of the chairs in the Blue Lodge; became a member of the Chapter and Commandery at Keokuk, and has occupied all of the offices in both capitular and chivalric Masonry. He is likewise a member of the Knights of Pythias fraternity and in that as in the Odd Fellows Lodge, to which he belongs, has filled all of the chairs. He holds membership in Tiphest Post, Grand Army of the Republic, which was named in honor of a comrade of Company H, who was the first member of the company to die. His has been an eventful career, and he has intimate knowledge of many of the important events which have shaped the policy, promoting upbuilding and formulating the history of Iowa. His influence has ever been a factor for good and his name is deeply inscribed on the keystone of the arch of its honored pioneers.

GEORGE B. STEWART.

George Bourdillon Stewart, a leading attorney of Fort Madison, Iowa, was born in the City of Burlington June 16, 1865, the son of Rev. George Dillon Stewart and Emily Stewart (Walker) Stewart. When about six years of age he removed with his parents to Omaha, Nebraska, where his father was pastor of the First Presbyterian church. At that place he first entered the public schools, and after his twelfth year continued his education in the public schools of Fort Madison, his father having removed to this city to assume the pastorate of the Union Presbyterian church, a position which he voluntarily resigned January 1, 1904, after a continuous pastorate of twenty-seven years. At the age of fourteen he entered the academy at Denmark, Lee county, the oldest incorporated institution of learning in Iowa, it having received its charter in 1843. After two years in that school he became a student at Lake Forrest Academy, near Chicago, and later at Cheltenham Academy, near Philadelphia. In 1882 he matriculated in the University of Pennsylvania, and pursued a course of study until his health failed, in his junior year, and he was compelled to defer all educational projects for about one year. During this time, however, he was not idle, but acted as editor of the Fort Madison Plaindealer, one of the older Republican newspapers of the city.

Having decided to devote his life to the profession of law, Mr. Stewart entered the law school of the University of Michigan in 1886, and was graduated with the class of '88. Immediately after his graduation he associated himself in partnership with Sabert M. Casey, and together they continued in the practice of law in this city until the death of Mr. Casey in 1903. At the present time Mr. Stewart occupies a handsome suite of offices in the Lee County Savings Bank building, where he enjoys a large and lucrative general practice. His position in the profession is now one of prominence, and he ranks as one of the better known attorneys of southern Iowa. He acts as attorney for a number of large corporations, among others the Street Railway Company of Fort Madison and the Iowa Farming Tool Company. He was general attorney for the Chicago, Fort Madison & Des Moines Railway Company until the merging of that corporation with the Chicago, Burlington & Quincy system. In March, 1898, he was appointed by President McKinley assistant United States Attorney for the Southern Iowa District, a position which he still holds. Necessarily, however, his principal activities are mainly local, and he has been connected in some capacity with all the important and celebrated law cases in Fort Madison since he began practice in this city.

On June 25, 1889, Mr. Stewart was united in marriage at Fort Madison to Miss Adele Kretsinger, who is a native of Chicago and the daughter of W. H. and Marie (Ramsdell) Kretsinger. Mr. Kretsinger was a native of Herkimer county and Mrs. Kretsinger of Utica, New York, and they located in Fort Madison in 1870. Mr. Kretsinger was president of the Iowa Farming Tool Company, of this city. To Mr. and Mrs. Stewart has been born one son, Alan Kretsinger Stewart, born in Fort Madison May 11, 1896.

Mr. Stewart is a Republican, and considers that he holds membership in that party by birthright. His maternal grandfather, Joel C. Walker, was a delegate to the Chicago convention of 1860 which nominated Abraham Lincoln for the presidency of the United States, and received from Mr. Lincoln appointment as collector of internal revenue for the Iowa district, a position which he held until after the accession of President Johnson. Not being in sympathy with the policies adopted by the latter, however, he was removed. Mr. Stewart cast his first ballot for Benjamin Harrison in 1888. While he has never aspired to public office, he has served his party a number of times as delegate to various conventions, and is an active and zealous worker in the ranks. Fraternally, he is a member of the Benevolent and Protective Order of Elks.

In his religious connection, he was reared in the Presbyterian faith, and became a full communicant in January, 1904. He has intimate connection with the material interests of Fort Madison, both through his profession and by direct financial interest, being a director and stockholder of the Iowa Farming Tool Company. He is recognized as a man of learning, integrity and great practical ability, and these qualities have won him success and the respect of all with whom he comes in contact.

JACOB HAISCH.

Among that valuable class of citizens known as German-American, none has been more worthy than Jacob Haisch, who was highly esteemed throughout Lee county, where he passed the greater portion of his life. Mr. Haisch was born in Germany, and coming to America at the age of fourteen years, he was later joined by his parents, who were farmers by occupation, and here he grew to manhood, but before he was eighteen years of age the great Civil War had begun and was well in progress, and with the consent of his parents he went to the front to fight the battles of his adopted country. In 1862 he enlisted at Keokuk in Company A, Nineteenth Iowa Infantry, under Captain John Bruce and Colonel Crab, and served for three years with the Army of the Gulf, enduring many hardships and taking part in much active service, among the more famous battles in which he was engaged being those of Prairie Grove, the siege of Vicksburg, Mobile and Spanish Fort. He was the bunkmate of Bendix Reimers, of Keokuk, and at New Orleans was sent home on account of sickness, which saved him from the fate that befell Mr. Reimers and others of his comrades, as they were taken prisoners at the battle of Sterling Plantation during his absence, and were held prisoners for six months at Tyler, Texas. He returned, however, and served out his three years' term of enlistment, being mustered out of the service at Mobile, in 1865, at which time he was under the command of Captain Sproatt and Colonel Bruce. He was a model soldier, who neither used intoxicating liquors nor tobacco in any form, and he regularly sent his pay home to his parents, who used it to purchase land, and upon his honorable discharge he returned home and took up the business of farming.

In 1869 Mr. Haisch was united in marriage to Miss Mary Krum, who was born in Germany and came to America when only one year old, and to them were born two sons and five daughters, as follows: Barbara, wife of Adam Seabolt; Kate, wife of Joseph O'Blenness; Emma, wife of George Voss; Lena, wife of Harry Wyatt; Flossie, who resides with her mother, and John and Jacob A., both of whom are dead. Mr. Haisch always provided with great liberality for all the needs of his family, as he was well able to do, he being very successful as a farmer and in all he undertook. At the time of his death he owned over 300 acres of excellent farming lands, which have since been apportioned among his daughters, with the exception of 103 acres now owned by

Mrs. Haisch. The death of Mr. Haish, which occurred in 1893, at the end of a year's illness, was caused by chronic diarrhoea contracted while in the army, and thus he gave his life for his country as many have been proud to do who were born upon its soil. He was universally respected as one of the leading farmers of Lee county and as a man of great ability and unimpeachable character, and had many friends who mourned his loss, and followed him to his final resting place in Oakland cemetery with sincere regret for the untimely end of his earthly career. He was a faithful member of the German Lutheran church, as is also Mrs. Haisch, his widow, and was a valued worker in Torrence Post of the Grand Army of the Republic, at Keokuk. He was a man of peculiarly modest disposition, and never cared to hold public office, but his friends and fellow citizens elected him a number of times to the office of school director, in which his practical ability proved of much benefit to the community. Mrs. Haisch is a pleasant lady of entertaining conversational powers, and her home is known as the center of a generous though quiet hospitality.

CALVIN T. MILLER.

Calvin T. Miller, who for a number of years has been well known as a general contractor of Keokuk, was born in Champaign county, Ohio, June 15, 1844, his parents being John and Sarah (Allen) Miller, the former a native of Pennsylvania and the latter of Ohio. Mr. Miller was descended from Pennsylvania Dutch ancestry, while his wife was of English lineage and was a grand niece of Ethan Allen, the distinguished patriot of Vermont. They were married in Ohio and became the parents of ten children: Calvin T.; Julia, deceased; John, of Ohio; Mary, the wife of Newton Byers, of Ohio; Jane, the wife of Will Nash, of Kansas; Newton, of Ohio; Ida, the wife of Daniel Gannon, of Keokuk; Milan, of Ohio; Rebecca, the wife of George Van Ostran, of Ohio; and Minnie, deceased.

Calvin T. Miller was reared in the state of his nativity, pursued his education in a district school and spent his boyhood days upon the home farm. In early manhood he responded to his country's call for aid, enlisting when but twenty years of age, in 1864, as a member of Company C, One Hundred and Thirty-fourth Ohio Infantry, under Captain Johnson and Colonel Armstrong, of the Army of the Cumberland. He spent some time in the vicinity of Richmond, Virginia, doing provost duty and on the skirmish line, and was discharged in September, 1864. In the year 1866 he removed to Macon county, Missouri, where he rented a tract of land and carried on agricultural pursuits. He afterward engaged with the Wabash Railroad Company for four or five years as a bridge builder, part of the time acting as foreman. In 1882 he came to Keokuk and for several years conducted the feed yard for the Wabash Railroad. He then entered into business relations with the Keokuk & Western Road on construction, hauling dirt and buildingwood, and erecting bridges, etc., for eight years. In 1902 he retired from connection with the railroad, has since done levee work, also handled sand and to some extent engages in farming, having a tract of land of thirty-three acres.

Mr. Miller was united in marriage on the 5th of September, 1865, in Mechanicsburg, Ohio, to Miss Florence Shepherd, who was born in Champaign county, Ohio, September 19, 1847, her parents being Jasper and Susan (Taylor) Shepherd. Her father, born in Ohio, was a representative of an old Kentucky family, while her mother was a native of Massachusetts. In their family were six children: Clarence, who resides in Kansas City, Missouri; Mrs. Miller; Josephine, the wife of Zepeniah Atterberry, of Texas; Edward, who is living in Hardin, Missouri; Elizabeth, the widow of Melvin Broeffle, and a resident of Atlanta, Missouri; and Birdie, the wife of Walter Baldwin, of Stanberry, Missouri. Four children have been born unto Mr. and Mrs. Miller: William C., the eldest, born July 15, 1868, resides near Alexandria, Missouri. He married Libby Sage, and has one daughter, Florence. Charles C. Miller, born July 15, 1872, married Nellie Turner, by whom he has two daughters, Frances and Mildred. He resides in Centerville, Iowa, and is employed as brakeman on the Keokuk & Western Road. Frederick A. Miller, born October 10, 1876, a brakeman on the Wabash road, wedded Mary Appleton, of Moberly, Missouri, and has one son, Fred Eugene. Jasper J. Miller, born January 21, 1882, married Hattie Appleton and lives in Keokuk.

Mr. Miller is a member of the Grand Army of the Republic, and his wife is connected with the Woman's Relief Corps and with the Eastern Star. They contribute to the support of the Methodist Episcopal church, of which they are members. His political allegiance is given to the Republican party and he has ever been progressive and loyal in citizenship, desiring the greatest good for the greatest number.

JOHN C. SCOTT.

John C. Scott, the present active and efficient Mayor of Montrose, Lee county, belongs to the number of the bright and earnest young men who believe in doing things, and are always ready to help forward any worthy enterprise. Such men are the life of the community in which they live. There are always enough to clog the wheels of progress; enough timid and irresolute souls to cling to the present rather than to dare the more splendid tomorrow. The men who dare the future, who are willing to take risks, and devise enterprises to enrich the the world, and help the town and the nation forward, are the real benefactors of their day and generation, and should long be remembered. Upon a small scale they are leaders in town and village; upon a large scale they are in legislative halls and executive chairs, and deal with great things, but the quality is the same: It is courage and faith in the men, and confidence in the future, and belief in the eternal order of progress. To this order belongs the present Mayor of Montrose. He dares and does, pushes things forward, and is a helping hand to whatever promises improvement in the existing order.

Mr. Scott was born in Harrison county, Indiana, in 1864, and secured a common-school education in Leavenworth, where he remained until he reached the age of twenty-three, being engaged in his earlier manhood in clerking. In 1887 he came into Iowa, and entered the employ of Walker Miller, at that time a very prominent civil engineer, in Fort Madison. This profession attracted him very much, and he began preparation for it as his life work, but he was offered an engagement in the bridge building department of the Santa Fe Railroad. This he later gave up, and in 1891 came to Montrose, where for some five years he was engaged in the hotel and restaurant business. For the last five years Mr. Scott has been associated with the Modern Woodmen of America, acting in the capacity of district deputy, his special work being in the building up of the membership of societies already established, though he was very successful in the establishment of Franklin Camp, No. 6032. For some eight or ten years he has been writing fire insurance, and practically handles all the business in that line in Montrose. Mr. Scott is a member of Park Bluff Camp, No. 853, Modern Woodmen of America, and of the Montrose Lodge of the Independent Order of Odd Fellows. He is also connected with the Daughters of Rebekah, of that order.

Mr. Scott was married in 1899, to Miss Alice Stephens, a daughter of J. C. Stephens, of Montrose, where she was born and reared. She is a prominent member of the Daughters of Rebekah, in which she holds a place on the Degree Team. In 1904 she was a delegate to the Grand Lodge, held at Mason City, where she acquitted herself very creditably. Mr. Scott has been previously married, having been united in matrimony in 1887, to Miss Dovie Conrad, who died in 1892, leaving one child, Claude C., who died in 1900, at the age of twelve years. Their remains rest in the cemetery at Leavenworth, Indiana.

Mr. Scott is a Republican, and is much interested in the working machinery of his party. He has been twice elected Mayor of Montrose, where his zealous public spirit is much appreciated. In 1897 he, with others, built the Montrose Hotel, a two-story brick building, on River street, which cost about $4,500, and is one of the conveniences of the town. Before his election as Mayor there had been no celebration of the 4th of July for nineteen years. He put an end to this apathy, and stirred up a feeling of patriotism, so that all entered into the great national holiday heartily and unreservedly. He has taken an active part in the location of several important business undertakings, such as the establishment of a button factory and a canning factory, and by general consent is a leader in all forward movements.

The mother of Mr. Scott is now living in Enid, Oklahoma, where her only daughter, Clara, the wife of James Isaacs, has her home. There also lives her other son, W. H. Scott.

The father of Mr. Scott was a farmer,

who was born at New Amsterdam, Indiana. He died about three hours before the subject of this article was born. As a fatherless lad J. C. Scott has had to make his way in the world, and may well be congratulated upon the very substantial results that have attended his active and industrious career.

JOHN INGERSOLL DAY.

Among the better and more prominent agriculturists, whose pleasant farm homes grace Denmark township, Lee county, and indicate the persistent industry and the thrift that have brought them success in their hard labors, may be placed the name of the gentleman, whose life history is given herewith to the readers of this volume. He has made a success of his vocation, and has long been widely known as one of the enterprising and intelligent men of this township. For many years his home has been in Iowa, and he has gathered about him a host of friends, who know him as a gentleman of the highest character. His estate is one of the first in the community, and it is through perseverence, honesty and industry, his three watch-words, that he has gained a very comfortable competence.

Mr. Day was born at Sheffield, Lorain county, Ohio, November 27, 1838, a son of John and Cornelia M. (Sackett) Day, both born and reared in Massachusetts. The father went from Sheffield, Berkshire county, where he was born and reared, when he was fifteen years of age, in 1816, to Sheffield, Ohio, where he met and married Cornelia Sackett, and there they lived and died.

John I. Day was their second child to reach maturity. He was given a good educational advantages, and was a student in Oberlin College. He remained at home and assisted his father upon the farm until 1859. That year he came west on a visit to Kellog Day, an uncle, who had been very successful in his labors in Lee county. Mr. Day was pleased with the country, charmed with its promise, and decided to make it his home. Back in Ohio he had already taught school two winters, and here he continued teaching, engaging as a clerk during the summer in the mercantile establishment of Day & Ingalls. About this time he contracted the "Pike's Peak fever," and in the month of October, 1860, crossed the plains with a cattle team, starting from Nebraska City, and safely making what was then a very dangerous journey. He remained in Colorado some four years, and then spent six years in Montana, after which he was ready to return to Denmark township, and resume the peaceful and uneventful life of the Iowa cultivator of the soil. While in the West he did various things to keep busy and earn money. In Colorado he was mostly engaged in mining, but in Montana did farming on quite a large scale.

Mr. Day was married in 1870 to Miss May Elizabeth Brown. She was a daughter of William Brown, and a sketch of her brother, E. H. Brown, appears on another page of this work. Her father was one of the early settlers of this county, and at one time was a considerable landowner, having title to four hundred acres.

The different heirs have been bought out

by Mr. Day until he now owns 250 acres of the old Brown farm. Part of the house in which he lives was the first frame house to be put up in Denmark township. All the details of the old farm property have been rearranged by him, the entire place greatly remodeled and improved, and the place is now pronounced one of the most desirable in the township.

To Mr. and Mrs. Day have come no children, but they have an adopted daughter on whom they have lavished tender care and affection. She was taken by them when only ten weeks old, and given their name, Lillian A. Day. She was born in North Carolina, and was a daughter of Mr. and Mrs. Peebles. Her mother died when she was but two weeks old. She is now the wife of Charles Wharton, and is the mother of one daughter, Mildred Day Wharton. Mrs. Day was born and reared in Denmark township, and received her education in Denmark Academy. She taught school for several years, and was married in the house in which her life has since been spent.

Mr. Day is a Republican in his political affiliations, and has been trustee of Denmark township for five years. He has completed one term as justice of the peace, and has proved himself a capable and impartial administrator of the law. He is a member of the Congregational church, and has served that body as trustee and as deacon for many years. Both he and Mrs. Wharton have served as trustees of the Academy, Mr. Wharton also filling the position of treasurer of that institution, from which both himself and wife were graduated.

Mr. Day is engaged in general farming, though he devotes much attention to dairying and the breeding of hogs and cattle for the stock markets. He is a wide-awake and enterprising farmer; and despite the weight of years, is still alert and vigorous.

MARTIN MURPHY.

Martin Murphy, who is now living retired, belongs to that class of citizens who win the admiration and respect of all by what they have accomplished through individual effort and along honorable lines. Mr. Murphy is entirely a self-made man and all that he has enjoyed and possessed has been won through well-directed labor, guided by sound business judgment. He was born in Ireland on the 11th of November, 1838, his birthplace being in Queens county, about thirty-three miles west of Dublin. His father, James Murphy, died in Ireland in 1855 and three years later his widow with her children came to the United States. She bore the maiden name of Helen Delaney and was born in Ireland, her people, however, coming at an early day to America and settling in New York. Those of the family yet living are Maggie, of Monroe county, Iowa; Julia, now of California; Kate, also of California, and Bridget, of New York. Patrick Delaney, one of the maternal uncles of our subject, had the contract for opening up Johnston street, the first street opened up in Keokuk. William Delaney, an uncle, was killed by the caving in of an embankment while Blondeau street was being opened up. It was their sister, Helen, who became the wife of James Murphy. She died in 1884 after a long residence in Keokuk. The living members of her family are Patrick Murphy, a resident of this city; Mrs. Maggie Furlong and Mrs. Annie Kelley, also of Keokuk, and Mrs. Mary E. Donnelly, of Chicago.

In his native country Martin Murphy acquired his education by attending the public schools. He afterward worked at a brick yard for eight years, for it was necessary that he start out in life on his own account when still quite young. He was twenty years of age when, on the 11th of June, 1858, he embarked on a sailing vessel, the "David Clinton," for New York, reaching that harbor after thirty-one days spent upon the Atlantic. He then proceeded westward by train to Keokuk and the same year began teaming for wholesale stores, continuing in that business until 1901. He at first had but one team, but later used four teams in the conduct of his business. He worked for Samuel A. Kerry for forty-four years, for A. Weber for thirty years, for J. F. Dougherty, forty-six years for the City Milling Company and the Warsaw Milling Company. In 1901 he traded his business to a Hamilton, Illinois, man for a farm in Clark county, Missouri, covering one hundred and twenty acres of improved land which he now rents. As the years passed by and his financial resources increased he made some investment in realty and in 1862 he built the home at No. 302 South Fourth street, which he has since occupied. He now owns two double houses and one single house in Keokuk.

In 1868 Mr. Murphy was married in Keokuk to Miss Jane Nelson, who was born in Couny Clare, Ireland, and in her girlhood days came to this city. They have three children: William, who is now engaged in merchandising in Chicago; James, a bookkeeper of Keokuk; and Anna, a successful teacher, who has been employed in connection with educational work in various schools in Lee county. Mr. Murphy is a member of St. Peter's Catholic church and belongs to the Catholic Mutual Protective Society. His political support is given the Democracy, for on becoming a naturalized citizen he concluded that the platform of that party contained the best elements of good government. He has never yet had occasion to regret his determination to seek a home in the new world, for he found the business opportunities which he sought and has gradually progressed toward the goal of success. He has also raised a good family, of which he has every reason to be proud. In the evening of life he is now living retired, enjoying a well-earned rest, the income from his property being sufficient to supply him with all of the necessities and many of the luxuries of life.

THOMAS J. CASE.

Those who are coming on the stage of action, and laying hold of the implements of industry and the weapons of power that the passing generation is laying down, should always think tenderly of them. The pioneers in the settlement of a community are entitled to peculiar reverence, as they have made possible comfort and ease by their sacrifice and hard labor. Because the men of the 'forties and 'fifties dared such large and noble enterprises, striking out into the prairies, and cutting loose from the great centers of trade and industry, that new centers might arise and new states be made, do we have the great West today in all its magnificent splendor. The men who settled southeastern Iowa were cast in a heroic mould, and should be long and gratefully remembered by those who come after and occupy seats of ease where they toiled and endured greatly. Among the few remaining of the old and sturdy pioneers is the man whose name introduces this article.

Thomas J. Case, who is now a resident of Vincennes, Des Moines township, Lee county, is a son of Horatio and Mary (Thomas) Case. He was born in Augusta, Kentucky, July 4, 1827. His father was born in Virginia, and was an early settler in Kentucky, where he followed the carpenter trade when he was not engaged in farming. He lived to be seventy-eight years of age, and finally passed to his rest in the village of Vincennes. The Thomas family lived near Augusta, Kentucky, and there the mother of Thomas J. Case was born and married. To Horatio Case and wife were born the following children: George W., James M., Walter, who died a youth; Lucinda, who married Elisha Harris, and later Daniel Comstock: Matilda, the wife of James Decker, died in Indiana; Thomas J., whose name introduces this article, and Augustus D., now a resident of Seymour, Iowa.

Horatio Case, in company with his son, Augustus, and his son-in-law, Daniel Comstock, came to Iowa, and effected a settlement in Des Moines township, in 1853. Three years later the subject of this sketch, and his wife came to what was then more a land of promise than of reality. Mrs. Horatio Case died in 1873, at about the age of seventy-three. The year that his father came to Iowa, James Madison Case went to California. George W. died in Indiana.

Thomas J. Case married Mary J. McBride, in Dearborn county, Indiana, November 24, 1850. She was born August 6, 1833, and was a daughter of Robert and Sarah (Fuller) McBride. Her father was born in Dearborn county, Indiana, and was a son of Hugh McBride. Sarah Fuller McBride was also a native of Dearborn county. They had but one child, and after his death she married John Foster, to whom she bore five children. This was while they lived in Indiana. They came to Iowa in 1856. George Foster, Mrs. Case's stepbrother, served in an Illinois regiment during the Civil War, and died of sickness. Lewis Foster, a half-brother, was also a soldier in the Union army. Samuel Fuller, a brother of Mrs. Case's mother, served in the Mexican War. Lewis Harrison, an uncle of Mrs. T. J. Case's mother, is said to have served in the War of 1812. Mrs. Foster lived to be about seventy years of age, and passed to her rest some twenty-eight years ago.

To Mr. and Mrs. Case were born nine children, of whom four lived to reach maturity: Augustus, who married Amanda Best, is a resident of California; Sarah E., the wife of W. W. Newberry, of whom a sketch may be found in another place in this work; Lewis, who married Belle Best, and is a farmer in California; Ann Frances died when seven years old; Thomas Elmer married Minnie Robertson, and lives in Des Moines township. Mrs. Case is a member of the Methodist Episcopal church, and very highly regarded by all who know her best.

Mr. Case took sides with the Democratic party in all matters relating to general and national topics, but in local questions has felt that the fitness of the candidate for the position was the determining issue. He has led a long and useful life, and now in his advanced years is much revered in the community where he lives.

ABRAHAM B. NEWBERRY.

Abraham B. Newberry, now deceased, was a son of James A. and Mary (Smith) Newberry, and was born in Orange county, New York, March 1, 1816. While he was still a lad his parents removed to the West, and made settlement in Missouri. In 1838 he came with his father and brothers from that state, and made a home for himself in what is now Des Moines township, Lee county, Iowa. Here he invested in land, and before his death became the proprietor of over 1,700 acres, which consisted mainly of very desirable farm land, and part of which was known in early times as the "half-breed tract."

Abraham B. Newberry was married in Des Moines township, January 1, 1842, to Miss Eliza Duty, a native of Newberry, Vermont. She was born October 24, 1824, and accompanied her parents, Israel and Mehitable (Sawyer) Duty, both Vermont born and bred. They located in Des Moines township in 1839, and became very prosperous. Farming was their life business. Her father died in Peaksville, Missouri. To the marriage of Mr. Newberry and Eliza Duty were born three children: Orson O., Charles, who married and lives in Argyle; Rosaline is now deceased.

After a long and useful life, Mr. Newberry passed to his rest at his home in Des Moines township, August 1, 1898, his widow surviving until 1904. He was an active and hard-working man, a good citizen and a kind neighbor, and those who knew him best, speak of him in the highest terms. He was largely engaged in stockraising, and was very fond of fine cattle and horses. To him, it is said, his neighborhood was greatly indebted for fine strains of equine blood. He was prominent in many ways in the community in which he lived, and from time to time held local offices of honor and responsibility. In politics he was a Republican, and in the more exciting times of the past was outspoken and active in his championship of what he considered the right. Living as he did not far from the border line of freedom and slavery, the political issues of the old days were forever taking on moral aspects, and he did not hesitate to meet the issue. In later days, when the passions of the Civil War had burned to ashes, he made politics a matter of men and principles, and sought for the best men to fill the positions, for which character and ability should be the main qualifications. He was a good and faithful citizen, and will long be missed from the community where his life was mainly spent.

JOSEPH P. POOLE.

Joseph P. Poole, one of the older native born citizens of Lee county, where he was born in Harrison township, October 16, 1840, enjoys the distinction of having served as a Union soldier throughout the Civil War, from the time of his enlistment in August, 1861, as a member of Company B, Third Iowa Cavalry, until his discharge in Georgia in 1865. He was mustered out at Jeffersonville, Indiana, and returned home war-worn and weary, but glad that he had been able to render effective service in behalf of the country he loved so well. As the years go by the value of that service becomes more apparent. As this country takes its place among the mightiest nations of the earth and exerts its influence for peace and order, justice and humanity, we shudder at the picture of what might have been, if the men of 1861 had not risen in their strength and asserted that the government of liberty should be preserved at all hazards. Mournful disasters of vast magnitude would have followed in the train of a divided Union and the progress of the world halted for hundreds of years. But thanks to the men of 1861 the world has written a history of advance, sometimes not compassed in centuries, since the day the rebel flag sunk in dust at Appomatox. The old veteran may be ragged and soiled, may be in the mire himself, but since it is a fact that he wore the Union blue, there is upon him a fadeless glory of what he dared and did in the days of trial and testing, when he fought and bled for God and humanity. And the world loves and honors and reveres them, rich or poor, wise or ignorant, for the cause they upheld and the flag they followed. Mr. Poole, whose name belongs to this honored company, did his duty on the field of action, and lives to see the wonder of the victory he helped to win as its remote effects sweep out into the whirlpool of the nations and make the whole world better and freer.

Mr. Poole remained at home with his parents until he was almost twenty-one, and went from the farm to the battle ground. After the war he came back to the parental roof, where he lived until the winter of 1866-67, when he was married. For about a year he lived on rented land near Big Mound, Lee county. After the expiration of this period he spent some years in the far West engaged in farming. The West did not please him as a home, and he finally came back to what he calls the "garden of the world," Lee county, and here he has maintained his home to the present time. For some years he was engaged in farming, and later he bought a home in the village of Primrose, in which he has made his residence to the present time.

In politics he is a Republican, and in local affairs seeks the best men for the positions to be filled, but in general matters he "votes as he shot."

The marriage of Mr. Poole occurred

in Primrose, Lee county, Iowa, in 1867, when Miss Rachel Holland became his wife. She was born in Ohio, and came into Iowa with her parents at an early date. They located in Lee county, and here her father, who was a tailor, followed his trade, but gave much attention to farming, having come into possession of a neat and attractive farm in Harrison township.

To Mr. and Mrs. Poole were born a family of eight children: R. May, at home; Edward, who died at Pilot Grove, Lee county, when one year of age; Myrtie J., the wife of Edward Glendenning; Benton F., a resident of Mt. Pleasant; George O. is resident of Tennessee; Charles E., now in Muscatine, Iowa; Claire, the wife of Albert J. Pool, a railroad man, of Ottumwa, Iowa; Edna O., at home and still a student in the local schools.

Mr. and Mrs. Poole have a pleasant and well-appointed home, to which their friends are always welcome, and their genial hospitable spirit counts all who come their way as friends. They are good people and highly esteemed in the community in which their quiet and useful lives are passing.

J. L. VANOSDOLL.

J. L. Vanosdoll, a leading merchant and one of the more prominent citizens of Montrose, Iowa, was born August 6, 1854, in Jefferson township, Lee county, the son of Richard and Emily Jane (Wilson) Vanosdoll, a full and complete sketch of whose lives and ancestry is given upon another page of the present volume, together with a detailed mention of the various members of the family. It was in the public schools of Montrose that Mr. Vanosdoll received his early education, and he also began early to learn the invaluable lessons of industry, working as a farmer and gardener until about his fifteenth or sixteenth year, when he took employment in a sawmill at Montrose, and during a period of eleven years discharged successfully all the duties of the establishment except those of engineer. At the end of this time he spent three years in Keokuk with the firm of Taber & Company, and later was with S. & J. C. Atlee, of Fort Madison, for two years, winning by careful work and faithful attention to duty the good will and confidence of his employers, and establishing for himself a reputation as a young man of unusual ability, enterprise and energy, thus laying the foundation for his future career.

On returning to Montrose Mr. Vanosdoll went into the meat business, which he followed for sixteen years, and the magnitude of the success he achieved in that venture is shown by the fact that at the expiration of this period he was able to abandon the enterprise which he had built up and enter upon a new business that has proved to be profitable in a still more gratifying measure; for in 1903 he established a grocery and men's furnishing store, to which he has since added a bakery department, and the new store is already recognized as the leading institution of the kind in this section of Lee county. Extensive and thoroughly modern stocks are carried, the appointments are of the latest and most approved style and quality, and the work of the various departments is systematized to an extent that commands unqualified admiration, while a rapidly and steady growing popularity attests the confidence of the general public.

On February 8, 1886, Mr. Vanosdoll was united in marriage with Miss Adele Le Matty, a native of La Harpe, Illinois, she being of French parentage and daughter of Joseph Le Matty, who as a partial invalid is retired from active life, and resides at Nauvoo, Illinois. To Mr. and Mrs. Vanosdoll have been born five children, these being Verda; Kenneth; Wanda, now deceased; and two which died in infancy.

As a member of the Republican party and a man of great public spirit Mr. Vanosdoll has played a very important part in the civic life of Montrose, having at one time held the office of Mayor, in which his administration was notable in local annals, and for a period of eighteen or twenty years acted as Recorder, while he is at the present time the municipal Treasurer, and was also once elected Justice of the Peace, although he did not accept the office. In a fraternal way he is widely known, being a member and Past Noble Grand of Cascade Lodge, No. 66, Independent Order of Odd Fellows, having, in fact, held all the offices of the lodge and acted as treasurer for a period of more than eight years, while he is also secretary and treasurer of Montrose branch of Falls City Council, No. 166, Mutual Protective League, in both of which orders he has been a constant and faithful worker. In addition, he is a member of the local organization of Daughters of Rebekah, in which Mrs. Vanosdoll also holds membership, and she has frequently been elected to the office of secretary and is now Noble Grand. Mr. Vanosdoll is closely identified with the substantial interests of Montrose, owning the buildings in which his stores are located and a pleasant home that is the center of a refined social circle, and he enjoys the respect of the community in which his career is passing because of the strict integrity which is observed in all his business and personal relations.

WINFIELD WEST NEWBERRY.

Winfield West Newberry is one of the younger representatives of a notable family in Lee county, and worthily sustains an honored name. While engaged in farming and always a hard worker, he is a well-informed citizen, and keeps abreast of the doings of the world. Agriculture is to him not a narrowing but a broadening occupation, and its opportunities for thought and reflection, its close contact with the order of nature, and its deep insight into the play of eternal forces, makes for a large and lasting culture.

Mr. Newberry was born in Des Moines township, Lee county, Iowa, February 29, 1856, a son of James W. and Edith (Benedict) Newberry, of whom a biographical sketch appears on another page of this work.

He was given a common-school education, and became an intelligent and thoughtful man. He remained under the parental roof until the time of his marriage, and assisted his father in the management and work of the family homestead. After he married he established his home on an eighty-acre farm, to the south of the southeast quarter of section 8, and here he has lived and labored until now he is known as a successful cultivator of the soil, and the owner of 147 acres of the choicest land. To this he has given close and constant attention with the exception of about a year in 1883 and 1884, which he spent in Sutter county, California.

Mr. Newberry was married February 7, 1877, to Miss Sarah E. Case, a native of Indiana, where she was born February 23, 1855. Her parents, Thomas J. and Mary J. (McBride) Case, were among the pioneers of Lee county, making their arrival here as early as 1857. They were honorable and upright people, and stood very high among the early settlers. An interesting sketch of their career appears on another page of this work, and shows that their character, general intelligence and industry, united with integrity and public spirit were mighty factors in their pronounced success.

To Mr. and Mrs. Newberry was born one child, Ida May, the wife of Dr. Ambrose W. Teel, a noted physician, of Kahoka, Missouri. Their wedding occurred May 18, 1899, and has proved in every way a fortunate one.

Mr. Newberry is a Republican in his political views, and has been a township trustee for fifteen years altogether. For two years he served as justice of the peace. He is much interested in educational matters, and for many years has been school director.

Mr. Newberry is awake to all public affairs, and anything that looks to the public good can always depend on him as an active supporter. He and his bright and charming wife have always drawn around them warm-hearted friends, and they are greatly attached to their friends and neighbors in turn.

JOHN S. FERGUSON.

That the life of John S. Ferguson, of Keokuk, illustrates a high and noble ideal of American manhood is due in part to a rigid discipline in the school of experience and honest labor during his early years, as well as to those personal characteristics which are peculiarly his own. Mr. Ferguson was born on October 15, 1830, in Beaver county, Pennsylvania, and at the early age of sixteen years became assistant to his father, who was George Ferguson, working with him at his trade of blacksmithing. George Ferguson early removed to Indiana, taking up his residence at the town of St. Omar, and later, when the subject of this sketch was eighteen years of age, again followed the star of empire westward. This time he purchased a farm of 160 acres at West Liberty, Muscatine county, Iowa, and here he did his work and lived his life and passed to the life beyond.

The young man was his father's co-laborer until three years after attaining his majority, at which time he married Miss Jerusha H. Odell, daughter of Thomas Odell, a farmer and Christian minister of Odell's Ferry, in the same vicinity. To them were born four sons and one daughter, as follows: George, who lives in the city of Keokuk and is the father of a family of three children: Elmer J., who has his residence at Galesburg, Illinois; Thomas D., also of Galesburg, and who for a full quarter of a century has filled the position of conductor on the Chicago, Burlington & Quincy Railroad; Clara, who with her six sons and daughters, lives with her father at his pleasant home in Keokuk; and Charles Henry, who is employed in Burlington, this state, where he and his wife have their residence.

At the beginning of the great Civil War Mr. Ferguson was living quietly on his farm of 160 acres in Marshall county, Iowa, which he had entered as a "homestead" five years before; but at the first call of his country for defenders he relinquished the care of his own business affairs, and offered himself as a recruiting officer to assist in sending men to the front. He was accepted, and during several months which he devoted to this service his influence and standing in the community were instrumental in raising a large number of troops. Then, in August, 1862, he himself joined the active forces, enlisting in Company F, of the Twenty-eighth Iowa Infantry. Three months after enlistment he was promoted to the office of first or orderly sergeant, which position he held until just before his discharge, when, in recognition of his distinguished and meritorious service, he was honored with a brevet colonelcy. With his company Private Ferguson went into camp at Iowa City, and later at Davenport, Iowa. Thence he was sent to Helena, Arkansas, and there first saw active service in battle. He arrived at Vicksburg, Mississippi, at the beginning of the siege, and was engaged there until the surrender of the city to General Ulysses S. Grant. Proceeding immediately to New Orleans, Louisiana, the regiment lost heavily in the battle of Lake Ponchartrain. Our subject was a member of the Red River expedition which, starting in March, 1864, fought its way over bitterly contested ground as far as Pleasant Hill, where a fierce engagement took place, as also one at Natchitoches. At Sabine Cross Roads he sustained the loss of his right arm, besides thirteen other wounds, and was, in consequence, taken prisoner by the enemy. He was held as a prisoner of war at Mansfield, Louisiana, utterly without medical assistance or care of any kind, suffering from hunger, and had for a bed only the bare floor of his prison. From the hardships of this terrible time his health has never fully recovered. When captured he was a fine specimen of physical manhood, his weight being 200 pounds; when released he weighed but 104 1-2 pounds.

At the end of the war Mr. Ferguson was transferred to St. Louis, Missouri, and thence to Keokuk, Iowa. Immediately upon his honorable discharge from military duty, although still suffering from the effects of wounds and privations, he went to Farmington, Iowa, and entered the Methodist Episcopal itineracy as a minister of the gospel. In this work he continued as long as his health would permit, which was a period of fourteen years. For three or four years thereafter he followed mercantile pursuits, keeping a store at Mount Pleasant, Iowa. Receiving the appointment as superintendent of Ashland National Cemetery at Jefferson City, Missouri, he held that position for six years, and was then transferred to a similar post at Keokuk, where he has since made his home. At present he is engaged in the real estate business, owning besides his own home considerable property in the city of Keokuk. In addition to his other duties he acts as notary public and pension attorney.

Mr. Ferguson is the present chaplain of the National Association of Prisoners of War, president of Missouri Prisoners of War, and chaplain of the Grand Army of the Republic, Department of Iowa. He is a member and Past Commander of Belknap Post, Grand Army of the Republic, has passed through the chairs of the American Benevolent Association, being now its chaplain; has passed through the chairs of the local lodge of Independent Order of Odd Fellows, and holds membership in the District Camp and State Canton of the latter order.

In politics Mr. Ferguson has been a Republican ever since the organization of that party, having cast his first vote for John C. Fremont for President. He has never cared for public office, but his popularity caused him to be elected sheriff of Muscatine county, Iowa, at the age of twenty-five years, and later he was elected justice of the peace in Marshall county. John S. Ferguson is an excellent example of a self-made man. His formal education was merely that of the public schools, and his advantages have been few; but an ever pressent readiness to follow the call of duty has led him upward along high paths of honor, and his reward is the respect and profound regard of his fellowmen.

NOBLE BLACKINTON.

Noble Blackinton, in whose life record there is much that is worthy of emulation and whose memory is dear to the hearts of a large circle of friends who knew and honored him during his active life, was one of the noble figures in the history and development of this section of Iowa, being known throughout Lee county and southeastern Iowa as one who was singularly devoted to all that might conduce to the moral and spiritual advancement of mankind, as well as being always among the first to aid any worthy movement for the material upbuilding of the community in which he made his home. He was born May 24, 1801, at Attleboro, Massachusetts, of old New England stock, one of a large family of brothers and sisters, and, fortunately, was reared to economy and toil, always two prominent conditions of health and longevity, as ordinarily they are also of virtue and usefulness in life, and indeed, the family was characterized by sobriety, strict temperance and frugality, qualities which especially marked the career of our subject, and was remarkable for longevity, his father laying aside earthly existence when eighty-four years of age, and one brother, who was a wealthy woolen manufacturer at the village of Blackinton, Massachusetts, attaining to the ripe age of eighty-eight years.

Mr. Blackinton in early childhood removed with his parents to North Adams, Massachusetts, where he received his education, and there he acquired, in addition to a knowledge of farm work, considerable skill in the trades of brickmaking, tanning and coopering, while the necessity of making his own way in the world was at the same time developing in him the qualities of perseverance, self-reliance and sound, discriminating business judgment. Later, he began to look about him for some more remunerative field of endeavor, some place of more abundant opportunity and wider scope for his individual effort, and very naturally making his choice in favor of the great West, he removed, when only twenty-four years of age, to Ashtabula, Ohio, and thence to Quincy, Illinois, at which latter place he was united in marriage to his first wife, and with her again removed in 1840, taking up his permanent residence in Denmark, Lee county, Iowa, where was passed the greater part of his long, useful and honorable life. Thus he became one of the very early pioneers of this great state, which was at that time only a territory and had a population of but about 30,000. Neither Illinois nor Iowa had then a mile of railroad, most of the 55,000 square miles of what is now the state of Iowa was then a vast area of scarcely broken waste. Keokuk had not a half dozen cabins, Fort Madison had only a single brick building, Burlington, though the territorial capital and the largest town in the territory, was but a small village, and Denmark had no church or academy, but simply a plain school house, which was the only public building.

Mr. Blackinton was twice married, and his first wife, who was a native of Boston, Massachusetts, died in Denmark in 1850, the mother of six children, of whom only two survived him, these being William N. Blackinton, of Denmark, and Mrs. Harriet Copp, of Nebraska. The latter died December 5, 1887. In 1866 he wedded Mrs. Anna Gooch, of New York, with whom he had become acquainted during her residence in Denmark at a previous period, and she still survives him. His was a deep religious nature, and having become a member of the Baptist church when only eighteen years of age, he maintained the connection throughout life, being one of the seven original members of the first Baptist church organized in Denmark, in the year 1848, and contributing liberally to the building of the first church edifice erected in the city, as he did also for the present home of the congregation to which he belonged. He also took a prominent part in securing a parsonage for the church, always gave lavish financial support to missionary work, and in 1852 when the first steps were taken in Iowa for the establishment of an institution of learning of higher grade, to be under the control of the Baptists of the state, and the preparatory school was opened in Burlington, he was made one of the board of trustees in control of the school and its property, an office to which he was re-elected from time to time for the remainder of his life—a period of thirty-four years. His contributions to the support of the institution were frequent and generous, and his place was seldom vacant at a regular or special meeting of the board, where his counsel, advice and encouragement were highly valued, both for their intrinsic merit and for the value which attached to his words as the utterances of a strong and cheerful nature. Thus he was faithful to every duty while life lasted. His death occurred at 10 p. m., on Thursday, September 15, 1887, and thus passed away a valued member of the community, one the story of whose life was a priceless bequest to his descendants and whose influence still remains potent for good.

WILLIAM N. BLACKINTON.

One of the most popular and widely known men in commercial, financial and political circles of Lee county, is William N. Blackinton, of Denmark, who conducts a banking and general mercantile business and for the last five years has occupied the office of postmaster at that place. Mr. Blackinton was born February 22, 1838, at Payson, Illinois, and is the son of Noble Blackinton, a sketch of whose career appears on another page of this volume. Coming to Denmark with his parents in 1840, he received an excellent education in the Denmark Academy, and in 1856 removed to Hancock county, Illinois, where he assumed charge of his father's farm at the early age of eighteen years, thus giving promise of that independent and enterprising spirit which has characterized his later life. To this work he devoted ten years, with gratifying success, and during that period he married Miss Roberts, of Hancock county, who died two years after her marriage, leaving one child, which died in infancy.

His business career in Denmark dates from 1866, at which time he returned to this place and engaged in a mercantile enterprise in company with George Epps, under the firm name of Epps & Blackinton, they conducting a general store for two and a half years, at the expiration of which period Mr. Blackinton sold his interest in the business. In 1870 he again became engaged in the business in partnership with Dr. A. Holland, the firm being known as Blackinton & Holland, and this connection was continued until 1884, when Dr. Holland disposed of his interest to Peter Sheric, and after seven years during which the firm bore the style of Blackinton & Company, Mr. Blackinton purchased Mr. Sheric's holdings in 1891. Since that date he has been the sole proprietor, and by his ability, tact, close attention to detail and well-known character of honesty, integrity and strict justice in all his dealings has succeeded in securing a very large and profitable patronage. The stock is a general one and among the largest and most complete in the county of its kind, and here Mr. Blackinton also conducts a small banking business for the benefit of his patrons and friends, an institution which has proved of great convenience to residents of the surrounding territory.

Mr. Blackinton's willingness to assist all worthy enterprises is evidenced by the fact that when the Lee County Savings Bank was organized he became one of the original stockholders and directors and is one of its largest depositors and that his counsel and advice have been strongly instrumental in raising the bank to its present high position among the leading financial institutions of southern Iowa, a credit to its founders and a monument to the ability, care and far-seeing sagacity of those who have made it what it is today.

In 1867 Mr. Blankinton wedded Miss Anna Hughes, born in Bumbury, Cheshire, England, in 1841, and they have one son, Fred L. Blackinton, who received his preliminary education at Denmark Academy, and later was graduated from Grinnell, after which he was for six years connected with the First National Bank of Chicago. Deciding, however, to adopt the profession of law, he entered Harvard University, and in two years completed the full course in the study of law—an achievement which must be considered truly remarkable. Mr. and Mrs. Blackinton occupy a commodious and luxuriously furnished home adjoining the store, all the appointments being of the most modern type and including an up-to-date system of plumbing, with hot and cold water and artistically executed open fireplaces in many of the apartments. Mrs. Blackinton is a pleasant lady of genuine culture, and in social circles has always been highly esteemed. She is a member of the Congregational church.

Although never an aspirant for political honors, Mr. Blackinton early recognized the duty of every good citizen to interest himself in affairs of government, and became allied with the Republican party, in whose principles he has always been a believer, and by the force of his example, his great influence in the community and by his counsel and faithful work in a private capacity has been of material assistance to his party in this section. In all walks of life he has been a positive force for good. Starting in a small way and working upward to greater things by his own strength of character, he has achieved a success which should be an inspiration to all younger men and to future generations. He is widely known throughout this portion of Iowa, enjoys the intimate friendship of many leading people of this and surrounding counties and is respected wherever known for his ability and the inflexible integrity notable virtues of his character.

REV. JOHN BURGESS.

The world passed favorable judgment upon the life of Rev. John Burgess, for there were many elements in his character which commanded for him universal confidence and esteem. The place which he occupied in the regard of those with whom he came in contact was a tribute to that genuine worth and true nobleness of character which are everywhere recognized and honored. He accepted life as one long course of spiritual warfare, and to him was vouchsafed a great victory over the forces of evil because of his conscientious use of great natural gifts and because of his infinite, unfaltering trust in a Higher Power.

John Burgess was born at New Market, Frederick county, Maryland, May 2, 1821, the son of William Pitt and Lydia (Griffith) Burgess. About the year 1826 the family removed to Mount Vernon, Knox county, Ohio. There the father conducted a general store, and at that place his death occurred.

After beginning his education in Mount Vernon Rev. Burgess attended Kenyon College for a time, and later completed his formal schooling in Norwalk Seminary. He was naturally of a somewhat thoughtful turn of mind, having a devout nature, and at Norwalk he was converted to the religious life. Being strongly impressed by the idea that his field of labor lay in the Christian ministry, he joined the North Ohio conference of the Methodist Episcopal church, receiving the rites of ordination at the hands of that body. In 1847 he married Miss Sarah Elizabeth Gray, daughter of John and Mary (Ponder) Gray, who was born in Milton, Delaware, July 8, 1826. Mrs. Burgess removed with her parents from her native state to Marion county, Ohio, about the year 1842. There her father followed his trade, which was that of blacksmithing, and he also purchased land on the present site of Upper Sandusky, after that section was vacated by the Indians. Mr. and Mrs. Gray both removed to Keokuk in their latter years, and here was the scene of their passing to the life beyond.

The first pastoral charge held by Rev. Burgess after his marriage to Miss Gray, in 1847, was that of the Pulaski and Bean Creek mission, in Williams county. The next year he was assigned to the Waterville circuit, and following that, the Orange circuit. He was then located at Lexington for a time, and at various other places in Ohio. Transferred to the Illinois conference, he held successively the charges of Grand View, Virden, Chatham and Chili. During his second year in Illinois he was appointed agent for the Jacksonville Female Seminary to sell scholarships and collect for the college. He procured a second transfer, this time to the Iowa conference, and was first sent to Springville, near the Missouri line. The following year he was stationed at Bloomfield, and the third year at Fairfield Station, and the next year had charge of the circuit at Brighton. At the beginning of the Civil War he enlisted for the service of his country and his faith, as chaplain of the Thirtieth Iowa Volunteer Infantry. He went to the front with his regiment, and remained until his health failed, when he applied in person to Gen. Ulysses S. Grant for a furlough. The general, however, on seeing the low state of his physical condition, gave him an honorable discharge instead. Arriving at home in February of 1863, and attending conference, he was placed in charge of Brookville circuit. After a year at that place he came to Keokuk and for three years acted as pastor of the Exchange Street church, then the oldest church of the denomination in the city. He was then made presiding elder of Albia district, but preferring pastoral work, he resigned after a time, and spent a year at Pella. Following that he was made pastor of Montrose and was appointed chaplain of the State Penitentiary.

Rev. Burgess's health was not of the best at that time, and for that reason and because oppressed by the weight of years, he assumed superannuated relations, and retired from the regular service of the church. He continued to preach occasionally, however, until the close of his long and useful life. He removed to Keokuk, purchasing property at the corner of Twelfth and Des Moines streets, where his widow still resides. In this city he pursued a course of study in the College of Physicians and Surgeons, taking an honorary degree, but did not have in view the practice of medicine. He also organized and for some time was pastor of the Free For All, an independent church attended only by men, and by this means was able to present the truth to many who, feeling themselves debarred by their style of dress, were not accustomed to attend divine worship. Services were held in the United States court rooms. He won the love of his congregation, and as a token of their esteem he was presented by them with a large and elegantly bound copy of the Holy Bible.

During his later years Rev. Burgess attained recognition as an author and literary man of prominence. He was the author of two books, published by the Methodist Book Concern, of Cincinnati. The first was a book of sermons, and enjoyed an extensive sale. His more recent and larger work was entitled, "Pleasant Recollections with Old Scenes and Merry Times of Long, Long Ago," and is a 12mo. of 460 pages. This volume, embodying, as it did, the ripe reflections of a lifetime of earnest thought and wide experience, was very well received, its sale being remarkably large.

Two sons and two daughters of Rev. Burgess survive their father. They are: William Crawford, who married Miss Anna Haines, and has two children, Edith and Ethel; Anna, wife of John Cale; Mary L., wife of John W. Harmon, has three children, Charles, Myrtle and Ralph; John Arthur, who married Miss Hattie Crowell, of Keokuk.

Rev. Burgess was an active member of the Masonic Order and of the Grand Army of the Republic. His lamented death occurred May 6, 1897. For more than fifty years he labored faithfully as a minister of the gospel, and his social, kindly nature endeared him to hosts of friends. Though he has passed away, yet his memory is cherished by those with whom he came in contact. He left his impress for good upon all who knew his high Christian character. His career was one long benediction, and the bright example of his life shall be an inspiration to lead the coming generations to higher things. The world is better because he lived.

Mrs. Burgess is a member of the First Methodist Episcopal church, and is an intelligent and pleasant lady of unusual ability.

NICHOLAS McKENZIE.

Nicholas McKenzie, who is serving as lockmaster of the lower lock at Keokuk, was born in Brooklyn, New York, October

18, 1840, a son of William H. and Rosanna (Riley) McKenzie, both of whom were natives of Ireland. The father was a stonemason by trade. He came to the United States in his boyhood days, but afterward returned to Ireland, where he married, and then brought his bride to the new world, settling in Brooklyn. Later removing to the West, he established his home in St. Louis, Missouri, and was there engaged in the construction of the first gas works of that city, following his trade of a stone and brickmason for some time. He afterward joined the Regular Army and was stationed at Jefferson Barracks prior to the Mexican War, in which he did effective service. While he was at the front his family made their home at Jalapa, Mexico, and in the City of Mexico. After the war he went to New Orleans, and thence up the river to Keokuk, arriving in this city on the 3d of August, 1848, but he died three years later, passing away on the 6th of August. He left three children to the care of the mother, who long survived him and died on a farm, the home of her daughter, Ann, in Lee county, on the 13th of August, 1897.

Nicholas McKenzie was the eldest of three children, his sister and brother being Ann and William McKenzie. He was but eight years of age at the time of his father's death. He attended school in Keokuk, being a student under General Torrence, of Civil War fame. At an early age he had to work and help support the family, being the mainstay of the household after his father's death. He was apprenticed to George Engelhart to learn the blacksmith's trade, but did not complete his term. He worked in a blacksmith's shop as striker or helper, then entered the government service in 1857 on a chisel boat and dredge on the river, being thus employed for about five years.

On the 27th of May, 1861, Mr. McKenzie enlisted as a member of Company A, Second Iowa Infantry, under command of Capt. R. H. Huston and Colonel Curtis. The regiment was attached to the Sixteenth Army Corps and he served for three years as a private, and afterward became corporal. He aided in the capture of Fort Donelson, Shiloh, siege of Corinth and several engagements with the troops under General Forrest. He did much scouting and skirmishing, and was mustered out at Louisville with his regiment, receiving an honorable discharge at Nashville. He did his full duty as a soldier and valiantly defended the stars and stripes wherever duty called him.

When the war was over Mr. McKenzie came to Keokuk, and three days later began as a brakeman on the Keokuk & Fort Madison Railroad, but after being employed in that way for three days he gave up his position on account of Sunday work, as he wished to hold that day sacred from secular labor. He then secured a position in the Rock Island shops, and was employed at his trade for about six years altogether. He then turned his attention to the grocery business and was proprietor of a store for about four years as a partner of his brother, William, who is now in St. Louis, Missouri. In 1876 he was made turnkey at a police station, and the following year began working for the government as a lock hand on the middle lock. He came to the lower lock in 1898, and was made lockmaster in 1904, which position he is now filling.

In October, 1864, Mr. McKenzie was married in the old St. Peter's church, by Father DeCailly, to Miss Grace McCaffrey, a native of Ireland, who was brought to the United States in her early girlhood by her parents, Hugh and Bridget McCaffrey, also natives of the Emerald Isle. Her father was a stonemason and built many house foundations and buildings. He afterward removed to a farm in Minnesota, about 1857, and he and his wife spent their remaining days there. They were members of the Catholic church. Mrs. McKenzie has three sisters, Mrs. Kate Swift, of Valley Junction, Iowa; Mrs. Ann McGinty, of Minnesota, and Mrs. Eva Rouse, of Elizabeth, New Jersey.

Unto Mr. and Mrs. McKenzie have been born eight children: Hugh, who is a butler on the government steamer "Lucia," and makes his home in Keokuk, married Kate Burk and they have two children, Lewis and Margaret; Rose is the wife of Howard Conable, a clothier, of Keokuk, and they have one child, Madaline; Frank, who is superintendent of the shipping department with a Kansas City millinery firm, married Ellen Downey, and they have two children, Marie and Grace; John, a cigarmaker, married Mary Roe and resides in Keokuk; Nicholas, a bartender, of the city, wedded Mary Trofter, and they have one child, Mary Louise. Will is employed in the office of the Iowa State Insurance Company. Joseph is connected with the millinery firm, of Kansas City. The family home is at No. 206 North Seventh street, and in addition to this property Mr. McKenzie owns a place on Palean street, which he rents. He belongs to St. Francis Catholic church, and holds membership relations with the Catholic Knights and with the Grand Army of the Republic, maintaining through the latter connection pleasant relations with his old army comrades, with whom he marched to the defense of the Union, following the stars and stripes upon hotly contested battlefields.

REV. MELVIN SCOTT ACKLES.

The consecrated energy and persistency of high purpose exhibited in the activities of Rev. M. S. Ackles indicate for him, although he is as yet a young man, a probable career of success, usefulness and honor. Melvin Scott Ackles was born at Arbela, Missouri, November 14, 1874. While the Ackles family came west from Pennsylvania, Mr. Ackles takes pride in the possession of a potent strain of Scotch characteristics inherited from his paternal grandmother, who was born on a Mississippi river boat during the journey of her parents from Scotland.

George Scott Ackles, the father, was born near St. Louis, and owned property that is now very valuable as constituting part of the city. He at one time was the proprietor of a large wood yard at that place, also a fine farm, being very well provided with worldly goods. In 1865 he disposed of his various properties in the vicinity of St. Louis, and removed to Hamilton, Illinois, where he had a horse-power sawmill and conducted a hotel near the levee, being very successful from a financial viewpoint. He afterward made some investments in which he lost a fortune. He is now retired from active participation in affairs, and has his residence at Warsaw, Illinois. The date of his birth is February 6, 1817. The mother of our subject is Hannah Elizabeth (Northcraft) Ackles, and hers is an old Missouri family, large slaveholders in ante-bellum days. A matter of interest is the fact that there recently died in Keokuk a former slave of the family, Aunt Rose Washington, at an age approximating a century.

Mr. Ackles began his education in the public school of Warsaw known as "the seminary," and was later a private student of theology for six years under the guidance of Revs. H. J. Frothingham and C. M. Taylor, pastors of the Warsaw Presbyterian church. At the age of eighteen he relinquished his studies, and took employment with the Roesler Stove Polish Company, and also spent two years with the Warsaw Pickle Company, supporting the family by his labor. During the four succeeding years he was engaged in retail grocery and clothing business at Warsaw, and at the end of that period came to Keokuk as agent for the Metropolitan Life Insurance Company. In recognition of ability he was promoted, October 28, 1901, after a short but eminently successful connection with the business, to the position of Assistant Superintendent, which he still occupies. In this capacity he is charged with the local affairs of the company throughout an extensive district, and during his incumbency has very materially increased the importance of his office.

In pursuance of a long-cherished ideal Mr. Ackles made an arrangement with the Sugar Creek congregation of the Christian church near Keokuk on October 17, 1900, to act as their pastor without compensation, as they were so few and he proposed to build up the church as a missionary work. At that time no formal organization existed, but six months later Rev. Ackles organized the congregation, and for two and a half years continued the work without compensation, erecting, during this period, one of the most beautiful—perhaps the most beautiful—church edifice outside the cities and towns in the State of Iowa. Since the completion of the new building one year ago he has received a nominal salary, but has continued his ministrations as he began them—for the love of the work. The society is now large and flourishing, the number of communicants, originally twenty, having been trebled.

October 3, 1899, Rev. Ackles was united in marriage with Miss Katie Herstein, daughter of Christian and Barbara (Uhl) Herstein, and gracing this union is one daughter, Mildred M., born November 23, 1901, and a son, Harold Scott, born May 20, 1904.

Rev. Ackles received his authorization as a minister of the gospel at the hands of the First Christian Church of Keokuk, the date being September 9, 1901, and the work of his life, were he free to choose, would lie in the service of the church. He is a young man of sterling character and unusual ability, and such a consummation would doubtless result in marked advantage to his denomination and the great cause for which it stands.

JOSEPH E. FORDER.

Joseph E. Forder, an honored veteran of the Civil War, now engaged in gardening, was born at Ribovelle, Alsace, France, December 4, 1834, but though born across the water there is no more loyal adherent of the stars and stripes among the native-born citizens of the United States. His parents were Joseph and Katherine (Sirrette) Forder, also born in Alsace. The paternal grandfather, who also bore the name of Joseph Forder, was a shoe dealer and his son, Joseph, became a shoemaker and shoecutter in a government depot where clothing was made for soldiers. In the maternal lines our subject comes of a family that has furnishing many representatives to military life. His grandfather, Francis Sirrette, had four brothers, three of whom were in the French army. The eldest was Francis Sirrette, who held the rank of major, and was with Napoleon in Moscow, and up to the battle of Waterloo, in which the great French commander met his first serious defeat. He was a cuirassier, was six feet and five inches in height and was ninety-two years of age at the time of his death. For a time thereafter our subject and his mother were with the widow of Francis Sirrette. August Sirrette, another brother, was in the French army as a lieutenant, and died in the service, while Maximilian was a captain.

After loosing her first husband Mrs. Kererine (Sirrette) Forder was married, in 1837, to Joseph Brucker, a wine inspector for the government, and coming to America they settled in Burlington, Iowa, in 1857. By her second husband she had four children, and by her first marriage there were one son and one daughter: Kate, deceased wife of Blace Ringer, of Burlington, Iowa, and our subject: The children of the second husband were as follows: Alexander, of Grand Island, Nebraska; Louis, of Buffalo county, Nebraska; Joseph and Frank.

Joseph Forder attended the common schools and a military academy in France, intending to become a soldier, but he crossed the Atlantic at the time of his mother's emigration. He learned the butcher's trade in his native country, and after reaching America began working on a farm in the vicinity of Burlington, Iowa, while later he was employed in the Barrett House, of that city, until he enlisted in the army. He was a member of the state militia for two years before the Civil War, belonging to the Ellsworth Zouaves, and in 1861 he enlisted in the First Iowa Infantry, with which he served for four months as bugler. He participated in the skirmish at Bunker Hill and others, and was mustered out August 10, 1861, after the expiration of his term of enlistment, re-enlisting the same year in the Twenty-fifth Iowa Volunteer Infantry, as bugler of the First Batallion.

He was at Arkansas Post, afterward in the seige of Vicksburg, and in the engagements at Haines Bluff, Champion Hills and other movements of that campaign. The regimen did much scouting and skirmishing and lost many men in action. After the seige of Vicksburg they camped at Black river bridge and there Mr. Forder became ill with fever, and was discharged and sent home. He next joined the Ninth Cavalry as chief trumpeter and served in Arkansas and went with Sherman through the seige of Atlanta, and on the march to the sea; also through the Carolina campaign, which terminated the war. He received an honorable discharge in March, 1866, after more than four years of active field service. The military spirit of his ancestors was manifest in his capable discharge of duty, his unquestioning loyalty and his fearlessness in the midst of grave danger.

When the war was over Mr. Forder conducted a meat market in Burlington for many years, and also went on the Burlington, Cedar Rapids & Northern Railroad as pit foreman in the roundhouse, occupying that position for about three years. He also worked in a packing house at Burlington for about two years, and then removing to Keokuk, conducetd a meat market for three years. Returning later to Burlington, he there engaged in gardening, and later came again to Keokuk and entered the service of the Chicago, Burlington & Quincy Railroad Company as foreman of the coach department, cleaning and inspecting the coaches. In Hamilton, Illinois, he was engaged in the meat and ice business, and on the 5th of November, 1898, he came once more to Keokuk, where he is now engaged in gardening.

In February, 1862, in Burlington, Mr. Forder was married to Miss Josephine Goodrich, who was born in that city in 1836, a daughter of Philander and Elizabeth (Ashmore) Goodrich. Five children have been born unto them: Philander and Flora, who died in childhood; Elizabeth, who passed away in early girlhood; Harry, who married Celia Weber and resides in Keokuk, and Frank, who married Myrtle Shaw and lives in Chicago. Mrs. Forder passed away in 1904.

Mr. Forder is a Catholic in religious faith; a Republican in politics, and fraternally a member of Belknap Post, Grand Army of the Republic, and the Odd Fellows Lodge, at Hamilton, Illinois. His has been a busy life, and now he is living in comparative retirement. He owns a house and lot on Ligdon street, in Keokuk. He still has in his possession his sword and bugle, and he nightly blows the retreat, which is to many of his neighbors the signal that the day is ended and the hour for repose has come.

DR. EDWARD C. FIEDLER.

Dr. Edward C. Fiedler, who is engaged in the practice of electro therapeutics and massage, having for twenty-five years been connected with the profession, while for fourteen years he has been located in Keokuk, was born in Germany in 1839 and when thirteen years of age was brought to the United States, the family home being established in Memphis, Tennessee. He there attended school and was afterward a student in the medical college at Memphis, in which he was graduated in the class of 1882. For five years he was in the hospital of the United States army of the Sixteenth Army Corps, being stationed at Jefferson Barracks in St. Louis for two years and during the remainder of the time in Arkansas. He practiced medicine in Arkansas during the succeeding three years and then locating in St. Louis he served for eight years as acting chief and captain on the police force. He joined the force through the urgent solicitation of some of his army friends who wanted him to organize a mounted force. He was made captain of the mounted force and was acting chief for a part of the time. On leaving St. Louis he went to Hot Springs, Arkansas, where he engaged in practice, giving massage and electric treatments. In 1878 he went to Memphis, Tennessee, at the time of the yellow fever epidemic in order to study the disease. He remained in the hospital there for two years and during that time was induced to enter college. In 1882 he left the hospital and returned to Hot Springs, Arkansas, where he remained until 1890, when he came to Keokuk and established an office at the solicitation of some of his former patients in Hot Springs. He is now located at No. 411 Blondeau street. He has an X-ray machine and all modern electrical appliances. He has never believed much in the use of medicines, but has labored for the alleviation of human suffering through surgical work and electro therapeutics.

At the time of the Civil War Dr. Fiedler was married and he has two children, a son and daughter, Mrs. E. J. Gable, whose husband is a physician at New Albin, Iowa; and Charles, of New York. Dr. Fiedler gives his political allegiance to the Republican party, but has neither time nor inclination for office, prefering to give his undivided attention to his practice which is constantly growing in volume and importance.

HORACE SAWYER.

In days of strength and youthful vigor it would be a disgrace for a man to retire from active life and labor. He is full of the zeal and strength that his Maker has given him for great purposes, and it is his to meet all that fate or fortune has for him, with a composed face and an unshaking spirit. It is work, and duty, and responsibility, and "give and take" the blows of adversity, or the favors of fortune. It is different when years have passed, and the hair is white and the back bowed to its burden. Rest is deserved after toil, and there is a fitness for a man to pause a little while before the Sunset Gates are opened, and enjoy the fruits of well-spent years. In old age the retired life is fitting and natural, and gives grace and dignity to the years. All this may be said of the gentleman with whose name this sketch begins.

Horace Sawyer, now a retired farmer, whose home is in the village of Denmark, a charming little hamlet of Denmark town-

MR. AND MRS. HORACE SAWYER

ship, was born in New Hampshire January 14, 1832, a son of Francis, Sr., and Lydia (Hibbard) Sawyer. The parents were probably natives of that state, and there they were married. When they came to Iowa they drove through from their far eastern home with a team, covering what was then an immense distance in a period of nine weeks. Here they settled in Washington township, near where the village of Sawyer subsequently arose. When the land came into market Mr. Sawyer entered different tracts in Washington, Denmark and West Point townships, until he had secured about 440 acres in all. Here he made his home some eight years, and then removed to the village, where he and his good wife spent the balance of their days.

While Mr. Sawyer lived in New Hampshire he ran a grist mill and a starch factory, in which he used potatoes as the material for the starch. He was a poor man, however, on his arrival in the West, and had to borrow money with which to enter his land. As time passed he became quite well-to-do, if not rich. Largely he was the architect of his own fortunes, and made himself what he was.

Francis Sawyer was the father of a family of ten children, as the following names show: Lovina, Lois, Lydia, Francis, Jr., Timothy, Clarissa, Martha, Alfred and Eldridge (twins), and Horace. The two oldest children died in the East; Lydia died in Massachusetts; Clarissa died while visiting in this county. The parents brought seven children with them.

Mr. and Mrs. Sawyer associated themselves with the Congregational church after their arrival in Lee county, and are remembered as among the most active members of that church. In politics he was first a Whig, and later became a Republican. Well along in years at the time he became a resident of Lee county, he was satisfied to make a home for himself and family, and did not become prominent, though he was known as an upright and honorable man and a good citizen in every way. (The remains of both himself and his excellent wife rest in the Denmark cemetery.) He was much interested in the cause of education, and gave liberally to the support of the Denmark Academy. He died in 1860, being at that time seventy-eight years of age. His widow, who lived to the same age, passed to her rest in 1867. A brother of Francis Sawyer was killed in the French and Indian War. The Sawyer family comes of English stock.

Horace Sawyer was but six years of age when he was brought by his parents into this county, so that practically it may be said that his entire active life belongs to Lee county. Here he attended district school, and for several winters was a student at Denmark Academy, living at home under the parental roof, and moving with his parents into the village of Denmark. When he was twenty years of age he started out for himself, his father giving him 120 acres in Washington township for the care of the parents during their lives, and on which he made his home until the year 1890. That year he left the farm, and retired to the village of Denmark, where he has since made his home. In the meantime he had brought the farm to a high state of efficiency, and made it one of the model places of the township. In Denmark he occupies the same spot where his parents lived, though having a new and modern house.

Mr. Sawyer was married in 1863 to Miss Mary A. Miller, a native of Dutchess county, New York, and a daughter of Henry Miller. Both her parents died when she was young, her father in Wisconsin, and her mother in Chicago. She was married in Jefferson county, Iowa, and though they have had no children they have reared several, and have always had them in the house. At one time Mr. Sawyer had added forty acres to his original farm, but he has sold it, and only retains ten acres in Denmark. He and his wife are members of the Congregational church, and in politics he is a Republican. At different times he has held local and minor offices, and is highly regarded by his neighors, who know him as a man of excellent parts and spirit. The family, of which he is a leading representative, is an old and honored one, gives its name to the pleasant little village of Sawyer, one of the thriving centers of country trade that are so convenient to the neighboring population and so interesting to the traveling student of human life and conditions.

LEWIS A. BERRYHILL.

Born at Rochester, Pennsylvania, November 2, 1842, Lewis A. Berryhill came west with his parents and located in Keokuk in the spring of 1855, and since that time has been a continuous resident of this city, an interested witness of her development and a loyal supporter of all measures calculated to promote her welfare. He is the son of John and Mary Anne (Allward) Berryhill. His father was born in Allegheny county, Pennsylvania, and died in Keokuk, March 14, 1887. Mrs. Berryhill, mother of our subject, was a native of Westmoreland county, Pennsylvania, and her death also occurred in Keokuk. They were the parents of eight sons and daughters, as follows: Anna E., wife of William Johnson, of Westmoreland county, Pennsylvania; Lewis A.; Sarah, widow of Robert Haines, resides in St. Louis; John H., a plasterer, resides in Keokuk; James Madison, also a plasterer, died in Keokuk in 1888, and William R., of Kansas City, Missouri, is foreman of a large plumbing establishment.

Our subject received his education in the schools of Keokuk, and as a boy and young man learned his father's trade of cabinetmaking, continuing in that occupation until August 29, 1861, when, imbued with a desire to serve his country in her struggle for survival, he enlisted in Company C, of the Third Iowa Cavalry, in which he was afterward commissioned as first duty sergeant in 1862. At the time of receiving his commission he was the only private who was able to drill the company. He afterward joined the One Hundred and Thirty-eighth United States Infantry, in which he was commissioned a lieutenant. His commission bears the signature of President Johnson, and was mustered out at Atlanta, Georgia, January 1,

1866, at the age of twenty-two, with the rank of captain, having been made captain of colored troops.

On his enlistment he first went into camp at Camp Rankin, Keokuk, after two months proceeded to St. Louis. Remaining at that place for one month the regiment then made a forced march to join General Curtis, at Pea Ridge. The first general campaign in which our subject was a participant was that executed by the Army of the Frontier, and this has become a matter of history. The second, of lesser importance, was an expedition from Helena, Arkansas, to Vicksburg, where he remained until the surrender of that stronghold, known as the Gibraltar of America. The stay at this place, however, was not continuous, as it was interrupted by a minor campaign against the Confederate General Johnson, during which the City of Jackson was captured, and from which the regiment returned on July 4th, the day Vicksburg fell. Ordered to Memphis, Tennessee, to destroy rolling stock on the Mississippi Central Railroad. Confederate troops were encountered at Granada, where an engagement took place. It was at Memphis that Mr. Berryhill had the pleasure of traveling down the Mississippi river for a short distance on the same boat with Gen. Ulysses S. Grant.

Mr. Berryhill was with the Army of the Frontier at Little Rock, Arkansas, when his original term of service expired, and was the first man of that army to re-enlist, leading a party of twenty-nine comrades to an officer's tent for that purpose at two o'clock on a bitter cold winter night. Through this action the entire regiment was led to re-enlist. Thirty days afterward he came home on furlough, but rejoined his regiment at Memphis in time to take part in a vigorous campaign in that region. Across the river from the city two battles were fought, those of the Big Blue and Little Blue Creeks, in which the enemy was routed. Proceeding to St. Louis, fresh mounts were secured, and at Gravel Springs, Tennessee, organization was completed for Wilson's raid on Andersonville. The following campaign including the battles of Ebenezer Church, which was a severely contested action. Other battles in which Mr. Berryhill was engaged were Selma, Alabama, and Columbus, Georgia. The severest in which he was engaged was that of Pea Ridge, where the regiment lost heavily. On July 7, 1862, there was a severe battle at Cotton Plant, in which his regiment took part. Mr. Berryhill was wounded at the battle of Guntown, in 1865. It was not until he reached Selma, however, that he suffered disabilities which deterred him from continuing in actice service. This occurred May 5, 1865. The Union infantry had made an assault upon the Confederate position, but suffered repulse, when Col. John W. Noble, at the head of a cavalry detachment, led a charge and captured the city after fifteen minutes of hard fighting. Among the captured munitions was a large powder magazine, which he received orders to guard personally, and to fire it and retreat in case Rebel reinforcements were sighted. While he was on guard, however, the magazine was fired from the rear, and in the explosion Mr. Berryhill sustained the loss of his sight, and suffered from total blindness for the ensuing four years.

Previous to the battle of Selma Mr. Berryhill acted as a member of a searching party in pursuit of Jefferson Davis, the president of the Confederacy, and the capture was made by members of his brigade.

Captain Berryhill was one of the organizers of Torrence Post, Grand Army of the Republic, and for five years was its commander, and also was the first commander of Belknap Post, serving two years. He is a man of much public spirit, and organized the first lodges of the Sons of Veterans and the Women's Relief Corps, in Keokuk. For a period of six years he was deputy marshal of the City of Keokuk, and proved himself a strong and aggressive officer, but at the same time acted with fairness and impartiality to all. For four years he was engaged in the mail service, but resigned the position. Although an active worker in the ranks of the Republican party and the organizer and captain of all the Republican marching clubs of Keokuk for the last thirty years, he has never sought office. He was, however, without his own solicitation, at one time nominated for an important public office by the largest majority ever received by any candidate in the City of Keokuk. Fraternally he is a member of the Knights of Pythias, and captain of the Uniform Rank.

On May 7, 1880, Mr. Berryhill was united in marriage to Miss Mary L. Noutney, daughter of Albert Noutney, and to them have been born five children, two of whom died in infancy. Those living are: John T., Fred, and George McKinley. Mr. Berryhill has been able to supply his sons with better educational advantages than he himself received, and the eldest son, John, who has already begun his independent career, is proving himself to be a young man of marked ability, and is rapidly forging to the front in his chosen calling. At present he holds a very responsible position with the Chicago, Burlington & Quincy Railroad Company, being located at Centerville, Iowa.

Captain Berryhill possesses great natural aptitude for all activities of a military nature. In 1876 he organized a drill regiment in Keokuk, which, after being under his care for the short space of six months, took part in a contest held at Burlington, in which regiments from all parts of the state participated, and won the prize as the best-drilled regiment present. It is probable that heredity played some part in endowing him with this talent. His grandfather, Thornton Allward, was aide-de-camp to General Washington, losing his life by a wound received from a poisoned arrow in an Indian fight. His father, John Berryhill, was a soldier in the Mexican War, as was also his father's brother, William, who performed distinguished service. One brother, John, enlisted for the Civil War at the age of fourteen, and suffered imprisonment in Andersonville.

Mr. Berryhill was for three years foreman of construction work on the government canal at this place. He has been connected with various public enterprises, and has a great many friends and a large circle of acquaintances, who respect him for his integrity, courage and talents. In the regretable troubles and disturbances which took place several years ago and resulted in the organization of the American Protective Association at this place. Captain Berryhill was forced to take a prominent part in opposition of many of his friends and neighbors, the excitement of the times rendering his efforts to prevent disorder unavailing. But the former bitterness has passed away in the light of a more perfect understanding between those concerned, and today no one enjoys to a greater degree the good will and high regard of all who know him.

THOMAS VALENTINE WILSON.

Thomas Valentine Wilson, whose name is familiar to the old residents of Lee county as native to the soil and reared in the community in which he was born, has seen the county transformed from a sunny and flowery prairie to the settled home of a great population, a result which his industrial habits and manly vigor have helped advance. In the history of a nation a period of fifty years has no great importance; time is an element of national greatness. In the making of the West, however, time has not been so important. In 1849 Iowa was but a fringe of settlement with promise as to the future; in 1904 it is an imperial state, with a splendid development not elsewhere accomplished in hundreds of years. Then Lee county was mostly uncultivated prairie with little towns and hamlets that hardly hinted future prosperity; now it is a rich and fertile part of a magnificent commonwealth. And all this easily within the life of the man whose name appears at the opening of this article. He has seen it, and has been a part of it.

Thomas Valentine Wilson was born on the farm where he has his home at the present time, February 15, 1849, and received his education in the district schools of Jefferson township, Lee county. He was reared a farmer, and to the cultivation of the soil he has devoted his life. The farm on which he is now living was secured by government entry made by his father and grandfather in 1833. Here they settled in March of the following year, and here the family has since resided. At the present time it comprises 123 acres of beautiful land, and its appointments are superior throughout. The farm house is of brick, and it is a fine and commodious structure in which Mr. Wilson is living. His father died April 4, 1870; and his mother, August 15, 1899. In politics Mr. Wilson is a Democrat, and in religion, a member of the Methodist Episcopal church.

Mr. Wilson was married to Miss Henrietta Schlagenbusch November 23, 1871. She was a daughter of John and Henrietta (Eppers) Schlagenbusch, and as a wife and mother is beyond criticism. To her union with Mr. Wilson have come eight children: William Alva, born October 3, 1872, married Miss Mary Bubner; Valley Lovinia, born May 30, 1876, she is now Mrs. Eugene Smith; Ethel Ottie, born February 15, 1878. She is Mrs. Granville L. Arnold, and the mother of two children, Uva Orvia and Orville Valentine; Geneva Salome, born August 11, 1880, and Thomas Valentine, born March 10, 1883. Ollie Ann, born March 3, 1885, is the wife of Louis Weisbruch. Herbert Elmer, born September 9, 1886; the next died an infant; Hazel Edna, born August 22, 1892, and Delbert Bryan, born July 22, 1896, are the two younger children.

Mrs. Wilson's father came to Lee county from Germany in 1852, but she was born in Braunsweig, Germany, February 3, 1853. The father settled in Jefferson township, where he died when Mrs. Wilson was thirteen years of age. Her mother entered into rest July 22, 1879. They were the parents of two children, one of whom is Mrs. Wilson, and the other a son, John, who was born February 23, 1858.

Mr. and Mrs. Wilson are quiet and unpretentious people, little given to display, but of genuine worth and character, to which their many friends bear ready testimony. They pay their debts, help the poor, speak the truth, and are always kind and generous. We write them among the solid and substantial citizens of the town, and commend their history as worthy of study.

ALBERT EDWARD FOULKES.

Albert Edward Foulkes, deceased, was accounted one of the most prominent and enterprising business men of Keokuk and was classed with the representative citizens who while promoting individual success also contributed in large and substantial measure to the public welfare. Because of his activity in commercial and industrial circles, because of his close adherence to business ethics and his sterling traits of manhood, he enjoyed the uniform confidence and trust of all, and his death, therefore, came as a public calamity in the city in which he had long made his home. Mr. Foulkes was born in Manchester, England, October 3, 1847. His parents died in that country, but the mother at one time was a resident of America, returning, however, to her native land, ere her demise. Sarah Foulkes, a sister of our subject, is now living in England and a brother, Joseph E. Foulkes, is a resident of Crawfordsville, Indiana.

Albert Edward Foulkes spent the first eighteen years of his life in the land of his nativity and then hoping to benefit his financial condition through the business opportunities of the new world he crossed the Atlantic and established his home in Keokuk, living with an uncle who had previously settled in this city. Here he learned the painter's trade and during the greater part of his life was connected with that department of industrial activity. He likewise learned the business of paperhanging and decorating and after being employed as a journeyman for some time he established a business of his own and in addition to contract work dealt in paints, oils, painter's supplies, wall paper and art goods. Gradually he developed a business of large and profitable proportions and at the time of his demise was senior member of the firm of A. E. Foulkes & Sons. He embarked in this business soon after his marriage, continuing therein for twenty-nine years and his services were called into requisition in many of the finest homes of the city. Selling his interests here, he spent the years from 1890 until 1893 in Ogden, Utah, after which he returned to Keokuk and again became a factor in the business life of Lee county. He based his business principles and actions upon strict adherence to the rules which govern industry, economy and strict, unswerving integrity, earning for himself an enviable reputation as a careful man of business known in his dealings for his prompt and honorable methods, which won for him the deserved and unbounded confidence of his fellow men.

In 1869 Mr. Foulkes was united in marriage to Miss Mary E. Frank, a native of Ohio and a daughter of John and Margaret Frank. Her father was a farmer of the Buckeye state, and after his removal to Lee county, Iowa, became a passenger conductor on the Chicago, Burlington & Quincy Railroad, occupying that position for a number of years or until his leg was crushed in a wreck. He then resumed agricultural pursuits and died upon his farm in Lee county. Mrs. Foulkes has one brother, Willard Frank, a resident of Peoria, Illinois. Unto Mr. and Mrs. Foulkes have been born seven children, who are yet living, John W. married Rosa Geiger and has one child, Mildred, who is with them in Keokuk. Albert E., who was born in Keokuk, Iowa, in 1872, was at one time in the employ of the Southern Pacific Railway as a fireman, but was transferred to the train service and while thus engaged he was killed at Promontory, Utah, while in the act of coupling cars, April 16, 1901. About four years before he had married Mrs. Chisholm, a former resident of Keokuk, and they were living in Ogden, Utah. Albert E. Foulkes was at that time but twenty-nine years of age. Joseph K. Foulkes, the third member of the family, enlisted as a volunteer in the Spanish-American War, becoming a private of the Fiftieth Iowa Regiment, and was encamped at Jacksonville, Florida. He married Nora Gregory and with his brother, John W., continued the business which was established by their father. Arthur L. is married and living in Ogden, Utah. Sarah, Edward S. and Mary A. are all at home, living with their mother at No. 620 South Seventeenth street in Keokuk.

Mr. Foulkes was always a stalwart Republican in politics, and while he never sought or desired office had firm faith in the principles of the party. He held membership in the Methodist church and belonged to the Independent Order of Odd Fellows, and the Modern Woodmen of America. He delighted in scientific research and was especially fond of the study of ornithology. Among his home treasures is a beautiful cabinet containing fifty-two varieties of native birds, stuffed and mounted and also some of the smaller animals. His work in taxidermy was of a superior order, the birds and animals being mounted true to nature. He was likewise a collector of geological specimens and his early finds in and around Keokuk and Hamilton now constitute a valuable collection. Mr. Foulkes died very suddenly in his home at Keokuk on Sunday, May 27, 1900, after an illness of only a few hours and his death was the occasion of deep and widespread regret through the city in which he had long resided. He was an upright, honorable business man in every respect and won the esteem of all and the love of many. In his family he was kind and devoted husband and father, his best characteristics being reserved for those of his own household.

CHARLES COLE ROBBINS.

Celebrated for his kindly nature, his good deeds and his loyal devotion to his family, his friends and his country was one, the subject of this sketch, who has but lately gone to his reward in the life beyond. In the reality of that future life he ever professed a firm faith, and for it he prepared throughout the days of his earthly existence. Mr. Robbins was born November 26, 1830, at Union, Broome county, New York. His father was Alan Robbins, who was by trade a stonemason. On the 29th day of February, 1852, he was united in bonds of holy matrimony, with Miss Louisa Johnson, a daughter of Isaac and Marsha (Short) Johnson. The place of her birth was at Cooperstown, Otsego county, New York, the date being January 12, 1831.

In 1857, after spending the first five years of their wedded life in the Empire state they journeyed westward, seeking new and larger fields of labor, and located at Fountain Green, Illinois, and here Mr. Robbins successfully followed his trade, that of wagonmaking, which he had acquired in New York. He was considered by all who had occasion to bespeak his services to be a workman of the highest grade of excellence, and it seemed to the young couple that a happy and prosperous career was opening out before them. Before the husband was fairly established in business, however, came the call of the nation for defenders, and in September, 1862, he enlisted in company A, of the One Hundred and Eighteenth Illinois Volunteer Infantry, and went to the front as a soldier, serving until the end of the war. He bore a part in the battle of Arkansas Post and in the siege of Vicksburg, but was overtaken by sickness early in the war, and was thereafter unable to perform active duty for a great part of the time. He participated, however, in the battle of Port Hudson, did much police duty, and at New Orleans was detailed to act as a clerk. His service was long and faithful and of value to his country, but he was a modest man, and upon the occasion of his being offered a commission he refused, preferring to remain a private soldier. Near the end of the war he visited his home on furlough, which had been granted him because of his illness. At the expiration of his furlough he reported for duty at Springfield, Illinois, but was advised to return home, as the close of the conflict was near. He complied, and did not return to the field.

Mr. Robbins's military service was long, faithful and honorable, and from the ill health resulting from its hardships he suffered for the remainder of his life. Indeed, it may be said to have changed the entire course of his life, as it was the direct cause of his being compelled to abandon his favorite ambitions, and thwarted his ardent desire to secure an education which should fit him for a place in the business world. He was at one time in a Chicago institution of learning, intending to pursue a commercial course but found his strength unequal to the task. Thereafter he supported himself and family by manual labor, and although eminently entitled to the aid of a soldier's pension, did not make application until several years after the termination of the war. His trade was resumed, and with a fair amount of success.

Unto Mr. and Mrs. Robbins have been born two daughters: Ellen L., who was born at Union, New York, is the wife of Lenton M. Strader, and they live on a farm near Orsburg, Nodaway county, Missouri. They are the parents of eleven children, five of whom are married, and there are four great-grandchildren. The second daughter, Inez M., was born at Fountain Green, Illinois, and is the wife of Zachary T. Bickford, who is a farmer. They have one child. Mr. Robbins was of the Methodist faith, and Mrs. Robbins and the elder daughter are members of the Baptist denomination. He was always faithful in the discharge of his political duties, in which he took a lively interest, having been a member and active worker of the Republican party since its inception. He was a member of Torrence Post of the Grand Army of the Republic, and during the year prior to his death was commander of his post.

As indicated, Mr. Robbins never recovered from the effects of hardships endured on the battlefields and in the camps of the South, and these were the sources of his last illness. After two years of continuous suffering he departed this life November 12, 1902, and is buried at Plymouth, Hancock county, Illinois. The funeral was conducted under the auspices of the Grand Army of the Republic. An ideal husband, a loving father and a faithful friend, his memory is held in honor and respect by all who knew him. Of him it may be truly said that none knew him but to love him, none named him but to praise.

BENTON POOLE.

In the vocation which this gentleman has chosen are to be found many of the most pleasant features and delightful experiences of life. It has its trials and troubles, but the farmer is independent. His work is in the free air, and health and comfort are at his command. He is his own employer, overseer and paymaster, and whether he drives his team a'field or feeds his cattle in the meadows, he is the true aristocrat and uncrowned king in these American days. Mr. Poole has made no mistake in devoting his life to agriculture and the substantial results that have attended his fifty-five years show that his skillful management and unwearied industry, together with his manifest integrity and kindly spirit were bound to win in the end.

Benton Poole, now one of the trustees of Harrison township, Lee county, and residing on his 140-acre farm, a half mile south of Primrose, was born in this township, September 28, 1849. His early education was secured in the district school, which was near at hand, and when quite young was able to render his father active assistance in the management.

Micajah Poole, the father of Benton, was born in Virginia in 1800, and when he was thirty-six years old made his home in Iowa. He left his native state at the age of ten years, to make his home in Indiana, and there he learned the blacksmith's trade, which he followed for many years. However, on coming to Lee county, he turned his attention to agriculture, and securing a half section of land in Harrison township, and Van Buren county, a quarter section in either county, was henceforth a farmer. This property was quickly and largely improved by him, and he at once put up a comfortable log house as a home for himself and family. In 1856, on receiving a good offer for his land, he accepted it and spent the following winter in Farmington. The next spring he bought a farm of eighty acres in Van Buren county, where he lived until 1869. That year he returned to Farmington, which henceforth was his home until his death in 1873. During his active life in this state he was a general farmer, though giving much attention to stockraising, ever proving himself an industrious man and a good citizen. In political matters he arrayed himself with the Republican party, and in religious affairs was associated with the Methodist church.

Rebecca (Rowlson) Poole, the mother of Benton, lived until 1884, dying at the farm in Harrison township at the age of seventy-six years. Born in Ohio, she participated in the trials and privations of the early days, and was ever of a cheerful spirit and a kindly disposition.

Of the ten children born to Micajah and Rebecca Poole the following may be noted: John R., deceased; Wyatt A., a resident of California; Milburn Z., deceased; William S., a resident of Muscatine, Iowa, and a farmer; Martin M., a resident of Washington; Joseph P., of whom a sketch appears elsewhere in this volume; Susan Mary died in infancy; Ewalt died in 1863, while serving as a Union solider in the Thirty-fifth Iowa Volunteer Infantry; Adaline, wife of Thomas Walker, a farmer in Oklahoma; Benton, whose career is the theme of this article.

Benton Poole remained at home until 1868, when he left home and for some years was engaged in the neighborhood as a farm laborer, being employed by the month. He was quite successful in his various enterprises, and when his father died he was able to enter into contracts with the other heirs, by which he secured their interests in the family homestead, becoming himself its sole owner. He continued farming until the death of his mother, but when she died he sold the Van Buren county tract, and purchased his present home in Harrison township, a fine and well-improved place, comprising 140 acres, well-improved and furnished with a handsome brick residence.

Mr. Poole is a Republican, and has served as trustee of the township two terms, and is now an encumbent of that position. He is an enterprising business man, and a public-spirited citizen, of whom many kind things are said in the community where he lives and labors.

Mr. Poole was married in 1876, near Farmington, Iowa, to Miss Carrie Townsend. She died about a year after marriage, leaving one child, who died an infant. Mr. Poole married for his second wife Miss Mary Stinson, by whom he had two children, neither of whom survived the perils of infancy. Mrs. Poole died in the fall of 1884, and Mr. Poole was a third time married, when Miss Mina Eyler became his wife. She was a native of Ohio, and to her union with the subject of this writing were born five children: Nellie A., Rollie, Everett, died when only six weeks old; Maree, and Clell. These children were all born in Harrison township, Lee county, and are growing into a very bright and charming family.

Mr. and Mrs. Poole have led a quiet and uneventful life, attending to their own affairs, but taking a kindly interest in all neighborhood relations. They have many friends, and are numbered among the solid and substantial people of Lee county.

ELIAS OVERTON.

Elias Overton, who is now numbered among the great and silent majority, was in his lifetime a man of marked character and more than ordinary ability. He belonged to an old North Carolina family, and was a prominent and influential man in the old pioneer days. Those were the days that tried men's souls, and in every privation and danger he proved himself a man, enduring the inevitable patiently and meeting the dangers of the frontier bravely.

Mr. Overton was born in Hartford county, North Carolina, January 12, 1807, and was a son of Asa Overton, who was born in the same county in 1771, and Kitty Thomas, who was also a native of Hartford county, where she was born in 1775. They removed to Randolph county, North Carolina, in 1811, and in the spring of 1837 made their home in Lee county Iowa. Here they both died in 1838, the wife passing first to the world beyond, and the husband followed on the twenty-ninth day of May. They left a family of seven children, all of whom are now laid at rest in the silent churchyard.

Elias Overton accompanied his parents in their western excursion, and as they were poor people he had but little opportunity for schooling. What little opportunity came his way was eagerly improved, and in his mature days he was regarded as a well-informed man. In early manhood he worked as a farm laborer, and when he was twenty-six years of age married Nancy York, a native of Randolph county, North Carolina, where she was born in 1811. Within thirty days after their marriage they removed to St. Clair county, Illinois, where he purchased forty acres, and began farming on his own account. In 1836 they changed their location, becoming residents of Lee county, Iowa, securing a farm in Marion township, on section 36, where he built a rail cabin for a home until he could erect a more substantial structure. Mrs. Overton did not long survive her settlement in Iowa, dying in the month of September, 1840, and leaving three children, of whom brief mention may be made: Alfred, born July 5, 1834, died March 11, 1863, as a soldier the Union army, of typhoid fever, at Columbus, Kentucky, where he was buried. He had enlisted as a member of the Fortieth Iowa Volunteer Infantry, and is remembered as a brave and loyal soldier; Eliza, born September, 1836, married Jesse Derr, and lives in California; Lurinda, born February 17, 1840, married Martin Derr, and lives in California; William died young. Mr. Overton contracted a second marriage in September, 1841, when Miss Eliza Bunner became his wife. She was born in Virginia, March 15, 1817, and is still living at Mount Hamill, in Lee county. To this union were born six children: Mary E., born in October, 1842, married C. C. McCord; she died in 1894; Arey L., born in May, 1844, is the wife of David Powell, of Cedar township; John T., born March 31, 1848, is now living on the old homestead farm in Marion township; Henry died in infancy; Marion T., born August 10, 1850, is a resident of Marion township, and is the subject of a biographical sketch that appears in another page of this volume; Sarah A., born September 27, 1852, is the wife of John Powell, and resides in the southwest part of Missouri.

Mr. Overton removed his home to section 27, Marion township, in 1854, and there he spent the remainder of his days, dying March 29, 1893. He was a very successful man in all his business deals and operations, seldom making a misdeal, and then soon regaining the lost opportunity. At one time he owned over 1,200 acres of land, nearly all being exceedingly choice for farming purposes, and attracting much attention as being uniformly of such high grade. In local affairs he was a man of more than ordinary standing, and was county supervisor and township trustee, and filled different school positions at various times. Both he and his excellent wife were members of the Methodist Episcopal church, in which they were highly regarded as people whose lives kept close to their professions, making religion sincere and practical in every case. Of him it may be said he was a good citizen, a kind friend and a helpful neighbor.

MARION T. OVERTON.

The man who makes conditions spell success for him in the toilsome career of agriculture well deserves recognition in any work devoted to the worthy and honorable characters of a community in which he has passed laborious years. The man who digs a competence from the earth and compels the sun and the rain to do his bidding, commits no wrong, but confers a favor upon the world. If he is a public benefactor who makes two blades of grass grow where one grew before, then the farmers, the men who raise the grain, and cultivate the vegetables, and breed the cattle, are the great benefactors of humanity. For without them the men who guide the flying spindles and watch the whirring wheels of modern industry could not exist a moment. They sustain the social structure, and trade and commerce but dabble in the things they produce. The subject of this article is a worthy representative of the noble profession of agriculture, and his career a proper theme for this history.

Marion T. Overton, of Marion township, Lee county, was born in this same township where his years have been spent in honest industry, August 10, 1850. His education was received in the district schools, and the first twenty-six years of his life were passed under the parental rooftree, where he assisted his father in his farm labors on section 27. In 1876 he established himself on section 28, where he engaged in the cultivation of a fine farm, consisting of 440 acres, which has since been icreased to 494 acres on sections 22, 27 and 28. In 1890-1 he added 388 acres on section 29. He has put up all the buildings, and has nearly all the land under active cultivation. He follows general farming, and guides his activities by an intelligent study of the markets of the world, that he may understand what will be the most in demand in the near future. Politically he is a Republican, and in his own community has filled several positions to the satisfaction of all who have had occasion to do business with him. He has served on the township board, and for twenty-two years he has filled the position of treasurer for his school district, a place he still holds. He is a member of the Methodist Episcopal church for many years, and has long officiated as one its trustees. For two years he has been a steward of that body, and is known as an active and efficient official. The Farmers' Mutual Fire Association, of Donnellson, counts him as a working member, and has numbered him among its directors since its organization.

Mr. Overton was married December 14, 1876, to Miss Mary J. B. Emmerson, a daughter of Michael and Sarah (Dodsworth) Emmerson, both natives of Yorkshire, England. Her father was born October 11, 1815, and when he had reached the age of thirteen years was set to learn the tailor's trade, at which he worked seven years. He then worked to secure passage to America, towards the destinies of the family were tending. He arrived in the United States in June, 1840, and made his way directly to Lee county, Iowa, where he located on section 20, Marion township. For several years he worked during the summer season as a farm hand, and spent the winters working at his trade in Morgan county, Illinois. About 1843 he bought an eighty-acre farm in Marion township, Lee county, Iowa, to which he added land from time to time, until he became the owner of 410 acres, which under his capable management, became a very desirable farm, and here he and his wife lived and died. In the meantime he made a visit to England, and renewed his intimacy with the scenes and friends of his early youth. He died March 10, 1895, his widow finishing her earthly career February 3, 1899, the remains of both being interred in the Clay Grove cemetery. He was a member of the Church of England, and she of the United Brtehren. In politics he was a Democrat, but never filled a public office. Becoming a very successful farmer he was naturally brought into public attention, but his modest and retiring disposition kept him close to the farm. He and his wife were greatly respected for their many sound and excellent qualities. His wife, Sarah Dodsworth, was born July 15, 1821, and accompanied her parents in their removal to this country in 1834, settling with them in Morgan county, Illinois. At the age of twenty-one she married John Emmerson, who enlisted in the Mexican War, and fell at Buena Vista, February 23, 1847. He left a widow and one son. In September, 1847, she married Michael Emmerson, and came with him to his home in Lee county, Iowa. To this union were born three children: Anna E., wife of Joseph Caldwell, of Mount Pleasant, Iowa; John S., who died young, and Mary J. B., who is Mrs. M. T. Overton.

One son, Richard W., survives her first marriage, and is now living in Morgan county, Illinois.

Mr. and Mrs. Marion T. Overton have become the parents of the following children: Elias E., born June 15, 1877, married Miss Minnie A. Paschal, and resides on the old Emmerson farm, in this township. They have one son, Charles F., born April 10, 1901; John T., the second son, born July 9, 1878, married Miss Lillian Paschal, and has his home on section 29, this township; Sarah Eliza, born January 3, 1883, died December 28, 1899; William W., born September 12, 1885, lives at home, as do Marion L., born September 5, 1887, and Frank S., born March 28, 1889. All the children were born in the home on section 28, and all have received their education in the local schools.

Mrs. Overton was born June 5, 1858, in the old home on section 20, and was reared, educated and married in this township, and here she has spent her entire life.

Mrs. Elias Overton, the mother of Marion T., was born March 15, 1817, and is still living, hale and hearty, notwithstanding her advanced age, at Mount Hamill, in Lee county. Elias Overton, the father of the subject of this sketch, whose career is noted under his own name in another place, died March 29, 1893, on the home place, and was buried in the Clay Grove cemetery.

The Overton family, as will be seen by the foregoing sketches is a notable one, and has been a pronounced factor in the making of this part of Lee county. Its various branches have been fruitful of honest lives and good deeds, and all were people of more than the usual force of character and strength of purpose. Marion T. Overton has been no unworthy bearer of the name, and his personal character as well as business standing is beyond question.

JOHN COSGROVE.

John Cosgrove, who has won both business and social success and today represents one of the leading commercial enterprises of

Keokuk, was born in Belfast, Ireland, on the 11th of November, 1847, and in the following spring was brought to the United States by his parents who established their home in St. Louis, Missouri. He was a youth of ten years when they located upon a farm in Hancock county, Illinois, and Mr. Cosgrove pursued his education in the district schools while in the periods of vacation he assisted in the operation of field and meadow. While in St. Louis he had been a student in the Brothers school. When a youth of sixteen he left home and came to Keokuk to accept a position in the wholesale and retail hardware establishment of A. Weber & Company. He had had no mercantile experience, but he manifested a willingness and desire to learn the business and his close application and ready adaptability soon won him recognition in deserved promotions. Gradually he worked his way upward and in each transition stage of his career found opportunity for further progress. For sixteen years he represented the house upon the road as a traveling salesman and in 1884 he became a partner in the firm and has since been actively connected with the control of the business. He is today the vice-president of the company which is conducting an extensive wholesale and retail hardware trade. The reputation which the house sustains is unassailable and Mr. Cosgrove added greatly to its record in this direction while upon the road.

In 1874 occurred the marriage of Mr. Cosgrove and Miss Mary C. Gregg, a daughter of M. Gregg, once a prominent merchant of Keokuk, but now deceased. The wedding was celebrated in this city and has been blessed with seven children: Cecelia, the wife of Louise Culkin, a resident of Carthage, Illinois; John Clement; Elizabeth; Stella; Hugh Bernard; Henry Edward, and Harriet.

Mr. Cosgrove is a member of the Knights of Columbus, having joined De La-Salle Council, No. 619, upon its organization. He belongs to Keokuk Lodge, No. 106, Benevolent and Protective Order of Elks, and to the Travelers' Protective Association. At one time he was president of the Keokuk branch of that organization and the local secretary and treasurer. He was also a charter member of the Keokuk Club, but is not identified with that organization at the present writing. He belongs to the Catholic Knights of America and was a state delegate to the national convention, held in Philadelphia, and also in Indianapolis—the only delegate from this state. He belongs to St. Francis Catholic church and was one of the members of the building committee, having in charge the erection of the handsome gray stone church at the corner of High and Fourth streets. His political allegiance is always given the Democratic party, and he was once a candidate for alderman, but the Republicans have the majority in this ward. He ranks high in the councils of local and state politics and frequently attends the national conventions.

Mr. Cosgrove owns a magnificent home overlooking the river, it having been built by Mr. Sanford and is situated at No. 101 North Second street. A local newspaper has said of him: "He applies himself closely to his business duties, but finds time to be genial, courteous and companionable among his associates in his home city and hundreds of visitors coming here who met him during his years on the road. Always in a good humor and with a kindly greeting for those with whom he comes in contact on business or in a social way, he makes friends readily and has no enemies." As a prompt and thorough business man, a fast friend, a genial associate, a good neighbor and a progressive and valued citizen, no man in Keokuk stands higher than John Cosgrove, who is accounted today one of the foremost representatives of social, political and business circles in Keokuk.

MARTIN F. REIGLE.

Martin F. Reigle, of Fort Madison, was born at Peru, Indiana, August 26, 1872, and is the son of John Reigle, who was born in Germany, and on coming to America located at Harrisburg, Pennsylvania. Later John Reigle was one of the early settlers of Peru, where he now lives, in his ninetieth year. For a time he was a locomotive engineer on the old Indianapolis, Peru & Michigan City Railway, but in the pursuance of the duties of this position had the misfortune to lose the use of one eye, and for ten years acted as a stationary engineer. Since twenty years ago he has been living retired. The mother of our subject is Elizabeth (Mortor) Reigle. She is living at Peru, and is in the sixty-eighth year of her age. Unto them have been born seven children, five of whom besides Martin F. are living. They are: Edward, Albert and Andrew, of Peru, Indiana; Frank, of California; Mrs. Thomas Moore, of St. Louis, Missouri; and Miss Lettie, of Kansas City.

Martin F. Reigle grew to years of maturity at the parental home in Peru, and at that place received his schooling. After leaving school he was variously employed until 1891, when he entered the employ of the Atchison, Topeka & Santa Fe Railway Company as a brakeman. He was assigned to duty on various sections of the road, making his first trip from Topeka to Emporia, then receiving a passenger run from Kansas City to Newton, Kansas, later traveling between Chicago and Kansas City, and since 1893 doing passenger work between Fort Madison and Kansas City. Since the latter date he has removed to this place, and on September 23, 1896, was here married to Miss Minnie Becker, daughter of Charles and Emilie (Muender) Becker. Charles Becker was born at Melberger bei Renne Kreif Huford, Germany, came to America and located at St. Louis in 1851, and there his marriage took place in 1854. He came to Fort Madison in 1856, and followed his trade of blacksmithing and wagonmaking until 1890, when he retired from active work. His death occurred in 1891. He was a member of the German Lutheran church. Emilie Becker was born in Halle, Prussia, Germany, December 26, 1834, and came to America in 1851. Her death occurred April 16, 1898. Unto Mr. and Mrs. Becker were born six children: Mrs. J. W. Meyer and Edward F. Becker, of Kahoka, Missouri;

Mrs. F. M. Reigle; Misses Emilie and Callie J., of Fort Madison; and Mrs. Fred W. Dodd, also of Fort Madison.

Mr. Reigle purchased pleasant residence property at 1015 Second street, Fort Madison, December 8, 1903, and in this he makes his home. He also owns a handsome residence at 1412 Fourth street. Believing Republican principles best fitted to maintain the general prosperity and well-being of the nation, he has always given his support, in important contests at the polls, to that party. In his fraternal connections he is a member of the Independent Order of Odd Fellows, and the Brotherhood of American Yeomen. Genial, ever courteous, and well-informed on all leading topics of the times, he is justly popular, and those among his friends who know him best predict for him honors, advancement and still greater successes than he has achieved in the past.

SYLVESTER T. WORLEY.

The expansion of trade interests and the evolution of business conditions are noticeable factors in American history of the present. In every community are found men of marked enterprise who are broadening the scope of their labors and meeting circumstances with an energy and discrimination that results in the development of extensive and important industrial and commercial concerns of value to their cities as well as to the individual. Of this class S. T. Worley is a representative who from a humble position in business life he has advanced until as a carriage manufacturer he occupies a prominent place in industrial circles in Keokuk.

Mr. Worley was born in Portsmouth, Scioto county, Ohio, on the 10th of January, 1832, and is descended from German ancestry. In the early development of Pennsylvania Henry and William Worley, natives of the Fatherland, crossed the Atlantic to the new world, establishing his home in Pennsylvania in 1669. The old family homestead near Philadelphia, which was obtained from William Penn, is still in possession of representatives of the family name. John Worley, grandfather of S. T. Worley, served as a spy and scout with the Colonial Army in the Revolutionary War. After the establishment of peace he removed to Ohio, becoming a resident of that state when the site of the City of Cincinnati was occupied only by a fort. Jacob Worley, father of S. T. Worley, was born and reared in Ohio and throughout his life followed the occupation of farming, save that during the second war with England he espoused his country's cause and rendered military service in defense of American rights. He married Elizabeth Truitt, a native of Delaware, the Truitt family removing from that state to Kentucky in 1789, the family home being established near Flemingsburg. It took three years to make the journey from Delaware on account of the Indians. Mrs. Worley's mother rode over the Alleghany mountains on a pack horse. The Truitt family was represented in the Civil War. Jacob Worley continued a resident of Ohio until his death, which occurred in the year 1849 and his widow afterward removed to Quincy, Illinois, where her death occurred in 1874. In the family were three daughters who reached mature years: Evelyn, the wife of James Hall, of Ottumwa, Iowa; Ann, who became the wife of H. Veach and died in Quincy, Illinois, and Lydia, the widow of Moses Hall, of Quincy, who was captain on a river steamer.

S. T. Worley was reared to manhood in the state of his nativity upon the old home farm and when twenty-one years of age he was married in 1853 at Portsmouth, Ohio, to Miss Caroline Pyle, who died in 1856, leaving two children, of whom Charles died in Keokuk at the age of thirty-six years. The other, Laura E., is now the wife of Seaberry Chandler, who resides upon a farm near Warsaw, Illinois. After loosing his first wife Mr. Worley was married again in Portsmouth in 1858, his second union being with Elizabeth J. Hicks. In 1860 he removed with his family to Quincy, Illinois. He had previously learned the carriage-maker's trade at Portsmouth and he conducted a shop there and upon his removal to Quincy, Illinois, he established a similar enterprise, which he conducted until his enlistment for service in the Cicil War. In June, 1862, his patriotic spirit having been aroused, he joined the army as a private, but was made lieutenant on the organization of Company A, One Hundred and Nineteenth Illinois Infantry, and on the death of Captain Holland he was commissioned captain of his company. The regiment was under command of Colonel Kinney and was assigned to the Sixteenth Army Corps, doing duty in Tennessee, Mississippi, Louisiana and Arkansas. Captain Worley participated in the battles of Champion Hills, Fort Derussa, Pleasant Hill, Moore's Plantation, Markville Prairie and Yellow Bayou. The ranks of the regiment had been so depleted that it numbered only 250 men at the time of the last-named engagement. All the officers in the regiment but three were wounded or killed and forty-seven men were killed in that engagement in about four minutes. Captain Worley and five others were the only officers who escaped. He participated in the battles of Tupelo, Mississippi, and in a two days' engagement at Nashville and was mustered out under special field order issued by General Thomas, department commander, in March, 1865. He was a brave and loyal soldier, careful of his men yet never hesitating to lead them wherever duty called and with a most creditable military record he returned to his home in Quincy.

In April, following, Mr. Worley came to Keokuk and established a carriage factory on First street, continuing business there until 1884, when he built on Johnson and Seventh streets. When his son attained a sufficient age he was admitted to a partnership and the firm was incorporated under the present style of the Worley Carriage Company. The present building is 50x80 feet and two stories in height with basement. From the time of the establishment of the enterprise it has constantly grown in volume and importance and the business has reached large annual figures, furnishing employment to a number of workmen and bringing a gratifying annual return. As his financial resources have made it possible Mr. Worley has become the owner of extensive farm and timber lands in Dent and Riles counties, he and his sons having bought 600 acres there.

Unto Mr. and Mrs. Worley have been born nine children: William, who is in partnership with his father; Emma, the wife of Paul Richardson, superintendent of the Keokuk Gas Works; Ida, the wife of H. B. Barnes, a farmer of Hannibal, Missouri; James, who died at Oakland, California, in 1900, at the age of thirty years and was laid at rest in the Keokuk cemetery; Harry F., a practicing physician of Oakland, California; Grace, the wife of Lewis Reinard, of Pheonix, Arizona, and Mary, the wife of Dr. N. B. Patty, of Syracuse, Nebraska.

While Captain Worley has led a very busy and useful life he has yet found time from his industrial interests to devote to those lines of activity which develop character and promote the moral growth of the community. He has long been a prominent member of the First Methodist Episcopal church and for twenty years has served on its board of trustees. He has been an active worker in the Sunday school for forty years, thirty years being a teacher of the young men's class and by example as well as precept he has done much to inculcate those principles which develop strong and honorable manhood and which work for the ethical ideas in all life's relations. Mr. Worley likewise belongs to Torrence Post, No. 2, Grand Army of the Republic, and he gives his political allegiance to the Republican party. His home is at the corner of Twenty-first and Orleans streets and he owns a small fruit farm of nine acres. It is his intention soon to retire from active business life, having through the long years of his connection with the trade of carriage manufacturing developed a business that has brought him gratifying success. To him there has come the attainment of a distinguished position in connection with the great material industries of the county and his efforts have been so discerningly directed along well-defined lines that he seems to have realized at any one point of progress the full measure of his possibilities for accomplishment at that point. Moreover, his entire career has been in harmony with the rules that govern unswerving integrity and honorable manhood and his entire career has won him not only the admiration but respect.

THE REV. FATHER JOHN TEGELER.

The Reverend Father John Tegeler, whose career forms the subject of this biographical study, belongs to the number of those ministers of religion who wait on the altars of faith with deep devotion and make their lives eloquent with good deeds and helpful words. As a priest of the Catholic church he has been faithful and devoted.

and as a citizen public spirited and awake to all social interests. He has shirked no responsibility that attended his divinely appointed labors, and has been a man of sympathy, godly counsel and ready charity. No needy soul turns unrelieved from his door. He chides, pleads and entreats for the better way, and is a living gospel of help and cheer. Such is the true priest of the everlasting church, "founded on the Rock," and such has been the ideal of the minister of Jesus Christ that has ever been cherished in the heart of the rector of St. James's Catholic church of St. Paul, Lee county. To wait on the oracles of faith, to declare the full gospel of his Master, to guide his people in the way of truth, honesty and sobriety, to watch, and lead and pray, and bear them on a tender heart has ever been his work and spirit, and for it he is known and revered, beloved by his own flock, and much respected by all in the community, who have come to prize him at his full worth, and to know how true and strong a man he is.

The Rev. Father John Tegeler, the present eloquent and devoted rector of St. James's Catholic church of St. Paul, Lee county, was born in New Vienna, Dubuque county, Iowa, March 19, 1859, a son of Gerhard H. and Frances (Belm) Tegeler. His father was a native of the town of Thine, Alfhausen, Germany. His mother was born in Rieste, Hanover, Germany. The father was born January 18, 1827, and his good wife August 24, 1824. When he was a young man he became a plasterer, and for many years followed that trade in the United States after his arrival on the American shore. When he was twenty years of age he crossed the ocean, and settled in Quincy, Illinois, where he was married in 1852. Some years later he removed to Dyersville, Iowa, where he purchased a farm, on which his family was reared, while he himself worked at his trade. Still later he purchased a home in Dyersville, Iowa, where he and his wife spent their last days in that peace and comfort that should attend the closing period of a true and noble career. He died December 27, 1899, and his widow December 9, 1900, and both are buried in St. Francis's cemetery, Dyersville, Iowa. They and all of their family were devout members of St. Francis's Catholic church, of Dyersville, Iowa. To them were born the following children: Henry, who married Miss Anna Burkle; Barney, who died young; Katie, the wife of G. W. Sudmeier; Gerhard J., who married Miss Anna Brunsmann; Barney, who married Theresa Beckmann; John, the pastor of St. James; Joseph J., who married Miss Maggie Eilers; Lewis, who married Miss Mary Steffin. All these children are living near Dyersville except the subject of this sketch.

The Reverend Father John Tegeler was born and reared on a farm. His primary education was secured in a district school, and the opportunities for health and physical culture, together with the building of nervous vitality and force, were his, and he profited by the privileges that were open to boys on what was still in no small measure the frontier. For one term he was a student in the Dyersville high school; and when he was twenty-one he entered St.

Joseph College, at Dubuque, Iowa, April 1, 1880, for the purpose of taking a classical course in that institution. He had at that time as the ambition of his life to become a priest, and for that purpose after his graduation in Dubuque, he was for two years a student at Mount Calvary, a Wisconsin college, from which he went to Cape Girardeau, Missouri, where he completed his theological studies with high honors, and was graduated in May, 1890. He was ordained to the priesthood on the 31st of the same month by the Right Reverend H. Cosgrove, of Davenport, Iowa, and soon after he was called to Bauer, Iowa, where he also had charge of a mission at Rosemount. In February, 1902, he was appointed rector of St. James's church, at St. Paul, Lee county, Iowa, and entered at once upon the sacred duties of that position with zeal and devotion. He arrived at his appointed field of labor, and on the following Monday broke ground for a new parsonage. By his untiring energy and push he has here erected a most modern home, in which 90,000 brick were used. It is modern in all its equipments, and has before it a fine lawn on which many trees have been set out. The building cost $5,000, and is a marked credit to the county.

St. James's church is a fine brick building, 150x60 feet, with a tower 175 feet in height. Father Tegeler has made many improvements in the house of worship, added much to its adornment, and today has one of the finest churches and the best appointed home in this section of the county. On his church rolls are carried the names of over 125 families, and connected with it is a parish school under the supervision of three sisters of the Order of St. Francis, P. A. They have the care of a hundred or more pupils, and the school is widely known for its fine spirit and thorough work.

Father Tegeler is a Democrat in his political views, though his profession demands all his thought and attention. He is widely read and deeply educated both in school and by travel, having been over much of the United States, and equally at home, in German, English and Latin. He is a polished and scholarly gentleman and bears himself everywhere with that kindly dignity and gracious manner that become his sacred calling.

BENJAMIN B. JEWELL.

Those who have to do with the banking interests of a community hold in their hands its most vital springs of action. The bank has become the heart of the business world, which has become so complicated that only those who are in daily touch can understand how vital to all commercial activities is the accommodation and facility afforded by the various banking institutions, both large and small. Mr. Jewell, whose name introduces this sketch, has been associated with the Keokuk Savings Bank for a long period of years in the capacity of general bookkeeper, and in that time has become intimately acquainted with the powers and privileges of the bank. Prior to his becoming connected with the Keokuk institution he was in business many years as a wholesale grocer, so that it is hardly too much to say that he is one of the most accomplished commercial men of southeastern Iowa. Kindly and courteous in his manner he is quick in his conclusions, and strong in his convictions. In the long period in which he has been in active life in Keokuk he has made a host of friends, and is universally pronounced one of the leading spirits of the city.

Benjamin Blackiston Jewell was born in Madison, Indiana, July 10, 1839, a son of William J. and Eliza A. (Blackiston) Jewell. The father was born in Baltimore, Maryland, October 1, 1812, and died April 12, 1891. He was a painter by occupation, and led a long and useful life. Eliza Ann Blackiston, to whom he was married at New Albany, Indiana, May 27, 1834, was born February 14, 1815, and died December 19, 1884. In their long and happy married life of fifty years, they were blessed with the birth of the following children: Harriet Eliza, who was born January 1, 1837; Benjamin Blackiston; Charles William; Sarah Elizabeth; Mary Margaret; John and James Edward.

Mrs. William James Jewell was the daughter of Benjamin Blackiston, who was born in Kent county, Maryland, in May, 1788, and who came west in 1819 to New Albany, Indiana, in 1819. He married Eliza Erskine March 28, 1814, who lived until November 1, 1868. They reared the following children: Eliza Ann, who was born February 15, 1815, and died December 19, 1884; Edward; Benjamin F.; Margaret; Sarah; Hester Caroline; Mary Susannah; James Edward and Elizabeth Jane, who were twins.

John Jewell, the grandfather of Benjamin B. Jewell, whose career is the theme of this writing, was born July 18, 1788, and is the earliest ancestor of the Keokuk bookkeeper, of whom there is an authentic record. He was a chairmaker and a painter by trade, and lived in Baltimore. He bore arms for his country when the English invaded that section of the nation in the War of 1812, and was in the engagement at Blandensburg. About 1818 he removed to Indiana, where he soon established himself in a paying business. Twice married, his first wife was Sarah Gregory, to whom he was united in matrimony October 4, 1810. She was born in 1789, and died September 5, 1819. To them were born: Mary, born July 11, 1811; William James; Susanna, February 4, 1814; Elizabeth, November 11, 1815, died January 3, 1900; Sarah Ann, August 23, 1817, died December 19, 1817; and John, September 5, 1819, died October 25, 1819. Mr. Jewell contracted a second marriage, December 21, 1819, when Miss Sarah Davidson became his wife. She was born May 1, 1796, and became the mother of the following children: Thomas Asa, born December 8, 1820, died September 20, 1821; Harriet; Charlotte; Amanda; Alfred D.; Sarah Eliza and Laura A. The father of these children died May 15, 1842.

William J. Jewell learned the painter's trade from his father, with whom he was associated in business for several years. This business he carried on after the death of his father, and for two and a half years made his home in New Albany. He then removed to Keokuk, where he arrived November 1, 1855. Here he resumed work at his trade, which he followed until about 1883. His death occurred on April 12, 1891. Mrs. Jewell died December 19, 1884.

Of the children of Mr. and Mrs. William J. Jewell, the following facts may be mentioned: Harriet E. married Thomas J. Hardesty, and is now a widow residing in Keokuk. Charles William died in childhood. Benjamin Blackiston is the subject of this article. Sarah E. has her home with her brother, Benjamin B. Mary M. is the wife of J. D. Graves, and is now living at Aspinwall, Pennsylvania. John is living in Keokuk, where his brother, James E., died in 1884.

Benjamin Blackiston Jewell, the subject of this article, received his early education in the public schools of Indiana. For a time he was a student in a private school, but when he was fourteen years of age he passed from the school room into active business, and was employed in mercantile pursuits until he came to Keokuk in November, 1855. For some two years he was a clerk in a retail store, when he took a position as bookkeeper. January 1, 1865, he became a member of the firm of S. Pollock & Company, wholesale grocers, a position he continued to fill for twenty-four years, and until the firm retired from business in November, 1889. He became connected with the Keokuk Savings Bank as general bookkeeper June, 1890. As a business man he is alert and capable, taking rank among the leading men of the city; and personally he has many friends both in and out of his commercial associations.

Mr. Jewell is a Republican in political matters, and takes a prominent part in all city matters. He has been treasurer of the City of Keokuk two terms of a year each, and for twenty-four years has been a trustee of the Keokuk public library, and chairman of books and catalogue committee for many years.

The long and useful career, which is briefly outlined above, abounds with incidents which illustrate the genuine worth and dignity of the character of Mr. Jewell. He has carried himself so carefully and well that as he advances into the midst of the years he writes a record of integrity and uprightness. His life is worthy of study and his business career worthy of emulation.

DAVID HOUGHTON.

David Houghton, now engaged in business as a barber at Montrose, Iowa, was born October 23, 1840, in Orange county, Vermont, the son of David and Elizabeth (Rowell) Houghton, both natives of Vermont, and is the sixth of eight brothers and sisters, of whom only three now survive, these being Melissa, wife of C. Hamma, of Sonora, Illinois; Pomelia, wife of William Dustin, of Oregon, and our subject. In 1841, the year following that of his birth, he came with his parents to Nauvoo, Illinois, they being converts to the faith of the Latter Day Saints or Mormons, and having sold their property in Vermont to follow the fortunes of the prophet, Joseph Smith. For his adherence to the new faith David Houghton, Sr., was disinherited by his father, a wealthy citizen of Vermont, but he nevertheless relinquished all his interests in his native state, including a very desirable position as manager of a large shoe factory employing sixty men, and set up a shoemaker's shop in Nauvoo, where he prospered, and by his industry built up a good business. He remained a Mormon all his life, and in 1848 went to Prairie du Chien, where he died the same year, while his wife died at the home of her son, David, in Montrose in 1871, she having been remarried to a Mr. Timmons and returned to Nauvoo, where she taught school after the occupation of that place by a French colony.

When ten years old Mr. Houghton left home in consequence of a quarrel with one of his schoolfellows, and went to live with a sister in Chicago, where he remained, working as a shingle packer for ten years, returning in 1854 to Montrose, and here he has since continuously resided. He worked for a time in the boat yard owned by John Bunker, and in the autumn of 1861 enlisted in Company B, Seventeenth Iowa Volunteer Infantry under Colonel Rankin and Captain Hoxie. In the spring of 1862 he went into camp at Benton Barracks, St. Louis, and after remaining there for two weeks proceeded down the Mississippi river to Shiloh, landing at that place just after the battle, but in time to participate in the battles of Corinth and Iuka. At Jackson, Mississippi, he was captured by Rebel forces and placed in Libby prison at Richmond, Virginia, whence after about fifty days he was paroled, and went to the hospital at Annapolis, Maryland, being detained there for a period of seven or eight months on account of suffering from gangrene in the right hand. After ninety days spent at Camp Tyler, Baltimore, subsequent to his leaving the hospital, he set out to rejoin his regiment, meeting it at Scottsboro, Georgia, and the next battle in which he was engaged was the second fight at Corinth in 1863, and while occupying a blockhouse at Tilden he, with the entire regiment, was captured by the soldiers of General Hood on October 13, 1864. Thence he was taken to Kahoba, then to Melon, Georgia, and later to the famous military prison of the Confederacy at Andersonville, where he remained a prisoner of war until April 1, 1865, a period of more than six months, during which he suffered great hardships. Released from prison, he was at Vicksburg at the time of the assassination of President Lincoln, and immediately thereafter started north, landing first at St. Louis, where for two weeks he was at Benton Barracks, and then returned to Montrose, and three days after his arrival here was called to Davenport, Iowa, where he was honorably discharged from the service of his country after a long and faithful devotion to duty on field of battle, in camp and in many perilous situations. After the close of the war he worked for some time as a freight handler on the Mississippi river, lighting freight over the Des Moines rapids.

On July 11, 1866, Mr. Houghton was united in marriage to Miss Mary Ann Ray, he then took up his present occupation, that of a barber, having learned the trade while a prisoner in Andersonville, and this he has ever since continued with great success. He has taken an active interest in public affairs as a member of the Republican party, having served two terms in the city council and also having been once elected to the office of constable, although he refused to accept the office. Fraternally, he is a charter member of Tip Best Post, No. 75, Grand Army of the Republic, while Mrs. Houghton is a member of the Woman's Relief Corps. They occupy a pleasant home at Second and Walnut streets, and enjoy the esteem and regard of a large circle of friends.

GEORGE WILSON.

In so new a country as the world west of the rolling waters of the Mississippi may be considered, it is somewhat difficult to form a proper idea of how young the old families may be. Such a term in Europe would mean hundreds of years, and many generations in New England. In Lee county it means perhaps the span, or less than that, of a human life. It is measured by what has been done rather than by what time has been required in the doing of it. Judged in this way, the Wilsons and the Drollingers are old families. They have seen a wonder-working in the planting of civilization in the wilderness accomplished, and in the doing of it they also helped.

George Wilson, the son of Hugh and Susan (Skyles) Wilson, was born on the banks of the Cumberland river in Tennessee, in 1809, and coming to Lee county in 1834, secured a tract of government land comprising 160 acres. From time to time he added to this until he owned 400 acres. His marriage occurred in Schuyler county, Illinois, July 22, 1832, and his wife died June 2, 1878, and he, March 20, 1891. Their eleven children were as follows: James, Susan, Elizabeth, Sarah, Jane, Louisa, George, Hannah, John and others who died in infancy. George Wilson was a Democrat and a member of the Methodist church. He bore arms in the Black Hawk War, and was remembered by those who knew him best and in his prime as a man of resolution and activity.

THE DROLLINGER FAMILY came to Lee county from Illinois and settled on the place which has been the family homestead since their marriage. Of this family all are now deceased with the exception of Benjamin Wesley, who is a son of Samuel and Rachel (Cook) Drollinger. He was born in Indiana December 4, 1830, where he was reared to the life of a farmer. His marriage to Miss Susan Laura Wilson occurred December 14, 1851. She was born in Commerce, Illinois, January 13, 1834, and was brought into Iowa when only three months old. Here she has since maintained her home. To this union have come nine children: George Monroe; Burrle Perry; Rachel Rebecca, who died at the age of four years; Emma Louise; Laura Caroline, who died at the age of two years; Frances Ellen; Mary Malvina; Benjamin Franklin, and Anna Luticia.

Mr. Drollinger is a Democrat, and has filled the office of treasurer for this district for the last twenty-five years. He is a man of whom good things are said, and is highly respected by the friends and neighbors of the community in which his peaceful life is passing. He is a member of the United Brethren church, where his honest character, upright dealing and truthful spirit gave strength to his religious profession.

Moses Justice, the great-grandfather of Mrs. Drollinger, was a veteran of the Revolutionary War and lived to be 101 years old.

JOSEPH GREGORY.

Joseph Gregory, formerly identified with building operations in Keokuk but now engaged in the raising of small fruit, was born in Indiana near the City of Indianapolis, March 27, 1839, and comes of Quaker parentage. His father, Silas Gregory, a native of North Carolina, was a prominent member of the Society of Friends. He followed the occupation of farming in Indiana for a number of years and afterward removed to Keokuk, Iowa. He first wedded Sarah Allen, who died in Indiana in 1862 and later married Miss Jane Hobson, who died in 1885 at Richland, Iowa. Silas Gregory was a gentleman of broad humanitarian principles, strongly opposed to slavery or to oppression in any form and he did much to counteract the unfavorable conditions of life that worked hardships for people in his locality. During the great famine in Ireland when so many were starving his feelings were on one occasion deeply touched by the song of an itinerant musician traveling over the country with a melodion. The chorus ran:

"Give me three grains of corn, mother,
Oh, give me three grains of corn.
It will keep the little life I have
Until the coming of the morn."

The song so touched Mr. Gregory and acquainted him with the conditions in Ireland that he forthwith entered upon the service of gathering quantities of corn from among his Quaker friends and the result was that many hundred bushels of corn went from his Indiana neighbors by boat, finally reaching Ireland, where it helped to sustain the famished nation. He was a great-hearted man of philanthropic nature and gave practical and generous assistance to the poor and needy. By his first marriage he had ten children, five of whom are yet living, namely: Eliza, the wife of Levi Pierce, of Kansas; Hulda, the wife of I. M. Hornaday, of Morgan county, Indiana; Joseph; John, of Indiana, and Albert, of Kansas. Those that are dead are William, Richard M., Rieley, Rebecca and Anice.

Joseph Gregory was reared on his father's farm, pursued a common-school education and assisted in the development and cultivation of the fields until the 9th of August, 1862, when he enlisted at Monrovia, Indiana, as a member of Company D, Seventieth Indiana Infantry, under Captain Johnson and Col. Benjamin Harrison. The regiment was assigned to the Army of the Cumberland and became a part of the Twentieth Army Corps in Sherman's campaign under the command of Gen. Joe

Hooker. The principal engagements in which Mr. Gregory participated were at Russellville, Stone River, Rocky-faced Ridge, Resaca, Cassville, New Hope Church, Kenesaw Mountain, Marietta, Peach Tree Creek and the siege of Atlanta. While at Chattanoga he was transferred to the First United States Veteran Volunteer Engineers and, remaining at Chattanooga, assisted in the erection of forts and stockades. He was mustered out there on the 30th of June, 1865, forty days before the expiration of his term of enlistment, but the war had ended and his services were no longer needed. He had joined the army as a private, but was corporal in the engineering corps. He was never wounded, but sustained injuries in the fall of 1862 and on account of this has for five years been disabled for active work in the line of his trade. Mr. Gregory was personally acquainted with Gen. Joseph Hooker and relates many interesting anecdotes concerning that commander when in the service. He also had a personal acquaintance with Gen. Benjamin Harrison, ex-president of the United States, whom he knew in Indiana.

For a year after his return to civil life Mr. Gregory suffered from malaria. He then went to Brookfield, Missouri, where he worked at the carpenter's trade and during three years of the nine years that he spent there he was carpenter for the Hannibal & St. Joseph Railroad Company. In 1874 he removed to Richland, Iowa, where he spent ten years as a carpenter and builder and then came to Keokuk, where he worked at his trade as a contractor. He was also for six years a stairbuilder with George Nunn, and he spent three years in business on his own account as a contractor and builder. In 1891 he purchased his present home and now has ten acres planted to small fruits. This gives to him a good annual income, the products of the place finding a ready sale on the market.

In 1859 Mr. Gregory was married in Mooresville, Indiana, to Miss Martha E. Harvey and they have six living children: Albinus Edwin, who is married and has a family, makes his home in Minneapolis, Minnesota, and is superintendent of construction for the Twin City Telephone Company, installing its plant; Annie Gertrude is the wife of Charles N. Hood, of Minneapolis, who is foreman of the Cable Supply Telephone Company; Amanda B. is the wife of W. H. Weed, a mechanic, of Keokuk; Lydia is the wife of William Davies, foreman of a printing establishment of Keokuk; Sadie married Charles Alden, who is employed by the Habinger Starch Company, of Cleveland, Ohio, and John Roscoe is foreman of the Missouri-Kansas City Telephone Company and resides at Springfield, Missouri. Mr. and Mrs. Gregory also lost one son, Charles Bert, who was killed by a street car when twenty-four years of age. He was superintendent of an electric light plant, but was killed while coupling cars on a run that he was making as motorman for a friend.

Mr. Gregory has been a valued representative of Iowa since 1874, exemplifying in his life the beneficent spirit of the craft. He is also a leading member of the Grand Army Post at Keokuk and is now acting as commander of Torrence Post. He attended the state encampment for two years and in 1903 he went as commander of Torrence Post. He is now a life member of the state department. His political allegiance is given to the Republican party and he has served by appointment on two occasions as ward registrar. He belongs to the First Methodist Episcopal church, of which he is a classleader and he has served as trustee and steward and also as superintendent of the Sunday school. He assisted in completing the church and in dedicating it as a member and trustee and has been very helpful in church work. He is a man of broad sympathies and the poor and needy have found in him a friend. In all life's relations he has commanded uniform confidence and respect and has made for himself a splendid reputation as a business man, as a soldier and as a citizen, while in his home and among his friends he has displayed the sterling traits of manhood that ever command good will and confidence.

FREDERICK W. SMITH.

The State of Iowa is greatly indebted to its citizens of German birth and blood who have done much to build it up to its present imperial proportions. They are a careful and conservative people, industrious in their habits, economical in their manner of life, and as a body are ever found on the moral side of every question. It is always safe to appeal to their better nature. Every great reform has found among them stanch advocates. They were the stoutest opponents of slavery; they are the most persistent friends of a uniform and general public education.

Mr. Smith, whose name appears above, is a noteworthy representative of an old German family, though he himself was born in Washington, Pennsylvania, November 9, 1851. His father, Joseph Smith (Schmitt), was born in Bavaria, in 1816, and when he was seventeen years of age emigrated to the United States. In Pennsylvania he followed the trade of a shoemaker, but on his removal to Lee county, Iowa, he secured land in Charleston township, and the remainder of his active life was a farmer. He is now retired, and is making his home with a daughter in Keokuk. At one time he owned a fine farm of 175 acres, but has long since converted it into cash.

Joseph Smith has led a somewhat checkered career, having had to face serious troubles when he was quite young. His father died when he was but six years old, and though his step-father proved a kind-hearted and capable man, was not as his own. He brought the family to America, and here the young lad left school at the age of fourteen years and set himself to learning the shoemaking trade. The family, consisting of mother, step-father and seven children, landed at Baltimore in September, 1834.

Joseph Smith became a young man and located himself in Pennsylvania, where he married Miss Henrietta Wittich, in January,

1839, in the City of Washington. Here he worked at his trade until 1854, when he removed to Iowa with his wife and their seven children. His advent was not encouraging for of his first two years in the state eighteen months were taken up by a severe illness. For some two years he did mason work upon the Washington and Jefferson College, then in process of construction; he was also employed in the erection of a female seminary at Washington, Pennsylvania.

In Lee county Mr. Smith bought land of Mr. Casey and a Mr. Eaton, and from others as well. These tracts of land he held until 1869, when he sold them to buy the "Henkel farm," in Van Buren township, of John McVey. Here for twenty years or more he was actively engaged in farming, leading a thoroughly industrious, honest and useful life. Ten children were born to him, all but one of whom are now living. His daughter, Agnes, who married John Anderson, died when she was twenty-eight years old, having become the mother of three children,—Carrie, George L. and Leroy. Mr. Anderson is also dead. Of the other children this may be noted: John W. lives in Sioux county, Iowa; Henrietta C. is the wife of Steven Beaty, of Farmington, Iowa; Mary E. is Mrs. Fred Geiser, of Keokuk, Iowa; Rosa is single, and is a nurse at Des Moines; Hannah L. Nenhoff lives in Chicago; Frederick W. is the subject of this writing; Samuel B. lives in Keokuk; Ella Hardwick has her home in California, and Nettie is Mrs. Henry Blagg, of Des Moines.

The mother of Mr. Smith lived to be seventy-two years of age, and her remains rest in Emberry cemetery, Van Buren township, Lee county. She was a woman of more than the usual force of character, and her memory is dear to those who knew her and loved her for many excellent qualities of heart and mind.

John W. Smith, the oldest brother of Frederick W., was a soldier in the Civil War, and served five years in the First Iowa Cavalry as a member of Company A, under the command of Captain Torrence. Upon the expiration of his first term of enlistment he re-enlisted, and when he was finally mustered out of service he was much broken in health, coming home seriously ill. After a protracted sickness he recovered, and is now living in Sioux county, Iowa.

Mr. Smith often says that the happiest moment of his life was when he was handed his naturalization papers, which gave him the full rights of an American citizen. He is well versed in the political questions of the day, being always an extensive reader of the English papers. His support is given to the Republican party, of which he is a stanch advocate.

Frederick W. Smith was given more than the usual educational advantages. In addition to the privilege of the public school, he enjoyed the opportunity of studying at Whittier College, an old and well-established institution of learning at Salem, Iowa. He became a capable and successful teacher, and for eighteen years found profitable employment in the school room. When he taught at Salina, Iowa, he did the work of two teachers, and had seventy-two pupils under his charge. In 1890 he retired from the teacher's calling, and buying his father's place in Van Buren township, has since been devoted to the cultivation of the soil. He has sold the Van Buren township farm, but reinvesting the proceeds in land, he now owns a splendid tract of 250 acres on which he has made his home since 1891.

On Christmas Day, 1884, Mr. Smith and Miss Sarah E. Brown were married in Summitville, Iowa, where the bride was born and reared, her birth occurring March 22, 1858. Her father, John J. Brown, was born in Utica, Michigan, August 29, 1830, and was a son of Andrew Brown, commonly called "Citizen" Brown, in recognition of his wide-awake spirit and public interest. At one time the grandfather owned a large warehouse in Keokuk, where his son, John, assisted him, doing "lighter" work, or carrying goods over the Des Moines rapids of the Mississippi river. It was impossible at that time for the river packets to ascend the rapids, something they were not able to do until the construction of the canal by the government. Mr. Brown became a wealthy man and purchased some 400 acres of land in Montrose township, though his home continued in Keokuk until his retirement from active business, when he removed to Clayton, Illinois, where he died. His wife was born at Johnstone, and came of Scotch parentage.

John J. Brown was married April 5, 1854, to Mrs. Elizabeth Null (nee Meltz), who was born in Calhoun county, Illinois, November 11, 1827, and was of German parentage. She died January 31, 1898, and he March 4, 1900. Both were buried in Hickory Grove cemetery, in Jackson township. Mr. Brown was a great reader and a wide student, being unusually well versed on all the questions of the day. He was a stanch Republican, but never sought official position. All his life he advocated good schools, and made his watchword their improvement. After his marriage he located on his father's farm in Montrose township, where he spent his subsequent life with the exception of a few years before his death when he removed to a farm he owned near Warsaw. Here his wife died, while his death occurred at the home of his daughter, Mrs. Frederick W. Smith, when he was making them a visit.

Mr. and Mrs. John J. Brown were the parents of the following children: Roy, of Lake Charles, Louisiana; Irvin J., a grocer at Salem, Iowa; Sarah, who is Mrs. Smith; Prior, a merchant in Summitville, Iowa; Horatio S., who is engaged in the same business at the same place; Amelia M., the wife of Albert Miller, a resident of Montrose township.

Mr. Smith is a member of the Independent Order of Odd Fellows at Farmington, and the Anti-Horse Thief Association, which organization he at one time represented at a state meeting in Des Moines. In political matters he is a Republican, and for some years served as a school director. He was elected as justice of the peace, and also as town clerk, but never saw fit to qualify for either position. Mr. and Mrs. Brown are the parents of a family of six children: Lizzie H., Willma A., John P., Alta M., Clyde F. and Daisy B. He is a man of fine education, broad views, and exercises a large influence for good wherever he is known. He belongs to an excellent family, and well sustains an old and honored name. He is a worthy citizen, and the pen of the historian finds in him, his career and family relations and associations a congenial theme. In Lee county, where so much of his active life has passed, he has a host of friends who will be glad to read of him and his.

THE NEWBERRY FAMILY.

The Newberry family, which is one of a few families which trace their genealogy back to the pioneers of Des Moines township, Lee county, was founded by ancestors of sound principles and sterling worth, persons who were mentally, morally, physically and spiritually superior—above the average. The traits of the progenitors of this family are largely reproduced by their descendants, who are now among the leading citizens of the township.

James A. Newberry, the ancestor of all the family now here, was born in Vermont, and when a young man removed to Orange county, New York, where he was united in marriage to Miss Mary Smith, who was born and reared in that state.

In 1821, James A. Newberry, with his wife and family, then consisting of four children, moved from Orange county to make his home in Pennsylvania. Later on in life he moved again and settled in Lorain county, Ohio, where he resided some years. Then, impelled by the spirit of unrest and ambition that sent so many of the boldest and the best from the East, they continued their way towards the setting sun, and located in Clay county, Missouri, on a tract of new and unimproved land. Two years later they made another removal, and took up a piece of raw land for a farm in Caldwell county. Here they resided for a short time, and then removed to the vicinity of Nauvoo, Illinois, and in 1838 they came to Des Moines township, Lee county. Here the sons secured land under pre-emption laws, but the father, well-advanced in years and having a competence, never became a landholder in Lee county.

James A. and Mary (Smith) Newberry were the parents of a numerous family: Jane, the oldest child, married Jacob Crandall and became herself the mother of eight children,—they lived in Panama, Shelby county, Iowa; she was ninety years old in May, 1904; John married Lucinda Williams, —they became the parents of four children, of whom three bore arms in the Civil War. He was for many years engaged in mining in Galena, Illinois, and died in 1856, at the age of fifty-six years, having never enjoyed robust health. Abraham B., the third child; James W. was the fourth child, and his sketch appears on another page of this record. Electa married George Wixam. She went to California at an early day and was there married, her husband being a man of ample means. Sallie Ann married James Pendleton and removed with him to Utah before the Civil War. They now live in Parawan, Iron county, in that state. Harriet married Seth Palmer and died in Montrose, where her remains now rest. She had no children. Mariah married George Morris, a stonemason. They went to Utah before the Civil War, and have reared a large family of children. She died about 1898. Esther married Edward Beebe, at Montrose, and went to California, where they were greatly prospered, becoming the owners of a large fruit farm. They were the parents of several children, and both are now dead. Pattie married George Hiatt, and lives in Parawan, Utah. They and the Pendletons made the journey to that distant country in company. Mrs. James A. Newberry died in 1842, at the early age of forty-six.

Mr. Newberry contracted a second marriage two years later, when Elizabeth Haskins, of Des Moines township, became his wife. She bore him four children: Alma M., a son who died March 12, 1904, in Decatur county, Iowa, leaving seven children; Joseph and Eber live in Mills county, Iowa; Joanna married Henry Winniger and lives in Missouri. Mrs. Elizabeth Newberry died in Mills county about 1858. James A. Newberry, while in this county, resided with his children until his second marriage. In 1883, at the venerable age of ninety years, he passed to his rest, having led a long and useful life. He was truly a pioneer and loved the freedom of a new country, where all had room and comfort.

CHRISTIAN TRUMP.

Christian Trump, who is one of the leading real estate owners and liverymen of Fort Madison, Iowa, was born in Charleston township, Lee county, June 25, 1849, and is the son of George and Katherine (Seyb) Trump. The father and mother were both natives of Germany, but were married in America, buying and locating on a farm in Charleston township, where they spent the remainder of their lives. The father's death occurred about 1887, and that of the mother in 1903, they being survived by nine children. They were early members of the Lutheran church, and were ever faithful to its teachings.

Christian Trump received his education in the schools of Charleston township, and assisted his father in the duties of the farm until his seventeenth year, when he began his business life by buying and shipping stock. In this he was so successful that he soon had sufficient capital to enable him to engage in mercantile business, and he began the conduct of a general store at Franklin Station. Here he continued for several years, but finally sold his interest to his partner, Mr. Best, and devoted all his time to dealing in live stock.

In 1883 Mr. Trump married Katherine Lang, of Franklin township, a daughter of Frederick Lang, who is one of the pioneers of the county and at the present time a general merchant at Franklin Center. For a year thereafter they made their home at Franklin. For several years Mr. Trump had been very active in Republican politics, and at this time he was appointed to the office of deputy sheriff, in which capacity he served for two years during Colonel Root's term as sheriff. At the same time he established himself in the livery business in Fort Madison, and continued dealing in horses, as well as contracting for grading

CHRISTIAN TRUMP

and heavy hauling, doing much work for the city, and building up his contracting business to large proportions. His many and successful enterprises brought him into contact with a large number of people, and wherever he went he made friends. A thing that shows his wide acquaintance and his standing in the community is the fact that he was elected to the office of sheriff of Lee county for two terms at a time when the party of which he was a member was in a normal minority of one thousand votes, and that in his first election he received the astounding majority of 293 and for his second term 297 votes. He filled his office acceptably, and retired with increased reputation.

During his term of office he continued his livery and horse business. The first building erected by Mr. Trump in Fort Madison was a livery barn on Locust street, and later he erected a fine business block, known as the Trump Block, at the corner of Locust and Front streets. He then converted his frame barn into a brick structure, with stone front and cement floor, facing south on Front street. This barn, in dimensions 50x150 feet, is the best in the city. Another large stone and brick barn, two stories in height, and now occupied as a feed and sale barn, stands at another corner of Locust and Front streets as a monument to the public spirit of Mr. Trump. He now confines his activities to the livery and sale business, shipping constantly large numbers of horses to all parts of the United States. Father died in 1884.

Mr. Trump's only fraternal connection is with the Independent Order of Odd Fellows, of which he has been a member for several years.

To Mr. and Mrs. Trump have been born two sons, Richard R., who has now completed his education at Elliott's Business College, at Burlington, Iowa, and Raymond F., who is at home. On August 16, 1892, the family sustained its greatest sorrow in the death of the wife and mother. Father and sons are members of the Evangelical Lutheran church. To Mr. Trump alone belongs the credit for what he has achieved. Starting empty-handed in life for himself, he has won his way to his present high position in the world by his own ability, energy and merit.

HOWARD M. DEWEY.

Howard M. Dewey is a farmer, and has his home in Sawyer, Washington township, where he was born January 23, 1852. His entire life has been passed in Lee county, with the exception of brief periods, mention of which will appear farther on in this sketch, and here he has achieved an enviable standing both as a man and a follower of the noble profession of agriculture. By industry and perseverance, joined to a close study of his calling, and an anxiety to produce the best results to his unflagging labors, he has won a commendable measure of success, and though not yet passed the prime of life takes high rank among the leading citizens of his community.

Mr. Dewey is a son of George Howland

and Chloe (Butler) Dewey. The father was born in Leroy, Berkshire county, Massachusetts, in 1816, and was a son of Asaph Dewey. He came to Iowa in 1838, and effected a location on section 18, Washington township. He attended the first land sale in Burlington, to which he walked from his home, and there he bought a quarter section at $1.25 an acre. He made some improvements on his land, but after a year had elapsed returned to Massachusetts, where he was married in 1839 to Miss Chloe B. Butler, a native of Pittsfield, in that state. The young couple made their way immediately to their western home, and there passed many honorable and useful years. They were both members of the Congregational church, and were highly respected for their many excellent qualities of heart and mind. Politically he was for many years associated with the Republican party, but in his latter years became somewhat prominently identified with the Prohibition movement. He long served as justice of the peace, and was at different times assessor of the township.

Mr. and Mrs. George H. Dewey were the parents of a family of ten children, of whom brief mention may be made: George H., Jr., born February 7, 1841, enlisted as a private in the Nineteenth Iowa Volunteer Infantry in 1863, died in 1871; Eunice S., born December 8, 1842, married N. F. Butler, and died in 1891; Asaph C., born April 8, 1844, was a soldier in the Civil War, being a member of the Nineteenth Iowa Volunteer Infantry, and is now living in Stone county, Arkansas. His wife, Mary Riggs, is dead; Sarah E., Mrs. William A. Tade, a resident of Van Buren county, Iowa, was born April 10, 1845, she died in March, 1881, her husband served as a captain in a colored regiment during the Civil War; James B., born November 29, 1846, died when only eight months old; Nancy W., born February 4, 1848, after the death of her sister, became the second wife of William A. Tade; Kate M., born August 11, 1850, married John Tade, lived in Nebraska, and is now dead; Howard M., whose name appears at the opening of this article; Siar Butler, born July 2, 1853, in Washington township, always made his home on the paternal estate, which he carried on in 1876, in company with his two brothers, Howard M. and Frank. He had a good common-school education, and was a man of more than ordinary gifts. On the 14th day of February, 1883, he was married to Miss Olga J. Kirk, a native of Pennsylvania, and a niece of Prof. Edson, who was for many years the head of Denmark Academy, and later a professor in Grinnell College. They had a family of six children: Charlotte C., Ethel B., Grace H., Ruth E., Kirk M. and Alice Irene. In politics he is a Republican, and in religion a member of the Denmark Congregational church, of which he has long been a deacon. He is the owner of forty acres of land in West Point township, and has in his home farm 190 acres. His specialty is Polled Angus cattle, in the breeding of which he enjoys more than a local reputation.

Frank M., born April 22, 1855, has his home in Cahoka, Missouri. George H. Dewey died in 1891, and his widow, June 8, 1894. After 1876 he lived a retired life.

Howard M. Dewey, whose name appears at the head of this biographical sketch, received a common-school education and lived at home until his marriage, February 14, 1881, to Miss Flora M. Sawyer. She was a daughter of Francis and Lucy (Baxter) Sawyer, and a lady of more than the usual character and attainments. Her father was born in Rindge, Cheshire county, New Hampshire, in 1815, and when he was eleven years old was taken by his parents to New Ipswich, where he was given a good education. In 1838, in company with his brother, he left home for the West, making the journey in a one-horse buggy. From Albany to Buffalo they availed themselves of the canal, then a popular route. After being on the road six weeks they reached Lee county, and made claim to the land on which the son-in-law, Mr. Dewey, now lives. Here he erected a cabin, and here he passed his remaining years. In 1840 he went back to his native state to marry Miss Lucy Baxter. She was born at New Ipswich, New Hampshire, December 7, 1816. She died in 1843. Three years later Mr. Sawyer married Miss Abbie Holt, who was born in Andover, Massachusetts, in February, 1828. She died May 27, 1898, leaving four children: Henry B., born January 30, 1849, is now deceased; Alfred, born in 1850, is also deceased; Perley F., born in 1856, died in 1871; Flora M., now Mrs. Dewey; Herbert, born in 1860, died in 1869. Mr. Sawyer became the husband of Miss Lucy Baxter in October, 1865. She was born in New Ipswich in 1821, and died May 27, 1898. Mr. Sawyer died September 11, 1897. He was a member of the Congregational church in which he had long served as a deacon. In farming he was very successful, and was known as a man of fine character and unusual merit.

Mr. and Mrs. Howard M. Dewey are the parents of three children: Perley Francis, born April 6, 1885; Arthur Howard, born October 7, 1890, and Daisy Helen, born October 25, 1893. The children are bright and gifted, and would do credit to any home.

Mr. Dewey is a very successful farmer and owns a fine farm of 250 acres, to which he has given the name of "Long Field Farm." While he is skilled as a general farmer, he makes a specialty of Polled Angus cattle, and is widely and favorably known as a stockraiser. In addition to his home farm he has a forty-acre tract of timber land in the township of West Point. Mr. Dewey is a member of the Congregational church, and was the first postmaster at Sawyer. Personally he is a man of irreproachable character and genial ways, and enjoys the respect and confidence of the community in which he lives to a very unusual degree.

MONTGOMERY MEIGS.

Among the more widely known residents of Keokuk, Iowa, is Montgomery Meigs, who has been in the service of the federal government since 1874 and is at the present time occupying the position of United States civil engineer, superintendent of the Des Moines Rapids canal and locks and superintendent of the Mississippi river improvements between Burlington, Iowa, and Hannibal, Missouri. He is of English ancestry, and is the son of Gen. M. C. Meigs, who was for a number of years quartermaster-general of the United States army, a position attained by simple force of merit and in recognition of distinguished services as a member of the engineering corps of the army, in which he had risen to high rank. General Meigs, who was a native of Pennsylvania, was a man of great talents and executive ability, and erected many public works which stand as a monument to his skill as an engineer, among these being the aqueduct in the City of Washington and the famous "Cabin John" arch, the largest structure of its kind on the globe. He occupied a high place among the leading public men of his time, enjoying a reputation of international scope, and although he never sought to stand in the limelight of publicity, his name is an important one in the history of his country.

Montgomery Meigs was born in the year 1847 in Detroit, Michigan, and passed the years of his boyhood and youth in the City of Washington, and there in the shadow of the national capital he grew to years of maturity in an atmosphere of large events and the society of many great and celebrated men of the time, meanwhile securing the foundation of his education in private schools of that city. Having determined, however, to attain to a high plane of usefulness and distinction in his father's profession, which he had also chosen for his own, he pursued further courses of study along special lines in the scientific department of Harvard University and in the Royal Polytechnich School at Stuttgart, Germany, from which latter institution he was graduated in 1869. Having thus acquired a magnificent training in the theoretical branch of his profession, he began his acquaintance with its practical side by starting at the lowest round of the ladder and gaining familiarity with its every phase by actual experience. The Northern Pacific Railroad was then in course of construction, and he first acted as rodman in a party engaged in surveying the route of that great transcontinental highway, later, becoming assistant engineer and finally resident engineer, and also taking and executing the contract for building a fifty-mile section of the road, terminating at Bismarck, in what is now the State of South Dakota. His whole connection with the building of the Northern Pacific road, including the preliminary survey and construction, lasted four years, a period which he now considers the most fruitful of useful experience in his entire career, and certainly he had cause to feel much satisfaction for his rapid rise to a position of trust and profit.

In 1875 Mr. Meigs accompanied the quartermaster-general, his father, as his secretary on a military mission to Europe, and in 1877 he was appointed United States civil engineer, stationed at Rock Island, Illinois, to conduct the improvements designed to aid navigation on the Mississippi river. He made an especial survey of the upper course of the river, and superintended the execution of innumerable improvements throughout its entire navigable length, namely from St. Paul to the Gulf of Mexico, thus performing a service to mankind which must rank as one of the notable achievements of his generation, it being due to his efforts more than to those of any other man that the present condition of this greatest of the world's waterways is due. Following the successful conclusion of this great enterprise he was assigned, in 1882, to the superintendency of the Des Moines Rapids canal, which had been opened in 1877, and of the river improvements which he had established between Burlington and Hannibal, a position whose duties he has since continuously discharged in a highly meritorious and efficient manner, and it may be safely said that no section of the river has received more conscientious and painstaking care than that intrusted to his charge, or that nowhere have the improvements been more perfectly maintained. When he assumed charge of the canal it was only partially finished, and he at once took steps for its completion along the most approved lines, building a dry dock at the middle lock, raising the walls of the two lower locks, constructing solid masonry sluices for the discharge of flood water into the river from the canal, building the boom at the lower lock, and, in a word, bringing the work to that state of perfection which has excited the admiration of all who have been privileged to inspect it. In connection with this work Mr. Meigs has built more than half a hundred barges for the government service, as well as two drill boats, three pile drivers and four building boats, and has built and named a fleet of twelve river steamers, as follows: "The Lucia," "Iris," "Ada," "Irene," "Pearl," "Marion," "Stella," "Louise," "Emily," "Ruth," "Fox" and "Grace."

At Rock Island, Illinois, in 1877, Mr. Meigs was united in marriage to Miss Grace Lynde, daughter of Cornelius Lynde, a leading banker and prominent citizen of that place, and during her residence in Keokuk Mrs. Meig's many graces of character won for her a host of friends. She died September 2, 1894, survived by six daughters, as follows: Mary, wife of Maxwell W. Atwater, of Baker City, Oregon; Louise, wife of Melvin Green, of Winchester, Virginia, and Misses Grace S., Alice McK., Cornelia L. and Emily F. The daughters of the family have all had the advantages of excellent training and education, and those of their number who remain residents of Keokuk adorn the most desirable social circles of the city. The present family home, which has been its place of abode continuously for twenty-five years, is what is known as the Judge McCreary homestead, at No. 618 Franklin street.

Mr. Meigs has borne a prominent part in the affairs of his adopted City of Keokuk, being at the present time a member and chairman of the Board of Education, a member of the Buildings and Improvements Committe and vice-president of the Keokuk Water Commission, a body whose labors have solved in a highly satisfactory manner the vexed problem of the city's water supply. Socially, he is a member of the Keokuk Country Club, and along the line of his professional work he is affiliated with the American Society of Civil Engineers and the American Society for the Advancement of Science. One important public service performed by Mr. Meigs, and one which has brought him a large measure of fame throughout the United States, was his proposal before the Good Roads Convention, at St. Louis, to which he was appointed the member for Keokuk by Judge F. T. Hughes, then mayor, to apply crude petroleum to the roads as a dust preventative, and in order to render ungraveled roads passable in all weathers. The idea was at once widely adopted, especially in the Western States, and is rapidly growing in favor, being found highly practicable and useful, and in all respects is fulfilling the claims of its originator, who is certainly entitled to the universal gratitude of this eminently utilitarian discovery. Thus it is manifest that the life of our subject has been one long period of service to his fellowmen, and while his business ability has enabled him to acquire a sufficient store of worldly goods, his chief riches consist of an honorable, upright and useful career, a possession which no accident of fortune can ever destroy or take away.

C. F. WAHRER, M. D.

Dr. C. F. Wahrer, of Fort Madison, physician and surgeon, has through his writings along professional lines become known to the medical fraternity throughout the country and through his efforts for the diffusion of medical knowledge and for the promotion of general education to the public at large.

A native of Baden, Germany, he was born July 19, 1850, and when three years of age was brought to the United States by his parents, who settled at Keokuk, Iowa, where the next eight years of his life were passed. He began his education in the public schools of that city, and following the removal of the family to Charleston, Lee county, he continued a public-school student there. He spent his early life upon his father's farm and after teaching in various district schools entered Whittier College, at Salem, Iowa, from which institution he was graduated. Immediately afterward he was elected professor of mathematics and filled that position, alternating with that of professor of natural sciences for a period of six years. He then became principal of the Salem public schools, and during the years thus spent he took up the study of medicine, pursuing his reading under some of the prominent physicians of that city. He afterward matriculated in the Medical College of Keokuk, and completed his course by graduation with the class of 1887. He immediately entered upon the practice of his profession at Mount Hamill, Lee county, Iowa, where he continued until 1893, when he removed to Fort Madison, where he has since engaged in general practice. During the latter years of his residence in Mount Hamill and until 1893 he was professor of pathology at the College of Physicians and Surgeons, of Keokuk, Iowa, and then resigned his position. In the years 1898 and 1899 he was persuaded to accept the professorship of therapeutics and at the close of the session he was tendered the chair of medicine, but resigned in order to devote his entire attention to his private practice, now grown to extensive proportions, making heavy demands upon his time and energies. He is a member of nearly all the prominent medical societies, including the Lee County Medical Society; the Southeastern Iowa Medical Society, of which he was president in 1902; the Iowa State Medical Society, of which he was vice-president in 1902, and also chairman of its various sections at different times—positions of distinctive honor. He has also been a trustee of this society for a number of years. He holds membership in the American Medical Association, in which he has held various positions of trust, the last being that of secretary of the section of the diseases of children. He has also been elected a member of the American Association for the Advancement of Science. In connection with his identification with these organizations he has traveled extensively throughout the United States and because of this and his writings on professional topics, there are few better known members of the medical profession, not only in his own state, but also throughout the United States. He is the author of many medical monographs, which he expects to publish in connection with other medical works.

Aside from his labors in connection with the science of medicine he has been interested in the advancement of musical and literary associations and has frequently delivered addresses upon medical, literary and moral topics and has identified himself with general educational matters.

Dr. Wahrer has been a lifelong Republican, but has never sought office. He is a member of the Presbyterian church and also belongs to the Independent Order of Odd Fellows and the Masonic fraternity, having in the latter attained the Knights Templar degree. He is also a member of Kaba Temple of the Mystic Shrine, at Davenport, Iowa.

Dr. Wahrer was married, July 11, 1876, near Richland, Iowa, to Miss Sara McCracken, who was born near Pleasant Plain, Iowa, and resided there during her girlhood. She acquired her education in Whittier College, in Salem, Iowa, and afterward became a teacher of history in that institution. While there she formed the acquaintance of Dr. Wahrer. Her parents were Hiram and Dinah (Hadley) McCracken, of Fairfield, Iowa. Dr. and Mrs. Wahrer had four children: Evelyn, who was born at Salem, Iowa, and pursued her early education in the public schools of Fort Madison, afterward attended Knox College, at Galesburg, Illinois, and the State Normal School, of Iowa. She is an accomplished scholar now occupying a position as one of the teachers in the high school of Fort Madison. She is also much interested in music. Carl W. Wahrer, born at Salem, Iowa, graduated from Rush Medical College, and after completing a two years' post-graduate course, became associated in the practice of his profession with his father, Dr. C. F. Wahrer. Within the last three years he has also illustrated a number of medical works, some of them being published by the press of Coblentz, Germany. August H. Wahrer, born in Salem, Iowa, died at the age of twelve years, and was buried at Fort Madison, Iowa; Frederick L. Wahrer, born at Mount Hamill, Iowa, was educated in the high school of Fort Madison.

It will be interesting in this connection

to note something of the family to which Dr. Wahrer belongs. He is one of the nine children, five of whom are living, born unto August and Rosina (Fiedler) Wahrer. The father was born in Baden, Germany, August 18, 1825, became a furrier and followed that occupation until his removal to the United States in 1852. He located at Keokuk, Iowa, and there followed his trade and also engaged in merchant tailoring, in which he continued until 1861, when he removed to Charleston, Iowa, where he carried on farming until his death, which occurred when he was seventy-six years of age. He was a fairly prosperous and successful man and was interested not alone in business, but also in church and educational affairs, being an active member of the Evangelical church. His wife died about five years prior to his demise, passing away at the age of sixty-seven years.

J. H. COULTER, M. D.

Dr. Coulter, who is a well-known figure on the streets of Summitville, Lee county, is an honored member of a noble calling, and well sustains the best traditions of his profession. It is a calling that demands the best in human nature, and confers its richest rewards only on those who take its vows of consecration, and live as brothers to all the world of the suffering and needy. It is the work of the physician to help and cheer. It is his to put courage into hearts that falter and faint, and strength into bodies weak and feeble. His shadow upon the threshold of pain should be a benediction upon the fevered brow of sickness, and in his touch a healing. Such men are very close to the heart of the race; and when they are once discovered, are revered and loved. The Summitville physician is a man after the best ideals of his profession, studious and learned, deeply versed in medical lore, but modest and unassuming, he is respected and esteemed wherever he is known.

Dr. Coulter was born in Adams county, Illinois, January 1, 1856, a son of Josiah and Mary J. (Dunlap) Coulter, natives respectively of Pennsylvania and Virginia. They were farmer people, the father died in Nebraska, whither they had gone in 1886 to settle on a ranch for stockraising, which they proposed to make their final home. The mother resides in Denver, Colorado. To them were born six children of whom the subject of this sketch was the oldest. The others were Emma, wife of A. J. Dunham, of Missouri; Mary, wife of Henry Vance; Samuel H.; Wilber, and Warren, both Nebraska stockmen, and Charles.

Dr. Coulter secured his education in the common schools and in his earlier life was engaged in farming near Tarkio, Missouri. From Nodaway county, in that state, he entered the College of Physicians and Surgeons at Keokuk, in 1887. In 1890 he was graduated from that justly celebrated institution, and immediately effected a location in Summitville, Lee county, where his high character and manifest ability commanded quick recognition and a profitable practice. For some nine years he has been county physician and also local physician for the local branch of the Du Pont Powder Mills. He is local examiner for the more noted life insurance companies, such as the Equitable, and the Mutual Life, of New York, the New York Life, the Pennsylvania and several fraternal associations as well, being an active member and local examiner for the Modern Woodmen of America. He is associated in the various medical societies of the day, and is a member of the American Medical Association, the Tri-State Association, the State Association, the Des Moines Valley Association, and the Lee County Medical Society. He takes much interest in the workings of these various organizations, but is especially active in the Tri-State Association and the Lee County Society. The doctor is a member of the Morning Star Lodge, No. 5, Knights of Pythias, at Keokuk, and of Summitville Camp, No. 4594, Modern Woodmen of America.

Dr. Coulter was married in 1881 to Miss Myra Dunham, who was born in Williamsburg, Indiana, in 1853. They were married in Maryville, Missouri. To them two daughters were born, Elsie and Nellie. Her father, Jerry Dunham, is dead, but her mother, Mary (Allen) Dunham, is still living.

Dr. Coulter has a very handsome and attractive home at Summitville. It comprises twenty-one acres, and on it are found 2,500 fruit trees. Here he has his office, and takes much delight in his leisure moments in superintending the improvements of his place, which is still continuing. All improvements have been made by him, and he is known as a public-spirited and wide-awake citizen, ready to make beautiful the community in which he lives.

The Doctor had to work his way through medical college, and his was no easy road to learning. He had saved some money in Missouri, but when he went to Nebraska with large plans he lost it all. In religion he is a member and a deacon in the Christian church, and his family are workers in the Sunday school. He was active in the building of the Summitville church, being on the building committee, and is now serving on the board of trustees of that organization. He is an occasional contributor to the medical journals. Politically he is a Republican.

The fact that Dr. Coulter is the only physician in Summitville is not as some might imagine a warrant of ease to him, but rather a call to constant study and close application to his profession, that he might keep abreast of its rapid development and be ready for all occasions. He has had to go through much trial and adversity in order to win his present prominence in his chosen calling, and only what has put him forward will sustain him. So he studies, and works, and gives his best to his great profession, which in turn is giving him honor and reputation as a healer of men and a doer of good in the world.

OSCAR O. TRACY.

The present age belongs pre-eminently to the young man, and he has shown his appreciation of the fact by the capable manner in which he has availed himself of its opportunities for advancement in all lines of endeavor. One of Keokuk's younger men who has manifested the possession of valuable qualities of aggressiveness, self-reliance and fidelity to duty in all matters intrusted to his charge, is Oscar O. Tracy, manager for the Western Union Telegraph Company. Mr. Tracy was born near Brighton, Iowa, August 14, 1871, the son of Mark Albert and Martha (Ohmart) Tracy, his father being by occupation a farmer and removing to Brighton from near Barnesville, and later, in 1872, to Pleasant Plain, Iowa; but in 1875 he came to Keokuk and was a resident of this city for a number of years, while at the present time he is located at Des Moines, and is employed in the car department of the Chicago, Rock Island & Pacific Railroad Company. The mother of our subject is the daughter of Christian Ohmart, and of Scotch-Irish extraction. She died at Brighton in 1872. Both are still remembered in Brighton as being people of sterling character, and they had many friends there who valued them for their kindly dispositions and sincerity of manner. To them were born one son, Oscar O., and one daughter, Amelia Belle, who is now the wife of Henry F. Schmidt, with the Keokuk drug firm of Wilkinson & Company.

Oscar O. Tracy removed to Keokuk with his parents in 1875, and has resided in this city continuously since that time. He received a good education in the common schools, and on the completion of his studies became a messenger in the service of the Western Union Telegraph Company, and while acting in this capacity he took advantage of his opportunities to familiarize himself with the art of telegraphy, in which he soon became expert and was promoted to the position of regular operator. His work having attracted the attention of his superiors, he was three years ago made local manager for the company, and in the conduct of this office he has displayed executive ability of an unusual order, a quality which, while advancing him in the favor of the public and proving of material benefit to the interests of the company which he represents, will doubtless be the means of his attaining still higher honors in future. In 1894 he wedded Miss May Antrim, who was born at Danville, Pennsylvania, the daughter of William and Hannah (Hammond) Antrim, both of Pennsylvania birth, and to Mr. and Mrs. Tracy has been born one daughter, Martha.

Mr. Tracy is well known in the fraternal circles of Keokuk, being a member of the Masonic order in Hardin Lodge, No. 29, and also of Keokuk Lodge, No. 13, of the Independent Order of Odd Fellows, in which he has held official positions and has been a prominent worker. In all matters of public concern he has taken a constant interest, and has given special study to politics, but has never formed any partisan connection, preferring to act with that increasingly important body of voters known as "independents," and believing that the best results may be obtained by deciding each question of public policy on its individual merits and not according to partisan bias. His religious connection is with the Methodist Episcopal church, of which he and Mrs. Tracy are members, and he is a liberal supporter of its work and a contributor to its various charities. He is a young man who is much esteemed in the business world of Keokuk, and enjoys the respect of many friends who have watched his upward course with interest.

STEPHEN H. KOTTENSTETTE.

Stephen H. Kottenstette, now deceased, was born at Fort Madison, Iowa, on the 18th of February, 1867, his parents being Peter and Theresa (Beine) Kottenstette. The father was born in Germany and in 1849 came to the United States, locating first at St. Louis, Missouri, where he remained until 1861. He there followed the cooper's trade, which he had learned in his native country. In the year mentioned he came to Fort Madison, Iowa, where he has since resided, being now about sixty-five years of age. Here he continued the work of coopering for a number of years and at this writing, in the fall of 1904, was employed in the S. & J. C. Atlee lumber yards. He is a member of the Catholic church, and in his political affiliations is a Democrat. He married Theresa Beine, who was born in Germany, and was brought to the United States when about eight years of age. The family landed at New Orleans and when on the way up the Mississippi river to Fort Madison, the mother died as did one of the sisters of Mrs. Kottenstette. The voyage across the Atlantic had covered sixteen weeks and the trip up the river was also a very hard and tedious one, while its difficulties were heightened by the sorrow induced by the death of the members of the family. Mr. Beine had to spend all the money which he had saved in order to bring his family to the United States and pay the expenses of the illness and burial of his wife and daughter. He was a shoemaker by trade, and after locating in Fort Madison, followed that pursuit for a long period, but about twenty years prior to his demise retired from active business cares. In the early days he suffered the hardships and trials incident to pioneer life, but as time passed by these gave way before an advancing civilization and Mr. Beine prospered in his work. He lived to the venerable age of eighty four years. Unto Peter and Theresa Kottenstette were born eleven children, nine of whom are yet living.

Stephen H. Kottenstette acquired his early education in the Catholic schools of Fort Madison, and also attended Johnson's Business College. After leaving school he clerked in the grocery store owned by Joseph Helling for five years and then started in business for himself as a grocer at No. 1202 Fourth street. At the time of his death he was in partnership with Frank Hermes as proprietor of a grocery store and he had succeeded in building up a large and lucrative business. Popular as a merchant, he enjoyed the full confidence of the business community and his success was due to his earnest desire to please his patrons, the excellent line of goods which he carried and his straightforward dealing in all business transactions.

On the 20th of November, 1892, Mr. Kottenstette was united in marriage at Fort

Madison to Miss Mary Pieper, who was born in this city and is a daughter of Frank and Elizabeth (Jaeger) Pieper, who still reside here. Her father was born in Prussia, in 1832, and there learned the carpenter's trade. In 1854 he started for America in company with his brother, William, now deceased. They took passage on the sailing vessel "Albert," which left the port of Bremen for New Orleans and thence they proceeded up the Mississippi river to Fort Madison. There was no railroad here at that time and in fact the city was only a trading post. Mr. Pieper began work at the carpenter's trade and when the Atlee saw and lumber mill was established in 1855, he obtained work in connection with that industry. For forty-seven years he was connected with that business and during the last years was foreman in the machinery department. He lost three fingers from his left hand and the fourth finger from his right hand, while working at the saw. He is now retired from active business life and his rest is well merited. As the years passed and his industry and economy brought him more capital he made judicious investment in property and now owns a valuable farm of 235 acres in Cedar township. He also owns a home at No. 1904 Division street at the corner of Walker street, and he likewise has ten acres of farm land in Madison township. He also owns three tenement houses and four lots on block No. 8 in Fort Madison, but his realty possessions indicate that his has been a life of business activity and usefulness. He was married in 1857, in Fort Madison, to Miss Lizzie Jaeger, and they became the parents of ten children, of whom six are living: William, who operates his father's farm in Cedar township, and married Lizzie Kottenstette, by whom he has six children, four sons and two daughters, Mary, the widow of Stephen Kottenstette, of Fort Madison, and the mother of three children: Lizzie, the wife of Frank Schilte, of Fort Madison, by whom she has five children; Anna, at home; Theresa, the wife of Frank Hermes, of Fort Madison; and Kate, at home. The parents and family are communicants of the Sacred Heart Catholic church, and Mr. Pieper belongs to the Old Settlers' Association.

His daughter, Mrs. Kottenstette, acquired her education in the Catholic schools of Fort Madison, and by her marriage became the mother of four children: Peter, who was born in Fort Madison, and is now eleven years of age; Frank, a youth of nine years; Edward deceased; and Robert, four years of age.

Mr. Kottenstette was a progressive young man, alert and enterprising in business and with ready recognition of possibilities and opportunities. He won success and also an honored name and it seemed that his death was most untimely, for he was filling a creditable position in both business and social circles in Fort Madison. In 1891 he built the pleasant home now occupied by his widow and there his death occurred on the 27th of May, 1902. He was a Democrat in his political views and belonged to Gate City Lodge, No. 288, Ancient Order United Workmen. Widely known and enjoying the full confidence and esteem of all with whom he had been associated the loss of Mr. Kottenstette was deeply deplored by his many friends who still cherish his memory. Mrs. Kottenstette still occupies the home which was erected for her by her husband and is rearing her children there. She, too, is well-known in Fort Madison, and the hospitality of many of the best homes of the city is extended to her.

THEODORE A. CRAIG.

Theodore A. Craig, a member of the Keokuk bar and a leader in local political circles, was born in Lee county, June 13, 1872, his parents being John H. and Alice (Read) Craig. His father coming to Keokuk about 1855, was one of the first practicing attorneys of this city and was associated in his profession with General Noble. He was a Democrat and took an active interest in the work of the party, frequently delivering campaign addresses in the county and state, although always refusing to become a candidate for office. He died in Keokuk in September, 1893, and is still survived by his wife. The four children of the family are also living: Read, who resides in Aurora, Illinois; Bertha R., who is teaching history in the Keokuk high school; Hugh H., an attorney of this city, and Theodore A.

Theodore A. Craig attended the common and high schools of Keokuk, and afterward continued his studies in Parson's College, of Fairfield, Iowa. On the completion of his literary course he entered the law office of John E. Craig and following his preliminary reading, which gave him a thorough knowledge of many of the principles of law, he was admitted to the bar on the 18th of January, 1899, before the supreme court, at Des Moines. He practiced alone for a year and then entered into partnership with John E. Craig, this connection being continued from June, 1900, until the 1st of June, 1904, when he again began business alone. His success along professional lines has been gratifying, and he now has a distinguished representative clientage. He presents his cause in a strong and forcible manner, displaying an excellent knowledge of the principles of jurisprudence and correct application of them to the points in litigation. For the past six years he has published annotations of the Iowa code, showing changes in the laws, supplying these to the attorneys of the state. Public spirited and interested in the great questions that concern the state and nation, he gives his political allegiance to the Democracy and served as Mayor of Keokuk from 1901 to 1903. He is a member of the Democratic Central Committe, and during campaigns delivers many addresses in support of the party candidates. He has often been chairman of the county convention and has been an attendant upon state and national conventions. Fraternally he is connected with the Modern Woodmen of America, the Ancient Order of United Woodmen and the Benevolent and Protective Order of Elks. Mr. Craig was married in April, 1902, to Miss Jean Blood, of St. Louis, Missouri, and they have resided at No. 503 North Third street. They have many warm friends in Keokuk and occupy an enviable position in social circles of the city.

FRANK H. JONES.

One of the most extensively known and highly respected citizens in the business world of Keokuk, Iowa, for a long period of years, was Frank H. Jones, who was born in Cass county, Ohio, January 30, 1843, the son of Benjamin and Eliza Jones, and came with his parents when about ten years of age to Keokuk, and here spent the remainder of his life in constant and useful activity along commercial lines. He was one of a family comprising four sons and one daughter, as follows: Edward H., now clerk in a bank in the Island of Porto Rico; Hezekiah, who died at the age of thirty years; Frank H., our subject; John, now a resident of Albuquerque, New Mexico, and Kate, wife of Newton E. Clark, of Newtonville, Massachusetts. While yet a mere boy Mr. Jones became a clerk in the hardware store of Cady, Jones & Peck, in which position he quickly won the favor of his employers, but at the beginning of the Civil War his enthusiasm for the cause of his country was so great that he determined to enlist in the Union army. Being opposed in this resolution, however, by his mother, he went in company with a friend to Chariton, Missouri, where was then stationed the First Regiment Iowa Cavalry, and enlisted in Company A, in which he continued until an injury caused by being thrown from his horse rendered him unfit for further active service, and he was honorably discharged. Later he became clerk to a sutler, a position in which he was paid a very high salary, and in this capacity accompanied the army througout its campaigns in the South until close of the war.

In 1865 Mr. Jones resumed his interrupted relations with his former employers, who gladly re-engaged his services, and he continued with them until they retired from business, when he formed a partnership with Samuel Dillon, and they established a men's furnishings business, the style of the firm being Dillon & Jones. This enterprise proved very successful, and its large prosperity was justly attributable in a very marked degree to the care, energy and sound business judgment of Mr. Jones, whose best efforts were ever devoted to its welfare, but after a time the connection was terminated by the sale of Mr. Dillon's interest to James Welch, the firm then becoming Welch & Jones. For a number of years, however, Mr. Jones conducted the business alone, and he continued to be actively associated with its fortunes until the hand of death removed him from the world of the living.

At Chariton, Iowa, on November 1, 1866, Mr. Jones wedded Miss Mary Elizabeth Moore, daughter of Samuel and Isabel (Burney) Moore. The Moore family were early arrivals on the frontier, and William Moore, grandfather of Mrs. Jones, came into contact with the Indians, by whom he was taken prisoner and held in captivity for three years. Shortly after his capture he was stripped of his clothing to undergo the ordeal of running the gauntlet, and as he stood at the head of the two ranks of savages armed with clubs and weapons ready to rain blows upon him, a squaw began the torture by thrusting a firebrand against his flesh; and this act of ferocity saved his life, for, seizing the squaw by the feet, he threw her down a steep, high bluff, on which the party was standing, and this so amused the Indians that they burst into laughter, and he was not required to run the gauntlet. He came to be greatly admired by the Indians, and after his return home he was visited each year by the chief of the tribe, who finally died at his home. Samuel Moore, who was one of a family of eleven sons and daughters, all of whom grew to maturity, was a farmer, and leaving Cadiz, Ohio, in 1853, he traveled westward by water, settling at Bloomington, Illinois, whence he again removed in 1865 to Keokuk, Iowa, and afterward to Chariton, this state. Later the family located in Grand Glacier, Arkansas, and it was at that place that Mr. Moore died in 1876, at the age of sixty-five years. Isabel Burney, mother of Mrs. Jones, was one of thirteen brothers and sisters, all of whom grew to maturity and married, and her paternal grandparents, who were of Scotch-Irish extraction, early settled in the neighborhood of Urichsville, Ohio, where they reached the land on which they established their home by cutting roads through the forest.

To Mr. and Mrs. Jones were born three sons and one daughter, as follows: Georgia Belle, wife of W. S. Phillips, of Keokuk; Charles E., clerk, and Frank M., manager of their father's estate, including the mercantile business left by him, and which they still conduct, and William S., who is a resident of Chicago. To the sons who manage the interests which he left in Keokuk has descended much of the prestige enjoyed by Mr. Jones during his life, and the responsibility attached thereto is an important one, for he occupied a recognized position of leadership, and was active in all good causes. He with his wife was a faithful member of the Congregational church, to which he was a generous and willing contributor for all its charities and philanthropic movements, and he took an active and helpful interest in the affairs of the Grand Army of the Republic, of which he was a member, while his public spirit and desire to fulfill the obligations of citizenship made him a loyal worker in the ranks of the Republican party. He occupied a desirable position as one of the earlier and more celebrated merchant promotors of Keokuk's welfare, while his enterprising disposition led him always to carry a large and seasonable stock of goods in his particular line; and he held his patrons by the strong ties of strictest integrity in his dealings and absolute frankness in all matters. Personally he was ever cheerful, courteous, considerate of others, and unfailingly kind to all. He died February 19, 1903, and his passing has been a matter for deep and sincere regret for many, as he numbered his friends by the score, and the hundred in this and more distant communities, and was universally respected for those high qualities which endeared him to those who now mourn a devoted husband and loving, indulgent father.

BYRON C. DAVIS.

The life of one who, beginning his business activities at an early age, passing through many changes of scene and fortune, achieving success, and always maintaining for himself an honored and respected standing in the community, can not fail to furnish an interesting study to the readers of this volume. Mr. Davis was born at Frankfort, Kentucky, July 30, 1846, and when nine years old accompanied his parents to Fort Madison. At the age of eleven years he began clerking in a dry goods store. After three years of faithful service he became second clerk of the Mississippi river steamer "Pomeroy," this step having been taken in 1860. During the following four years he was employed on the "Pomeroy," "Kate Cassel," "New Boston," and "Keithsburg," and in January, 1864, he went to Chicago and entered school, having a high regard for education, and wishing to perfect himself in certain branches of learning. Here, however, his patriotism and a knowledge that his country was in danger triumphed over his desire for self-advancement, and he enlisted as a soldier in the One Hundred and Forty-seventh Regiment, Illinois Volunteer Infantry, under Capt. A. C. Bardwell and Col. H. F. Sickles. Assigned to the Army of the Cumberland, the young soldier was not destined to participate in any of the more important battles of the war, but passed through a year of hard and exhausting service, mostly skirmish duty, and sustained hardships from which his health suffered much in after years.

Mustered out of the ranks at Savannah, Georgia, and receiving his arrears of pay at Springfield, Mr. Davis visited New York city for a short time and then returned to Chicago, where he accepted employment as a traveling salesman for Day, Tilden & Company, wholesale dealers in notions and fancy dry goods. For three years he continued in this work, the latter part of the period being spent with the firm of Dunlap Brothers, when he was seized with a violent attack of rheumatism, which rendered him unable to perform any work for seven years, during which he remained at home. This affliction, which also led to a heart affection of a serious nature, was a recurrence of the same disease contracted while doing military duty in the South.

About the year 1879 Mr. Davis had so far recovered his health as to enable him to resume active life, and he entered the employ of McDonald Brothers, of La Crosse, Wisconsin. For seven years he was engaged in rafting and towing logs and lumber from Stillwater to St. Louis. This work he abandoned in 1885 for the purpose of establishing himself in the retail shoe business in Fort Madison. After successfully conducting this enterprise for two years he disposed of it, selling to D. T. Brown, and was engaged in clerical employment until 1903, when he repurchased his former business.

On January 30, 1879, at Fort Madison, Mr. Davis married Miss Mary Elizabeth Brown, daughter of Daniel T. Brown, of this place. As Mr. Brown has been long identified with the business interests of the city it seems fitting that he should receive mention. He was born in Athens, Ohio, August 27, 1822, and removed to Iowa in 1856. Until attaining his majority he acted as a clerk, but then established a general store, which he sold before coming to Lee county. In Denmark township, this county, he bought a farm, which he operated until 1870, when he became the proprietor of a store for the sale of books, wall paper, sewing machines, etc. Here he built up a large business, but sold it in 1882. Later he opened a shoe store, which he has since sold to his son-in-law. His marriage to Miss Maria Dean Foster, who was born at Athens, Ohio, took place in October, 1845, and unto them have been born six children —William E., of Fort Madison; Charles P., of Clark county, Missouri; Mrs. B. C. Davis, of Fort Madison; Augustus P., of Fort Madison, Iowa; Frank R., who is in Mexico, and Herbert D., who is in Washington, D. C. Mr. Brown is himself the only living member of a family of eight children, of whom he was the youngest. He has long been a member of the Presbyterian church, and in politics has always affiliated with the Republican party. He owns a commodious residence at 629 Fourth street.

Mr. Davis, our subject, is the son of William H. Davis, a physician, who served during the Civil War as assistant surgeon of the Twenty-first Missouri Volunteer Infantry. His death occurred at Corinth, Mississippi, July 27, 1862. At one time he was engaged in professional practice in Fort Madison, and at another period of his life was a contractor, having built the levee along the river front. At the time of his enlistment in the Union forces he was conducting the McFarland Hotel on Front street. The wife and mother was Margaret (Davis) Davis. She died October 12, 1888. Four of their sons and daughters survive them, Byron C. Davis being the eldest. They are: William H., who was murdered at Pine Bluff, Arkansas, February 22, 1879; Mrs. Margaret J. McDermith, of Fort Madison, a widow; Charles J. Davis, of Jefferson City, Missouri; and Holmes Lee Davis, actor and musician.

Of the union of Mr. and Mrs. Byron C. Davis have been born four children, as follows: Daniel Churchill, born October 17, 1882; Bessie, born December 11, 1883; Frank Brown, born December 11, 1885, and William Lynn, born September 19, 1887.

Mr. Davis is a member of the Presbyterian church, and fraternally has membership relations with the Masonic order, the Grand Army of the Republic, of the local post of which he is a charter member; the Knights of Pythias, Independent Order of Odd Fellows, Ancient Order United Workmen, the Druids and the Brotherhood of American Yeoman. At the present time he is acting as deputy state fish and game warden, and holds the honorable office of president of the board of education of the City of Fort Madison. The family home is at 409 Fourth street. Mr. Davis is well liked and popular, with a wide circle of friends, and well deserves mention in the history of the city in which a great part of his life has been passed.

WILLIAM H. HOPKIRK.

A long career of highly useful public service, first on the field of battle and later in the no less honorable field of education, combined with a character of inflexible integrity and broad human sympathy, such are the claims to consideration possessed by the man whose name stands at the head of this article. William H. Hopkirk was born in Jefferson county, Iowa, October 13, 1843, the son of John and Jane (Nicholson) Hopkirk. The father, who was a farmer, was born in Scotland, April 1, 1808, and emigrated to America in 1828, and the mother was a native of England, her natal day being February 8, 1810. Their marriage took place in Jefferson county, this state.

William H., our subject, was reared in the work of his father's farm, acquiring during his early years those lessons of diligence and application which have since carried him to positions of usefulness. At the beginning of the Civil War, although scarcely more than a boy, he resolved to aid in the great struggle upon which his country was then entering, and enlisted in Company M, of the Fourth Iowa Cavalry, under Colonel Winslow and Captain Whiting. His regiment formed at different times a part of the departments of Mississippi and Tennessee, and the young soldier was destined to experience much hard and active duty. Among the more imporant battles in which he was engaged were those at Guntown and in the rear of Vicksburg. During his regiment's Missouri campaign he was prostrated by malarial fever, and was assigned to hospital. He was mustered out of the military service June 22, 1865, at Davenport, Iowa, having served through the entire course of the war.

On leaving the army Mr. Hopkirk resumed his education, entering Iowa Wesleyan University, at Mount Pleasant, from which institution he was graduated with the degree of Bachelor of Arts, in 1872. He then began his life work of teaching. For many years he acted as principal and teacher at Burlington, being teacher of science in the high school at that place for ten years. For an interval of two or three years he was engaged in business with his brother at Lockbridge, but returned to teaching, and spent five years as principal of schools at Agency and five years in a similar position at Montrose, thus completing a total of twenty years devoted to educational work with scarcely an interruption. In 1894 he came to Fort Madison, and engaged in the insurance and real estate business, in which he still continues. He occupies handsome offices in the Marquette building.

At Burlington, Iowa, June 27, 1877, Mr. Hopkirk was united in marriage with Miss Etta Cowles, who was born in Massachusetts March 15, 1854. Unto them have been born five children, as follows. Ruth, now deceased; Jessie L., student in the State Normal School, at Cedar Falls; Clarence C., graduate of Fort Madison high school, class of 1904; Roland, attending the public school, and Howard.

Mr. Hopkirk's father died in Jefferson county in 1876. He was the father of five children, two of whom, besides our subject, survive him. They are: David, of Fairfield, Iowa, and Mrs. Isabel Sampson, of the same place. He was well favored of fortune, leaving to his family at his death 480 acres of fertile and improved land in Jefferson county.

Mr. Hopkirk and his family are active workers in the Presbyterian church, and he is a member of the Knights of Pythias, the Independent Order of Odd Fellows, and the Grand Army of the Republic. In memory of his school days he holds membership in the Alumni Association of Iowa, Wesleyan University, and in the Greek Society of Phi Delta Theta. Politically he adheres to the principles and organization of the Republican party, and is an especially warm admirer and supporter of President Roosevelt. Warm-hearted, genial, and a ready reader of character, he is popular with a large circle of acquaintances, and enjoys the general esteem.

ELIZABETH PENNARTZ.

Elizabeth Pennartz, of Fort Madison, was born in Germany, October 3, 1847, and came with her parents to America at the age of ten years. She is the daughter of Frank and Margaret (Kolkmann) Otte, the father being a linen weaver in his native land and an engineer in a woolen mill at Quincy, Illinois, where he spent the latter part of his life and where he died.

Before going to Quincy the family lived for a time at West Point, Lee county, and at that place our subject was married to Hubert Pennartz, a farmer, in 1866. On account of ill health they later left the farm and removed to Fort Madison, where Mr. Pennartz conducted a billiard hall on Front street, and in this city he died in 1895. He was a member of St. Mary's Catholic church and of the Catholic Mutual Protective Association. To them were born nine children, as follows: Bertha, wife of Frank W. Sloan, of Chicago; Margaret, who died at the age of four months; Marie, wife of Cassimere Wolpers, Doctor of Medicine, Doctor of Dental Surgery, Chicago; Magdalen, wife of Winter Hupp, of Des Moines, Iowa; Katherine, wife of William Maize, of Fort Madison; Anna, wife of Peter Kron, of Fort Madison; John Joseph; Clara, who died at the age of twenty years, and Richard Hubert, student.

Since her husband's death Mrs. Pennartz has been practicing midwifery and acting as a nurse. She was graduated from the Chicago School of Midwifery, August 28, 1896, and from the Chicago School of Anatomy and Physiology, February 22, of the same year, receiving diplomas from both schools, and passed the state board examination at Springfield, Illinois.

Fraternally Mrs. Pennartz is a member of the Brotherhood of American Yeomen. The family home is at 1304 Third street, and notwithstanding the care of its supervision and her other duties, Mrs. Pennartz has always given the closest attention to the advancement of the individual members of her family. The four older children were educated at St. Mary's parochial school, and the others in the public and high schools of Fort Madison. Mrs. Pennartz is a woman of strong character, and her children are fortunate in the inherited abilities which are enabling them to win success in the world. She enjoys the respect, confidence and esteem of a wide circle of acquaintances and friends.

SARAH MARIA BENBOW.

The name which forms the title of this article is well worthy of a place in the present volume as the representative of a family widely known in connection with the more important interests of Lee county—a family which in its history exemplifies in the most admirable manner the triumph of those qualities of enterprise, sound judgment and unwavering integrity which have caused men of English race to win supremacy in all departments of the world's activity.

Mrs. Sarah Maria Benbow was born on the 12th day of August, 1835, in London, England, the seventh child of William Cole and Sarah Cole. The father was also born in London, the only son of Richard and Sarah Jourdon Cole. Richard Cole was a designer of patterns and embosser, and manufacturer of silks, and accumulated a considerable fortune. His son received a liberal education at Edinburgh and Oxford Universities, and afterward studied law at Lincoln's Inn, where he was admitted as a barrister-at-law. He was married to Sarah Gosling, and having imbibed the spirit of freedom and being a firm believer in Republican institutions, he decided to emigrate to America with his wife, seven children and his parents, and started on the long journey. The voyage across the ocean took over four weeks, during which voyage his father died and was buried at sea. They landed at New York city and from there journeyed westward by the slow Erie canal boats to Buffalo, thence by lake to Racine, in the Territory of Wisconsin, arriving there on the 14th day of February, 1842. The next spring they moved to Yorkville township, Racine county, and settled upon a large tract of unimproved prairie land, entered by Mr. Cole from the government, and there established their new home on the border of civilization, a great change for a family born and raised in the City of London. The children being young, quickly adapted themselves to their new surroundings. It was here that Sarah Cole, at the age of seven years, commenced to attend school. Fortunately such advantages as the school offered were supplemented by parental instruction and discipline in a refined home and under the guidance of liberally educated parents. Under these influences she grew to womanhood and on the 24th day of April, 1854, was united in marriage to John William Benbow, a native of England, born in Staffordshire, the eldest son of William Benbow and Ann (Bagley) Benbow, who resided near Dudley. At the age of nine years the parents, with their family, emigrated to America, crossing the Atlantic ocean, which voyage took over five weeks, landing at New York city in June of 1840, where they immediately took up their westward journey by way of the Erie canal and Great Lakes, at that time the most convenient mode of travel to the great Mississippi valley, and finally settled in Yorkville township, Racine county, Territory of Wisconsin. It was here also that John attended school, and while growing to manhood experienced the frontier life of a new and undeveloped country, and with these surroundings he developed a strong character and vigorous constitution, and it was here that he first met Sarah Cole. After their marriage they.

too, followed the wave of emigration westward and finally settled on a farm in Lee county, Iowa. Afterward they moved to the City of Fort Madison, Iowa, where Mr. Benbow engaged in business as a dealer in grain and seeds and carried on this business up to the time of his death, which occurred on the 29th day of March, 1890, resulting from an injury sustained from being run over by a railway train while walking along the railway track from his place of business to the depot. He was an energetic, aggressive and honest man, commanding the respect and confidence of those who knew him. He left surviving him his devoted wife, one daughter and six sons, whose family ties have kept them close together, all the children having married and settled near their old home. William Henry Benbow was married to Harriett A. Rice, now deceased, leaving an only daughter, Fay Sarah Harriett Benbow. Horatio Frederick Benbow was married to Emma Sowden, to whom was born one son, John Glenn Benbow. Henrietta Sarah Benbow was united in marriage to John Benjamin Williams; they have two daughters, Sarah Henrietta and Vida Williams. Edgar Charles Benbow was united in marriage to Edith Minnie Heitz; they have been blessed with two daughters, Edith Stella and Hazel Florence, and one son, Earl William Benbow. Alfred James Benbow was married to Emaline Okell, they have three daughters, Margaret Helen, Martha Marie and Esther Drake, and one son, Alfred Lusk Benbow. John Lincoln Benbow was married to Happy Melissa Plumer. Albert Richard Benbow was married to Freda Lazetta Salmon, they have one daughter, Charlotte Ruth Benbow.

The mother is still the center of this large family circle and looks back with great pleasure upon the many rugged hardships overcome and difficulties surmounted during her active and strenuous life in caring for and watching over the interests and welfare of her family and still takes a keen interest in everything that is going on in the busy world.

H. C. LANDES.

H. C. Landes, who, since 1851, has resided in Keokuk and is now filling the position of justice of the peace, was born in Circleville, Pickaway county, Ohio, January 7, 1832. The Landes family is descended from Pennsylvania German ancestry, and the parents of our subject were natives of the Keystone state. The father, Joseph Landes, served in the War of 1812, and died in the year 1864, while his wife, who bore the maiden name of Eve Weaver, passed away in January,. 1877, in Montgomery county, Iowa.

H. C. Landes acquired a public-school education and came to Iowa in 1851, when but nineteen years of age. He has resided in Keokuk continuously since the 20th of December, of that year. He is a baker by trade and in the early period of his residence in Keokuk he worked for U. Raplee, in whose employ he remained until 1854. In December, 1854, he was a clerk in the postoffice, under Colonel Patterson; in 1856 he left the employ of the postoffice and entered into partnership with James F. Dougherty in the baking business one year. He was also for several years foreman for Patterson & Timberton Pork House. In the spring of 1860, while being employed in a mill he suffered an accident, having his ankle crushed and this defeated his desire to become a soldier at the time of the Civil War. He, however, was a sutler with the Twenty-fifth Missouri Infantry, which was afterward consolidated with Bissell's Engineering Corps. He was stationed at Johnsonville, the terminus of the Nashville & Johnson Railroad during the construction of that line. Returning to Keokuk in 1865, he soon afterward went to Charleston, where he conducted a restaurant for a year and then again came to this city, in 1866. In 1870 he accepted a position on the police force as turnkey. In 1874 he was elected justice of the peace, but resigned that position the following year, and again became a member of the police force, acting in that capacity until 1884. He afterward conducted the Fulton market in connection with his son for three or four years, and on the expiration of that period, turned his attention to market gardening, which he followed until 1901, within the city limits. He afterward purchased a restaurant, which he conducted until January, 1903, when he qualified again as justice of the peace, and is now acting in that capacity.

Mr. Landes is a Republican in politics, and has always been deeply interested in the success and growth of his party. All matters of public moment have elicited his attention, and along many lines he has been active in support of measures for the general good. He served as an independent fireman in early life, and was the last president of the Young American Fire Company, which was organized in 1856, and disbanded in 1876, when the paid department was instituted. In 1878, while he was a member of the police force, he was one of the principal promoters of the movement, whereby the police held Sunday afternoon services with Rev. John Burgess, as pastor. The services continued for one hour and none but men were admitted. It was held in the council chamber and this custom was kept up for about three years. A choir was organized, of which Mr. Landes became a member. They paid John Wyckoff, the leading singer, five dollars for his Sunday services and paid the preacher whatever remained from the collection above incidental expenses.

On the 29th of April, 1854, Mr. Landes was married at Francisville, Missouri, to Miss Mary Louise Rogers, of Keokuk. She was born in Clinton county, Ohio, and with her father came to Iowa in 1846. They have one child, William H., of Chicago, and he has one daughter, Mamie Edna, who is now the wife of John W. Raymond, of Burlington, Iowa, by whom she has twins, Clarence and Bernie. The Landes home is in Belknap boulevard, in the fifth ward, of Keokuk. Mr. Landes was reared in the Lutheran church, but now attends the Unitarian services, while his wife is a member of the Methodist Episcopal church. For more than a half century a resident of Keokuk he witnessed much of its growth, progress and improvement and has taken great interest in what has been done, having always had firm faith in its future.

ARCHIE VERMAZEN.

Archie Vermazen, who, starting out in life for himself at a very early age and with a brave spirit and strong determination, meeting the difficulties and obstacles that lay in his path, has worked his way upward to success, and is now classed with the leading agriculturists of Lee county. The experiences of pioneer life in the Wild West have been his, and for many years his portion was that of unremitting toil, but his persistency of purpose and capable management have made him today one of the prosperous agriculturists of southeastern Iowa. He was born in Holland, in the province of Gilderland, January 25, 1844, his parents being Archie and Augusta (Von Hafton) Vermazen. His maternal ancestors were connected with the nobility of that country. His father, of Huguenot extraction, was an active business man of his native province, where he conducted a bakery and also dealt in grain. In 1857 he came to the United States with his family including his wife and nine children. That the means of travel in those days bore little resemblance to the transportation methods of the present is indicated by the fact that fifty-two days were concerned in making the trip from Havre, France, to New Orleans. He came up the river to Keokuk, arriving in April, 1857, and in that city the father established his home. Being at that time well advanced in years, he did not enter active business there, but subsequently removed to a farm and died in Charleston township, in December, 1875. His wife survived him until 1900, passing away at the advanced age of eighty-nine years.

Archie Vermazen was, with one exception, the youngest in a large family. He acquired good educational privileges in Holland, attending school without vacation until coming to Iowa. Here he also continued his studies and gained a good command of the English language. Not long after arriving at Keokuk he found employment with a farmer in Clark county, Missouri, receiving for his services but seven dollars per month. Later he was paid eight dollars per month, and did practically a man's work. He managed to save something from his meager wages, and he continued employment as a farm hand until 1859, when he accepted a position in a bakery in Keokuk, and later was in the office of Dr. Sanford, of that city, until about 1861. In the fall of that year he enlisted in the Second Iowa Infantry, but his parents not giving their consent he could not be sworn in. A very dissimiliar experience to anything that he had previously known came to him, however, in the spring of 1862, when he joined an expedition that left Summitville for eastern Oregon. He drove an ox team on that long journey over the plains and the mountains, reaching his destination in September. About that time many emigrants were killed, but the party with which Mr. Vermazen traveled escaped without loss of life. During the fall and winter of 1862 he was on a ranch in eastern Oregon, and in the spring of 1863 went to the mines in Idaho, which had but recently been discovered. There he spent two years in mining, sleeping in a stockade over night on account of the hostility of the Indians. The difficult experiences of frontier life in these mining camps is to him not a matter of history, but a matter of personal experience. He was successful, however, and returned from the mines to eastern Oregon, where he first located. There he conducted a trading post and stage station on the edge of the Umatilla Indian reservation, under the name of Swift & Vermazen, Mr. Vermazen, however, having exclusive management of the business, which he successfully conducted for four years. While there he was elected sheriff of Umatilla county, but his business being worth much more to him than the office he succeeded in getting out of it on account of not being of age. This was during the exciting period in the formation of the great northwestern country, when there was a large lawless element attracted thither by the hope of being able to prey upon the fortunate miners and business men. Mr. Vermazen took a firm stand in favor of law and order, and in connection with other citizens of worth, aided largely in promoting the material unbuilding of the district and in upholding its moral, legal and political status.

Desiring to return home in 1868, and knowing it unsafe to cross the plains, he went down the Columbia river to Portland, thence to San Francisco and from that port sailed to New York by way of the Nicarauga route, and returned from the eastern metropolis to Lee county. In the spring of 1868, however, he again left home and made a settlement in Dakota, but that was the year of the great grasshopper scourge there, and he abandoned his business interests in the North and returned to Lee county, determined to make it his permanent abode. Here he has since lived, and his years have brought him prosperity because of his business adaptability and the excellent use he has made of opportunity. He first purchased a farm in Charleston township, on which he lived for five years and then turned his attention to the conduct of a general store in the village of Charleston, which he successfully conducted, building up an extensive trade from a small beginning. He also added agricultural implements to his stock of goods and erected a store building there 22x100 feet, all of which was devoted to the conduct of his enterprise. For twenty-six years he represented the mercantile interests of Charleston and gained a wide and favorable acquaintance throughout the county as a merchant of progressive spirit and known reliability. In the meantime he began dealing in lands and carried on quite an extensive real estate business. He also built a good home in the village and there lived until his retirement from commercial circles, when he removed to his farm, comprising 556 acres of land adjoining Charleston. This he now manages, the farm being devoted to stockraising purposes. As in his other business ventures he displays keen discernment, unfaltering perseverance and great diligence, and these qualities have been the essential factors in bringing him the splendid success which he enjoys.

In his political views Mr. Vermazen has always been a Democrat and has taken an active and helpful interest in political and other public affairs in his township and county. He was first elected justice of the peace while still upon the farm and held that office until he declined further election for the office, his long retention therein indicating the fact that his decisions were always characterized by strict impartiality. He has served as township clerk and township assessor for some time, and as delegate has attended various county, congressional and state conventions. Before his term of assessor expired he was elected county supervisor and held the office for six years, serving as chairman of the board during the greater part of that time, and in the period of his incumbency a large number of substantial improvements were made. He was postmaster under President Cleveland's administration during both his first and second terms, and received credit for his efficient service. His fraternal relations connect him with Joppa Lodge, No. 136, Free and Accepted Masons, of Montrose; Potowonok Chapter, No. 28, Royal Arch Masons, of Fort Madison, and Charleston Lodge, No. 89, Independent Order of Odd Fellows, in which he has filled every office, and for fifteen years was treasurer.

On the 31st of December, 1868, Mr. Vermazen was married to Miss Emma Sapp, of Charleston, a daughter of John W. Sapp, who at one time lived in Kentucky, afterward in Ohio, and thence came to Iowa. They have two living children: James H. and John A. The former is now engaged with his father in the stock business, and is also a member of the firm of Vermazen Brothers, who succeeded their father in the mercantile business. He was married to Miss Mae Griswold, of Jefferson township, and they have three children: Hazel Marian, Helen Marr and Lloyd Griswold. John A. Vermazen, who is manager of the mercantile establishment of Vermazen Brothers, wedded Grace Griswold, of Jefferson township, and they have two children: Mildred Bessie and Archie James. Mrs. Vermazen is a member of the Baptist church, and Mr. Vermazen attends the services and contributes generously to that church, although he was reared in the Presbyterian faith. He has traveled extensively in this country and also in Europe, for he spent the summer of 1897 visiting the home of his boyhood and other countries and places of interest. While there are many self-made men in America the history of such a one never fails to prove of interest and often furnishes an incentive for renewed effort on the part of others. Every individual feels a delight in victory, and when the conquest is over unfavorable conditions and the competitions of the business life the result is certainly most creditable. Mr. Vermazen, starting out in an independent business career at an early age, has proven in his life record that prosperity and an honorable name may be won simultaneously.

WALKER WILSON.

Walker Wilson, a resident of the township of Montrose, Lee county, Iowa, for more than forty years, donned the Union blue almost immediately on the outbreak of the Civil War, and was long a gallant soldier at the front, ever bearing himself bravely, and writing a record of which his many friends are justly proud. A generous government well remembers his sickness and privation, and his name is on the roll of those it loves and honors, ever ministering to their needs with a liberal hand.

Mr. Wilson was born in Gettysburg, Pennsylvania, October 2, 1835, a son of John and Rebecca (Walker) Wilson, both natives of that state. Soon after his birth his parents removed to Athens, Tennessee, where they maintained a home some years, after which they moved to Lowell, Iowa. In 1844 they came to Lee county, where their remaining years were spent.

Walker Wilson secured his schooling in the log structures then the common type of the educational temple in Tennessee and Iowa, and early took charge of the parental homestead. On the formation of the First Iowa Cavalry he became a member of Company A, June 13, 1861, and participated in the long and honorable career which was had by the members of that gallant organization, a record that was a credit to the state and an inspiration to all who loved the starry banner they so gallantly followed. The captain of the company in which he went out to the front was a Mr. Torrence, who afterward became a colonel. Many of the other officers rose to high command, the entire body of troops being noted alike for its bravery on the field, general efficiency in all the details of war, and self-reliant action in the face of danger and surprise. It was organized at Keokuk as an independent command, and went into service with its own horses, arms and general equipment. Mr. Wilson was in the regiment for three years and four months, and during that time did duty in Missouri, Arkansas, Texas, and several other states, participated in a number of severe engagements, mainly at Prairie Grove, Little Rock and Camden. Much of the time the regiment was engaged in fighting guerrillas, principally those under Price and Quantrell. While in the service he contracted rheumatism, chronic diarrhea and hemorrhoids, and on account of their after effects, is the recipient of a handsome pension from the government.

After returning to the pursuits of peaceful life Mr. Wilson was engaged in cooking on the steamboats for some twenty years, being employed both on government boats and the Northern Line steamers. At differnet times he was also employed in this capacity on rafters, and everywhere was regarded as an efficient and reliable man. For the past seven years he has been incapacitated for any kind of active work. He is a cheerful and genial character, and has many friends in the community, with whom he loves to recount his old-time experiences and memories. The nearest he came to being wounded during the Civil War, was when his horse was struck on the neck by a spent Minie ball, that glanced from the brass pommel on his saddle, and ranging upward, gave him a close call for time and eternity. Mr. Wilson is a member of Tip Best Post, No. 75, Grand Army of the Republic, and is now holding the position of chaplain in that organization. Once when the State Encampment was held at Cedar, he was appointed commander. In politics he is a Republican.

Mr. Wilson was married in 1856, at Sand Prairie, Lee county, to Miss Mary Jane Douglass, who died in 1858, leaving one child, James, who is now a resident of Fort Madison. Her remains were interred on Sand Prairie.

In his youthful days, Mr. Wilson heard

Joe Smith, "the prophet," preach in Nauvoo Temple many times during the period that the Mormons held sway in that region, and he well remembers the destruction of the Temple by fire. He knew many of the reputed bandits that flourished along the river in the early days, among them being Hodges, Barney, and perhaps eight or ten more. They lived in cabins about eighty rods from his early home, and there were quiet enough. When they finally left the neighborhood young Wilson and his chums thought they might have left something, perhaps some coin in their cabins, thoroughly overhauled the buildings, but only seventy-five cents rewarded their labors. He remembers when the Mormons were driven out of Nauvoo, and the subsequent arrival of the Icarian fraternity from France; and it is his opinion that many of the crimes and depredations charged to the Mormons were in reality wrought by the bandits that then enjoyed such immunity on the river. He saw the hanging of the two Hodges at Burlington in 1848, who had been condemned for murder at Davenport. At an early day he was a member of the Anti-Horse Thief Association, and was a very active defender of law and order. Mr. Wilson has a good standing in the community for his manifest honor and genuine integrity.

FRANK COYNE.

One of the prominent representatives of practical agriculture in Lee county, is Frank Coyne, a resident of Jefferson township, where he has a beautiful home and a well-improved farm of 320 acres. Mr. Coyne traces his ancestry to Ireland, his paternal grandfather having been a native of that country, but his own place of birth is Springfield, Missouri, and the date November 6, 1854. He is the son of William and Lavina (Oberly) Coyne. The father was born in Philadelphia, Pennsylvania, and there grew to manhood, acquiring meantime the trade of plastering. Hearing of the superior opportunities to be found in the great West, and wishing to avail himself of its advantages, he came to Iowa some time between 1840 and 1850, locating at Fort Madison, Lee county, where he successfully followed his trade, and later met and wedded Miss Oberly, who was also a native of Pennsylvania. She came with her parents, Mr. and Mrs. Andrew Oberly, to Fort Madison in 1840. Mr. and Mrs. Coyne removed after a time to Springfield, Missouri, where they continued to reside until the father of our subject was appointed, under the administration of President Buchanan, to a position in the office of the auditor of the postal department at Washington. The family then returned to Lee county, locating upon the farm now owned by Mr. Coyne. At the beginning of the Civil War the father became a member of the Confederate Army, but at its close returned to a position in Washington, which he held until 1870, when he came to live with his family in Jefferson township. His death occurred here in 1875. The mother still survives, and is living with her son.

Frank Coyne, the subject of this review, secured a good education in the public schools, and enjoyed the additional advantage of learning the work of the farm by practical experience with its details. When the farm on which he resides was acquired by his mother in 1870, he assumed sole charge of its management and operation, and in 1900 he himself purchased it. This he was enabled to do by the success which had come to him as a result of his energy, care and foresight in the conduct of the business. All the improvements have been made under his supervision, and the farm is one of the finest and best equipped in this portion of the county. Here Mr. Coyne conducts general farming and stockraising and is also somewhat interested in buying and shipping grain and live stock. On January 25, 1877, he was united in marriage to Miss Eliza Cale, of Jefferson township, daughter of the late Joseph Cale, who died in 1904. They have two daughters and four sons, these being Mabel, William, Howard, Nellie F., Frank, Jr., and Harry.

In his political faith Mr. Coyne is a firm believer in the declared principles of Democracy, and has served his party as a delegate in various conventions, but has never aspired for public office. He feels a deep interest in the cause of education, taking an active part in the betterment of the public schools, and has been a director of Liberty district, No. 4, for a period of twenty-five years. He was reared in the Episcopal church, and still holds membership in that body at Montrose. He is enterprising, public spirited and progressive, and his loyalty to his convictions and absolute integrity in his dealings have inspired respect for his character on the part of all with whom he comes in contact.

FRANK ROSS WATERS.

Frank Ross Waters, who is engaged in the real estate business, in Keokuk, was born in Philadelphia, Pennsylvania, July 10, 1854, his parents being Henry and Sarah (Pollock) Waters. The father was a contractor and on coming to the West settled in Keokuk, where he resided for many years, his death occurring in 1901. His wife had previously passed away.

Frank Ross Waters spent the days of his boyhood under the parental roof, pursued his education in the public schools of Philadelphia and learned the carpenter's trade in that city. He went to Kansas in the spring of 1869, when fifteen years of age, settling in Osborn county, where he secured a claim, making his home thereon until 1872. He owned a quarter section of land and in addition to his agricultural pursuits followed carpentering. In 1872, however, he removed to Keokuk, where he continued as a journeyman carpenter until 1876, when he returned to his native city, there residing until 1880, when once more he established his home in Keokuk. Here he was employed as a bench worker in the coach building department of the shops of the St. Louis, Keokuk & Northwestern Railroad, occupying that position continuously until 1889, when he met with an accident which has disabled him from active work as a carpenter since that time. He fell from a scaffold on a building about forty-five feet and his ribs were broken. He was in St. Louis at the time, having gone there for business purposes, and for fourteen months he was confined to his home. Being unable to resume work at his trade, he spent five or six years upon the road as representative for the Taylor Manufacturing Company, of St. Louis, and for the Horn Vinegar Company, at Keokuk. He was also for two years traveling solicitor for the Constitution-Democrat, of Keokuk, and was also solicitor of Gates City for two years, while in 1899, he turned his attention to the real estate business, in which he is now engaged. He handles both farm and city property and has secured a good clientage, negotiating many important real estate transfers, which have not only added to his individual income, but have also been a factor in the improvement of the city.

In April, 1878, when in Philadelphia, Mr. Waters was married to Miss M. A. Weaver, and their children are Harry, who married Miss Calista A. Boatman, and is now foreman in a laundry; Clara, who is serving as forelady in a laundry; Edward, who is cutter in the Irvin-Philips Co., of Keokuk; Anna, at home; Maggie, George, Nellie, Mary and Emma, in school. Mr. Waters is a prominent representative of the Modern Woodmen of America. He has served for seven years as clerk of Camp No. 622, of Keokuk, and attended the clerks' meeting, in Indianapolis, in 1903. He is likewise a Mason, belonging to Eagle Lodge, No. 12, Free and Accepted Masons, of which he is junior deacon, and has been secretary of the Court of Honor since he became one of its representatives. He is also identified with the Knights and Ladies of Security, and attends and supports St. John's Episcopal church. In politics he is a Republican, and was a candidate before the county convention for nomination for county recorder. He has served for two years on the board of registration in the first ward, and is a notary public. He has resided in Keokuk during the greater part of the time for more than thirty years and his interest in its upbuilding and improvement has led to active co-operation in many measures for the general good.

FRANK DIETZ.

Frank Dietz was born in Jackson township, Lee county, on the 16th of May, 1859, his parents being Edward and Martha (Gray) Dietz. The father's birth having occurred in New Albany, Indiana, on the 25th of January, 1822, while his wife was born on the 29th of December, 1829, at Lexington, Kentucky. They were married in Keokuk, Iowa, on the 16th of June, 1849, the father having been a pioneer settler of this city, arriving in the early '40s. A bricklayer by trade, he became a contractor in that line and erected many of the large buildings of the city. In later years he owned a garden spot in the Nassau addition to Keokuk, and lived a quiet life at his home, being comfortably situated with his family around him. He passed away in 1896, at the advanced age of seventy-four years, while his wife died on the 8th of March, 1892. She belonged to the Methodist Episcopal church, to which her husband gave his support and both were people of high respect, enjoying the confidence and good will of many friends: In their family were ten children, of whom eight are now living, but Freeman and William have passed away. The others are George, who is pilot on the government boat "Lucia" and makes his home at Keokuk; Clara Belle, the wife of John Merrick, who is employed in the sawmill of the Tabor Lumber Company, at Keokuk; Ella, the wife of Emery Brain, who for twenty-four years was a bugler with the United States Regulars, now retired on a pension, living in Wichita, Kansas; Charles L., who is now assistant storekeeper for the Chicago, Burlington & Quincy Railroad Company, at St. Joseph, Missouri, and who for four years was alderman of Keokuk; Harry, a twin brother of Charlie, who is engaged in business in Keokuk as a member of the firm of Harrison & Dietz; Emma, the wife of George Heartlyne, who is connected with the railroad service in the State of Washington; and James, a teamster of Keokuk.

Frank Dietz acquired his education in the public schools of Keokuk, and after putting aside his text-books he secured employment in a sawmill, where he remained for fifteen years. On the expiration of that period he was appointed to a position on the police force in 1899, serving under Mayors Dougherty and Craig, as captain of a night force. For several years he has worked at the carpenter's trade. His political allegiance is given the Democracy and he takes an active part in conventions, putting forth every effort in his power to promote the growth and insure the success of the party. He belongs to the Independent Order of Odd Fellows, with which he has been identified for sixteen years and for four years he has been connected with the Modern Woodmen of America.

On the 11th of May, 1880, Mr. Dietz was married to Miss Sarah Hamilton, of Keokuk, who was born in Lee county, but was reared in Lewis county, Iowa, by her grandmother, her mother, Mrs. Hamilton, having died during her infancy. Her father is now in the Soldiers' Home in Marshalltown, Iowa. Mr. and Mrs. Dietz have an adopted daughter, Elouise, who was born January 15, 1897. Their home is at the corner of C and Estes streets in West Keokuk, and was erected in 1884.

FREDERICK B. KREHBIEL.

Frederick B. Krehbiel, one of the respected and well-known citizens of Fort Madison, where he is leading a life of retirement at his pleasant home, 1401 Sixth street, is one of Lee county's native sons, having been born at West Point, January 4, 1851. There he acted as assistant to his father in the farm work and applied himself to acquiring an education in the public schools until his nineteenth year, when he decided to begin his independent career. Going to the village of Denmark, this county, he learned the trade of blacksmithing, which he followed at that place for twenty-eight years, achieving, by his energy, honesty and devotion to his work, an important financial success. After learning the trade he bought the shop of his employer. On terminating his business at Denmark in March, 1896, he purchased a farm of 378 acres in Pleasant Ridge township. The land at that time was only partially improved, but Mr. Krehbiel has since placed the entire tract under cultivation, and also erected some of the present buildings. Here he remained for a period of eight years, engaged in general farming and the raising of high-grade stock, in which he met with a considerable degree of success. In 1903, having decided to retire from active life, he resigned the management of the farm to his son, and removed with his family to Fort Madison, where he purchased the present home and has since resided.

In his religious relations Mr. Krehbiel is a member of the Mennonite church of Lee county, and politically, he is a lifelong Republican. He has not, however, possessed time or inclination to engage actively in partisan politics, or to do more than cast his ballot in favor of honest government.

Mr. Krehbiel is a son of John Charles and Katherine (Raber) Krehbiel. His father was born in Rheinpfalz, Bavaria, Germany, June 9, 1811. At the age of fifteen he learned the trade of a miller, and continued in that occupation in his native land until 1832, when he emigrated to the United States and followed it for one year in Butler county, Ohio. He then returned to Germany and on April 12, 1837, was married to Miss Annie Wohlgemoth, who was also a native of Rheinpfalz, the date of her birth having been March, 1811. On the day of their marriage they sailed for America. They made their home in Butler county until the autumn of 1839, when they decided to seek the greater opportunities of the West and became pioneers of Lee county, Iowa, erecting their cabin of logs at West Point. At that place the wife died the following year, leaving two children: John J., now a resident of Newton, Kansas, who was born in Ohio, May 3, 1838, and Hannah M., born in Lee county, November 26, 1839, now the widow of Daniel Hertzler, late of Mount Rich, Kansas.

On July 31, 1846, Mr. Krehbiel's father was remarried, his second wife being Katherine, daughter of Christian Raber, an early settler of the county. She was born in Baden, Germany, April 8, 1826. In the autumn of 1849 John Charles Krehbiel was ordained pastor of the Mennonite church, a position he retained until the time of his death. In 1857 he removed to the village of West Point, where he purchased a half interest in the sawmill known as the Krehbiel & Risser mill. Of his second marriage were born ten children, as follows: Annie M., wife of Edward Brown, of Denmark, Lee county; Christian W., deceased; Frederick B., the subject of this review; Katherine B., deceased; Elizabeth, wife of John Trowbridge, of Denmark; Daniel S.; Sarah M., deceased; Sarah R., wife of Lewis Bretz, of Deer Creek, Oklahoma; Charles W., a resident of McPherson Center, Kansas, and Henry E., of Lingborg, Kansas. The father of the family died at West Point, February 26, 1886, at the age of seventy-five years. He was successful in business; was very public spirited, and was generally respected. He was elected to a number of township and county offices and performed their duties with efficiency and honor. He was buried at West Point. Mrs.

Krehbiel, mother of our subject, died when Mr. Krehbiel was ninteen years of age. She died at the age of forty-four, and is also buried at West Point. Mr. Krehbiel was united in marriage at West Point, this county, to Miss Lena Linhard, who was born in Franklin township, the daughter of George and Louisa (Haessig) Linhard. Her father was born in French Alsace, in 1823, and emigrated to the United States when twenty-eight years of age. He first located in New York state, where he remained four years, coming to Franklin township, Lee county, in 1856. There he purchased land and engaged in farming for a number of years, but a few years before his death he sold the farm and removed to Missouri, near Kirksville, where his death occurred, February 27, 1899, in the seventy-fifth year of his age. His widow is still living, at the age of seventy years, and resides with Mr. Krehbiel. She was the mother of eight children, as follows: Lena, Mary, who died in 1886; George, who resides at Lyons, New York; Phillip, a resident of Adair county, Missouri; Emma, wife of Dr. D. N. Coon, of Fort Madison; Lula, wife of O. M. Hutchinson, of Adair county, Missouri; William, of Adair county, and Ella, wife of Russell Bartlett, of Adair county.

To Mr. and Mrs. Krehbiel have been born three children, all of whom are natives of Denmark, Lee county. They are as follows: George J., born May 14, 1877, resides on his father's farm, in Pleasant Ridge township, and on February 2, 1903, he married Miss Mayme Figgen, a daughter of Lawrence Figgen, late of Fort Madison. They have one child, Lawrence F., born November 13, 1903, in Pleasant Ridge township. Alice K., daughter of Mr. and Mrs. Krehbiel, was born April 22, 1882. She is now the wife of John A. Heberer, a farmer, of Washington township. They have one child, Doratha Lee, born August 6, 1904, and Addie L., twin sister of Mrs. Heberer, resides with her parents.

Mr. Krehbiel has been a witness of many improvements in general conditions in Lee county, has viewed its rise, in fact, from an almost primitive state to the proudest position in the commonwealth. Moreover, he has borne a worthy part in the general advancement, as his ability has enabled him to do. He is a man of strong character, and has won success by his own efforts and this achievement has gained for him the respect of all, while his genial disposition has made him many friends.

LINDSEY GREEN PITMAN.

Lindsey Green Pitman, the oldest resident of West Point township and a member of one of the oldest pioneer families of Lee county, Iowa, was born in Laurel county, Kentucky, December 22, 1822, a son of Lewis and Martha (Green) Pitman. His father, Lewis, was a son of Richard Pitman, who was a pioneer of Kentucky and first settled in Woodford county, but later removed to Laurel county, where he died. In the fall of 1834 Lewis Pitman left Kentucky with his family, traveling in wagons drawn

MR. AND MRS. LINDSEY G. PITMAN

by ox teams, and in the spring of 1835 they arrived in West Point township, this county, and settled on the east bank of the creek which flows past the present site of the village of West Point, taking up their residence on a claim which Lewis Pitman later entered as a "homestead" from the government, the tract consisting of about 160 acres, to which 200 acres were added by purchase later. Here the father of the family continued to reside until 1862, when his death occurred, and he was buried in the cemetery on the old Pitman homestead farm. He was one of the first representatives of the Methodist faith in this section of the county, and throughout his life was a conscientious worker and very prominent member in the church, which he assisted in every possible way, giving generously of his means and personal efforts. The Pitman family is truly entitled to the name of pioneers, for when they settled in Iowa there was but one other family in the territory comprising the whole of the present township of West Point, and they were compelled to forego many of the advantages offered by older communities and to make many sacrifices of comfort, convenience and personal advancement.

The first wife of Lewis Pitman died in Kentucky, as did also his second companion, and it was his third wife who accompanied him to Iowa. By his first marriage he was the father of three sons, Lindsey Green, Granville and Green, to all of whom was vouchsafed long life, the first death of one of these three occurring as late as September 29, 1902, and all were residents of this county. By his second marriage Mr. Pitman had one child, which, however, died young, and his third wife, Parmelia Love Warren, who died in Lee county in 1875, was the mother of eleven children, of whom four are now living, these being Martha, wife of B. R. Essex, a resident of California; Minerva, wife of A. Knowles, of Iowa; Stephen D., of Van Buren county, Iowa, and Eliza, wife of John Bonnell, of Fort Madison, Iowa. The founder of the family in Lee county was in his political affiliations a Whig, and was a man of considerable natural gifts, being very successful in his business of farming, and being widely known as of an energetic and enterprising disposition.

Our subject began his education in his native State of Kentucky, and concluded his studies in Lee county, being a pupil in the public schools, while at the same time he worked on his father's farm and became proficient in agriculture, as is shown by his later success. He remained at home until attaining his majority, after which he was employed for a year as a farm laborer, and subsequently worked by the job until the time of his marriage in 1851 to Miss Rhoda Whiteaker. Mrs. Pitman was born March 21, 1831, in Vermilion county, Illinois, a daughter of John and Dorcas (Campbell) Whiteaker, both natives of Tennessee, where they were married and whence they removed to Illinois. In May, 1834, they located at Augusta, Iowa, building and conducting a store at that place until 1842, when they removed to Jefferson county, and later to Fort Madison, Lee county, running a store at the latter place on the west side of Pine street, between Front and Second streets, for a number of years. Later they went to Missouri, but at the beginning of the war between the states returned to Fort Madison, the father there retiring from active business, and making that city his residence until his death, which occurred in 1884, when he was eighty-nine years, four months and twenty-six days old. He was a man of ability, and was widely known.

After his marriage Mr. Pitman established a home upon the farm of 190 acres which he had previously purchased, and here he has ever since resided, and by judicious management has been able to add to the original tract until he now owns 470 acres of high-grade farm lands in an admirable state of intensive cultivation, a fact which unmistakably proclaims the possession of business ability of no mean order. Moreover, all the improvements which now grace this immense farm are of his own inauguration, as it was entirely without buildings or other improvements when purchased, and the credit is his alone. Among the first white inhabitants of this section, to which he emigrated when the country was yet a desolate and pathless wilderness, he has seen the land emerge from primitive conditions to one of the most favored spots on the continent of America, covered with cities and villages, churches and schools, furnishing the necessaries and luxuries of life to thousands of residents and pouring forth a steady stream of wealth to sustain the workers of many a distant metropolis and foreign land, he has borne a large and important part in bringing about these remarkable changes, this marvelous and incomparable development, this miracle which has made the barren wilderness to bloom and bring forth fruit abundantly.

Unto Mr. and Mrs. Pitman have been born three sons and one daughter, as follows: John Lewis, who died in infancy; Alice, wife of Monroe Marsh, who lives in Pleasant Ridge township, Lee county, and has three children, William, Bertha and Lucia; Asbury Lee, who married Miss Sarah Cloud, and has one daughter, Cora, lives with his parents and manages the farm, and George G., who died in infancy. This family has enjoyed all the advantages of a sound Christian training, for both Mr. and Mrs. Pitman are consistent adherents of the Methodist faith, and are members and supporters of the Pitman Chapel congregation, whose house of worship Mr. Pitman helped to build, and which he has always supported in a liberal manner, contributing to the work of the church in all its various branches. To his duties as a citizen he has been no less faithful and attentive, taking part in the political affairs of county, state and nation as a member of the Republican party, whose principles approximately represent his views of American governmental science.

At the present time Mr. Pitman is not actively engaged in the pursuits which engrossed his energies during the greater part of his life, having relinquished his regular occupation a number of years ago, and is now living in ease and retirement, as befits one of his years and achievements. Mrs. Pitman is a gracious lady of pleasing presence, and although she suffered an accidental injury some eight years since which renders it impossible for her to move about without the aid of a wheel chair, she has preserved in the face of misfortunes her accustomed cheerfulness of demeanor, and around her centers the affection of young and old. Mr. Pitman is an example of well-preserved physical manhood, and in this connection may be cited a fact of remarkable interest in regard to the Pitman family: Mr. Pitman's father had eleven children of whom the oldest and the youngest died in the fall of 1846, but from that time until September 29, 1902, no deaths occurred among the remaining nine, and at that time the aggregate of their ages was 657 years, or an average of seventy-three years, there being now but five living, four having died within two years after the first died in 1902. Mr. Pitman, himself, has now long past the allotted span of three score years and ten, being eighty-six years of age, and the life thus prolonged has been filled with success and honor, while its latter years find him enjoying the respect of all and the friendship of many because of his kindly nature and the sterling manhood of his character.

GEORGE A. HART.

George A. Hart, who follows the trade of blacksmith and wagonmaker, at Fort Madison, is a native son of Lee county, having been born in Pleasant Ridge township, March 26, 1843. He is the son of John H. and Phoebe (Thurston) Hart, who were married at East Greenwich, Rhode Island, and removed to Lee county in 1839, where the father purchased land and engaged in farming until his retirement. At that time they again removed, going to Denmark, this county, and later to Butler, Missouri, and there John H. Hart died in 1870, at the age of fifty-six years. The demise of his wife preceded his, she having passed to the higher life in the year 1851, at the age of forty.

Our subject is one of a family of eight brothers and sisters, as follows: Jane, wife of Robert Henry, of Mount Ayr, Iowa; Thomas H., of Fort Madison; Ray S., of Denmark, Lee county; George A.; John T., who died in a military hospital at St. Louis, in 1864; Ariadna, wife of T. F. Whitmark, of Lee county; Lorin, deceased; and Lewis, deceased. After the death of his first wife John H. Hart was again married, this time to Emily Green, who died in 1891, leaving three children: Phoebe L. (Root), now deceased; Manley D.; and Jessie, wife of Frank Murphy, of Stronghurst, Illinois.

The Hart family originally emigrated to America from Ireland at an early date, and Mr. Hart traces his genealogy through the maternal line of Thurston as far back as 1640, when two brothers of the name settled in America, coming from England.

The patriotic record of the Hart family is indeed an inspiring one, and truly extraordinary. After acquiring a knowledge of books in the district school, George A. Hart, with four of his brothers, left home at the age of eighteen years to aid his country in the great struggle of the Civil War, and enlisted in company "F," of the First Iowa Cavalry, under Captain James O. Gower, and Colonel Warren. He was assigned to the Seventh Army Corps, and served two years, or from August 1, 1861, to July 11, 1863. He was engaged in battles at Blackwater and at Silver Creek, as well as numerous skirmishes and arduous duty against guerrillas or "bushwackers" in southwestern Missouri. His service ended at Duval's Bluff, where he was mustered out.

After returning from the war, Mr. Hart began acquiring the trade of blacksmithing, working as a journeyman until 1868, when he established himself in business at Denmark. Here he continued for about twenty-five years, with a large measure of success and in 1891 he took up his present location in Fort Madison. On October 1, 1867, he was married at Fort Madison to Miss Leonora C. Burton, a native of Vermont, and to them were born four children, one of whom, Dorr, is now deceased. The others are: Glenn T.; George Emmet, student of medicine at Keokuk, and assistant to his father during vacations; and Nellie B., wife of William F. Moore, of Des Moines county, Iowa. Mrs. Hart died November 1, 1883, at Denmark, and is there buried. December 28, 1885, Mr. Hart was married to Miss Ellen Young, who was born in Lee county in 1844, and is a daughter of Lyman Young, of New York state.

In his political faith, George A. Hart is a stanch and loyal member of the Republican party. Fraternally, he is connected with the Grand Army of the Republic, and is a charter member of Camp No. 460, Modern Woodmen of America, of Denmark. He owns his place of business and family residence at No. 1005 Second street. By a long career of industry, integrity and just and generous dealing Mr. Hart has made his own way successfully, and has earned for himself the respect of a large circle of friends.

W. L. RAY.

One who has served his nation well, both during the dark days of armed conflict and in times of peace, is W. L. Ray, of Fort Madison. He was born in Washington county, Iowa, January 16, 1841, the son of Archibald Ray, of Ohio, and Tabitha (Custer) Ray, also a native of Champaign county, Ohio. The parents were married in Wayne county, Indiana, where the father was a farmer. They are now both deceased. To them were born ten children, but only two survive—W. L., who is the third child, and Mrs. Almeda Mason, of Weeping Water, Nebraska.

Mr. Ray, our subject, was married in 1878, at Farmland, Indiana, to Miss Mary E. Mills, a native of that place and a daughter of Elisha and Barbara (Lever) Mills, both of Indiana. They removed to Red Oak, Iowa, where they remained for three or four years, at the expiration of which period they removed to Fort Madison. Here Mr. Ray was appointed by Warden George W. Crossley, April 17, 1885, a guard in the Iowa State Penitentiary, a post which he has filled with honor and ability for twenty years.

In 1861, when the government at Washington was calling for volunteers to crush out the great rebellion of the Confederate States, Mr. Ray enlisted, on October 2, at Mount Pleasant, Iowa, in Company D, of the Fourth Iowa Cavalry, under Colonel Asbury B. Porter. The part which he bore in the subsequent struggle was long and arduous. A list of the battles in which he was engaged is given herewith, and it presents a record both remarkable and impressive. They are: The battle of White River, Arkansas; Tallatt's Ferry, Brown's Ford, Mount Olive, Big Creek; Vicksburg, Jackson, Canton, Brownsville, Mechanicsburg, Bear Creek, siege of Jackson, Livingston, Big Black Bridge, Baker's Creek, Clinton, Ripley, Brice's Crossroad, Harrisburg, Guntown, Tallahatchie, Memphis, Independence, Big Blue, Osage Plantation, White's Station, and a number of skirmishes. At Raymond, Mississippi, May 12, 1863, he was wounded, receiving a gunshot wound in the left leg, and twelve days later was taken prisoner while in hospital. As a prisoner he was taken to Parole Camp at Benton Barracks, Missouri, and he still treasures among his most cherished possessions his parole of honor, dated May 24, 1863, and signed by Christian Foster, surgeon of the Fifty-eighth Ohio. He rejoined his regiment October 4, 1863, at Vicksburg, and was discharged December 4, 1864, it being then foreseen that the end of the war was near, and that the service of the Western armies would be no longer required. He served three years, two months and three days in the Army of the United States, and during that time he never used a dose of any medicine, and never suffered any disability except from the wound before mentioned—a fact which indicates the possession of great physical powers.

Unto Mr. and Mrs. Ray have been born one son and five daughters, as follows: Lona May, born March 8, 1880; Harry L., born August 31, 1881, married Miss Edith Alvina Little and lives in Fort Madison; Myrtle, born June 26, 1883; Mabel, born February 18, 1885; Effie Belle, born November 6, 1887; and Dora, born March 20, 1895.

Mr. Ray, by his honorable course under all the circumstances of life, has won for himself a place of high esteem in the community, and has made friends of all who know him well.

JOSEPH TROJA.

To record the life and deeds of men who have borne an honorable share in the upbuilding of county, state and nation is the duty and the highest privilege of the historian. Joseph Troja, who for many years, has been well known in connection with the best interests of his adopted city, was born in Westphalia, Germany, on May 4, 1844, and there grew to manhood. His father being a stockfarmer, the young man was engaged in that work until twenty-two years of age, when, in company with his brother, Frank Troja, he set out to seek his fortune in the new world. Embarking on board a sailing vessel at Bremen in the year 1866, he landed in New York, traveled thence westward by rail to Rock Island, then by river boat to Fort Madison, where he arrived in the early part of July.

For a short time after coming to America Mr. Troja was employed in the work of farming, but having secured an education in his native land of Germany, he shortly afterward accepted a position in a hotel, which he continued to fill for about a year and a half. For this service he received but fifteen dollars a month, but at the end of the time, by rigid economy, had managed to save a sum of money approximating $600. With this capital he embarked in the grocery business, forming a partnership with Adrian Stolwick, and the arrangement continued for two years, at the expiration of which time Mr. Stolwick died, and his interest became the property of John Troja, a brother of our subject. Under the firm style of Troja Brothers the business was continued with success and profit for about fifteen years.

In 1885 Mr. Troja sold his interest in the business to his brother and partner, and for a time lived retired, but has since been engaged in various enterprises. For about six years he was connected as proprietor with a stone quarry and brickyard in Hancock county, Illinois, just across the Mississippi river from Fort Madison. In a financial way his ventures have brought him excellent returns.

On April 2, 1872, Mr. Troja was united in marriage to Miss Margaret Helling, who came to Fort Madison in 1855 from the neighborhood in which the Troja family resided in Germany. The ceremony was performed by Father Hare, also a former neighbor in the Fatherland. Of this union were born twelve children, five of whom grew to maturity. These are: Anna, born June 18, 1874, wife of William Mansheim, farmer, of Washington township; John, born June 5, 1879; Louis, born February 7, 1881; Rena, born March 7, 1886; Samuel, born June 25, 1892. William, another son, died in Fort Madison, at the age of twenty-three years. His death was caused by accident, he having fallen from a wagon. During the Spanish-American War he served as a private, stationed at Jacksonville, Florida. His demise occurred April 7, 1900.

Three brothers and three sisters of Mrs. Troja reside in Lee county, namely: Bernard, Joseph and William, and Theresa, widow of Henry Krotmeyer; Mrs. Henry Decker and Mrs. Herman Krieger.

After a study of American political principles Joseph Troja early became a supporter of the Democratic party, and cast his first vote for Horace Greeley. He is a member of St. Joseph's Catholic church, and contributed to the fund raised for the building of the present structure. To sum up chronologically his connection with the material interests of Fort Madison, he was for two years engaged in business on Front street, the remainder of the time in Second street, and his was the first business house in Second street with the exceptions of a tailoring shop and the Metropolitan Hotel. His career has been long, honorable, successful and a credit to the city, and has won him the respect of a large number of friends and acquaintances. He is in the best sense a self-made man, and of this he has reason to be proud.

EDWIN URFER.

One of the rising and better known of the younger farmers of Lee county is Edwin Urfer, who holds the office of assessor of Jefferson township. Mr. Urfer was born in Jefferson township, September 22, 1877, the son of Christian and Martha (Ezelle) Urfer. The father of our subject is a native of Switzerland, but came to America as a young man, locating in Pennsylvania. Desirous of taking advantage of the unexampled opportunities offered by the great West, he removed to this section about the year 1845, becoming one of the pioneers of West Point township, Lee county. There he married Miss Ezelle, a native of this county, and engaged in farming. He shortly purchased a farm in Jefferson township, however, and here he passed the active period of his life, and is now living retired. To Mr. and Mrs. Urfer was born one son, the subject of this review. They were for many years members of the United Brethren church, but latterly Mrs. Urfer has become connected with the Presbyterian denomination.

Edwin Urfer was early inspired with enthusiasm for learning and knowledge, and has enjoyed unusual educational advantages. After completing the work of the public schools he entered Johnson's Business College at Fort Madison in order to become acquainted with commercial forms and principles. Later, he pursued a course of study at Denmark Academy. He has since supplemented his early training by keen observation and wide reading, he being the possessor of a large and well-selected library, one of the finest in the county, both along general and special lines. Upon the completion of his schooling he was for a time associated with his father in the work of the farm. With a view, however, to broadening his business experience, he purchased a stock of general merchandise at Veile, this county, where he at once erected a new building and conducted a mercantile enterprise. In addition he handled agricultural implements extensively, and for two years operated a well-drilling outfit. He continued the successful conduct of his business at that place until 1903, when he sold it and assumed charge of his father's farm. In the meantime he had made outside investments which have since proved profitable, including a farm of 320 acres in Butler county, Kansas, well-improved, with good buildings and very productive. In the work of his father's farm he is meeting with his usual success, applying himself to the business with energy and assiduity and making a close study of agricultural problems.

On January 10, 1900, Mr. Urfer was united in marriage with Miss Caroline Queisner, daughter of August Queisner, of Jefferson township, and of this union have been born one son and one daughter, Harold and Blanche.

In his political affiliations Mr. Urfer is a firm and stanch supporter of Democratic principles, and one of the intelligent and active workers in the party ranks. In 1900 he was elected assessor of his township, and having shown himself a capable public servant was re-elected in 1902. The county board of supervisors having issued instructions for the discovery and assessment of property hitherto concealed, Mr. Urfer made considerable effort to carry out their wishes, and during the four years of his incumbency the assessment for Jefferson township was larger than ever before. He is a young man of ability and integrity, and is generally respected, and as he is eminently fitted by his social qualities and loyalty for winning and keeping friends, it seems not too much to predict for him a career of honor, usefulness and success.

FRANK J. SCHENK.

Frank J. Schenk, now deceased, for many years a resident of Keokuk, displayed in his life record many sterling traits of character. He was born in Baden, Germany, March 9, 1827, and acquired a good education in the schools of his native country. He entered upon his business career as an apprentice to the shoemaker's trade, and when he had served his term of indenture began work as a journeyman, being thus employed in the Fatherland until 1850, when, believing that he might have better business opportunities in the new world, he crossed the Atlantic and established his home in Keokuk, after a brief residence in St. Louis, Missouri, where he was married. He worked faithfully at the bench for many years, or until he was obliged to give up his trade on account of failing eyesight. As his financial resources increased he made judicious investment of his capital, becoming the owner of farm and city property, the latter including several tenement houses. At length he sold this property in order to purchase the Central Dry Goods Store, which had been established by his son, Frank Joseph Schenk. He made this purchase but two years prior to his death and left it to his widow, who is, therefore, closely associated with commercial interests of Keokuk, this being the largest dry goods emporium of the city. In the early days, when the canal and locks were being built along the Mississippi river, Mr. Schenk conducted a shop at Sandusky. Throughout his active business career he did repair work, as well as made shoes, and he carried a small stock of ready-made shoes. For three years prior to his demise, however, he was ill and unable to work.

In St. Louis, Missouri, Mr. Schenk was married to Miss Louisa Camuf, who was born in Baden, Germany, and went to St. Louis, Missouri, in 1852, when fifteen years of age. There she gave her hand in marriage to Mr. Schenk in 1855, and almost immediately afterward they came to Keokuk, where she has since lived. Unto Mr. and Mrs. Schenk were born eleven children, seven of whom survive, namely: Mary, the wife of Peter Kennedy, of Keokuk; Frank J., of this city; George; Albert, who managed the store for about ten years, but went west a year ago for his health; Charles, Catherine and Margaret. Four children, George, Charles, Margaret and Catherine, are in the store. The business conducted under the name of the Central Dry Goods Store was established by Frank Joseph Schenk; was purchased from him by his parents, and is now the property of Mrs. Schenk, who also owns a half interest in the building. Charles Schenk is acting as manager of the business. After leaving school the sons learned the dry goods trade and the establishment is now the leading house of the kind in Keokuk, having a very large patronage and catering to the best class of trade.

Mr. Schenk never engaged in military service, either in his own country or in America, being exempt from army life in Germany because of deafness. He had a strong attachment for his adopted land and her free institutions and rejoiced in both local and national advancement. He held membership in the Catholic church, and when he was called to his final rest in November, 1893, at the age of sixty-seven years his remains were interred in the Catholic cemetery. He never had occasion to regret his determination to seek a home in America. Crossing the Atlantic at the age of twenty-seven years, he entered upon his business career here with little capital, but his entire life was characterized by close application and unfaltering energy. This proved an excellent basis upon which to build success, and while he never became weatlthy gained a cosy little home and comfortable competence, and left his widow in very pleasant financial circumstances. He never sought to figure in public light, but was content to give his energies to his business affairs and to the enjoyment of the pleasures of the home, and he derived his greatest happiness in promoting the happiness of his wife and children.

In his political relations he was a lifelong Democrat. He was a man who always held out a helping hand to those that were unfortunate.

HENRY VOIGT.

Beginning his active career without capital, in a new and foreign land, ignorant of the customs and even of the language of the people, and rising by natural talents and unaided personal effort to a position of prominence and importance—such is the history of one whose life work it is a pleasure to trace and to record for the inspiration of future generations. Henry Voigt was born in Westphalia, Germany, October 12, 1841, the son of C. H. and Engel (Marten) Voigt, of Prussia, Westphalia, and came alone to the United States in 1858 to enter the grocery business at Pittsburg, Pennsylvania, with a brother, William, who was a prior emigrant from Germany and still lives in Pittsburg.

Mr. Voigt had received a good education in his native land, but in order to acquire American methods attended a night school during the first year of his residence in this country, clerking in the grocery store in daytime. He also attended business college. In this way he made rapid progress, and after four years spent with his brother he was able to accept a position as bookkeeper in the banking house of Ira B. McVeagh & Company, with whom he continued for ten years. In 1873 he organized, at Pittsburg, the firm of Voigt, Ward & Company and the Independent Glass Company, of which he was partial owner. Labor troubles, however, marred the success of the enterprise, which was operated on a grand scale, having a pay roll of $1,800 per month.

Before terminating his residence in Pittsburg Mr. Voigt rose to a prominent position in society and politics, as well as in business, his name being recorded in the Blue Book of Pittsburg for the year 1880, and he having served for three years as treasurer of the South Side. He was also urged by his friends to accept nomination for the state legislature, but refused for business reasons.

Mr. Voigt was married in Pittsburg in 1869 to Miss Sophia Schultz, who was a native of Germany. She died in 1886, at Pittsburg, leaving five sons and one daughter. The latter, Bertha, is now deceased, she having died at the age of twenty-one years, four months after her marriage to William Englert, who also died three months later. The sons are: Otto, of Pittsburg; Harry, of Cleveland, Ohio; Arthur, of Pittsburg; Arno, of Altoona, Pennsylvania, and Ralph, of Fort Madison.

The residence of Mr. Voigt in Fort Madison dates from 1894, when he came to this city at the solicitation of a sister, Mrs. Spreen. Having been engaged in active business ever since leaving his father's farm at the age of sixteen years, he soon became dissatisfied with passing his days in idleness, and in order to supply employment for his otherwise unoccupied time he established a seed, grain and flour business under the name of the Fort Madison Feed Store, Voigt's Sons, proprietors. In this enterprise he is financially interested, in association with three of his sons, namely, Otto, Arno and Ralph.

Mr. Voigt makes his home with his sister, Mrs. Sophia Spreen, widow of Henry C. Spreen, a former soldier and a pioneer of Fort Madison. He also has another sister living, Mrs. Dora Spreen, of Pittsburg. In his religious affiliation he is a member of the Evangelical church, and politically he is a firm adherent of the principles advocated by the Republican party. He is a man of strong character and broad ideas, and his energy, uprightness and genial disposition have won him admirers and friends.

JAMES McQUADE.

James McQuade, of Keokuk, was born in Scotland in 1835. His parents never left their native land and in fact were never more than ten miles away from their place of birth, Wigtown. Their son, John McQuade, has become wealthy through the conduct of a floral business in New Jersey. The youngest son of the family is still living in

Scotland. James McQuade spent the first sixteen years of his life on the family home and during that period attended the public schools, acquiring a good common-school education. He then bade adieu to friends and native land and started for America, taking passage on the "Queen of the West," a sailing vessel, which weighed anchor in the harbor of Liverpool and after nineteen days spent upon the Atlantic reached the harbor of New York on the 19th of March, 1851. The next morning he left for Newburg, New York, where he had acquaintances, twenty-five of his former schoolmates being in that locality. The succeeding morning he secured a job at shoveling snow from the sidewalks and the money paid him being so large in comparison with what he would have received in his own country he thought himself rich. For five years he remained at Newburg and worked for one year on the Hudson river boat, "Columbia," as a hand and after that as mate. Attracted by the opportunities of the West, however, he started for Keokuk and on the 3d of March, 1857, reached his destination. Here he obtained employment in the machine shop of the Rock Island Railroad Company and in 1858 he went upon the road as foreman. Soon afterward he was promoted to the position of engineer, in which capacity he served for three years and then returned to the shops, working as a machinist for twelve years. During the period of the Civil War he was an engineer dispatcher for the Keokuk-Des Moines Valley Railroad, now a part of the Rock Island system. He left the road while receiving a salary of one hundred dollars per month at the time the line was purchased by the Rock Island Company. He then bought ten acres of land in the Nassau addition to Keokuk and has recently refused $5,000 for this property. His time is devoted to the raising of small fruits and he has a good business, finding a ready sale on the market for his products because of their excellence in size and flavor.

Mr. McQuade was married in Newburg, New York, in 1855, to Miss Louise Palmer, who was born in Dutchess county, that state, and died in Keokuk in August, 1894, her remains being interred in Oakland cemetery. They had five sons and a daughter: John, a resident of Tacoma, Washington; Samuel, of Keokuk; Alice, who died at the age of sixteen years; Jane, who is living in Tacoma; Charles and Robert, both of Keokuk. The sons residing in Tacoma are longshoremen and are very successful there. Both Samuel and Charles are with the Tabor Company as engineers and Robert is at home.

At the time of the Civil War Mr. McQuade enlisted as a member of the Home Guard and participated in the battle of Athens, Missouri. This occurred because of the delay of the trains occasioned by Confederate troops. A train was then made up in Keokuk and carried the Home Guard to Athens, where an engagement occurred, the Home Guard winning the victory. Mr. McQuade acted as engineer of that train. Fraternally he is a member of the Eagle Lodge, No. 12, Free and Accepted Masons, with which he has been identified for over forty years and in his life he has exemplified the beneficent spirit of the craft. He served both as junior and senior warden in early days. He was reared in the faith of the Presbyterian church, but is not a member of any denomination. As he has saved from his wages he has made judicious investment of his earning in property and he now has real estate on Fifth street and also a storeroom occupied by the Cereal Company, of Keokuk. Coming to the United States empty-handed he has gradually advanced in the business world and all that he has acquired came to him as the result of earnest, persistent effort.

WILLIAM HARMON.

One of the residents of Keokuk whose reminiscences are most valuable in a work dealing with the historical development of Lee county is William Harmon, who was born in Harrison county, Indiana, May 15, 1830. The family is remotely of German origin, but the first member of whom there is accurate record is Abraham Harmon, who came from Tennessee in the pioneer days to Indiana, where he was manager of a gristmill owned by General William Henry Harrison. It is still remembered that his instructions were to "take toll from the rich and give it to the poor," thus leaving no profit for the owner.

William Harmon's father was John Harmon, who was born at Jonesboro, Tennessee, May 30, 1807, and died July 13, 1893. He was reared in Harrison county, Indiana, in territorial times, and remembered the massacre of nine families in his neighborhood by the Indians. In 1829 he married Miss Stacey Witt, who became the mother of our subject. She died in the fall of 1839, and he remarried, his second wife being Miss Butler, whose death occurred in Keokuk. He came west in 1841, locating in Keokuk, where he took up land on the half-breed tract. Indians still occupied the vicinity and the settlement consisted of one frame house and three log houses. His experience was wide. Previous to the Civil War he served as a soldier twelve years under the old military law of South Carolina, and when General Jackson called out the troops to combat threatened secession in that state he took the field with his regiment. In Keokuk he was a member of the "Gray Beards," or Thirty-seventh Iowa Volunteer Infantry, assigned to post duty, which was very severe service. Two of his sons gave their lives to the Union cause, and are buried near the battlefield of Shiloh. In 1836 he, with his father-in-law, traveled from Indiana to Illinois by three-horse wagon, camping on the way. It was a large party, and the men of the party walked the whole way, taking turns, however, at riding one of the horses and driving. Although then but six years of age, our subject remembers the journey distinctly.

On account of his wife's ill health John Harmon built a flatboat, and took his family for a trip down the Mississippi river. She failed to improve, however, and died six miles below Alton, Illinois, in the American bottoms. He then revisited Indiana for a year, after which he returned to Keokuk, and with the exception of two or three years' residence in Clark county, Missouri, here passed the remainder of his life. He voted for Andrew Jackson for President of the United States, but was in politics a Whig and Republican. He was the oldest member of the First Methodist Episcopal church of Keokuk. He is buried in Prouty Mound cemetery.

When William Harmon came to Keokuk, Lee county was a wilderness. For the first year he lived in a primitive "shanty," having the bare earth for a floor. The family cleared away the forest from a tract of land and for a while did some farming. In 1845 they removed to what is called Prouty's Mound on the banks of the Des Moines river, where for four years they conducted a ferry. The territorial government required no license for ferrymen, but on the formation of a state government a law was passed providing for license formalities, and the privilege which the Harmons enjoyed was secured by a politician, thus depriving them of that source of income.

Mr. Harmon as a boy conceived an interest in the statement frequently made that the American Indians in burying their deceased warriors and chiefs followed the custom of burying with them their arms and other valuable possessions. To test its truth he, with others, examined many Indian graves, and he asserts that the theory is evidently without foundation, as no arms or implements of any kind were ever found. He has also closely observed the floods of the Mississippi river, and is convinced, though alone in his contention, that the famous "flood of fifty-one" has not since been equaled. Throughout the three weeks of its duration he was engaged in rescue work at Alexandria. He and his father owned a boat, and with this they saved a great deal of valuable property, often entering houses in which water stood shoulder-high, and diving to recover household goods.

July 30, 1851, Mr. Harmon was united in marriage to Miss Sarah R. Wickham, daughter of Slattriel Wickham. She was born near Zanesville, Ohio, March 7, 1832. They are the parents of the following sons and daughters: Mary Ellen, born April 22, 1852, died January 22, 1854; Stacey Drusella, born January 31, 1854, died March 16, 1854; Nancy Ann, born September 6, 1855, died April 9, 1886; John William, born September 23, 1857, and Charles, born March 9, 1861. Both sons live in Keokuk, occupying homes in the immediate vicinity of the father's residence at 1820 Oak street.

With his father and brother-in-law Mr. Harmon early purchased a ninety-acre tract of land on the Des Moines river in order to secure the timber, and later it was cleared and cultivated. He sold his share in 1855.

On March 1, 1862, leaving a wife and three small children to answer the call of patriotism, Mr. Harmon enlisted in Company E, Seventh Iowa Volunteer Infantry, under Captain (afterward Colonel) Parrott, and went into camp at Camp Lincoln, Pittsburg Landing. Thence proceeding to Corinth, he arrived there three days after the battle, and at this place he first saw active service, taking part in skirmishes. His health failed, and for three weeks he was in Monterey Field Hospital, and later in Quincy Hospital. On recovery from his illness he was placed upon detached service, in which he continued for about eighteen months, first coming to Keokuk to join a body of 100 men detailed to guard the city. For a time he was acting sergeant, and frequently took out squads of soldiers at night to guard the fords of the Des Moines river, as Keokuk was menaced by Rebel guerrillas and Southern sympathizers. This service ended, he rejoined the active forces in the field, and followed General Sherman in his famous march to the sea. He was honorably discharged March 6, 1865, at Goodwin's Mill, South Carolina, but continued with the army for a period of twenty-five days thereafter. Although gifted with a fine physical constitution, Mr. Harmon still suffers from the hardships of his army experience.

After the war he was variously employed for rather more than a year. He ran a dray in Keokuk for four years, having a ten-year contract to do hauling for a foundry. The company for which he worked suffered financial failure, but a new company was organized, and he secured another contract for five years.

Mr. Harmon owns a pleasant home in town and seventy or eighty acres of island land in the Des Moines river—land formerly owned by his father. He has retired from active pursuits. Although self-educated, never having received any schooling, he gives much time to reading, and is thoroughly informed on current topics and events. In his religious connection he is a member of the First Methodist Episcopal church, as is also Mrs. Harmon, and has been an active worker since ante-bellum days. He has acted as class leader and steward, and having in a marked degree the gift of language, formerly was a very successful exhorter. His sons and their wives are also members of the church. He is a member of Belknap Post of the Grand Army of the Republic. Politically he has always been a loyal and consistent Republican since the organization of that party. His first vote was cast for the Whig candidate for President. William Harmon has many friends in Keokuk, and no man is more respected for his earnest Christian character and his unwavering fidelity to the right as he sees it.

Mr. Harmon died suddenly while in his fields gathering corn, on Friday afternoon, November 11, 1904. At the time of his death he was Keokuk's oldest resident in point of continuous residence.

WILLIAM SHEPHERD.

William Shepherd, one of the widely-known and influential citizens of Van Buren township, Lee county, Iowa, where he owns and operates a fertile farm of 280 acres, was born December 17, 1842, at Lowhesket, Northumberland, England, the son of William and Mary (Turner) Shepherd, and when only seven years of age came with his parents to the United States, and proceeding directly to Iowa, located in the City of Keokuk. There the father, who was originally a farmer, worked by the day for a number of years as a well and cistern digger, but in 1864 removed to Van Buren township, where he purchased 160 acres of land, upon which he erected a house, made improvements and established a home for himself and family, while he also bought additonal land, so that at the time of his death, which occurred in the eighty-fifth year of his age, he owned a farm of 240 acres. He was a man of business ability and very popular among his neighbors, being several times elected on the Democratic ticket to the office of road supervisor, in which he performed valuable service; and in his religious connection he was a member of the Episcopal church, as was also his wife, whose death occurred two years after his own at about the same age. They were the parents of seven sons and daughters, of whom our subject is the only one now living.

Mr. Shepherd received his education in the public schools of Lee county, and during his boyhood assisted in the work of the home farm, while at a later period he was for several years employed in packing houses at Keokuk and Des Moines, but in 1865 he took up farming as an occupation, since which time he has operated the farm formerly owned by his father. Here he is engaged in general farming and more especially in stockraising, giving particular attention to Shorthorn cattle, Poland-China hogs and French coach horses, with which he has had remarkable success, one of his horses in particular taking first prize two years ago at the Lee county fair. His farm is excellently maintained in every respect, and all the improvements have been installed by himself, including good, substantial barns and a pleasant and commodious dwelling house. Besides attending with ability and careful consideration to the business of his farm, Mr. Shepherd finds time to study public questions, taking an active part in politics as a member of the Democratic party, and for the past five or six years has served his community with impartiality and strict fairness as justice of the peace. In his younger days he, for nineteen successive years, held the highest office in the gift of his township, that of trustee, and today he enjoys the respect and confidence of his fellow citizens to a still greater degree than when he held that important position.

On February 15, 1865, Mr. Shepherd was united in marriage to Miss Mary Slaughter, who was born in Alsace, France, and with her parents came to the United States when three years of age, first locating in the State of Kentucky and later removing to Keokuk, Iowa, where the father died at the age of fifty-one years and the mother when seventy-seven years of age and were both buried there. Mrs. Shepherd is the daughter of Antone and Catherine (Roth) Slaughter, both of whom were born in France and were, like herself, members of the Catholic church. To Mr. and Mrs. Shepherd have been born seven children, as follows: Harry, who is a farmer of Van Buren township; James, who is an engineer and resides in Montana; Ella, a teacher in the schools of Van Buren township, resides with her parents; Mamie, wife of Thomas Hayes, of Charleston township, has three children, James, Cecelia and Agnes; Gertrude, who is the wife of William Case, of Muscatine, Iowa, has one child, Loraine; Andrew, who resides at home, and one child who died in infancy.

As an early resident of Iowa, Mr. Shepherd has been an interested witness of nearly all the vast and wonderful improvements which have marked the progress of Lee county from a rude and inhospitable region to its present proud position as one of the richest farming communities of the Mississippi valley, and in this great development he has borne a goodly share, as he still continues to do. For this and for the honorable course he has pursued in all his dealings with his fellowmen he has the respect of all who know him, and is widely known throughout Lee county as a man of marked talent for business and agricultural pursuits on a large scale and as one who has succeeded by his own efforts and ability.

JONATHAN MERRICK.

Jonathan Merrick, who for over thirty-four years has been connected with the Tabor Lumber Company, was born in Washington county, Ohio, July 11, 1846. His paternal grandfather was a native of New Jersey, and on his removal to the West purchased a farm in Monroe county, Iowa, where he spent his remaining days, dying at the advanced age of ninety-three years. His son, Seth Merrick, was born in New Jersey and after removing to Ohio was married there to Miss Margaret McMeckin, a native of Pittsburg, Pennsylvania. Seth Merrick became a mate on an Ohio river steamer, following that pursuit in early life. In 1858 he removed with his family, then numbering his wife and six children, to Iowa, settling in Lee county, and his remaining days were devoted to agricultural pursuits. He died upon a farm in Des Moines valley, January 1, 1902, while his wife passed away on the 8th of December, 1880. Their children were as follows: Mary C., the wife of James Rigney, a farmer of Lee county; Harriet Emily, the wife of Eli Jaquin, a resident farmer of Lee county; Jonathan, of this review; Harvey, of Macoupin county, Illinois; Jared, of Keokuk, and Rebecca Jane, deceased.

Jonathan Merrick was a lad of twelve years when he accompanied his parents on their removal to Iowa. His education began in the public schools of Ohio, was continued in the public schools of this state, and he assisted in the development of the home farm until 1866, when he started out in life on his own account, entering the employ of the Tabor Lumber Company, in the sawmill. He has remained in this position almost continuously since, and has been log weighman for about twenty-seven years. For an interval of three or four years, however, he was away from the mill and devoted his energies to farming, but at the end of that time he returned to the mill. His faithfulness to duty is well indicated by his long continued service, and his trustworthiness stands as an unquestioned fact in his life record.

On the 24th of March, 1875, Mr. Merrick was married in Keokuk, Iowa, to Miss Clara Belle Dietz, who was born in this city, September 3, 1854, a daughter of Edward and Martha (Gray) Dietz. Her father was born in New Albany, Indiana, January 25, 1822, and his wife, a native of Lexington, Kentucky, was born December 29, 1829. They were married in Keokuk, June 16, 1849, and became the parents of ten children. Further mention of their history is made in connection with the sketch of Frank Dietz on another page of this work. Unto Mr. and Mrs. Merrick were born five children: Maggie Belle, born February 1, 1876, is the wife of A. J. Patterson, a railway clerk, at Keokuk; Harry Lewis, born August 15, 1880, is a farmer; Grace May, born September 26, 1892; Edward Seth, born May 5, 1886, and Edith V., born May 23, 1891, are all at home.

Mr. Merrick purchased six and two-thirds acres of land in the Nassau addition in 1898, and in 1900 built thereon his present home. This was the old family homestead and the purchase price was $4,000. He has planted the place to small fruit, and it is now a very attractive and comfortable home. Mr. Merrick is a member of the Independent Order of Odd Fellows; has filled all of the offices in the subordinate lodge and is now a Past Noble Grand. He belongs to the Second Presbyterian church, in which he is serving as an elder, and in politics he is a Republican, but though urged many times to accept the position of alderman he has always refused, having no political aspiration, although he is deeply interested in the welfare of his party and of the general community at large.

WILLIAM L. BARRETT.

No man is more intimately and vitally connected with true progress than he to whom is intrusted the training of the coming generation. In his hands largely rests the future destinies of the state and nation. It is fitting, therefore, that to such service every community should assign its best talents—that at the head of the schools should be placed those characters which are capable of the highest and most intelligent devotion to the general welfare. William L. Barrett, principal of the Fort Madison high school, has consecrated his life to the important work of education, and for that reason, and by reason of the zeal and ability displayed in his chosen field, he is here entitled to extended mention.

Mr. Barrett was born at Nevada, Story county, Iowa, December 27, 1870, the son of John T. and Margaret (Seabalt) Barrett. John T. Barrett was born at Russellville, Ohio, July 5, 1842, and died at Kellerton, Iowa, September 4, 1900. The date of his marriage to Margaret Seabalt was March 18, 1869. She died October 30, 1874. She is survived by two sons, the younger being J. C. Barrett, who is also a resident of Fort Madison, and is a guard at the state penitentiary. The father was remarried September 14, 1876, to Miss Margaret Silvers, and of this union have been born six children. Mrs. Margaret Barrett is at the present time a resident of Kellerton, Iowa.

W. L. Barrett, the subject of this sketch, began his education in a district school, but his enthusiasm for further intellectual advancement led him to enter Drake University, at Des Moines, at which institution he matriculated in 1888, and was graduated with degree of B. D. S. C., in 1895, after having completed two separate courses of study, the scientific and the didactic. His professional activities since that time have been continuous and of broad scope. He has taught physics and algebra in the Polk County Institute; reading and history in the Ringgold County Institute; history, civics and economics in Henry county; and reading, history, grammar and physiology in Lee county. He first began teaching in the rural schools of Ringgold county, came to Primrose, Lee county, in 1893, as principal of the graded school, became principal of a graded school at Birmingham, Van Buren county, in 1896, and came to Fort Madison as principal of the high school in 1899.

August 11, 1902, at Des Moines, Iowa, Mr. Barrett was united in marriage with Miss Bertha E. Lightfoot, daughter of Amos Lee and Ella (Grommon) Lightfoot, of Fort Madison. Mr. and Mrs. Lightfoot were the parents of six children, five of whom survive, as follows: Charles A. and William T., of Chicago; Edwin Lee and Benjamin H., of Fort Madison; and Mrs. Barrett, who was born in Delaware county, February 27, 1876, and at the time of her marriage was a teacher in the eighth grade of the Fort Madison schools. She is a graduate of Fort Madison high school, and has attended the State Normal School at Cedar Falls, the Epworth Seminary at Epworth, Iowa, and Iowa Wesleyan University at Mount Pleasant. For four years she was a teacher in rural schools, and for two years taught sixth, seventh and eighth grades in the Fort Madison schools.

Mr. Barrett is descended of Revolutionary ancestry through the maternal line and the family name of Silvers. The Barrett family was originally Irish, the founders of the American branch having been three brothers who emigrated from Ireland together. The line of descent has been traced in unbroken succession to them.

Mr. and Mrs. Barrett are members of the Christian church, and Mr. Barrett is a member and very active worker in the Young Men's Christian Association, being one of the directors of the organization. Strong in his individuality and earnest of purpose, he is peculiarly adapted to work of this nature, and his sterling character and talent for leadership are qualities that seem destined to carry him to distinction, and perhaps to eminence, in the field of education.

ROBERT LANGE.

One of the most progressive farmers and influential citizens of Green Bay township is Robert Lange, who is a representative of a well-known pioneer family. Mr. Lange himself is a native son of the township, but his father and mother were of German birth, both having been born in Prussia. His natal day was October 4, 1854, and he is the son of Harmon and Christina (Batthalt) Lange, who, in order to profit by the superior resources and environment of the New World, emigrated from their native land and settled in Green Bay township, Lee county, in 1852. Here the mother still lives, at the age of eighty-three years, and here the father spent the remainder of his life. He was enterprising, progressive and successful, and was highly esteemed for the substantial virtues of his character by all who knew him.

Robert Lange secured his education in the public schools of his township, and as a boy and young man learned farming under the direction of his father. On September 25, 1889, he was united in marriage to Miss Ellen Miller, who was born at Burlington, Iowa. He then rented a farm on what is known as "the bluff," in this township, successfully cultivating it for a period of eight years, at the end of which he purchased his present farm of 155 acres, and has since resided here. This farm consists of rich bottom lands, and is in a high state of cultivation and thoroughly well developed. It has undergone many improvements since passing to the ownership of Mr. Lange. The house, which is very commodious, has been remodeled, and new barns and other buildings have been erected to accommodate the products of the fertile soil, and all the equipment is modern throughout.

To Mr. and Mrs. Lange have been born nine children, one of whom died in infancy. Those living are: Carl A. R., Harry F. H., Caroline C. L., Robert P. E., Herbert J. A., Edna M. A., Nelson L. A., and Arthur P. F. Mr. Lange enjoys a gratifying measure of popularity and public favor. He has held the office of road supervisor, and in 1901 was elected trustee of Green Bay township, an office in which his business ability proved valuable to his constituents. Fraternally, he is a member of Independent Order of Odd Fellows, of Wever. After a careful study of questions of government and politics he early decided to support the Democratic party, as most nearly embodying his ideal of American principles of liberty and justice, and to this allegiance he has ever since been unwaveringly loyal, his work in the ranks being recognized as of much benefit to the local organization. As one enjoying a high reputation for honor, integrity and complete grasp of practical questions, his service and influence have been particularly valuable.

WASHINGTON NEWBERRY.

Washington Newberry, a noted resident of Des Moines township, Lee county, where he has long followed the occupation of farming with much success, was born in the same township where he still maintains his home, August 13, 1848, a son of James W. and Edith A. (Benedict) Newberry. The Newberry family is identified with the founding of the township, and from the beginning has taken a prominent part in its affairs. It has contributed a number of prominent and influential characters to the citizenship of Lee county, and its name has always been high. Washington Newberry has worthily sustained that name, and lived an upright and honorable life.

The subject of this sketch was given a common-school education, beyond which very few young people went at that time, and remained at home until he reached the age of twenty-two years. At that age he took charge of his father's farm in Scotland county, Missouri, which he partly fenced. There he broke seventy acres of raw prairie, and was there for about three years, when he returned to Des Moines township. Here he married, and settled on his present farm property, consisting of eighty acres, the southeast quarter of section 8, and also twenty acres of timber in the west part of the township. He is a general farmer, but gives his attention mainly to stockraising, in which he has met with very satisfactory results.

Mr. Newberry was married December 24, 1874, to Miss Ella F. Washburn. She was born November 7, 1854, in Des Moines township, a daughter of Stephen S. and Melissa H. (Sprott) Washburn. Her father was born in Leeds county, Canada, and came into Iowa Territory in time to be classed as one of the very early pioneers of Lee county. Melissa H. Sprott was a daughter of James and Annie Sprott, who came from Pennsylvania and settled near Keokuk in 1845. Her father bought land and became prominent and influential. He was called "Colonel Sprott," and was a member of the legislature at one time. Mrs. Newberry remembers him as coming in a buggy and a "stovepipe hat" when she was a little girl. He came to their house in a buggy, a thing then very seldom seen; and wearing a "plug hat," another rarity. He brought blooded sheep into Lee county, and did much to improve the general stock level at that time. The family came from Pennsylvania by the river route.

Mr. and Mrs. Newberry have two sons: Arthur Devere, who graduated from the Keokuk College of Physicians and Surgeons in 1898, and is now practicing his profession in Kingston, Iowa. He is a man of imposing physique, stands six feet and two inches in his stocking feet, and weighs 325 pounds. His appearance is fine, he makes a good impression, and is commanding a large practice. Their other son, Van Werden Clark, is station agent of the Santa Fe Railroad at Argyle, Iowa. He married Miss Jessie Marshall, a daughter of John Marshall, of Fort Madison, who was an early settler in that city. To this union has come one child, Lloyd Devere, who was born August 31, 1904.

Mr. Newberry is a man of fine standing, irreproachable character and personal popularity. He is quiet in his ways, reliable in all his transactions, and is known as a good citizen.

JOSEPH E. NEWTON.

A prominent and prosperous citizen, a native son of Lee county, and at the same time one who has witnessed the growth of the State of Iowa from a wild and sparsely inhabited region to its present magnificent proportions, is Joseph E. Newton, of Pleasant Ridge township. Mr. Newton was born August 13, 1842, on the farm on which he now resides, and is the son of Orson Newton, of Vermont, and Harriet (Bullard) Newton, of Massachusetts, who celebrated their marriage in this township. Orson

Newton came to Lee county in 1836, and staked off a claim of 160 acres of wild land, which he later entered as a "homestead," and continued to occupy for the remainder of his life, clearing the land, adding improvements, and working his way upward in the world until he, together with his son, our subject, at one time owned 750 acres of fine agricultural lands, most of this being located in Adams county, Iowa. When he emigrated from his native state, in 1836, and settled in Pleasant Ridge township, his entire possessions consisted of fifty cents in cash and an ax, but with dauntless energy and iron will he set out with this small capital to win for himself a recognized place among his fellowmen, and in this he fully succeeded, achieving a position of prominence and influence and being many times honored by calls to serve the public in responsible capacities, among these being the office of trustee of his township. In politics he was a Whig and later a Republican, and was prominent in both parties, while in his religious connection, to which he was ever faithful, he held membership, in the Congregational church of Denmark, and he took a special interest in the public schools of his community, which were largely under his care and direction during the greater part of his life. The comforts of life he provided for his family without stint, as far as lay within his power, and the residence building now occupied by his son was erected by him in 1850, although since enlarged and remodeled along modern lines. He died in July, 1894, at an age of more than eighty-two years, and his wife was laid by his side in the Denmark cemetery three years later at the age of seventy-seven.

Mr. Newton paid $1.25 per acre for 160 acres in 1836, borrowing money for which he had to pay 25 per cent. One-half of it was timber land.

Joseph E. Newton, who is at the present time the only surviving member of his father's family of three sons and two daughters, received in his early youth a good common school education, which he has since enlarged by extensive reading, and at the same time he was thoroughly trained in the principles and practice of agriculture, acquiring knowledge and proficiency by personal experience, so that while yet a young man he became, like his father, a successful farmer, and to this occupation he has devoted his entire life, pursuing it as a trade and as a business. He now owns 290 acres of most productive farming land, which is operated under his direction, and this yields him a large annual return, and among the improvements installed by him is a substantial barn, just erected, which is forty by fifty feet in dimensions, while all the buildings are tastefully painted and in an excellent state of repair. He has all his life been a resident of the farm which he now occupies, and, taking a natural pride in maintaining it in the most perfect condition, has given quite a little attention to its external appearance, his house, especially, being surrounded by beautiful and attractive grounds.

When Mr. Newton was ten years of age, his father one day brought in a large hollow log to place in the fire-place, and in the log was a large blacksnake which the father killed with an old-fashioned shovel ten feet long.

In 1869 Mr. Newton was united in marriage to Miss Mary Anderson, who was born in the City of New York, a daughter of John and Sarah Anderson, natives of Scotland. Mrs. Newton came to Burlington, Iowa, in 1863, but her parents remained in New York, and never removed to the West. She is a pleasant lady of fine Christian character, and is a faithful member of the Baptist churh at Burlington, Iowa. Unto Mr. and Mrs. Newton have been born one daughter, Hattie, and one son, Joseph Orson, who both remain members of the parental household.

While Mr. Newton has always been a practical farmer, he has also made a study of the subject on its theoretical side, and has been three times elected general superintendent of the West Point Agricultural Society, and has been a director of the society since its formation, an office which he still holds. On the other hand he has not taken a narrow or contracted view of life, and while giving due weight to his own special calling, he has always manifested a willingness to perform the duties which devolve upon him as a citizen, and is widely known as one of the leading Republicans of Lee county, having been an active and helpful worker in that party for many years, as in his opinion the best way of promoting the cause of good government. He has never actively sought public office, but has represented his community a number of times in county conventions, and for a period of four years had the supreme direction of the Republican party's organization in this section as chairman of its township committee, a capacity in which he performed much valuable service and displayed executive ability of a high order of efficiency. Indeed, it may be said of him that in every relation of life in which he has been called upon to play an important part, he has proved himself equal to the occasion, and that while as a public character the pages of his record are fair, stainless and inspiring, the history of his private relations with men is one of unfailing honor, uprightness and strictest rectitude—an ideal mode of life which has made him rich in the friendship of many and the respect of all.

RICHARD VANOSDOLL.

Prior to the great Civil War, which claimed the sacifice of his life, the subject of this review, Richard Vanosdoll, was a well-known agriculturist of Montrose township, Lee county, Iowa, where he owned a small farm. He was born March 21, 1825, in Pennsylvania, of which state his parents were also natives, and was undoubtedly of Dutch lineage, a descendant of those early settlers from Holland, to which the great commonwealth owes so much of its wealth and splendid material prosperity. He early emigrated to the West, in order to take advantage of the opportunities offered by the rich country, which was then almost unoccupied, becoming a pioneer of Lee county, Iowa, and on October 10, 1850, he was united in marriage, the exact location being four miles north of Montrose, to Miss Emily Wilson, Rev. David Crawford, of the Methodist Episcopal church, performing the ceremony. To Mr. and Mrs. Vanosdoll were born three sons and two daughters, as follows: John L., of Montrose; William Henry, who died in childhood, July 24, 1853; Clara B., wife of Charles Allen, of Montrose; Charles, and Sophia R., who died January 5, 1894, at the age of thirty-one years.

At the opening of the Civil War Mr. Vanosdoll believed it was his duty to join the forces which were to fight the battles of his country, and enlisted in Company A, Thirteenth Regiment Iowa Volunteer Infantry, as a private soldier. While in the field he was seized with the dread disease known as chronic diarrhœa, and was assigned to the hospital at Keokuk, but while on his way to that place he died, April 26, 1863, and was buried at Milliken's Bend, Arkansas, where his remains rest. He was a man of much force of character, and was esteemed by all who knew him for his generous and genial disposition, and was universally respected for the uprightness and strict integrity that characterized him in all his dealings.

The death of her husband left to Mrs. Vanosdoll the sole care and support of four small children, and although the responsibility was in no sense a light one, she accepted her trust in a spirit of true Christian fortitude, and performed her new duties with energy and determination. Selling the farm home she removed to the village of Montrose, where she gave her children the best of home training and the inestimable advantage of a good education, thus fitting them to cope with the problems of life in whatsoever sphere they might find themselves called upon to labor, and in this village she still resides. She was born in Pennsylvania, February 7, 1834, the daughter of John and Rebecca (Walker) Wilson, and with her parents first removed to Tennessee, coming to Lee county when about eleven or twelve years of age. Here her father bought land and farmed in Montrose township, and he died on the home farm, February 28, 1849, while the mother died in the village of Montrose. Two brothers of Mrs. Vanosdoll were soldiers of the Civil War, these being Walker and Harry Wilson, now of Montrose. She is a devout and faithful worker in the Methodist Episcopal church, to whose support she generously contributes, and is a charter member of the Montrose Lodge, Daughters of Rebekah, and also a chater member of the Woman's Relief Corps, in the history of whose work in this community she holds an honored place. She receives a widow's pension from the United States government, and owns a comfortable home in Montrose, where she spends her declining days in comparative ease, and although she has accomplished more than the her share of arduous and useful work during a long life, she is surprisingly well preserved for one of her years.

EUGENE G. BULLARD.

An enterprising business man of Fort Madison is Eugene G. Bullard, proprietor of the Gen City Livery. A native son of Lee county, he was born in Jefferson township, three miles west of this city, July 24,

1863, the son of James Bullard, Sr., now deceased. James Bullard, Sr., was the son of Theophilus Bullard, of Virginia parentage, and was born in Jacksonville, Morgan county, Illinois, May 22, 1825. He traced his genealogy through various families of England, Ireland and Germany, who combined to produce a race having many admirable traits of character. Two of his grandfathers, by name James Bullard and Thomas Armstrong, were soldiers of the War of 1812. The former, at the close of the war, settled on a farm in Brown county, Illinois, where he spent the remainder of his life. Thomas Armstrong was a master mechanic, and erected many iron furnaces and forges near the place of his residence in Tennessee.

Theophilus Bullard, father of James Bullard, Sr., was a millright, and built his first mill in Morgan county, Illinois, on the Morvester creek in 1824, supposed to have been one of the first mills in Illinois. He was a volunteer soldier in the Black Hawk War, serving all through the Indian troubles, and at the end of the war removed with his family to Burlington, Iowa, arriving March 12, 1834. He acquired five farms in the Black Hawk Purchase, and was the first justice of the peace in that section, while Iowa was yet a territory, holding the office twenty-five years. He also made the first local survey in this part of the country. The date of his birth was March 17, 1798. He married, at Nashville, Tennessee, Lucy Armstrong, who was of Virginia birth and parentage.

James Bullard, Sr., was the second child of the family. He was educated in the public schools, and remained at home until his marriage, in Jefferson township, of which, in passing, his father was one of the organizers. He married Miss Sarah A. Wallace, who was born in Northumberland county, Pennsylvania, June 1, 1834, and came to Iowa with her parents when a young woman. Of this union were born seven children, only two of whom survive, these being Robert Rolio, a farmer, of Green Bay township, and Eugene G., the subject of this sketch. Mrs. Sarah A. Bullard, the wife and mother, died June 25, 1884. She was a consistent and faithful member of the Baptist church. Mr. Bullard was a successful farmer and stock breeder, and lived in a beautiful home, located on a 300-acre farm of fertile Mississippi bottom lands. He was universally respected, and had many friends. In politics he was a stanch Democrat.

Eugene G. Bullard: The subject of this review was reared on a farm, and received his education in the public schools. Not content, however, with the learning thus gained he resolved to pursue a course of practical investigation into modern business methods, and with this object in view attended Johnson's Business College, at Fort Madison—with what success his subsequent career has amply shown. For a number of years he was associated with his father in the livery business in this city. On his father's death, in February, 1896, however, he assumed sole charge of the enterprise, and has continued in this capacity ever since, with the exception of two years spent in farming. He is the proprietor of the building and equipment, valued at $9,000. He also owns the old home farm of 160 acres in Jefferson township, which he rents, and is interested in the New York Gray Silver Mine, in Park county, Colorado, and in the Comstock, Le Roy, Big Chief and Cody mines, in Lake county, Colorado.

On January 25, 1893, Mr. Bullard was united in marriage to Miss Mary M. Finnerty, and they occupy a pleasant home at No. 403 Second street. Unto them have been born two sons and two daughters, as follows: Velma E., born February 4, 1894; James Everett, born September 16, 1895; Patrick Le Roy, born May 3, 1897; and Naomi Jane, born August 9, 1902. Mrs. Bullard is a native of Jefferson township, the date of her birth being January 21, 1871, and she is the daughter of Peter Finnerty, a native of Galway, Ireland, and Jane (Shay) Finnerty, born in Cleveland, Ohio. Mr. Finnerty died in June, 1887, at the age of forty-eight years, and Mrs. Finnerty has since remarried, being now the wife of a Mr. Newberry, and residing at Quincy, Illinois. Mrs. Bullard has two sisters, Anna L., wife of Theophilus Bullard, and Cecilia J., wife of Dr. Wahrer. She is a member of St. Joseph's Catholic church and of the Ladies' Auxiliary.

In his political faith and activities Mr. Bullard is a Democrat, and fraternally he sustains membership relations with the order of Knights of Pythias and with Claypoole Lodge, No. 13, Free and Accepted Masons; also being in the Masonic order, a Knights Templar. He has many friends, and is a man of marked executive ability, progressive and enterprising. It is safe to predict, in the light of his past achievement, that for him the future holds much success and honor.

GEORGE W. TUCKER.

One who for many years has been identified very prominently with the agricultural interests and the public life of Lee county is George W. Tucker, the subject of this review. He was born in Dearborn county, Indiana, June 13, 1855, and is the son of John W. and Sarah (Spicknell) Tucker, who were married at Lawrenceburg, Indiana, and came to Lee county in 1857, purchasing land in Green Bay township, where they continued to reside until the father's death, June 29, 1893. Sarah Tucker survived her husband a number of years, her demise occurring in March, 1903.

Mr. Tucker is one of a family of five brothers and three sisters, as follows: Richard, who has his home in the State of Kansas; George W., Charles C., of Green Bay township, Lee county; William H., an engineer, of Hannibal, Missouri; Nettie, now deceased, who was the wife of Scott Littell; Kate, wife of James Scott, of Burlington; Emma, widow of Lee Cadwallader, a former teacher in the high school of Fort Madison, and Frank, a farmer, of Green Bay township.

George W. Tucker received a good common-school education, but in order to further prepare himself for the successful business career which has since been his, he entered Pearson's Business College, at Fort Madison, and pursued a course of commercial study. In 1876 he began farming, believing that in this field of endeavor lie rich rewards for those who conduct their efforts with energy, care and the scientific application of business principles. His expectations have been fully justified, in his own case, at least, by the event, as his vigorous prosecution of the enterprise has brought him much material prosperity.

Mr. Tucker is well known and liked throughout Lee county, and this popularity caused him, in 1897, to be elected to the office of sheriff, in which he continued successfully for four years. He also acted as deputy sheriff for a period of two years, and has held most of the offices of his township. On his election he removed to Fort Madison, where he has since resided, having purchased a home at 411 Second street. He still retains, however, his agricultural interests in Green Bay township, where he owns 500 acres of land, which he rents. In addition he holds title to some valuable property in the City of Fort Madison.

At Burlington, Iowa, June 13, 1876, Mr. Tucker was united in marriage with Miss Clara Miner, a lady of German extraction, who was born May 12, 1855, in Des Moines county, this state. Unto them have been born six children, as follows: Etta May, wife of Herman Lange, of Green Bay township; Charles C., of Fort Madison, who married Miss Elsie Badley; Susie, wife of Charles S. Tucker, an engineer, of Blackwell, Oklahoma; John W., of Fort Madison, who married Miss Josephine Schlemer; Nathan J., and Frankie Kate. John W. and Charles C. are engaged in the hardware and implement business in this city, and are meeting with gratifying success.

Mr. Tucker is now living retired from active business life enjoying the well-earned fruits of his labors. He still maintains, however, active connection with the various social and fraternal bodies in which he holds membership, and is a valued factor in their affairs. These are: The Independent Order of Odd Fellows, the Benevolent and Protective Order of Elks, Knights of Pythias, Modern Woodmen of America, and the Forresters. In politics he has always given hearty and loyal support to the Democratic party, believing that its principles are best calculated to secure the general welfare in harmony with the spirit of American institutions. Personally he is of a genial and generous disposition, and these characteristics, together with his uprightness and justice in all his dealings, have made for him many friends.

BENDIX REIMERS.

One citizen of Keokuk, who is especially entitled to mention in any work which claims to comprise those who have rendered valuable service to city, state or nation, is Bendix Reimers, the subject of this sketch. He was born July 10, 1826, in Holstein, Germany, and is the son of Marx and Marguerita Reimers, who both died in Holstein. There was a family of seven children, but only one other of these came to America. This was George, who was for some time in the grocery business in Keokuk, but is now deceased.

Mr. Reimers early exhibited a spirit of patriotism, and for three years took part in the war of his native land against the Danes as an artilleryman, operating in Jutland and Schleswig. Much of this fighting was of the most severe character, it being related that on one occasion Mr. Reimers's battery was engaged in continuous action for two days and nights. Six years after the conclusion of his military service the longing to try his fortunes in the new world led him to embark for America. Landing in New York in 1857, he came direct to Jackson township, Lee county, Iowa, where he located, six miles from Keokuk, and pursued the business of farming for five years.

Then came the call of his adopted country for defenders against rebellion and treason, and Mr. Reimers, a second time intrusting himself to the fortunes of war, enlisted, August, 1862, in the Nineteenth Iowa Infantry, Company A, under Colonel Bruce, and went into camp at St. Louis. Among the more important engagements and campaigns in which he took part were the siege of Vicksburg, the battles at Mobile, Prairie Grove or Fayetteville, Arkansas, Van Buren and Sterling plantation. At the latter place he was captured by the enemy and was taken as a prisoner to Tyler, Texas, where he remained for six months, suffering great hardships, from the effects of which his constitution has never fully recovered. The regular ration of the Union prisoners was but a pint of corn meal per day, and they were utterly without shelter from weather and storm until, after much labor, they were able to build a few miserable huts of brush and bark. At length the prisoners were taken to Shreveport, Louisiana, on their way to some other point to be exchanged, but the execution of this plan was slow, and Private Reimers, with two others, escaped from custody at that place, and started, during a heavy rainstorm to work their way back to the Union lines. Relying on a pocket compass for guidance, they traveled through the swamps for several nights and days, often compelled by the presence of Confederate pickets to go into hiding and to deny themselves food and drink, and often losing their way. Finally, however, by representing themselves to be Texas troopers, they secured food at a plantation and learned the location of the Rebel troops. Thus enabled to avoid danger, they came up with a colored regiment of Union cavalry, which they accompanied on an expedition up the Red river, and Mr. Reimers rejoined his regiment at Brownsville, Texas. By this exploit he saved himself many weary weeks of captivity, as his comrades at Shreveport were not released until four months later. After a short stay at New Orleans he accompanied his regiment to Mobile, where he was located until the end of the war.

In all his experience of war, Mr. Reimers was never wounded, and received but one assignment to hospital, which occurred at Springfield, Missouri, lasting one week. He was mustered out of his country's service July 10, 1864, at Mobile, Alabama, and received his discharge at Davenport, Iowa. He then returned to Lee county, and worked by the month until he had accumulated the sum of $1,500, when he purchased a farm of forty acres, near Keokuk, where he resided for about ten years, at the end of which time he removed to this city. It was during this time that he was united in marriage to Mrs. Anna Schilling, and to them have been born five sons and daugnters, as follows: Marx, who is a letter carrier in Keokuk; Mary; William, who is employed in a meat market in this city; Bendix, employed in a shoe factory; Anna and Eva. The children of Mrs. Reimers's first marriage are Louise, who lives at home, and Bertha, living in Misosuri.

Mr. Reimers holds membership in Torrence Post of the Grand Army of the Republic, and was connected with the Grange when it was in existence at this place. He is a member of the Lutheran church, and in politics has given his support to the Republican party ever since coming to America. He is a self-made man, and what he has of worldly goods has been acquired by his own efforts and ability. For this he deserves the highest credit.

HENRY GEORGE HAESSIG.

Henry G. Haessig, the well-known cigar manufacturer, of Fort Madison, Iowa, is a native son of Lee county, having been born in this city December 16, 1866. His father, George Haessig, was born in Germany, and came at an early date to Fort Madison, where he was a contractor and builder, and attained a degree of prominence in the city's affairs. In politics he was affiliated with the Democratic party, and for two terms represented the third ward in the city council. He was a member of the Lutheran church. The mother was Christiana (Rhode) Haessig. Both parents are now deceased. Unto them were born, besides the subject of this sketch, seven sons and one daughter, as follows: George G., Charles, William, Edward, who died September 6, 1904; Albert, Otto, Oscar, and Amelia.

Henry G. Haessig was educated in the public schools of Fort Madison, and in 1881 entered the cigar factory of L. B. Reader, in whose employ he continued for sixteen years, or until 1897, when he bought the cigar manufacturing business of Charles Jones, and has since conducted the enterprise independently. In this venture he has met with very gratifying success.

August 13, 1889, Mr. Haessig was married to Miss Pauline A. Meyers, of Fort Madison, and of this union has been born one child, a daughter, Margaret, her natal day being December 30, 1895; two daughters died, Marie and Catherine.

In fraternal affairs Mr. Haessig has taken an active part, being a member of Benevolent and Protective Order of Elks, of Fort Madison Commercial Club, and of the local Cigar Makers' Union. Of this latter body he was one of the organizers, and for eight years was its treasurer. In politics he has always given his support to the Democratic party, and for one term served his township as its clerk. He was one of the organizers of Company F, of the Iowa National Guard, in 1887, and was at that time appointed a corporal, later attained the rank of sergeant, and at the time of his resignation in 1894, was captain of the company.

The factory, where nine workmen are

continuously employed, is located at 835 Second street, and the pleasant and commodious home of the family is at 1034 Second street. Mr. Haessig is one of the most active younger business men of the city, taking a leading part in all progressive movements, and while these qualities are bringing him personal success and adding to his popularity in a marked degree, they are at the same time a powerful factor in building up the material prosperity of the community.

Mrs. Haessig was born in Fort Madison August 3, 1867, a daughter of John B. and Catherine E. (Pliesser) Meyers. Both were born in Germany and as young people came to Fort Madison, where they were married and here resided till their deaths. For many years their home was at 1034 Second street, which was erected by them in 1867. Mr. Meyers died July 21, 1885, and Mrs. Meyers passed to her rest July 1, 1889. They were members of St. Mary's Catholic church. They were the parents of six children of whom only Mrs. Haessig and Louis B. Meyers now survive.

THOMAS H. DONNELL.

Thomas H. Donnell, a well-known farmer of Charleston township, was born on the farm on which he now resides, the date being September 15, 1861. He is the son of William A. Donnell, a native of North Carolina, and Celestia (Hamilton) Donnell, who was born in New York. As a boy William A. Donnell, father of our subject, removed with his parents to Illinois, and in 1838 he came to Iowa, and entered 160 acres of government land. This tract he increased by means of further purchases, becoming one of the most extensive landholders of this section of Lee county. Among his holdings was the site of the present village of Donnellson, which he himself platted in 1871. In the business of farming he was eminently successful. His political affiliation was with the Republican party, and he was very popular throughout the county, being for a number of years county supervisor, and holding the office of trustee and other minor positions. He took a great and intelligent interest in public affairs, and was esteemed for his ability and integrity. He was a member of the Cumberland Presbyterian church. Mr. and Mrs. Donnell were the parents of four sons and four daughters, as follows: Jane, deceased; Laura, deceased; George, now a resident of Melbourne, Iowa; Philo, deceased; Ida, wife of William Benjamin, of Donnellson; John, of Mount Pulaski, Illinois; Thomas H., our subject, and one child who died in infancy.

Thomas H. Donnell received his education in the public schools of his district, and while growing to years of maturity learned the work of the farm by actual experience of its duties. He has always resided on the farm on which he was born, and in 1890 he became its owner. Here he conducts general agricultural operations and makes a specialty of stockraising, giving particular attention to Shorthorn cattle and Shropshire sheep. Keeping only small herds, he strives for high quality, and has received various premiums for his exhibits at county fairs. The farm consists of 160 acres of fertile lands.

In 1881 Mr. Donnell was united in marriage to Miss Emma Spilkey, who was born in Illinois, and to them have been born two daughters, Ethel and Orion. The family occupies a very pleasant home, in which they are surrounded by the material comforts and many of the luxuries, and it is a center of hospitality for many friends. Mr. Donnell is a firm believer in Republican principles and a stanch supporter of that party's policies and chosen leaders, but has never cared for public office, though he enjoys wide popularity. By choice he devotes nearly all his time to agricultural pursuits. He has, however, served a number of terms as supervisor, and has been elected whenever nominated. He holds membership in the Modern Woodmen of America at Donnellson, and has borne a prominent part in the affairs of that order. He is a man of much business ability, and by the exercise of his natural talents has achieved success and attained to an important station in the community in which he lives.

GEORGE W. JUDY.

One of the leading farmers of Jefferson township and one known throughout the county for his ability, social qualities and sterling character is George W. Judy, the subject of this sketch. He was born in West Point township, this county, May 27, 1851, the son of Henry and Elizabeth Emmett) Judy. The father, who has the distinction of being the oldest living pioneer of Lee county, still lives on the original farm that he purchased from the government in 1834. He was born in Ohio, and as a young man came to the West, locating at Fort Madison when there were only four families at that place. When the government holdings of land were thrown open to settlement he purchased the first tract of 160 acres at $1.25 an acre. This he improved and from time to time added other purchases until he now owns a half section of land. He underwent all the hardships incident to pioneer life, and is entitled to much credit for the part he has played in the development of natural resources in Lee county. As illustrating the lack of adequate transportation and the remoteness of market facilities in the earlier days, he recalls that he has hauled dressed pork to Keokuk by wagon and that he received for his load only $1.25 per hundredweight. Indians occupied the country in places at that time, and he remembers having frequently seen the celebrated chief Black Hawk. He married Miss Harriet Cooney, daughter of Dr. Cooney, a pioneer physician and owner of a ranch near Franklin. His second wife was Elizabeth Emmett, daughter of George Emmett, of West Point township. In politics he has been a Republican since the formation of that party. He has lived continuously in Lee county longer than any other person now living, although Captain Washington Galland was here for some time before him. At present he resides on the home farm, and is in his eighty-eighth year.

George W. Judy received during his boyhood and youth a good practical education through the medium of the public schools, and learned the lessons of faithful application to duty in the work of his father's farm, in which he continued until attaining his majority. He then rented land, and began farming on his own account. In this venture he was so successful that in 1876 he was able to buy a farm near Veile, in Jefferson township. This he occupied for twenty years, making important improvements, and in 1896, desiring to extend his operations, he purchased his present holdings of 160 acres. Here he engages in general farming and in stockraising, specializing somewhat, however, in the raising of sweet potatoes and melons, and has attained a very substantial measure of financial success. He has made improvements in the condition of the farm since purchasing, having planted a large orchard of carefully selected fruits, modernized the house and erected a large barn for storage purposes.

On March 14, 1872, Mr. Judy was united in marriage to Miss Lucinda Ann Hart, daughter of Jacob and Sarah (Dukes) Hart. Mr. Hart is a native of New York, but as a child removed with his parents to Pennsylvania, and later in life he settled in Jefferson township, where Mrs. Judy was born. To Mr. and Mrs. Judy have been born nine sons and daughters, as follows: George Thomas, who is in the express business in St. Louis, Missouri; Sarah Elizabeth, wife of Charles Arthur, of Plymouth, Illinois, has two children, Helen and George; Cora A., wife of William Brown, of Montrose township, has one child, Raymond L.; Laura, wife of Victor Griswold, living near Harrison, Arkansas, has one child, Lloyd; Frank, a farmer, of Jefferson township; Joseph, John Logan, Charles G. and Roy Allen, who are at home.

Mr. Judy is a lifelong Republican, and has served that party frequently as delegate to important conventions. For some years he has also acted as chairman of its township committee, but has never been himself an aspirant for public office. He was formerly connected with the Independent Order of Odd Fellows, but has allowed his membership to lapse. He attends and supports the Presbyterian church, of which Mrs. Judy is a member. He is enterprising, public spirited and a believer in progress, and his influence and activities have been valuable to the community in which he lives. Gifted with a capacity for friendship and a pleasing personality, devoted to strict integrity and eminently just in all his dealings, he has won for himself the general respect and made many friends who prize his kindly regard.

JOHN W. TUCKER.

Although but a recent addition to the business and commercial forces of Fort Madison, John W. Tucker is proving himself a factor to be reckoned with in forecasting the future prosperity of the city. Mr. Tucker was born in Green Bay township, Lee county, October 21, 1878, the son of George W. Tucker, of this city. He was educated in the common schools of his township, and also attended Johnson's Business College, at Fort Madison. During the incumbency of his father, George W. Tucker, as sheriff of Lee county, John W. Tucker served two years as turnkey and two years as deputy sheriff, and later served a further two years as deputy sheriff under Sheriff John M. Kenney.

In 1904 he, with his brother, Charles C. Tucker, purchased a half interest in a vehicle and implement business which had been established in Fort Madison the previous year, and in this connection he still continues. The style of the firm is now Tucker Brothers.

On October 10, 1900, Mr. Tucker was united in marriage with Miss Josephine E. Schlemer, and they have their home at No. 205 Second street. Mrs. Tucker is a native of Fort Madison, the date of her birth being April 5, 1882, and is the daughter of Henry and Mary (Kern) Schlemer. The mother died November 22, 1902, and is buried in Fort Madison. Henry Schlemer, father of Mrs. Tucker, is an attorney of this city. Three sisters, Elizabeth, Minnie and Carolyn, remain at home.

Mr. Tucker is a member of the Independent Order of Odd Fellows, in which he has occupied offices of honor, having passed all of its chairs, and is in his political views and associations, a Democrat. He is a young man of promise, and is rapidly acquiring that reputation which rewards energy, integrity and alertness to the demands of the times.

CHARLES DOERR.

A prominent representative of that valuable class of citizens known as German-American is Hon. Charles Doerr, of Fort Madison. Mr. Doerr was born in the duchy of Nassau, Germany, January 13, 1831, and there received the thorough training that fitted him for his later successes in business and public life. Enthusiasm for knowledge and learning carried him through the public and high schools with credit, and gave him an education well-grounded and fully rounded, and as a provision against unforeseen circumstances he learned the trade of stonemason.

He is the son of Philip and Katherine (Tresbach) Doerr, the father being also a stone worker—a master mason. The family came to America in March, 1851, stopping in New York, and in the autumn of that year removed to Vermont, where father and son plied their trade. At Shaftsbury, that state, occurred the death of Katherine Doerr, mother of our subject, in 1852, and she is there buried. She is survived by one son and one daughter, the latter being Jeannette, who was married to John Koehler, and after his death became the wife of George Anthes, but is again a widow. She resides in Minneapolis, Minnesota.

Coming to Fort Madison in 1855, Charles Doerr, in partnership with his father, began the business of building railroad bridges, which they carried on extensively and with success for two years. Then in March, 1857, he forsook the hammer for the pen, and became a copyist, doing this

CHARLES G. DOERR

work at the court house until 1860, when he was appointed deputy county clerk. Two years later, in recognition of his talents, integrity and ability, he was elected by the Democratic party as county clerk of Lee county, and in 1864 was re-elected to the same office, but was "counted out" by a technicality. In June, 1866, he was reappointed county clerk, and this was followed, in the fall of the same year, by another re-election to the office, and this, in turn, by a repetition of the honor in 1868. On the expiration of his term as county clerk he purchased, in 1871, a ferry line across the Mississippi river, which he operated for six years, when he sold it and entered the real estate business, in which he still continues. He was not permitted, however, to remain in political retirement, and in 1884 was called to represent Lee county in the legislature, serving through the Twentieth General Assembly of Iowa with distinction. Further honors awaited him, and in 1885 he was appointed by President Cleveland postmaster of Fort Madison. His other public trusts include the office of justice of the peace, to which he was elected in 1895, and which he still holds, and his membership in the school board for a period of twelve years. In addition he is probably the oldest notary public in the State of Iowa, having acted in this capacity continuously since 1858.

Mr. Doerr was married at Fort Madison on August 20, 1857, to Miss Katherine Magerkurth, who was born at Kindenheim, Rhenish Bavaria, April 30, 1837. She came to America when thirteen years of age. Unto them were born nine children, as follows: Emma, who died at the age of three and one-half years; Charles P., manager and vice-president of an electric lighting company of Aguascalientes, Mexico; Jeanette, familiarly known in the family as Nettie, who is at home; Edward, who was a mining engineer in the City of Mexico, and died October 4, 1904, at San Antonio, Texas, while on his way home from Mexico; Philip O., who died March 24, 1900, at thirty-two years of age, and who was a contractor for freight transportation in Mexico; Albert, a mining engineer at Asientos, Mexico, having spent four years in the school of mining at Freiberg, Germany; Kuno, with the American Smelting and Refining Company, of Aguascalientes, Mexico; Elsie D., wife of Dr. C. L. Bennet, of Aguascalientes, Mexico, and Katherine, who is at home. The wife and mother died December 2, 1899, and is interred in the city cemetery of Fort Madison. The death of Mr. Doerr's father occurred February 21, 1899, he passing away at the age of ninety-one years and six months.

Mr. Doerr, in his fraternal relations, is a member of the Blue Lodge, the Chapter, the Commandery and the Mystic Shrine of the Masonic order, and has been an Odd Fellow since May 6, 1854. In his religious faith he is a member of the Evangelical Lutheran church. With the development and progress of Fort Madison his public spirit has placed him in intimate connection throughout the greater part of his life. He has erected a number of residence buildings in the city, and also was the builder of Concordia Hall, for thirty years the principal opera house. He has owned considerable property here, but recently disposed of the major portion. He has still, however, a number of investments in Mexico. The life of Hon. Charles Doerr is one more illustration of the truth that "America means opportunity," and that the best prizes of fortune are for those who strive conscientiously, uprightly and with fixity of purpose.

JOHN BENNETT.

John Bennett is an honored veteran of the Civil War who, for fifteen years, has been unable to engage in work on account of ill health, brought on by his army service. He was born in Clark county, Indiana, May 2, 1844, a son of James A. and Sarah A. (Howard) Bennett. The father was born in Charleston, South Carolina, and is still living at the advanced age of eighty years, but the mother died in 1900. Both lived with their son, John. Their children were as follows: Missouri, the wife of Dr. A. Rogers, of Kansas City, Kansas; John, of this review; Lizzie A., who became the wife of Robert A. Junk, and died in 1902, and George B., who was drowned while swimming in the Mississippi river, in 1892.

John Bennett was a lad of ten summers when his parents removed from Indiana to the vicinity of Augusta, Illinois, and there he was reared upon a farm, until 1856, when the family home was established in the vicinity of Bentley, Illinois. There John Bennett assisted in the cultivation of his father's farm until the spring of 1861, when he enlisted as a member of Company F, Fourteenth Illinois Cavalry, and he was afterward transferred to the United States navy on the steamship "Silver Lake," plying on the Mississippi, Ohio and Tennessee rivers and took part in several naval engagements on the first named. He was wounded in the head by a gunshot at the battle of Shiloh, and also wounded in the right hand. He took part in many of the engagements along the Tennessee, was also at Vicksburg, Mississippi, the main duty being to guard the river. When his three years' term had expired Mr. Bennett re-enlisted in 1864, becoming a member of Company I, One Hundred and Forty-fifth Indiana Infantry, with which he served in the Army of the Tennessee until the close of the war. He was with Sherman in the Atlanta campaign, participated in the battle of Chattanooga, and was mustered out at Louisville, Kentucky, after which he returned to Augusta, Illinois, with an honorable military record, for he had been a brave and fearless soldier.

The same year Mr. Bennett came to Keokuk, where he conducted a grocery store for about three years. He afterward worked in an egg and butter house for a time, but was at length obliged to abandon his position on account of ill health, and for the past fifteen years has been connected with no business enterprise. He draws a pension of thirty dollars per month.

Mr. Bennett is a member of Torrence Post, No. 2, Grand Army of the Republic, and belongs to the Baptist church, with which he has been identified for thirty-five years. In his political views he is a Republican. He owns a home at No. 1526 Carroll street, and has been a resident of Keokuk almost forty years. He has ever been interested in public progress as well as local advancement and throughout his entire life has manifested the same spirit of loyalty and patriotism which he displayed on Southern battlefields.

WILLIAM MULLIKIN.

Men of marked ability, forceful character and upright purpose leave their impress upon the world written in such indelible characters that time is powerless to obliterate their memory, or sweep it from the minds of men. The force of their example spurs others to emulation, and what they have accomplished is an inspiration to those who come after them, while their sterling virtues live on forever in the hearts of those who have known and loved them, and is cherished in the annals of the community in which they lived and labored as faithful citizens.

William Mullikin, who was for a long term of years one of the leading landowners and representative agriculturists of Lee county, was a native of Indiana, the date of his birth being July 5, 1843, and by the death of both his parents he was left an orphan at a very early age. He was reared by a Mr. Peter Cuddeback, of near Montrose, Lee county, and there he grew to manhood and received a common-school education. While yet quite young he decided to begin his career by striking out into original paths of endeavor, and went to California, where he engaged in farming and other enterprises for two years, acquiring, by his ability thus early manifested, enough money in that short space of time to enable him on his return to Lee county to purchase a farm of eighty acres in Montrose township. Shortly after his return he was united in marriage, in September, 1864, to Miss Mary Jones, who was born in Youngstown, Ohio, June 7, 1846, and came to Lee county at an early day with her parents. Mrs. Mullikin is the daughter of Clement Jones, a successful farmer, and Unity (Bostic) Jones, both now deceased, the father dying in 1860, and being interred in Montrose cemetery, and the mother, whose death occurred in 1887, being buried near Dumas, Missouri. They were excellent people, highly esteemed in the communities in which they lived, and generally respected for their many virtues.

To Mr. and Mrs. Mullikin were born twelve children, of whom now survive five sons and two daughters, as follows: Charles, who married Miss Pearl Brickley, is engaged in the grocery business at Springfield, Missouri, and has one daughter, Clara Belle; Ora, widow of James Doyle, has two sons, Earl and William; Laura, wife of John Renwald, of Keokuk, has six children, Raleigh, William, Mary, Clarence, Paul, Lawrence; William, who is a farmer in Montrose township, Lee county, married Miss Anna Wirtz, and has three children, Nellie, Clara, Gladys; Wilkinson, who married Miss Agnes Hassett, resides in Keokuk; Clarence, who married Miss Alida Vermazen, is a resident of Jackson township, Lee county; Ida, who is the wife of Charles Lupton, of Kansas, has three children, Norman, Elizabeth, Myrtle; Nellie, wife of Phillip Glazier, of Keokuk, has one child, Raymond, and Grover, the youngest member of the family, is a student in the public schools of Keokuk.

Mr. and Mrs. Mullikin resided on their farm in Montrose township for some time after their marriage, but later removed to another farm near the village of Montrose, where they continued to make their home for a number of years, and there Mr. Mullikin acquired, by industry, care and the exercise of business tact and foresight, about 600 acres of very valuable land. In 1886 he purchased a farm of 141 acres in Jackson township, to which the family returned and there resided until Mr. Mullikin's death, which occurred in February, 1902. Mrs. Mullikin removed to Keokuk in April, 1904, and now considers this city her home. Mr. Mullikin gave almost his entire attention to farming, although he for a time bought live stock extensively, and shipped to eastern points. He was very successful in all his efforts, and besides his large real estate holdings in Montrose and Jackson townships he acquired 320 acres of land in Missouri, and a tract of 173 acres in Illinois. The manner of his death was peculiarly sad, and one which was a terrible shock to the family and to the community, which honored him for his great ability and his upright character; it was, in effect, almost beyond the shadow of doubt an assassination. He was sitting in his own home at half past eight o'clock in the evening, when a shot was fired from the darkness through the window, taking effect in the brain, and death was almost instantaneous, he having expired before Mrs. Mullikin, who was with him in the room, could reach his side. No clew to the identity of the perpetrator of this awful and cowardly crime has ever been successfully followed, although the widow does not abandon hope that in time full justice will be done, and this is a hope in which she is joined by all who have at heart the fair name of the community.

Mr. Mullikin was a man of large and generous nature, and was very public spirited, and while he never aspired to public office, he was not the man to shirk civic responsibility, and for a time served as a member of the school board, in which capacity his good judgment and practical grasp of affairs were of much value to his constituents. Politically he gave his support to the Democratic party, and was one of its most highly esteemed members, both on account of his wide influence and for his active co-operation. In his fraternal relations he was prominently connected with the Masonic Order for many years, being a member of Joppa Lodge, at Montrose, and his obsequies were conducted according to the beautiful and impressive ritual of the order, the funeral being attended by a large and distinguished concourse of citizens prominent in Masonic circles throughout southern Iowa. As he was universally respected for his achievements and for the shining virtues of his character, so also was he universally mourned, and his loss was deeply felt by all who knew him. He was laid at rest in Hickory Grove cemetery. To his children he was ever indulgent, and to his wife a kind and devoted husband, always making her truly a partner in his affairs and profiting by her advice and counsel in almost all matters of importance in which he engaged throughout the term of their wedded life, and the wisdom of this course was amply vindicated by the success which attended everything he did.

WILLIAM COLVIN.

William Colvin, a venerable resident of Montrose township, has his farm home on section 35, of that township, where his home has been for more than forty years, beloved and respected by his friends and neighbors, alike for his modest character, genuine worth, industrious habits and kind heart. As a link he binds the remote past to the living present, and from his childhood days recalls visions of Revolutionary heroes, Indian fighters, shadowy figures on a painted canvas, but greatly daring and nobly winning, in the storm periods of the making of the West and Northwest.

Mr. Colvin was born in Lincoln county, Kentucky, August 6, 1826, a son of Joseph and Nancy (Turner) Colvin, natives of Virginia, and born and bred to a farming life. They died before the Rebellion in Kentucky. To their union were born thirteen children, of whom William was the fourth in order of birth. He is now their only living child.

Mr. Colvin was married in 1847 to Miss Katherine Van Arsdall, a native of Mercer county, Kentucky, where she was born December 12, 1830. Her father, John Van Arsdall, was born in Virginia, where he was reared to farming. With his wife, Mary Westerfield, he came west to make his home in Montrose township, Lee county, where both he and his good wife passed to their rest some years ago. They were the parents of a family of seven children, of whom Mrs. Colvin was the third in order of birth. She has four brothers living: William, Charles, Smith and Alonzo. To Mr. and Mrs. Colvin have come nine children, two of whom are now dead; Melissa is the wife of Austin Wright; Amanda is the wife of John Boyd, a resident of Montrose township; Mattie married William Grimes, and is now dead; Green married Miss Lucy Rice, and has his home in Fort Madison; Mary married Z. Boyd, and is now dead; Sadie is the wife of Frank Davis, and with her husband, has her home on the old homestead; Nannie is the wife of Robert Grimes, a resident of Montrose township. There are twelve grandchildren and one great-grandchild in the family, so that a numerous progeny perpetuates this honored name.

William Colvin owned a small farm in his native state, but after his marriage sold it and came into Lee county in 1854. For some three or four years he lived on Montrose Bottoms, but in 1860 came to his present home, where he owns ninety acres of land, on Lemon Lee creek, a stream fed by springs, amply sufficient the season through for all stock watering, and similar purposes. When he secured this handsome farm there was already constructed a small cabin, which he replaced some five years later by a commodious and attractive house. Here for many years Mr. Colvin and his good wife have lived, honorable and worthy people, anxious only that they may do what good they can in the place where the Author of their being has placed them. They have courted neither the applause nor the favor of men, only seeking to be honest and square. They have been lifelong members of the Christian church, of Summitville, and their deeds have brought no blush to their profession. In his more active years he has filled a number of local positions carrying considerable responsibility, such as road supervisor and school director, and everything entrusted to him was well done. In politics he has taken the Republican side, and generally acted with that party, though not in any sense a zealous partisan. He is now in his seventy-ninth year, and is still hale and hearty. If the necessity arises he is sure he could still do a day's work. As it is he does what he wishes and keeps a good appetite.

An uncle of Mr. Colvin, one Charles Colvin, served in the Revolutionary War, and is well remembered by the subject of this sketch. The uncle was a bachelor, and he would visit at the home of his brother, and when there would take his little nephew on his lap and tell him such horrible stories that the little chap was afraid to go tto bed. Along with this was a wealth of Revolutionary lore that would be of vast value if it could now be recalled and preserved to the world.

The golden wedding of this modest and unassuming couple was celebrated with enthusiasm on August 11, 1897. It was a surprise very cleverly managed by the children. The old folks were spirited away for a time, and when they returned to their home it was in possession of a numerous company, who had come bearing congratulations and numerous gifts of golden love, such as a gold watch for the father, gold spectacles for the mother, and many similar gifts. Friends had spread a fine repast, and among those present to enjoy it were not only the local friends, but those from Keokuk, and many other places as well. Peter Colvin, a minister from California, and a nephew of the aged husband and father, was fortunate enough to be present at this rare event.

CHARLES C. TUCKER.

One of the younger business men of Fort Madison who is achieving a position of prominence is Charles C. Tucker, who is a dealer in farm implements, hardware and vehicles. Mr. Tucker is the son of George W. Tucker, a sketch of whose life appears elsewhere in this volume, and was born on a farm in Green Bay township, Lee county, October 22, 1874. After completing his education in the public schools he assisted in the work of his father's farm until his marriage, when he rented land, and conducted farming operations independently until 1900, when he removed to Burlington. There he, in association, engaged in the sale of buggies and agricultural implements for a period of two years, at the end of which time he located in Fort Madison, establishing himself in the enterprise which he still conducts.

December 25, 1895, Mr. Tucker was united in marriage with Miss Elsie Badley. Mrs. Tucker was born in Green Bay township, May 10, 1874, and is the daughter of Uriah Badley, now a resident of Burlington. Her mother is deceased.

Mr. Tucker's political affiliation has always been with the Democratic party, and fraternally he is a member of the Independent Order of Odd Fellows. Thoroughly imbued with the spirit of modern enterprise and progress, and endowed with the talent for making and holding friends, his pathway to success seems clear and assured.

WILEY B. RAY.

Wiley B. Ray, proprietor of a livery stable in Keokuk, was born at Knoxville, Tennessee, October 25, 1833, his parents being William and Harriet (Parmer) Ray. His grandfather, William Ray, was reared in Virginia and went to eastern Tennessee with the first white settlers, assisting in driving out the Cherokee Indians, and reclaiming the wild land for the uses of civilization. He was a frequent companion of Daniel Boone in his hunting expeditions, and on one occasion when they were out in the Indian country together, they built their campfire against a log and also left their guns leaning against the log, while they, for safety, slept some distance away in the bushes. In the morning, missing their guns, they rushed to the place where they had built their fire and found both gunstocks burned off. Boone took his tomahawk, cut down a walnut tree and restocked the guns—a task that required two or three days. William Ray was married three times and was the father of twenty-five children. Two of his sons fought with Jackson at the battle of New Orleans, January 8, 1815. His family scattered, most of them settled in the West and Northwest. His death occurred about 1844, when he was eighty-five years of age.

William Ray, son of William Ray, the explorer and Kentucky pioneer, was born on his father's farm, near Knoxville, Tennessee, in 1806, and was the twenty-second child. He was a farmer and became a prominent citizen of his community, serving as sheriff of his county while James K. Polk was circuit judge of that district. In politics he was a Whig. He continued a resident of Tennessee until March, 1843, when he gave his brother four slaves that his father had given him and made preparation to come to Iowa. In company with others he constructed a houseboat 25x90 feet, with six compartments, one for each family, with opening for ingress in the roof—one for each chamber. There were two sweep oars and a great steering oar, and in this boat they descended the Holston, Tennessee and Ohio rivers to Cairo, where they sold the boat, proceeding by steamer to St. Louis and thence by another boat to Keokuk.

Iowa. Mr. Ray and his family settled on the Des Moines river in the timber, near Farmington, and secured a piece of land, about six acres of which had been cleared and a cabin built. He cleared the timber from about forty acres in order to make a farm. There were no Indians living in this locality, but many passed through on their way to hunting grounds farther west. Mr. Ray was one of the first settlers of his locality and took an active part in promoting the pioneer development. He died May 10, 1848, at the age of forty-two years. He was married in Tennessee to Harriet Parmer, about 1827. The Parmers were from North Carolina. Daniel Boone was the leader of a company from that state, but when they reached Knoxville, being worn out with the journey, the Parmers and some others halted and remained near Utica, Tennessee, while the others proceeded on their way to Kentucky. The mother of Harriet (Parmer) Ray was living there in 1885, a hale and hearty woman of ninety-five years. Game was not always plentiful and therefore the family was at times without meat.

William and Harriet (Parmer) Ray were the parents of nine children, two sons and seven daughters: Rebecca Ann, who married Robert Davis; Mary Jane, the wife of Thomas Renwell; Wiley B., Martha, wife of Edward Stevens; William, who married Joanna Ensenminger; Isable, who married Jonathan Holmes; Mrs. Sarah Sawyer; Senath, who died unmarried, and Cynthia, who died in infancy.

Wiley B. Ray had but limited opportunities for attending school. He lived at home until 1848, and then worked as a farm hand for others for two years. From 1850 until 1854 he owned and drove a hack in Keokuk, and in the latter years went to St. Paul, Minnesota. In June of that year he was one of a party of thirty civilians who started with military escort under General Canby, Lieutenant Wells being in immediate command, to survey the railroad line west from Minneapolis. They were among the Sioux and other tribes of Indians, proceeding to the headwaters of the streams running into the Pacific. They returned the following February, part of the way with snow shoes, dogs and sleds. They had plenty of trouble with the Indians, and a guard was often stationed at night to prevent an unexpected Indian outbreak. After again reaching Keokuk Mr. Ray once more drove a hack.

In 1858 Mr. Ray went to Missouri, and in 1860-61 he and a partner built a bridge across the Platt river, near Ringgold, Platt county, taking the stone from the quarry and the lumber from the woods, and receiving $16,000 for the work. They were often shot at by bushwhackers while thus engaged in bridgebuilding. Mr. Ray came again to Keokuk in the fall of 1861, and has since made this city his home. For a number of years he owned a transfer line and did a profitable business. He also conducted a wood and coal yard until 1883, when he established his livery stable, and has since been in this line of business, covering twenty-one years. He has both a livery and feed stable, and receives a good patronage. His barn is located at No. 408 North Fifth street.

On the 31st of May, 1860, Mr. Ray was

married to Miss Emily Gilbert, at St. Joseph, Missouri. She was born thirty miles from Baltimore, Maryland, in 1840, a daughter of Thomas and Lorena Gilbert, and died twent-six years after her marriage. For his second wife he chose Emma Clark, the wedding taking place December 28, 1886. She is a native of Keokuk and a daughter of Charles Clark, a native of England, and a butcher by trade, who settled in Keokuk in 1853. There are three children by this marriage: Emily, William and Jesse Ray. Mr. Ray is a Republican in politics, but has never been an aspirant for office, prefering to give his undivided attention to his business interests, in which he has prospered, owing to close application and untiring diligence.

ELIAS HAIL ENSLOW.

In the settlement of the West the pioneers had to face many trials and difficulties. They had gone far from the conveniences and privileges of civilization. Markets were remote, and communication difficult. The prairies were like the ocean, and the roads primitive in the extreme. Distances now measured by hours then required many days, and the journey from Fort Madison to Chicago was a tax on a stout heart. Schools were few and far between, and when located were of very inferior grade. But the hearts on the frontier were brave, and nothing discouraged the builders of the great states that are now mighty empires in themselves. They improved the land, bridged the rivers, built the roads, planted what are now great cities, and in due time came the railroad and the tlegraph and the mail to bring the ends of the country together. The East and the West, at least, were next-door neighbors; space was eliminated; time was annihilated. To the prairies of Iowa came the art and refinement of New England; learning was no longer strange and the schoolmaster was abroad in the land. The Empire state beyond the great river had come to its own. The men who helped in this great transformation should always be reverently remembered. It was no slight task, the building of an empire, that they undertook. Among them, and entitled to an honored place, is the man whose name heads this article. He is now dead, but in his day he played a man's part in the settlement of Lee county, and he is remembered in Pleasant Ridge township as a man of fine character and upright spirit.

Elias Hail Enslow was born in Tuscarora, Schuylkill county, Pennsylvania, June 8, 1826, a son of Thomas and Catherine (Noss) Enslow. He was but a small child when his parents came to Pleasant Ridge township, where they settled in the timber, but soon removed to the prairie, making a home on section 23, where the family home has been maintained to the present time. Here passed to their rest the father and mother in due time, and their ashes, with those of the other members who have been called home, are to be found in the family burying ground, long retained on the old homestead.

Mr. Enslow was given a common-school education, such as the frontier schools of the time afforded; but he had a thoughtful and reflective mind, an observant disposition, and kept close watch on the passing world, so that in due time he became what might be fairly and justly termed a well-educated man, an education largely acquired by himself, but none the less genuine and real. As the oldest child in the family he was early called upon to form critical and decisive opinions, and was mature beyond his years. For many years he lived at home, and when he began for himself bought a forty-acre tract of his father, as the nucleus of a very fine estate. He bought land on several subsequent occasions, until he was the owner of a fine farm, consisting of 250 acres. In later years he disposed of a part of his extensive real estate holdings, and at the time of his death had reduced his farm to 160 acres.

Mr. Enslow was married December 2, 1859, to Miss Sarah A. Lee, a native of Ohio, and a daughter of Edward D. and Matilda (Frederick) Lee. The mother was born in Virginia, and the father in Genessee county, New York. They were married in Ohio, of which state they were pioneers. In 1839 they removed to Fort Madison, where the husband and father found employment as a carpenter, and was engaged in the construction of the first court house erected in Lee county. Mr. Lee remained in Fort Madison only about a year, and after spending two more years in Farmington, Van Buren county, returned to Ohio. They did not long continue in Ohio, but coming back to Iowa, secured a farm near Farmington, on which both father and mother lived and died. Mrs. Enslow was educated in the district schools, and profiting by her opportunities has become a lady of intelligence and broad views. Though now advanced in years she is still alert and vigorous to all the passing interests of the community in which she lives and the welfare of her children and their children, who enfold her in loving care.

Mr. and Mrs. Enslow were the parents of a large family, brief mention of which may be made as follows: Ella M., the wife of John Morgan, and the mother of John, Grace, Elmer, Helen and Alonzo; Alice, the wife of Charles Miner, a resident of Fort Madison; Mary L., the wife of David Conro, of Schoharie county, New York, and the mother of George Edward, Hester Ann and Floyd. She has by her first husband, William Flemming, two daughters, Ada and Maude; Miss Ada Lee, Maud Alice, Katie Belle died of consumption when a young woman of seventeen; Edward P. died when twenty-four years of age; William Chase, who lives in Pleasant Ridge township, married Miss Frances Blum, and is the father of five children; Lucia, Agnes, Arthur, Alvin Lee and Alma Lea, the last two being twins; John F. lives at home with his mother and runs the farm, he married Miss Carrie Colton, by whom he has had two children; George Fremont and Sadie Jane; Elias Fremont died at the dawn of early manhood, and two others who died in infancy, Benjamin H. and Lizzie Maude.

In religious matters Mr. Enslow was a member of the Presbyterian church, as was his father before him. Mrs. Enslow is connected with the Cumberland Presbyterian church, and her walk and conversation bring no discredit upon her faith and profession. After his death she took charge of the family homestead, and conducted it with marked success until her son became of age to take the burden from her shoulders.

The Enslow family have given Lee county some of its best citizens. They have been trained to honesty, industry and thrift, and taught lessons of integrity, worthily sustaining an honored name.

WILLIAM D. PATTERSON.

The legal profession affords opportunity for the development of the finest character and the exercise of the noblest powers of thought and reason. It may be followed in a narrow and selfish manner, but the man who makes the law a means of self-aggrandizement alone or mainly, is regarded with doubt and aversion. The lawyer should cultivate public spirit, he should place the right above profit and loss, and be ever ready to espouse the cause of innocence against the oppressions of the strong and brutal. It is a calling in which ideals should have a very large place, and though the materialistic tendencies of the present time make constant assault upon his idealism the true lawyer is always seeking to live in the upper regions of his nature. Such men the world loves and honors, and when it discovers them will not readily give them up, but holds them in honor and reverence. Among these men is numbered the distinguished gentleman whose name introduces this biographical review. He is an able lawyer, an honorable man, and is regarded as a credit to the Lee county bar.

William D. Patterson, attorney at law, Keokuk, Iowa, is a native of that city, his birth occurring October 9, 1857. He is a son of John A. and Elizabeth (Wilson) Patterson.

The first of this branch of the Patterson family came from the North of Ireland, and settled in Jefferson county, Ohio, where he lived a farmer. His wife was an Armstrong, and they had a family of fourteen children. She lived to a great age.

John A. Patterson was the first of a family of fourteen children born to his parents in Jefferson county, Ohio, and learned the carpenter trade in Pittsburg, Pennsylvania, whence he came to Iowa, in 1852. He settled at Keokuk, where he has since followed his trade. His wife, Elizabeth Wilson, was a daughter of Henry and Mary (Burbridge) Wilson. Both families came from Virginia, but spent some years in Kentucky. They were later settled in Pickaway county, Ohio. The Wilsons accompanied Dr. Galland in his removal to this state. Mrs. Elizabeth Patterson, who was born January 18, 1829, died on Easter Sunday, 1899. Henry Wilson was a farmer, and was first located for himself near Carthage, Illinois, whence he removed to Monticello, that state, and opposite Keokuk, where he worked at the shoemaker's trade. Still later he settled on a farm six miles west of Keokuk, which is now occupied by Joe Lupton. When Keokuk had become something of a town, Mr. Wilson became one of its residents, and was killed while handling logs. His widow did not long survive his death. At one time he owned a part of the "Half Breed Reservation," which now constitutes part of the city of Keokuk. The title was made out to him by an Indian, but it was so indefinite in its description by metes and bounds that he could not locate it after years, and finally lost it. Eleven children were born to Mr. and Mrs. Henry Wilson. The two oldest died while young. Lucinda married Jonathan Wycoff. Samantha is the wife of Thompson McCleary; Nancy married Hugh McCleary, a cousin to Thompson; Elizabeth, the mother of the subject of this article, was the next child in the family. Mary J., is the wife of R. W. Alvord. Mattie is the wife of Benjamin Harrison. William H. lives in Chicago. Andrew J., is in Nebraska, and Samuel is dead.

John A. Patterson and wife were the parents of a family of five children: Ida; William D.; Charles, who died at the age of twelve years; Mabel, who died at the age of twenty-five years; and Robert J., of Keokuk.

William D. Patterson received his education in the public schools and Miller's Commercial College. He read law with Gilmore & Anderson, eminent attorneys at Keokuk for three years. Under their advice and instruction he became deeply versed in the basic principles of the profession, and imbibed a large enthusiasm for the law in its higher phases and applications. He was admitted to the bar in 1880, and served for some time as an attorney clerk. For a time he was associated with J. C. Davis, who is now a resident of the capital city. In 1884 he began the practice of his profession for himself, and has been alone in his career. He carries on a general law practice, and devotes himself to all branches of his work. Although he is a Republican, and is regarded as a reliable party worker, he takes no part in the political affairs of the city, preferring to devote all his thought and energy to the work of his profession. The law as he regards it is a jealous mistress, and will not tolerate any divided allegiance. Others may give attention to many outside large or petty interests, but for Mr. Patterson his great calling is so magnificent a field of labor that it more than exhausts all his strength and energy. He is not a member of any secret or fraternal society, and while genial and courteous in his manners as a gentleman should always be, he keeps one thing before him, and that is his life work, the practice of the legal profession.

CHARLES A. BUTZ.

On the roll of useful and substantial citizens who have borne their part honorably in the industrial life of Fort Madison appears the name of Charles A. Butz. Mr. Butz was born in Greene county, Pennsylvania, April 13, 1858, and is the son of John

P. and Mary (Ledwith) Butz. John P. Butz, the father, who was born at Brownsville, Pennsylvania, was a physician and practiced his profession in that state and in Indiana, his death occurring at Vevay, Indiana. He was of the lineage known as Pennsylvania German. Mary L. Butz, mother of our subject, was born in Greene county, Pennsylvania, and died in Milwaukee in 1902. They were the parents of two children, the younger being Jessie, wife of Harry McGill, of Milwaukee, manager of the Postal Telegraph Company.

Charles A. Butz was reared in Vevay, Indiana, to which place he removed with his parents from Pennsylvania in his early years, and there he acquired a good education in the public schools. He left his home in 1887, and, going to Chicago to seek broader opportunities, entered the employ of the Western Union Telegraph Company as bookkeeper. Continuing in that work for three years, he engaged himself at the termination of that period as fireman on a passenger locomotive of the Santa Fe system, running between Chicago and Fort Madison. In this capacity he continued for six years, or until 1896, when he accepted a position as engineer with the Morrison Plow Company, of this place, by whom he is still employed.

At Fort Madison July 18, 1891, Mr. Butz was united in marriage to Miss Ella Atlee, daughter of Samuel J. and Elvira V. (Norton) Atlee. The marriage of Mrs. Butz's parents took place December 25, 1866, the ceremony being performed by Rev. T. E. Bliss. Samuel J. Atlee was born March 12, 1838, and died in Memphis, Tennessee, October 14, 1873, the victim of a yellow-fever epidemic. At the time of his death he held the office of deputy United States marshal. He was born in Pennsylvania, spent the days of his boyhood and youth in Fort Madison, and was married to Elvira Norton in Memphis. During the Civil War he was captain of Company D, of the Seventh Regiment Iowa Volunteer Infantry, participating in important engagements, was taken prisoner by the Confederate forces, and suffered a six months' imprisonment in Libby prison. Although the hardships and deprivations of that time had serious effects upon his health, and although many of his comrades succumbed to the wretched and terrible conditions of prison life, he survived. He possessed strength of character, ability and an affectionate nature. Elvira V. Atlee, mother of Mrs. Butz, was of Virginia birth, her natal day being January 27, 1844. She died July 21, 1877, while on a visit to relatives of her husband at Fort Madison.

Mrs. Butz became a resident of Fort Madison in 1881. She is the eldest of a family of three, the date of her birth being November 29, 1867. The others are: Marion, born January 17, 1869, became the wife of Charles Whyte, of Jerseyville, Illinois, and has one child, Geraldine; Nettie, born August 20, 1872, married Robert Cattermole, of Abbotsford, Wisconsin, son of the Mr. Cattermole who was for many years a pork packer in Fort Madison.

Mr. Butz is a member of the Ancient Order United Workmen, in which order he has held the office of foreman, and in his political connection he is a believer in the principles of the Republican party, supporting its nominees in all cases where important issues are at stake. In January, 1904, he purchased a pleasant and commodious home at No. 611 Fourth street. The family formerly occupied a residence at 909 Fourth street. Mr. Butz is a man of genial disposition, respected for his strict integrity in all his dealings, and has many friends who speak his praise. He is well worthy a place in this volume.

CHARLES CLINTON TUCKER.

Charles Clinton Tucker, a member of one of the older families of Lee county and at the present time assessor of Green Bay towwnship, is well known to a large circle of friends and acquaintances who will be interested in a sketch of his life and family history. Mr. Tucker was born in Dearborn county, Indiana, September 6, 1852, the son of John W. and Sarah (Spicknall) Tucker, and removed with his parents to Green Bay township, this county, in his early childhood. There the father entered as a "homestead" one-half section of land, which is still in the possession of the family. Both parents are now deceased, and are interred in the Beebe cemetery. Active and consistent members of the Methodist Episcopal church, identified with the progressive interests of the community in which they lived, becoming large landholders and very well-to-do in a pecuniary way, they enjoyed the general respect and esteem, and the record of their characters is a precious heritage to be handed down to succeeding generations in loving remembrance and veneration. They were the parents of eight children.

Mr. Tucker, the subject of this sketch, received his initial knowledge of books, and indeed his entire formal education, in the public schools of his township, but this training he has added to by a life of reading and observation, and by his lively interest in public questions has become well versed in current topics. Until 1876, the year in which he attained his majority, he assisted in the work of his father's farm, thus receiving a practical training which has since proved valuable as the basis of later successes. In 1876 he was united in marriage with Miss Alice Hyter, a native of Green Bay township, and they have four children, as follows: George, a farmer, who married Miss Blanche Puckter and has two children, John and Vida; Fred O., who married Miss Maude Liddle and has two children, Frank and Clinton; Samuel, who married Miss Liddia Lange and has one child, Lloyd; and Vida, who is the wife of Harry Peel.

Mr. Tucker is the proprietor of 430 acres of fertile and productive lands, among the best in this section of the state, upon which he has placed many modern improvements. A large and handsome dwelling and well-kept grounds attest the progressive spirit of the owner. Here Mr. Tucker conducts general farming, and also makes a specialty of the breeding of stock. His present prosperity is the result of his own efforts, he being one of that valuable class of citizens who are entitled to the name of self-made men. He attends and supports the Christian church, of which Mrs. Tucker is a member, and fraternally he holds membership in the Independent Order of Odd Fellows at Wever, of which lodge he is Past Grand, and in the Benevolent and Protective Order of Elks, at Fort Madison. His political faith is that of the Democracy, whose principles he believes best calculated to secure the greatest good to the greatest number, and of whose chosen leaders he has ever been a loyal and able supporter. He has served his party as delegate to all conventions of importance for a long term of years, and in 1900 he was chosen by public suffrage to the office of assessor of Green Bay township, a testimony to his ability; popularity and party services. This position he still holds.

Mr. Tucker is a man of rare foresight and discernment in affairs of business, and his social qualities have made him many friends who regard him as a man of sound judgment and one who is disposed to deal justly in all relations of life. He is a worthy representative of a family who did much toward the upbuilding of Lee county in pioneer days.

JOSEPH A. LUPTON.

To record the life stories of men who have gained large and lasting success by their own unassisted efforts is the most important task of the historian, and the record of their achievements forms the proudest pages in the chronicles of mankind. To this class of useful citizens belongs Joseph A. Lupton, who now resides on his large and prosperous farm of 400 acres on section 19, Jackson township, Lee county, Iowa, and who was born July 12, 1827, on a farm in Highland county, Ohio, the son of David and Ruth (Adams) Lupton, both of Virginia, in which state they celebrated their marriage. In 1844 he accompanied his parents to Lee county, and here the father rented land and farmed, but afterward bought land in Putnam county, Missouri, where he died in 1889, his own demise having been preceded by that of his wife, which occurred in 1879. In 1853 Mr. Lupton bought land in Putnam county, on which he resided for a year, but at the end of that time he returned to Lee county, and has since resided in Jackson township, with the exception of a period of six years during which he lived in Butte county, California, where he owned a farm in the Sacramento, conducting agricultural operations and hauling the products of his land up into the mountains, where he was able to dispose of it at a profit.

At the home which he now occupies Mr. Lupton was united in marriage in 1852 to Miss Anna Lancaster, who was born in Liverpool, England, June 14, 1835, and came to the United States in 1847, making the voyage on the sailship R. D. Shepherd, which set sail February 13th, and landed at New Orleans, March 17th, after a remarkably long and tedious voyage, during which they were becalmed for two weeks in the Gulf of Mexico. Thence the family ascended the Mississippi river on the steamer Lucy

Burton to Lee county. The father of Mrs. Lupton was John Lancaster, of Penrith, Cumberland county, England, and while in Liverpool he was a wholesale butcher, but in America he pursued the occupation of farming, owning land in Jackson township, where he died on September 29, 1850. His wife survived him until 1856, and her death was caused by a railroad wreck while en route to California, occurring on the Isthmus of Panama, where she is buried. The family consisted of five brothers and sisters, of whom only two are now living, the other being Sarah E., wife of Samuel Snow, of Santa Rosa, California. Mrs. Lupton received her education in England and in Williams's school in Keokuk, and after the completion of her studies was a teacher for one year, 1849-50, in the Oakwood school. To Mr. and Mrs. Lupton have been born six sons and three daughters, as follows: David A., residing in Kansas, who married Miss Jennie Sparks and has three children, James, Ellis and Francis; Sadie; John C., who now manages his father's farm; Louis E., who died at the age of thirty-nine; William H., who died at twenty-four years of age; Mary B., wife of W. W. Howells, a farmer, who has three children, Thomas, Anna Belle and Mabel; Anna Ruth, who resides with her parents; Charles N., who married Miss Ida Millikin and has three children, Norman L., Anna E., and Myrtle R.; and Asa F., who married Miss Nora Osgood and has one child, Paul.

Mr. and Mrs. Lupton have been for twenty years faithful members of the Westminster Presbyterian church at Keokuk, being ranked among its most generous and constant supporters and always contributing liberally to its charities, in which they take a deep interest, and Mrs. Lupton in a member of its Circle No. 14. Mr. Lupton is an extensive reader and student of public questions, being an influential member of the Republican party in this section, and was at one time called upon by his fellow citizens to assume the duties of township supervisor, which office he held for eight years with credit to himself and to the benefit of those who elected him and the public in general, while he also served as director of the public schools for one year. At the present time, however, owing to the weight of advancing age, combined with feeble health, he is living retired from the earlier activities of his career, enjoying the well-earned ease and comfort which have come to him as the result of careful, wise management and long and faithful devotion to duty. He is of a marked patriotic spirit, which may be explained by citing the fact that he is a distant relative of that grandest among the grand figures of American history, Abraham Lincoln, as his grandmother Adams was a sister of Nancy Hanks, the mother of Lincoln. Another interesting bit of family history is that William Lupton, of London, England, an uncle of David Lupton, father of our subject, was one of the eight men who met in Baltimore, Maryland, in 1819, and organized the first lodge of the Independent Order of Odd Fellows in the United States. Mr. Lupton takes a keen interest in matters of family and local history, and relates many anecdotes and facts which are of value as illustrating the manners and customs of an earlier day.

EDGAR C. COBB.

Edgar C. Cobb, who for many years was identified with building operations in Keokuk and who made an unassailable reputation in business circles, was born in Burlington, Vermont, on the 18th of November, 1837. His father, Richard Cobb, was a native of England, but his mother, Mary A. Cobb, was born in Canada and they were married in the latter country. The father served as a soldier in the Mexican War and his sympathies were with the Union cause at the time of the Civil War, but he was too old to enlist. He carried on farming for a long period in Jackson county, Iowa, and subsequently conducted a hotel in the town of Andrew in that county. He was one of the pioneer residents of the state and aided in laying broad and deep the foundation for the present development and progress of the locality, in which he made his home. In the family were the following named: Farnsworth, who is a veteran of the Civil War, and died October 10, 1904 in Sac City, Iowa, from wounds received in the army; William A., who also served as a member of the Union army and is now residing in Huntsville, Washington; Mrs. Josephine Willey, of Council Bluffs, Iowa; and Mrs. Hannah Bryan, of Sioux City, Iowa. Edgar C. Cobb the other member of the family, remained a resident of New England during the first fourteen years of his life and then accompanied his parents on their removal to Jackson county, Iowa. His education was acquired in the public schools of Vermont and of this state, and he is also a graduate of the Maquoketa Academy of the class of 1857. He remained at home until about nineteen years of age, when he started out in life for himself and became an apprentice to the carpenter's trade in Galena, Illinois. While thus engaged he took up the study of medicine and in 1858 he entered the medical school at Nashville, Tennessee, from which he was graduated in the spring of 1860, with the degree of Doctor of Medicine. He afterward purchased a drug store at Nashville, but this was later confiscated by the Rebels in the name of the United Confederate States of America, and Mr. Cobb was left with only the clothing that he wore and what money and valuables he had on his person. Then under sixty days' armistice, he came north and enlisted in the United States army, becoming a member of Company I, Twelfth Iowa Infantry, under command of Captain Vanduze and Colonel Wood. The regiment was attached to Prentice's division and Mr. Cobb served for three years and four months, participating in a number of hotly contested engagements, including the battles of Shiloh, Duvall's Bluff, Memphis, Nashville, Atlanta, Corinth, Pittsburg Landing, Fort Blakely and siege of Vicksburg, together with many minor engagements. He was wounded on the advance on Corinth, his eyes being burned with powder and one put out. He also sustained a gunshot wound in the right leg, which took off a portion of the patella. When injured in the eye he went into the hospital at Shiloh, where he remained for two weeks and later was put aboard a boat and sent to Keokuk. It was here that Sergeant Hughes placed him in the drug room of the Estes

House Hospital, where he remained for three months and then having recovered he again joined his regiment at St. Louis, and went on down the river. They left the boat at Pittsburg Landing preparatory to taking part in the fight at Vicksburg. On various occasions he was detailed as medical store keeper and also as assistant surgeon and at Vicksburg he was detailed for duty as assistant surgeon in General Prestice's Hospital. He was mustered out on Dauphin Island in the Gulf of Mexico, after the battle of Fort Blakely, and with a most creditable military record returned to his home.

On again reaching Keokuk, Dr. Cobb entered upon the practice of medicine, in which he continued for six months, when he opened a drug store in the Keokuk Medical Building, continuing in that business for one winter. Finding, however, that professional duties and the sale of drugs was not entirely congenial he entered the Rock Island Railway shops as a journeyman carpenter, being thus employed for two years. On the expiration of that period he began contracting and house building and from 1875 until 1898 was closely associated with building operations in Keokuk. In the latter year, however, his left eye began failing and he was forced to give up the work. He was the architect and builder of many modern structures in the city, however, and elsewhere in the state. He both designed and built the court house at Perry, Iowa, erected the Limberg, Essex & Frazier Building in Keokuk, the school house at Warsaw, Illinois, and many residences and business blocks in this city and surrounding districts.

In the fall of 1858 at Nashville, Tennessee, while attending school there, Mr. Cobb was united in marriage to Miss Mary A. Maddox, who died October 20, 1889, in Keokuk, Iowa, at the age of forty-seven years, one month and seventeen days. She left two children, William, an architect, of Alton, Illinois, who is married and has three children; and Jessie, the wife of E. A. Meyer, a barber, of West Keokuk.

Mr. Cobb is a valued member of the Independent Order of Odd Fellows, with which he has been identified since attaining his majority and he is now serving as outer guard in the Keokuk lodge. He also belongs to the Grand Army of the Republic, and in his political views is a stalwart Republican. He has ever endorsed the principles which he believed would contribute most to the welfare of county, state and nation and has always been fearless in advocating any measure or movement which he believed to be right. In business his strong executive force, keen foresight and unfaltering energy proved the foundation for his success and gained to him a comfortable competence.

HON. DAVID A. YOUNG.

The subject of this review is an honored and highly respected citizen of Des Moines township, Lee county, Iowa, where his neighbors have called him to represent them in the State Senate. He is a man of broad and progressive views, and in the state where there is such wide diffusion of political knowledge and such general prevalence of sound political sense, he has won an enviable standing as a leader and statesman.

Mr. Young was born in Burnside, Hancock county, Illinois, January 16, 1852, a son of the Rev. William and Juliette (Toms) Young. The remote American ancestor of the Young family settled in Canada long ago. David Young, the grandfather of David A., made a home on the Toronto river, forty miles below the Canadian city of that name, being a farmer and much interested in milling. He was the father of a family of five children: Justus: Hettie, first the wife of Warren Bain, and after his death, the wife of David Lyons, of Galland, Lee county, Iowa; Polly, wife of John Wilson, of Hancock county, Illinois; John and William. The grandmother passed away in Hancock county, Illinois, many years ago. The Young family removed to the United States about 1840, and settled near Burnside, Illinois, where the children in due time made homes for themselves. The grandfather died in 1868, at the age of seventy-five.

The Rev. William Young was born December 5, 1831, and secured his education at the hands of the teachers of the public schools. He was reared on the farm, and was closely associated with the vocation of farming. In 1864 he was licensed to preach by the Missionary Baptists, and three years later was ordained at Charlestown, Iowa, where he had a notable work. He was also pastor of a church at Croton, and other churches where he did a great work. Mr. Young was an earnest preacher, who wrought a good work in the days of his active ministry. He married Juliette Toms, who was born in Illinois, and to their union came two children: David A., and Juliette, who married Isaac Schafer, a resident of Des Moines township, Lee county. Mrs. Young died when David was only four years old. The Toms family came of English ancestry, and have made a good record in past years.

Rev. William A. Young was later married to Miss Lydia Swisher, a native of Pennsylvania, the wedding occurring August 23, 1857. To this union were born ten children: Edward; Dr. James A.; Ida M., the wife of Dr. Brownfield, and now deceased; John; Daisy M., wife of J. Ross Kelsy; five died in infancy. Rev. and Mrs. Young both died in 1881, the mother on the 18th day of June, and the father on the 25th day of March, at the residence of his son, David. He was a man of serious convictions, gifted with fine oratorical power and good sense. He was a strong Prohibitionist, voted the Democratic ticket until 1864, when he cast his vote for Abraham Lincoln. Much devoted to his work, he attained much success in his sacred calling, and his converts were numerous. Dignified and firm in his bearing, he was powerful in prayer. It is said that he had no enemies, but on the contrary legions of friends.

David A. Young received his education in the public schools in a very large degree, and early proved himself a hard worker, being employed on the United States canal, on the farm and in a saw mill before he was twenty-one. He was married early in life, to Miss Sarah J. Wright, October 1, 1872. She was born May 27, 1849, at Keokuk, the daughter of M. D. and Mary Ann (Clark)

Wright, of Summitville. Her parents were very early pioneers of Keokuk, where her people have become quite numerous. Mr. Young took charge of a part of Mr. Wright's farm, and was thus engaged for a period of three years. In 1876 Mr. Wright sold out his real estate and the family removed to Rice county, Kansas. Mr. Young located in Van Buren township the following year, where he bought a farm. For some four years he devoted himself to buying and selling the desirable farms of Lee county, then settled on section 8, Des Moines township, where he has since remained. Here he owns a farm of 332 acres, a highly improved and exceedingly valuable place. For twenty-four years he has been a public salesman, and during that time has sold a very large amount of property.

Mr. and Mrs. Young have had born to them four children, three of whom died in infancy. William M., the only one that has survived, married Miss Addie J. Rumbaugh, the daughter of Rev. Alexander Rumbaugh, of Des Moines township. They live on a farm adjoining his father's place, and have two children, Willa J. and David A.

David A. Young has devoted much attention to stockraising, and his reputation as a stockman is not confined to Lee county. He has taken much interest in political affairs since he was a young man, and has done much work in behalf of his friends, though not going into the campaigns as a public speaker. He has attended nearly all the state and county conventions as a delegate since he was twenty-one, and was elected as justice of the peace in 1890, a position he filled four years.

Mr. Young was solicited in 1897 to become a candidate for the State Senate on the Democratic ticket, a compliment rendered his conceded abilities and fine character. He accepted the nomination and was elected. In 1901 he was re-elected, being the first senator ever elected for two full terms in this district. In the General Assembly he has secured the passing of nine bills for the direct benefit of his county. He has always been a Democrat, and is a straightforward and upright man. In him are reflected the characteristic traits of his father, and he worthily sustains an honored name. He is of a fine and sympathetic personality, and is a pleasant and courteous gentleman on every occasion. In religious matters he is connected with the Missionary Baptist church, and well maintains his father's faith. His wife and son are closely associated with him in all the activities of his earnest life, and are also members of the same denomination. The entire family is regarded as one of the most honorable and upright in Lee county, where their name commands respect and admiration.

GEORGE RUMP.

One of the native sons of Lee county, who is deserving of a place in this volume on account of his record as a distinguished citizen and successful business man, is George Rump, of Fort Madison. He was born in Pleasant Ridge township, this county, on

April 19, 1842, and is the son of John G. Rump, who was born in Oldenburg, Germany, December 1, 1801, and of Katherine (Pisch) Rump. The marriage of his parents took place in Pleasant Ridge township, January 27, 1838, the ceremony having been performed by Esquire John Burns, J. P.

John Rump came to America about the year 1835, and entered a claim of government land in Pleasant Ridge. Later, when opportunity offered, he sold this claim, and purchased another tract of land in the same township. It was here that the mother of our subject died on March 23, 1847, and was buried in West Point cemetery. In the family were six children, of whom George Rump was the third, the others being Elizabeth, who died at ten years of age, having been born September 2, 1849; John, who lives at West Point; Mary, wife of William Hamelman, of Kansas City, Kansas; Katherine, who was born March 28, 1847, and died in infancy; and Anna, who also died in infancy. Mr. Rump's father, John G., was remarried July 1, 1847, to Mary Lutmer, since deceased. In politics John G. Rump was a lifelong Democrat, and in his religious connection a member of the Christian church. His death occurred December 6, 1871.

George Rump acquired his schooling during the territorial period of the history of Iowa, principally in a rural public school, but attended for the space of one year the village school of West Point. He has, however, made up for the meagreness of his early educational advantages by a life of intelligent observation combined with reading and a study of public questions. At the age of eighteen years he began the independent work of his life by leaving the home of his youth and securing a position in the City of St. Louis, where he acted as clerk in a grocery store for a twelve month. Returning to West Point, he was employed at manual labor for a few months, and as a result of these various occupations, together with thrift and economy, he was able to accumulate and save about one hundred dollars. With this capital he came to Fort Madison, and established himself, November 1, 1861, at the age of nineteen years, in the dry goods and grocery business at what is now 1436 Fourth street. After successfully operating this enterprise for two years, he formed a partnership with his father-in-law, H. E. Borchers, they combined their stocks of goods and continued the business under the firm style of H. E. Borchers & Company. Mr. Borchers owned the principal interest at the time of his death, which occurred about the 29th of April, 1857. The following year, pending the settlement of the estate, Mr. Rump acted as manager at a salary of fifty dollars per month. He then bought the business, continuing to conduct it at the Front street location until August, 1871, when he removed to 715-17 Second street, and there he remained until 1900, when he disposed of his holdings by sale. When he sold the stock, which then consisted exclusively of dry goods, it was valued at $4,500. He has since been living a retired life, occupying his time with the supervision of his various property interests. He is to some extent interested in real estate, being owner of 240 acres in Washington and Madison townships, all of which he rents.

He also owns residence property on Fifth street, Fort Madison, and a commodious business structure, two and one-half stories in height, on Second street. At 826 Second street he built in 1899, furnishing the plans himself, a magnificent home costing in the neighborhood of $7,000.

As a token of the high esteem in which he is held by his many friends Mr. Rump was elected in the year 1870 to the office of city treasurer of Fort Madison, and was five times re-elected. He has also held the office of director of the public schools, as well as many similar positions of trust and honor. In politics Mr. Rump has always been a member of the Democratic party, believing its principles to be for the greatest good of state and nation. He holds his church membership in St. Joseph's church.

On May 13, 1861, was solemnized by Rev. Father Haetenberger, at Fort Madison, the marriage of George Rump and Miss Mary Engelkur. The date of Mrs. Rump's birth was January 6, 1845, and the place St. Louis, Missouri. To them have been born eight children, all of whom are living. Of there, George H., the eldest, born January 25, 1865, married Miss Lena Schneider, and they live in Fort Madison, where he is in the flour and feed business; Henry W., born January 16, 1868, married Katherine Hesse, and is a member of the Fort Madison firm of Rump & Seamers, grocers; John H., born December 3, 1869, conducts an ice business in Fort Madison; Louis H., born December 4, 1871, and William F., born January 10, 1874, are partners in the local grocery firm of Ellis, Rump & Company; Ella was born February 17, 1876; Clara, October 30, 1878, and Minnie June 18, 1882. Sons and daughters all acquired their education in St. Joseph's school, and in addition the sons received preparation for the active part which they have since taken in the city's affairs at Johnson's Business College.

George Rump has borne no inconsiderable part in the upbuilding of Fort Madison. Two large two-story brick business blocks were erected by him in 1871 at 715-717 Second street, and in 1888 another was added, being No. 719. In the execution of these enterprises he has gained for himself worldly goods and reputation, and has demonstrated anew the truth that most benefits himself who benefits others as well.

THOMAS COLLIER.

One of the leading and best known railroad men of Keokuk is Thomas Collier, now retired and living at his pleasant home at 916 Grand avenue. He was born March 28, 1841, at Lowell, Massachusetts, and there received his education in the public schools. When fifteen years of age he was apprenticed in the machinist's trade at Taunton, that state, but the shops being closed on account of the financial panic of 1857, he decided to avail himself of the opportunities of the West, and at the early age of sixteen he came to Peoria, Illinois, and secured a position as fireman on the Toledo, Peoria & Western Railroad. When but nineteen years of age he was promoted to the position of engineer, which he filled with credit to himself and to the satisfaction of the company until 1868, when he went to New Orleans. There he had charge of a train on the New Orleans, Jackson & Great Northern Railroad, known as the "Jackson route." In 1876 he re-entered the employ of the Toledo, Peoria & Western Railroad Company as an engineer, in which he continued for a period of four years.

Mr. Collier came to Keokuk in 1880, at which time he entered the service of the Missouri, Iowa & Nebraska Railroad Company, now known as the Keokuk & Western. Here he rounded out his railroad career, continuing until December, 1903, when he was compelled on account of an attack of nervous prostration, to relinquish the work. His life as an engineer extended over more than forty years, twenty of which were spent in the passenger service, and while his experience included a number of wrecks, he never sustained a personal injury in an accident.

At New Orleans he was married in 1870 to Miss Margaret Hannon, who died the following year, leaving one daughter, who is a trained nurse and resides at Hammond, Michigan. At Peoria in 1876, he wedded Miss Hettie Teal, and unto them have been born eight sons and daughters, seven of whom survive, as follows: Harry, who is connected with a wholesale grocery business at St. Joseph, Missouri; Lucy, who is a stenographer; Hattie, Thomas, Byron and Wilfred. Mrs. Collier is the daughter of Henry Teal, who is a machinist in the employ of the Toledo, Peoria & Western Railroad Company at Peoria. Two sisters of Mrs. Collier, Ellen and Emma, are also residents of that city.

Mr. Collier is of English ancestry, his parents having come to America from Manchester, England, where the father was a cotton worker. He followed the same occupation in Lowell, Massachusetts. His death occurred at Fall River, Massachusetts. Mr. and Mrs. Collier and family have occupied their present home for about fifteen years. The situation is one of great beauty, overlooking the Mississippi river. They are members of the United Presbyterian church at Keokuk, in which Mr. Collier has acted as trustee for many years. In his political faith he is a Republican, and takes an abiding interest in public questions. Fraternally, he is a member of the Brotherhood of Locomotive Engineers, having, for a long term of years, been an officer in the Keokuk Lodge of that order. He is widely known in railroad circles, and has many friends in Keokuk, who respect him for the upright and honorable course in life and for his force of character.

ATSTIN N. WRIGHT.

Austin N. Wright, who is one of the oldest residents of Lee county, who was born within its limits, is a man well-deserving of a place in the pages of this work, both because of his successful career and because, as one of those who in the nation's time of need went unselfishly to her defense, he has fulfilled the highest duty of a citizen. Mr. Wright was born near Sandusky, Lee county, May 13, 1838, the son of James and Mary (Chenoweth) Wright, both of Indiana. His parents were married in Indiana, came to Lee county in 1837, and bought land in what was known as "the half-breed tract." John Wright, the grandfather, also came at the same time, together with his six sons and two daughters, and bought land in the same tract.

Mr. Wright obtained his first knowledge of books in the public schools of his district, acquiring a very good education. Not less valuable were the lessons learned in the work of the farm, which called for hard and faithful application to duty, as well as the exercise of judgment, foresight and business ability. On his father's farm it was that those qualities were formed which were to make him successful in after life, and there he grew to manhood, remaining until January, 1864, when he enlisted for the service of his country in Company B. of the Twenty-third Iowa Volunteer Infantry, under Captain Walker and Colonel Glasgow. His period of service covered approximately nineteen months, and while Mr. Wright's regiment constituted part of the Western Army and took part in no celebrated campaigns, the spectacular scenes of the combat having by that time shifted to the East, he was called upon to perform much hard and important service. The regiment did duty along the Red river in Texas, Arkansas and Mississippi, and at Mobile, Alabama, played a prominent part in the capture of Spanish Fort.

On March 1, 1868, Mr. Wright was united in marriage with Miss Melissa Colvin, and they have one son and five daughters, as follows: Hattie, a dressmaker; Kathryn, who is a clerk; Minnie, a teacher; Effie, who is employed as a milliner; and Ernest and Blanche, who are still pursuing their education in the schools of Keokuk. Mrs. Colvin is the daughter of William and Catherine (Vanosdall) Colvin, of Kentucky. Her parents were married in their native State of Kentucky, and came to Iowa in 1854, purchasing land near Sandusky, Lee county, where they still live. She has one brother, G. H. Colvin, a farmer near West Point, and three sisters, Amanda, wife of John Boyd, of near Montrose; Sarah, wife of Frank Davis, of Montrose township; and Nancy, wife of Robert Grimes, also of Montrose township, Lee county.

Mr. Wright conducted farming operations on his father's land until 1879, when he bought a farm of his own. Later he sold this, however, and resumed charge of the old home farm, which he continued till the time of his father's death. He then sold his inherited interest, and removed in 1895, to Keokuk, where he purchased residence property at No. 1228 High street and has since lived. Of his father's family three brothers and one sister survive, the others being John T., of California; Samuel B., of Keokuk; and Isabella, wife of F. J. Walker, of Keokuk. Mr. Wright holds membership in the Grand Army of the Republic, an honor which can not be too highly esteemed. He is a man of much force of character, and enjoys the respect and friendship of those who know him well.

JOSEPH A. NUNN.

The family name of Nunn is old in Fort Madison, and is indelibly associated with much that is interesting and significant in her history. Joseph A. Nunn, the subject of this review, was born in Marion county, Indiana, March 12, 1841, and is the son of John A. and Charity (Edgell) Nunn, the former a native of Ohio and the latter of Indiana. John and Charity Nunn were the parents of six children, of whom Joseph A. is the only survivor. Their marriage took place in Indiana. The family removed to Missouri in 1842, and at Sweet Home, Clark county, that state, the father taught school until the spring of the following year, when they came to Des Moines township, Lee county, where a farm was purchased and cultivated for eight years.

Selling the farm in 1851, John A. Nunn removed to Montrose to engage in the mercantile business. Appointed deputy county clerk in 1855, he again changed his location, this time to Fort Madison, where he served as deputy county clerk, deputy sheriff, and when the law establishing the office of superintendent of schools became effective he was elected as the first superintendent of Lee county. He was an educated man, well-fitted for the duties of his position. In addition he was known as an expert penman, having taught penmanship, as well as one term of school, in Indianapolis. At one time he was engaged in mercantile business in Fort Madison, and served a number of terms as mayor and treasurer of the city. Religiously he was a very active member of the Methodist Episcopal church, in which he held offices of trust, and to him usually fell the duty of entertaining visiting celebrities, including Henry Clay Dean, Dr. Thomas, I. P. Teeter, and Frank Evans. He was widely known and universally popular. He was twice remarried after the death of his wife, first to Mrs. Harshey and again to Mrs. Preston. His death occurred in Fort Madison.

Joseph A. Nunn, our subject, began his business career as clerk in a store, after leaving the farm, and conducted a grain business in Fort Madison from 1865 to 1867. He then engaged successfully in real estate business for a time, also acting as special traveling adjuster for a number of insurance companies. In 1876 he was appointed deputy to Sheriff Higgins, of Keokuk, and also acted as deputy during his father's incumbency of the office of sheriff. Then in 1880, in recognition of his high personal character and his valuable services as an officer of the law, he was elected sheriff of Lee county, which office he held for a period of four years. At the expiration of this term he purchased a farm in Washington township, where he resided for three years, but continued traveling, however, in the interest of insurance. In 1888 he returned to Fort Madison, and has made his home in this city continuously since. One of the great difficulties Mr. Nunn has had to overcome in making his own way in the world is ill health, and few would have succeeded in spite of this handicap as thoroughly as he has done. For six years he was compelled to retire altogether from active business, but in 1902 was again able to resume the care of his realty and insurance interests.

At Fort Madison April 18, 1866, Mr. Nunn was united in marriage with Miss Elizabeth McCalmont Espy, of Franklin, Pennsylvania. She was born February 22, 1841, and her lamented death occurred April

26, 1903. Unto Mr. and Mrs. Nunn were born ten children, all of whom are living. They are: John Espy, who is associated with his father in the insurance business and is also assistant county surveyor; Ralph A., who is engaged in insurance work in St. Louis; Mary Luella, a music teacher; Emma Josephine is the wife of Edward Whitcomb, of Fort Madison, and they have four children, Ruth, Fay, Jessie, Luella; Thomas Emmet, who married Lena Inkman, of Fort Madison, and has one child, Ruth Elizabeth, wife of Breton L. Sater, of Henry county, a farmer, is the mother of two children, Helen Marie and Joseph Murace; Charity Edgell, wife of Ralph K. Davis, druggist, of St. Louis; Joseph A., of Fort Madison; Louise, of St. Louis; and Louis B., of Fort Madison.

Mr. Nunn is, in his fraternal relations, a member of Claypoole Lodge, No. 13, Free and Accepted Masons, of Damascus Commandery, Knights Templar, of Keokuk, and is a charter member of Gem City Lodge of Knights of Pythias. In his political life he has always been a loyal supporter of the Democratic party and a firm believer in its basic principles. The family are members of St. Joseph's Catholic church, as was also the deceased wife and mother. The residence is at 1033 Sixth street.

The ambition of Mr. Nunn's earlier years was to become a member of the profession of law, and at one time he pursued a course of study which prepared him for entrance into the law school of the University of Michigan at Ann Arbor, but the failure of his health prevented consummation of the project. He has gone forward, however, with determination to win over all obstacles, and his life has been highly successful in the best senses of the word. He has a large circle of friends who respect him for his energy, loyalty and upright character and admire him for his talents and achievements.

CHARLES N. RABER.

Charles N. Raber, who is now residing on his pleasantly situated farm of 100 acres on section 17, Jackson township, was born November 24, 1857, at Warsaw, Illinois, and is the son of Christian Raber, a native of Baden, Germany, who came with his parents to the United States when five or six years of age and settled in Ohio, where the grandfather, who was a farmer and distiller, spent the remainder of his life. Christian Raber, father of our subject, early came westward to Iowa, and here he learned the trade of coopering and after his marriage removed to Warsaw, Illinois, where Charles N. Raber was born, and where he remained until our subject was about twelve years of age, when he returned to Iowa and for three years managed what is now the White Oak vineyard. This was a very large and important enterprise, and included the making of wine, the vintage of the year 1871 being 71,000 gallons. On relinquishing this employment Mr. Raber's father removed to the Sanford farm north of Hamilton, Illinois, and two years later to the small farm on which he now resides, the location being on the Hilton road near Keokuk. He is now in the sixty-ninth year of his age.

While at his father's home last referred to, Mr. Raber was employed in connection with a dairy, driving a wagon for Mr. Ingersoll and Mr. S. Putnam, and on their removal to California he bought the business, which he conducted for eight years, but at the end of that time, finding the enterprise unprofitable, was obliged to discontinue it, and for a time rented land and engaged in farming. Later, on the return of his father-in-law, Mr. Putman, from California, he again worked for him in the dairy business until February, 1899, when he purchased of Frank Harshman the farm on which he now resides, and here he has since made his home continuously, conducting farming operations to some extent, but on account of ill health sub-renting a portion of his land.

On February 15, 1883, Mr. Raber was united in marriage to Miss Edith Putnam, and to them have been born six children, of whom two died in infancy, and those living are Arthur, employed in a packing house at Omaha, Nebraska; and three daughters, Elcy, Ethel, and Mary, who are members of their father's household. Mrs. Raber and the two oldest daughters are members of the Sugar Creek Christian church, while Mr. Raber is devoted to the cause of right and justice in all their aspects, and has always been a believer in the duty of the citizen to make a study of questions affecting the public and to assist, with whatever ability he may possess, in their solution. He has never aspired to the holding of public office, although at the solicitation of friends he has for two terms faithfully discharged the duties of road supervisor, but in order to perform his part in local government he has been very active in the work of the Republican party, and at the present time holds the important office of chairman of its township committee. He is well known throughout this section, and is esteemed by all who know him for his thoroughly conscientious attitude in all the affairs of life, especially in matters touching the welfare of others.

FREDERICK SCHWITE.

A prominent retired representative of the building interests of Keokuk is Frederick Schwite. Mr. Schwite received a good common-school education in his native land, having been born in Germany. The date of his birth was January 30, 1833, and in 1854 he set out for America, resolved to try his fortune in the New World. He made the trip in a sailing vessel, embarking at Bremen and arriving at New Orleans after a voyage of nine weeks' duration. In the winter of that year he came north by boat on the Mississippi river, and arrived at Keokuk March 1, 1855. Here he worked at his trade as a stonemason, which he had learned in Germany, until he became somewhat acquainted with local conditions, when he began contracting for stone work. Among the principal structures erected by Mr. Schwite are the church edifice of B'Nai Israel, the Ayers building, the Pond Cold-Storage building, a number of other business houses and many residence buildings.

Although successful in his undertakings from the first, when the Civil War began Mr. Schwite abandoned his growing business, and volunteered for the service of his adopted country. Enlisting at Keokuk under Captain Rice, he was drilled here by Colonel Juliet, a French officer, after which he proceeded to St. Louis, where on May 1, 1861, he entered Company H, Fifteenth Missouri Infantry, and served with the Army of the Cumberland for the long period of three years and three months. Among the more noted battles in which he was engaged were those at Pea Ridge, Corinth, Mill Creek, Kentucky; Murphreesboro, Chattanooga, Resaca and Atlanta. During the greater part of the year 1863 he was rendered unfit for duty by illness, having contracted malaria. For about two months he was an inmate of the general field hospital at Stevenson, Alabama, and was also for a time in Louisville, Nashville and Jefferson Barracks hospitals. His term of enlistment expired while he was at Atlanta, and being still incapacitated by illness, he was honorably discharged. At Big Shanty, Georgia, while doing guard duty at night he had the misfortune to fall into a ditch, not being able to see his way in the darkness, and sustained injuries from which he has never recovered. For this cause and in recognition of his faithful services, he receives from the United States government a monthly pension of seventeen dollars.

On leaving the army Mr. Schwite returned to Keokuk, and resumed building and contracting. This calling he pursued with much success until 1900, when on account of the increasing weight of years he decided to retire from active business life. Since that time he has been living in well-earned ease at the home which he has built at 1422 Morgan street.

At Keokuk in 1857, Mr. Schwite married Miss Minnie Mishol, who, like himself, was of German birth. She is now deceased, her death having occurred in 1903, and is buried in the Catholic cemetery of Keokuk. To Mr. and Mrs. Schwite were born five sons and three daughters, as follows: Charles, Frederick, William, Edward, Harry, now deceased; Sarah, Nellie and Kate, who is the wife of William Carrlin, of Keokuk. The family are members of Saint Francis de Sales congregation of the Catholic church.

The parents of Mr. Schwite are both deceased, their demise having occurred in Germany. The father was a contractor and builder. One brother, Charles, is a resident of Keokuk, where he follows the trade of stonemason.

Mr. Schwite is a member of Torrence Post, Grand Army of the Republic, of Keokuk. He has many friends, and is popular for his upright and honorable career and for the generosity and friendliness of his nature.

W. E. HARRISON.

W. E. Harrison, whose intense and well-directed activity has been one of the forceful factors in the industrial life of Fort Madison, is the president of the Fort Madison Chair Company, manager of its works. He was one of the original private firm of four members out of which grew the present organizations. This original firm was composed of Captain J. T. Soule, Dr. J. A. Smith, W. H. Kretsinger and Mr. Harrison, and was in the business of manufacturing farming tools, employing convict labor. It dated from as far back as 1867. In 1876 was effected the incorporation of the Fort Madison Chair Company, and since that date the two branches of the business have been conducted under separate managements. The volume of business conducted by the original concern was quite large, as it employed all the convicts in the Fort Madison prison. In the reorganization of 1876 only Mr. Harrison and Dr. Smith became interested in the chair company, Mr. Kretsinger taking the tool manufacturing business. The present stockholders are W. E. Harrison, James C. Brewster, the estate of Joseph A. Smith, J. H. Kinsley and H. P. Gibbs.

W. E. Harrison was born at Rodney, Mississippi, November 22, 1846, and is the son of E. H. Harrison, a native of New Jersey, who came to Keokuk in 1859, and was engaged in business there as a banker and as a wholesale merchant until his death in 1877. The mother was Marie E. (Lewis) Harrison. She was born in Loudoun county, Virginia, and the date of her death was July, 1894. There were three children—W. E. Harrison, Mrs. J. L. Root, of Keokuk, and L. R. Harrison, of New York city.

Mr. Harrison received his education in a private classical school at Keokuk, and in the State University at Iowa City. May 2, 1877, he was united in marriage at Fort Madison, to Miss Elizabeth Hamilton, who was born in Pittsburg, Pennsylvania, August 4, 1854. Unto them has been born one child, a daughter, Helen Hamilton Harrison, the date of her birth being February 8, 1878. Her education has been conducted at Rockford, Illinois and at Chicago, she being a graduate of Chicago Musical College. Miss Harrison has unusual talent as a violinist, and her ability in this direction has been favorably remarked upon by eminent critics. The family home is at 313 Elm street.

Mr. Harrison was reared in the Unitarian faith. In politics he is a consistent Republican, giving his support to that party in all issues of importance. He comes of old and patriotic ancestry. The founder of the family in America was Richard Harrison, Sr., who was one of the founders of Bradford, Connecticut, in 1644, and his son, Richard, Jr., was one of the founders of Newark, New Jersey. Our subject takes a just pride in the fact that he is a descendant of Lynn Gardner, who commanded the first fort erected on the New England coast, Fort Saybrook. His grandfather, Stephen Harrison, was one of the heroes of our early national life, having been a soldier of the Revolutionary War.

W. E. Harrison is a stockholder in the Lee County Savings Bank, but otherwise he has few interests at present outside his manufacturing business, although in the past he has been connected with other manufacturing interests, and it is almost entirely due to his untiring care and watchfulness that the chair company owes its present proportions. One hundred and fifty men are constantly employed, comprising both free and convict labor, with an output of about forty dozen chairs per day, or an aggregate business of about $100,000 per annum. In terms of carload lots the product of the factory is approximately 150 cars per annum. The company has resident agents in California, commission agents in Missouri, Iowa and Illinois, and salaried salesmen in Kansas, Nebraska and Texas. While acquiring for himself material wealth Mr. Harrison has, in fostering this important industry, done much for Fort Madison, and richly deserves the reputation for ability and strict uprightness, as well as the wide popularity, which he enjoys.

JAY W. FAULKNER.

Especial honor belongs to those who in time of war served the nation's need and in days of peace have contributed by strength of arm and toil of brain to the building up of her prosperity and her proud position among the empires and peoples of the earth. Along these lines runs the life history of the subject of this review. Jay W. Faulkner was born April 3, 1846, at Fort Wayne, Indiana, and there passed his boyhood days and secured his schooling. He is the son of George and Eliza (Blake) Faulkner. The father, a carpenter and joiner, was born at Rochester, New York, and died at Hamilton, Indiana, about the year 1855. The mother was born at Canandaigua, New York, and died in 1894 at Goodland, Indiana. Unto them were born six children, of whom two survive, these being our subject and John Faulkner, of Michigan, a master mechanic in the employ of the Chicago & Lake Huron Railway Company. Two of the brothers lost their lives in war, Henry being killed at Chickamauga, and James, who was a member of the Eighth Iowa Cavalry, dying at Fort Henry, Tennessee.

At the age of twenty years, Mr. Faulkner entered the Pittsburg, Fort Wayne & Chicago railway shops for the purpose of learning the trade of machinist; but this work not proving suited to his tastes, he abandoned it, and became a locomotive fireman for the same company, running between Fort Wayne and Valparaiso. In this capacity he continued for five years, at the end of which time he was promoted to the position of engineer. In 1879 he severed this connection, and engaged with the Santa Fe system as engineer of construction work out of Trinidad, Colorado. After assisting in the construction of 350 miles of track from Trinidad to El Paso, Texas, and Deming, New Mexico, he was assigned to duty as a passenger engineer between Mattoon and Wallace, was later transferred to the Topeka-Nickerson run, and in February, 1887, was sent to the eastern division of the system at Streator, Illinois. Here he did construction work until the road was completed to Chicago, when he took the first passenger train over the division—from Fort Madison to Chicago—on January 1, 1888, and this has been the scene of his labors ever since, he having charge of train No. 7, the Fast Mail, and No. 8, the California and Texas Express.

In his railroading experiences Mr.

Foulkner has met with mishaps, as is the fate of all men of his calling, but no shadow of blame has ever attached to him because of accident. On March 18, 1888, while running train No. 7 out of Chicago, he was shot in the right hand by bandits in an effort to rob his train. In consequence of this encounter it became necessary to amputate two fingers of one of his hands, but he brought the train into Fort Madison on time, and in a personal letter from Superintendent Nixon received thirty days' credit of salary for his heroic action. He acted as engineer for the train conveying President Roosevelt from Chicago to Peoria, and for the character of his services received a letter of commendation from Trainmaster C. L. Short. He also possesses a commendatory letter from Superintendent Nixon for his successful and rapid run of a train bearing the President and board of directors from Chicago to Shopton, Iowa, December 8, 1897. This letter speaks especially of his effective handling of the air brakes.

At the beginning of the Civil War, Jay W. Faulkner, then a mere boy, enlisted at Fort Wayne, September 23, 1862, under Captain Hoy and Colonel Zollinger, and was assigned to the First Brigade, Second Division, of the Twenty-third Army Corps, under the command of General Schofield. He took part in ten general engagements, besides skirmishes. On December 15, 1864, he was wounded by a gunshot, having his right hand crippled, and was discharged on account of the resulting disability May 8, 1865, returning home in September.

In addition to having real estate interests in Indiana, Mr. Faulkner owns a farm of 160 acres in Shawnee county, Kansas, and is a stockholder in the Ideal Farm Implement Company, manufacturers, at Knowlton, Iowa. This company manufactures the Climax Corn Cutter and Shocker, a combination hay rake and loader, and the Eureka Kaffir Corn and Sorghum header, and Mr. Faulkner is the inventor of these machines, having worked out his plans, made tests in the fields, secured the patents and organized the company with a capitalization of $50,-000 while at the same time making his regular runs as a passenger engineer.

Mr. Faulkner is a member of the Brotherhood of Trainmen, and has similar relations with the Improved Order of Red Men. In politics he is a Republican, having been a member of that party all his life. Indeed, his first vote, at or near Decatur, Alabama, when he was a member of the Union army, was cast for Abraham Lincoln before he attained his majority. He was, in fact, but eighteen years of age. This early loyalty to principles in which he believed has been characteristic of him in all the relations of life. His ability and talents have brought him success, and his just and genial disposition have brought him friends and a wide circle of acquaintance and popularity. He is a citizen of whom Fort Madison may well be proud.

JOHN LEISY.

John Leisy, the Keokuk representative of the Leisy Brewing Company, of Peoria, Illinois, of which he is a partner, was born in this city, March 17, 1862, his parents being John and Christina (Showalter) Leisy. The father was born in Germany, July 4, 1835, and came to America in the year 1856, settling at Franklin Prairie, Lee county, Iowa, where he engaged in farming for one or two years. He then removed to Keokuk and forming a partnership, established a brewery conducted under the name of Baehr & Leisy Brothers, his brother Isaac being also interested in the business. There were several brothers of the family who came to the United States, most of them after John Leisy's arrival, namely: Abraham, Jacob, August, Isaac, Rudolph and Henry. Isaac Leisy afterward became the proprietor of an extensive brewery in Cleveland, Ohio, while Abraham and Jacob became residents of Lee county, Iowa, and Abraham is yet living near Dover, this state. Rudolph, Henry and August Leisy went to Nebraska and were stock dealers and bankers, of Wisner.

Unto John and Christina (Showalter) Leisy were born four sons and a daughter: Gustav, Edward, John, Lena, wife of Jacob Schwellbacher, of Peoria. The father, John Leisy, Sr., died in 1873, and following his demise his brother, Randolph, managed the business in Keokuk. Gustav, Edward and John Leisy, of this review, entered the brewery as soon as old enough, learned the business in every detail, and as soon as able took charge of the plant, which they conducted with success until the Prohibition law went into effect, when the brewery was closed down. The brothers went to Peoria, Illinois, in June, 1884, and there established a large brewing plant under the name of the Leisy Brewing Company, and since the 4th of July of that year John Leisy has had charge of the distributing depot at Keokuk. He is a partner with his brothers in the business, which has become a profitable enterprise, with a large annual output and profitable sales.

Mr. Leisy was married October 8, 1901, to Margaret Weisemann, a daughter of Charles and Anna Weisemann.

JACOB C. McCABE.

Jacob McCabe, a scion of old and honored pioneer stock of Iowa, and now a leading resident of West Point township, Lee county, was born September 13, 1836, in Preble county, Ohio, and is the grandson of Warren McCabe, of Sussex county, Delaware, who was one of the pioneers of Preble county and successfully conducted a farm there at an early day, his death occurring in the seventy-fifth year of his age. The father of Mr. McCabe was Arthur McCabe, who was born in Sussex county, Delaware, August 18, 1810, and when fifteen years of age removed with his parents to Eaton, Preble county, Ohio, remaining at the parental home until twenty-one years of age, when he went to Lebanon, Ohio, where he engaged in the manufacture of fanning mills and in October, 1835, married Miss Susan Christ, daughter of Jacob Christ, of Stanton, Augusta county, Ohio. The mother of our

JACOB C. McCABE AND FAMILY

subject was born July 16, 1817, and removed with her mother, whose maiden name was Mowery, to Preble county, where she was married to Mr. McCabe. They soon after their marriage purchased a small farm near Eaton, on which they resided until the autumn of 1836, when, deciding to imitate the example of their forefathers, they came westward to cast their fortunes in new and undeveloped territory, settling in West Point township, Lee county, Iowa, and here Mr. McCabe passed the remainder of his life as a hard-working farmer, in which vocation he was very successful, and accumulated 400 acres of very fine agricultural lands. He and his wife were connected with the Methodist Episcopal denomination, being members of the Pitman Chapel congregation, of which he was one of the trustees, and whose present place of worship he helped to build. Both lie buried in the cemetery of the chapel, and their memory is yet recalled by the survivors of the generation that followed them, for they were famous for their open-handed hospitality, their generous support of all good causes and their lofty Christian character.

Jacob C. McCabe gained his early knowledge of books in the public schools of West Point township, an education which he has since very materially increased by extensive reading and observation ,and while still quite young began to assist his father in the work of the farm, which was in those days a far more difficult and arduous occupation than at the present time, for the task which is now easily performed in a few hours by highly perfected machinery, then required long days of laborous toil; the mower, binder, thresher and hay-loader, as well as many other modern conveniences, were uninvented, and the sickle, the scythe, the cradle, the flail and the walking plow were the main implements of husbandry. And in this hard school Mr. McCabe learned the lessons which fitted him for his later success in life, continuing to employ himself on his father's farm until his twenty-third year, when he was united in marriage to Miss Mary Ann Edwards, a native of Ohio and daughter of Joseph Edwards. Mr. Edwards was born in the State of New York, and early removed to the vicinity of Lebanon, Warren county, Ohio, where his boyhood was passed, and where he married Miss Huldah Marie Hathaway on November 4, 1823, and they continued to reside in Ohio until 1854, when they removed to Iowa, locating in West Point township. Here they made their home until 1875, and then retired from active life and removed to Fort Madison, where he spent the remaining years of his life. Mr. Edwards attained the advanced age of seventy-three years and three months. Mrs. Edwards was a native of New Jersey, the date of her birth being January 2, 1802, and died in Missouri at the home of her granddaughter.

To Mr. and Mrs. McCabe have been born one son and two daughters, as follows: Theodora, who died at the age of six years; Arthur, who resides upon his father's farm, of which he has the management, married J.; Hulda, wife of Hervey Hazen, son of Hon. J. B. Hazen, ex-representative of Lee county, resides in Pleasant Ridge township, Lee county, and has three children, Arthur, Ruby Pearl, and Harry. After his marriage Mr. McCabe purchased a small farm of eighty acres, and by industry, care, frugality and keen business foresight and the exercise of sound practical judgment has added to the original purchase until he now owns 267 acres comprising some of the finest farm land in Lee county, and while thêre were almost no buildings on the land when he became its proprietor, he has erected a large and substantial dwelling house, commodious barns, and other buildings, and has introduced modern improvements in every branch of the business. The land is now devoted to general farming and stock raising, and is in charge of Mr. McCabe's son, to whom it is rented, while he himself lives retired from active life in the enjoyment of social intercourse with friends and neighbors. He continues to take a deep interest in public affairs, and while he has never cared to hold public office, he has given much attention to political questions, being active in the work of the Republican party. He has also displayed constant readiness throughout his long and useful life to aid all charitable and philanthropic movements, and in fact has contributed generously of his means and personal services to every project calculated to advance the moral and spiritual condition of mankind, and he and Mrs. McCabe are faithful members of Pitman Chapel congregation of the Methodist church, of which he is a trustee, while both are widely known in Lee county as people of the most exemplary Christian character, and have a host of friends who hold them in respect and affection.

WILLIAM SCOTT HAMILTON.

In all the various activities of modern life no function is more important to society than that performed by the man who holds and directs the threads of the complicated relations which bind its members one to another—in a word, who studies and interprets its laws. For those who elect to serve their fellowmen in this capacity, bright rewards are waiting. This truth is finely and adequately exemplified in the life and career of one of the native sons of Lee county.

Mr. Hamilton was born on a farm near Fort Madison, this county, his natal day being February 2, 1857, and is the son of John Scott and Sarah (Miller) Hamilton, who were pioneers and people of prominence and standing in the community. The father was a native of Pittsburg, Pennsylvania, and it was in that city that he received his education, and later took up the study of law and was admitted to practice in the courts. Although a man of great intellectual gifts, he was willing to renounce the prospect of honors which he knew awaited him, in the cause of patriotism, and at the beginning of the Mexican War he tendered his services to the nation. At the close of the conflict he married Miss Sarah Miller, and continued to reside in Pittsburg until 1851, when they removed to this county. Here he was one of the leading practitioners of Fort Madison and a prominent member of the Democratic party of his state, having been a member of the state legislature at the time of his death. His death, the circumstances of which were directly connected with his public activities, was the result of an accident, and was caused by the explosion of a cannon used in celebrating the election of President Buchanan, who was a personal friend of Mr. Hamilton's. The death of Sarah Miller Hamilton occurred in 1903. Both were members of the Presbyterian church, and Mr. Hamilton was of the Scotch-Irish stock which has given to our nation so many of its most highly useful and distinguished men.

William Scott Hamilton received his preliminary education in the public schools of Fort Madison, and later continued his training at Knox College and at Amherst College, having been graduated from the latter institution with the class of '76. During his college life he was prominent in athletics, especially in gymnasium work, and took part in one of the first regattas, that of 1874, the event having been inaugurated only in 1872. His fraternity membership is in the Society of Delta Kappa Epsilon, and also Phi Delta Theta, being one of the few men in the country who is a member of two Greek letter societies. During the year following his graduation from college he acted as principal of the high school of Fort Madison, and the two succeeding years were spent in European travel. On his return to America he began the study of law with John Scott Ferguson, a prominent attorney of Pittsburg, Pennsylvania, and was there admitted to the bar in 1880. In 1883 he located in Lincoln, Nebraska, and during the fifteen years of his residence at that place succeeded, by virtue of strict attention to his chosen work and by the exercise of natural talents of an unusual order, in securing one of the largest and most profitable clienteles in the city. It was in 1898 that he returned to Fort Madison, the home of his youth, and here he immediately assumed an extensive practice. His brother, J. D. M. Hamilton, having received appointment to the position of claims attorney for the Atchison, Topeka & Santa Fe Railway Company, Mr. Hamilton formed a partnership with him, and this connection was maintained until the removal of the former to Topeka, Kansas.

After the dissolution of the partnership with his brother, Mr. Hamilton continued his work alone in Fort Madison, with his usual success. He is at the present time attorney for the Atchison, Topeka & Santa Fe Railway Company, and, exclusive of the duties of his official position, the volume of his legal business is among the largest in the county. The enviable nature of his standing here is reflected in the fact that he is president of the Fort Madison Bar Association. Since returning to Lee county he has confined his activities to strictly professional lines, but while a resident of Lincoln he sustained quite a marked degree of prominence in the politics of the city, acting with the Republican party, serving his ward as its representative in the city council and being elected to the office of city attorney. As chairman of the Republican congressional and county central committees he was, of necessity and by force of his decided opinions in matters of politics, largely instrumental in shaping and determining the policy of the party in that section.

Fraternally Mr. Hamilton became a member of the Masonic order in Lodge No.

54, at Lincoln, Nebraska, and now holds his membership in Claypoole Lodge of the order at Fort Madison. At Lincoln he was also a member of the Knights of Pythias, was Chancellor Commander of his lodge, and Grand Chancellor of the State of Nebraska.

In February, 1878, Mr. Hamilton was united in marriage with Miss Belle V. Casey, daughter of the late Judge J. M. Casey, a sketch of whose life and genealogy appears on another page. To them have been born three sons and two daughters, as follows: Ruth, wife of H. D. Everingham, of Fort Madison; J. M. Casey, now a member of the Iowa State University; John Scott, who is a graduate of Fort Madison high school; Sabert, now in high school; and Sarah. The family occupies a beautiful home on Sixth street. Our subject is an attendant and supporter of the Baptist church, of which Mrs. Hamilton is a member.

William Scott Hamilton is a broad-minded man, honorable and honored, and in every relation of life, political, social and professional, merits the high regard which he uniformly receives, and is thoroughly deserving of that success which has always attended his efforts.

ROBERT H. HART.

Robert H. Hart, overseer of the poor farm of Lee county, Iowa, was born in 1865, near the City of Springfield, Sangamon county, Illinois, and when thirteen years of age came with his parents to Lee county, where he received his education in the common schools, and grew to manhood in the practice of industry and devotion to the task at hand. He is the son of Samuel and Penina J. (Neece) Hart, both natives of Sangamon county, and they made their home in Keokuk with the father, who was a school teacher, until his death, in 1885. The mother, who is still living, is now a resident of Hamilton, Illinois, and has been remarried, her second husband being C. W. Self. The family was composed of five children, of whom three are now living, the two besides our subject being Curtis M., of Summitville, Iowa, and Otis, of Hamilton, Illinois.

Mr. Hart was employed as a laborer all his active life until being appointed to his present important position, and since the age of seventeen has been engaged in the work of the poor farm in various capacities, with the exception of two or three years spent in other work. For a time he lived in Keokuk, where he was foreman of the Rees-Sansone Bag Factory, in which position he achieved considerable success and demontrated himself to be the possessor of unusual executive ability and talent for the management of large affairs. His connection with the Lee county poor farm dates from 1883, when he entered its service as a farm hand under the administration of Overseer Avis Miles, and later he became an attendant in the insane ward, while for two years he acted as cook. On April 1, 1904, he was appointed to the office of overseer on the retirement of Frederick Korschgen, who had filled the position for the previous eighteen years, and who recommended the appointment of Mr. Hart as being eminently fitted for the many arduous and complex duties involved in the management of this great institution, and as meriting promotion by reason of his long, faithful and highly efficient service in other capacities.

On January 28, 1886, Mr. Hart was united in marriage to Miss Hannah Isabel Laurinson, who was born in Lee county, the daughter of William and Melissa (Phillips) Laurinson, the former of whom, her father having died when she was five years of age, and the mother having since twice remarried, first to H. H. Thompson, and subsequent to his death to J. W. Wiley, with whom she now resides, in Oregon. To Mr. and Mrs. Hart have been born two children, a son, Sherman E., and a daughter, Hazel H.

Mr. Hart is a very prominent member of the Democratic party in Lee county, and a loyal supporter of its chosen leaders and zealous worker in its ranks, having served as delegate to county and state conventions for the past ten years, and having, while a resident of Montrose township, acted for three years as chairman of the township committee, performing in this capacity much valuable work for his party. Fraternally he has extensive connections, being a Master Mason of Lodge, No. 136, of Montrose, a member of Keokuk Lodge, No. 13, Independent Order of Odd Fellows, and of Camp, No. 4594, Modern Woodmen of America, of Summitville, of which he is Camp Banker; and of the Keokuk Lodge of the Knights and Ladies of Security.

In the insane ward of the Lee county poor farm under Mr. Hart's charge are three male and sixteen female patients, while for the remainder of the institution the proportions are thirty-eight and twenty-three, male and female respectively, a total of eighty inmates. The farm, which contains 250 acres, has been substantially improved during the last few months, the buildings and fences thoroughly repaired and the external appearance of the farm much altered for the better in many respects. Mr. Hart is doing excellent work and giving splendid service as overseer, and will doubtless, by reason of his ability and his familiarity with the farm, be retained for a long term of years. He is ably assisted by his wife in caring for the unfortunates who come under his charge, and their mutual efforts promise to elevate the institution to a standard of efficiency that will reflect credit upon themselves and upon the public spirit of the citizens to whom it owes its support.

THOMAS KENNEDY.

Thomas Kennedy, who is now residing on his highly improved farm of 160 acres on section 7, Jackson township, Lee county, was born June 6, 1849, in Birmingham, Pennsylvania, the son of Edward and Elizabeth (Linnihan) Kennedy. Both parents were natives of Ireland, the father having been born in County Tipperary, emigrating thence to the Keystone state, where his marriage was celebrated, coming west in 1852 and locating temporarily in Lee county, and after a six months' residence here removing to Clark county, Missouri. Although a carpenter by trade, he engaged in farming in Clark county, where he purchased a tract of 640 acres of land, of which, however, he later sold all except 120 acres, on which he lived in the successful pursuit of his vocation until his death, which occurred in 1865. His wife survived him many years, the date of her demise being 1889. To them were born five sons and daughters, as follows: John, who is now a resident of Montana; James, who occupies the home farm in Clark county, Missouri; Thomas, our subject; Ellen, deceased; Mary, the wife of John Clark, of Clark county, Missouri.

In Clark county, Missouri, our subject received his early education in the public schools, and grew to manhood's estate in the practice of the virtues imposed by the necessity of independent effort, for he was but fifteen years of age when the death of his father deprived the family of its head and left him as the main protector and support of its younger members. He met the duties thus cast upon his youthful shoulders with that ability and fortitude which have marked his whole career, applying himself to the task before him with energy, assiduity and careful, considerate judgment, and achieving a success of which any man might well be proud. For twelve years he devoted himself to the care of the family, remaining at home until his twenty-seventh year, and it was in 1877 that he came to Lee county, where for the first two years he cultivated rented land and at the end of that time purchased his present large farm, on which he has since resided continuously. Here he has introduced many improvements, has brought the land to a high state of productivity, and has established a pleasant home in which he enjoys the fruits of his long life of worthy and honorable toil, having erected a substantial and handsome residence in 1898. He successfully carries on farming according to accepted modern theories, and makes a specialty of raising stock for the general market.

At St. Peter's church, Keokuk, November 19, 1877, Mr. Kennedy was united in marriage to Mrs. Kate Gorman, widow of John Gorman, who was born in Ireland, coming to Keokuk August 19, 1869, and was for a time employed as an engineer on the Rock Island Railway. At Santiago, California, whither he had gone for the benefit of his health, Mr. Gorman died December 15, 1874, survived by one son and one daughter, the elder being Mary, now the wife of Edward Bevering, of Keokuk, and she has four children, Mary, Edward, Gorman and Margaret. John, the son, is now engaged in railroad work in California, and is a veteran of the Spanish-American War, having served as a soldier in the Philippine Islands as a member of the First Regiment of Idaho Volunteer Infantry. Mrs. Kennedy was born at Zanesville, Ohio, December 26, 1846, and removed with her parents to Clark county, Missouri, in 1856. She is the daughter of Peter and Ann (Riley) McGuire, who were married in the city of New York, whither the father had emigrated from his native country of Ireland, and the deaths of both parents occurred in Clark county, where they had always made their home since coming to the West. To Mr. and Mrs. Kennedy have been born six children, Edward Paul, Joseph T., Maude Ann, Vincent, Grace Catherine and Alice, and all the members of the family are members of St. Peter's Catholic church of Keokuk.

All his life Mr. Kennedy has shown himself the possessor of a civic virtue which is especially valuable in a country enjoying a republican form of government, namely, public spirit, and he has ever displayed a lively interest in all matters affecting the welfare of the communities in which he has resided, taking part in political action as a member of the Democratic party and frequently serving that organization as delegate to the county conventions. In Lee county he has been elected to the offices of road supervisor and school director, and in Clark county, Misosuri, he served a period of eight years as road overseer and four years as constable, exhibiting in these various positions the same attention and faithfulness to duty which have made him successful in private life and which have won him the good opinion of his acquaintances, neighbors and friends.

WILLIAM SKINNER.

Through a long term of years William Skinner was a resident of Lee county, and was classed with the leading agriculturists of this portion of the state. He had to enter business life handicapped to some extent by an over-generous temperament which often led him to sacrifice his own material interests to those of his friends, and yet he achieved a success that many might envy. He had the force of character, the strong purpose and the laudable ambition that enabled him to win prosperity, and, moreover, his life was characterized by unfaltering honesty and by unremitting loyalty to duty, so that his name became honored and respected by all who knew him. His life record covered almost ninety years, and he left behind him a name and a memory that are cherished and revered.

Mr. Skinner, who was the son of David Duncan Skinner, was born April 5, 1795, in Franklin county, Pennsylvania, and there he was reared in the work of the farm, which occupation he followed throughout his life with eminent success, and also received a limited education by attending for a short time the subscription schools which were then in vogue. But although this was the whole extent of his formal schooling, his remarkable mental acuteness and the broad quality of his understanding, together with his incessant desire for knowledge and self-development, led him to become a great reader and a deep student of affairs and to acquire a vast and accurate store of information, which rendered him a man of mark and distinction in any society. It was amid the environments of his native state that his mind expanded to its full proportions, for he remained in Pennsylvania until his forty-ninth year, and there he began his active career, and there also he wedded Miss Margaret Wilson, of which union were born two sons and two daughters, these being Anne, Harriet, Wilson and Daniel.

The month of March, 1839, witnessed the arrival of Mr. Skinner in Lee county, and here he entered a great deal of land from the government, as well as purchasing a number of claims, so that at one time he owned 500 acres of rich farming lands; but through acting as security for numerous friends, he lost the greater part of his extensive real estate holdings, although at his death he was the owner of a very fine farm. Mr. Skinner was married twice, he being, after the death of his first wife, united with Miss Eleonora Farree, daughter of Cornelius Faree, and they became the parents of six children, as follows: Isabelle and Mary, now deceased, and Sarah, Susan, Josephine and John. Mr. and Mrs. Skinner traveled life's journey together most happily for many years, but on February 14, 1885, the hand of death removed him from the sphere of mortal existence, and she did not long survive him, her own demise occurring January 11, 1888. The husband was of Scotch and English parentage, while the wife was of French and German extraction, and was a native of Hagerstown, Maryland, where she was born July 25, 1812, and whence after the death of her father she removed to Ohio, where she met and married Mr. Skinner. She was a woman of character and pleasing personality, and was beloved and respected by many friends in the communities in which her life was passed. At his death our subject left to his daughter, Susan, 144 acres of the original "homestead" tract, on which she still resides, and which she personally manages and superintends. Miss Skinner was born on the farm on which she has ever since made her home, and was educated in the public schools, and at the old academy at Fort Madison, after which, for about twelve years, she followed the profession of teaching, being highly successful and taking high rank in that pursuit. She not only possesses education, culture and unusual business ability, but is rich in those social qualities which win friendship and high regard.

His agricultural interests Mr. Skinner entrusted largely to the care of a superintendent, his own time being given principally to public affairs, and he was a very active and influential member of the Democratic party, in whose principles he thoroughly believed and whose chosen leaders he always supported with great ability and unfailing consistency. A man of strong mentality, vast information and ever true to his convictions, he never hesitated in the expression of his real views on any subject of general importance, and never wavered in their support, and it has been said of him that in the many political discussions in which he took part, he was always prepared with a winning defence, and that his undisputed leadership among men was in its fundamentals an intellectual one. He also occupies a prominent position in the affairs of the Masonic Order, of which he was a member of long standing, and according to the sublime morality of its teachings he regulated his life, for his character was one of exalted honor, honesty and the strictest integrity in all its phases. By his death Lee county lost one of its most honored pioneers and distinguished citizens and one whose memory is universally held in esteem, but is dearest of all to the survivors of his own family and to the daughter who gave her life to his care, for these know by intimate personal association all the wealth, the strength and the beauty of his character.

HARVEY ALEXANDER SKYLES.

A worthy representative of one of the hardy pioneer families and of the more progressive agricultural element of Lee county, is Harvey A. Skyles, who is now serving his third consecutive term as trustee of Jefferson township. Mr. Skyles is a native son of the county, his birth having occurred in Jefferson township, November 24, 1860, and is the son of Thomas and Elizabeth (Conlee) Skyles. His father, Thomas Skyles, who is at the present time the oldest living resident of this township, was born in Greene county, Illinois, and came to this locality with his parents in 1836, when but three years of age. Here he has passed his life as a successful farmer, and has been honored by election to the various township offices, including that of trustee. In matters of politics he is a lifelong Democrat, and his loyalty and ability have been of material benefit and assistance to his party. The grandfather, Benjamin Skyles, was born in August, 1810, and died in 1901, at the age of ninety-one years, his funeral taking place on Christmas day. The mother of our subject was born near Mammoth Cave, Kentucky, a daughter of Reuben Conlee, who came to Iowa in 1836, and settled in Jefferson township in 1840. He became a member of the first state legislature of Iowa, and his death occurred in Iowa City during its first session.

Engaged in the work of his father's farm, Harvey A. Skyles grew to manhood amid surroundings well fitted to form and impart those strong, self-reliant and energetic traits of character which have since made him successful and respected. Meanwhile he was acquiring in the public schools of his township a good and thoroughly practical education, and this he has supplemented by a life of intelligent observation and reading. On March 17, 1897, he was united in marriage to Miss Letha Stewart, daughter of Francis Stewart, a well-known pioneer of Jefferson township. Immediately after his marriage Mr. Skyles purchased 152 acres of good land near Veile, and there he has since been successfully engaged in the business of farming. He also gives much time to dealing in farm produce, buying and shipping for the general market, and by the exercise of judgment, foresight and careful calculation, has by this means secured very gratifying financial rewards.

Mr. Skyles has on all occasions manifested a very progressive tendency, and has never failed to support any proper project for the material and moral advancement of the community in which he lives. He was one of the organizers of the Veile Telephone Company, and on the first election of officers was made president and general manager and bore an active share in the installation of the line and system. In his fraternal connection he is a member of the Modern Woodmen of America, and politically he is a firm believer in the principles advocated by the Democratic party and a stanch supporter of its chosen leaders, having in addition served his party as delegate to various important conventions. He enjoys a high degree of popularity, and has received a number of public trusts, including the offices of school director and road supervisor, and in 1898 was elected trustee of Jefferson township. Having fulfilled the duties of this important position with great credit and to the public satisfaction, he has been twice re-elected.

Mr. and Mrs. Skyles are active members of the Methodist Protestant church, and bear a valued part in the social life of the community. They have two children, Vida and Verna. The subject of this review is one of the leading younger men of his township, and has many friends throughout Lee county who recognize his ability and predict for him a future of usefulness and honor.

REV. CHARLES HANCOCK, M. D.

Rev. Charles Hancock, M. D., a widely known and respected citizen of Lee county, Iowa, and at the present time a resident of the village of Denmark, was born in Worcester county, Massachusetts, April 11, 1833, the son of Levi and Fanny (Thompson) Hancock, both natives of the Bay state, where they passed their lives and whence they passed to that better life beyond. He received his academic education in the state of his birth, and later took up the study of medicine at the University of Michigan, Ann Arbor, from which institution he was graduated with the degree of Doctor of Medicine, in March, 1858, but did not, however, engage in practice at that time, having decided to devote at least part of his life to the Christian ministry, for which he possessed many natural qualifications, and in which, as the event proved, he was destined to accomplish a highly useful work. With that object in view he next entered the Chicago Theological Seminary, where he pursued a three years' course of study, and was graduated in 1861 with a magnificent equipment for the task which he had mapped out for his future endeavors. During the seven years immediately succeeding he was engaged in the work of ministry in the State of Illinois, with the exception of an interim of one and a half years which he spent among the Union soldiers in various parts of the South as a member of the Christian commission.

It was in the year 1868 that Rev. Hancock removed to Iowa, and in this state he continued in his ministerial labors until 1881, which date marks the beginning of his residence in Denmark, Lee county. He then took a course in Keokuk Medical College in order to recall the results of his earlier researches in the same field, and in a short time built up a large and profitable practice in Denmark and vicinity, remaining an active member of the profession until

1903, when he availed himself of the prerogative of long and conscientious service and retired.

In the spring of 1867 Rev. Hancock was united in bonds of holy matrimony with Mrs. Mary E. (Green) Bonney, who was born in Boston, Massachusetts, where she became the adopted daughter of Isaac Field and wife, and with them came to Iowa in 1838, and settled upon the property on which she and the Doctor now reside. Deacon Field was a prominent business man of Boston, but came to the West on account of his health, and here purchased a great deal of land at an early day, which, however, he afterward sold, and also built the large and fine brick dwelling-house which is now the residence of Dr. and Mrs. Hancock. He was one of the original movers in the founding of Denmark Academy, to which he gave generously of money and personal services, an active and constant worker in the Congregational church, whose present place of worship he helped to build, and in which he for many years officiated as a deacon. Both himself and his wife were earnest, faithful Christians, and although they had no sons or daughters of their own, they reared a number of orphaned girls, giving them the benefits of education and sound religious and domestic training. Mr. Field attained to the age of eighty-four years, at the end of which he was laid at rest beside his wife in Denmark cemetery, and the influence for good which they exercised while on earth is potent still, while their memories are lovingly enshrined in many hearts.

Mrs. Hancock's first husband was Jones Bonney, for whom the Grand Army of the Republic Post, at Denmark, is named, and who was the first soldier from Denmark to meet death in the Civil War. After his death his widow entered the hospital service as a nurse, and went to the front, doing valuable and self-sacrificing work in both Kentucky and Arkansas; and the rare character of her devotion is shown in the fact that she was the only woman to enter that service from this section of the county, if not from a much greater territory.

Rev. Hancock has ever given much thought and study to affairs of public interest, and since attaining his majority has been a member of the Republican party, having cast his first ballot for Abraham Lincoln for president of the United States. Since coming to Denmark he has borne a prominent part in the affairs of the community, having for twelve years held the office of clerk of Denmark township and acted as township health officer for a number of years, while in the Congregational church, of which both he and Mrs. Hancock are members, he has been a deacon for more than eighteen years, and superintendent of the Sunday school for more than twenty years, and is the treasurer of Denmark Academy, a member of its board of trustees, and a member of the executive committee and of the committee of inspection. Thus his activities bear no taint of self-seeking, but have all been calculated to benefit the community which claims his citizenship and for the good of humanity at large. He may well look back over a life given to the arduous labors of two of the most noble and altruistic professions known among men, and trace with satisfaction the record of his life. Successful in all he has attempted, having done much for the general welfare, widely known, universally respected, enjoying the friendship of many and the affection of those who know him best, the ideal conditions of his later years are equaled only by the sterling virtues of his character. The names of Rev. and Mrs. Hancock are precious to many, for theirs have been careers beautiful in service and sacrifices, rich with lessons for coming generations, and many will trace fondly this unassuming chronicle of their lives, the rubric of their years.

JAMES X. WILSON.

For more than seventy years the Wilson family has been associated with the annals of Lee county, Iowa, and during that long period its record has been an honorable one. Its various members have been noted for their industry and integrity; and while these characteristics have given them standing in the business circles of the community, their kindly disposition and general good fellowship have made and retained for them a host of friends. Men can not live the friendly life without finding friends; and those who live neighbors, find neighbors everywhere. "We see what we are." The Wilsons have been good neighbors, kind friends and honorable men for long years, and they have delighted in the friends they found and the neighbors that abounded. While these principles are true of all, they seem especially illustrated in the career of the Wilson whose name heads this article.

James X. Wilson, son of Thomas and Mary Gilkey (Justice) Wilson, was born on the farm where he is now living, February 13, 1847. His education was secured in the local schools, and he was reared a farmer. In politics he was a Democrat, and at one time served as trustee. In religion he is a member of the Methodist Episcopal church, and has led a consistent Christian life.

Mr. Wilson was married October 7, 1870, to Miss Hannah Elizabeth, daughter of Granville and Adaline (Langford) Arnold, a union that has proved in every way happy and fortunate. It has been blessed by the birth of four children: Clayborn, Elmus, Rhoda Elzira, Sabert C. and Susan, all of whom are now living. Mrs. Wilson died October 8, 1899, and Mr. Wilson was married again, February 24, 1904, when Esther Susanna Cogburn became his wife. She is a daughter of Abner and Elizabeth (Byers) Cogburn, and the widow of James Henry Mason, by whom she had two children: Alonzo, who died when seventeen months old, and Laura Isabelle.

Thomas Wilson, the father of James X., came to Lee county from Hancock county, Illinois, in 1833, having previously lived in Missouri. Mr. Wilson secured a quarter section of land by government entry, and proceeded to improve it as a farm home. Hughey Wilson, the father of Thomas, also took up land, and the entire tract of land as secured by father and son is now held by the two Wilsons, James X. and Thomas Valentine, both of whom are hard-working and industrious farmers. Thomas Wilson was born in Tennessee, but spent the most of his earlier years in the State of Kentucky, where he received his education. When a young man he came to Illinois, and then removed to Missouri, whence he soon returned to Illinois, and settled in Lee county, in 1833, as already noted. He had a brother-in-law, Richard Dunn, who served in the War of the Revolution.

The first Mrs. James X. Wilson was born in Clark county, Missouri, December 20, 1821, and died October 8, 1899. Granville Arnold and Adaline Langford were married June 15, 1848. She died September 3, 1857. Mr. Arnold was again married to Susan Jane Thompson, March 15, 1860. He was born December, 1821, and she October 16, 1831. Their children were as follows: Hannah Elizabeth, born June 24, 1849; Georgia, January 1, 1851; Benjamin Langford Arnold, February 7, 1853; Calvin Elmer Arnold, September 28, 1855; Mary Alice, January 16, 1861; William Andrew, August 22, 1862; Emma Louise, August 20, 1864; Sarah Ida, March 3, 1867, and Granville Lewis, February 19, 1873.

Mrs. J. X. Wilson was born in Knox county, Missouri, June 9, 1864. The father was born in Morgan county, Illinois (being the first white child born in that county, fifteen miles from Jacksonville), May 8, 1819. He died December 7, 1889. The mother was born August 17, 1826, and died April 24, 1867. To this couple were born six children: Sarah Jane, Margaret Arseneth, Harold Byers, Armina Drusella, Esther Susanna and John Nathan. Mrs. Wilson was first married and became the mother of two children: Laura Isabelle, who is now Mrs. Amber Smith, was born July 12, 1886, and Alonzo Abner, born November 17, 1888, died April 30, 1889.

Hugh Wilson, grandfather of this subject, was a native of Kentucky, and married Susanna Skyles Schuyler, and their children are as follows: Salley, born November 7, 1801; Elizabeth, born April 11, 1804; John, born November 2, 1806; George, born July 22, 1809; William, born August 17, 1811; Thomas, born April 15, 1814; James, born September 4, 1816, and Polly, born about 1818.

WILLIAM A. ROSS.

That America, and especially that portion of it known as the West, is synonymous with opportunity, finds once more an illustration in the career of William A. Ross, who is at the present time occupying the position of county recorder of Lee county, Iowa, with offices at Fort Madison. Coming to the United States from a foreign land, without financial resources and deprived from the first of all possibility of aid or encouragement from family or kindred, he has by care, industry, energy and strict integrity and uprightness in all relations of life achieved for himself an honorable place in the community of which he is a valuable and valued member. Mr. Ross was born in County Antrim, Ireland, his natal day being October 4, 1843, and is the son of John and Elizabeth Ross, who, with their son and one daughter, sailed from Belfast, Ireland, March 2, 1853, and after a voyage of eight weeks landed at New Orleans, May 2. In the latter city all the members of the family were overtaken by that dread scourge of tropical and semi-tropical climates known as yellow fever, and in the autumn of that year Mr. Ross found himself bereaved of father, mother and sister, he himself being the only survivor of that fatal visitation.

Reduced by this terrible calamity to the necessity of self-support at the age of only ten years, the native strength and resolute quality of his character were his only capital. Accepting, however, the lessons of adversity, he struck out boldly for more distant regions, determined to make misfortune the means of a more perfect development of his natural powers. Recovering from his illness he came up the Mississippi river to St. Louis, and later to Keokuk, where he apprenticed himself to a farmer, that being the occupation pursued by his father. The gentleman with whom he formed this connection was Mr. N. McCullough, of Franklin, Lee county, with whom he contihued for a period of ten years and thirty-three days, at the end of which time he again sought new fields of labor, locating thirty-six miles west of the City of Des Moines, where he took employment as a farm hand and continued to devote his energies to farm work until the outbreak of the Spanish-American War in 1898. At the beginning of that now historical conflict Mr. Ross, harkening to the call of duty and patriotism, volunteered as a nurse for the army service, and being immune to the attacks of yellow fever, the disease from which the American forces suffered most, was able to perform much needed and highly valuable service, visiting for the purpose the islands of Cuba and Key West. He is a member of the Red Cross Society, the only member of that honored and world-famed organization in Lee county.

In 1899 Mr. Ross returned from the sanguinary scenes of war and once more resumed his residence in Franklin township. It was in the following year that he became assistant postmaster at LaCrew, and in 1902 he received the appointment as postmaster, a position for which he proved himself eminently fitted, discharging its many duties to his own great credit and the thorough satisfaction of the public. Mr. Ross also added to his other activities the functions of a notary public. He owns the business block at LaCrew in which the postoffice is located, and is otherwise identified in a substantial manner with the material interests of that community. Possessing a lively interest in all matters of vital importance to the public, he is well informed as to current topics and modern tendencies, and appreciates the value of ethical ideals in all relations of life, knowing that the moral interests of humanity are in no degree less important than the material and visible. He is a member of the Presbyterian church, in which he has long been a faithful and assiduous worker, and has held the office of trustee.

In 1865 Mr. Ross was united in marriage to Miss Carrie A. McMillan, and to them have been born six sons and one daughter, as follows: Albert Lee, George F., Edwin C., Jesse A., Mary M., William G., and LeRoy. Politically Mr. Ross gives his allegiance to the Republican party, is an active and efficient worker in its ranks, and as a result of the high honor and esteem in which he is held by his party, he was elected in 1904 to the office of county recorder of Lee county, a position for which he is fitted by the facts of his character and experience. Having carried the greater number of his enterprises to their desired terminations, enjoying the general respect and the friendship of many of Lee county's best people, and having, above all, developed his natural powers along lines best fitted to benefit both himself and others with whom he comes in contact, his may be called a successful life in all the best senses of the word. A self-made man, the architect of his own fortunes, he is a typical example of a strong personality developed in the free sunshine of American institutions.

THOMAS S. PAGETT.

An ideal type of success is exemplified in the career of Thomas S. Pagett, who is now retired from active pursuits, but was formerly a prominent representative of Keokuk's business and commercial life, and by his energy and aggresive, enterprising spirit, contributed much to the upbuilding of the community in which he resides. Mr. Pagett was born December 25, 1823, in Warren county, Ohio, and is the only living representative of his family. Born and reared on a farm in an undeveloped country, he received only the limited educational advantages afforded by the rural schools of that day, but he possessed a self-reliant disposition, and at the age of twenty-one years we find him leaving the parental roof and securing employment in the City of Cincinnati, making his own way in the world unassisted. Here he worked at the trade of coopering, having mastered that vocation in his boyhood.

On February 6, 1844, Mr. Pagett wedded Miss Elizabeth Cox, who was born in Warren county, Ohio, September 2, 1826, and in 1849 they removed to Mount Holly, Ohio. In Mount Holly Mr. Pagett successfully conducted a cooperage business until 1855, when he came west and located at Keokuk, making the latter part of the trip on the river by way of St. Louis. Here he was employed for the first year by Connoble & Smith, wholesale grocers, after which for a period of two or three years he conducted a cooperage shop for Albers & Austin, and then, in partnership with George Holt, he established the New York Grocery Store. After two years he sold his interest to Mr. Holt, and began a cooperage business on what was then justly considered a large scale, employing six workmen continuously. The work was all done by hand, and the material was secured from the neighboring forests. Mr. Pagett's shop was an institution of importance among the early industries of Keokuk, he supplying barrels to the pork-packing houses of the city, and he continued its operation for over twenty-one years. The shop is still standing, a monument to the success of its founder. In 1874 Mr. Pagett went into the pork business on Main street for one season, and during this time handled one thousand head of hogs. He shortly went into partnership with Mr. Keiser, they buying and curing hams and shoulders. They continued in business together for four years, at the end of which time they suffered the loss of their stock by fire—a loss amounting to about $12,000. Later Mr. Pagett purchased stock in a canning factory and for a number of years acted as overseer in the department of peeling and packing. Some five or six years ago he sold his interest in the company, and since that time has been living in retirement, enjoying the well-earned fruits of a life of honorable and useful activity combined with sound business judgment and foresight.

To Mr. and Mrs. Pagett has been born only one child, who died in infancy, at Mount Holly, Ohio. To three nephews, however, they have given a home, rearing and educating them as their own children. These are William, of Tacoma, Washington; Harry, who is employed in Keokuk with the commercial agency of Dunn & Company, and Wilfred, who is at the present time in the South.

As a result of a fall last winter Mr. Pagett sustained a painful injury, the bone of the leg being broken; and in consequence he has since that time been confined rather closely to his house. He is a member of the Westminster Presbyterian church, and in his political affiliation he holds with the Republican party, believing the principles advocated by that organization eminently suited to the maintenance of the general welfare. His long and honorable career in Keokuk has won for Mr. Pagett many admirers, and his personal qualities of tact, geniality and strict uprightness and integrity in all his transactions have brought him a host of friends. He still takes a lively interest in the well-being of his adopted city, and in return no one is held in more fitting honor by its citizens than he.

ELI R. OILAR.

Eli R. Oilar, who is now living in retirement on his farm on section 28, Jackson township, is well known in Keokuk and vicinity, and has many friends throughout Lee county, whose esteem he has won by his record as a citizen and a man, for he is one of those who, in the dark hour before the dawn of perfect civil liberty on the American continent, risked their lives and their all on the field of battle in the cause of liberty and national union. He is a native son of Iowa, and was born in Muscatine county, April 24, 1842, the son of Andrew and Charlotte (Warnick) Oilar, and his father, who was a farmer, was a native of Indiana, where he was born in 1796. He served through the War of 1812, came to Lee county in 1844, and purchased land in Jackson township, where his death occurred in 1854. Thus he was one of the earlier pioneers of Lee county and the West, one of that rugged and forceful class of men who developed the land and sowed the seeds of our present civilization. His wife, who was a native of Greenbriar county, Virginia, died in 1882, at the home of her son, our subject, at the age of eighty-two years. She was the mother of nine children, of whom four still survive, as follows: Andrew, Frances, Batheba and Eli R., the subject of this sketch.

Mr. Oilar obtained his education in a public schools conducted in a log school building, a structure typical of the times, and in subscription schools which were held at the homes of the various pioneers of the neighborhood, and in this manner he acquired a knowledge of "the three R's," and at the same time, however, a taste for reading, which enabled him in after life to enlarge upon his early training. As a boy and young man he also applied himself diligently to the work of the farm, a task which, under pioneer conditions, was potent in developing the manly qualities of enterprise, perseverance and self-reliance in a high degree.

At length, however, his country's call summoned him from peaceful pursuits, and in 1862 he enlisted in the First Iowa Cavalry Regiment under Captain McQueen and Colonel Thompson, in which regiment he re-enlisted in 1864 and served until February, 1866, being mustered out of the service at Austin, Texas, and receiving honorable discharge at Davenport, Iowa, after a long and perilous military career. With the exception of the battle of Prairie Grove, Missouri, which was a severely contested engagement, his duties were largely those of a scout, and in this capacity he met with many hardships and dangers in the states of Missouri, Arkansas, Mississippi, Tennessee, Louisiana and Texas. As an instance of the deprivations of a soldier's life, it is mentioned that while in camp near Camden a scarcity of provisions was met by issuing to each soldier a single ear of Indian corn, from which he was under the necessity of making both supper and breakfast. This they ground, mixed with water and baked into what is known as "Johnny cakes," and in default of something better were fain to relish it heartily. During the course of the war he lost four mounts in battle, three horses being shot under him in one day at Brazos river, while he himself escaped unhurt. But while never sustaining a wound he was seized with an attack of smallpox during the summer of 1864, and in consequence was for a long time immured within the cheerless walls of a military hospital at Memphis, Tennessee, an experience which was in all probability more trying than all the privations and dangers of the camp and battlefield combined.

At the close of the war Mr. Oilar returned to the work of his mother's farm, and in the following year, 1867, he was united in marriage to Miss Sarah O'Blenness, who was born in Ohio, Janurary 2, 1850. To Mr. and Mrs. Oilar have been born one son and five daughters, as follows: Marietta, the wife of Albert Lingle, connected with the work of the Wabash Railroad Company, at Kansas City, Missouri; Lucretia, wife of Thomas Lee, a farmer, has three children, Goldie, Vera and Wilma; Fred, married Miss Tillie Raber, of Keokuk, and Abba, married Frank Bugh, who is employed in the works ot the Illinois Central

Railroad Company, in East St. Louis, Illinois; Irene, wife of Walter Adams, a farmer, of Jackson township, Lee county, Iowa, and Gertrude, who lives at home.

In 1868, the year following his marriage, Mr. Oilar purchased a farm of forty-four acres in the Hogthief creek bottoms, part of a tract formerly known as Gardendale. and designed to form a suburb of the City of Keokuk, and here he has resided continuously since. For a number of years he was engaged in the dairy business, running two wagons, which supplied milk to customers in Keokuk, and he has, of course, given some attention to farming, but in recent years has been debarred from active business by physical disabilities originally incurred in war, and now sub-lets his land to neighboring farmers. From a grateful country he receives a pension of twenty-five dollars a month, and taking this in connection with his other sources of income, he finds himself comfortably well-to-do, and looks back over the years of his life well spent with the equanimity which comes of duty done and the good will of friends who approve his course. Politically Mr. Oilar affiliates with the Republican party as most nearly representative of his ideas of governmental science, and in his fraternal relations he is an honored member of Belknap Post, of the Grand Army of the Republic, and of the American Benevolent Association. He has never cared for personal distinction in any form, and in consequence does not seek public office, but realizing the responsibilities which attach to citizenship, he has for a number of terms accepted the position of director of the public schools, which he now holds, and in this capacity his services have been eminently satisfactory to all concerned. Indeed, the record of his life is one of uninterrupted success, and this, together with the respect which belongs to a strong and upright character, entitle him to a place of honor among this roll of Lee county's distinguished sons.

HENRY RINGS.

One of the more prominent younger farmers of Lee county who have won recognition by the exercise of energy, business acumen and force of character is Henry Rings, trustee of Franklin township. Mr. Rings is a native son of his township, having been born here April 17, 1761, the son of Daniel Rings. He received a common-school education in both the German and English languages, and has since done much to broaden his knowledge by a study of subjects of public and general interest as well as by contact with the world of actual affairs. His boyhood, youth and early manhood were passed in the usual manner of those who are trained in the life of the farm, assisting in his father's work and acquiring the lessons of experience without which the knowledge of books is of little value.

In 1882 Mr. Rings was united in marriage to Miss Anna Handrich, a native of Franklin township, Lee county, and daughter of Jacob Handrich, a sketch of whose life appears on another page of this volume.

Immediately after his marriage he established himself upon the farm which he now occupies, renting and farming it successfully for seven years. He then purchased a farm of sixty acres on section 16, this township. At the end of three years, however, he sold that farm and returned to his present location, purchasing the farm, which consists of 197½ acres of fine land. Here he has made many improvements, and conducts a general farming business, and by close study of the markets and careful attention to detail in the management of his operations has been successful to a very gratifying degree.

Mr. and Mrs. Rings are the parents of eight children, the eldest of whom, Alma, is the wife of Herbert Wilhelm, and resides upon a farm in the western part of Franklin township. All the others remain at home, and are as follows: Rosa, Arthur, Herbert, Harry, Seymour, Clyde and Ermine. One child died in infancy. The family are members of the Mennonite church. In his political allegiance Mr. Rings has always been an admirer and supporter of Democratic principles, and has been active in promoting the supremacy of that party. He is interested in public affairs, and has often been honored by election to office at the hands of his neighbors, friends and acquaintances. For a number of terms he served as director of the public schools, and in the autumn of 1903 he was elected for a term of three years to the highest office within the gift of the township, that of trustee. This position, which is one requiring business qualifications of a high order, he has so far filled to his own credit and the satisfaction of his constituents, and doubtless the bestowal of further honors will reward his able and conscientious service. He is a young man of progressive tendencies, and enjoys a reputation for integrity and the strictest uprightness in all his dealings, while his genial good nature has made him popular. He has many friends.

FRANKLIN R. SEITZ.

Franklin R. Seitz, now deceased, was one of the honored pioneer settlers of Franklin county, arriving here at an early day, when the district was largely unimproved. In fact it was considered a far western region, and the greater part of the land was still in its primitive condition. The forests stood in their primeval strength, many of the streams were unbridged, and the land was uncultivated. Mr. Seitz joined the early settlers in laying the foundation of the present prosperity and progress of the country, and well does his name deserve to be inscribed upon the pages of the history of this portion of Iowa.

He was born March 2, 1831, in Lancaster county, Pennsylvania, and there spent the days of his childhood and youth. There also, being of an energetic and ambitious turn of mind, he set himself to learn a trade, that of ship carpentering, in which he attained a high degree of proficiency. After coming to Keokuk he continued his work as a carpenter, in which he was very successful, and thus very materially contributed to the advancement and upbuilding of the community in which he lived.

In Jackson township, Lee county, November 13, 1855, Mr. Seitz was united in marriage with Miss Anna M. Pore, the ceremony being performed by Rev. W. Y. Cowles. Mrs. Seitz was born June 14, 1836, the daughter of John and Julia (Gorgas) Pore, both of whom are now deceased. Her father was a farmer and was of German extraction. Unto Mr. and Mrs. Seitz were born three children, as follows: John Gorgas, born July 29, 1856, follows his father's trade of carpentering; Ada Jane, born August 31, 1859, died September 11, 1883, aged twenty-four years and eleven days; Franklin R., born March 13, 1868, is a carpenter, residing at Davenport, Iowa. He married Margaret Davis, and they have two children, Harry and Mamie.

Mr. Seitz was a public-spirited man, and had a high sense of duty and patriotism. At the beginning of the Civil War he commended his family and material interests to the care of Providence, and went to join the Union army in its heroic struggle for the saving of the nation. He enlisted in Company A, of the Second Iowa Volunteer Infantry, under Capt. William Wilson, and for three years served his country as a soldier, undergoing all the hardships and privations of camp and field life, and participating in important battles. It was during his term of military service that he contracted the dread disease known as chronic diarrhœa, which made him an invalid for the remainder of his life and resulted in his death four years after the close of the war. The date of his demise was June 30, 1869, he being then thirty-eight years, three months and twenty-eight days of age. He passed away in the very prime of life, and his loss was keenly felt by all who knew him. He was a member of the Baptist church, as is also his widow, and in matters of politics he acted with the Republican party.

The death of Mr. Seitz occurred in Jackson township on a farm which he purchased at the close of the war. By his death the care and responsibility of rearing and educating the family of three children fell to the widow. The farm was operated under her supervision, and she continued to reside there until about 1890, when the family having attained to years of maturity, she removed to Keokuk. Here she owns a pleasant home, at 1407 Fulton street, as well as residence property on Blondeau street. Through the efforts of friends she has secured from the government a pension of twelve dollars a month, with an initial payment of $900. Two brothers of Mrs. Seitz were also soldiers of the Civil War, these being Samuel and William Pore, both members of the First Iowa Cavalry. Samuel is a resident of Rothville, Missouri, and William, of Denver, Colorado.

Mr. Seitz, the subject of this sketch, was a man of the purest and most admirable private character, honest, honorable and generous always, and in his public relations the fact that he sacrificed himself for his country in her hour of distress speaks more loudly than any words could do, "for greater love hath no man than this, that he lay down his life for his friends."

WILLIAM C. POTTS.

One who has achieved success entirely by his own efforts and reared for himself a noble edifice of reputation is the subject of this review. Mr. Potts was born in Monmouth county, New Jersey, near the scene of the famous battle of Monmouth, June 21, 1835, and is the son of Richard and Ann (Borden) Potts, both of whom were born in New Jersey. The grandfather was Thomas Potts, also of New Jersey. Richard Potts was a tanner and farmer. He died on a farm in New Jersey in 1853, and the mother at the same place in 1863.

William C. Potts received his education in the common schools of his native place, and there began life as a farmer, at which occupation he continued until 1858. At that time he decided to seek larger opportunities in the new country which was then known as "the West," and went to Peoria county, Illinois, where he rented land and continued farming for ten years. Again removing to new fields of labor in 1868, he came to Fort Madison, where he took a position with the Potowonok Milling Company. By this firm he was employed for fifteen years at various places as bookkeeper, shipping clerk and weighmaster, and on terminating the connection he engaged independently in the insurance business for three years. In 1895 he became bookkeeper and collector for the Fort Madison Water Company.

In 1863 took place the marriage of Mr. Potts to Miss Fanny Tebow, at Princeville, Illinois. She died in 1865, leaving one child, Anna, who was born December 23, 1865, and is now the wife of W. A. Caldwell, of Wood River, Nebraska. Mr. Potts has since remarried. At Fort Madison, in 1867, he was united in bonds of matrimony with Miss Fanny Toors, who was born in Lee county, September 17, 1846, and died April 29, 1896. Four children survive her, as follows: Caroline E., born April 6, 1873, is a trained nurse, and is located at Quincy, Illinois; Emma G., born February 14, 1876, is a clerk at the office of J. P. Cruikshank; Richard, born January 28, 1879, holds a position with the painting force of the Santa Fe Railway system, and Isla Pearl, born November 20, 1884, is still at home. Mrs. Frances (Hardin) Toors, mother of the deceased Mrs. Potts, makes her home with Mr. Potts, spending the winters with her son, Taylor Toors, of Little Rock, Arkansas. She was born at Brighton, England, in 1820, and came to Lee county in 1841 with her husband, John W. Toors. He was born on Long Island, was reared in Cincinnati, and died during the progress of the Civil War. He was of Dutch ancestry. They were the parents of two sons and one daughter besides Mrs. Potts. These are: R. L. Toors, died in May, 1904, in Mexico; Taylor Toors, of Little Rock, Arkansas, and Miss Mary Toors, for the past thirty-five years teacher in the public schools of Lee county.

Religiously Mr. Potts is a member of the Presbyterian church, of which he has served as trustee, and in a fraternal way he is in similar relations with the Order of the Knights of Pythias. In politics he early became convinced of the superiority of the principles advocated by the Republican party, and his first vote was cast for John C. Fremont, first Republican candidate for the office of President of the United States. Since that time he has voted for every Republican presidential candidate. He has never sought public office, but has allowed his friends to use his name as candidate for alderman and for assessor. The Republican party being in the minority, however, no chance of election was possible.

Mr. Potts has a commodious home at 915 Fifth street. The welfare of his family has ever been his first care, and all his children have received excellent educations in the Fort Madison high school. His ability and social qualities have made him many friends, and his reputation is of the kind that might be envied by the most highly honored.

MORRICE E. WAITE.

One of the oldest locomotive engineers of the Santa Fe system is Morrice E. Waite, who resides at No. 2522 Webster street, Fort Madison, Iowa. Mr. Waite is a native of Spencer, Worcester county, Massachusetts, where he was born May 15, 1847, and received his early education in the public schools. He assisted in the work of the home farm until twenty years of age, when he decided to begin his independent career and win his way in the world by his own efforts. Learning of the rewards awaiting industry and ability in the great West, he came as far as Aurora, Illinois, in 1868, and began work as a fireman for the Chicago, Burlington & Quincy Railroad. After three years and four months' faithful and efficient service he was promoted, in October, 1871, to the position of engineer, and continued with the company in that capacity until January 7, 1887. He then entered the employ of the Santa Fe Railroad Company, with headquarters at Fort Madison, and in this city he has since resided, having erected a very pleasant dwelling about five years after his removal here. He is in the passenger branch of the company's service, and his route is between Fort Madison and Kansas City.

Mr. Waite, in his fraternal relations, is a member of the Masonic order, his local connection being with Stella Lodge, No. 440, of Fort Madison, and also of the Brotherhood of Locomotive Engineers, Division 391, of Fort Madison. In matters of politics he is a believer in the principles of the Republican party and a loyal supporter of its standard bearers, especially when important issues are at stake. He is a member of the Christian Science church, and actively connected with its work, the meetings of the society being held at his home.

Morris E. Waite is the son of Josiah and Emmeline (Farnam) Waite. His father, who was a currier by trade, was born at Millsbury, Massachusetts, where he lived for many years. He was also engaged in the pursuit of his calling for a number of years at Northbridge. He came to Fort Madison in 1890, and here his death occurred in 1892 at the home of his son in the seventy-third year of his age. He was a man of business ability, and achieved considerable material success. Mr. Waite's mother died in Florida in 1881, at the age of fifty-three years. She was a native of New York state. Mr. Waite is the second of a family of five brothers, the others being Charles, who lost his life in the Battle of the Wilderness; Jonas, of Charlton, Massachusetts, who was for many years station agent for the Boston & Albany Railway Company, but is now retired from active pursuits; Jerry W., who is engaged in orange culture at Lemon Grove, California, and Fred D., who resides at Palmetto, Florida, and is superintendent of an orange grove at that place. All were born in Massachusetts.

On April 24, 1871, Mr. Waite was married to Miss Sarah J. Willis, and to them have been born five children, only one of whom, Carrie, is living. She was born at Galesburg, Illinois, and was educated at Fort Madison. The deceased were: Charles, born at Mendota, died at the age of six years; Kittie, born at Aurora, died in infancy; Freddie, born at Galesburg, Illinois, died at three years of age, and Ella, also born at Galesburg, died at the age of five. Mrs. Waite is a faithful member of the Christian Science church and a woman of deep religious nature. She was born in Racine county, Wisconsin, the daughter of Joseph W. Willis. Mr. Willis was born in Cayuga county, New York, December 15, 1825, and at the age of two years removed with his parents to Yates county, New York, where he lived until 1846. He then came west, locating at the town of Raymond, Racine county, Wisconsin, where he engaged in farming. In 1862 he enlisted in Company H of the Twenty-second Wisconsin Volunteer Infantry, and served his country throughout the remainder of the war, being discharged June 28, 1865, at Milwaukee, Wisconsin. He was assigned to detached service for the greater part of the time, but accompanied General Sherman on his famous march to the sea. On March 25, 1863, he was taken prisoner by the enemy at Brantwood, Tennessee, eight miles from Nashville, and conveyed to Libby prison, but was released through an exchange of prisoners which took place the following day. During the time of his military service Mr. Willis's eyesight began to fail, and has since deteriorated steadily until he now suffers from total blindness. After the close of the war he engaged in the ice business at Aurora, Illinois, continuing in that occupation for twenty-four years. On sustaining the loss of his sight he retired from active participation in affairs, and since 1900 has resided with his son-in-law, Mr. Waite. He is a member of Grand Army Post No. 20, at Aurora, Illinois, and his religious affiliation is with the Christian Science church. He was married to Miss Mary B. Cole, who was born in London, England, and came to America when fourteen years of age. She died July 30, 1861, and is buried at Racine, Wisconsin. To them were born seven children, as follows: Sarah J., wife of our subject; Martha, who died at four years of age; Eveline H., who died in infancy—at the age of six months; William C.; James H., of Moline, Illinois; Mary E., of Missouri, and Edward, who died in infancy. Mr. Willis was remarried, the second time to Kate Fitch, who was born in Delaware county, New York. She died May 21, 1900, at Aurora, Illinois, and is buried at that place.

MATTHIAS GARMO.

Matthias Garmo, of Garmo & Company, of Keokuk, is of distinguished Revolutionary ancestry, his grandfather having been a French officer who accompanied General La Fayette to America and served under him in the War of American Independence, later deciding to become a citizen of the country which he had helped to free from British domination, and settled in New Jersey. There his son, the father of our subject, was born, and he in his turn took part in the second War of American Independence, serving as a cavalryman in the War of 1812 and sustaining a sabre wound which afterward caused his death. He was a man of powerful and muscular frame, and in his earlier life followed the trade of a bloomer or forgeman, but during the larger fraction of his life was a commission merchant at Hackensack and at Paterson, New Jersey. He was thoroughly American in all of his sympathies, and procured an act of the New Jersey legislature changing his name, which was originally De Garmo, to its present form, thereby following the example of the descendants of General La Fayette and eliminating the evidence of his aristocratic descent.

Matthias Garmo was born in Sussex county, New Jersey, in the year 1836, and there received his education in the public schools. Orphaned, however, by the death of his mother when he was but fifteen years of age and the death of his father two years later, he resolved to begin the active work of life, and became an apprentice to J. W. Inglis, a carpenter and joiner, of Paterson, New Jersey, and later accepted employment with the York & Erie Railway Company as a millwright at Jersey City, New Jersey. In this latter line of effort he was signally successful, and was able to command a salary of two hundred dollars a month, but finding that the position did not offer as much opportunity for individual initiative and independent enterprise as he desired, he resigned, and in 1864 came to try his fortune in the West, locating at Burlington, Iowa, where for three years he conducted a planing mill business in partnership with C. S. Quick. At the expiration of that period he accepted the position of manager of a planing mill and sash, door and furniture factory for McGavic Brothers & Davis, of Keokuk, in which he continued for five years, and then the firm of Garmo & Hume was formed and conducted the same line of business until the latter part of the year 1888, after which Mr. Garmo was connected with the firm of Henderson Brothers for three years. In 1891 he re-established himself in the planing business in partnership with B. C. Taber, the firm style being Garmo & Company, and this business has been continued very successfully ever since, the mill operating throughout the entire years and furnishing employment to an average of fifteen men. To this work Mr. Garmo gives his exclusive attention, although he has other interests, among these being his membership in a local company owning a lead and zinc mine with very promising prospects in the wonderful metal producing region of Jasper county, Missouri.

At Paterson, New Jersey, in 1862, Mr.

Garmo was united in marriage to Miss Mary J. Smith, a native of that state and of old Holland ancestry, the daughter of a family of farmers. To Mr. and Mrs. Garmo have been born two daughters, of whom one, Fannie, survives, and is the wife of W. H. Palmer, of Keokuk, they having one child, Greta, twelve years of age. The other daughter, Lillian, was the wife of John Dollery, and they are both now deceased, leaving one son, Clyde, who has been reared as a member of Mr. Garmo's family, and is now in his seventeenth year. The family home is a commodious residence at No. 418 South Eighth street, erected by Mr. Garmo in 1878.

Our subject has always been in sympathy with any movement designed to advance the moral and ethical interests of society, and never fails to encourage such as are worthy by all means in his power. He was formerly a member of the Methodist Episcopal church, and although he has since allowed his connection to lapse, he still contributes to its support, as he does also for the various other denominations. In like manner his public spirit has led him to assume an active part in political affairs, and he was one of the leading organizers of the gold wing of the Democratic party in Keokuk in the celebrated presidential campaign of 1896, though he is now a supporter of President Roosevelt, considering that the true principles of good government are in a large measure represented by that distinguished president. He is also very prominent in the fraternal world of Iowa, being a charter member of Keokuk Lodge of the Knights of Honor, having held all its official positions, and for the last nine years been Grand Treasurer of the Grand Lodge of Iowa, an office which he now holds and in which his able financial administration has made him many admirers in this and other states. In fact his life has been a success in almost all its phases without an exception, and while his business ability has enabled him to win for himself a substantial reward for his labors and has brought him a very comfortable competency, the useful enterprise which he has established in Keokuk has been a factor in the development of the city, and for this he is entitled to credit. A self-made man, working his way upward from humble circumstances to his present enviable position, the keynote of his career may be summed up in one word, integrity, a trait of character which has won him the general respect and made his name synonymous with sound and irreproachable business methods wherever he is known.

BENJAMIN F. McINTYRE.

Benjamin F. McIntyre, who having reached the age of seventy-seven years, has now practically retired from active business life and is enjoying a well-earned and richly merited rest, was born in Adams county, Ohio, on the 15th of September, 1827. His father, William McIntyre, was also a native of the Buckeye state, but the paternal grandfather came from the north of Ireland. The mother bore the maiden name of Ellen

Montgomery, who was born in Kentucky, while her people were of Scotch lineage, so that Mr. McIntyre is of Scotch-Irish descent. The father died when the son was but five years of age and the mother, remaining true to his memory, never married again, but passed away in Keokuk in 1855, at the age of seventy-five, a short time after coming from her Ohio home to this city. Benjamin F. McIntyre was the youngest in a family of nine children and the only one now living, although all reached advanced years. He had one brother, William Newton McIntyre, who served as a soldier in the Civil War as a member of an Illinois Regiment, and died in Hancock county, Illinois, in 1899.

The common school afforded Benjamin F. McIntyre his educational privileges and he was reared in Ohio. After putting aside his text-books he learned the carpenter's trade, and at about the age of twenty-two years went to Kentucky, working for seven years in Maysville, Mason county. He arrived in Keokuk in 1854, and for many years continued an active representative of building interests here and to a limited extent he yet engages in the use of tools, although he has in recent years lived practically retired. He worked on the government canal at Keokuk and on the government arsenal at Davenport. His business interests, however, were interrupted by military service, for in September, 1862, in response to his country's call for aid he joined the Union Army at Keokuk as a member of Company A, Nineteenth Iowa Infantry, under Capt. John Bruce and Colonel Crabb. The regiment was with the Army of the Frontier during the first six months of his services, and was afterward in the seige of Vicksburg, and at Yazoo City was ordered to join the Gulf Department, on the Rio Grande, in Texas, under General Herron, and was held in readiness for any emergency. With his command Mr. McIntyre participated in the engagements at Prairie Grove, Arkansas, the seige of Vicksburg and the seige and capture of Yazoo, Mississippi. For about nine months he was encamped in Texas. In the latter part of the war he participated in the engagements at Fort Morgan, Alabama, and the seige and capture of Spanish Fort and Fort Blakeley. The latter fort was captured on the night that President Lincoln was assassinated, and the news reached the army the following morning. The regiment went into camp at Mobile, Alabama, and soon afterward Mr. McIntyre, having been mustered out under General A. J. Smith, returned to Davenport and was honorably discharged. He enlisted as first orderly sergeant, and six months later was promoted to the rank of second lieutenant, and when three months had passed was commissioned first lieutenant. While at New Orleans he was granted a leave of absence and returned home, where he suffered greatly from a severe attack of malaria. So ill was he that his leave of absence was twice extended, and he remained at home for sixty days, after which he rejoined his command at Brownsville, Texas. In addition to the engagements mentioned the regiment participated in several skirmishes, including one at Pensacola, Florida. They marched long distances through the South and experienced the usual hardships that fall to the lot of a soldier, but Mr. McIntyre was ever true and loyal to his duty and never faltered in performance of any task assigned him in his effort to preserve the Union.

Returning to the North Mr. McIntyre resumed work at carpentering and made that his life occupation, being connected with building operations in Keokuk through long years, and evidences of his handiwork are yet seen in many of the substantial structures of the city. He is a member of the Grand Army of the Republic, and for fifty years has been a representative of the Independent Order of Odd Fellows. He has held all of the positions in the subordinate lodge; has attended the Grand Lodge on several occasions, and on the 23d of February, 1903, he received the gold jewel from Keokuk Lodge, No. 13, in honor of his completed half century of membership and active work. Only eight such jewels are found in the State of Iowa. The No. 50 upon the medal is set with twenty diamonds. He was representative to the Grand Lodge at Clinton, and also attended the Grand Lodges at Davenport, Keokuk and Rock Island. He has likewise been a member of the Knights of Pythias fraternity, and his life accords with the beneficient spirit of these various fraternal organizations. He voted for the first Republican nominee, John C. Fremont, and has never faltered in his allegiance to the party and its principles, but has throughout the years continued to give it stalwart support.

On the 30th of September, 1850, Mr. McIntyre was married in Maysville, Kentucky, to Miss Emeline M. Williams, who died March 6, 1890, after a happy married life of almost forty years, her remains being interred in Oakland cemetery. They were the parents of four children, of whom three are living: Mary, the wife of A. J. Jenkins, of Keokuk; Harry, who died at the age of thirty-two years; Emma B., and Katherine, who has charge of the queensware store owned by Duncan & Schell. Mr. McIntyre resides at No. 1013 High street, where he has a pleasant and comfortable home. In his business career he never had special advantages nor was assisted by any fortunate combination of circumstances, but he has worked earnestly year after year, and his unfaltering diligence has been the keynote of his success, so that he is now numbered among the substantial citizens of his adopted county. At all times his course has been such as to command uniform confidence and esteem, and he has gained that warm personal regard which arises from true nobility of character and kindliness of spirit.

JASPER K. MASON.

Jasper K. Mason was born in Kirksville, Missouri, September 10, 1840, and died in Keokuk, Iowa, June 17, 1903. He had lived for many years in the latter city and had gained a large circle of friends here. Having completed his education in the public schools, he was apprenticed to the trades of cigarmaking and coopering, in Warsaw, Illinois, after which he came to Keokuk, where he continued to make his home until his death, with the exception of one year. He had remained here but a brief period, however, when the Civil War was inaugurated, and about a year later on August 14, 1862, when he was twenty-two years of age, he enlisted as a private in the Nineteenth Iowa Infantry for three years. He was discharged, however, with the rank of sergeant before that time because of disability caused by wounds which he had sustained. His jaw was terribly injured and one of his ribs broken by a spent shell. He was captured at Morganza Bend, but managed to make his escape on the night of November 14, 1863. Later he was captured and cast into Libby prison, but he managed to escape a second time by tunneling under the barricades. His experiences were of a most thrilling character, and he wrote a book concerning them, which was published and read with much interest by thousands of veterans. In the anniversary edition of Gate City, in 1902, there was also a long and interesting account of his vicissitudes and hardships while in the army. He served until June 22, 1865.

Mr. Mason returned to the North and resumed business. He was married in Warsaw, Illinois, in 1867, to Miss Rachel L. Markley, who was born in Arkansas, and in 1865 became a resident of Missouri. She spent a short time in Warsaw, and there formed the acquaintance of Mr. Mason. A year after their marriage they came to Keokuk, and he was variously connected with the business interests of the city through the succeeding thirty years. For ten years he conducted a grocery store, enjoying a flourishing trade, in West Keokuk. He was afterward appointed deputy United States oil inspector, in which capacity he served for fourteen years, when he resigned. After retiring from the grocery business he was engaged in the real estate and insurance business for some time.

Politically Mr. Mason was a Republican, deeply interested in the growth and success of his party and recognized as one of its leading workers in local ranks. He represented the second ward of the city council in 1879 and 1880, and as a private citizen he contributed to and supported those measures which had for their object the permanent good of the city. He capably served for about eight years as a member of the soldier's relief commission for the City of Keokuk, and he was prominent in his fraternal relations, being a member of Torrence Post, Grand Army of the Republic, for many years, in which he filled nearly all the offices and became commander. He belonged to Eagle Lodge, No. 12, Free and Accepted Masons, the Commandry and the Mystic Shrine, and also the Eastern Star, and although he affiliated with no religious denomination he was a warm personal friend of Rev. D. R. C. McIlwin, pastor of St. John's Episcopal church, whom he requested to conduct the funeral services when he should be called away. He recognized and appreciated true worth in others, and so lived as to develop a character in keeping with high ideals and honorable, manly principles.

Mrs. Mason, who survives her husband, was married when sixteen years of age. Theirs was a close and congenial companionship, causing his loss to be all the more deeply felt. Mrs. Mason joined with him the Order of the Eastern Star and served as Worthy Matron. She is also a past president of the Torrence Woman's Relief Corps and has served as Senior Vice-President of the state organization, while for two years she was instituting and installing officer for the state of the Corps. For two years she was delegate from the State of Iowa to the National Convention of the Woman's Relief Corps, at Philadelphia and at Washington. She belongs to the Baptist church, and her kindly spirit and ready sympathy have prompted her to take active and helpful part in church and charitable work. She makes her home at No. 200 South Eight street, Keokuk, and in addition to this property she owns realty in Colorado Springs, Colorado.

RHODA WILLIAMS.

Rhoda Williams, widow of John M. Williams, has long been a well-kown resident of Jackson township, and is a member of one of the old and representative families of Lee county. Her late husband was a native of Indiana, having been born in that state in 1832, and on coming to Iowa, purchased a farm of eighty acres in Lucas county, near Chariton, but located in Wayne county, where he engaged very successfully in the vocation of farming until January 10, 1863, when he decided to offer himself for the service of his country in the Civil War, which was then draining the best blood of the land, and enlisted in the First Battery of the Iowa Light Artillery. Assigned to duty as a teamster he was never actively engaged as a combatant in battle, but for eighteen months he performed hard, faithful and often dangerous service, proving himself a valuable and efficient member of his corps and winning the esteem of both his equals and superiors in military rank.

On returning from the war Mr. Williams first went to Keokuk, where Mrs. Williams was then making her home with her father, and shortly afterward he sold his lands in Lucas county and purchased a farm of forty acres in Jackson township, Lee county, on which Mrs. Williams still continues to reside, and whence he carried on farming operations during the remainder of his life. He possessed much ability, had a wide acquaintance, and enjoyed the friendship of many who respected him for the sterling qualities of his character—his energy and the strict honor and integrity which marked him in every relation of life. He was a member of the Baptist church, and was a true and devout Christian, being faithful to his religion until his death, which occurred in 1879. He was buried in Hickory Grove cemetery. A public-spirited citizen, a kind husband and indulgent father, ever generous, sympathetic and true, his loss was in every sense a calamity, and one which no favor of fortune can ever repair.

To Mr. and Mrs. Williams were born four daughters and one son, as follows: Atha, now the wife of John Cruse, of Vincennes, Lee county, and have four children, Mabel, Gennetta, Robert and John; James, who married Miss Anna Jaquin and resides with Mrs. Williams; Anna, who is the wife of William Colvin, of Mooar, and has four children, Lulu, Georgia, William and Vernon; Lucretia, who is the wife of Thomas Taylor, of Mooar, and has two daughters, Ruth and Beatrice, and Margaret, who is the wife of George Colvin, of Keokuk, and has three children, Wilfred, Inez and Enid. Left by the death of her husband with the sole care of five children, the eldest only seventeen years of age and the youngest five, Mrs. Williams has exhibited much strength of character and Christian fortitude, meeting and fulfilling her difficult obligations with extraordinary ability, and proving herself equal to the unexpected and trying situations arising from her station in life. She is of a highly respected family, and was born in Mercer county, Pennsylvania, in 1838, coming to Lee county with her parents in 1852. She is the daughter of James and Martha McCleary, who were natives of Ireland and celebrated their marriage in that country before their emigration to the United States, and both are now deceased. Mrs. Williams is a member of the Christian church, in which she is an active and very helpful worker, doing much to advance the cause of religion in her community and setting by her own life an example of humble Christian piety, faith and charity, and is also a leading worker in the aid society of the church, of which she is president. She has merited the admiration of all, and of her it may be truly said that to few or none in this section has come a greater measure of esteem.

PETER S. SCHEFFLER, Sr.

One of the most highly successful farmers and business men of Lee county and southern Iowa is Peter S. Scheffler, who owns 280 acres of high-grade farming land and forty acres of timbered land in Franklin township, where he resides, and in addition a section of valuable land in the State of Texas. Mr. Scheffler was born January 25, 1836, in southern New York, a son of Antoin and Mary Scheffler, both natives of Germany, whence they emigrated to America when young. Soon after Mr. Scheffler's birth his parents decided to remove to the West in order to reap the benefits of early occupancy of the new country, and drove over the mountains of Pennsylvania, through Ohio, and penetrating Indiana, settled on the banks of the Wabash river, remaining there until 1840, when they again traveled westward, and came to Lee county, Iowa. Here they first located at St. Paul, Marion township, and remained for two years, at the end of which time they entered a tract of government land as a "homestead," in West Point township, where they lived the remainder of their lives, working as farmers until the hand of death removed them from the scenes of this world. The father of our subject was widely known as a man of high and forceful character, being still remembered by many of the older inhabitants. He was a pioneer of his religion as well as of his race, for he was the first to erect the symbol of the Christian faith, the cross, both at St. Paul and at West Point.

Mr. Scheffler received in the pioneer community in which his fortunes fell a very limited educational opportunity, attending a rural school in an old log cabin which was used both as a school building and as a residence for the schoolmaster. But the acquirement of other knowledge largely compensated for the lack of knowledge of books, for when quite young he learned the trade of coopering, and worked at it during the winter months for twelve years, while at the early age of fourteen he was taught to drive an ox team to a plow to break up the soil for planting and to swing the cradle in the harvest field, and to do other hard work usually assigned in these days to strong men or performed by the aid of modern machinery. He was thus variously employed until he reached his twenty-sixth year, when he was married, in 1862, to Miss Christiana Engleman, who afterward died, leaving six children, as follows: Peter, a resident of Lee county; Emma, who married Samuel Tackler, and resides at Moline, Illinois; William, Edward, Clara, wife of Mr. Wm. F. Hutchins, who resides in New York state, and Albert. Mr. Scheffler was subsequently married to Miss Elizabeth Furrer, who is also now deceased, and is survived by one child, Ida, wife of Mr. Albert T. Faith, of Wellington, Kansas. She is buried, as is also the first Mrs. Scheffler, in the Everhart cemetery, near the home farm.

In 1862, just after his marriage, Mr. Scheffler rented a farm in Franklin township, where he was so successful in farming that in only five years, or in 1867, he was able to buy a farm of 200 acres, being part of the large farm he now occupies, and to the original purchase he has since added eighty acres of farm land and forty acres of timbered land of high quality and value. When he bought the farm it was in a very dilapidated condition and almost entirely without improvements, but by care and good management, combined with energy and enterprise, he has greatly improved it in all respects, fencing the fields, erecting new buildings and repairing the old, and bringing the land under cultivation according to modern methods, so that at the present time the whole establishment would compare favorably with any in southern Iowa. He conducts general farming on a large scale, and is especially interested in stock feeding, giving particular attention just at the present time to registered Durham and black Polled Angus cattle, for which his farm is widely known. He often feeds as many as 1,000 head of cattle, as well as large numbers of hogs, and at the present is feeding 500 head of hogs, which, in accordance with his usual custom, will be shipped direct to the Chicago market.

For a period of more than twenty years, however, Mr. Scheffler devoted himself mainly to the threshing business, which netted him very handsome profits, and for a time he was associated with his brother in running the mill at Donnellson, Iowa, which was also very successful. In fact every enterprise in which he has engaged has been successful in a high degree, owing to his careful attention to detail and his remarkable business ability, his foresight and quickness to see an opportunity and his confidence in his own power to carry to a satisfactory issue any matter to which he applies his talents. He has given his attention principally to business affairs, and has never aspired to the tenure of public office, but at the same time he never fails to discharge the duties of a citizen, voting for a candidate according to his personal fitness for the position which he seeks and without regard to partisan bias or affiliation, as he believes it to be in this way that the interests of good government are best advanced. In his religious connection he retains the faith of his forefathers, being a member of St. Mary's Catholic church, of West Point, and has observed a lifelong fidelity to the teachings of his denomination. But the true key to his character lies in the fact that he is a self-made man, that he started in the struggle with the world equipped only with his own strength and ability, and that he has by his own unaided efforts raised himself to his present honored position in the community. For this he deserves great credit, the more so because his methods have always been marked by the strictest honesty and integrity and that he has been fair, upright and impartial in all his dealings, and, indeed, these facts in his career have won for him a high reputation for honor throughout Lee county, and he is universally admired and respected for what he has achieved.

HENRY J. DOERING.

One of the self-made men who have assumed substantial and respected positions in the business and social circles of Fort Madison, by reason of their own efforts and merits, is Henry J. Doering. Although he is a young man, he has been engaged in useful activity evere since his boyhood, and it is probably due to this early training in habits of industry, management and economy that he has achieved success.

Mr. Doering was born in Germany, February 3, 1867, and is the son of George and Mary (Harold) Doering. The father was born in the German Kingdom of Saxony; came with his family to America in 1869. He was by trade a painter and paper-hanger, and during the winter, when it was not possible to follow this occupation, he was engaged as a butcher. Mary Doering, mother of our subject, died in Fort Madison, May 20, 1897, and is buried in the Catholic cemetery. They were the parents of six sons and daughters, all of whom are still living. They are: Henry J., Mrs. Mary Hunt, Peter, John, Joseph, Valentine, all of Fort Madison.

Henry J. Doering was educated in the common schools and in Saint Mary's parochial school. As a boy he was his father's assistant in the work of painting and paper-hanging, and when young began his connection with the market business as his father's assistant. Thus, by the time he attained to years of maturity he was already schooled in the principles of business, and was acquainted with all the intricacies of his own individual occupation. At the present time he has a thoroughly modern equipment and market at 1737 Third street, and enjoys a large and growing patronage. He is the owner of his business location and building, valued at $3,000, and in 1888 built a beauti-

HENRY J. DOERING

ful residence at 1810 Third street, valued at two thousand dollars.

Mr. Doering's religious connection is with the Sacred Heart church, and he is a member of the German Roman Catholic Benevolent Society, of Saint Mary's; of the Sacred Heart Literary and Benevolent Society, of which he is president, and of the Volunteer Fire Company. He is also at the present time secretary of branch No. 118, of the Roman Catholic Mutual Protective Association. In his political faith he is a firm believer in the doctrines advocated by the Democratic party, and a loyal supporter of its leaders.

On July 30, 1889, in St. Mary's church, was celebrated the marriage of Henry J. Doering and Miss Catherine Dettmer. Mrs. Doering is of German parentage, and was born in Fort Madison. Unto them have been born one daughter and three sons, as follows: Eda Margaret, born November 20, 1895; George Philip, born September 29, 1898; Edmund Henry, born October 2, 1901, and Peter Joseph, born January 23, 1904.

Mrs. Doering is the fifth of a family of eight sisters. The others are: Mena, Eda, Bertha, wife of Fred Struck, of Burlington, Iowa; Josephine, Rosa, wife of Edward Kueser, of Burlington; Mary, wife of John Hillesheime, of Fort Madison, Iowa, and Dorothy.

Mr. Doering has many friends who wish him well. Steadily working his way upward in spite of many difficulties, he commands the respect of his fellowmen by his honorable course and unfaltering perseverance.

FRANK MILLMEYER.

Frank Millmeyer, who was one of the early pioneers of Lee county, and later became one of its leading and successful farmers, claimed Germany for his native land, having been born in that country in the year 1838, the son of Frank Millmeyer, Sr., and from Germany he accompanied his parents to America when only two years of age. On the arrival of the family in America they came to Iowa and located in Fort Madison, but later removed to the country, where our subject was reared on a farm and learned by actual experience of its difficult duties all the details of farming, thus fitting himself for his later successes in that line of effort, and acquiring that strength of character which made him a man among men.

April 14, 1874, Mr. Millmeyer was united in marriage with Miss Catherine Hoenig, who was born in West Point township, Lee county, March 15, 1854, the daughter of Casper and Mary (Wolf) Hoenig, and a full account of whose genealogy will be found under the name of Frank Hoenig on another page of this work. Mrs. Millmeyer is a member of one of the early pioneer families of this county, her parents having settled in Lee county in the year 1850, and she has a family of nine, as follows: Anna, who died at the age of twenty-one years; John, Tracy, who is a resident of St. Louis; Mary; Lizzie, wife of Albert Bullard, of Fort Madison; Catherine, Paulina, Dora, Fred and Clara. The father of the family died November 1, 1888, and the mother January 31, 1889, and it was felt that in their passing the community sustained a deep and irreparable loss, for by the loftiness and purity of their lives they exerted great influence for good.

In 1880, six years subsequent to his marriage, Mr. Millmeyer purchased a large farm of 215 acres in Jefferson township, and on this the family has resided continuously since. He managed it with rare discrimination, bringing to bear upon its problems a singularly clear and accurate foresight and a sound judgment, while he devoted himself to the work with energy and enthusiasm, overlooking no detail and never omitting to improve the slightest opportunity to the best of his ability, thus winning a large success. He gave his attention to general farming and also to some extent to stockraising, and this has been continued by his family. Although a member of the Democratic party, Mr. Millmeyer never aspired to public office, but contented himself with performing conscientiously the first and most important duty of a citizen, that of casting his vote in favor of good and honest government after mature reflection upon the issues at stake. His death occurred in a singular manner, he having left home in a boat for the City of Nauvoo, and many days later was found drowned, the date of his demise being about November 10, 1898, and was buried November 26, 1898, a day on which all those who knew him well experienced a profound sense of loss, for he was one whose long career of worthy endeavor and unfailing allegiance to everything that was best won the universal respect and endeared him to many, so that the grief at his death was at once general and sincere. Mrs. Millmeyer, who is a lady of unusual ability and fine strength of character, continues the management of the farm with success.

CASPER SWINDAMAN.

One of the highly respected and substantially successful citizens of Lee county is Casper Swindaman, now residing on his farm of 353 acres in Charleston township. He was born in St. Louis, Missouri, January 6, 1849, and as a child removed with his parents to LaSalle county, Illinois, where he received a good education in the public schools of that day.' From Peru, Illinois, he removed to Iowa in 1870, and located at Sandusky, where he conducted a butcher shop for the United States government, furnishing the workmen on the Des Moines Rapids canal with their meat supply. In 1877 he removed a third time, renting a part of his present farm, and occupying it for several years. Later he purchased 200 acres, which he has since increased. Here he has erected a large and substantial dwelling-house, as well as other necessary buildings, and has introduced many modern improvements. All except forty of the 353 acres are under cultivation, and the business consists of stockraising and general farming.

Mr. Swindaman is in his political adherence a member of the Republican organization, as he believes the ascendency of that party necessary to the continued prosperity and well-being of the nation. He is influential in the ranks of his party, and at the present time holds the office of trustee of his township, being in his second term. He is also public school director, a position which he has held for a number of terms, discharging its duties with that strict fidelity and practical ability which characterizes all his acts. Religiously he is a member of the Catholic church, and in his fraternal relations he is connected with the Independent Order of Odd Fellows.

In 1875 Mr. Swindaman was united in marriage to Miss Amanda McCord, a native of Lee county and daughter of Joseph C. McCord, one of the pioneer settlers of Iowa, he having come to Lee county from Ohio at an early date. He is now deceased, his demise having occurred about ten years ago. To Mr. and Mrs. Swindaman have been born seven sons and two daughters, all natives of Charleston township, and all educated in the public schools of that township. They are: Lawrence J., Joseph C., who is engaged in railroad work; William A., Walter, a machinist for the Santa Fe Railroad, and resides at Fort Madison; Charles, Frank, Eddie D., Genevie, wife of Simon Griswold, of Fort Madison and has one child, Grace; and Katie.

Mr. Swindaman is of German descent, being the son of Lawrence and Catherine (Kirn) Swindaman, both natives of Baden. They emigrated to America in 1838, and were married in St. Louis, Missouri. The father was a farmer during the latter part of his life. He died at the age of seventy-seven years, at Marysville, Kansas. The mother survives at the age of eighty-one, and resides at Marysville. Mr. Swindaman is well known throughout the greater part of the county, and no doubt this modest review of his life will be read with interest by his many friends, who respect him for his ability and his upright character and esteem him for his genial and social disposition.

CHRISTIAN HARTMANN.

In the career of many a humble emigrant from the Old World who has braved the ocean voyage and the perils of a transfer to an alien people and a strange land, there is material for more tender and touching stories and studies of the heart and life of man than ever have been penned. For the sake of a home and a career the timid have become bold and the weak strong Fathers and mothers have left a land endeared by generations of melting memories; and with streaming eyes have sought a land of promise that their children might have room to rise in the world, as the good God had endowed them with strength and character. The young have come that the old might die under their own roof; and friends that those they loved might have opportunity for freedom and growth. Prosaic enough the outer life, and matter of fact enough the daily career, but the heart glows with its own riches and the inner life has its own illumination. To leave the home land and go among strangers is an act of courage, and may rival the bravery of the soldier on the field of battle. It requires enterprise to contemplate such an adventure, and the men who remove to the New World are very largely men of character and nerve. They come because they crave a larger field and are bound to thrive. Of such is the man whose name introduces this article. He is of an energetic, pushing disposition, and in spite of serious reverses has won a very fair measure of prosperity, and though still in the prime of life has had a somewhat varied and extensive experience.

Christian Hartmann was born in the Kingdom of Baden, Germany, August 24, 1858, and is the only child of John and Catherine (Messmer) Hartmann. He received his education in the schools of his native community, and after the solid manner of his countrymen was trained a baker. When he was nineteen years of age he was called to do military service, and for two years was "with the colors." When released from the army the young soldier proceeded to carry out plans he had carefully formed, and became an emigrant to the great republic over the seas. So glowing were the tales of success and so inspiring the opportunities as described by those who had already made trial of the land and people that he, too, must go. On his arrival in the United States Mr. Hartmann spent about a year in the City of New York, and then removed to Chicago, where for thirteen years he was engaged in his work as a baker, for which, as already noted, he had been thoroughly trained.

After being at work so long a time Mr. Hartmann was prostrated by a serious and prolonged illness. Before he had recovered he had lost all his property, and was left where he had begun years before. On the advice of friends he left the big city, and for a time lived in Burlington, Iowa, where he worked at his trade. In the fall of 1896 he became a resident of Fort Madison, and here for some four years he was busily engaged as a baker, working on good wages and saving his earnings. On the 21st of November, 1900, he was able to carry into effect long-cherished schemes of doing business for himself, and started a bakery and lunch room at No. 115 Pine street. He had $500 of his own, and ran into debt $1,100 more. It was taking large chances, but two years later he had paid it all, and owned his stock and outfit without a dollar of debt. He purchased the building in which he was doing business, November 21, 1903, and today it is said that his entire fortune amounts to over $10,000, all of which has grown out of his original investment of $500, with his pluck and energy. He has a large country trade in lunches, gives employment to two bakers, two boys, and a clerk, and looks forward hopefully to a still more profitable future.

THOMAS J. SIMPSON.

It is always a pleasure for the historian to trace the record of the military service of the gallant sons of the Union who rallied to the defense of their imperiled country in the great days of 1861 to 1865, and bore amid storms of shot and shell the starry banner to an overwhelming victory at the last. They were true men who left the plow and the shop and the study, to don the soldier blue, and fight and die on the Southern plains for the government of the people by the people. When, as is the case with Mr. Simpson, his services at the front exhausted his strength and vitality, and left him such a wreck that for twenty years or more he has not been able to do a stroke of work, the sacrifice was complete, and it is a life laid on the altar of duty. Our country has many such, and honors them all with equal love and reverence.

Thomas J. Simpson was born October 8, 1841, in Tennessee, and was brought by his parents up the Mississippi river on a steamboat in 1843, landing at Montrose in the month of May.

Harmon Simpson, his father, was born in South Carolina, and was married in Tennessee to Miss Margaret Trainor, who was born in Warren county, Kentucky. To this union were born nine children: Thomas J. was the fourth in order of birth, and four children are now living, including him: Mary, the widow of Nelson Cooper, lives in Montrose; Margaret, wife of James Wright, is a resident of Burlington; John D. is also a resident of Burlington. Mr. Simpson was among the earliest settlers of Montrose township. Two thousand Indians were then camped on ground now owned by Zachariah Owens. Mr. Simpson was friendly with them, and traded and mingled with them to his own profit and their convenience. He did butchering for the settlers, ran a farm and died January 4, 1861.

The maternal great-grandfather of Thomas J. Simpson, a Mr. Cummins, served in the Revolutionary War. The mother of Mr. Simpson died May 19, 1888. After the loss of her husband she never remarried, and both she and her husband were buried in the Montrose cemetery. They were members of the church of Latter Day Saints, and both saw the prophet, and his brother, Joseph, and Hiram Smith, after their assassination at Carthage. They lived in Nauvoo about two months. They were converted by an elder preaching in Tennessee, in company with several families.

Thomas J. Simpson was a student in a subscription school before the day of public instruction. His first work was plowing corn at fifty cents a day. Before the opening of the canal at the Des Moines Rapids he worked as a "rafter of freight," loading and unloading cargoes during the summer season for some ten or eleven years.

At the time the Civil War broke out Mr. Simpson was employed as a farm laborer, receiving monthly wages. In January, 1862, he enlisted in Company B, Seventeenth Iowa Volunteer Infantry, and served Uncle Sam as a private until September 12, 1862. Capt. William Hoxie was in command of his company, and Col. J. W. Rankin of the regiment. He was mustered into service at Keokuk to serve three years or during the war. His regiment was assigned to the Second Brigade, Third Division, the Fifteenth and Seventeenth Corps, Army of Tennessee. He took part in the seige of Corinth, the battles of Iuka, Champion Hill, and Chattanooga, and received an honorable discharge at Keokuk, September 12, 1862, on account of disability. He re-enlisted February 25, 1864, as a private in Company C, Third Iowa Volunteer Cavalry, under Captain Wilson and Col. J. W. Noble, and was attached with his regiment to Winslow's Brigade of Cavalry, a part of the Army of the West. He participated in the Guntown expedition and the battle of Cupolo, Mississippi, as well as in many skirmishes of less importance. He was honorably discharged at Davenport, Iowa, in July, 1865, on account of the close of the war. He was in the hospital at Hamburg for six weeks on account of poisoning, and was brought with others to the Estes House Hospital, at Keokuk, where he was treated for three months and then discharged in 1862. During his second enlistment he was under hospital treatment two months at Memphis, and was then transported to the Simpson House Hospital, at Keokuk.. From this institution he was sent to Davenport, where he received his discharge as noted above. The sickness from which he suffered and from which he is still troubled, resulted from the poisoning already noted, and assumes a form of epilepsy. On account of this serious disability he is a pensioner of the United States, and well deserves every cent he receives from the hands of a grateful country.

Mr. Simpson enlisted in the Regular Army at the close of the war, and was stationed at Fort Wadsworth, Dakota, then on the far frontier. The soldiers were very much occupied for some months in keeping the hostile Indians from predatory excursions into Minnesota. They burnt brick and built houses at the Fort. He was in the Regular Army for three years, nine months of which were spent in Galveston, Texas. After the expiration of his military service Mr. Simpson presently came back to Montrose, and was engaged for some years in hotel work, also being employed in the sawmill four summers and three winters, then taking up again the hotel work, which he followed for a time. He became disabled and for five years was an inmate of the Soldiers's Home, at Marshalltown, Iowa. When this period had passed he was given a pension, and with the bounty of the government came back to Montrose, where he bought a home, and has since led a quiet life. For twenty years or more he has not been able to do a stroke of work. He owns a place on First street, which comprises a half block. He boards with the family that live in the house. He is a member of Tip Best Post, No. 75, Grand Army of the Republic, where he now holds the position of Officer of the Day. In religious matters he is associated with the Reorganized church of Jesus Christ, Latter Day Saints, which he serves as a deacon of the Montrose branch. In politics he was formerly a Democrat, but of late years has voted the Republican ticket as the party for a poor and laboring man.

Mr. Simpson has been much handicapped in life by a frail physique, and his poor parentage. He has had to work out from childhood, a fact that interfered with his early schooling. His memories are vivid and interesting. He has recollections of the mob of 300 who came to drive the Mormons out of Nauvoo in 1846, and burning of the Mormon Temple at Nauvoo, in November, 1848, which was attended by some 20,000 people. When the Temple was burned the light was so bright at Montrose that one could see to pick a pin from the ground. The Icarians, a communist organization, came from France, and they proposed to restore the Temple as a place of worship, but it was destroyed by a cyclone. The Icarians left, and their place was taken by a German settlement. At the present time nearly all the Nauvoo country is occupied by Germans and their descendants.

JOHN HARDWICK.

John Hardwick, who is one of the older residents of Montrose, and a most active and enthusiastic worker in the local organization of the Grand Army of the Republic, comes of an old Kentucky family long established in the "dark and bloody hunting ground."

His ancestors have left traditions of their experiences in those far-away days when the beautiful and inviting forests of that region rang with the war cry of the savage, and the wild beast, and the wilder man of the wilderness made life a perpetual round of dangers. Now a land of peace, song and story keep green the memories of the old pioneers who fought their way to the possession of a land fair and fertile after many years of blood and strife. John Hardwick himself knew little of this, as he was removed to the Indiana shore when but a babe, and reared in a more settled community. It is, however, in his blood, and he is proud of what his forefathers did in reclaiming the wilderness and making possible the great state.

John Hardwick was born in Kentucky, November 13, 1834, a son of Edward Hardwick, who was born in Kentucky, and of Mattie Hooker. His parents were married in that state, but early removed to Indiana, where they found a home in Clark county, where the father devoted part of his time to farming. Our subject learned the harness trade at Lexington, Indiana, at which he worked five years. He served in the Civil War, and was company saddler while in the army.

The mother brought the family to Lee county, Iowa, and settled them on a farm, while the father remained in Indiana, but after the passing of a year or more returned to him. They removed to Lee county in 1851.

John Hardwick was married March 4, 1855, to Miss Martha A. Scott, a native of Wheeling, West Virginia, where she was born in 1839. Her parents made the journey by boat to Lee county in 1847. Her father, Luke Scott, was born in Maryland, and Rachel Frazier, her mother, was a native of Virginia, where they were married. He was a farmer at this time.

Mr. Hardwick was engaged in farming for a time after his marriage, and was then appointed mail carrier from Keokuk to Charleston, Charleston to Bentonport, and Charleston to Franklin, making his trips sometimes on horseback, and sometimes by teams, though hiring much of this work done, and taking star route contracts from the government. He and his brother, Mitchell, were engaged on different routes by way of Keokuk, Montrose, Keosauqua and Mount Pleasant daily, by way of Salem.

In 1864 Mr. Hardwick enlisted in Company C, Third Iowa Cavalry, having William Wilson for captain and a Mr. Noble for colonel. The field of service for the command was extensive, covering Alabama, Mississippi, Georgia, Texas, Tennessee, Missouri and West Virginia, fighting weeks at a time for day and night. Mr. Hardwick was company saddler, while in the service. He participated in important engagements in Guntown, Salina, and Ripley, Mississippi. Much of their service was on the skirmish line around Memphis. At Guntown the regiment met a severe defeat, and there Mr. Hardwick received a wound that nearly cost him his life, being struck on the head by an exploding shell, a piece of which struck him on the left side and that part of his head is still insensible to feeling. A gunshot grazed his left wrist and right arm, but he had no hospital record. At one time he had the measles and was assigned to the hospital, but escaped by eluding the guard, and sought his tent. He was marked on the records as a deserter, but was pardoned by Colonel Noble, and missed no fight in which his command was engaged, though not obliged to bear arms because of his position as company saddler. His service with the company covered about nineteen months in all, at the hardest time of the war.

When the strife had ended and the great host dissolved in peace, Mr. Hardwick engaged in farming in Pike county, Missouri, where he owned a farm on which he spent three years. In 1869 Mr. Hardwick returned to Keokuk, Lee county, and here he remained a year. In 1870 he came to Montrose under engagement with Healy, Felt & White, to take charge of the extensive stables connected with their sawmill, and for many years he had the care of over thirty horses. Since 1882 he has been unable to work, and "has taken life easy," as the saying is. His home is in the village of Montrose, and he has built the most of it himself. Here he owns four lots and is quite fore-handed.

As already noted, Mr. Hardwick is a devoted member of the Grand Army of the Republic, being sergeant of the Tip Best Post, No. 75, and is a constant attendant at state and county encampments. His wife was a charter member of the Woman's Relief Corps, an organization not now in existence. In politics he is a Republican.

Edward Hardwick, the father of the subject of this sketch, served in the Black Hawk War, and his son, Hiram, served in the Mexican War. This son is now living in Pike county, Missouri, and has attained the age of seventy-six years.

Mr. and Mrs. John Hardwick are the parents of five children: William M., general manager of a grocery business, married Miss Bertha Jones, of San Francisco, and is the father of one child, Perry E.; Ida Belle, the wife of Seth A. Beemer, of Almer, Ontario, and the mother of four children, Ivy B., Emory, Delia and Gilesbie H. Mr. Beemer is in the employ of a canning company. Perry E., twice married, but has lost both wives by death. He is the father of two children, Mamie D. and Ida B., and is now employed in a mill at Victoria, Louisiana, as a sawyer. John E., a resident of Kansas City, is unmarried. Della May, wife of C. W. Kendall, of Montrose, a carpenter, and now marshal and street supervisor by appointment. The motherless children of Perry Hardwick are with their grand-parents, Mr. and Mrs. John Hardwick, where they have a pleasant and happy home.

The subject of this sketch lived in 1862 and 1863 in Salem, Henry county, where he ran a stage route. While there he fed a company of recruits for the Union army three weeks. Both he and his excellent lady are highly respected by all who know them. They are closely connected with the Methodist church, though never formally uniting with it, and are numbered among its most earnest supporters.

JACOB YOTTER.

Jacob Yotter, who is a prominent retired contractor of Fort Madison, deserves a place in this volume of history because of the fact that, starting alone in the world, and working his way without any outside aid and without any other capital than his own ability, industry and determined purpose, he has raised himself to a respected place in the community and achieved success of a substantial character. Born in Byrne, Germany, October 15, 1835, he came to America with his parents when about nine years of age. The voyage was made in a sailing vessel, and occupied forty days. The family first stopped at Keokuk, Lee county, and went thence to Charleston, where the father bougth a farm. Mr. Yotter, the father, died in West Point in 1864, and is buried in the city cemetery at that place, and the mother is buried at Warsaw, Indiana.

The early boyhood of Jacob Yotter was passed on the farm, and there he grew up in the acquirement of those habits of thought and action which proved invaluable to him in his after life. With a view, however, to broadening his field of activity, he left the farm at the age of fifteen years and began to learn a trade—that of brickmason. At this and similar work he continued to employ himself successfully until about three years ago, when he was obliged by the duties of public office to devote his time to other affairs in the interest of the city. He first located at West Point, where he lived for three years, working at his trade. In 1888 he came to Fort Madison, where he built a home at 821 Sixth street, and here, for more than sixteen years, he has been in business as a carpenter, and while amassing for himself a goodly share of material wealth, has erected a large number of public edifices, which add to the appearance and reputation, and consequently the prosperity, of his adopted city. Specimens of his work are the two church structures of the Methodist Episcopal denomination, as well as that of the English Lutherans, in Fort Madison, and the convent at Nauvoo, Illinois. He has built in all about fifteen churches and a number of residences. The volume of his business was always so large that he was compelled to employ constantly a force of five or six experienced workmen.

Mr. Yotter was married in September, 1860, at West Point, to Miss Anna Carston. Thirty-one years of wedded life were theirs ere her death occurred at Fort Madison in the year 1901. Five children survive her, as follows: Frank, who married Miss Minnie Robers, of Hannibal, Missouri, and follows his father's trade; Charles, who married Miss Gussie Best, and has his home in Indiana; George, who married Minnie Deloshman, of Fort Madison; John, located in Minnesota; Sophy, and Rosena, who is employed as a clerk in Eitman's shoe store.

One incident of our subject's career is worthy of mention as showing his willingness to perform any duty which may appeal to him as for the public good. During the Civil War he was sworn into the service of the United States at Nashville, Tennessee, and was with the Union troops for one year, acting as blacksmith's helper. He is a member of the Methodist Episcopal church, and in politics gives his support to the Democratic party. Fraternally he is connected with the Ancient Order of United Workmen. He has never sought public office, but during his residence at West Point was called by his fellow citizens to serve them in the office of alderman, and three years ago was appointed by the city council of Fort Madison to be street commissioner for this city, which position he still occupies.

In 1900 Mr. Yotter met with a most regretable accident in the form of a fall on an ice-covered sidewalk, which caused a sprained wrist, and later resulted in bone cancer which made necessary the amputation of the arm at the elbow. In other respects, however, he is perhaps a better specimen of physical manhood than most others of his age, and the high standard of his character is attested by the fact that of him all good men speak well. It is with pleasure that this sketch of his life is here presented.

CHARLES KAMMERER.

The Kammerer family has long been represented in the business and social circles of Lee county, by men of solid worth and character, not inclined perhaps to show and display but honest and upright. The name was known here as early as 1847, and during the almost sixty years now intervening it has been kept clean and free from stain.

Charles Kammerer was born in Delaware, Ohio, February 12, 1846, and is a son of Gotlieb and Dorathea (Conrad) Kammerer. The father was born in Germany, where he was reared in what was once the Kingdom of Wurtemberg. He early emigrated to this country, and in 1843 made his home in Ohio, then the favored resort of home-seekers from the old world. In 1847 he joined the westward-moving throng of pioneer settlers and located himself and his family in Lee county, where he spent the remainder of his days. For many years he followed the butcher trade, in which he was quite successful, accumulating a very comfortable competence, and commanding the confidence and respect of all who knew him. He died December 1, 1888, and his widow the following year.

Charles Kammerer for a time followed in his father's footsteps and was also a butcher, and for a period of four years was associated in that business with a Mr. Buescher. Thinking an out-of-door occupation would be better for him, in company with his brother Albert, he carried on the family homestead for four years, and then with this same brother he went into a butcher shop in Fort Madison. This was an undertaking which proved highly successful, and the two brothers were still together in business when Charles died, September 10, 1896.

Mr. Kammerer was a Democrat, and took a somewhat prominent part in local affairs. He held the position of trustee of Green Bay township for two terms, and was looked upon as one of the leading spirits at the various gatherings of the faithful of the party.

The subject of this sketch was married February 11, 1879, to Miss Amalie Lachman. She was born in Erie county, New York, and is a daughter of Edward and Anna (Bruhne) Lachman, both natives of Germany, but married in the City of New York. Of their four children, Mrs. Kammerer is the eldest. Mr. and Mrs. Kammerer were the parents of four children who are now living, and one child who died an infant. The four living children are as follows: Henry G., Nelson C., Lena D. and Harry E.

Mrs. Kammerer still survives and is the recipient of tender care and solicitude from a wide circle of friends and relatives. She is a lady of more than the usual force of character, and her kindly disposition and ready sympathies make her a strong figure in the community.

HON. JAMES BLAKENY PEASE.

Of recent years there has arisen a wide-spread discussion concerning the question of what really constitutes success, and while some aspects of the matter seem destined to remain unsettled, all ages and peoples have agreed that there are two modes of action which are entitled to the name "success" beyond dispute. The first of these is a life of piety and honesty, and the second is a career of distinguished service to the state or nation. To both of these the Hon. James Blakeny Pease has conscientiously and intelligently devoted himself throughout the course of his long and useful life. He was born in Washington county, Pennsylvania, January 24, 1817, the son of Andrew and Mary (Blakeny) Pease. The father was born in Maryland, and as a boy was brought by his father, Nicholas Pease, to Washington county in 1769. Nicholas, the grandfather, was born in Germany; came to the United States when seventeen years of age, and reared a family in Washington county. There the father of our subject was often engaged in garrison duty as a protection to his community against the raids of the Indian savages, and at one time took part in a battle of some importance at Sandusky, Ohio, June 4, 1782. He passed his life as a farmer in Washington county. His second wife, who became the mother of Hon. James P. Blakeny Pease, was Mary Blakeny, daughter of James Blakeny, who was of Irish descent, and who married Ruth Drennan in Ireland, later coming to America, and making his home in Washington county.

Nicholas Pease was a communicant of the Lutheran church; Andrew adopted the Presbyterian faith, in which his wife, Mary Blakeny, was reared.

James Blakeny Pease was educated in the select and common schools, taking his Latin in the former. He was his father's assistant in the duties of the farm until the death of his parent in 1844, when he married Miss Elizabeth McCullough. They continued to live upon the home farm until 1851, when they removed to Lee county, Iowa, and settled in Marion township. There the wife died in 1856, leaving five children, of whom three survive, the eldest son, Samuel G., having died of typhoid fever at Memphis, Tennessee, during the Civil War. Those living are: Frances M., widow of Henry V. Evans; Anna B., wife of Lebbeus Clark, of Mills county, Iowa, and John McCullough, of Cedar township, Lee county. On coming to Iowa Mr. Pease bought a farm of 320 acres, upon which he lived until 1865, when he sold it, and the following year purchased a fine grain and fruit farm in Van Buren county. In 1859 he married Miss Catherine L. Crawford, who died in 1865. The ensuing fifteen years were devoted to agricultural pursuits at the farm in Van Buren county. In 1880 Mr. Pease purchased a home in Fort Madison, and here he has since continued to reside. He has been engaged in manufacturing to some extent, but has now retired from active business.

In politics Mr. Pease was reared as a Democrat, and has continued throughout his life a firm adherent of the political tenets of Thomas Jefferson. He has served his party and his state in prominent and important capacities, and few men are better known in the state of Iowa for zeal and devotion to the public welfare than James B. Pease. Few men have done more effective service in placing the commonwealth in that proud position which she occupies today among her sister states. In 1856 he was elected to represent Lee county in the state legislature, and in 1873 was elected from Van Buren county to the state senate on the Anti-Monopoly ticket. While a member of the legislature he held the position of chairman of the Committee of Reform Schools, and took a leading part in the regulation and betterment of those institutions. Another service for which he merits peculiar honor was the part he played in the support of the bill to regulate the exorbitant charges of railroad companies. Since 1880 he has not been especially active in politics, but has, however, served a number of terms as justice of the peace in Fort Madison.

October 17, 1867, Mr. Pease married Mrs. Catherine Brownlee, nee Clark. Catherine Clark was born in Washington county, Pennsylvania, December 16, 1826. She was a daughter of Joseph and Catherine

(Andrews) Clark. Her grandfather was Joseph Clark, a pioneer of Washington county, Pennsylvania. There the father of Mrs. Pease lived and died, he being a farmer all his life. Mrs. Pease was educated in Washington Seminary, and was first married to Mr. Samuel T. Brownlee, who died in March, 1854, leaving three children: Nelson, who lives upon the old homestead; Adeline, now Mrs. Colin M. Reed, of Washington, Pennsylvania, and Samuel, a farmer of Lee county, Iowa.

They are members of the Presbyterian church, of which our subject has been an elder for forty-five years, he having been a charter member of Sharon congregation, and being the only one of the eight original members now living. He organized the congregation in 1851, and helped to build the church edifice. There he was elected an elder, and has served in the same capacity in Fort Madison since 1880. Here he assisted in the building of the present church. During his earlier years he acted as Sunday-school superintendent and as teacher in the prison Sunday-school, at this place. In Van Buren county Mr. Pease was one of the organizers of the Grange. At the present time his principal work, outside the home, is the service of the church. To correctly estimate the life work of Mr. Pease would be to determine his usefulness in many lines of activity, for business, civil and religious interests have all been promoted through his labors, profited by his wise judgment and benefited by his championship. To him justly belongs the distinction of being called one of the most representative men and honored citizens of Fort Madison.

W. C. WILLARD.

W. C. Willard, a well-known and highly successful farmer of Washington township, Lee county, Iowa, is a native son of his township, where he was born April 18, 1850, the son of Sidney R. and Angelina (Richards) Willard. Mr. Willard received his early education in the district public schools and also attended Denmark Academy, meanwhile learning thoroughly and in detail the management and work of his father's farm, a branch of his training which was destined to play a large part in the success which he afterward achieved. When twenty-two years of age he removed to the City of Des Moines, where he engaged in the real-estate business for two years, the first year being spent in erecting buildings which were disposed of the second year at considerable profit. Thereafter he remained at the parental home until his twenty-eighth year, at the same time, however, cultivating his farm, and this has since been the principal business to which he has devoted his abilities.

Mr. Willard has added greatly to his original farm, until now he owns 130 acres in the farm on which he resides and in addition 404 acres on sections 12, 13 and 14, a total of 535 acres of extremely high-grade farming lands which compare favorably for productive quality with any in Lee county or southern Iowa and constitute him one of the principal landholders of this section. Here he conducts general farming operations on an extensive scale and engages largely in cattleraising and feeding, applying to the care and promotion of his vast interests the latest approved and scientific methods and manifesting a thoroughly modern spirit that accounts in some measure for the gratifying results which he has been able to obtain. When he purchased the home farm it was unimproved, but he at once erected the necessary buildings, put up fences and made many other important alterations, to which he has since added very materially in many respects. He removed to the farm soon after his marriage, and has made this his place of residence continuously since. On September 26, 1888, he was united in marriage to Miss Frankie Shephard, a native of Green Bay township, Lee county, and daughter of John H. Shephard. Mrs. Willard was educated in Knox College, after which she successfully pursued for a time the profession of teaching, and is a lady of many social graces, enjoying popularity among a large circle of friends. The union of Mr. and Mrs. Willard has been graced by the birth of two children, these being Helen Effie, born April 21, 1892, and Clarence Shephard, born July 16, 1898.

Mr. Willard has ever exhibited a praiseworthy devotion to all worthy causes, and is a generous contributor to the work of the church, being a member of Lost Creek Christian church, as is also Mrs. Willard. In his party affiliations he is a member of the Democratic party, in which he is a prominent and well-known worker, having at one time been elected to the highest office in the gift of his township, that of trustee, in which his business ability was employed to the benefit of his constituents. In the attainment of his present prosperous estate he has had many obstacles to overcome, and what he has accomplished has been done without assistance, being entirely the result of his own force of character, so that he is fully deserving of that old but expressive title of self-made man. These facts in his career have made him many admirers, while his genial disposition and absolute integrity and fairness in all his dealings have won for him the general respect and a large number of sincere friends.

HENRY CATTERMOLE.

Henry Cattermole, whose name holds a prominent place in the early annals of Fort Madison, Iowa, and who has now passed to his reward, was born in London, England, September 10, 1803, a son of William and Susan (Thompson) Cattermole. His parents reared to maturity a family of eight children, five of whom came to the United States, and all of whom are now dead.

At an early age Henry Cattermole learned the butcher trade, which he followed until his coming to the United States in 1825. On arrival on these shores he was for a time engaged in a mercantile enterprise at Rochester, New York. This proved unsuccessful, largely owing to his confidence in pretended friends, by whom he was grossly deceived, if not robbed. In 1830 he removed to Cincinnati, Ohio, where two years later he was married to Miss Elizabeth Cattermole, a sister of Arthur C. Cattermole, whose sketch appears elsewhere in this volume. She was a lady of many excellent traits, and the union proved in every way a happy one. Mr. Cattermole was here engaged in a mercantile business, which proved fairly successful, but which, however, he disposed of to take up a similar undertaking at Appanoose, Illinois, where he remained until 1841. That year marked his location in Fort Madison, Iowa, where he set up a dry goods and pork-packing establishment. This proved largely successful and grew upon his hands from year to year to such an extent that in 1859 he formed with his brother-in-law, Arthur C. Cattermole, the mercantile firm of H. & A. C. Cattermole, a firm which had an exceedingly creditable history, and which continued unbroken until 1871, when the senior member of the firm retired in favor of Arthur C. Cattermole. This was done largely on account of the infirmities of advancing age, though other interests were also influential in inducing him to retire from the packing house.

As early as 1856 Mr. Cattermole had demonstrated a financial ability that made its impression on the banking interests of the city and that year he connected himself with the banking house of Knapp & Eaton. In 1858, when that institution gave way to the Fort Madison branch of the State Bank of Iowa, and the Fort Madison National Bank was organized, he became one of the original stockholders of the last-named corporation, and served as one of its directors until January 30, 1872. That year its charter was suspended, and the Bank of Fort Madison was organized under the state law. Mr. Cattermole was one of its original stockholders, and later became its sole proprietor. It was very successfully conducted by him until April 6, 1875, when he sold it to Charles Brewster and Joseph A. Smith. After thus disposing of the Bank of Fort Madison Mr. Cattermole, in company with others, the following year organized the German-American Bank, with himself as its president, and his cousin and brother-in-law, A. C. Cattermole, as the vice-president, positions they both retained as long as they lived.

Mr. Cattermole was universally conceded to be one of the substantial men of Lee county, and was highly regarded alike for his known integrity, his genial spirit, and his generous heart. In early life he was associated with the Whig party, but on the formation of the Republican party he became one of its zealous and active workers. In his later years, however, he was a Democrat.

Ever a firm believer in the religion of Jesus Christ, Mr. Cattermole lived a life that brought no blush of shame to his professed faith. He was an attendant and a liberal supporter of the Episcopal church.

Upon his death, Mr. Cattermole left in his will the sum of $10,000 for the building of a training school. As the sum was not sufficient to meet the requirements of the bequest this section of the will was set aside, and his widow later put up a beautiful library building, which with its contents and equipment cost $30,000. It was erected in 1893, and is called the "Cattermole Memorial Library." It is a neat and attractive building, and is greatly admired by all who visit the city with an interest in the higher things of life. Mrs. Cattermole was much interested in its construction, but was called home before it was finally completed. Her last words were: "I wish that I could see it." It is of brick construction, and stands on Pine street, between Second and Third streets.

Mr. and Mrs. Cattermole were people of the best character, the kindliest spirit, and ever regarded themselves as accountable to Almighty God for the proper use of the wealth He had put into their hands.

EDWARD HILLS BROWN.

It was a boast of old that if the mountainous states of New England were of little value when considered from an agricultural point of view, they were of great value in raising men. And truly the men that New England has contributed to the making of the West have been of the large-hearted and the strong-brained order, men of might and men of mind, and who can tell the story of their achievements in these vast regions taat are now great and populous states! What would Minneapolis be without the State of Maine? Or southeastern Iowa without its splendid draughts of manhood from New Hampshire and Vermont? Of a thousand communities in the West the same thing is true,—the men of thought and action, the strong and forceful pioneers were born and bred in the rough and rocky East. Among them is not to be lightly reckoned the esteemed and honorable man, Edward Hills Brown, whose name introduces this article.

Mr. Brown, long a resident of Denmark township, and now living in the village of that name, was born in New Ipswich, New Hampshire, May 9, 1836, a son of William and Lucy (Taylor) Brown, both born and bred in that state. The year of his birth his parents sought a home in Iowa, arriving here October 26, 1836, making the journey with a two-horse carriage. They were a little over six weeks on the road. Immediately on his arrival he entered upon government land and eventually became one of the largest land owners of the county, and at the time of his death, which occurred in January, 1877, being worth over $30,000. In his native state he had been a merchant, but misfortunes had attended him and he had come a poor man to the land of promise. He lived to seventy years of age, and his widow, who survived him many years, was almost ninety when she was called away. He was devoted to farming and the dairy interests, and in the early days ran a threshing outfit so that he was familiarly known as "old thresher Brown." Coming as he did from the moral heart of the country, it was to be expected that he should take strong ground as a determined opponent of human slavery. This he did, and was for years an earnest and enthusiastic abolitionist. In religion he was a member of the Congregational church.

Of the eight children born to William

and Lucy Brown, four were boys and four were girls: William died at the age of sixty-three; Charles has his home in Alabama; Edward Hills forms the subject of this biography; George, born in Lee county, is now dead; Eliza is Mrs. Day; Harriet married Newton Mills and lives at Houston, Texas, where he has a very valuable business; Lucy lives with her sister; Ellen S. married a Mr. Tibbetts, and has her home in Eldon, Iowa.

Edward Hills Brown received his education largely in the district school, though he was for some time a student in Denmark Academy, an institution quite noted in the early days as a school of high grade, and the finishing "alma mater" of many of the young people, who were afterward to become famous in local or general affairs. While still quite a lad he was active in helping his father bring their prairie farm under cultivation, and make it productive of ease and comfort. After the fashion of the times he married early, becoming a husband when only about twenty years of age. His wife, Ellen Dudley, was born in New Hampshire and came into Lee county when she was sixteen years of age. To this union were born the following children: Arthur A., who lives at Summer, Missouri, and is the father of a family of four children; Clarence, also a resident of Missouri, has a family of six children; Ettlee married William Taylor, and is now a widow with three children living; Charles lives in Mt. Pleasant, Iowa, where he follows the occupation of a well digger, and is the father of five children. Mrs. Brown died in 1888, and her ashes are interred in the local cemetery.

Mr. Brown was married a second time, Mrs. Ann M., widow of John M. Deimer, becoming his wife. Mr. Deimer was a blacksmith by trade, and was working in the town at the time of his death. To this marriage were born: Louis P., now a resident of Mt. Pleasant, and the father of one child; Albert John and Cora Elizabeth, who are at home.

After his first marriage Mr. Brown rented a farm, which he afterward bought. He sold it in 1863, and with his wife and two children went to Denver, Colorado. In crossing the plains he saw only two small herds of buffaloes, though he was six weeks on the way. He remained in the mountains only one summer, and while there was engaged in brickmaking, which proved then more profitable than gold digging. When he came back to Lee county, after his wife's death, he bought a place in the village and gave up active farming. In politics he always took a very independent position, and voted for the men he thought most qualified to meet the duties of the positions they sought. In religion he has associated himself with the Advent body, and early united with the church of that faith at Mt. Pleasant.

Mr. Brown was very early an advocate of the dairy interest as a relief for the farmers who suffered greatly from the low price of grain, and the excessive cost of transportation. As early as 1850 he ran a cheese factory that required the milk of a hundred cows for its successful operation, and for more than thirty years he was devoted to this progressive enterprise. Though not now in active business he is still prominent in all local affairs and his experienve and standing, together with his well-known probity, give weight to all he says.

ROBERT CHESTNUT.

Robert Chestnut is the name of a venerable resident of Lee county, Iowa, whose home is on section 32 of Green Bay township, where he is now passing the closing years of an unusually protracted and useful life. Far down the hill the shadows fall and stretch away behind, yet his heart still sings of youth, and the crown of years rests but lightly on him. Though his life is a link to bind us to the remote past, he is still hale and hearty and bears himself with that vigor and buoyancy that mark a peculiar vitality. His natural force is still unabated, and his mind clear and vigorous; so that conversation with him is a privilege and an instruction. Such men are rare in any community, and especially so in any region where a single life may unite the wilderness and the peopled state, so that always they are reverently regarded by the thoughtful.

Mr. Chestnut was born in Mercer county, Pennsylvania, May 20, 1811, a son of Andrew and Mary Chestnut. He lived in his native county until the month of March, 1824, when he removed to Burlington, Iowa, coming by way of the Ohio and the Mississippi rivers to that city at a time when it consisted of a single frame house and a few shanties. With two other men he went to Augusta, where the three put up a saw and gristmill on the Skunk river. Before coming to this county he had learned the carpenter trade, a business much in demand in a new country. After the construction of the mill he put himself up a carpenter shop and prepared to follow his trade. A sudden rise in the river swept it away, and Mr. Chestnut was so discouraged at the unexpected reverse that he gave up all thought of immediate resumption of work at his trade, and coming into Green Bay township bought the improvements a settler had made on section 32, and when the land came into market he secured it, and became the owner of a fine farm of 120 acres. In 1836 he completed the title, and has since made his home here, though for a number of years he worked at his trade in Augusta. In later years when carpenters became numerous and wages fell away to very small figures he gave up the trade and devoted himself entirely to his farming operations which, taken together, have proved highly remunerative and satisfactory.

The present house which he makes his home was built by Mr. Chestnut in 1850, prior to which a log cabin answered for family shelter. The orchard which has flourished for so many years he brought from Pennsylvania, to which state he had returned for a visit in 1830, and carrying back to his pioneer home both seeds and sprouts, out of which came in time a magnificent fruitage that was the delight of the country for miles around.

Among the memories that crowd the mind of Mr. Chestnut are those of Indians in the early days. He has seen at one time as many as twenty canoes going up the Skunk river, and, though they were undoubtedly friendly, it was a thrilling sight to contemplate them as representatives of a fast-vanishing race. It is possible that they seldom presented themselves to the pioneers in that light. Rather at their best they were a nuisance; and at their worst, "painted and hideous devils, just let loose from hell." Mr. Chestnut has seen and talked with Keokuk and Black Hawk. With the latter he made the journey from St. Louis to Burlington on the steamboat, and Keokuk was the first Indian he ever saw. When he first came to Lee county game was scarce, as the Indians had driven it away by their close hunting. The skeletons of elks and buffaloes were still numerous, and he says he was here a year before he saw a rabbit.

Mr. Chestnut was married in August, 1838, to Miss Mary Haynes, and to their union were born three boys and three girls, of whom only two are now living: Napoleon B., who lives upon the farm and is engaged in its cultivation; Elden Lore married Matilda Farmer, and is a resident of Colorado; his wife is now devoting herself to the care of her venerable father-in-law, whose own wife passed to her final rest in the month of January, 1900. Her ashes repose in the Tierney cemetery. Mr. Chestnut is a Democrat, and is proud of the fact that his first presidential vote was cast for General Jackson. To his original 120 acres of land he has added ten acres, and still retains the ownership of the entire tract, which is regarded as very valuable.

Illustrating the fruitfulness of much of the wandering and unwise journeyings of the western settlers, who went here and there and everywhere in search of a fortune, which they might better have secured by staying at home and attending strictly to business, Mr. Chestnut left home May 10, 1852, and crossed the plains, reaching California, his destination, the night before Christmas of that year. He went as far as Salt Lake on the direct route, and then journeyed south for a thousand miles to escape traveling in the mountains by winter. He was gone from home twenty months, and when he returned found for almost two years of hardship and privation he had cleared only $2.10.

Mr. Chestnut is still a hale and hearty man, and scarcely a day is permitted to pass without his doing something around the house or yard. Yet the long years are behind him, his friends are proud of him, and his children tenderly cherish and care for him. A beautiful setting for the closing period of a noble career.

JULIUS EICHHORN.

Julius Eichhorn is a notable representative of an old Saxon family, and though himself born in this country, he has manifested in the course of a peculiarly active and interesting career many of the most interesting traits of his paternal race and blood. He has been industrious to a marked degree, and has never shown any disposition to shirk hard work or avoid his full share of the labor to be done. He has been prudent and economical, and while not miserly or stingy, he has never shown any disposition to waste his money in foolish extravagance. He has kept his word and his pledge has been like a bond. Kind to the poor, and with an ear always open to the cry of the needy, he has ever been a good neighbor, a generous friend and an upright citizen. These are the virtues that belong to the Saxon blood, and these characterize the career of the man whose life deeds and achievements are the subject of this biographical history.

Julius Eichhorn, a prominent farmer and breeder of Percheron horses for twenty-two years, and a respected citizen of West Point township, Lee county, Iowa, has his home on section 12, of that township, was born in this same part of the county where he now lives, on section 7, August 28, 1851, a son of Charles and Barbara (Holzberger) Eichhorn, both of whom were born in Saxony, Germany, though married in the United States. The father was highly educated in music, and well versed in the classics, being far above the common run in the extent and variety of his information, his strength of character and refinement of soul. He came to this country in 1835, making the ocean voyage in a sailing vessel, a trip that was slow and dangerous, being more than six months on the water. His feet first pressed American soil in the City of New York, where, however, he did not remain but journeyed at once to Saginaw, Michigan, where for two years he was employed in a brewery. For about the same period he lived in Burlington, Iowa, after which he purchased 150 acres of partly improved land in West Point township, Lee county, and here he spent the balance of his days in its cultivation. He lived to be a very old man, and kept his health and strength to the last, the direct cause of his death was the effect of a kick received from a horse when he was over eighty-five years of age.

Charles Eichhorn was accompanied in his removal to America by his father and mother, then both advanced in years. They died in Lee county and were buried in the West Point cemetery. Charles Eichhorn was a hard-working man, and passing through the hardships of the early days came out well and strong, and possessing a fine farm. Of a fine character and a social spirit he was popular with his neighbors, and had many friends in the community. Before coming to this country he taught the violin, of which he was a master, and after his arrival in this county was a leader of the band that on many occasions furnished music for Joe Smith and the Mormons. He was well acquainted with Smith, and also with both Black Hawk and Keokuk, celebrated Indian chiefs. He served in the militia as a private, and assisted in the expulsion of the Mormons from Nauvoo and Illinois at the call of the government. In the early days he had many exciting experiences, and his family still preserve his rifle, his faithful friend in times of trial and danger. In early life he was a Democrat, later he became a Whig, and in the organization of the Republican party, became its ardent supporter.

To Charles and Barbara Eichhorn were born the following children: Henry and

Adolphus, who are dead; Julius is the subject of this sketch; Amelia, who is dead, and August were twins; Edward; Charles, who is dead, and Barbara. Both father and mother are now dead, and the green grass waves over their graves in the West Point cemetery. He was over eighty-five, and she also lived to advanced years, when they died.

Julius Eichhorn received his education in the local schools, and remained at home until he was over thirty years of age. In 1881 he was married to Miss Anna Onstott, who was born upon the place they now occupy as a home, on section 12, West Point township, a daughter of John and Rachel (Bean) Onstott, of whom a sketch may be found on another page of this work. After their marriage Mr. and Mrs. Eichhorn lived for eight years in Pleasant Ridge township, two years in Washington township, and then removed to Missouri, where they remained until 1901. That year they returned to West Point township, and settled where we find them today, living on what was the birthplace of Mrs. Eichhorn. Mr. Eichhorn has always owned the different farms on which he has lived, and he still owns the Missouri place, a finely cultivated farm of 240 acres, as he does the farm on which he makes his home, which comprises 171 acres.

Mr. and Mrs. Eichhorn have one child, Ella, who is at home a bright young woman, a charming belle of the community, and a great comfort to her parents' hearts. The family is associated with the Presbyterian church in Missouri, and in politics he is a Republican. His Missouri place he rents, and his own home farm he devotes to general agriculture, raising what seems to be in most demand, and always aiming to meet the market. Mrs. Eichhorn has her father living with her, and finds much pleasure in ministering to his last days. The Eichhorns are good people, honest and substantial in every way, and it is a pleasure to the historian to render them this sincere tribute of praise.

JOHN ONSTOTT.

John Onstott is one of the oldest citizens of Lee county, and was among its very early settlers, his residence here dating from 1835. In that time he has seen a revolution wrought in agricultural and industrial conditions as great as passing of the world from winter to summer. The old hard conditions that made life so dreary have passed away, and men who work have opportunity to breathe and enjoy the passing days. With what infinite labor was accomplished the farm labor of the pioneer days! And how easy the work of the farmer of the present day! A multitude of labor-saving devices and improved machinery are at his command. He rides where once he walked, and is at ease where once he did the hardest work. It is a new world in which the farmer lives, and "the end is not yet."

John Onstott, who has passed through many strange and wonderful experiences in his seventy years in Lee county, was born in Muskingum county, Ohio, January 22, 1820, a son of Henry and Rebecca Onstott.

The father was born near Pittsburg, Pennsylvania, and when quite young became a resident of Muskingum county, Ohio, where he spent his life. The Onstott family is of German descent, and shows many of the characteristic traits of its ancestry in its industry, integrity and moral worth.

The subject of this writing was the second member of a family of five children born to his parents, all of whom are now living. His education was mainly secured in his native community, and in May, 1835, when he made his advent in Lee county, in company with his uncle, he was quite a strong and sturdy lad. The uncle made his home in West Point township, and here John Onstott attended school, making his home with his uncle until he started out for himself in 1840. He bought grain, and building a flat boat would descend the river with it to New Orleans, where he would sell both grain and boat. Each trip would call for the building of a new boat. He spent several winters in New Orleans, and saw and learned much in that gay southern metropolis. He was in that city when peace was declared between Mexico and the United States, having with him 100,000 bushels of oats and 500 bushels of corn. At that time oats were ten cents a bushel and corn fifteen cents in Lee county, so a very handsome profit was his.

In 1840 Mr. Onstott purchased the farm on which his son-in-law now resides, and five years later he married Miss Rachel Bean, a native of Indiana and of English descent. She remained on the farm as long as her husband continued on the river, and though she found it at times lonesome and discouraging she was determined that things should go well at home while he was building the family fortunes in the river trade. In 1852 Mr. Onstott concluded to devote himself exclusively to the farm, which from that time has been his home. In 1850 he built the handsome brick edifice that has been the family home to the present time. His wife died in 1901, and all that is mortal was laid away to rest in Pitman cemetery, an old burying ground of West Point township. They were both devout members of the Methodist church, and during a long connection with that organization did much to increase its power and usefulness. He has been a Republican since 1855. Prior to that he had been a Democrat, but when the cleavage of the country came according to the new ideas, he chose to vote with the progressive elements of the country, and voted for General Fremont.

Mr. and Mrs. Onstott were the parents of a family of ten children, of whom eight are now living: James, of Des Moines; George, in Colorado; William, in Kansas; Samuel, at Mt. Pleasant, Iowa; Jasper L., in Norwalk, Iowa; Anna, the wife of Julius Eichhorn, of whom a sketch appears on another page; Robert, in Kansas; Mary, the wife of P. R. Bruce, of Palmyra, Iowa.

Mr. Onstott began life with no capital but a strong heart, a clear brain and a good bodily endowment. He has been industrious, calculating and keenly alive to all the possibilities opening before him, and he has achieved a very fair competence. As one of the self-made men of the passing generation, he possesses the respect of the community in which he lives to an uncommon degree, for his manly qualities and upright character are not questioned. Some eight years ago he injured his knees, since which he has been an invalid, and is compelled to depend upon crutches for his movements about the house.

DANIEL F. MILLER, Sr.

Daniel F. Miller, Sr., was born in Maryland in October, 1814, his parents removing to Ohio while he was still young. His education was secured principally in the Ohio schools, and at Pittsburg where he attended school when about fifteen years old. For some three years he was a teacher in Allegheny, and for some three years was engaged in reading law in the office of an eminent lawyer of that date. In 1839 he removed from Pittsburg to Fort Madison, where he practiced his profession for twenty years, and then made Keokuk the scene of his professional activities. In 1843 he was elected to the General Assembly and in 1851 was elected as a member of the national house of representatives, in which he served one term as a member of congress. At one time he was elected presidential elector, and was also a candidate for judge of the supreme court on the Democratic ticket. At one time he was a candidate for the United States Senate and was so voted for by the Democrats in the General Assembly, but as his party was in the minority was not elected.

During his active career Mr. Miller had one of the largest criminal practices in the state, and his success was marked. He married Rebecca Phillips in 1841, in Pittsburg, and became the father of ten children, of whom only four are now living.

The life of David F. Miller was as opportune as it was able. He was born into the world at a season befitting a nature that was adventurous, brave, enduring, loving and great-hearted. He was naturally equipped for a life of difficulties. The pioneer era was comforting to his spirit, and he engaged in it with the enthusiasm of the school boy. For half a century he was a commanding figure in Iowa, and its lawmaking was largely influenced by him, as well as its law-giving and its literature and morals. He was also a marked figure in its social life. In all of these he was a strong personality and his work was very strengthening in its splendid example to all who cherished intelligent ideals. His heart was pure, his mind grand and intent, and his brain a lexicon and a cyclopedia. It was in literature that Mr. Miller manifested the possession of the very highest powers. He was a great lawyer and jurist by profession; and, somewhat of necessity, in his professional work there was a bare hint only of the imaginative faculty that would have made him famous. All his life he had but touched on the field of literature because he held to ideals that could not be cherished in any other manner.

One can not go anywhere, however, in American literature and find a more perfect example of the exaltation of the human heart than is afforded by Mr. Miller's plain-tive story in verse of "The Indian Girl," "The Wild Rose," the object of the literary passion of his youth, an ideal of natural and womanly loveliness, untouched by art or consciousness, and as pure as a dream of heaven. He was an artist of experience, and came from the puncheon seats of the country district school to give to the world some of the best examples of formative thought then in existence. He knew how to chasten, and how to prune, and how to modulate. He could make a classic with the stroke of a pen. His sentences were like the running water. All the good law libraries have his standard work on rhetoric, and it is a book that is frequently referred to by the courts. Intelligent men everywhere hold but one opinion as to its value.

DANIEL F. MILLER, Jr.

The legal profession in the City of Keokuk, Iowa, has long had a brilliant following, and some of its more distinguished representatives have won a national reputation. Others, who have not been fortunate enough to attain so wide celebrity, have still been noted for their mastery of the fundamental principles of their great work, and have been noted for their forensic ability, voluminous learning and analytic powers. The bar at Keokuk is regarded as second to none in the state, and there the gentleman with whose name this article begins occupies no subordinate place. He is prominent in the city as a lawyer who understands the principles of right and justice, and who may be depended upon to apply those principles as a matter of equity and right to the details of common life. Courtly and urbane in his manner, his knowledge of the law is broad and accurate and his personal character high.

Daniel F. Miller, Jr., was born in Washington township, Lee county, Iowa, May 27, 1851, being a son of Daniel F. and Rebecca (Phillips) Miller, and was taken by his parents in 1859 to live in Keokuk, where his earlier education was obtained in the public and private schools of that city. He was a student at a later period of the Christian Brothers' College at St. Louis, and also of the Iowa State University, from the law department of which he graduated in due time. He immediately located at Fort Madison, where he established himself in the practice of his profession. Shortly afterwards, however, he entered into professional associations with M. B. Davis, under the firm name of Davis & Miller, which became, some years later on the dissolution, the firm of Miller & Sons, the subject of this sketch moving to Keokuk for the purpose of practicing his profession in that city.

Mr. Miller was elected county attorney in 1887, and the firm of Miller & Sons was dissolved, to be reformed six years later, when Mr. Miller retired from official position and resumed his practice. On reorganizing the firm it was called Miller & Son, and here Mr. Miller continued in his legal work until the death of his father, which occurred at Omaha, in December, 1895, whither he had gone to visit his children. Since that time Mr. Miller has practiced law alone in Keokuk. His practice is a general one, and during his long and continued career he has had a leading part in many of the more noted civil and criminal cases that have been tried before the courts in this part of the state.

Mr. Miller enjoys the possession of a very complete library of legal works, and his mind is thoroughly informed as to all legal propositions. His judgment commands the high esteem of both the bench and the bar, and there are few who can safely undertake to controvert his positions. He is a member of the Lee County Bar Association where, as everywhere else, he is popular and respected. In religion he is a member of the Catholic church, and in politics a Democrat. He is also associated with several fraternal orders of the city, where his genial character and companionable ways command a host of warm friends.

Daniel F. Miller and Miss Lillie A. Archer were married February 27, 1878. She was born and reared in Keokuk, and is a daughter of Col. S. M. Archer, who commanded the Seventeenth Iowa Infantry during the Civil War. He lived and died in Keokuk, where he sustained a high reputation as a business man. Mr. and Mrs. Miller are the parents of four children: Daniel F., who is now connected with the editorial department of the Chicago Tribune; Mary Elizabeth; Archer C., a student in the high school, and Lillian, also a student in the public school. The last three are at home, and all were born in Keokuk.

The son, whose career we have somewhat hastily noted in this article, is a worthy successor of his father and walks in the same broad way of professional ability, literary excellence and personal character. A brilliant name suffers no deterioration at his hands.

SAMUEL F. RICHARDSON.

It is indeed seldom that the pen of the historian is privileged to assume a more agreeable task than is here found in writing the life chronicle of the subject of the present review, an old and highly respected citizen of Green Bay township, Lee county, Iowa, a man who has played a worthy part in the upbuilding of the community of which he is an honored member, and one whose ambitious and enterprising spirit has made him successful in all he has undertaken. Samuel F. Richardson was born February 6, 1833, in Miamitown, Hamilton county, Ohio, the son of David Richardson, the father was born in New Jersey and the mother, whose maiden name was Foster, was born in Maryland. They were married in Hamilton county, Ohio, near Cincinnati, whence they soon afterward removed to Hancock, Indiana, where they remained until 1846, and then came to Lee county, Iowa, locating upon a farm near Ivanhoe Park at Fort Madison. There David Richardson purchased a farm of 262 acres at ten dollars an acre, and to this farm he devoted the efforts of his remaining years, placing it under cultivation and operating it very successfully.

Samuel Richardson, our subject, was the

fifth of a family of six children, and was a child four years of age when he removed with his parents to Indiana, and but thirteen years of age when he came with them to Lee county. He received a good common-school education in the public schools, as well as a careful home training, and was reared to the business of farming, early learning its lessons thoroughly by hard practical experience, following the plow and the harrow and wielding the cradle and flail, tilling the soil, sowing the seed and reaping the ripened harvest in its season. Thus engaged in the occupation which was to be his life work he continued until his twenty-first year, when, in company with a party of eleven others, he set out for the Pacific coast on a trading expedition, taking with him a herd of 250 cattle for sale. Starting April 21, 1854, he traveled overland across the plains, arriving, on August 25, at Sacramento river, in California, where he disposed of his herd at a price exactly double the investment, and then made the return journey by ship to Aspinwall, across the Isthmus of Panama by rail, then by ship to New York, and thence through the Dominion of Canada by rail to Fort Madison, after having been absent for a year.

Following this first independent and highly successful venture, Mr. Richardson worked on his father's farm for a year, at the end of which he bought a farm of 200 acres across the Mississippi river in Illinois, but after three years he sold it and removed to his present farm of 200 acres, which was formerly the property of his father-in-law, and here he has resided ever since. As a result of his intelligent efforts and direction, the land has been brought under the rule of modern improvements, fine large barns and necessary buildings have been constructed on the farm, and an elegant and commodious dwelling of brick has been erected, surrounded by beautiful grounds and stately shade trees. He has given much attention to farming, and for many years has made a specialty of the rearing of thoroughbred Shorthorn cattle and high-grade Clydesdale and Hambletonian horses, a pursuit which has made his stables famous far and near and in which he has done much to increase the reputation and prestige of these valuable breeds of stock in the middle West.

On September 21, 1856, Mr. Richardson was united in marriage to Miss Caroline Hyter, a daughter of Abraham and Nancy A. (Phares) Hyter, who were natives of Maryland and New Jersey, respectively, but settled in Green Bay township in 1845, and here spent the rest of their lives. Mrs. Richardson, who is the only survivor of a family of eight brothers and sisters, was born in Dearborn county, Indiana, October 1, 1833. To Mr. and Mrs. Richardson have been born four sons and five daughters, as follows: Angeline, who died in infancy; Roscoe A., who is the present manager of his father's farm; William F., who died at the age of ten years; Clement Clarence, who died when five years of age; Clara, whose death occurred in childhood; Alice, who married Charles Willard, of Washington township, Lee county, and has one child, Earl Grover; Ida, deceased wife of Charles Parker, who is survived by a daughter, Lulu; and Caroline, wife of Clyde Sheppard, who resides in Green Bay township and has one son, Samuel Clyde.

That Samuel Richardson enjoys the respect and confidence of his neighbors and fellow citizens is amply evidenced by the fact that he has, on various occasions, been called upon to serve the public in numerous capacities of honor and trust, among these being the important office of trustee of Green Bay township, in which he gave an eminently business-like and highly satisfactory administration, and he has also at the request of friends acted as director of the public schools, an office in which he was able to render valuable assistance to the cause of education, in which he is a firm believer and to which he has ever given all the encouragement in his power, realizing that the public-school system is the foundation stone of our national liberties, and that a wise oversight of the training of youth is the price of our continued greatness as a people. He has also played an important part in the political life of Lee county, taking part in public activities as a member of the Democratic party, for whose success he has consistently labored throughout his career without hope of reward, and in whose counsels his voice has carried weight and authority. He believes its principles to be more thoroughly in accord with the fundamental spirit of American institutions than that of any other party, and that he is therefore morally obliged to assist in its struggle for supremacy; and it is conceded that no small share of the party's success in this section of Iowa is due to his efforts and personal influence. On the other hand, he has not neglected the higher interests of humanity, and Mr. and Mrs. Richardson are members and generous supporters of the Christian church, taking an interest in all its work and assisting the cause of religion by every means in their power. Mr. Richardson's life has been one of constant usefulness and success, and in all his dealings with his fellow men he has striven to be strictly honest and impartial, always seeking to guard against doing any man an injustice, preserving at all times an upright, honorable and absolutely unwavering course of integrity—a mode of life which has brought its own reward in the esteem of all who knew him as he is. In his career as a farmer and a business man, his qualities of foresight and ready appreciation of an opportunity, added to an unfailing perseverance in all circumstances, however adverse, have brought him worldly wealth and enabled him in his later years to retire from active affairs and to enjoy in ease the fruits of a life well spent.

JOHN HENDERSON CRAIG.

History is held by writers and readers as a mighty mirror, reflecting the images and deeds of great men, and some of these heroes are pictured with such overtowering proportions that they monopolize the thought and admiration of the world.

It is one province of biography to correct the exaggerated and unjust discriminations of history and give a due proportion of praise to some of those who aided in elevating those heroes to their high historical plane and by manly deeds, honest lives and eloquent words added to the progress and glory of our common country.

To portray human actions and characteristics with honest fidelity should be the aim of the biographer. And as a man worthy of high position and the dearest memory in the annals of Iowa and the Union we shall unhesitatingly place as compeer with the great men who have preceded him, Keokuk's honored and lamented citizen, John H. Craig.

The subject of this brief sketch was born on a farm near Claysville, Washington county, Pennsylvania, July 31, 1824, of which county his parents were also natives. His early years were spent upon the farm, pursuing the usual duties of a farmer boy about the old homestead but receiving a good common-school education. These advantages were supplemented by courses in chemistry, philosophy, rhetoric and algebra. He studied later under the instruction of the pastor of his church. As early as at the age of fifteen years Mr. Craig left the farm, taught school one term and then attended the West Alexander Academy at West Alexander, Pennsylvania, for a period of four years. Completing the academic course in 1845, he engaged in teaching at the academy for a year, when he entered the junior class at Washington and Jefferson College, from which institution he was graduated in 1848, meeting the expenses of this collegiate course by acting as a tutor of Latin and Greek in the college.

In the spring of 1849, Mr. Craig commenced the study of law with Hon. T. M. T. McKennen, ex-secretary of the interior and ex-member of congress. He had, however, so closely confined himself to his studies in school that his health forbade his continuing them further, so, in the spring of 1850 he went to Natchez, Mississippi, where he devoted himself to literary pursuits and teaching. In the fall of 1853 his health being perfectly restored, he returned to his Pennsylvania home. The following year he went to Wheeling, Virginia, now West Virginia, and resumed his law studies.

The death of his father occurred about that time and he returned home to settle the estate. Afterwards he entered the law office of Hon. William Montgomery, of Washington, Pennsylvania, congressman from that district. Here he pursued his studies one year and was admitted to the bar in 1856. After the death of his mother, in November of the same year, Mr. Craig concluded to seek his fortunes in the West, having now no very strong ties to bind him to his native state.

In the following spring, 1857, he came to Iowa, stopping in Keokuk to visit friends. During this visit he was induced to form a law partnership with Judge R. P. Lowe, afterwards governor of Iowa, and John W. Noble, who rose to distinction as a general in the War of the Rebellion, became secretary of the interior in President Benjamin Harrison's cabinet, and now a prominent lawyer at St. Louis, Missouri. The fall of that year Judge Lowe was elected governor and the partnership was dissolved. Mr. Craig, however, continued in active practice until about 1888, when his health precluded the possibility of continuing professional pursuits.

During his practice he was associated with different attorneys. The last firm with which he was connected was that of Craig, McCrary & Craig, composed, besides himself, of A. J. McCreary and John E. Craig, a nephew. He was an earnest student, a conscientious lawyer, a finished orator, a valued citizen, and above all an honest man. He was a magnetic pleader at the bar, and never allowed a difficult point of law to go unmastered. In life he bore the fame of being one of the ablest attorneys in the West and was regarded all over Iowa as a brilliant lawyer.

The first important case with which Mr. Craig was connected was that of Nash and Redoubt, charged with the murder of Harrison, partner of the late Patrick Gibbons, in which he ably assisted in the prosecution, and he was connected with many of the important cases in Lee county and other counties of the state and in the supreme court of the state.

In politics Mr. Craig was a stanch Democrat but always declined to be a candidate for office though many times solicited to break the rule of his life. In educational matters he always took the deepest interest and was for sixteen years or more a member of the board of education of Keokuk. He was the president of the College of Physicians and Surgeons, one of the oldest and best-known medical colleges of the West, for a number of years prior to his death. For about thirty years he was attorney for the Iowa State Insurance Company, having made a special study of Insurance laws. He was a consistent and devout member of the first Westminster Presbyterian church and until he became broken in health was a constant attendant at the services, always taking an active part in religious matters.

Mr. Craig was of fine literary taste and culture and would have taken rank with the best in that field had he chosen to enter it more largely. Some of his lectures were gems of the platform. But he was the kind of genius who hid his brilliant attainments from the world rather than proclaim them from the housetops. His writings and poems were never published but many of them are preserved as precious family relics in happy memory and as evidences of the power of the man.

John H. Craig was married December 24, 1863, at Madison, Wisconsin, to Miss Alice Read, daughter of Hon. Daniel Read, who was for many years connected with the State University of Indiana, was later president of the State University of Wisconsin, and who at the time of his death was president of the State University of Missouri. Mrs. Craig survives her husband with the following children: Daniel Read Craig, superintendent of construction of the Northwestern Telephone Company, of Illinois; Miss Bertha R. Craig, teacher of history in the Keokuk high school: Theodore A. Craig, attorney in Keokuk, and ex-Mayor of the city, and Hugh H. Craig, attorney and member of the board of education of Keokuk. Mr. Craig was also eminent as a husband and father. He loved his home and family. Their welfare and happiness were his delight. The great lawyer, the busy citizen, the untiring student was never too engrossed in the affairs of life to turn the ear away from the call of wife or child. His home was his loved paradise on earth, where rest and comfort and happiness came as a benison.

After an illness existing over four years, during which time he was incapitated for the duties of his profession, Hon. John H. Craig passed away peacefully Monday, September 18, 1893. Mr. Craig was first stricken during the March, 1888, term of the district court and while addressing a jury he sank to the floor and was borne to his home. From this attack, which the physicians said was caused by the rupture of a small blood vessel in the brain, he recovered sufficiently to resume the duties of his profession until in January, 1889, he suffered another attack while sitting at his home. At the time it was thought this attack would prove fatal, but he again rallied so that he was able to walk about. From that time, however, his life work was over and the great legal mind and eloquent tongue ceased their labors, until after more than four years "he drew the drapery of his couch about him and lay down to pleasant dreams." The end had come.

Citizens of every class and creed felt with moistened eye the great loss that had befallen the city. The State of Iowa echoed the lament from Keokuk. The Keokuk bar passed resolutions of regret and eulogy as did also the Iowa State Insurance Company and the Keokuk School Board of which he was so long a member and presiding officer. The press of Iowa, of Pennsylvania, the commonwealth which gave him birth, and of other states gave high tribute to the goodness and greatness of Mr. Craig.

WILLIAM EITMAN.

William Eitman, who is now deceased, was born in Germany, near Bremen, February 22, 1831, and came to this country in 1848; was on the ocean sixty-eight days, it requiring that time to make the voyage in a sailing vessel from his native city to New Orleans, where he transferred himself and his belongings to a Mississippi river steamboat to journey to St. Louis, Missouri. He learned the marble-cutter's trade and found employment in this line at various places along the river, in Quincy, Burlington and Muscatine, and returning to Burlington in August, 1856, he engaged in the grocery business for several years, later entering into business with T. W. Barhydt, and in 1862 he arrived in Fort Madison.

The young lad, only sixteen years of age when he left his Fatherland, had now become a man of thirty, a keen and shrewd business man, and ready for the whirl of fortune, or the decree of fate. He had worked hard, saved his money, and was ready for such important commercial enterprises as circumstances might open to him. In Fort Madison, in 1862, he opened a shoe store in company with T. W. Barhydt, with whom he continued business for ten years under the firm name of T. W. Barhydt & Company, after which Mr. Eitman became sole owner of the business, which he carried on under his own name until his death which occurred February 28, 1900.

Mr. Eitman was a devoted member of the Independent Order of Odd Fellows, and it is not too much to say of him that he lived up to the best principles of this fraternity, in whose welfare he was deeply interested. Politically he was a Republican, and was known as a broad-minded, patriotic citizen, anxious to promote the best interests of his adopted country. For this purpose he used his political rights, to put good men into office and promote wise and helpful political measures, and not merely to gain partisan advantage or to put the men on the ticket into office.

Mr. Eitman was married in Wapello, Iowa, August 19, 1856, to Miss Johanna Hintzen, who was born in Germany, September 3, 1837. She came to this country in company with her parents when about eleven years old. She is still living, as are four of the five children born to her marriage with Mr. Eitman: Clara, the wife of D. W. Evans, clerk in the Inter-State National Bank, Kansas City, Missouri, and the mother of two boys,—Harold and Russell; Emma, the wife of F. E. Lofgreen, died December 10, 1890, at the age of thirty years, leaving two daughters,—Josephine and Laura; William H. lives at home; Laura, a stenographer with S. & J. C. Atlee Lumber Company; Francis, manager of the store since the death of Mr. Eitman. Laura and Francis are graduates of the Fort Madison high school, and are young people of more than the average intelligence and general knowledge.

The Eitman family are members of the First Methodist Episcopal church of Fort Madison, and their sincere devotion, high character and clean and wholesome living make their membership doubly significant. The family home is at the corner of Third and Walnut streets, and it is the center of an invigorating and enkindling social life that exerts an uplifting and refining influence on all who come within its sunny atmosphere.

Mrs. Eitman has a sister and a brother in Louisville, Kentucky, Mrs. Frances Laufer and J. H. Hintzen, where she was reared herself, the family later removing to Wapello, Iowa, where occurred the death of her mother August 12, 1864. Her father died in Louisville, Kentucky, January 17, 1880.

The parents of the subject of this writing never came to this country, but lived and died in their German Fatherland. They had a large family, and one of their sons, Frank, is a resident of Muscatine, Iowa. Another son, Herman, lives near New Hanover, Missouri; and a daughter, Rebecca, in Missouri.

The remains of Mr. Eitman are at rest in the family lot in the city cemetery of Fort Madison. The mother and three children occupy the commodious home at the Corner of Third and Walnut streets. The store is at No. 717 Second street.

The father of Mrs. Eitman was born in Germany in 1800, and was trained to business as a wholesale manufacturer and dealer in cloth. By a series of misfortunes he lost his property and came to the United States in 1848, to mend if possible his broken resources. At the time of his settlement in Louisville that same year, he was a man well-advanced in years, being some forty-eight years old. His energy, industry and thrift carried him through many a difficulty, and at last he did recoup, in a measure at least, his wasted fortunes.

Mrs. Eitman's grandfather, Adolph

Ludwig Von Gustorf, was a man of education, and was employed in the Royal Schools of Prussia as an instructor.

Of Mr. Eitman, personally, it may be said that he was a man of good and clean history, living a life upright and honest, and presenting to the world an example of industry, integrity and unaffected kindness and human sympathy, good for all to imitate and follow.

GEORGE F. JENKINS, M. D.

Dr. George F. Jenkins, president and professor of principles and practice of medicine, physical diagnosis and clinical medicine in the Keokuk Medical College, College of Physicians and Surgeons, at Keokuk, has been identified with this institution for a quarter of a century. He has won more than local renown because of the successful results which have attended his life work when viewed from the professional standpoint and the medical fraternity as well as the general public accord him high rank as a physician and surgeon. He was born in Clark county, Missouri, in July, 1842, a son of Robert and Elizabeth (Rambo) Jenkins. The family is of Welsh lineage and the ancestry in America can be traced back to David Jenkins, the great-great-grandfather of Dr. Jenkins, who became a resident of Lancaster county, Pennsylvania, in the year 1700. Through several generations the family was connected with the iron works of Conestoga, Pennsylvania, being among the oldest representatives of that great iron industry of the Keystone state. The mill and plant at Conestoga were in possession of the family for one hundred and thirty-seven years, terminating in 1837.

Robert Jenkins, father of Dr. Jenkins, was born near the old ancestral home in Lancaster county and became an emigrant to the West, settling in Clark county, Missouri, in 1837. There he made his home for a long period, rearing his family in that county. His wife's ancestors came to the United States with a Swedish colony about 1665 and were colonial settlers of Chester county, Pennsylvania. Her grandfather, Ezekial Rambo, espoused the cause of liberty at the time of the Revolutionary War and did valiant service for the colonists. Mr. and Mrs. Jenkins were married in Pennsylvania, but the greater part of their married life was passed in Missouri. They were members of the Presbyterian church and were promoters of the substantial development and progress of their locality.

Dr. Jenkins began his education as a student in the public schools of Clark county, Missouri, afterward attended the high school at Alexandria and then entered the Commercial College at St. Louis, subsequent to which time he entered upon preparation for the medical profession in San Francisco, California, in 1865. He was a student there in the Toland Medical College, now the medical department of the University of California and, returning to Missouri, he matriculated in the Missouri Medical College at St. Louis, from which he was graduated with the class of 1867.

The honorary degree of Master of Arts was conferred upon him by Parsons College, at Fairfield, Iowa, in 1884.

Dr. Jenkins located for practice in Keokuk, entering upon a successful career in this city. Realizing that in the professions as well as in the great industrial and commercial departments of activity, success and advancement are due to close application, thorough preparation and thorough understanding of the work to be done, Dr. Jenkins has always remained an earnest and conscientious student of the science of medicine, continually broadening his knowledge and also contributing to the sum total of information and experience which have made the labors of the profession partake almost of the nature of the marvelous. From the time of his graduation down to the present (1905) he has continued in the general practice of medicine and surgery in Keokuk and today stands at the head of the medical fraternity in his adopted city, having few peers and no superiors. A valuable part of his services in behalf of humanity has been in the line of medical education. In 1879 he was elected to fill the chair of diseases of children in the College of Physicians and Surgeons, occupying that position until 1882, when he was made professor of the principles and practice of medicine and clinical medicine in the same institution. He filled the latter chair until 1890, and was also president of the faculty during that period. In the year mentioned he assisted in the organization of the Keokuk Medical College; was elected its president and also chosen for the chair of principles and practice of diagnosis, retaining that connection with medicine, clinical medicine and physical the school until 1900, when the consolidation with the College of Physicians and Surgeons was consummated under the name of the Keokuk Medical College, College of Physicians and Surgeons. In the new institution he was elected to fill the same positions, and is not only president and professor in the college, but also dean of the faculty. Associated with physicians and surgeons, whose abilities have gained them much more than local reputation and whose work and writings have made them known to the profession throughout the country, Dr. Jenkins has labored persistently and effectively for the development of the skill and the raising of its standards. In 1898 a dental department was established, of which he was also chosen president, and in 1901 a department of pharmacy was founded, with which his official connection is the same. Both of these departments have proved to be successful adjuncts to the institution, and excellent work is being carried on therein. A capable faculty has been secured and the buildings assigned to its departments have been well equipped with every facility to advance the useful and practical work of the students.

Dr. Jenkins was also largely instrumental in the founding of St. Joseph's Hospital, at Keokuk, and from the organization has been chief of its medical staff Keokuk has benefited by his professional labors aside from his work as private practitioner and educator, for he has given close study to its sanitary conditions, and has served as president of its board of health. He became a member of the Keokuk Medical Society in 1868, and was honored with its presidency for two terms. He also belongs to the Lee County Medical Society; has been a member of the State Medical Society since 1869; has held various positions therein, and has been chairman of sections, which includes preparation of papers read before the society. He was also elected its president in 1891. In 1873 he became a member of of the American Medical Association; has attended the majority of its sessions, and was elected to its house of delegates in 1901, while in 1903 the association conferred upon him the honor of election to its vice-presidency. His writings have been valued contributions to medical literature. He is the author of a number of articles which have been published in the leading medical journals of his day, including the Medical and Surgical Reporter, of Philadelphia, the Journal of the American Medical Association, and the Transactions of the Iowa State Medical Society. In Keokuk, in addition to his general practice, he has been for many years first medical examiner for the Northwestern Mutual Life Insurance Company, of Milwaukee, for the New York Mutual Life, the New York Life, the Equitable, the Connecticut Mutual, the Pennsylvania Mutual, the Mutual Benefit, the Aetna, of Hartford, the Pacific Mutual, and the Travelers' Life Insurance Companies, of Hartford, the Preferred Accident Insurance Company, of New York, the Iowa State Traveling Men's Association, and others.

Dr. Jenkins was married December 29, 1870, to Miss Charlotte Elizabeth Van Wagenen, of Fulton, New York, a daughter of Captain Van Wagenen, a representative of one of the old Holland families of the Empire state, established along the Hudson in colonial days. They have four children, of whom the eldest is Marcia L., the wife of Hazen L. Sawyer, of Keokuk; Florence E. is the wife of Harry Boyden Blood, of Keokuk; George Van Wagenen, who acquired his literary education in Parsons College, pursued the work of the sophomore year in Keokuk Medical College, and in 1898 he enlisted in Company A, ——Iowa Regiment, at Fairfield, Iowa, for service in the Spanish-American War. He was sergeant of his regiment, and died of typhoid fever contracted in camp at Jacksonville, Florida. Katherine E., the youngest, is at home. Dr. and Mrs. Jenkins are members of the Presbyterian church, and their social prominence is equal to his professional standing. His professional duties and his work in connection with the college, however, leave him little leisure time. He has carried his investigations far and wide into the realms of scientific knowledge, and has made researches along original lines, wherein experience and deductive thought have brought him knowledge that the profession recognizes as valuable to the great humanitarian work that claims the attention of the medical fraternity.

ARTHUR HOSMER.

A history of Lee county, and the City of Keokuk, Iowa, lacking the name of Arthur Hosmer, and giving no space to the Hosmer family of that city, would omit some of the most important factors in the development of the southeastern part of the state. For Mr. Hosmer is one of the most venerable of the pioneers of the city who is still left to the new century, and others of the family were also engaged in the industries and enterprises of a very early day at this point. At that time they had won an honored standing, and have maintained a good name and a high character through the intervening years.

Arthur Hosmer was born in Niagara county, New York, February 5, 1815, and was reared to manhood under the parental roof, securing a good education in the local schools, and assisting his father in the care of the family homestead. When he became a young man he taught school for a time, and then removed to Ohio, secured the appointment of general manager in the improvement of the locks on the Muskingum river, then being done under contract, by his uncle, S. R. Hosmer. Arthur Hosmer subsequently became a contractor on the public works on the Hocking river, and later still was owner of a large cotton mill at Zanesville. In 1857 he removed to Keokuk, and in the month of November of the year following secured a large interest as a stockholder in the old State Bank of Iowa. He was elected, September 15, 1864, a director to fill the place made vacant by the death of B. F. Moody. When the bank was changed to become the State National Bank of Keokuk, May 22, 1865, he was one of its original directors, and in January, 1868, was chosen vice-president. As such he served until April 11, 1877, when on the death of James F. Cox he was called to the presidency of this very important financial institution, a position he retained until his retirement from active business, March 26, 1889.

During this long and honorable career Mr. Hosmer won the unreserved confidence of the business men with whom his lot was cast, and was trusted without question. Though he opened his heart to but few, and they his most intimate friends only, as a financier he was eminently forceful and successful. His personal characteristics were those of the scholar and the gentleman. He has always had a pleasure in fine books and in broad reading, showing himself on many an occasion a thorough student and an apt critic. Refined in his tastes, charming in his manners and habits, all his life he has commanded the warm friendship and esteem of the best elements of the community.

Mr. Hosmer, in the spring of 1865, made investments outside of his banking interests, the most important being the purchase of the old sawmill plant which, under his management, became an extensive lumber and milling establishment, and was operated by Hosmer-Taber & Company with marked success. Later he retired from the firm, which then became Paul & Taber, and the business has descended through their successors to the present time. Mr. Hosmer was afterward associated with T. F. Baldwin in the operation of a lumber yard. Mr. Baldwin retired from the business and Mr. Hosmer carried it on alone until he was able to take in his sons, Lewis and Arthur, whom he put in charge until the closing of the establishment in 1881. Mr. Hosmer has, however, always regarded himself as a banker, and has never neglected any detail of the work which he felt was his as a trusted leader and representative of the financial interests of the City of Keokuk. Mr. Hosmer died July 11, 1891. His father, Titus Hosmer, was a Revolutionary soldier, a native of Connecticut, though married in New York to Helen Brown, a daughter of the Empire state.

Arthur Hosmer was married in Zanesville, Ohio, August 18, 1847, to Miss Adeline C. Love, a daughter of John S. and Mary (Vermillion) Love, of Fairfax county, Virginia. Her father was a mail contractor and the proprietor of a plantation on which he maintained many slaves. There Mrs. Hosmer was born August 19, 1823. Her family were of Scotch extraction, her grandfather coming from Scotland, where the family had long been known. Her father died when she was young, and her people removed to Ohio about 1831.

Thomas Hosmer, the remote American ancestor of the family, was a son of Stephen and Dorothy Hosmer, of Hawkhurst, County Kent, England, settled at what is now Cambridge, Massachusetts, as early as 1632, where three years later he was admitted a freeman of the settlement. In June of the year following he removed to Hartford, Connecticut, where his name appears as one of the original settlers of that community. On the records it appears that sixty acres of land were assigned him January 14, 1639. His first wife, Frances, died February 5, 1675, and he married for his second, Mrs. Katherine Wilton (a name now spelled Wilson), the widow of Lieutenant David Wilton, of North Hampshire, and formerly of Windsor. The records of the minister at Windsor at the time is as follows: "May 6, '79: Goodman Osmer, of Hartford, and the widow Wilton, that had been wife to David Wilton, were to be married at Hartford." Mr. Hosmer died at Northampton, where he was buried. His tomb bears this inscription:

"Thomas Hosmer: Aged 83 years. He Died April 12, 1687."

ALBERT LEE CONNABLE.

Among the many prominent and successful men of southeastern Iowa none stood higher for business integrity and personal honor than Albert L. Connable. He was born upon the old homestead of his father and grandfather in Bernardston, Massachusetts, August 10, 1811. His father was Ezra Connable, born in Bernardston, November 12, 1779; and his mother before marriage was Abigail Stevens, born in Warwick, Massachusetts, in 1784. It was an extensive family and the name as found in a book of the genealogy of the family is spelled in thirty-eight different ways, from "Cannabell" to "Cunnable." The first immigrant of the family was John Cunnabell, who came from London, England, and located in Boston, Massachusetts, about 1674. Ensign John Cunnabell was prominent in the War of the Revolution, and in 1779 was chairman of the committee of safety and correspondence, a highly important position in the Revolutionary War. Other members of the family became prominent in those stirring and patriotic days, and several of the name or blood have gathered varied laurels in the later days of the republic.

There is room for mention of only two of these: "George Cunnabell Howard," whose real name was George Howard Cunnabell, was a poet of some pretentions and a prominent actor. He gained early popularity by the unique distinction of bringing out the first dramatized representation of Mrs. Stowe's entire work of "Uncle Tom's Cabin." The work was dramatized by another but Cunnabell was the original "St. Clare," his wife the original "Topsy," and his daughter, Cordelia, the original "Eva."

Mary Ann Dennison Connable, a sister of A. L. Connable, subject of this sketch, was a woman of excellent qualities and proved herself a fitting companion for her gifted husband, Rev. Asbury Lowrey, D. D., of Ohio, an eminent minister of the Methodist Episcopal church in the early days, a member of the Cincinnati conference for forty years, author of "Positive Theology" and "Possibilities of Grace," and editor of a magazine, "Divine Life," in New York City, after extensive travel in Europe and the Holy Land.

Albert Lee Connable was a sturdy man of business. He left his eastern home in 1831, before he had reached his majority, and spent nearly a year in traveling. In 1832 he reached Eaton, Ohio, where he was afterwards joined by his three sisters, and engaged in the business of contracting and staging, remaining there until 1843. In that year he removed to Fairfield, Jefferson county, Iowa, where he was married, October 9, 1849, to Sarah Hurst Finney, daughter of Louis Hourth Finney and Annie (Hurst) Finney, born in Baltimore, Maryland, November 15, 1822. Her parents removed from Baltimore to Columbus, Ohio, thence to Indianapolis, Indiana, and Fairfield, Iowa.

Mr. Connable removed, in 1848, to Keokuk, Lee county, Iowa, where he resided to the time of his death. At Fairfield he was extensively engaged in farming and wool growing. In 1848-9 he was a contractor on the Keokuk and Des Moines Slack Water Navigation Canal to the amount of $350,000, a very large sum for a contract in that early day in Iowa. He then engaged in a wholesale grocery and iron store for ten years. Then he engaged extensively in pork and beef packing, which was a prominent industry in Keokuk at that time, which he continued for seven years. In 1873 he retired from active commercial pursuits, giving his entire time to superintending his numerous farms and buildings in and around Keokuk. Mr. Connable had great faith in real estate values.

He was one of the incorporators of the Iowa State Insurance Company in 1856 and continued a director in that institution until his death; was a director in the Keokuk Savings Bank from the date of its organization, December 19, 1867; also a director in the Water Works Company and the Keokuk Water Works Company and the Keokuk Canning Company. Besides his possessions in and around Keokuk he owned about 12,000 acres of land in the northwestern part of Iowa.

Mr. Connable served three years in Jefferson county and three years in Lee county as county supervisor and was a model official. Having an aversion to holding office, these were the only times he could ever be induced to serve the people in public place. He stood high in the communities where he resided and was at all times regarded as a man of the strictest integrity, an exemplary citizen and a careful and remarkably successful business man. He was a faithful and consistent member of the Unitarian church.

Mrs. Connable died January 21, 1885. She was a good woman and a housewife in the true sense of the term. It has been said of her that "nothing ever tempted her from her home. She mingled little in society, but will long be remembered for her many acts of kindness which were always given in a quiet, unobtrusive way."

Mr. Connable went peacefully to his last rest at his home in Keokuk, Apri 15, 1894, regretted and mourned by the entire community.

Ezra Connable, the father of the subject of this sketch, had seven children: Caroline Abby, Albert Lee, Charles Denison, Mary Ann Denison, Elizabeth Frances, Augusta Sophronia and Samuel Charles.

The children of Albert Lee Connable, three in number and all living are as follows: Albert Ezra Connable, born October 16, 1851, married Miss Rose Florida Franklin, of Keokuk, is an extensive farmer and resides at Hamilton, Illinois, opposite Keokuk. They have three children, all living, as follows: Sadie, who married Ira W. Wills, wholesale grocer, Keokuk; Lucile, who married L. C. Judd and they reside in the City of Mexico, and a son, Franklin Connable, who lives at Houston, Texas. Edwin Hurst Connable, born November 23, 1885; unmarried; large farmer at Gregory's Landing, Clark county, Missouri. Howard Lee Connable, born January 14, 1858; married Miss Rose McKenzie, of Keokuk; successful clothing merchant in Keokuk for a number of years and a director in the Keokuk Savings Bank, in which his father served in the same capacity from its organization. They have one little girl, Madaline.

Mr. A. J. Mathias, the present cashier of the Keokuk Savings Bank, who had as close personal and business relations with Mr. Connable as any man in Keokuk or elsewhere, was asked to give his estimate of him, and without hesitation he said to the writer:

"One personal characteristic of Mr. Connable was his modesty. He never was self-assertive, but had firmness to sustain any action he contemplated. He was very courteous in manner, at all times civil, rarely displaying temper or giving vent to vexation—was benignant. He was amiable and pleasant always; was a good conversationalist upon topics he understood; had a clear vision of the incidents of everyday life and calmly pursued the even tenor of his way. He was a good judge of human nature and rarely made mistakes in his estimate of men. He had a fine faculty in dealing with people. He loved justice and tempered his judgment with kindness and mercy."

GEORGE DEXTER RAND.

It was written of the renowned Athenian, Aristides, that

"To be and not to seem, is this man's maxim;

His mind reposes on its proper wisdom,

And wants no other praise."

These lines may be aptly applied to the subject of this brief sketch. And we are told that "a distinguished character of antiquity was questioned as to what constituted best means of national defense; he answered,—men. The interrogatory was repeated again, and even the third time; and he replied with emphasis,—men." In remembering the career of George D. Rand, these sayings came vividly to mind. "To be and not to seem" appeared to govern his actions by intuition. And if men, in the true sense of the term, constitute the best means of national defense, a country blessed with such sons may have no cause to doubt its high destiny.

George Dexter Rand was born at Quincy, Illinois, February 9, 1838, coming from an old and prominent family. Attending the home schools in boyhood, at the proper age and advancement he entered Asbury University, Greencastle, Indiana, from which he was graduated with becoming honors. This famous old university was the alma mater of many remarkable men, among them Oliver Perry Morton, the eminent war governor of Indiana and United States Senator, also a prominent candidate for nomination for the presidency in the national Republican convention in 1876, and others of almost equal fame.

Closing his university labors, with commendable ambition for success in life, young Rand entered into a business career and spent his earliest business life in Colorado, then reckoned in the very wild West. The Civil War approached, the bullets of the South were sullenly answered by the bullets of the North. Mr. Rand was appointed assistant paymaster in the volunteer navy, a position of high honor and trust for so young a man. In this capacity he served up to June 30, 1864, when he was appointed assistant paymaster in the regular navy, his commission being signed by Abraham Lincoln, President, and Gideon Wells, secretary of the navy, a marked promotion and a distinct endorsement from a high source of the able and honest manner in which he had kept his former trust.

After the close of the Civil War he engaged in active business, and in 1880 moved to Keokuk, Iowa, being an active member of the extensive operators, the Carson-Rand Lumber Company. He managed the large business of the Keokuk branch for several years, until the withdrawal of the corporation from this field.

Mr. Rand was not a politician. While firm and steadfast in his political convictions he envied not the place-hunter and sought no political preferment. His home and office were his abiding places. With a kindly recognition for rich and poor alike, he was genial and companionable. A few chosen friends, however, were more pleasing to his naturally reserved temperament than are indiscriminate mingling with the world, and yet he respected and loved the world and enjoyed its enjoyments. He had a big heart—laughed with the world and wept with it. His silent charities and bountiful benevolences were countless, and yet they were mostly hidden rather than paraded. The poor of Keokuk lost a friend indeed when suddenly the life of George D. Rand went out. And they quietly yet deeply mourned him.

Not many years after his coming to Keokuk he was elected mayor of the city. He did not want the position, but his friends urged and he consented. His administration was wise, conservative and commendable. It was during his official career that Rand Park, named for him, and one of the most beautiful and attractive parks in any city the size of Keokuk, was completed. A great fight was made against it, but now the people see the wisdom of Mayor Rand's course and Rand Park is the pride of the city—a noble and undying monument to him and his administration. He was urged to accept a nomination for re-election but firmly declined.

During the latter part of his life he had his office at the State Central Savings Bank, of which he was vice-president at the time of his death. He was also a director of the Keokuk National Bank and of the Iowa State Insurance Company, and interested in a number of other corporations and enterprises.

For some time he had suffered from heart trouble but had continued, except at rare periods, to visit his office daily in attendance upon his large business interests. November 12, 1903, he returned from his office about the noon hour and suddenly expired soon after being driven to his home.

Mr. Rand was a member of the Military Order of the Loyal Legion of the United States and at a stated meeting of the Commandery of this organization held January 12, 1904, at Des Moines, Iowa, resolutions in memoriam were adopted from which the following paragraphs are taken:

"Companion Rand lived a sunny life, was pleasant to everyone from the lowest to the highest. It seemed he had no cloudy days. His life all sunshine. He died as he lived.

"To the living one of the family and relatives we tender our deepest sympathy and love, and we shall always treasure in our hearts the memory of our departed companion."

And the people of Keokuk, and of many other points where he was known, joined in the above sentiment of treasuring in their hearts the memory of George D. Rand.

The body was taken to St. Peter's Catholic church, and after a Requiem High Mass, which was remarkable for its beauty and solemnity, his remains were removed to Greencastle, Indiana, where his body was interred with all the honors and love of a host of friends and relatives.

While a student at the Asbury University he met Miss Sara McGaughey, daughter of the Honorable Edward W. McGaughey, of Greencastle, Indiana, and was married to her, his first love, who survives him. She is an amiable, cultured woman, combining the sturdy, commendable qualities of our foremothers with the sensible acquirements of the twentieth century and is foremost in all good works in a quiet, unostentatious way. Mr. and Mrs. Rand were born companions as well as husband and wife. So inseparably were the twain linked that death of her husband must have been a terrible blow. But of Spartan courage, strong and sensible and Christian, instead of pining and complaining in the world's way, she took her heart-breaking grief to the Great White Throne, and the whisper came, "Peace, be still; He doeth all things well."

Mrs. Rand continues to reside at the beautiful Rand home in Keokuk, and is active in pursuit of various secular and religious duties. She is a prominent member and president of the Keokuk Woman's Club, in which her counsel is invariably sought on all questions. Scarcely a benevolent, or other enterprise, in which women are engaged, is inaugurated that Mrs. Rand is not consulted, because of her acknowledged intelligence, executive ability and wisdom, her aptness in such matters, her gentle womanly courtesy, and the charitable tendency of her very nature. Withal, she is a model home woman, warmly and graciously attached to the cares and duties of her household.

Her father, Edward W. McGaughey, was the son of Arthur O. McGaughey and Sarah Bell. The father was born March 3, 1788, and came from Johnstown, Pennsylvania, to the West when a young man, with a company of "Rangers," presumably a militia company, armed for protection. He married Sarah Bell, about 1810, at Corydon, Indiana. The family consisted of six children, William B., Edward W. (father of Mrs. Rand), Thomas D., Mary Jane, John and Harriet. Mary Jane McGaughey was the first white child born in Putnam county, Indiana. Arthur McGaughey was the clerk of the first court held in th[illegible] county. The first case taken to the suprem[illegible] court was by him. He held the [illegible] clerk twenty-three or twenty four ye[illegible] an[illegible] lived on a farm about three mil[illegible] on[illegible] Greencastle up to the time of his death [illegible] 2, 1857. His wife was a wom[illegible] character and keen intellect and w[illegible]ell known for her independent and [illegible]less frankness and energy in the discharge [illegible] her duties. Many incidents o[illegible] interes[illegible] might be recited of this good mother of the early days, illustrative of these marked trai[illegible] of her character. She wa[illegible] staunch member of the Baptist church.

Edward W. McGaughey, father of Mrs. Rand, was born in Putnam county, Indiana, January 16, 1817. He was principally self-educated, as he entered his father's office as deputy clerk at a very early age. He was married to Margaret Matlock, January 18, 1838, at Greencastle and signed his own marriage license, "Arthur McGaughey, clerk, per E. W. McGaughey, deputy." His father opposed the marriage on account of his youth. In March, 1835, he was admitted to practice law in Putnam county at the age of eighteen. In 1842 he made his first race for office, that of state senator, and was elected. He resigned the following year to make his first race for congress, his opponent winning on the close margin of three majority. He was elected to the twenty-ninth congress, taking his seat in 1845, and also the thirty-first congress. He was defeated at the next election. He was nominated by President Taylor, governor of the territory of Minnesota, but he had been a strong opponent of the Mexican War and the senate failed to confirm his appointment. His rejection caused great excitement and indignation among the Whigs of Indiana. His triumphs at the bar, his prominent record in politics and his firm, consistent character as a citizen, as shown in the newspaper files of the day, would form a volume of interest and value, too varied and voluminous, however, to have even an outline in this short sketch. He left his native Indiana home to reside in California, where he died in San Francisco, August 6, 1852, of Panama fever.

RICHARD BRYAN BURCHAM WOOD.

The Wood family traces its origin to England. From that country came its ancestors to the United States. The records of the family show that before the Revolutionary War three brothers of the name came over from Great Britain and the war coming on took active part on the side of the patriots against the mother country.

The ancestors of Richard B. B. Wood came as far west as Kentucky and Indiana from Maryland. His grandfather, Seeley Wood, married Mary Ann Hahn, of Bardstown, Kentucky, a daughter of a pioneer of that locality. They resided in southern Indiana. He was a soldier in the War of 1812, his wooden canteen, copper kettle, flint-lock musket and other relics of that war remained long in the family. He was killed in his early manhood by the fall of a tree. He left a widow and two small children, Richard, who died before his majority, at Huntsville, Alabama, and Christian Hahn Wood, father of the subject of this sketch. The widow afterwards married Jacob Woodring, and five boys and one girl were added to the family.

Christian Hahn Wood was born January 19, 1819, and was married to Sarah Katharine Slack, November 28, 1841. She, too, was from a pioneer family of the locality. Her mother, Letitia Bush, was born also in Hardin county, Kentucky, in Indian times, which gave to Kentucky the name of "the dark bloody ground." She married Reuben Slack from another pioneer family. This couple was blessed with two sons and one daughter besides Mrs. Wood, mother of the subject of this sketch, who was the youngest child. Soon after her birth the father died. The widow afterward married Thomas Cofer, a prosperous planter, her father being an extensive farmer and landowner, besides possessing numerous slaves. By this marriage three daughters and two sons were added. Soon after the birth of the last of these children, Mr. Cofer died.

Christian H. and Sarah K. Wood had two children born to them, Richard B. B. Wood, whose birthday was December 19, 1842, and Mary Letitia Wood, born September 5, 1845, both born at Elizabethtown, Kentucky, the county seat of Hardin county. The father died March 20, 1846, when only twenty-seven years and a few months old. The family at the time of his death continued to reside at Elizabethtown.

Rich'd B. B. Wood, as he signs his

name, whose birth date is given above, was delicate in childhood, but attended school almost constantly during the ten months' school terms of each year. His first two teachers were women; the other two were men, including George H. Yeaman, afterwards a member of congress from a Kentucky district and later a minister to one of the South American states by appointment from President Lincoln, and Fayette Hewitt, who was afterwards a prominent officer on the staff of Gen. Albert Pike, of the Confederate army, and after the close of the war State Auditor of Kentucky. Mr. Wood never attended a public school but once and that for a three months' term, taught by Mr. Yeaman. When about thirteen years of age he rested from school duties by advice of the family physician on account of a partial failure of his eyes by overstudy, and with his mother and sister visited relatives in Iowa for a year, in 1856-7, notably the coldest winter ever experienced in the state. Returning to Kentucky in the latter year, he did not resume his studies, except what he could learn around a country newspaper office, acting as carrier for the weekly paper of the town, "The Elizabethtown Intelligencer," the junior editor of the paper being George W. Parker, afterwards a prominent lawyer and state senator of Illinois and later president and general manager of the Cairo Short-Line Railroad, with residence and headquarters at St. Louis, where he now resides in affluent retirement. Mr. Wood took no steady employment on the paper, but did odd jobs and benefited by the exchanges, but was even too small and delicate to aspire to the position of "printer's devil."

On the 17th day of August, 1857, he went into the mercantile establishment of Cunningham & Matthis with an oral agreement to remain with the firm for a period of three years. When the three years had ended he resigned his position and in September, 1860, entered St. Joseph College, Bardstown, Kentucky, as a student. Up to 1857 all his life his mother and maternal grandmother had resided together, both being widows and the grandmother in affluent circumstances. Besides her town residence, she owned considerable landed property and a few family negroes. In that year the grandmother died, when his mother bought a home for herself and children. It was a happy little trio, linked together by the tenderest cords of affection. The ordeal was trying to separate from those who claim all his love, and from whom he had never before been separated for scarcely more than a day, even though the distance was only about twenty-four miles.

The time at college was spent studiously and profitably and pleasantly, too, with a long visit from mother and sister in the meantime.

But war clouds gathered. Still they gathered thicker and faster. There were 250 students in the college, with only three or four from the Northern states, the remainder from Kentucky and the other Southern states and a scattering attendance from Mexico, Spain, Cuba and France. The political kettle boiled and bubbled. In January, 1861, he about concluded to return home as it was inevitable that the college must suspend and the tumult was so great and the times so unsettled that profitable study was impossible. There was a brass band serenade at the old college a short time before he left when the air resounded, amid the night vigils, with the inspiring strains of "Dixie" and "The Girl I left Behind Me," calculated to fire the student-heart and unfit him for the accurate duties of the study hall and class room. So he left the old college of fond memories and hied himself to his "Home, Sweet Home."

He secured a position as deputy county clerk, which he filled for a time. In September, 1861, when Gen. Lovell H. Rousseau's Federal forces, the first to appear in that locality, entered on the north side of the town, without time for farewells or the slightest preparation Mr. Wood mounted a Kentucky mare and with three companions set his face toward the South. At Woodsonville, in Hart county, on the classic banks of old Green river, he remained with Gen. Simon Bolivar Buckner's Confederate army a short time with no other thought than that he would enlist in the Confederate army, as soon as he could determine the organization to which he preferred to attach himself.

He has told with perceptible feeling of the trivial incident which led to his failure to enlist as a Confederate soldier. Reared in tenderness, petted by mother, grandmothers and aunts, and even great-grandmothers, he had never seen much of the rough side of life. His clothing was always carefully watched over by a patient and painstaking mother and he knew comparatively nothing of the little vexations which sometimes confronted other boys less happily situated. He wore on his hurried trip to the South a pair of light-colored cassimere trousers, such as were worn by the young men in the South, in the spring and fall. But somehow just above one of the knees of those trousers a rent appeared, torn about an inch two ways, leaving a flop and a gap, to his mind, like the mouth of a Kentucky cave. His pride revolted at the sight of this tatter. Discussing the matter to himself, he determined, life or no life, to steal his way home to replenish his wardrobe and his purse. With two friends the journey through the by-ways and underbrush was commenced. All manner of dreadful stories of outrages at Elizabethtown were heard along the road. Without meeting a Federal soldier they finally arrived at the outskirts of Elizabethtown and rode boldly into the little suburb of Claysville, where one of his companions lived, and there found his mother and sister too frightened to return to their home, away from which they had been during his absence. He then remembered that a few months before he had received a pleading letter of advice from an old bachelor uncle, brother of his mother, charging him under no circumstances to enlist in either army; to stay with his mother and sister; loyalty to them was loyalty to humanity and God; they had no other protector. Here was a test and his mind was made up if it were possible for him to remain. He and one of his companions concluded they would reconnoitre. They ventured into town to the outskirts, at least, and there they met a brother to his companion who wore the epaulettes of a Federal major. He knew they had been gone and where. He greeted them cordially, insisting on their going down in town with him and on their remaining at home, assuring them of safety. These words, the almost forgotten letter from his uncle and the frightened and unsettled situation of his mother and sister, settled the matter, at least for the time or so long as he could live in peace on the northern side of the line

The only newspaper in the town had suspended on account of the war, the editor and publisher both being in the Confederate army. The office was still there idle. A paper was started in the summer of 1862, under a partnership composed of the possessor of the plant under a mortgage, a practical printer and Mr. Wood, not yet twenty years old, who was to be the editor. It was a weekly paper and took up the name of the suspended paper, "The Elizabethtown Democrat" In a short time, however, members of the Nineteenth Illinois Regiment concluded they knew more about running a paper than those conducting "The Democrat," so they moved in and published "The Zouave Gazette." "The Democrat" politely and generously suspended publication.

On October 7, 1862, he was married to Miss Lauretta Ellen Culley, daughter of Judge James DeWitt Culley, an old citizen of Elizabethtown, the ceremony being performed by Rev. Samuel Williams, of the Presbyterian church. She was born at Elizabethtown, December 20, 1845. Her birthday is in the same month as that of her husband and within one day of his, making him three years and one day her senior. When they were married he lacked from the date of their marriage to his next birthday anniversary of being twenty years old, and she lacked the same time of being seventeen years of age. Her father was of Irish descent and was born in the State of New York. Her mother was Miss Lauretta Jane Buckner before marriage, member of one of the oldest families in Kentucky. She died when Mrs. Wood was only a few months old.

After his marriage he taught a term of three months in a country school near Elizabethtown and afterwards a five months' private school in Elizabethtown. He then entered mercantile pursuits and the spring of 1865 found him at Nashville, Tennessee, as first clerk in the leading restaurant of that city, The Donegana, remaining there three months and was there when Lee surrendered and when Lincoln was assassinated. While there he also did occasional newspaper work and was correspondent of the Louisville Democrat. Returning to Elizabethtown he engaged in the confectionery and grocery business. He did not like it and sold out.

In 1866, with Capt. Frank D. Moffitt, native of Brookville, Indiana, a returned Confederate officer, under the style of Moffitt & Wood, they commenced the publication of "The Weekly Banner," being the first paper printed in the town after the War of the Rebellion. Captain Moffitt was elected police judge and soon retired when the firm was changed to Wood & Culley, the junior member of the firm being Freeland H. Culley, also a returned Confederate, and a brother of Mrs. Wood. After a few months this firm sold out, Mr. Culley purchasing a newspaper plant at Fayette, Mississippi. Afterwards Mr. Wood engaged in further local newspaper work and as a newspaper correspondent for the Louisville Courier and other papers. At the time he received his licensę to practice law in 1868 he was one of the editors and publishers of the "Kentucky Telegraph," at Elizabethtown, but retired to open a law office, having been elected city attorney for a term of one year, to which position he was re-elected for a second term. At the conclusion of this term he was elected justice of the peace to fill an unexpired term and also appointed examiner for Hardin county, by the judge of the circuit court, continuing in the meantime his law practice.

Before these terms expired he engagd as proofreader on the "Louisville Daily Evening Sun," a sprightly paper started after the war by Will S. Hays, the songwriter, and Charles D. Kirk, a returned Confederate and noted war correspondent, under the non de plume of "Se De Kay." The latter had died and Hays had retired before Mr. Wood went to "The Sun." In a few months he was promoted to chief editor, and the editor-in-chief resigning soon after, Mr. Wood, who had the esteem and confidence of the management, was left in full charge of the editorial department.

In 1872 he returned to Elizabethtown, and shortly afterwards engaged in job printing and conducted a campaign daily, which did effective work as shown by the election returns.

March 25, 1873, his only sister, Mrs. Mary Letitia Quiggins, died, leaving one small son, John Wood Quiggins, still a resident of Kentucky. This sad happening in the family was the cause of his coming to Iowa, where the only sister of his mother resided. He always claims that he did not come west to grow up with the country, as Horace Greeley advised, or to better his condition, which he didn't, but for the sake of the health and happiness of a mother much grieved over the loss of her only daughter. He still has the fondest memory of old Kentucky and her people.

Bloomfield, Davis county, was the first point at which he located in Iowa, arriving there October 26, 1874, and expected to resume the practice of law there, but a newspaper opening seemed to present itself at Drakeville, in the same county, and there he made the venture with a small weekly paper, "The Drakeville Sun." Mr. Wood said afterward that he got a great deal more fun than money out of his first newspaper venture in Iowa, and that "the Drakeville people expected a man to run a paper on wind and furnish the wind himself." The town was too small even in the progressive West for a newspaper, and after a year's time, in which he spent more money than he received from his business, he returned to Bloomfield. Here he entered the "Bloomfield Democrat" office, his name appearing as editor during the campaign in which the proprietor, T. O. Walker, was a candidate, heading the Democratic state ticket for secretary of state. Capt. J. A. T. Hull, the present prominent Iowa congressman, was editor of the Bloomfield Republican, and also a candidate for secretary of state on the Republican ticket. During these days, too, Will Van Benthusen, who became prominent as a managing editor both in Chicago and New York, and whose death occurred only a short time ago in the latter city, was the youthful junior editor and publisher of the "Bloomfield Commonwealth," and the acknowledged wag of the press gang. Afterwards, although not an Odd Fellow, he was engaged as editorial writer on "The Odd Fellows' Banner," a thriving weekly printed at Bloomfield, which he accompanied in November, 1877, to Cedar Rapids, Iowa, to which point the paper was removed, but returned in about four weeks and again engaged on "The Democrat." The last of November, 1878, he answered personally a telegram from "The Daily Constitution," of Keokuk, which paper was seeking a successor to Thomas W. Eichelberger, who had tendered his resignation There were several applicants on the ground and elsewhere, and after a few days' quiet contest Mr. Woods was selected to succeed Mr. Eichelberger as city editor and paragrapher, the paragrahing being the manufacture of funnygraphs for the daily, enough in the six days to make a long column or more for the weekly, a very popular feature at the time. He remained with "The Constitution" about a year. After a short time, with comparatively no capital, he started "The Daily Evening Democrat," but the press contracting to do the printing broke down completely in a very short time and the venture had to be abandoned for the lack of funds to replace the press, and in the face of the most promising prospects.

He worked on the various papers in Keokuk, sometimes regularly and at other times as a sub-writer and as a special correspondent. He was working on the "Gate City" as night editor when J. C. Thompson and P. R. Nelson conceived the idea of commencing the publication of "The Daily Democrat." Mr. Wood had under advisement the acceptance of a proposition to go as editor of a paper in southwestern Missouri. Mr. Wood had not heard of the proposed new Keokuk paper until Mr. Nelson came to "The Gate City" office and offered him the position as editor. After a little parley he accepted. Afterwards the paper was reorganized by a company of seven and corporation papers were filed. Mr. Wood was president and editor under the new arrangement, and P. R. Nelson business manager. Mr. Wood soon resigned and sold his interest. Soon the paper changed control and Mr. Wood was again engaged as editor and again resigned, and though importuned by Frank Madden, who now had a controlling interest, to return to the editorship of the paper he irrevocably declined on the terms offered, and worked for "The Constitution" and "The Gate City" in various editorial posititons, frequently subbing for Sam M. Clark during his absences from the city, and also acted at different times as editorial writer, managing editor and city editor of "The Constitution."

A short time after Warwick & Ranson bought "The Democrat" Mr. Wood engaged as editorial writer and assisted Mr. Ranson in the local department. In the meantime he resigned the duties of editorial writer, but continued on the local page. He was holding a place on "The Democrat" when that paper bought "The Constitution" and the two papers merged. He continued his duties with the merged papers until he had been with "The Democrat" and the consolidated papers eighteen months to a day, when he resigned to commence the publication of "The Keokuk Chief," a weekly paper. This he afterwards sold and it soon became an afternoon paper, "The Daily Chief." On this paper he was working when it was purchased and merged with "The Constitution-Democrat." Since then Mr. Wood has done work on the different Keokuk papers at times, including "The Standard," and is now engaged in newspaper correspondence and feature story writing. One other Keokuk paper on which Mr. Wood did editorial work a number of years ago was "The Labor Tribune."

In early days Mr. Wood was addicted to flirtations with the muse and has written some rather meritorius verses, some of which were published in George D. Prentice's old Louisville Sunday Journal, and he is quite proud of the fact that he had personally from the lips of Mr. Prentice, nestor of the Kentucky early day poets, most flattering commendation of his work. Those specially in the mind of Mr. Prentice were "Phantom" and "Pattering Rain," which had just appeared in "The Journal." He has also written other verses since coming to Iowa, among these a song, "The Wild Rose of Iowa," which has been set to music and published. It is a pretty, patriotic song, a fitting tribute to Iowa, his adopted state.

Mr. Wood was born in the same county which gave Abraham Lincoln birth and Mr. Lincoln's good stepmother, Mrs. Johnson, nee Bush, was a blood relative of his early Kentucky ancestors.

There was a streak of Presbyterianism in some of the older members of the Wood family, though both of his great-grandmothers and his father and mother were Methodists. His paternal great-grandmother was a Presbyterian and died in 1866, at the age of ninety-six. At the time of her death Mr. Wood's daughter, Ida Fitzhugh, was about six months old, making five gererations alive, a rare happening. Mrs. Wood's paternal grandparents were early settlers and suffered the many trïals of pioneer life, her grandmother being for some time a prisoner with warlike Indians, of which sad experience she would never talk. These paternal grandparents were uncompromising Presbyterians, as was her father. Her maternal grandparents were Baptists, yet her uncles and her aunts departed from that faith, one uncle, Dr. Edmund P. Buckner, being a physician and a prominent and popular Methodist divine in Kentucky. On account of his health he practically gave up preaching, confining himself to the practice of medicine. Some of her aunts were also Methodists. Mr. and Mrs. Wood are Presbyterians and so are several of their children.

Mr. and Mrs. Wood have been the parents of ten children, as follows, six of whom are living: John Burcham Wood, born in Kentucky in 1863, lived but a few moments after birth; Ida FitzHugh Wood, born in Kentucky, February 24, 1866, married Samuel Hendricks Selman, of Bloomfield, son of Dr. J. J. Selman, prominent in state affairs in pioneer days, and a native of Alabama, died in 1804. They have one daughter, Marie, in her fourteenth year. Mr. and Mrs. Selman recently returned from a residence of two years at Colorado Springs, Colorado, and now reside at Bloomfield, Iowa; Christian LaRue Wood, born in Kentucky, April 11, 1868, painter and cartoonist, of Houston, Texas; William Claude Wood, born in Kentucky, March 7, 1870, a very bright and promisinig boy, died at Keokuk, Iowa, August 17, 1886; Richard Warfield Wood, born in Kentucky, August 21, 1872, married Frances Chiles, of Illinois, has two children, Lillian, aged three years and an infant son; Richard Francis, resides in St. Louis, Missouri, and is district sales manager for two large Eastern establishments.

All the above Kentucky children were born at Elizabethtown.

John Young Brown Wood, born July 8, 1870, at Bloomfield, Iowa, is a member of the newspaper fraternity and doing newspaper work in Louisiana. He has written many popular dialect and other verses. He has also done some clever cartoon work and frequently pleases audiences as chalk-talker, illustrating his lectures with rapidly drawn pictures or caricatures; Howard Walker Wood, born at Bloomfield, Iowa, March 26, 1878, did some newspaper work before his majority and developed early a marked literary taste, but before he was graduated from the Keokuk high school, in 1898, he was offered a position with the Keokuk Savings Bank, which he accepted with the understanding that his work was to begin at the close of the school term. He was graduated with honor and was class poet. In his junior year he was entered in an oratorical contest for a gold medal, in which his two opponents were members of the senior class of the high school. He won the medal amid the plaudits of a very large audience of the representative citizens of Keokuk, at the Keokuk opera house. He entered the bank after graduation and is now assistant teller in that institution; Lawrence Culley Wood, born in Keokuk, Iowa, March 22, 1880, recently resigned a position with the Iowa State Insurance Company, Keokuk, and now assistant in the office of his brother Richard W. Wood, at St. Louis; Burnham DeWitt Wood, born in Keokuk, and died there; Lauretta Ellen Wood born May 16, 1884, in Keokuk, and died there November 13, 1892, of diphtheria. She was the family pet and pride, and her death brought great grief to the household.

COLONEL WILLIAM PATTERSON.

It is told of Oliver Cromwell that he had a mole on his face, and when sitting for a portrait the artist asked if it should be omitted from the picture. "Paint me as I am!" vehemently replied the man. The individuality of Col. William Patterson was of that noble caste that to paint him just as he was will give the truest and best delineation of his fine qualities. He was a courageous pioneer and a grand old citizen.

Colonel Patterson was a prominent character in Lee county, Iowa, and a detailed biography of his life would form an interesting history of the entire locality adjacent to his Iowa home. Coming from sturdy honest pioneer stock, of large and commanding stature, he stood a strong, living monument to the worth of honest manhood and life of sterling, active Christian qualities. He was born in Wythe county, Virginia, March 9, 1802, was the son of Joseph and Jane Patterson, and is of Scotch descent. When about five years old his father moved to Kentucky, settling in Adair county, where he received a common-school education, attending school during the winter months and assisting on the farm in the summer. He had a fondness for farming and in early manhood intended to make that his life vocation, but subsequent events caused him to abandon that determination, and he drifted into mercantile pursuits.

On April 2, 1822, Colonel Patterson was married to Miss Eleanor Johnson, both being in their twentieth years. Eleanor Johnson was born in Anna Arundel county, Maryland, April 21, 1802, and in early childhood moved with her parents to Adair county, Kentucky. Her father died soon thereafter, and the mother of Colonel Patterson died in his boyhood. Joseph Patterson, the father, married the mother of Eleanor Johnson, and the two families became as one. Thus Colonel Patterson and his wife had known each other from childhood. In 1829 they left Kentucky and settled in Marion county, Missouri, but after a residence there of three years removed to Sangamon county, Illinois. In 1837 they moved to West Point, in Lee county, Iowa, which was then a portion of Missouri territory. Colonel Patterson became tired of farming and in 1846 the family located in Keokuk. He opened a store in connection with furnishing boats with provisions. Keokuk at that time had only from one hundred and fifty to two hundred inhabitants, and the village was built on the edge of the river. The hill upon which the city now stands was covered with timber and underbrush.

After engaging in the mercantile business in Keokuk Colonel Patterson, as an experiment, began in a small way to pack pork. In 1848 he sold his store and engaged exclusively in the pork-packing business, which he followed for over thirty years. The firm for a considerable time was Patterson & Timberman, the latter dying in 1879. The packing operations grew to 20,000 hogs per annum. Colonel Patterson took an active part in shaping affairs in early Iowa days. He was elected a member of the first legislature of the Territory of Iowa, in 1838, and was influential in settling the disturbance about the boundary line between Iowa and Missouri, which was strenuously agitated at that time. He was commissioned a colonel of militia by Governor Lucas, of Iowa, and in 1839, during the border troubles, was ordered by Maj.-Gen. I. B. Brown to report with one company at Farmington, Iowa. The company was sent to the front, but by the efforts of Colonel Patterson and some of his colleagues in the legislature, bloodshed was averted, the militia was disbanded and soon the boundary line between Iowa and Missouri was established by congress according to the claim of Iowa. Colonel Patterson served in nine regular or special sessions of the Iowa legislature, was three times mayor of Keokuk, and for seven years postmaster in that city. He was a member of the constitutional convention, which convened at Iowa City in 1857, and was for a long time president of the Des Moines Improvement Company. For over nine years he was president of the Keokuk National Bank, a position he held at the time of his death.

Colonel Patterson was one of the principal movers in the work of building the First Westminster Presbyterian church, of Keokuk, one of the most substantial and commodious edifices in the city, built of stone, and subscribed liberally to the enterprise. For over sixty years he had been of the Presbyterian faith. In 1837 he was elected an elder of the Old School Presbyterian church, at West Point, Iowa, and was the first Presbyterian elder ordained in the state. He was a wise, able and conscientious Christian man, a recognized patriarch in the church. Firm yet mild, many interesting stories are told of his rebukes to members whom he thought had deviated from rectitude. He had no patience with hypocrisy or shams.

When he located in Keokuk goods were received by river only; that was the only means of transportation and these goods were distributed over the sparsely settled surrounding country by means of ox teams and wagons. Colonel Patterson was, therefore, identified with Keokuk from its earliest history, from the inception of its first infant industry, up to the time when it had grown into a prosperous little city, and the greater part of the time intervening was spent by him in ceaseless activity.

In 1881 he had a limb broken, which gave him much trouble and forced him to retire from active business life. The use of crutches became necessary, and consequently he remained most of the time in the quiet of his beautiful home. Almost up to the time of his death his general health was quite good, his mind clear, and in pleasant weather would ride down in town to greet his many friends. He was still a notable figure at church, where at the Sunday services he was helped by a faithful attendant to a large arm-chair near the pulpit.

Socially he was pleasant and affable, one of the old-style gentlemen, intercourse with whom was calculated to make men and women proud of their ancestry, the early manhood and womanhood of the country. Reading was one of his chief pleasures, and he kept a strict watch on the current events of the country. He was one of nature's noblemen, a large-brained, big-hearted, honest man.

April 2, 1872, Colonel Patterson and his wife celebrated the fiftieth anniversary of their wedding. This golden wedding was a notable event in Keokuk.

On April 2, 1880, just fifty-eight years from the date of her marriage to Colonel Patterson, Mrs. Patterson, ripe with years and full of Christian hope, was called from earth and passed over the river to the eternal city, lighted by the glory from the Master's throne.

Saturday evening, March 9, 1889, the eighty-seventh anniversary of his birth, an informal surprise reception was tendered to Colonel Patterson at his home by a number of his friends and admirers for the purpose of grasping his hand and extending warm and heartfelt congratulations. As a matter of history in this connection it will be interesting to perpetuate with his memory the following list of those who were among the number present on this notable occasion, many of whom long since were numbered with the dead, while others still live to call to memory with reverence the last time they mingled in social communion with this great and good man. The list follows: Rev. and Mrs. John B. Worrall, Mr. and Mrs. William Fulton, Mr. and Mrs. Alex Collier, Dr. and Mrs. E. E. Fuller, Mr. and Mrs. W. J. Fulton, Mr. and Mrs. D. A. Kerr, Colonel and Mrs. Samuel T. Marshall, Mr. and Mrs. David W. McElroy, Mr. and Mrs. W. A. Patterson, Mr. and Mrs. Arthur H. Moody, Capt. and Mrs. A. H. Evans, Mr. and Mrs. D. Steele, Capt. and Mrs. L. D. Sheppard, Mr. and Mrs. M. L. Boyles, Dr. and Mrs. George F. Jenkins, Mr. and Mrs. Richard B. B. Wood, Col. and Mrs. A. Hosmer, Dr. and Mrs. H. A. Kinnaman, Mr. and Mrs. Ed Crossan, Mr. and Mrs. E. T. Albert, Mr. and Mrs. John Dickie, Mr. and Mrs. S. L. Hagny, Mrs. H. Brownell, Mrs. Mary A. Creel, Mrs. Henry Huiskamp, Mrs. Amanda Hughes, Mrs. Eliza Martin, Mrs. Martha McQuee, Mrs. George B. Smythe, Mrs. Margaret Starkwater, Miss Sallie Carver, Miss Nannie P. Fulton, Miss M. Lizzie Fulton, Miss Rachel Worrall, Miss Ellen J. Martin, Miss Eleanor J. Patterson, Miss Anna M. Ringland, Miss Cora H. Pittman, Miss Lucia Pittman, Judge James M. Love, Judge Edward Johnstone, D. J. Ayres, A. J. Wilkinson, John Carver, G. W. Pittman, A. E. Johnstone, Col. H. B. Blood, L. H. Ayer, Dr. William Burkett, George H. Comstock, John H. Freeman, Maj. D. B. Hamill, Dr. E. B. Ringland, George D. Mann, Adam Hagny, Robert D. Fulton, Joseph C. Patterson, and G. R. Pettet.

Only a few months after this memorable reception, this kindly tribute to Colonel Patterson, he was called to his reward. He died peacefully at his home, October 23, 1889, greatly lamented, not only in Keokuk, but wherever Colonel Patterson was known. He lived to a ripe old age, far beyond the three score and ten, and his lengthened days were days of usefulness and peace. And the world is better that he lived.

Colonel and Mrs. Patterson were the parents of eleven children, three of whom died in infancy. Those who lived to manhood and womanhood were the following: Mrs. Mary A. Creel, born in Kentucky; Mrs. Eliza D. Marshall, born in Kentucky; William Albert Patterson, born in Kentucky; Joseph C. Patterson, born in Kentucky; Sabert T. Patterson, born in Missouri; Mrs. Margaret Starkwather, born in Illinois; Miss Eleanor Patterson, born in Iowa; Thomas B. Patterson, born in Iowa.

Of these only two survive, Mrs. Starkwather, who resides at the old home place, and Sabert T. Patterson, unmarried, and also a resident of Keokuk.

CHRISTIAN SMITH.

Christian Smith, one of the early settlers and highly respected citizens of Primrose, Lee county, Iowa, was born July 18, 1843, at Braunschveid, Germany, and emigrated to America in 1854, landing at New Orleans and coming up the Mississippi river to the City of Keokuk, whence he proceeded to Harrison township, and with his mother and stepfather located on a farm. His father died in Germany, and the mother afterward remarried, coming to America with her second husband, and her own death occurred only seven years ago, in the seventy-second year of her age.

Mr. Smith received a good education in the public schools of Primrose, working on the home farm during vacations, and when he was eighteen years of age he began to acquire the blacksmithing trade, which he has followed ever since. He learned the trade in Franklin township, Lee county, and then removed to Farmington, Iowa, where he continued to pursue his new calling for a period of five years with great success; but at the end of that time he returned to the scenes of his boyhood, establishing a blacksmith shop in Primrose, where he has carried on the work of his trade continuously from that day to the present time. In addition he has to some extent engaged in the wagonmaking business, and also conducts a general repair shop He enjoys the patronage of a very large territory, and by reason of his skill, his careful and conscientious attention to his work in all its details, and the unwavering integrity and honesty of all his business transactions and personal relations he has reaped a very full and gratifying measure of success. His shop is the only one in the village, and is fully equipped with the latest apparatus for doing thorough and finished work, for it is one of Mr. Smith's favorite maxims, that "what is worth doing is worth doing well." He has purchased a tract of three and a half acres of land for residence purposes, and on this has erected a fine two-story dwelling adjoining the shop, this being one of the best residences in the city, both for convenience and external appearance. Although Mr. Smith takes a deep interest in public affairs, and is a loyal member of the Democratic party, he has never cared to hold public office; on the other hand he has always been devoted to the cause of education and the public schools, and for this reason he has been elected and re-elected by his friends to the office of school director year after year for a long period, and has invariably discharged the duties of that important position to his own credit and the benefit of those who depend upon his judgment for its proper conduct. In fact he is a constant advocate of all that tends to advance the interests of the community in which his career is being passed, and is a faithful member and supporter of the German Lutheran church.

On December 15, 1868, Mr. Smith was united in marriage to Miss Henrietta Wendt, who was born in Germany and came to the United States in the same vessel in which Mr. Smith made the voyage, locating with her parents in Harrison township, Lee county, her father being a farmer. Both her parents are now deceased, and are buried in Harrison township. To Mr. and Mrs. Smith have been born two sons and five daughters, as follows: Ida, who is the wife of Prof. L. Antrim, of Mount Pleasant, owner of Mount Pleasant Academy, and a professor in the institution, has two children Etta May and Florence; Amelia, who is the wife of Edward Jack, a railroad man, of Farmington, Iowa; Sophia, who resides with her parents; William, an employe of the telephone company at Primrose; Charles, who is in the electric light business at Centerville, Iowa; Emma and Elda, who reside with their parents. All the children were born at Primrose, and there received excellent educational advantages, while Charles and Emma also attended Mount Pleasant academy.

J. G. HURLEY.

J. G. Hurley, one of the old and venerable residents of Montrose township, Lee county, whose years but emphasize the regard his intellectual acquirements and moral standing command, has had a long and useful career, in which his best faculties and strongest powers have been freely placed at the service of the public. As a man of thorough education and deep training he has ever regarded his best as a gift to be used for the public benefit, and felt that the highest privilege of knowledge is to communicate it in turn to darkened minds. It is the glory of light to give light, and the right of the intellectual to stir up in ignorant minds a thirst for knowledge. So Mr. Hurley has always lived and worked. Born and bred a farmer, he has been a teacher of marked ability and wide influence; and while he has cultivated the soil he has also cultivated the youthful mind, and commanded the respect and confidence of every element in the community at all interested in the improvement of the youth.

Mr. Hurley came to Montrose township, April 2, 1882, from Pike county, Illinois, where he had lived since 1846. He was born near Knoxville, Tennessee, May 3, 1831, and early removed to Illinois. In the spring of 1870 he went to California, and made an extensive visit with a brother who had already settled in that country. For some two years on his return he was engaged in farming and in teaching in Bureau county, Illinois, after which he returned to Pike county, where he continued teaching. He has taught extensively, but was reared a farmer, and has farmed in Lee county since 1882.

Mr. Hurley has taught in Montrose, and at one time was principal of the Montrose village schools. He has also taught several terms in the district schools of that township.

Mr. Hurley's educational acquirements are of a very high character, and his standing among teachers is fine. He began his studying in the public school, and completed his schooling in Asbury University at Greencastle, Indiana. He has taught in town and country work, and has everywhere acquitted himself creditably. From S. M. Etter he holds a state certificate, issued September 1, 1877, at Springfield, Illinois. He has done good work in county institutes in Illinois. A recommendation issued to him from the superintendent of Pike county schools, in which it is stated that Mr. Hurley is though to be the best mathematician in the state. Prof. Hippen, at that time the teacher of Latin and Greek, declares Mr. Hurley to be a better English scholar than himself. Mr. Hurley takes special delight in mathematics and English grammar.

Mr. Hurley is a son of Jonathan Hurley, who was born in Delaware in 1782, and was reared by Nathaniel Carolton. He lived to be ninety-six years old, dying April 25, 1878. The mother of Mr. Hurley was Rebecca Hicks, distantly related to Governor Hicks, of Maryland. She was born in Maryland, June 26, 1788, and died in Pike county, Illinois, December 14, 1851. Her people owned slaves in North Carolina at an early day, and her paternal grandfather was widely noted for his broad and liberal scholarship. Jonathan Hurley was drafted two or three times during the War of 1812, but escaped the perils of war.

J. G. Hurley was married July 31, 1862, in Montrose township, Lee county, to Miss Lydia J. Boyd, who was born in Ohio, and came to this state when she was but twelve years old. At the present writing she is still living. To her marriage with Mr. Hurley were born five children: W. C.; Frank A.; Lulu B.; Ruth M., who is now a teacher in the Montrose high school, and Nettie G. Three children are dead: J. G., who died at the age of eight years, in 1871; J. B., who died in 1866, was eleven months of age, and Katie, who died in 1883, was but fifteen months old. None of the children are married.

At one time Mr. Hurley was a member of the Independent Order of Odd Fellows as well as the Independent Order of Good Templars, but is not now connected with either society. He is an active member of the Methodist church, and is devoted to its welfare. In politics Mr. Hurley is a Bryan Democrat, though he was a Republican until the passing of the Credit Strengthening Act of 1869. In Bureau county, Illinois, he was elected tax collector on the People's ticket. In 1896 he was appointed township commissioner of Montrose by the Democrats.

Mr. Hurley owns a splendid estate of 120 acres, on which he is engaged in both general farming and truck and fruit culture. He has many acres devoted to strawberries, potatoes and tomatoes. Of the last he had over seven hundred bushels the last summer. He is an intellectual, thoughtful and successful farmer, and has met with a large success. Always a hard-working and industrious man, he is reaping the rich reward that attends industry, integrity and manliness.

HARRISON F. MILLER.

One of the early settlers and well-known citizens of Harrison township, Lee county, Iowa, where he now resides on his farm of 120 acres, in section 18, is Harrison F. Miller, who was born on November 3, 1830, in Hardy county, West Virginia, and there he received his education in the common schools and learned the work of agriculture by assisting on his father's farm. In April, 1856, however, he removed to Muskingum county, Ohio, where for ten years he engaged in farming, and at the end of that period he again removed westward, locating in Clark county, Illinois. After farming at that place for six years, during which he achieved considerable success, he came to Iowa in 1871, renting land for a time in Harrison township, and later he purchased a fine and productive farm of 120 acres. On this farm he has made nearly all the improvements and established a comfortable and pleasant home for himself and family, and here he has resided continuously ever since, engaging in general farming and to some extent in stockraising, with signal success.

Mr. Miller is a member of a family comprising seven children, of whom only three are now living, and is the son of Corbin and Amanda Frank Miller, both of whom were natives of West Virginia, and resided in that state until removing to Ohio in 1856, whence he later came to Iowa and farmed for a short time, or until his death, which occurred in the eighty-second year of his age on the farm now occupied by his son, our subject, and he is here buried, while his wife, whose death preceded his own by several years, is buried in Illinois.

In 1855 Mr. Miller was united in marriage with Miss Catherine Miller, daughter of Aquilla B. and Rebecca (Fravel) Miller, who were born in West Virginia and removed about the year 1856 to Clark county, Illinois, where the father continued his occupation of farming, and where they both passed the remainder of their lives. To Mr. and Mrs. Miller have been born two children, a son and a daughter. Florence, the elder, who was born in West Virginia, is now a resident of Missouri, and the wife of Mills Coleman, a very prosperous and enterprising citizen of that state. Corbin B., who is a farmer by occupation, owns a farm of 100 acres in Harrison township, on which he resides, and is very successful in the conduct of his affairs. He married Miss Clara Grimm and to them have been born three daughters and one son, all natives of Harrison township. These are Bertha, Ethel, Stella and Elmer, the latter of whom died at the age of five years.

Although Mr. Miller's father was a member of the Democratic party, he is himself a staunch Republican, believing thoroughly in the applicability of that party's principles to modern conditions, and while he has never sought public office for himself, he has rendered valuable service to the local branch of his party, always evincing a strong interest in public affairs, and being a consistent advocate of all worthy movements having for their object the promotion of the community's interests. As a farmer he has been highly successful by reason of his business ability and his attitude of readiness toward opportunities, coupled with a sane, sound judgment and keen foresight that have enabled him to carry his ventures to the desired issue; and as a man and a citizen he enjoys the general respect because of his honorable and upright methods in all matters in which he comes into contact with his fellowmen.

ISAIAH McKEEHAN.

One of the early settlers of Lee county and now among the most influential and substantial citizens of Harrison township, is Isaiah McKeehan, who has been an interesting witness of the development of this section of the state from a condition approximating that of a wilderness and has borne his part in advancing the material and moral interests of the community. He owns a farm of eighty acres besides another tract of 120 acres. Mr. McKeehan was born in the City of Lafayette, Indiana, on April 10, 1838, and when only two years of age removed with his parents to Iowa, making the entire journey by wagon and ox teams. The father purchased land in Harrison township, making for himself and family a home in that new and wild region, and here our subject received his education and assisted in the hard work of the home farm.

Mr. McKeehan is the son of Benjamin and Minnie (Hawk) McKeehan. The father was born in Kentucky, and came to Indiana when a young man. He engaged in farming all his life, and when he came to Harrison township purchased eighty acres of land which he cultivated until his death, adding to the original purchase, however, until he owned 240 acres, all of which he placed under cultivation. His was a progressive disposition, and he availed himself of all modern improvements in the accomplishment of his work. His death occurred in 1891, when he had attained the age of eighty-five years. In politics he was a member of the Democracy, and was elected to various township offices. The mother's demise occurred some years before that of her husband. Both are buried in Harrison township. They were the parents of nine children, only two of whom are now living, the other being Mrs. George Smith, of Fort Madison.

Our subject remained a member of his father's family, assisting in the work of the farm, until his twenty-fifth year, when he purchased his present farm in section 16. The land was at that time wild and unreclaimed, but has been transformed by Mr. McKeehan's energy and industry into a marvel of fertility and productiveness, excellent buildings have been erected, and modern improvements now take the place of the crude implements and equipment known to agriculture when the country was new. Here the proprietor conducts general farming and stockraising, and has met with much success to reward his industry and exercise of keen foresight and discernment.

In 1861 Mr. McKeehan was united in marriage to Miss Sarah J. Meyers, who was born in Ohio and came to Iowa with her parents in 1852, locating at Primrose, Harrison township, Lee county. Her father was Fred Meyers, who was a blacksmith and followed his trade at Primrose until his death, which occurred when he was eighty-four years of age. The mother died at the age of eighty years. To Mr. and Mrs. McKeehan have been born seven children, as follows: John, residing on a farm of eighty acres in Harrison township, married Miss Rebecca Alexander and has three children, Bertha, Ray, Mary; Laura, now deceased, was the wife of Frank Saunders, and is survived by three children, Bert, Glenn, May; Ida, wife of William Hanson, a machinist and pattern maker in the Santa Fe Railroad shops at Fort Madison; Nellie, who is at home with her parents; James, residing on the former home of his grandfather, married Miss Nannie Methews, and has one child, Viola; Rose resides in Montana, and Clyda, the youngest of the family, is also making her home in Montana. The children were all born and educated in Harrison township.

Mr. McKeehan has been until recently

a member of the Democratic party, but has transferred his support to the People's party. He takes a deep interest in matters and questions of public policy, but devotes his time exclusively to business pursuits, and does not aspire to public office, being content to cast his vote in favor of honest government.

FRANK OERTEL.

Frank Oertel, who was born in Keokuk, Iowa, November 28, 1862, has taken a position in the business world of southeastern Iowa, which can only be secured by genuine worth and real manhood. The confidence of the community is not easily won, nor is it long retained by sham and pretense. Integrity of the life must go with the appearance of honesty, or the fraud is soon exposed. A man whose "word is as good as his bond," and in whose "hands may be left uncounted gold," is a treasure in any community, and when discovered and identified beyond dispute, is trusted and honored without measure.

The man whose name introduces this article is widely known as that kind of a man, whose word may be trusted and statement accepted in any case. His reputation is high, and what he says is regarded as settling any dispute. Simple and modest in his ways, unpretending in his disposition, and thoroughly reliable and trustworthy in his character, he is regarded as one of the leading business men in the City of Keokuk, and as he is still in the prime of life, what he has accomplished is but the forerunner of what he will do if health and strength are spared him.

Frank Oertel is a son of John Oertel, who was born in Germany, where he married Miss Elizabeth Genter. They came to this country at an early day, and established a milk dairy and general farm near Keokuk years ago. He died August 30, 1890, and his widow, who has attained the age of seventy-eight years, is still living. The subject of this sketch attended the local schools where he secured his education, and when quite young assisted his father in his farming operations. In company with his brothers he carried on the homestead farm for two years after his father's death; and then in company with them was engaged from 1882 to 1890 in a very extensive meat business. The last-named year he bought out the interest of his brothers in the business, and from that date has conducted it alone. Mr. Oertel has met with marked success, and employs advanced methods in his work. For twenty-two years he has now been in business, and in that time has greatly prospered, not only establishing a large and growing industrial enterprise, but winning for himself an enviable name and standing where he has been so long and favorably known. He buys live stock, which he kills and dresses himself, so that his patrons are always sure of receiving the best the market affords, good sound meats, and sold at a reasonable price. Mr. Oertel also retails ice, and in this line has secured a good patronage for himself. His home is at No. 1724 Johnson street, where his father lived before him.

Mr. Oertel and Miss Emily Hessbacker were married in March, 1885. Their only child, Frank, who was born December 9, 1887, has been blind from his birth. For the past nine years he has been in the state school for the blind at Vinton, where he is still engaged in studying and preparing himself in music and piano tuning to make his own way in the world, if fate should so demand.

Mr. Oertel has had three brothers and one sister,—John, Fred, William and Lizzie, who is the wife of Sigmund Hamilton, and lives in Illinois. Politically he is a Republican. In business matters Mr. Oertel has been greatly prospered. He owns sixty feet front at No. 1328 Main street, where his business establishment is located, with four large rooms for business operations and slaughter house, stable and ice house in the rear, which he built in 1894. He does a very considerable business in wholesaling to smaller dealers, and his retail store was not opened for several years after he began operations.

Mr. Oertel is a daughter of Cornelius Hessbacher, who was born in Switzerland, but who came to the United States in early life, and locating in Cincinnati, Ohio, where he married his third wife, Rosina Stroble, a native of Baden, Germany, and removed to Keokuk over fifty years ago. He was a machinist, and for many years before his death in that city, in 1868, he was an invalid. Before her death she married for a second time, becoming the wife of John Marks. She passed to her final rest June 30, 1900, and Mr. Marks, April 16, 1892. Mrs. Oertel has one sister, Matilda, the wife of Edward Etle, of Keokuk. She is a contributor to the German Lutheran church, in which her son was christened, though born a Catholic. She takes much interest in the business affairs of the family, and is bookkeeper at the store. For six years she and her husband have worked very close together, and they have built a business that rests on a very solid foundation, of which they may be justly proud.

FRANK E. STANNUS.

Frank E. Stannus, who was born in Keokuk, Iowa, January 24, 1858, a son of John Stannus, worthily sustains a name to which his father gave standing for many years in the earlier history of southeastern Iowa. The father was at one time a wholesale dealer in groceries, and was also largely engaged in pork packing. During the Civil War he held a position in the custom house and had charge of all the ammunition passing through this port for the government. During the palmy period of Keokuk he was one of the leading men of the place, and at one time became very wealthy. The fortunes of the stock market, however, proved adverse to him, as they did to others, and he lost, it is said, as much as $100,000. In 1876 he went to the Black Hills, hoping to recover his wasted resources in lumbering and mining but with small results. During the war he made up a volunteer squad and served in the "battle of Athens." In politics he was a Republican, and was appointed surveyor of customs by President Lincoln. This office was lately held by Sam Clark, but has now been removed to St. Louis.

John Stannus was born in Wheeling, West Virginia, and was the son of parents who came from Ireland when they were young. He came to Keokuk in 1843, and became a carpenter and contractor, and as he was energetic and aggressive he pushed business, making money rapidly. He was a sportsman of much enthusiasm, a rifle shot of marked excellence and bore the nicknames of "Audubon" and "Ironclad." He shot game, but would never sell it, preferring to give it to his friends, and had contempt for those who sold game, calling them "pot-hunters." On one occasion he crossed the Mississippi for a wager of fifty dollars, that he would not get his feet wet. The river was very low, and he actually did cross as he wagered he would at Price's creek. He died at Central City, in the Black Hills, in 1895, and his remains now rest in Oakland cemetery. His wife, the mother of Frank E. Stannus, was Martha Hamilton, who was born and reared in Keokuk.

The subject of this article, Frank E. Stannus, remained at Keokuk under the parental roof, where he attended the public schools, and studied out a career for himself, until he reached the age of fifteen years, when he started out in a wholesale and retail business in which he was engaged for twenty-two years. In October, 1873, he began a retail oil business, and in 1895 gave it up, after having reaped very substantial results. After several years he established "The Economy Rug Works," in 1900; and four years later purchased a similar plant at Quincy, Illinois. His investments in real estate are now three dwellings and a business house on Main street.

Mr. Stannus takes much interest in fraternal matters, and is a trustee in Keokuk Lodge, No. 13, Independent Order of Odd Fellows, and for twelve years has been a member of the building committee of the Modern Woodmen of America. For two years he held the office of alderman from the Third ward, and in the council was chairman of the street committee one year, and of sidewalks two years. For five years he represented the central committee in city and county in the Republican organization.

Mr. Stannus was married to Miss Lizzie Young, of Warsaw, Illinois, in 1881. Of the four children born to their union, two are living: Edward F. is practicing dentistry and taking a medical course in a school at Quincy; Etta C. is a child at home. John Young, the father of Mrs. Stannus, is a retired business man of Warsaw. Her mother is dead.

Mr. Stannus is the third member of a family of six living children, who were born to his parents: William J., a ranch-owner in South Dakota; John J., a resident of Central City, South Dakota; Albert L., a resident of Spearfish, South Dakota; Mrs. Milton C. Brenn, of Spearfish, South Dakota, and Mrs. A. R. Clemmons, also of Spearfish, South Dakota.

As will be noted from this outline the

family have long taken a prominent part in the upbuilding and development of the country wherever they may be found. The grandfather and the father have proved themselves wide-awake and public spirited, and the new generation, whether in Dakota, or Chicago, or elsewhere, shows the same moving, and is progressive and earnest.

FRANK M. FULLER, M. D.

Dr. Frank M. Fuller, a practicing physician of Keokuk, was born in the city which is yet his home on the 29th of September, 1867. His father was Dr. E. E. Fuller, a physician and druggist who died in the year 1897, and his mother, who still survives, is now living in Quincy. In their family were five children: Charles M., who is now foreman with the Baker Medicine Company, of Keokuk; Mrs. E. F. Keith, of San Francisco; David G., of Chicago; Mrs. J. L. Tapp, of Quincy, Illinois, and Frank M.

Dr. Fuller, of this review, comes of a line of physicians the profession being represented in each generation from 1737 down to the present time. He pursued his early education in the public schools, passed through successive grades until he had completed the high-school course and subsequently entered Parson's College at Fairfield, Iowa, in which he was graduated on the completion of the classical course in 1888, the degree of Bachelor of Arts being then conferred upon him. In 1891 he received the Master of Arts degree from the same institution. He entered upon his business career in connection with his father and was associated with him in the conduct of a drug store for seven years. When determining to engage in the practice of medicine he entered as a student the Keokuk Medical College and therein completed the regular course by graduation with the class of 1897. He then practiced until the fall of 1897, when he accepted the chair of chemistry in the Keokuk Medical College. Later he went abroad and pursued a post-graduate course in the Metropolitan School of Medicine in London. Upon his return he resumed the practice of medicine and also his college work, in which he actively continued until 1901, when he again crossed the Atlantic and this time pursued a course in the University of Vienna and in the Vienna Polyclinic. He has been very successful in his practice, owing to his careful and comprehensive preparation and his devotion to the duties of the profession. He has a large private practice and in addition has long been connected with educational work in the Keokuk Medical College. At the present writing he occupies the chair of diseases of children in the nurses' school and of clinical diseases of children in the hospital in connection with the college. He belongs to the American Medical Association, the Iowa State Medical Society, the Tri-state Medical Society, the Southeastern Iowa Medical Society, the Des Moines Valley Medical Society and the Lee County

Medical Society, the latter society of which he is the president.

In 1897 Dr. Fuller was married to Miss Anna Ballinger, who was born in Keokuk and they have one child, Madison Ballinger, born August 17, 1903. Fraternally Dr. Fuller is connected with the Masonic Lodge and with the Ancient Order of United Workmen. He is a Republican in his political views and has been somewhat prominent locally in the ranks of his party. He served as alderman from the Fifth ward for four years, has been president of the board of health for four years and city physician for two years. He was also a director in the Keokuk public library and manifests an active and helpful interest in whatever pertains to the welfare and progress of his native city. He resides at No. 524 North Third street, where he has a pleasant and attractive home and his genial, social nature has gained him warm friendship, while his professional skill and ability have placed him in the front ranks among the representatives of the medical fraternity in his native county.

INDEX.